Absolutism and Ruling Class

ABSOLUTISM
and
RULING CLASS

The Formation of the
Russian Political Order
1700–1825

John P. LeDonne

New York   Oxford
OXFORD UNIVERSITY PRESS
1991

Oxford University Press

Oxford   New York   Toronto
Delhi   Bombay   Calcutta   Madras   Karachi
Petaling Jaya   Singapore   Hong Kong   Tokyo
Nairobi   Dar es Salaam   Cape Town
Melbourne   Auckland

and associated companies in
Berlin   Ibadan

Library of Congress Cataloging-in-Publication Data
LeDonne, John P., 1935–
Absolutism and ruling class : the formation of the Russian
political order, 1700–1825 / John P. LeDonne.
p.   cm. Includes bibliographical references and index.
ISBN 0-19-506805-X
1. Soviet Union—Politics and government—1689–1800.
2. Soviet Union—Politics and government—1801–1825.
3. Despotism.   4. Political leadership—Soviet Union—History—18th century.
5. Political leadership—Soviet Union—History—19th century.
I. Title.   DK127.L43   1991
306.2'0947—dc20   90-20057

9 8 7 6 5 4 3 2 1

Printed in the United States of America
on acid-free paper

For MYROSLAVA

PREFACE

This book studies the social foundations of the modern Russian political order during its long formative period from the sudden emergence of Russia on the stage of European politics at the beginning of the eighteenth century to the consolidation of its position as the dominant European power after the victory over Napoleon. It also raises some questions about the traditional approach to the study of Russian political history. There is still a certain static quality about much of Western scholarship because the importance of the ruler has been overemphasized and that of the ruling class, which alone could make his power effective, has been neglected. The ruler is seen as the authority that not only formalized long-term policy but also made it. Various authors have challenged this view in one form or another,[1] and I have shown in an earlier book[2] that Catherine's great reforms served above all the selfish interests of the nobility rather than the higher precepts of enlightened absolutism propagated by hardworking monarchs in the name of Reason.

The need remains, however, for a systematic study of Russian political institutions in the eighteenth century as the resultant of social, economic, and cultural forces over which the autocrats had little or no influence. It is necessary to study the methods by which they ruled and the purpose of their rule, and this cannot be done without an awareness of the issues involved in making and carrying out policy. I have presented some of them in *Ruling Russia*, and it is now my task to discuss these same issues in the much broader context of an entire century during which three major reforms sought to institutionalize a consensus between ruler and ruling class. Peter's reforms created a remarkable system of central and local agencies, but the local infrastructure was dismantled after his death. Catherine's reforms spread an elaborate provincial structure but closed most central agencies. Finally, Alexander's reforms built a new and permanent edifice of central agencies on the foundation of Catherine's local agencies that lasted, with significant changes in the 1860s, until the Revolution.

One of the major issues to be faced is the need to acknowledge the existence of a Russian ruling class. The legacy of a concept of Russian history in which the autocrat, whether a great man, a mental weakling, a child, or a woman, even a foreigner, exercised absolute power has been oppressive in defiance of common sense. It is seldom, if ever, asked whether the service class of the history books, denigrated as a servile class, was not in fact the ruling class of the country. Servility to the principle of autocracy there undoubtedly was, but it worked as a faith capable of turning a heterogeneous nobility into a powerful ruling class governing a dependent population with a no less despotic control.

Humility and arrogance all too often go together; so do servility and unrestrained power.

I choose the term *ruling class* rather than *ruling elite* because of its wider implications as a numerically much larger social group, even if it constituted an insignificant proportion of the total population. The concept is not new, of course. Plato and Aristotle used it; Gaetano Mosca was its major exponent in the 1890s; Klyuchevskii and Miliukov had no doubt that Russia had its ruling class; and it has informed a number of recently published essays on Athenian, Roman, and British society.[3] Suzanne Keller defines a ruling class as "a group of families who have more or less monopolized access to the most important elite positions of society and who are able to transmit their rewards and opportunities to their descendants, thereby dominating society in the present as well as in the future."[4] I define it in this book as a social group with a definite function to perform, which is to rule; with privileges giving it a status sharply different from the rest of the population; with a consciousness of its privileged status and leadership function; and one in which internal unity is maintained by de-emphasizing professionalism and occupational separateness and emphasizing the primacy of power unlimited by law, both between superior and subordinate within the ruling class and above all in relations between ruling class and dependent population. I include in the Russian ruling class of the late seventeenth century what Richard Hellie calls the "upper service class" and the "middle service class,"[5] and in that of the eighteenth century what is usually called the hereditary nobility. I reserve the term *ruling elite* for the top stratum of the ruling class, as we shall see in Part 1, that is, for those individuals in the landowning nobility and the political apparatus whose agreement on the foundations of the social and political order was not only a prerequisite to the maintenance of order and stability but a crucial ingredient of the consensus without which the ruler's will could not be translated into effective policy.

Robert Dahl has addressed searching questions to the supporters of the ruling class theory in a modern democracy, and Robert Aron and Suzanne Keller have been careful to distinguish between these societies and either preindustrial societies or modern dictatorships.[6] The ruling class theory is perhaps more applicable to preindustrial Russia than to any other similar society because of its association with a highly centralized system of administration, the prevalence of military values, the combined ownership of land and human beings, and the inseparability of the public function from private considerations by individuals, clans, and patronage networks. As a result, the resources of the treasury were kept accessible for private gain, and private activities were associated, if not actually identified, with the exercise of public power. The ruling class of the Russian Empire well into the reign of Nicholas I was coterminous with its civil society, sharply distinguished from the dependent population by the fact that only membership in the hereditary nobility gave a monopoly on the ownership of human beings and a quasi-monopoly on the ownership of land as well as access to positions endowed with public power.[7] It thus met Dahl's basic test—a well-defined group that made its will prevail in any contest with any group in the dependent population from which, it must be emphasized, it continued to co-opt some of its members in order to maintain the legitimacy of its rule.

It is no less important to refine our concept of bureaucracy. If it is possible to raise the question whether a bureaucracy can exist in a Communist political system, it is surely worth asking whether one existed in eighteenth-century Russia.[8] Bureaucracy is a concept used indiscriminately in Western and Soviet scholarship alike to include anyone occupying an official post, although, strangely enough, it seldom includes army officers. The son of a modest and despised priest or merchant is a bureaucrat; so is a Potemkin or a Zubov. Mikhail Safonov even refers to a "bureaucracy of grandees" (*vel'mozhnaia biurokratiia*) as if the combination were not a contradiction in terms.[9] From this indiscriminate lumping of offspring of various origins in a single organizational construct, unjustified and misleading conclusions have been drawn about the nature of political power in Russia.

A bureaucracy requires the existence of a certain social homogeneity; the recognition of rights and duties among superior and subordinate alike; a clear system of appointments and promotions, with a salary pegged to each rank; full-time work by its members; and insulation from political interference capable of playing havoc in the name of sudden imperatives disdainful of abstract and permanent rules.[10]

If we follow these criteria, we are in a position to reassess our understanding of the Russian bureaucracy. I apply the term only to what I call in Part 1 the secretarial and clerical staff in ungraded positions or in graded positions that did not confer hereditary nobility, and this only with substantial qualifications, the most important being that staff's lack of rights, low social origin and status, and total dependence on the whims of superiors. By contrast, members of the ruling class in graded positions constituted a political apparatus of army officers and political managers to whom few or none of the criteria defining a bureaucracy applied. Therefore, I do not think it is possible to characterize the Russian imperial government in the eighteenth century as a bureaucracy. It was instead a highly political system in which relationships were not dominated by external and formal criteria but by highly personal ones, subject to the vicissitudes of the politics of patronage groups. In view of the considerable privatization of public power at the time, I have called the secretaries and clerks the collective household staff of the ruling class.[11]

Russian absolutism as a system of government came into its own in the seventeenth century. The preceding century had marked the completion of the territorial integration of principalities and republics under the political hegemony of Moscow, but the violence that attended the reign of Ivan IV showed how insecure the ruler's position remained and how essential was the destruction of all political opposition before reality could be said to match the theory of autocracy. The disintegration of the political order after the tsar's death, however, showed forcefully that an autocracy without an adequate social base was a house of cards. A social base was necessary to provide the legitimacy without which no ruler could operate, and it established, by its very existence, a political program giving the exercise of power a purpose and a limit. The early steps taken in the sixteenth century, notably the allocations of *pomest'ia* and the restriction of the peasantry's freedom of movement, remained too narrow in scope and had been overshadowed by the political struggle over the supremacy of the ruling house.

The new Romanov dynasty embarked on a forceful program of action to consolidate its position. The double marriages of the first two tsars and the marriage of the third brought into the inner sanctum of power families that became the core of extended political families around which patronage networks grew to form the building blocks of Russian politics for more than a century. The massive allocation of *pomest'ia* by pretenders to the throne and by the Romanovs after 1613 was designed to reward and to recruit supporters, and implanted the social base in every corner of the realm, a calculated endeavor to share the spoils of victory reminiscent of the princely *druzhina* of old who rewarded loyalty with land and positions. In the seventeenth century, however, landowners had their own interests—to bind the peasantry to their properties if not to their persons in a country where the population density was three or four persons per square kilometer while it had already reached forty in contemporary France.[12] A convergence thus naturally developed between a dynasty seeking a social base to make its power effective and landowners in need of central government support to protect their holdings, enserf the peasantry, and subjugate the towns. The pact binding ruling class and autocracy in the *Ulozhenie* of 1649 formed the foundation of Russian absolutism until the abolition of serfdom in 1861.

In 1649 the Romanovs earned the legitimacy of autocratic rule by recognizing the land grants made by their predecessors, continuing the policy of allocating *pomest'ia*, and accepting the transformation of the conditional grants into permanent tenures: *pomest'ia* and *votchiny*, both liable to service obligations, became interchangeable. The formal abolition of the legal distinction between them in 1714 revealed that Russian absolutism was grounded on the private property of the ruling class, even though the traditional refusal to recognize private property in land continued to compete with the new policy and remained a source of tension between the ruling house and the ruling class until the 1750s.[13] Moreover, the ruling class won from the autocracy the confirmation of earlier decrees banning all peasant movement until further notice and the abrogation of time limits beyond which fugitive peasants would no longer be returned to their owners, an issue that had pitted great landowners against small holders, the former eager to populate their extensive properties with the fugitive peasants of their less-endowed brethren.[14] The freezing of the social order resulted in the strangulation of towns and the subjugation of the urban population to the economic power of the landowners.[15] It also established an unshakable bond between the autocracy and the ruling class and made both prisoners of the same social order.[16] Common interests precluded the ruling class from ever challenging the autocracy of the ruling house.

The turbulence of seventeenth-century social history challenges at first glance this picture of relative unity in the ruling class, but Novoselskii has discovered a process of "interpenetration" between the upper and middle service classes that transformed them into a nobility conscious of its privileges.[17] Complaints against the greed and violence of "the strong" were manifestations not only of intense competition for landed property and peasants but also of an anxious search for an identity that could be acquired only by sharply demarcating the ruling class from those immediately under it—the so-called lower service class of *streltsy* and others—who had to be relegated to the dependent population. This is what Richard Hellie calls "the conscious rise of the middle service class."[18] In this process the upper service class began to fan out from Moscow into the districts, but the middle service class moved to Moscow in increasing numbers, while claiming to be dispossessed. These new parvenus pressured the government to dispossess in turn petty landowners outside the middle service class—the so-called *odnodvortsy*—and complete their juridical separation from the ruling class by subjecting them to taxation in kind and money from which the ruling class had gained exemption. The essential point is that disagreements, even conflicts, within the ruling class were not over key political choices, and social mobility did not bring outsiders ready to challenge the compact between absolutism and serfdom but, on the contrary, outsiders who insisted on strengthening both.

The dispersion of the ruling class across a vast and constantly expanding territory necessitated, for both the protection of the landowners and the effectiveness of autocratic rule, a vertical integration of the ruling class into a command structure run along military lines. The militarization of the ruling class already had a long history, but it was reinforced in the seventeenth century by the fact that an essential element of the program of Russian absolutism was to roll back the Swedes and the Poles, against whom the very founding of the Romanov dynasty had been an act of national defiance. Both were better equipped and better trained than the Russians, and both were heretics. A program of military westernization was therefore a fundamental necessity. At the same time, the progressive breakdown of the "symphony" between the Orthodox church and the ruling house to the latter's benefit heightened a political intolerance facilitating the integration and the development of a consensus in spite of the assertion by the ruling class of its dominion over the dependent population. Centralized agencies (*prikazy*) created in the preceding century and voevodas of military origin carried out all over the country the terms of the compact: the maintenance of serfdom in return for the intensification of taxation and the building of a military machine that both strengthened the autocracy and promised an undiminished abundance of spoils. These *prikazy*, run at first by secretaries managing the properties of the ruling house, became the executive agencies of tsar and ruling class, and were led in the seventeenth century by members of its top stratum, who were often the tsar's relatives.

The systematic buildup of Russian absolutism inevitably caused strains in church and ruling class. The Treaty of Westphalia, signed 1 year before the publication of the *Ulozhenie*, confirmed the supremacy of Sweden in the Germanies, and Charles XI (1660–1697) proceeded to integrate in a centralized

Swedish empire the Baltic provinces over which the Russians had fought a bloody war under Ivan IV. The Thirteen Years' War with Poland (1654–1667) ended with what might rightly be called the country's first partition.[19] To achieve this success and prepare for what loomed as an inevitable showdown with Sweden, a mercenary army of foreigners rendered increasingly obsolete the heavy cavalry of the ruling class mobilized in emergencies to cope with Tatar raids. The creation of a separate and alien military establishment[20] within the ruling class became a threat to the unity of that class and to its compact with the ruling house. Moreover, these preparations for war brought into the country foreign and heretical influences that encountered the xenophobic intolerance of church and ruling class, contributed to the Schism, and forced nobles to face the challenge to their ignorance and self-righteousness. These strains also brought into question the ability of the *prikazy* to improve the efficiency of absolutism beyond a certain point. Some *prikazy* were closed or consolidated under the guidance of a small number of boyars, but their top-heavy edifice contrasted unfavorably with the undeveloped structure of local government.

Such were the factors that led to the crisis of the 1690s, to which Marc Raeff and James Cracraft have drawn attention.[21] The concept of crisis is not to be understood in apocalyptic terms, as the collapse of a traditional world of values and the revelation of a new one, but rather as the emergence of a consensus that the traditional order had become inadequate to cope with the new tasks imposed by circumstances, and that the resulting strains must be overcome to prevent the destruction of the political and social compact that guaranteed the legitimacy of the ruling house and the ruling class. The task facing Russian absolutism on the eve of a long war with Sweden was to create a "redeployed and recharged apparatus"[22] of domination, and it called for the masterful leadership of a great tsar.

The long century from 1700 to 1825 presents a considerable internal unity. It began with a reaffirmation of the compact between ruling house and ruling class. Early defeat in war called for a general mobilization of the ruling class to staff the officer corps of a conscript army; foreigners were swamped in a native force of noblemen and commoners. As reward for answering the call to serve for life under the leadership of a tsar who claimed unlimited power to govern as his conscience alone dictated, the ruling class subjected the peasantry to a rigorous census that extended and systematized the serfdom declared half a century earlier to be the foundation of the new order. The compact between Peter and a ruling class in full expansion affirmed the latter's duty to support the great cause of national construction through which Russian absolutism forced its way into the concert of European nations and began to share in its growing enlightenment. The tsar's example generated what was called during the contemporary reign of Louis XIV a "contagion of obedience"[23] in which the majesty of the ruler devolved upon every member of the ruling class, despite the inevitable tension between the impetuosity of the ruler and the cautiousness of the ruling class.

After Peter's death, rights began to gain ascendancy over duties, as his successors lacked his drive and charisma, and changed circumstances favored relaxation and brought to the ruling class the stimulation of Western thought and the comforts of Western enterprise. Catherine's reign was one in which the rule of a woman and a foreigner was accepted in return for the full acceptance of private property in land, the ultimate intensification of serfdom, and expansion into neighboring states. Her reign marked the "golden age of reconciliation"[24] between the ruling house and the ruling class, and left an indelible memory in the political consciousness of the ruling class. All the promises of the *Ulozhenie* were finally realized. But it also dangerously shifted the center of gravity from the national capital to regional headquarters of army and civilian administration, and it is undeniable that a new crisis was brewing at the end of her reign.

That is why Paul's reign was a logical outgrowth of his mother's, despite the sharp contrasts between them. Alexander was faced with a task similar to that which his great ancestor had successfully solved: to reaffirm the compact with the ruling class in order to harness its energies and intensify absolutism to cope with that of Napoleonic France. By then, however, the terms of the contract had changed. There was nothing left to be gained from serfdom, and voices were already heard against its immorality and inefficiency.[25] The ruler could only offer commissions in a rapidly expanding army and positions in a newly centralized civilian apparatus whose size compelled bureaucratization. With the reign of Alexander, the old network of families that had governed Russia for more than a century began to disintegrate, and a serfdom without growth potential could no longer hold together ruling house and ruling class. An estrangement between the two slowly but inexorably began, which ultimately undermined their legitimacy and destroyed both in the same cataclysm.

This book traces the evolution of Russian government in the long century during which Russia completed the transition from a medieval to a modern political order. Part 1 describes the constituent elements of Russian society and its political apparatus, and offers a model of that society as a command structure led by a ruling class. Part 2 analyzes the reforms of the central government and local administration and the impact of military reforms on these changes during the reigns of Peter, the empresses, and Alexander. Each of the next three parts begins with a description of central and local agencies. Special attention is devoted to an analysis of the concept of police in Russia and to the scope of its authority in Part 3, to penal and civil law in Part 4; only the briefest exposition of civil law is feasible, but it provides a starting point for the study of this completely neglected field. The book concludes with an analysis of taxation and budget making, two areas also potentially rich in insights into the nature of Russian society and government, yet completely ignored in Western scholarship.

Much of the research is based on the Collection of Laws of the Russian Empire (First Series, 1649–1825). There exists a strange misperception that the collection contains chiefly normative acts of no great use to students eager to learn how institutions really worked. This is true for most of the documents published after the 1810s, but it is certainly not the case for eighteenth-century documents. Many of these consist of Senate reports to the ruler. They present not only the essentials of an issue but often contain considerable factual material as well. Some even give a historical survey describing how past intentions were never realized. My research is supplemented with references from other collections, likewise seldom used, such as the *Russkii Arkhiv* and *Russkaia Starina*, which published either archival documents or articles based on them, including provincial archives. Taken together, this political–administrative and "existential" material constitutes a fully adequate base for a work of this scope. A few unpublished archival references have been used to support some specific points.[26]

It has been my good fortune to know Marc Raeff, the founder of eighteenth-century Russian studies in this country, and to be able to discuss with him on many occasions a number of essential questions to which I seek an answer in this book. I have benefited immensely from his encyclopedic knowledge of European history, from his friendly encouragement in times of doubt, and his readiness to give new interpretations a generous hearing. To him and to Istvan Deak I extend special thanks for recommending me to Oxford University Press. I am greatly indebted to Edward Keenan, always ready to challenge established ideas and open up new vistas, and to Richard Wortman for his pertinent and incisive comments. My thanks also go out to other scholars who have read the manuscript and made valuable comments: James Cracraft, Gregory Freeze, and George Yaney.

This book could not have been written without financial support from the Harriman Institute at Columbia University; from the Guggenheim Foundation; and from the Kennan Institute, Wilson Center, Washington. I owe a special debt of gratitude to the Russian Research Center at Harvard University, which has also given me a home, to its director, Adam Ulam, associate director, Marshall Goldman, and administrative officer, Mary Towle. The manuscript was efficiently typed by Rose DiBenedetto, Christine Porto, and Michele Wong. Last but not least, its quality was much enhanced by the dedicated editorial work of Ruth Mathewson and Charles McAndrew. To all these individuals and institutions I extend my heartfelt thanks.

Cambridge, Mass.   J. P. L.
November 1990

CONTENTS

I

SOCIETY

1

The Structure of Russian Society

The Nobility as Ruling Class

Eighteenth-century Russian society was dominated by a small and conspicuous ruling class, enjoying a monopoly over the exercise of political power. The monopoly was buttressed by privileges that conferred status upon the ruling class and sustained an awareness of its mission. Access to the ruling class, restricted and broadened in accordance with circumstances and the perception of needs, remained open to members of a dependent population consisting of clergy, townsmen, and peasants. Their upward mobility kept rejuvenating the ruling class and legitimizing the exercise of its power. Russian society was thus a command structure in which the ruling class collectively owned half the population and controlled the destiny of the other half, exercising its power through the agency of interconnected patronage networks, and governed the dependent population in pursuance of selfish ends, the maintenance of the status quo, and the maximization of military power.

It has been a recurrent theme in Russian historiography that the nobility was a service nobility, but the wrong conclusions have been drawn from this indubitable fact. To emphasize the nobility's bondage to service is also to define it as a political class. Serving the ruling house was the core of its ideology, but identification with a patron and integration into a patronage network were the essence of a nobleman's politics. Hereditary nobles alone were members of the ruling class, citizens of a Russian political order whose characteristic, to paraphrase Aristotle, was to share in the administration of justice and in other civic offices, while townsmen and peasants and even clergy were merely the servants of that order, excluded from membership in it.[1]

The exercise of power was in no way directed against the ruler and could not be, since there existed no widely perceived and fundamental conflict of interest between the ruling house and the ruling class, both deriving their material well-being from the exploitation of the dependent population, unrestrained by moral considerations, although occasionally toned down by a healthy understanding of their self-interest. Disputes were settled by considerations of the litigants' positions in the hierarchy; taxation was almost exclusively the burden of townsmen and peasants. If there was an unwritten contract between ruler and ruling class until well into the nineteenth century, the same

3

obtained between ruling class and dependent population. The permanence of a
social and political consensus gave the exercise of power the harshness and
cynicism[2] that were the hallmark of Russian politics during the eighteenth
century and well beyond the reign of Alexander I.

This power was exercised with little distinction between public and private
interests.[3] Landowners, if they resided on their estates, stewards if they did not,
together with their secretaries and clerks, possessed over the serfs, even if
custom and self-interest dictated caution, the full power to try, to punish, to
tax, and even to interfere in their most private lives. Members of the apparatus,
given command over the remainder of the peasant population and over townsmen, treated their charges with the same mixture of paternalism, brutality, and
greed. Consensus and political unity at the top blocked any challenge to the
exercise of power at lower levels, save running away and outright rebellion,
both marginal phenomena.

The ruling class at the end of the seventeenth century consisted of an
apparatus in which military and civil functions were not yet clearly distinguished and a political infrastructure of serf owners residing in provinces and
uezds.[4] This political infrastructure was approaching a stage of consolidation
after a full century of turmoil when it was drastically shaken by Peter's policies
and transformed into a new military apparatus, leaving the country bereft of
any political presence. It gradually reconstituted itself during the two generations following Peter's death and crystallized in the 1780s, when the reforms
created a political machinery of elected landowners to supplement a now
extensive civilian apparatus.

The ruling class, in turn, was arranged on three concentric levels, cutting
across the military and civilian establishments as well as the political infrastructure. Its leading group included the high command of the army (marshals,
generals, and lieutenant generals) and the civilian high command of senators
and ministers (real privy councillors and privy councillors), all in grades one
down to three. This leading group also included landowners owning more than
100 male serfs. It has been estimated that 5,636 landowners, or 8.7 percent of
the total, owned 1.7 million serfs, or 58.9 percent of the total, in the 1720s. By
the 1770s this top layer of landowners had grown to perhaps 8,000, or 16
percent of the total, owning more than 80 percent of the serfs. In 1834 some
13,170 serf owners, still 16 percent of the total, still owned 80 percent of the
serfs.[5] These three elements in the leading group naturally overlapped, since
most high-ranking officers and civilians were large landowners as well. One
should also include here members of court families without landed properties.
Lacking a complete list of the members of this group, I estimate that they
numbered fewer than 6,000 individuals in the 1720s, about 8,500 in the 1770s,
and some 14,500 in the 1820s. I shall call it the ruling elite of Russian politics.

The second level included the managerial staff of the ruling class in positions graded four to eight. The upper-management people were in grades four
to six: majors general who commanded several regiments and colonels who
commanded regiments; presidents of colleges, governors, and members of
colleges and chambers after the reforms of the 1770s. Lower-management

positions in grades seven and eight were filled by field officers in the regiments and voevodas who managed towns and uezds. Landowners owning between 20 and 100 serfs must be included here. The third level included the battalion and company staffs and landowners with fewer than 20 serfs.[6] They had no equivalent in the civilian establishment but they often filled police and supervisory positions after transferring from active military service. Here again there was considerable overlapping, with many members of the apparatus having no land in the early nineteenth century and large landowners having ranks below those their economic standing would require. Any individual entered the ruling class when he received the appropriate rank—fourteen in the army or eight in the civilian apparatus—but any landowner was ipso facto a member of the ruling class because he shared in the exercise of power of which his class had a monopoly, and access to the officer corps and the civilian apparatus was guaranteed if he chose to seek it.

The ruling class and upper-management positions belonged to the direct patronage network of the ruler. He appointed members of the elite just as the medieval prince had once appointed his *druzhina* but in the eighteenth century often from families related to the Romanov house, and the managers on the recommendation of the ruling elite. The delegates of the elite in the College of War and the Senate appointed in turn to lower-management positions as well as the battalion and company staffs and the police apparatus in town and countryside.

The nobility was the ruling class of the empire not only because it fulfilled a definite function—the exclusive exercise of political power—but also because it possessed a status corresponding to its mission and a consciousness of its leadership role. Status is the right to certain privileges, and the distinguishing mark of the hereditary nobleman was the right to own serfs. The allotment of inhabited land (*derevni*) in conditional tenure—the *pomest'e* system—both as a reward for past service and as an inducement for outsiders to join the apparatus, was premised upon a fundamental assumption that membership in the ruling class gave a prescriptive right to own the peasants settled on that land. Indeed, the ownership of human beings became such a status symbol of the ruling class that successful entrepreneurs from the dependent population who could gain access to it sought to obtain the privilege as a mark of social distinction.[7]

This privilege was hardly ever granted to other than members of the ruling class. *Gosti* were forbidden to own serfs after 1666. Factory owners obtained permission in 1721 to bind serfs to their factories, but these serfs did not become the personal property of the owners. However, the absence of separate courts until the 1780s, the politicization of justice, and the conceptual confusion in the law of property fostered widespread evasion. We learn from the imperial order of October 1730—which forbade the practice—that even peasants had been buying, selling, and mortgaging land and serfs. Holders of positions below grade eight—except secretaries—were forbidden in February 1758 to own inhabited land, and the charter of April 1785, which created the new category of personal nobles, renewed the prohibition. Ownership was observed in the breach, however, and it was found necessary to insist in the Digest of 1832 that purchases of serfs by merchants and personal nobles after October 1804 and June 1814, respectively, were null and void.[8]

From this exclusive right to own serfs there followed important economic advantages and privileges. The original purpose of the *pomest'e* had been to guarantee the nobleman an income sufficient to provide for his military equipment, his retinue, and a standard of living corresponding to his standing in the apparatus. The justification of serfdom was to facilitate the exploitation of the peasantry in order to finance the cost of "westernization." The growth of the economy throughout the eighteenth century was accompanied by an intensification of serfdom, and the demobilization of the ruling class at a time when the grain trade was being liberalized and a decade after the abolition of internal custom duties set the stage for the expansion of corvée labor and the demesne economy.[9]

These advantages were strengthened by the imperial order of March 1762, which granted the nobility the monopolistic right to the labor of serfs, a right shared since 1721 with factory owners; and by the decrees of June and September 1782, which awarded the nobility the ownership and unrestricted use of minerals and forests on their properties.[10] The government's economic policy during the reign of Catherine was directed at enhancing the economic status of the nobility vis-à-vis the dependent population at a time when capitalism was beginning to penetrate the countryside. At a time when free or hired labor had not yet developed as an effective competitor of serf labor, the ownership of serfs, land, and resources gave the nobility an enormous advantage. Flax, hemp, wool, and hides were processed on the estates, and transportation to the market was part of the corvée obligations.

Although the development of such a large country was bound to benefit more than the numerically insignificant ruling class, the enhanced status of the nobility left the enterprising members of the population at a severe disadvantage. The Noble Charter of April 1785 confirmed the privileged position of the nobility in the economic life of the country.[11] The growth of a self-sufficient manorial economy stifled the growth of an urban economy, and nobles capable of engaging in the wholesale trade of their production had to register in the appropriate guilds, where they competed with the less-favored merchants. We can be sure, then, that merchants with sufficient capital and respectability would wish to escape from that dependent status and seek a patent of nobility as a reward for services rendered to the crown, chiefly by offering favorable terms in government contracts and by intermarriage with noblemen.

Not all landowners had the means to engage in large-scale agricultural and industrial production, but almost all could benefit from the monopoly over the production of vodka given to landowners in July 1754.[12] The sale of vodka provided a ready source of cash, perhaps the single most important source in a nobleman's life, and conspicuous consumption in pursuit of westernization reinforced his status vis-à-vis non-nobles. As vodka producers, noblemen also served as tax agents of their treasury. The vodka delivered to government-owned stores was then sold to the dependent population, including their own serfs. Finally, they were exempt from the capitation, which became, as the century wore on, the badge of social disfranchisement, but they collected it from their serfs together with the quitrent, which they kept for themselves, while their brethren in the apparatus collected both capitation and quitrent from the state peasantry.

Thus, the advantages derived by the hereditary nobility from its monopoly over serf labor and the privileges it assumed to maintain this monopoly gave it the status of a ruling class. These economic privileges were accompanied by judicial privileges. Immunity from corporal punishment was granted by the charters of 1785. It was also given to merchants in the first two guilds, but a nobleman could be tried only by his peers, that is, by other members of the ruling class—while everyone else was tried by noblemen—and could be expelled from the ruling class for criminal actions only by the ruler's personal decision.[13]

It is difficult to accept a certain historical interpretation that the seventeenth-century nobility was not conscious of its leadership role. It is true, as Turgot wrote in his eloquent memorandum of 1775 to Louis XVI, that the society of his day—and this would have been even truer in the preceding century—was one in which cross-sectional ties were little developed, leaving everyone absorbed in his own interests and engaged in a "perpetual war of claims and undertakings," without any concept of common interest.[14] This very absorption in parochial interests, however, was evidence of an awareness of distinct interests and of a standing vis-à-vis other social elements in need of recognition and protection. Girgorii Kotoshikhin recognized this much in the 1660s when he wrote in passing that service gave freedom from "slavery and peasantry,"—that is, that joining the ruling class gave a freedom enjoyed by no one else. The upsurge of the nobility—a pan-European phenomenon in the eighteenth century—proceeded from this fundamental assumption and reflected the growth of class cohesiveness.[15]

Three assumptions shaped the consciousness of a member of the ruling class: that his position did not depend on education and competence, even though these might be useful, because its only justification was the exercise of power; that each member must have his own particular empire, a definite area allotted to his responsibility; and that he must exercise utmost power over this empire.[16] There developed as a result a common language among members of the ruling class, imbued with pride of place and the conviction that their parochial interests alone were of national significance.

To serve—that is, to be assigned tasks that gave control over men—was less a stifling obligation than the justification of a nobleman's existence.[17] The seventeenth-century boyar said he would rather be dead than be without a charge (*to im smert', chto im bez mest byt'*), and the poet Derzhavin found it offensive and depressing a century later to be kept out of the government (*ne u del*).[18] This perception of constituting the ruling class of the country was strengthened by the knowledge that the nobility had always been a social formation with a military mission wrapped inside a political function. The

Noble Charter praised the nobility for learning discipline and assuming the habit of command, and Alexander's policy of restricting access to the officer corps by non-nobles emphasized that field (*stroevye*) officers—those who commanded troops distinguished from those in the supply services—must be of noble origin. A nobleman thus served primarily in the army, where he exercised unconditional power over noble subordinates and peasant soldiers; or he served in the civilian apparatus, where he exercised a similar power over the dependent population; or remained on his estate, where his power over his serfs was nearly absolute.

The emphasis on the exercise of power created a certain ambivalence toward education and training. The eighteenth-century nobility was not known for its eagerness to master the liberal arts and sciences. It was drawn to foreign language because French and German provided a code common to the entire ruling class, unintelligible to the dependent population, and the Corps of Cadets intended for noblemen taught dancing and fencing as well as mathematics and natural sciences. As late as Alexander's reign, few nobles attended Moscow University, and none taught there; Karamzin, in his poem entitled "A Phenomenon," recognized Grigorii Glinka's appointment as the first noble professor of Russian. In the provinces, nobles still considered ignorance and boorishness as their birthright at the beginning of the nineteenth century and openly claimed they cared little about scholars since nothing was better than Holy Russia, a clear statement of the preeminence of politics over intellectual life.[19]

If foreign languages provided a code for members of the ruling class to communicate among themselves, fashions likewise gradually set the nobility apart and sharpened the consciousness of its superiority. The shaving of beards—even if it encountered resistance among the conservatives—was a traumatic departure from tradition, the symbolic postscript to the mobilization of the ruling class to bring Russia into the modern world. Western dress, balls, the mixed company of men and women in society, and travel abroad all helped in time to uproot the ruling class and even to alienate it from a world once held in common with the dependent population. Enhanced consciousness brought arrogance and deepened contempt, and by the end of serfdom every squire, in the passionate words of the priest Belliustin, regarded himself as an aristocrat to whom all must subordinate themselves, who treated his hunting dogs better than his peasants, and whose "horrendous vanity" it was dangerous to expose because "landlords scream loudly and their voices can easily carry all the way to St. Petersburg." Townsmen were likewise dismissed as so many *muzhiki* in urban garb.[20]

But the consciousness of separateness had been rising among other social groups as well. The *nakazy* of the 1760s already expressed class antagonism against merchants and factory owners, an antagonism reflecting the perception that a conflict was emerging over resources and access to capital. Some contemporaries sensed the tension, and one wrote that even to banish a general and a merchant in the same *kibitka* was an affront to the nobility's pride.[21]

The exercise of power by the ruling class—through subtle patronage networks, unrestrained by institutions—was also challenged by an influx of priests' and merchants' sons into the personal nobility and by their pressure to obtain access to the military and civilian apparatus, a pressure that another long period of war and the increasing complexity of administrative tasks made difficult to contain. The *nakazy* already reflected the resentment of the apparatus at the intrusion of these despised effluences from the dependent population,[22] and the decree of August 1809, claiming that a certain level of education must determine access to the higher levels, was a slap at one of its most cherished beliefs. The fall of Speranskii and the "aristocratic" reaction represented the counterattack of a ruling elite on the defensive against a policy of bureaucratization the ministries were in the process of launching.

Ruling Class and Society

The Russian ruling class was not a caste, and serfdom did not preclude social mobility. Quantitative studies are almost nonexistent, but there is enough evidence to suggest that the ruling class rejuvenated itself by the constant assimilation of individuals from the urban population and from the peasantry, as well as from the borderlands. Caste-forming tendencies may have been at work toward the end of the seventeenth century,[23] and a similar claim may perhaps be made for the end of Nicholas I's reign. In both cases, however, these tendencies emerged on the eve of a social upheaval that accelerated social mobility and must be seen as exceptions confirming the general rule that Russian society from the reign of Peter to that of Alexander I remained remarkably free from debilitating social prejudices capable of undermining the legitimacy of the nobility as its ruling class.

The Romanov house led the way. If marriages with Dolgorukovs and even Apraksins and Saltykovs were unions befitting a royal family, those with Streshnevs, Naryshkins and Lopukhins would have been misalliances by the standards of French and English royalty. Women of noble but modest means were brought into the ruling house along with their relatives and protégés, who, in due time, joined the ranks of the ruling elite. Tsar Peter married a servant girl captured in the camp of the enemy who had first been the booty of Menshikov, his closest collaborator. Favorites, as a rule, were no exception. Biron's father had been a mere cornet in Polish service; Razumovskii was the grandson of a rank-and-file cossack; Orlov, Potemkin, and Zubov belonged to undistinguished provincial families. Only with Paul did Russian tsars begin to shun their nobility—thus paving the way for their own ultimate isolation—and marry into European families of royal or princely blood.

The nobility likewise did not disdain its social inferiors when interests and feelings were involved. Toward the end of the eighteenth century, Fedor Tolstoi (great-grandson of Petr Tolstoi, one of the leading figures of Peter I's reign) married Stepanida Durasova, the daughter of a Moscow Old Believer merchant. The wife of Guard major Gerasim Skvortsov in the 1770s was the daughter of a Pskov merchant.[24] Nobles married peasant women as well. This is all the more remarkable since concubinage was rampant in the countryside, and lords all too often took advantage of the powers serfdom gave them over the serf population. Mikhail Apukhtin, for example, grandson of a *stolnik* (1686–1692), who had been granted estates in what later became Orel gubernia, married there in the 1760s one of his serf girls—but later committed bigamy with another woman. A former page, expelled from the court for some offense, lived in Kursk gubernia in the 1810s married to a "common woman." The most famous of these marriages with serf women was that of Nikolai Sheremetev, chamberlain, senator, and former director of the Bank for the Nobility, well known for the serf theatrical troupe he gathered on his Moscow property; in 1800 he married its most beautiful actress, whose portrait can still be seen on the walls of the theater.[25]

How often these marriages took place is difficult to say, but they were not rare, as we learn from an 1807 decision referring to the doubts "often" encountered by the Senate about the legal status of peasant women who had married noblemen and later married non-noblemen husbands. Under the law, a man gave his status to his wife. A nobleman's wife who was not of noble origin thus automatically became noble. The Noble Charter of 1785 had provided that noble status, that is, membership in the ruling class, could be lost only as a result of a criminal sentence confirmed by the ruler. The imperial order of December 1807 allowed such noblewomen to retain their status but upheld the prohibition against transferring it to their second husbands and to their children by the second marriage.[26]

Access to the ruling class was also granted by the ruler as a favor to successful merchants who had contributed substantial sums to its treasury in the form of deliveries of goods at lower than market prices or, increasingly, in the form of higher bids for government contracts, chiefly to sell vodka. The Stroganovs, patrons of the arts under Alexander I and relatives of the Romanovs, were descendants of a prosperous merchant (*imenityi chelovek*). The Demidovs were descendants of a family of industrialists from Tula who also made a fortune in the Urals. The practice of bringing merchants—themselves former peasants of recent memory—into the ruling class accelerated under Elizabeth and continued under Catherine, when merchants' sons were admitted into the Guard regiments or when their fathers got decorations, like the Cross of Saint Vladimir. At the end of the eighteenth century, ennobled merchants owned two-thirds of the enterprises and produced more than half of the copper and over two-thirds of the pig iron. Vodka farmers were often ennobled—a process that sapped the vitality of a nascent bourgeoisie and kept it firmly subordinated to the ruling class.[27]

Such elevation was done on a much wider scale by the nobles themselves. We shall see presently how the military and civilian apparatus provided channels for advancement and opportunities for rejuvenation of the ruling class. The charter of 1785 called upon the nobility in each uezd to elect representatives who would meet in committee under the chairmanship of the gubernia marshal to draw up a register of hereditary nobles in the gubernia. Nobles had to submit evidence of their status; the committee voted to accept it by unanimous vote or by a majority of two-thirds, and the register, once approved by the gubernia assembly, was printed in three copies, one for the archives of the assembly, another for the gubernia board, the third for the Senate's heraldmaster. Patents of nobility, it seems, were issued by the assembly. Abuses, however, soon crept in, as noble assemblies showed little discrimination about the social origins of prospective nobles. In gubernias and uezds where tax farmers were almost the only individuals with a source of ready cash, money must have talked loudly to convince nobles that it was in their interest to accept fraudulent evidence. Moreover, assemblies were not eager to send their registers to Petersburg, if only to protect themselves against disturbing questions. By 1813, however, all but five of the twenty-six gubernias had sent them. Paul, meanwhile, had reasserted, and Alexander confirmed, the autocrat's exclusive right to issue patents of nobility. It is not clear whether his decision had a retroactive effect, making null and void locally issued patents. If it did not, hundreds and perhaps thousands of families had joined the ranks of the nobility without any right to it. At any rate, it was still found necessary as late as 1834 to order a general review of the operations of the membership committee.[28]

Military service in wartime was one of the fastest roads to promotion and social advancement because it provided continual occasion for distinction, and regular casualties among the officers necessitated rapid promotions from below. In Russia, where the ruling class remained in a state of permanent mobilization until the 1760s and the army fought long and costly wars during the reigns of almost every ruler from 1700 to 1815, the officer corps, generation after generation, drew upon the dependent population to replenish its ranks, and by so doing, enhanced its legitimacy and strengthened a general consciousness of its role as the core of the ruling class.

Even before the general mobilization of the ruling class in the 1700s, there had been a constant pressure from below to admit into it people from the dependent population (*tiaglye liudi*) in town and countryside, as well as children of priests. These pressures could not be resisted despite official prohibitions because the growth of the political order and its military establishment neutralized the caste-forming tendencies in an age of social consolidation. The interminable Northern War that began in 1700 and did not officially end until 1721, together with the creation of a standing army of soldiers and officers that developed as a mirror image of Russian society—all officers being noble and almost all soldiers non-noble—intensified pressures for admission into the officer corps. Peter, out of conviction and by necessity, was compelled to emphasize merit revealed in courage on the battlefield and distinction in the exercise of command responsibilities, qualities that recognized no social differences, in Russia or elsewhere.[29]

A sample of the officer corps in 1721 reveals the extent of social promotion within the army. It shows that 62 percent of the officers came from the nobility, another 11 percent from the lower ranks of the old Muscovite army—*streltsy*, cossacks, gunners, and so on, some of them nobles—and 14 percent from other social groups, that is, the dependent population of townsmen and peasants. These figures, however, do not tell the entire story. The contribution of the other social groups to the officer corps in the cavalry was negligible—the Muscovite army had traditionally been a heavy cavalry. In the infantry, however, they contributed 23 percent of the officers, over 30 percent if we add the contribution of the former *streltsy* and similar "old formations" (*starye*, also *preszhnye*, *sluzhby*)—the so-called lower service class of the seventeenth century. It is true that these officers of non-noble origin were all junior officers— only 1 of the 299 was a field officer.[30] Whether their junior status was the result of their recent promotion or of the ruling elite's conscious policy of keeping them in the lower ranks is difficult to say: only a study of their subsequent careers would show whether access to higher officer ranks was open to them. It is nevertheless suggestive of the extent of some social mobility in the army during Peter's reign that nearly a third of the infantry officers were of non-noble origin.

The promotion of non-noble soldiers and noncommissioned officers continued after Peter's death and accelerated during the destructive Crimean campaigns of the 1730s and the bloody battles of the Seven Years' War, when officers killed on the battlefield had to be replaced on the spot by whoever was available and capable, regardless of social origin.[31] Promotions also served to create patronage networks and imposing retinues. The promotion of non-nobles often meant the admission of a second male into the nobility, since the Table of Ranks allowed a new officer to select one of his sons, born before his promotion, to join him in his new status.[32] We know, for example, that the son of a regimental priest, who had become the confessor of Petr Shuvalov, the Chief of the Artillery, was first a sergeant, then a captain, in the artillery and settled down in the 1770s as a landowner in Orel gubernia. A Captain Fedor Bodganov, who incited peasants to revolt in Lifland gubernia in the 1770s, was the son of a miller and was married to a domestic of Count Manteufel. Petr Kotliarevskii, a lieutenant general at 29 and a leading figure in the army of the Caucasus in the 1810s, was the son of a village priest. These examples were no exceptions, as we learn from the nobles of one of the uezds of the future Kaluga gubernia, who complained in 1767 that "many people" from the clerical estate (*pod'iachii chin*) and various other groups had been promoted to junior and field-officer ranks, used their new status to get rich "improperly," then bought villages and peasants and caused great "distress" (*utesnenie*) to the old nobility resenting the arrival of parvenus who claimed social equality with it.[33]

These complaints by the more conservative members of the ruling class had no effect, if only because the strength and legitimacy of that class had always resided in its ability to absorb some of the most capable, ambitious, and ruthless elements of the dependent population. Potemkin's tenure as president of the College of War, replacing the staid and cautious Zakhar Chernyshev and followed by the short and irresponsible rule of the Zubov brothers, was characterized by a generous policy of admitting townsmen and sons of clergy and, most probably, peasants as well, into the officer corps. An Orel merchant, for example, married to the daughter of an Orel priest, was made an officer in the 1780s—a purely formal favor that nevertheless admitted him into the hereditary nobility. Other merchants who had never served at all were given officer ranks following their appointment as adjutants to a general on active service or admission into the Guard. This gave them the right to buy peasants and land and allowed them to retire as landowners. Andrei Abakumov, among other cases, the son of a Toropets merchant, was registered as a noncommissioned officer in the Preobrazhenskii Guard regiment in 1787, was promoted officer, and became in 1816 Chief of Supply of the First Army, then Provisionmaster General.[34]

Paul's decision to concentrate in his chancery all promotions to officer and all grants of patents of nobility was unable to check the constant pressure from below for admission into the officer corps. The power to promote was removed from various commanders in chief, but the tsar became dependent on his inspectors, some of them from the Gatchina officer corps of crude and brutal men, who now began to build their own patronage networks. The situation got so out of hand that Semen Vorontsov, whose aristocratic prejudices may have led him to exaggerate, claimed in March 1802 that officers from the nobility had been replaced by children of innkeepers, postmasters, and petty traders.[35]

Yet it has such an officer corps of captains, lieutenants, and ensigns, whose social composition had undergone a revolutionary transformation, that fought Napoleon's own officer corps, likewise the product of a revolutionary upheaval, at Smolensk, Borodino, and Maloiaroslavets. Fatezh, an insignificant uezd center in Kursk gubernia, a town known until then chiefly for its turnips and its dirt, became famous for the number of shopkeepers (*meshchane*) who entered the officer corps during the war and even became generals, and may have been no exception.[36] The appearance of these new officers promoted from the ranks of simple soldiers struck some contemporaries after the war of 1812. Because they wore epaulettes and some even were majors, they were received by the owners of estates on which their companies were billeted, even though "some were very strange."[37] The restrictive legislation of Alexander's reign, which sought to stem the influx of men from the dependent population into the ruling class, merely succeeded in preventing a flood.

Access to the ruling class by promotion in the civilian apparatus was less welcome and much more difficult. Nevertheless, it is easy to detect in various Senate decisions and imperial orders a sense of resignation at the ruling elite's inability to resist pressures from below. At the same time, the civilian apparatus competed with the army for limited resources, especially after the creation of the colleges in 1718 and the establishment of gubernatorial and voevoda chanceries. The demand was consequently great for clerks and secretaries but was dampened by a reluctance to admit not so much individuals from the dependent population as people required to pay the capitation, once its payment became the symbol of social degradation, and exemption from it—for nobles, clergy, and, after 1775, merchants of the first two guilds—one of social respectability. On the other hand, appointments to clerical and secretarial positions after the introduction of the Table of Ranks gave the ambitious and those capable of joining a patronage network the chance to be promoted eventually to college assessor in grade eight and enter the ruling class. The conflict between the reluctance of the ruling elite, the demand for qualified people, and the eagerness of outsiders to gain privileged status runs through eighteenth-century legislation on social mobility in both the military and the civilian apparatus.

Unease at the growing presence of non-nobles in the secretarial staff must have motivated the imperial order of January 1724 forbidding the appointment of non-nobles to secretarial posts without Senate approval because subsequent promotions practically guaranteed access to the rank of college assessor, and it is difficult to agree with Troitskii's interpretation that it improved the chances of lower-class people to enter the hereditary nobility.[38] If indeed those chances improved, it was in spite of that order. In the 1730s, for example, governors and even voevodas appointed clerks from among people paying the capitation and promoted them for a variety of reasons, including generous bribes, to secretarial positions and even to grade eight. This was forbidden in May 1737 and May 1742, but the shortage of clerks made these prohibitions a dead letter: only four of thirty-one gubernia secretaries in 1752 were of noble origin; the others were former *raznochintsy*,[39] that ill-defined social pool in which sons of priests, old soldiers, emancipated serfs, and whoever could not fit into the established social categories found the minimal sense of a common identity. The addition of stages through which clerks had to pass before their promotion to secretarial ranks was an attempt less to "bureaucratize" the clerical staffs than to ease the pressure of lower-class elements to enter the nobility.

Despite the reluctance of the elite, the apparatus kept absorbing members of the dependent population and training the more ambitious to assume managerial positions. One of Artemii Volynsky's recommendations in his reform project of 1740 was to somehow induce the nobility to enter the secretarial and clerical staff (*prikaznii chin*) because "everyone" working in the chanceries belonged to the lower (*podlye*) classes. Thirty-two years later the Senate "once more" forbade all central and local agencies to hire people listed on the capitation rolls and to recommend for promotion to grade fourteen those already hired. The prohibition applied as well to their children, whose familiarity with chancery work would qualify them for rapid promotion.[40]

The shortage of clerks and secretaries was aggravated by the local government reform of the 1770s and the ministerial reform of the 1810s. It was taken for granted that more outsiders would have to be taken in, provided they came from the "free population." This was unenforceable. The Saratov governor, for example, complained to the procurator general in 1781 that vacancies had to be filled with the children of garrison soldiers and "various kinds of people paying the capitation," with the excuse that they had been hired "temporarily."[41] In addition to sons of priests, who had nowhere else to go, townsmen applied for admission, taking advantage of the exemption from billeting soldiers given to those who entered the apparatus. Such was the case of a Saratov merchant who applied to the civil chamber and was hired as a clerk with his son. The son was promoted to the upper ranks of the secretarial staff (after

1785, everyone in grades fourteen to nine became life nobles) but did not break the barrier to hereditary status. Gavril Dobrynin was more fortunate. Born in Sevsk near the Ukrainian border, the son of a priest, he became the secretary of the local bishop, then left to try his luck in Bielorussia as others, under Alexander, would try theirs in Georgia: an entire cemetery in Tiflis was apparently reserved for those who did not make it to college assessor. In Mogilev he met a merchant, a domestic, and a clerk from his native town, who had already become life nobles. He was promoted to grade fourteen in 1777 and ended his career in the 1810s in the post of gubernia procurator in grade six, with two coveted decorations, Saint Anne and Saint Vladimir.[42] For many who reached manhood between 1775 and 1815, life could be a fairy tale indeed.[43]

Russian Society as Command Structure

If we accept the proposition that the hereditary nobility, slowly but steadily replenished by the co-optation of individuals from the dependent population, was the ruling class of the empire, we are prepared to examine its corollary—that Russian society as a whole was a command structure in which each level was both subordinated to the next higher level and in a position to control the destiny of the next lower level.

Kliuchevskii once wrote that the tsar was the "commander in chief of the Great Russian national army" and that boyars remained until the end of the seventeenth century his voevodas, dispatched on special missions to take command of regiments and towns, who spent their time in the Duma between missions.[44] Less than two generations after Kliuchevskii, Stalin used similar terminology in his famous speech of March 1937 when describing the constitution of the Party, led by a high command of "generals" (top-grade leaders), followed by so many "officers" (middle-grade leaders), and "non-commissioned officers," the General Secretary being presumably in the post of commander in chief. Military words appear in civilian official documents throughout the eighteenth century to reveal a conception of governing at all levels of the ruling class as the issuance of orders requiring unconditional obedience. Even the church became the "Synodal command" and seminarians its soldiers.[45] Reality could not quite be shaped to conform to the ideal of a society under martial law, but it remained a fundamental assumption that it could.

Such a view of the political process was, however, in full accord with the traditional attitude toward the purpose of governing. Sergei Solov'ev saw the medieval prince as a political leader extorting booty from the population and sharing it with his retinue (*druzhina*) in order to keep its allegiance and legitimize his power. Alexander Gradovskii was struck by the insistence on the part of the political apparatus in "old Russia" on "receiving much and giving nothing in return," and it is all too evident that even the massive transformation of Russia has not questioned a hallowed tradition that the purpose of governing is to extract the maximum resources from the population in order to sustain the privileged position of the ruling group and the expansion of military power.[46]

Serfdom, that "abominable system" without which the Russian economy would be thrown into chaos, to paraphrase Frederic II, was the foundation of the Russian social and political order.[47] Whatever differences existed among high and low members of the ruling class, a consensus bound them in that belief among themselves and collectively with the Romanov house for more than two centuries. The inviolability of serfdom precluded the growth of divergent interests and kept tsar and ruling elite the inseparable constituents of a ruling class whose grip on the political life of the country was unchallengeable. The politics of the ruling class was the politics of patronage, and the search for dominance, incarnated in the rise of favorites, implied the glorification of the principle of autocracy, as every ambitious politician, unable to find a power base in society outside the ruling class, took refuge behind the unlimited power of the autocrat to consolidate his position. The losses of favor, the banishments, and the confiscations of property, which maintained a permanent circulation of wealth among the ruling class, were less the result of the ruler's capricious actions than of an internal process of rejuvenation within the ruling class. Such politics, however, fostered a climate of insecurity and a spirit of intolerance favoring the strong and forcing upon the less fortunate of the moment an unconditional obedience.[48]

If the ruling class was bound to its commander in chief by a quasi-military discipline, it demanded from the dependent population a peremptory conformity to its wishes. The Russian absolute monarchy was based on a foundation of local tyranny—*Und der König absolut, wenn er uns den Willen tut*, as the Prussians put it.[49] Serfdom became more and more oppressive during the eighteenth century. The *Ulozhenie* of 1649 bound the peasant to the land of his lord, who could not sell one without the other. By 1725, however, serfdom had become an only slightly mitigated form of slavery: peasants were now seen as the personal property of their lords, who could sell, banish, or resettle them at will.[50] Catherine, whose youthful idealism was turned by long exposure to the harsh reality of Russian politics into shameless cynicism, told Diderot in 1773 that landowners did as they pleased, that there was nothing conditional in the relationship of masters and subjects, but that "every master with some common sense will spare the cow in order to milk it at his pleasure without exhausting it."[51] Peasants who were not the property of landowners were the collective property of the apparatus, which collected the quitrent from them just as landowners collected it from their serfs, and the deplorable condition of these peasants in the 1820s was an eloquent testimony to the exploitation they had endured at the hands of government-appointed stewards and local squires.

The grip of the ruling class over the urban population was no less complete and arbitrary, and was maintained by institutional devices.[52] Townsmen sought to escape the yoke of the local agents of the ruling elite between 1699 and 1727 and between 1742 and 1775, when the local agencies of the registered population were allowed to take their grievances directly to a central agency, yet this central agency was always headed by a leading member of the elite, not a representative of the urban population. Catherine's reforms strengthened the apparatus of control over towns and townsmen by placing the police under a Senate appointee and vesting the review of judicial decisions over townsmen in appointed chambers and the governor. Although Alexander's government admitted some participation by the first two merchant guilds in the judicial chambers, municipal government passed under the authority of the minister of internal affairs, the corps commander of the nobility, and state peasants found their "protector" in the finance minister—both ministers among the most powerful members of the ruling elite.

Moreover, the dependent population itself was a command structure, and its ruling group—the heads of patriarchal households—exercised a tyranny that was no less oppressive than that of the ruling class over its subjects. Such households, like serf estates and armies, were total institutions claiming comprehensive control over the destiny of their members. The almost despotic authority of these patriarchs rested in turn on the "power-assertive" relationship characteristic of Russian parents' attitudes toward their children. Patriarchs formed a ruling stratum in which membership was primarily a function of age; they conceived their interest to be the exploitation of other members of the household, especially in arranging marriages, that is, building patronage networks among the peasant community, in controlling the sons' freedom of movement, and cursing the children when all else failed.[53]

Russian society taken in its totality was thus a huge command structure in which social and family relationships were dominated by considerations of power. Authority was created not by wealth but by position within a hierarchy determined by age, seniority, and co-optation. Translated into power through exploitation, the assertion of a primary, even exclusive, claim over scarce resources, it gave wealth and honor. At all levels of such a society the tyranny of the superior was accepted because it justified the subordinate's tyranny over his own subordinates, leaving no room for the assertion of individual freedom, economic initiative, and social autonomy.

Such a society fostered the cult of military values and encouraged resort to military personnel to carry out tasks that elsewhere would be the responsibility of civilian authorities. Several features characterized premodern Russia as a militaristic society, notably the existence of an ideology supportive of military ideals, propagated by the educational system, manifested in heavy emphasis on military ceremony, the large share of the budget devoted to military expenditures, and a readiness to commit armed forces in foreign and domestic conflicts.[54] The parallel with Prussia readily comes to mind, with one major difference, however. The Prussian officer corps, servants of a tradition inspired by memories of the Teutonic Order, was a brotherhood separate and distinct from the country's civilian apparatus, cohabiting with it in a state of latent tension. The famous phrase that Prussia was not a country with an army but an army with a country was a striking commentary on this almost alien status of the military in the political order.[55]

Such a dichotomy did not exist in Russia, at least until after the abolition of serfdom. The service class, as it is called in history books, had nothing of the

Prussian tradition of an order that had fought its own battles and created its own legend. It had always been the ruling class of the country, possessing collectively and together with the ruling house the near totality of the country's wealth and carrying out its military mission within the framework of its own political mandate. From this subordination of military tasks to political imperatives there followed a refusal to accept a professionalization of the officer corps as creating an unacceptable division within the ruling elite and a threat to the integrity of the political leadership. This politicization of the officer corps is a theme running through the memoirs of General Langeron, the French émigré who served in it some 40 years. It was evident in the favoritism shown in the promotion of officers and in the privileged role of the Guard in staffing divisional and regimental commands, and John Keep has shown how a willingness to risk professionalization in the wake of the Napoleonic Wars—with the creation of main staffs a major step toward that end—was cut short by Nicholas I when the Decembrist uprising made its implications quite clear.[56]

Nevertheless, the impact of war—the Northern War, the Seven Years' War, the protracted struggle with Napoleon—gave the military an enormous stake in the councils of government and a dominant presence in society. So did the fact that Peter's and Paul's reigns, at least at their inception, were military coups against the constellations of power in which these tsars had been brought up. The role of the two regiments of the Guard in the 1690s, its vast expansion under Paul and Alexander, and the long shadow cast by a general of artillery over the entire government during the first 25 years of the nineteenth century testified to the existence of the military as the social foundation of a triumphant autocracy and to the rise of a military apparatus that, although politicized, began to develop its own set of values.[57] And these values could only reinforce that spirit of intolerance and the demand for unconditional obedience that serfdom had been relentlessly spreading throughout the social and political order.[58]

The Table of Ranks opened with a statement that military men took precedence over their civilian peers and gave all officers the status of hereditary nobles, while those rising in the civilian apparatus had to wait until they were co-opted into grade eight, the equivalent of an army major.[59] Even under Catherine, when the civilian apparatus vastly expanded and military values were somewhat denigrated—as had been the case under Elizabeth—civilian ranks below grade eight were still called "civilian junior officer ranks" (*shtatskie ober-ofitserskie chiny*), so that the gubernia secretary could pretend he had become an officer. Officers had prestige; some behaved like princes, even if "they did not have a shirt on" (*goly kak bubny*), and the proximity of a regimental commander was a safeguard against the arrogance of a voevoda.[60]

This prestige was not an artificial creation and often reflected an experience and knowledge of the world that civilian duty in the monotonous interior of Russia could never match. General Alexander Rumiantsev (1680–1749) fought in Finland, on the Prut, and in Pomerania, traveled to Constantinople, Vienna, Amsterdam, and Paris, served in the Ukraine and in Transcaucasia. The memoirs of Andrei Bolotov (1738–1833) vividly describe the discovery by a boy from Tula of the strange and fascinating world of Riga and Königsberg, his visit to the then-small Winter Palace where he thought he was in paradise, and his happiness at wearing his first corporal uniform at the age of 10. It was characteristic that he picked children from the local *meshchane* to be soldiers in his squad.[61] Growing up in such a world, marked by constant drill, inspections, and transfers every spring from one part of the country to another, instilled a spirit of obedience and a habit of command—together with a great deal of nomadic restlessness—which many a nobleman would then take to his estate and his civilian post when he retired.

The general mobilization of the ruling class in the 1700s had created a lasting shortage of personnel in the civilian apparatus—hence the concern, still in evidence 100 years later, over an influx of candidates from the dependent population: by November 1760 the curator of Moscow University, Ivan Shuvalov, had recommended the establishment of a separate promotion hierarchy (*liniia*) for nobles who had managed to avoid serving in the army. Most provincial officials in the mid-1750s had transferred from the military. The overwhelming majority of governors until the 1760s were former colonels promoted from a regimental command to that of a gubernia. The signatories of the *nakazy* of 1767 were for the most part lieutenants, captains, and majors, and the Noble Charter insisted that nobles who took part in elections and were elected to local offices have officer ranks.[62] It would remain the legacy of Peter's policy that the Russian countryside was ruled by retired or demobilized officers.

The local reforms of the 1780s multiplied the number of posts, subdividing—perhaps unwittingly—the civilian apparatus between appointed members engaged in collecting funds and keeping accounts on the one hand and those elected to take charge of police and justice on the other. A survey of several provinces in 1822 reveals that the internal structure of the army had been transplanted into the provincial administration, with marshals, judges, captains, and sheriffs representing the "line" (*stroi*), the civilian treasurers and accountants, the noncombatants (*nestroevoi*).[63] The importance of military training and values thus remained very great among those who policed and punished the dependent population and demanded from it the obedience to which army life had accustomed them.

The rigidity and severity of this command structure, however, were mitigated by the pervasive influence of patronage networks. These networks are characteristic of political systems in the process of state formation; in eighteenth-century Russia it was still impossible to speak of a Russian state in the sense of a complex of abstractions representing interests extending beyond those of the Romanov house and the ruling class. They provided the only access to career mobility until the imposition, and above all the observance, of formal criteria of selection and promotion divorced from the candidates' social origins.

Patronage networks bound together patron and client in a relationship satisfying to both. In a society imbued with a static view of the social order, where economic development throughout the eighteenth century strained serfdom's potential to its utmost before falling victim to its debilitating influence in the first half of the nineteenth; where means of livelihood were problematic for most of the population, including members of the elite; and where the absence of a legal tradition made recourse to the law superfluous and counterproductive, the resulting general insecurity placed a premium on personal relationships that cut across institutional frameworks.

A noble seeking to rise in the world needed a patron to introduce him to those with the power to advance his career. With a position came a salary and also the ability to do small favors, for which "gifts" were expected in order to supplement the usually meager salary. The client then brought his relatives to share in his success, a first step toward building his own modest patronage network. The patron needed clients—a full antechamber of petitioners enhanced his "honor" in the ruling elite. Clients placed in strategic positions in the central apparatus and in the provinces were a source of information, otherwise scanty in a country without a developed periodical press. The clientele did not need to be limited to members of the elite. Personal nobles were the most in need of a patron, and merchants seeking noble status had the additional advantage of being in a position to offer "gifts" as well as services. Patronage networks were thus largely based on the self-interest of all parties and much less on the obedience of some to the command of others.[64]

They helped bridge the immense social distance between high and low members of the ruling class and between members of that class and outsiders. Some resorted to desperate methods to find a patron for their children. Others cultivated their talents and patiently waited for the chance of their life. Gavril Derzhavin, from an unknown Kazan family, vegetated for years in the Guard until Grigorii Orlov, the favorite, got him promoted to corporal at the age of 20. Unable at first to win Potemkin's protection, he was able to get Viazemskii's, and his tempestuous career began. Arakcheev's father did not have the funds to register his son in the Corps of Cadets, but its director waived the requirement and introduced the future favorite into the powerful Saltykov clan. Speranskii, a priest's son, owed his meteoric rise to the patronage of the Kurakins.[65]

Civilian appointments were made by the Senate in general assembly and after 1811 largely by ministers, military appointments by the College, then Ministry of War, except those in grade six and above, made by the ruler on the recommendation of the Senate or ministers or at his or her discretion. The great majority of appointments were thus made on the recommendation of military commanders, governors, and governors-general. Dmitrii Mertvago owed his career to the patronage of Osip Igelstrom, the governor-general of Bielorussia; Alexander Bezborodko and Petr Zavadovskii to that of Petr Rumiantsev, the governor-general of Little Russia. These governors and governors-general, on the other hand, sometimes owed their appointments to their loss of favor with a powerful patron. Derzhavin's governorships resulted from Prince Viazemskii's attempts to remove him from the capital, Timofei Tutolmin became governor-general of Olonets after falling out with Grigorii Potemkin, and Mikhail Kakhovskii was sent to Nizhni Novgorod after a similar quarrel with Valerian Zubov.[66]

This permanent upward and downward flow of careers certainly explains the major shake-ups punctuating Russian political life. The observer might wonder, for instance, why 153 senior appointments, transfers, and retirements were announced by six imperial orders on a single day, August 16, 1760,[67] unless he is aware that a realignment of Russian politics had been taking place during the preceding 2 years, resulting in the removal of a procurator general who had been in office for 20 years; or why fifty-nine governors, vice-governors, and chairmen of civil and criminal chambers—45.4 percent of the total—changed positions between 1791 and 1793,[68] unless he remembers that these were the years of Prince Viazemskii's debilitating illness, which forced his retirement in September 1792 and caused his death in January 1793. In both cases the overthrow or death of the procurator general as the chief dispenser of patronage resulted in a major shake-up of the entire apparatus.

The initiative did not always come from the top. Influential families had taken root in the provinces by the 1770s—the Makarovs in Vologda, the Molostvovs in Kazan, the Chicherins in Kaluga—with useful ties and relatives in Moscow and Petersburg and with their own local patronage networks. In endogamous Smolensk gubernia "almost half the nobles" were related in the 1810s to Elizabeth Engelhardt, the daughter of a Passek, and the gubernia marshal was a personal acquaintance of the tsar.[69] Family ties bound clerks in the capital with clerks in provincial and uezd centers, and heads of patriarchal households used unmarried daughters as pawns in their own patronage games.

The existence of a national network of families and client systems made a mockery of the rigid hierarchy established by legislative texts in a constant search for administrative order and "regularity." It explained why the Russian government, more than any other, was a government of men and not of laws. The consolidation of the political infrastructure during the reign of Catherine also marked the completion of this national network and its transformation into an imperial one. This achievement went a long way in explaining the success of Catherine's policies and guaranteed the legitimacy of the autocracy for another century.[70]

2

Social Groups

Nobility

The nobility was the smallest yet the dominant class of Russian society. Detailed and comprehensive surveys of its size and territorial distribution before 1782 are lacking. Kliuchevskii estimated that the capital nobility consisted of 6,385 males in 1681. Since the nobility of Petersburg and Moscow gubernias constituted about 30 percent of the total nobility of the twenty-six gubernias of central Russia in 1782 and 1816, the size of the Russian nobility in 1681, if the same ratio applied, would have been about 19,000 males. We know that it was 37,000 in 1744 and 53,360 20 years later. By the end of Catherine's reign it had grown to 68,320 males (1795), and the census of 1816 reported a total size of 96,600 in Russia proper. Nobles constituted a minuscule proportion of the total population: about .58 percent in the 1680s, .54 percent in 1744, .56 percent in 1782, and .83 percent in 1816. They were found in all twenty-six gubernias but were heavily concentrated in those of the two capitals and in Smolensk gubernia, where a more visible nobility remained a vestige of Polish social tradition. Indeed, the combined nobility of these three gubernias constituted 36.5 percent of the total in 1782, 44.8 percent in 1816. Elsewhere, the strength of the nobility varied from a high of 4,350 nobles in Iaroslavl gubernia to a low of 130 nobles in Olonets gubernia in 1782, from 6,644 in Kursk gubernia to 333 again in Olonets gubernia in 1816. The average in twenty-six gubernias was 1,473 nobles per gubernia in 1782, 2,317 in 1816.[1]

At the end of the seventeenth century the Russian nobility was a ruling class consisting of individuals expected to serve whenever called in military and civilian administration and enjoying hereditary status. It was divided into three strata. At the very top was a ruling group sitting in the Duma and consisting of boyars, *okolnichie*, and the so-called Duma nobles. Boyars were those with the greatest authority and prestige, and were appointed to their rank by the ruler, whether they belonged to aristocratic families of long lineage or were of less distinguished birth. *Okolnichie* were of a lesser rank but similarly elevated; the Duma nobles often came from the lesser nobility. The ruling group staffed the high command of the army, presided over the most important *prikazy*, and went on tours of duty as voevodas in the larger towns. Boyars, in addition, were close to the ruling house, related to it in various ways, and often served as

22

tutors (*diad'ki*) to the ruler's sons; their wives were nurses (*mamki*) to his daughters.

The second stratum was that of the Moscow nobles, so called because they served in the capital and chiefly at court. They formed the major pool from which Duma nobles were drawn. We find among them *stolniki*, who served at the tsar's table, and *striapchie*, who served him in various capacities and administered his properties. Their number was very large—more than 1,500—and many of Peter's councillors came from their ranks. We also find among them the *zhiltsy*, who guarded court palaces, treasuries, and storerooms, and often came from the provincial nobility, thus serving as the intermediaries between the world of Moscow politics and that of provincial ambitions. All these together began to be called *tsaredvortsy* at the beginning of Peter's reign. We find them serving as presidents of the lesser *prikazy* and as voevodas in towns of secondary importance.[2]

Finally, the great mass of nobles belonged to the third stratum, the provincial nobility or the nobility of the provincial towns (*gorodovoe dvorianstvo*). They had been granted patents of nobility by the ruler, usually in return for military service in wartime, together with a land allotment (*pomest'e*) commensurate with the value of that service. Among these provincial nobles we find the so-called *deti boiarskie*, literally sons of boyars, more accurately minor nobles. Originally the sons of boyars, impoverished by the division of inheritance generation after generation, they had become by the end of the seventeenth century an intermediate group on the periphery of the provincial nobility through which non-noble servicemen like *streltsy* and cossacks, who came from the urban population and the peasantry, were incorporated into the ruling class.

The impact of 20 years of war upon this loosely integrated social organism was tremendous. There was a general mobilization of the ruling class after the first battle of Narva into the Western-style infantry and cavalry regiments that had replaced the Muscovite heavy cavalry manned exclusively by nobles. Field promotions to deal with battlefield losses increased social mobility. All these changes accelerated the internal integration of the ruling class until its three constituent elements could be fused into a single nobility, or *shliakhetstvo*, a term borrowed from the Polish, first used in 1712; it was replaced by *dvorianstvo* after 1762.[3]

The Table of Ranks of January 1722 ratified that consolidation. At first a table of graded positions granting specific ranks to their holders, it became a table of ranks largely dissociated from the hierarchy of positions. The Table sharply distinguished between military and civil service and followed the Muscovite tradition in giving the former privileged status. All officers, whatever their social origin, became noblemen, while nobles who served in the ranks remained noble. Those who chose a civilian career had to wait, if they were of non-noble origin, until they reached grade eight before being brought into the ruling class.[4] It was as if the entire provincial nobility of Muscovy had been drafted into the officer corps, leaving the lower ranks of the civilian apparatus to be filled with non-nobles.

Membership in the nobility was hereditary. The Charter of April 1785, however, gave lifelong nobility to individuals occupying positions on the Table of Ranks below grade eight, while the equivalent military rank continued to confer hereditary status.[5] Thus, the entire civilian apparatus was brought into the nobility, but a nobility now divided between full-fledged and second-class members. Nevertheless, the life nobility grew so fast that its numbers even exceeded those of the hereditary nobility by 1816—48,854 life nobles, 47,746 hereditary nobles, a 10.5 percent decline from the 53,360 registered in 1782, due to migration into the southern borderlands (Ukraine and Northern Caucasus). Within Russia proper a substantial relocation had taken place from the central and especially the northern region toward the southern gubernias and those along the mid-Volga. By contrast, life nobles were concentrated in Petersburg gubernia (39.2 percent) and Moscow gubernia (12.5 percent)—more than half of them thus lived in the provinces of the two capitals in the northern and central regions, against 8.4 percent of the hereditary nobles.[6]

The ruling class, called into existence by the need for an armed force in permanent reserve for military emergencies and for a police apparatus to administer the country in peacetime, always had some form of corporate organization. This organization served the dual purpose of channeling orders from the ruling group and petitions from the rank and file on the one hand, and providing the nobility with local leadership on the other.

The nobility in the seventeenth century was organized along territorial lines. The Moscow nobility lived in and around Moscow and was mobilized separately from the provincial nobility, or, as the expression went, *po Moskovskomu spisku*. The provincial nobility was organized into companies (*sotni*) in the administrative center of the territory in which they lived, usually an uezd. There were the Novgorodians, the Suzdalians, the Kalugians, and so on. The nobles of a town were mobilized in sections (*po dvorovym spiskam*) or collectively (*po gorodovym spiskam*) and reported to Moscow. The *sotni* chose their own officers (*golovy*) to command them in wartime. The nobility was thus a territorial army ready at all times to answer the call for mobilization.

In peacetime, those nobles who lived in a town formed associations and elected deputies (*vybornye*) from among those who were better provided with lands and peasants. They were their corporate agents, settling disputes and forwarding petitions; one of them, the *okladchik*, concerned himself specifically with military matters. They also made sure that sons of noblemen presented themselves for service at the age of 15 and were properly registered. Inspections (*smotry*) were made by voevodas or specially appointed boyars, and service records were kept in the *Razriad*, where the Moscow nobles were required to report for inspection and registration. These noble associations possessed corporate rights. They elected, often from retired nobles, a local judiciary of *gubnye starosty* and police officials called *syshchiki*, who fought brigandage and pursued runaway serfs. They also took possession of the property of nobles who died intestate.[7]

The relatively peaceful world of the provincial nobility—except along the southern border, where Tatar raids were a permanent menace—was threatened by the creation after the 1650s of regiments structured after the Western model of a standing army and was shattered by the Northern War. The new regiments followed a radically different principle of functional organization—infantry and cavalry—without a territorial base, and the Northern War imposed a general mobilization for an entire generation.[8] Some eighty regimental staffs became by the 1720s the new corporate associations of a nobility gathered into a modern officer corps commanded by boyars, *okolnichie*, and *stolniki*, made generals and colonels. These associations promoted noncommissioned officers into the officer corps, voted to recommend candidates for promotion to their commanding generals, commanded former serfs and peasants in wartime, and used them in peacetime as domestics and dependents.

This general mobilization of the provincial nobility,[9] monitored by periodic inspections, some conducted by the tsar in person, was effective until the late 1710s and left without any corporate organization the few nobles who managed to escape the call. An attempt was made to recreate provincial agencies, a few elected nobles sitting together with the voevodas after 1702 and with the governor after 1713.[10] It failed, however, chiefly for lack of human resources, while martial law, under which the country found itself after 1708, transformed the officer corps and its representatives, the governors and commandants, into a political apparatus governing towns and countryside. The increasing resistance to sending young nobles to inspections, once the outcome of the war was no longer in doubt, the stationing of the regiments all over the country for the purpose of feeding them directly from the land, the election of land commissioners (*zemskie komissary*)[11] to mediate between the dependent population and the regimental officers meant a return of the provincial nobles, now in uniform, to reassert themselves as the ruling class of the country.

The restoration of a territorial army in the 1720s—part of a trend of reversion to Muscovite practices—was incompatible, however, with the strategic need to concentrate troops in certain sectors to maximize striking power against potential enemies, and was abandoned after Peter's death. The corporate organization of the ruling class became once again almost exclusively military and nomadic but glorified by association with exotic places and regiments with prestigious names. This left most of the country without a substantial political infrastructure, prey to violence and extortion.

The recognition in the 1750s that a political infrastructure was fundamental to social stability, at a time when the ruling class had become large enough to fill all officer vacancies, convinced the government that the demobilization of the officer corps was at last both possible and necessary.[12] The imperial manifesto of February 1762 gave the nobility the choice between remaining on their properties and entering the army or the civilian apparatus. It marked the culmination of a trend that had begun 40 years earlier,[13] and it split the corporate organization of the ruling class into two communities: the functional world of military and civil management and the territorial brotherhood of landowners. Its logical consequence had to be the recreation of corporate agencies for the landowners. Uezd marshals were elected in 1767 along with delegates to the Legislative Commission,[14] but the completion of the reform

was delayed for nearly 20 years by the Turkish war and the administrative–
territorial reorganization.

As the central administrative headquarters of the nobility in the seventeenth century, the *Razriad* kept rolls of the nobility and cleared appointments;
the *Pomestnyi Prikaz* kept registers of the nobles' properties and settled disputes over sales and inheritance. These agencies were virtually abolished in the
wake of the reform of 1708, and governors became territorial commanders
over those nobles who had managed to avoid being drafted into the field army.
The Senate's chancery took over coordination. Beginning in 1722, the responsibilities of the *Razriad* as personnel agency were vested in the heraldmaster's
office, closely linked with the Senate; those of the *Pomestnyi Prikaz*, in the
College of Landed Affairs.

The completion of the local government reform in the early 1780s paved
the way for the recreation of a corporate organization of the nobility on a
territorial basis. Nobles were instructed to meet every 3 years during the winter
months—usually in December—in the gubernia capital to constitute an assembly of the nobility. Not everyone, however, was allowed to attend and to vote.
Members had to be at least 25 years old, own some real property (*derevnia*),
and have been in the service with the rank of junior officer, from ensign to
captain. The assembly was summoned and closed by the governor, and met for
the dual purpose of listening to proposals the governor might present for its
consideration and to elect personnel to staff the new agencies of local government created by the reform.[15]

These assemblies were thus conceived from the very beginning as general
meetings of retired company commanders and subaltern officers on a gubernia
basis to hear instructions from the governor as their divisional commander and
delegate of the procurator general, chief dispensor of patronage and chief
executive officer of the ruling class. In view of its military origin and constitution, those assemblies remained as receptive as ever to orders from above,
while the ruling class expanded the network of local agencies in order to
consolidate its control over the dependent population. Nevertheless, elections
were often tempestuous events, creating disquiet at the highest levels of government and prompting the minister of the interior, Aleksei Kurakin, to demand
in 1809 that attempts by provincial nobles to turn their assemblies into "a state
within a state" be suppressed by invoking drastic disciplinary powers against
both the governor and the assembly.[16]

Each assembly was required to elect a substantial number of delegates to fill
the elective posts, some for each uezd, others for the gubernia as a whole. Each
uezd had a marshal, a uezd court, and a land court of three members each. In a
gubernia of twelve uezds this required eighty-four noblemen. Two gubernia
agencies, the upper land court and the court of equity, required another twelve
members, raising the number to a total of ninety-six. The upper land court of
ten assessors was abolished by Paul in 1796, but nobles were allowed in
September 1801 to elect two members to the civil and two to the criminal
chamber; this left 90 elective posts. The entire assembly, it seems, elected

delegates to the gubernia agencies, while the representatives of each uezd voted separately to elect candidates to uezd positions. Candidates had to own real property large enough to yield 100 rubles of revenue a year, and their election required the governor's confirmation.[17] Candidates did not usually run for office, although the practice was not unknown, especially where a powerful landowner wanted his candidate to be chosen. In accordance with the electoral law of December 1766 governing elections to the Legislative Commission, every member of the delegation was voted on, and the winner was the one who got the largest number of votes. It was thus possible for the assembled nobles to vote one of their number into office against his will.[18] We know that elections were well attended in the early years after 1785, largely because the experiment was new and took place at a time when the center of gravity of Russian society was shifting from Moscow to the provinces, and that the elite often took part in the elections. We also know that they were poorly attended during the reigns of Paul and Alexander.[19] This was principally because a large number of nobles had to be elected and local politics compelled reluctant noblemen to assume responsibilities that sometimes put them on a collision course with the governor, and because there was no room for initiative in a local society whose ruling class saw the maintenance of the status quo as its major duty.

The key post was that of marshal (*predvoditel'*). Uezd marshals had been in existence for 20 years before the charter took effect. In some ways they were the descendants of the *Landrichter* of the 1710s and the land commissioner of the 1720s. At first elected for 2 years, their terms were extended to 3 years by the Organic Law of November 1775 and were renewable. This law also created the post of gubernia marshal but gave it no superior standing: all marshals were placed, merely for purposes of identification in such a rank-conscious society, in grade seven, the equivalent of a lieutenant colonel in the army. It was not until 1818 that gubernia marshals were raised to grade five. Governors, as a rule, were majors general. The assembly chose two candidates for gubernia marshal; the governor confirmed one of them in office. In 1794, for example, the 170 nobles of the Vladimir assembly voted 164 to 6 in favor of Brigadier Taneev and 101 to 69 in favor of Major Alenin, both uezd marshals. Taneev was confirmed and remained uezd marshal as well. Some marshals, Nikolai Savelov in Mozhaisk, for example, served for a decade or more.[20]

The marshals' responsibilities were never spelled out in detail, and Kochubei complained in 1814 that there were too many misunderstandings between them and the governors, who accused the marshals of encroaching upon their prerogatives.[21] They were the true politicians of the gubernias and uezds, with bands of followers in their uezds and good connections in Moscow and Petersburg. When the Kursk governor refused to confirm Vasilii Tiutchev as uezd marshal on the grounds that he was under police surveillance for stealing hunting dogs, smuggling vodka, and harboring fugitives, his supporters gathered signatures and got Petersburg to overrule the governor.[22] After 1802 the Ministry of Internal Affairs assumed jurisdiction over assemblies and marshals, and the minister replaced the procurator general as corps commander of the nobility. From then on, elections were confirmed by the minister, on the governor's recommendation. He also inherited the unpleasant responsibility of having to choose between the governor and the gubernia marshal, who increasingly became the spokesman for the nobility of his gubernia and an interlocutor unwelcomed by both governor and minister. Marshals were key links in a vast patronage network connecting capital and province, and their political influence was greater than the governors'. The infamous General Lev Izmailov, for example, was gubernia marshal in Riazan from 1802 to 1814. When the governor refused to recommend the confirmation of his reelection in 1805, Izmailov turned to the minister, who refused to be convinced. He then forced the issue by appealing to the tsar in person, asking to be put on trial to clear his name. The tsar had the governor removed.[23]

Townsmen

The exact size of the urban population was, and remains, uncertain. Economically stunted towns could not impose themselves upon the consciousness of the ruling class as territorial entities and exercise a liberating influence upon the countryside, shaping a new society with their own interests and mores, and creating an urban culture transcending the dominant values of an agrarian order. As a result, only certain individuals performing a number of functions were considered members of the urban population and were registered on official rolls, while others, such as nobles and peasants, were ignored as outsiders even though they were permanent residents. An awareness of the town as a sui generis territorial creation began to influence governmental policy during the reign of Catherine, part and parcel of that broad discovery of the Russian land so characteristic of the period, but never to become strong enough to overcome traditional prejudices.[24]

The persistence of these prejudices was due in large part to the remarkable stability of the social order. The registered urban population equaled 3.5 percent of the total population in 1719, 3 percent in 1744, 2.9 percent in 1762, returning to its 1719 level in 1795, and reaching only 4 percent in 1815. If it had not been for the territorial reform, which raised the number of uezd centers from 177 to 321 and the size of the registered population from 230,062 males in 1762 to 358,193 in 1795, that urban population might have been even smaller at the end of the eighteenth century than it was at the beginning.[25] Moreover, the provinces with the largest urban concentration showed few changes between the first and the seventh censuses. Moscow gubernia, still the economic hub of the country in 1815; Orel gubernia, Russia's link with the Ukraine; Tver gubernia, Moscow's link with the Baltic—these three provinces were among the top six during the entire period. Kaluga's importance steadily declined, Tula and Iaroslavl' had fallen off the list by 1815, but Petersburg and Saratov emerged as new centers on the Baltic and the Volga. The combined population of the six (out of twenty-six) provinces made up 35 percent of the total urban population in 1719, 42 percent in 1762, and 44 percent in 1815.

This registered urban population consisted of the so-called *posadskie liudi*, people residing in the *posad*, a term referring to the area of the town that lay between the walls of the fort and the outer land walls. They included entrepreneurs, factors, clerks, petty merchants, unskilled laborers, and artisans. Where the economic development of the town was sufficiently advanced to result in some degree of social differentiation, these people were apportioned among three legal categories (*stat'i*). The poorest individuals, hawkers of wares and manual laborers, made up the third and largest category, each *posad* deciding how to fill the other two. The most enterprising merchants with far-flung interests were registered in a nationwide corporation, called the *gostinnaia sotnia*, of about eighty families at the end of the seventeenth century. They owned flour mills and vodka distilleries, sold salt, fish, and leather, and engaged in the Persian trade through Astrakhan.[26]

At the top of the urban pyramid were the *gosti*, the most prosperous merchants, whose names were kept on a roster drawn up by the ruler. It was an unstable list because Russian economic development had not yet succeeded in creating foundations on which credit would prosper and wealth create more wealth in an ever-expanding network of integrated exchanges. Only one family in four was able to perpetuate its standing beyond one generation. The roster contained thirty-one names in 1710, only thirteen in 1713. *Gosti* were engaged in the European trade through Arkhangelsk and in the Siberian fur trade. They produced salt, iron, and potash, and supplied grain, flour, and vodka to the government. In rare cases, enterprising individuals were rewarded with the title of "distinguished people" (*imenitye liudi*), like the Stroganovs, for example, granted an enormous salt concession in the Urals by Peter I.[27]

This internal differentiation of the registered urban population matched that of the ruling class. *Gosti* and members of the *sotnia* were scattered across the land. It was therefore inevitable that the general mobilization of the ruling class should affect the townsmen in a similar way, but it was not until the 1720s that the "rebuilding of the crumbling house of the Russian merchantry" was completed.[28] The instruction of 1724 combined *gosti, sotnia* members, and the three *stat'i* into a single category of townsmen (*grazhdanstvo*), which it then divided into two major groups, the active ("regular") and disfranchised ("irregular") townsmen. The latter corresponded to the third *stat'ia* and were now called "base" (*podlye*) people, subordinated to the political will of the active townsmen. These were in turn divided into two merchant guilds (*gil'di*), depending on the nature of their mercantile and entrepreneurial activities.[29] No monetary value was yet placed on assets to distinguish between the two guilds, but it had already been established in May 1722[30] that those wishing to register in the *posad* must keep a trade turnover of 500 rubles a year. The first guild thus incorporated the successors of the *gosti* and *sotnia* members; the second guild absorbed the first and second *stat'i*. Guild members were henceforth called merchants (*kuptsy*). The "base" people (the term did not yet have the pejorative connotation it later acquired) included the so-called *raznochintsy*, a literal description of "people of various social origin"—sons of priests, emancipated domestics and peasants, coachmen (*iamshchiki*), and miscellaneous clerks who hired themselves out to write petitions and represent plaintiffs before the voevodas.[31] Base people who engaged in various forms of manual labor registered in craft guilds (*tsekhi*).

The legislation of 1724 remained the foundation of government policy toward the urban population beyond the reign of Alexander I. Later amendments adapted it to changing conditions but did not modify its substance. The manifesto of March 1775 replaced the base population with *meshchane* by declaring merchants unable to declare assets of at least 500 rubles expelled from the merchantry, and the Senate order of May divided the remaining merchants into three guilds, distinguished by minimum assets of 500, 1,000, and 10,000 rubles. The resulting purge broke up the existing merchantry of 222,767 members into 24,470 *kuptsy* and 194,160 *meshchane*.[32]

The Municipal Charter of April 1785, published on the same day as the Charter to the Nobility, restored the title of "distinguished townsman" (*imenityi grazhdanin*), reserved for shipowners and merchants declaring assets over 50,000 rubles (the upper limit for first-guild merchants), for bankers, and, incongruously enough, for scholars and artists. The manifesto of January 1807 retained this honorific title for scholars and artists and gave the top layer of the first-guild merchantry the title of "merchant of the first category" (*pervostateinyi kupets*). This in effect restored the Muscovite distinction between the *gosti* and the three categories of merchants. The Supplementary Statute of November 1824 retained the distinction, calling the elite of the merchantry *negotsianty* as well. At the bottom of the social scale it divided *meshchane* into trading *meshchane* and *posadskie*, to separate those engaged in trade from the others.[33]

The core of the urban population thus consisted of the guild merchants. Applicants for membership in the first guild had to declare assets valued at between 10,000 and 50,000 rubles. These qualifications were raised during the reign of Alexander I to keep pace with inflation; by 1825 a minimum of 50,000 rubles was required. Membership was reserved for those engaged in foreign and domestic trade, both wholesale and retail, as well as entrepreneurs who built and managed factories and industrial plants and owned seagoing ships. The statute of 1824 emphasized mercantile activities and continued to recognize the right to engage in tax farming and bid for contracts to supply the army and the government.[34] Second-guild merchants had to declare assets valued at a minimum of 5,000 rubles in 1785 and 20,000 rubles by 1825. They were barred from foreign trade and from owning seagoing ships but competed with first-guild merchants in wholesale and retail trade in towns and at fairs, such as those of Kursk (*korennaia*), Makar'ev (later Nizhni Novgorod), and Irbit in the Urals. The statute of 1824, however, gave these merchants the right to engage in foreign trade, providing a merchant's turnover did not exceed 300,000 rubles a year, barred them from engaging in banking and insurance, and restricted their capacity to contract to a total of 50,000 rubles. Merchants from these first two guilds were the elite of the merchantry. The charter gave them the right to travel in a coach-and-pair (*kareta paroiu*)—sumptuary laws were still in effect to check the progress of a money economy in erasing social differences—and, most important, immunity from the capitation and corporal punishment.[35]

Third-guild merchants were less respectable. They were given no legal immunity and were forbidden to ride in coaches but were granted the no-less-covered exemption from the capitation. Their assets, valued at a minimum of 1,000 rubles in 1785 and 8,000 in 1825, came from retail trade in towns and countryside within the uezd in which they were registered. They competed less with the merchants in the other guilds than with peasants, who also owned mills (*stany*), engaged in handicrafts, and operated small riverboats. The statute of 1824 continued to recognize them as small producers and contained a long list of light industries—textile, construction, and so on—in which they were allowed to operate. They were not only small producers but also small traders. They were allowed to own taverns, inns, and dramshops (*traktiry, gerbergi, postoialye dvory*) as well as public bathhouses (*torgovye bani*). The statute was more specific than the charter and in some ways more restrictive. Third-guild merchants were identified more clearly as the middlemen for merchants of the first two guilds, who delivered to them Russian and foreign goods, and for trading peasants, that is, peasants authorized to bring their goods to town for resale by the merchants. Legislation was treading a fine line here, which actual practices must have ignored, but it served to protect the self-respect of the guild members. These merchants were also factors for those of the other two guilds and were therefore allowed to transport food products (*s'estnye pripasy*) directly to Moscow and Petersburg. Their capacity to contract, as suppliers and tax farmers, was limited to 20,000 rubles.[36]

If merchant guilds can be looked upon as horizontal associations of traders and owners of means of production, craft guilds must be seen as vertical structures of masters and apprentices engaged in actual production and subordinated to guild merchants to whom they sold the product of their work, whether hats, bricks, or candles. The charter, of which Article 123 was entitled a Statute on Crafts and consisted of 131 paragraphs, left the relationships between the two kinds of guilds unclear. It merely stated that craft guilds were open to anyone who wished to practice a trade (*remeslo*) or handicraft (*rukodelie*) in the town, and that their members were included among the *meshchane*. This implied that only those whose assets were valued at less than 1,000 rubles could join a craft guild, and allowed two kinds of craftsmen to join, those on the rolls of the registered population and outsiders, chiefly peasants. The statute of 1824 recognized the right of merchants in all three guilds to join craft guilds. This could only complete the integration of guild elders into the management of the factory, since third-guild merchants were forbidden to employ more than thirty-two workmen.[37]

Despite the expansion of the political infrastructure in the provinces, the growth of an administrative and military apparatus in the towns, and an influx of trading peasants swelling the urban population far beyond the level registered on the rolls,[38] the government remained unwilling at the end of Alexander's reign to look upon this urban population as a human community operating within a territorial framework. The explanation, no doubt, must be found in the basic fact that the nobility, reorganized after 1785 along territorial lines, had no interest as the ruling class of Russian society in fostering in its midst the growth of territorial complexes that sooner or later would challenge its dominion in one gubernia after another. A fragmented urban population, whose nobles and peasants were only temporary members retaining their ties to a larger community and whose chief figures were the governor in the gubernia capital and the policemaster or sheriff elsewhere—in any case a delegate of the minister of internal affairs—was a guarantee of continued dominion and stability.

The nobility's dominion was made even more secure by the internal instability of the guilds. When a nobleman rose by promotion in the Table of Ranks, his achievement was permanent, and only in the army was a nobleman degraded to the ranks. Even then, he remained a nobleman. The acquisition of real property or capital affected his standing among his peers but not his status in society as a member of the ruling class. Membership in the guilds, by contrast, depended on hard work, luck, and the vagaries of the market. *Meshchane* rose to become merchants and gained coveted privileges, but merchants were degraded back to *meshchane* by the same impersonal forces that had promoted them. With neither a territorial base in their control nor a permanent status recognized by law and impervious to changes in their economic standing, the merchants were the most volatile elements in Russian society and the most conscious of indignities suffered at the hands of the ruling class. No wonder that the most cherished goal of a merchant was to escape his guild by gaining access to the nobility, in which he would begin another laborious progression.[39] The internal structure of the nobility resembled in fact that of the merchantry, but at a higher social level: nobles in grades fourteen to eight were the equivalent of the third-guild merchants, those in grades eight to six that of the second-guild merchants, and those in grades five and above the counterpart of the first-guild merchants and their "distinguished" elite.

The refusal of the ruling class to look at the town as a territorial complex meant that it was impossible to speak of a unified municipal administration representing more than the registered population and operating for the benefit of the town as a whole. The management of the police, the single most important urban responsibility in the eighteenth century, was more often than not in the hands of an outsider—first the voevoda, then the sheriff. Nobleman and peasants were tried and taxed by their own communities and leaders, and the undeveloped urban economy created no strong pressures on them to participate in a common effort, thereby reinforcing the prejudices of the ruling class and creating a vicious circle from which there was no escape.

Registered townsmen were represented by the heads of patriarchal households (*dvory*) in a general assembly called the *mirskii skhod*, the meeting of the collectivity (*mir*); the fact that these and other terms were also used in villages shows that the world of the townsmen remained little differentiated from that of the peasant. The assembly chose the *zemskii starosta*, apportioned taxes among members of the collectivity, and voted punishment for undesirables, including banishment to Siberia or to the army when the community was required to supply its quota of recruits. The assembly also elected *tseloval'niki* —people who kissed the cross as a form of oath—for a variety of purposes, notably collecting taxes and selling vodka. The common office of *starosta* and *tseloval'nik* was called the *zemskaia izba*. Each of the three *stat'i* had one or more *starshiny* (elders), depending on the size of the *stat'ia*, and *starshiny* and *starosta* formed a kind of unofficial council handling only affairs of the registered population.[40]

The mobilization of the merchantry began in 1699, when the isolated communities and *stat'i* of townsmen were ordered to elect at their assemblies new representatives called *burmistry* for the management of financial and judicial affairs, meeting in the same *zemskie izby* but no longer subordinated to the voevodas who, in the process of "feeding themselves," had often made a point of squeezing the merchantry into bankruptcy before the end of their tour of duty. Although the *burmistry* were no more than the old *tseloval'niki* under a Germanic name, the novelty was in the creation of a *Ratusha* or Chamber (*Palata*) in Moscow to provide an administrative and corporate headquarters for the registered population now mobilized on a nationwide basis. Following the territorial reform of 1708, the Chamber lost its role as national head-quarters and became the corporate agency of the urban population of Moscow gubernia—the largest—while *burmistry* and *starosty* continued to be elected elsewhere but were now subordinated to the governors.[41] Ten years later, in 1718, when colleges were being created and plans were being made to give them local agencies, the government began a campaign to convince the townsmen, in the largest towns at least, to create *magistraty*, modeled after the Riga *magistrat*. In February 1720 Iurii Trubetskoi was appointed senior (*ober*) president over all *magistraty*. In January 1721 he was given an office called the Central (*Glavnyi*) *Magistrat* in Petersburg and supplied with an instruction. Three years later, local *magistraty*, called *ratushi* in the smaller towns, were given their own instruction.[42]

The *magistrat* was a collegial *zemskaia izba* at a time when collegiality was seen as the most efficient principle of administration. In the larger towns like Petersburg, Moscow, Arkhangelsk, Vologda, and Novgorod, it consisted of a president, four burgomasters, and four councillors (*ratmany*). Its size declined with the size of the town, and in the smallest towns, no different from villages, the *starosta* remained the chief figure. The elders probably became members of the *magistrat* or selected someone to replace them. This was expected in a patriarchal society, and indeed the instruction of 1721 required the *magistrat* to be elected from among "people of the first *stat'ia*, well off and intelligent," those in fact whom the government would hold responsible for the tax arrears of their communities and for failure to meet contractual obligations. Their choice required the confirmation of the Central *Magistrat* The *magistraty* thus became the permanent executive committees of the assemblies, ratifying their decisions, acting as their intermediaries with the government, and thus part of a national network subordinated once again to a central headquarters accoun-table to the Senate.

The post-Petrine period was not favorable to the development of towns (the percentage of the registered population being less in 1762 than it had been in 1719), and the broad picture is one of desolation, except in some of the provincial centers transformed into gubernia capitals by the local government reform of the 1770s. The reform and the charter of 1785 compelled the government to take a new look at "municipal" administration. The urge to legislate, however, was set against the impossibility of imposing a uniform statute upon a situation in the field so disparate that even gubernia capitals had nothing in common with uezd centers, many of them villages baptized as towns for administrative convenience. The result was a municipal statute (*gorodovoe polozhenie*),[43] applicable to Petersburg, Moscow, and a few gubernia capitals, irrelevant everywhere else.

Since there never was any doubt that the police would remain in the hands of an appointed member of the apparatus, the task of the statute was to distinguish between the administration of justice and the management of the municipal economy, and to vest responsibility for each in separate agencies. The registered population earning at least fifty rubles a year met in general assembly to elect—following the same procedures as in the assembly of the nobility—a duma (*obshchaia duma*), consisting of a mayor (*glava, golova*) and deputies representing the merchant and craft guilds, the *meshchane*, and the distinguished townsmen. The duma then chose among its members an executive committee of six members (*shestiglasnaia gorodskaia duma*), chaired by the mayor. Its main responsibility was to develop the urban economy and raise revenue. The *magistrat* in each uezd capital of two burgomasters and four councillors, all elected by the assembly, became a lower court for the registered population. Elections required the governor's confirmation. With the abolition of the Central *Magistrat* in 1784, duma and *magistraty* were subordinated to the gubernia board and the governor, a paradoxical situation at a time when the government was seeking—or claiming to seek—the development of a "third estate" and was about to launch a radical program of urban reconstruction. *Starosty* remained in existence, but only as heads of urban historical districts (*slobody*).[44]

If there was a certain consistency in the reform, it foundered on the poverty of the merchant class, its refusal to assume additional administrative reponsibilities, and the very inappropriateness of such an elaborate administrative structure, which continued to assume an identity of interests between the registered and the total population. Duma were never elected in most towns, *magistraty* continued to manage the affairs of the registered population, and in the smaller towns *starosty* remained in charge, as they had been since Muscovite Russia.[45]

Peasantry

The peasantry, it hardly needs to be said, constituted nearly all of the Russian population. There were in 1719 on the territory of the twenty-six post-1785 gubernias 5.5 million male peasants, or 93.2 percent of the total male population. At the beginning of Catherine's reign the percentage actually rose to 96.1 percent. By 1795, when the fifth census registered 9.5 million males, or 93.1 percent of the population, it was obvious that there had been very little change in the course of 75 years. The reign of Alexander, here as in much else, witnessed the beginning of a change, but the 10.5 million males in 1815 still made up 91.3 percent of the total.[46] These few figures tell us much about the constitution of the social order. When combined with figures illustrating the stability of the fiscal base, they project the compelling image of an almost unchanging world. This in turn goes a long way to explain the permanence of the ruling families and the unchallengeable sway of the ruling class throughout the eighteenth century.

The internal composition of the peasantry likewise underwent very few changes. The censuses divided it into four categories: the serfs of landowners, those of the treasury, called state peasants in the nineteenth century, those of the crown, and those of the church. The percentage of serfs owned by landowners was 57.6 percent in 1719 and 57.6 percent in 1795 but declined slightly to 55.3 percent in 1815. There is some question, however, about this classification. Since the Synodal administration and the black clergy—bishops and monks—were no more than the ideological apparatus of the ruling class, their peasants should be combined with those of the treasury, as indeed they were in the census of 1815. Peasants of the crown, on the other hand, were the private property of the Romanov house and should be added to those owned by landowners. It then follows that 66.7 percent of the peasant population was privately owned in 1719, 62.9 percent in 1795, and 61.6 percent in 1815.

"Peasants of the treasury" (*kazennye*) was a general term for the other third of the peasantry whose origins were the most diverse. Since time immemorial, the provinces north of the Volga had been the land of the *chernososhnye* peasants, so called because they lived on "black lands," not immune from taxation. Serfdom had made limited inroads into those provinces because soil and climate made agriculture unproductive almost everywhere. In the eastern provinces, chiefly Kazan and Nizhni Novgorod, the native, non-Russian population of Tatars, Votiaks, Mordvy, Chuvash, and Chermiss had been incorporated into this category of peasants, who paid the quitrent to the treasury in return for continued residence on lands that had passed under treasury control after their annexation in the sixteenth century.[47]

Other peasants were assigned a definite function. The defense of the southern border against the steppe nomads remained a high priority well into the eighteenth century, and *odnodvortsy* (homesteaders) had been settled along a succession of lines guarding the outer limits of Russian colonization.[48] Descendants of *deti boiarskie* given an estate barely large enough to support them, they divided their time between farming and service on the line. Their claims to recognition as noble were consistently rejected after 1719. Related to them were the "settled [*pakhatnye*] soldiers" in Orel, Kazan, and other gubernias.[49] The mass of "state peasants" in central and southern Russia consisted of declassé landlords and descendants of lower service people (*sluzhilye liudi po priboru*), formerly called *streltsy, pushkari,* and *cossacks,* who were not incorporated into the nobility by Peter's reforms; and of peasants settled on lands that had once been the tsars' patrimony, who paid the quitrent to the treasury, not to the agency responsible for the administration of court peasants. Mention must also be made of the peasants attached (*pripisnye*) to copper- iron- and salt-works, shipyards, and gun factories in Petersburg, Olonets, Tula, and the Urals.[50] As for the peasants of the church, they were found almost everywhere, but 51.6 percent of them in 1719, 45.3 percent in 1795, were concentrated in the six provinces of Moscow, Petersburg, and Novgorod, Vladimir, Tver, and Iaroslavl.[51] Taken as a whole, the peasants of the treasury were heavily represented in the northern and southern regions, where their share approached 50 percent of the peasantry in 1719 and 1795. In the central region, however, it ranged from only 17.6 percent in 1719 to nearly 20 percent in 1795.

These peasants were considered free men, but only in the sense that they were not the personal property of other men. They were no more bound to the land than the serfs and could be transferred en masse to other parts of Russia or to its borderlands by administrative order. They could not be sold but were given away to landowners by imperial orders, even though this practice was increasingly limited to the borderlands. They did not own the land on which they were settled but paid the quitrent for the right to use it and could not pass it on to their heirs or give any part of it as dowry to their daughters. Like the serfs, they could not travel without a passport, which had to be renewed at regular intervals. Until the 1770s they were at the mercy of the voevodas, who shamelessly exploited them as their major source of livelihood. After the reforms they fell prey to the greed of "directors of economy" and vice-governors.[52]

Nevertheless, they possessed a degree of liberty not granted to privately owned serfs. They were not subject to the petty tyranny of owners and their stewards. They owned not only personal property but also real property—after 1801—in the form of houses, shops, stores, land, and capital. They could marry without the approval of a landowner. They pledged allegiance to the new ruler while serfs did not, at least after 1741. They testified in court. They elected "assessors" to the land court and the uezd court to sit with a nobleman in police investigations and at the trial of their peers. They were, in short, second-class citizens, the collective property of the apparatus, with limited rights, but without the petty and arbitrary supervision of a landowner, his steward, and his wife.[53]

Among the privately held serfs, it is necessary to distinguish three groups. Landowners' peasants, the largest group, were descendants of peasants settled on properties held in hereditary tenure (*votchiny*); of those attached to properties held in conditional tenure (*pomest'ia*), which had gradually turned into hereditary properties before the traditional distinction between the two was abandoned in 1714; of state peasants granted to individual landowners as a reward for services; and of fugitives who by hook or crook were registered by census takers as belonging to private owners, a practice suspended in 1781.

The percentage of private serfs in the three regions was remarkably stable across an entire century. In the northern region they made up 42.2 percent of the peasantry in 1719 and 39.8 percent in 1815, in the southern region 47.2 percent and 48.4 percent, respectively. In the nine central gubernias of the central region, which contained 58 percent of the serf population in 1719 but only 47.6 percent in 1815—the result of transfers to the more fertile southern provinces—the serfs made up 72 percent of the peasantry in 1719 and 74 percent in 1815. The highest percentages of serfs in this region were found in Kaluga gubernia in 1719 (85 percent), in Tula gubernia in 1815 (85 percent), the lowest, in Moscow gubernia in both 1719 and 1815 (59.7 percent and 66.5 percent respectively).

A second group consisted of peasants of the imperial family. Their number actually declined slightly from 506,000 in 1719 to 480,000 in 1795, and their share of the total peasant population declined from 9 percent to 5 percent. By 1815, however, their number had risen to 666,000, or 6.3 percent of the peasant population, possibly as a result of the incorporation of some church peasants and serfs on bankrupt private estates. More than half of these peasants of the Romanov house were found in the central region in 1719, chiefly in Vladimir, Moscow, Kostroma, Nizhni Novgorod, and Smolensk gubernias, and another 25 percent were in the northern region. By 1795 they were almost equally distributed among the three regions. By 1815, however, almost three-fourths (73 percent) were again found in the same gubernias of the central region and in the north, chiefly in Viatka gubernia.[54]

The third group consisted of the so-called *dvorovye liudi*, often improperly translated as "domestics" or household serfs, in fact the household staff. These serfs, especially on large properties, which could afford to be as self-sufficient as possible, did include domestics and lackeys living in the lord's household but also his clerks, craftsmen, gardeners, and cattle hands. They did not pay the capitation, and their share was apportioned among the field serfs.

Large household staffs were a characteristic feature of Russian serfdom. Great lords kept hundreds of such serfs, others as many as they could afford. They formed a kind of brotherhood, guarding access to the lord and his family, distrustful of outsiders and haughty toward them. They trained their young masters to demand the appointment of large staffs of clerks and adjutants when they entered the apparatus and helped them to bring into public life the same cavalier attitudes of detachment and contempt with which they had been familiar at home. These domestics also corrupted the environment, spreading denunciations and taking bribes. Their excessive number created a climate of idleness around the lord's person conducive to every vice. Their influence was at its most perverse when gifted serfs, trained by their masters to become actors, painters, and musicians, suffered degrading humiliation among such jealous and superstitious slovens.[55]

Serfs were the slaves of the nobility, little different from the chattel slaves of American plantation owners.[56] Their function had been to keep their masters in a state of constant readiness for military service in the seventeenth century and to provide the resources in money and in kind to facilitate the "westernization" of the nobility in the eighteenth. It did not follow that a serf was bound to the land. He was instead bound to his master, who moved him whenever necessary from one estate to another and sometimes resettled entire villages over long distances. He was indeed a piece of "movable property." Moreover, he was in effect outside the jurisdiction of the "state," as Catherine II recognized when she nonchalantly confessed that landowners on their estates were doing as they pleased.[57] Most landowners must have agreed in their hearts with one of their number who told his serfs that he was emperor on his estate and their God in this world.[58] The contention that this was not the case because serfs paid the capitation and were drafted as recruits and therefore recognized as legal subjects is based on a misinterpretation of the Russian political order. Resources from direct taxation—the capitation and the quitrent—were split three ways. The quitrent, paid by all peasants, went in part to support the nobility on their estates, in part the apparatus of noblemen who governed the country. The capitation, likewise paid by all peasants, went to pay for an army of noble officers and conscripts from the dependent population. These resources were extracted from the dependent population for the single purpose of supporting the ruling class and were distributed in accordance with a simple division of labor.

Once it is acknowledged that serfs were the personal property of their owners, all of them noblemen, their lack of the most elementary rights must be taken for granted. The lords punished them at will, and the claim by some that Russians were forbidden to kill their serfs while Polish landowners recognized no such inhibition was no more than self-righteous mummery—witness the properly "legal" beatings, mistreatments, and banishment without proper clothing resulting in death, whether on the estate, on the long journey to Siberia, or to the regiments in the field. Lords were allowed to banish their serfs to settlement and even to hard labor to eliminate those who stood up to them. They interfered with the private lives of their serfs and married them off against their will, despite the church's prohibition against such marriages. The murder of a serf by another was treated as a civil action, the owners suing each other for compensation, and serfs could not testify in court against their lords. Servants, always under the eyes of the master and his wife, were of course the worst victims of the lawlessness permitted in the social system.[59]

This is not to claim that lords and serfs were constantly at war with one another. Lawlessness does not necessarily entail violence, and the brutality inherent in serfdom was mitigated by patriarchal relationships facilitating access to the source of power, fostering benevolence and responsibility toward dependents, demanding humility and repentance in them but applauding generosity and mercy among the lords. Without these redeeming qualities, the ruling class would have been an army of occupation and would have lost the legitimacy it needed to rule for so long. Serfs had no property rights. Yet peasants were traders, producers, and entrepreneurs in the towns, usually not under their own name. If they did operate under their own name, there was never any doubt that their earnings and assets were the property of their masters.[60] Finally, the symbol of the serf's defenselessness was that he could be sold. This explains why the attempts to limit the evils of serfdom began with restrictions on the right to sell men, women, and children. Their effect was insignificant. It was noted in 1807 that serfs were still brought in chains to markets like domestic animals and sold individually. As late as 1813, the State Council continued to accept the sale of serfs even when no land was sold and established a nationwide price in notarized transactions of 200 rubles for a male, 100 rubles for a female.[61]

The size and variety of the peasant population, the immensity of the country, and the multiformity of patterns of settlement make it difficult to describe how villages, estates, and various other and larger communities of peasants were administered. Any overall picture must of necessity be a composite. A village, even a small one, was a territorial community with its own representatives and elders, but it was not uncommon to find villages whose serfs belonged to several and even scores of landowners.[62] The inevitable conflict between territorial administration and vertical channels of command—not unlike those preventing the unity of municipal administration— must have sundered the unity of village life. This cannot be treated here, however, and we must limit ourselves to situations in which villages remained undivided.

Villages, let us assume, were part of an estate. Their delegates, heads of patriarchal households sometimes called "wise and old peasants" (*dobrye i starye muzhiki*), met in a general assembly called the assembly of the community, the *mirskii skhod*. Twenty-seven peasants might attend on one estate, 15 on another, from 30 to 115 on a third, representing thirty villages. At the larger meetings, proceedings were controlled by a small group of elders. The assembly's decisions took the form of resolutions (*prigovory*), probably passed by voice vote. These decisions were of three kinds: to elect representatives to run the affairs of the villages between assemblies, to apportion taxes and discuss crop rotation and the repartition of fields, and, finally, to impose punishment on undesirables, including banishment. The assembly also discussed events affecting the community, complaints against the elected representatives, and even suits among peasants. They selected peasants to be sent as recruits and gave permission to individual peasants to leave the community to work for a salary in the towns or on riverboats. The assembly was to a large extent the governing body of a closed world in which the apparatus took little interest beyond the collection of recruits and taxes. Its core consisted of the *starosta*, the treasurer, village elders, and the richer peasants, often called "peasants of the first *stati'ia*" (*pervostateinye*).[63]

The chief executive officer of the collectivity of villages was the *starosta*, sometimes chosen by the landowner, sometimes elected by the assembly for 1 year or more, even for life, from among the "best people," the richer peasants. He summoned the assembly, carried out its decisions, supervised field work, collected taxes, and released funds for local expenditures. His status was enhanced by the fact that he was also the landowner's eye in the peasant community, could play one off against the other, and derived considerable benefit from the Janus-like role that made him indispensable to both. *Starosty*

were also called *burmistry* or *vybornye*, but the titles were not always interchangeable, although it is not clear what role the *burmistr* played when a
starosta was in place.

The closest associate of the *starosta* was the *tselovalnik*, the treasurer who
kissed the cross, a peasant sometimes chosen against his will, since fiscal
irregularities were punished with fines, whipping, banishment, or the draft.
Like the *starosta*, he was chosen from among the wealthier peasants. Election,
here as among the nobles and merchants, was not only a reward for ambition
but also a punishment imposed by the community, a devious way to protect the
community from the exactions of landowner and voevoda. Depending on the
size of the community, there might be more than one treasurer. *Starosta* and
treasurer operated from a common office called the *prikaznaia izba*. The chief
figure in each village was the *sotskii*, also chosen by the assembly, so called
because he was responsible for 100 households, and assisted by deputies in
charge of 10 households (*desiatskie*), often purely fictitious figures without any
relationship to the exact number of households. They and the elders of the
villages—they must at times have been the same people—represented their
villages in the assembly.[64]

Upon this basic administrative pattern landowners and the apparatus
clamped a superstructure adapted to rule over communities of serfs and
peasants of the treasury. The landowner, rewarded for his military service with
a *pomest'e*, later the officer returning to his *votchina* after exacting unconditional obedience from his soldiers, brought to the administration of his
property a military style that did not always succeed in breaking the authority
of peasant representatives but always tried. The result varied from one estate to
another, but on the whole it was a standoff between arbitrary will and inertia.

If the landowner resided on his estate, he managed his property with the
help of the *starosta*. If he resided in Moscow or Petersburg—this was often the
case with the wealthier landowners—he might appoint a steward (*prikaz-
shchik*), an outsider, perhaps a landless nobleman, even a serf, often a foreigner. The steward represented the landowner and very often exercised his
powers in his own interest and against his master's. The essence of management was to keep *starosty*, treasurers, and *sotskie* in a state of fear, and the
steward kept a register of all peasants on the estate and a file on each, like the
service record (*formuliarnyi spisok*) in the army and the apparatus. He
watched over the personal life of the peasants, granted permission to marry,
married off reluctant serfs, and tried to limit the consumption of vodka. The
steward was likely to insist on the appointment of *starosty* and *sotksie* in order
to extend his authority into the villages. No wonder that he was often hated, as
he went about carrying out lengthy instructions written in a distant capital. If
the estate was large, the steward and his clerical staff made up the estate
management office (*votchinnoe upravlenie*), where the desk—covered with a
red cloth, a copy of the *Ulozhenie* of 1649, and the mirror of justice on the
wall—reminded peasants that the landowner was their true governor and
voevoda. Wealthy families like the Sheremetevs, who possessed several large
domains, maintained a management headquarters (*kontora*) in Moscow or

Petersburg from which the lord himself supervised the operations of his stewards.[65]

Other peasant communities were managed according to their social classifications. Peasants of monasteries, among whom stewards had earned an infamous reputation, were secularized in 1764, and their 20,000 villages placed under sixty, later ninety-three, appointed "treasurers," one for every 215 villages, responsible to the College of Economy through four regional headquarters. Villages of court peasants were run by "managers" (*upraviteli*), appointed from among retired officers, whose responsibilities were similar to a steward's. In 1774 these peasants were enjoined to elect *starosty* to replace the managers, and the *starosty* were made responsible to seven regional boards (*kontory*) accountable to the Chancery for Court Peasants in Petersburg. *Odnodvortsy* were run by managers appointed by the College of War. "Peasants of the treasury" were at the mercy of voevodas. The local government reform placed all peasants but the serfs under a "director of economy," a member of the treasury chamber. Beginning in 1797 their villages were gathered into *volosts* of no more than 3,000 males run by an elected head (*golova*) operating through a network of village *starosty*. By 1825 the serfs of the landowners had passed, together with their masters, under the jurisdiction of the Ministry of Internal Affairs, the "state" peasants under that of the Ministry of Finance, and the court peasants under that of the Department of Court Properties.[66]

3

Political Apparatus and Bureaucracy

The Officer Corps

Russian society, consisting of a small nobility ruling over dependent townsmen and peasantry, was governed by a political apparatus representing the interests and embodying the values of the ruling class. At the end of the seventeenth century, this apparatus exercised both military and civilian responsibilities indiscriminately, but the creation of a standing army and 20 years of war resulted in a functional separation of the military from the civilian apparatus, although officers were thrust into leading positions in civilian administration during Peter's reign and for a long time thereafter.

There was no professional officer corps in Muscovite Russia. Nobles reported for duty in *sotni* commanded by headmen (*golovy*), and *sotni* were combined into tactical units called regiments commanded by military voevodas appointed by the tsar. The creation of a regular army entailed the adoption of a permanent officer corps ranked in accordance with Western, notably Swedish and Prussian, models. The responsibilities of the higher ranks were described in the Military Code (*Ustav*) of March 1716, and officer ranks were listed in a separate column of the Table of Ranks of January 1722.[1]

The size of the officer corps remains undetermined. Toward the end of Peter's reign it was about 5,000, at the beginning of Catherine's about 9,000, at the end about 16,000, and about 27,000 at the end of Alexander's reign in 1825.[2] It cannot be determined with accuracy by using the table of organization of the army because many officers served outside the regular chain of command and because of the widespread practice, at least during the latter half of Catherine's reign, to appoint supernumerary (*sverkhshtatnye*) officers in regiments and battalions.[3]

The officer corps was divided into three strata: the general officers, usually referred to as the *generalitet*, and field ("staff") officers, and the junior officers. The *generalitet* came into being as a political force at the end of the Northern War and is sometimes mentioned at the accession of a new ruler on the same footing as the Senate and the Synod, the three constituent parts of the political apparatus that bestowed legitimacy and vouchsafed the execution of government policy.[4] Its privileged position was underscored by the fact that the pay of its members was earmarked as a separate item in the military budget.[5] The *generalitet* authorized by the table of organization of 1720 consisted of twenty-two marshals and generals; that of 1763 authorized eighty-four.[6]

Field marshals, in grade one, stood at the top of the military hierarchy. Peter created two for the first time—Sheremetev and Menshikov—as a reward for distinction on the battlefield. After the creation of the College of War, one became its president, while the other was placed in command of the most sensitive military sector. After 1725, however, the rank was given from time to time on an honorary basis to a favorite of the ruler. The practice became more prominent under Elizabeth when the number of marshals rose to four and even six, including political marshals like the Razumovskii and Shuvalov brothers. In 1736 it was fixed at three, and the empress Catherine never exceeded that number.[7]

Full generals, called "generals en chef" (*anshef*) until the reign of Paul and generals of infantry, cavalry, or artillery thereafter, ranked below the marshals. There were five in 1720, eight in 1763. The Chief of the Artillery was a full general. Generals commanded divisions in the eighteenth century, army and separate corps under Alexander. Lieutenant generals—five in 1720, twenty in 1763—also commanded divisions and distant separate corps in Siberia, Orenburg, and the Caucasus. They and the generals often doubled up as governors-general in the borderlands. Majors general, finally—ten in 1720, fifty-three in 1763—commanded brigades and even regiments, and are often found among the governors. Marshals, generals, and lieutenant generals formed the hard core of the high command, formulating military policy, co-opting outsiders into the officer corps, and controlling promotions, at least until 1797. Majors general were the executive officers of the military establishment, its managers in the field and the provinces. The rank of brigadier—in grade five—fell into disuse during the eighteenth century and was abolished by Paul.[8]

The second stratum of officers included the so-called "staff," or field officers (*shtab-ofitsery*), from colonel in grade six to major in grade eight. As a rule, regimental commanders were colonels throughout the eighteenth century but often generals after 1800. The regimental staff consisted of a lieutenant colonel and a major who commanded battalions. The table of organization of 1731 distinguished between first and second majors, both in grade eight. The distinction, intended to slow promotion to the higher grades and to introduce some discipline among unruly majors who refused to recognize the seniority of their equals, was abolished by Paul in February 1798. Artillery officers ranked one grade higher than their army colleagues, guard officers two grades higher; a guard major was the equivalent of a colonel in the army.[9]

Junior officers (*ober-ofitsery*) from captains in grade nine to ensigns in grade fourteen—the lowest—made up the third stratum. Captains were company commanders. Their subordinates were called captain lieutenants in grade ten. No army rank was placed in grade eleven: lieutenants and sublieutenants were in grades twelve and thirteen. Beginning in 1731, captains in the cavalry were called *rotmistry*, and captain lieutenants second *romistry*. The latter were renamed staff (*shtabs-*) captain and staff *rotmistry* in January 1797. Artillery sublieutenants were called *shtyk-yunker* until February 1797. The one- and two-grade differential between army officers on the one hand and artillery and guard officers on the other applied to junior officers as well.[10]

All officers were noblemen, but not all noblemen joining the army became officers. The process by which a member of the ruling class entered the military apparatus varied with his social standing. A modern army requires a competent officer corps, and war is the most demanding teacher. Indeed, the emphasis on merit had been one of the reasons behind the abolition of *mestnichestvo* in 1682, under which command positions were assigned in accordance with a complicated system of precedence among established families. The tense situation during the first decade of the eighteenth century did not permit the government to neglect the quality of its officer corps, and those who failed in battle, even if they belonged to the best families, were harshly treated.[11] Peace was in sight, however, after 1710, and tradition, marked by an intense politicization of the military apparatus, began to reassert itself.

The imperial order of February 1714 recognized that young nobles were being promoted to officer who had been noncommissioned officers for a few months at the most and had never served in the ranks. To give them a minimum of military training, they were required to serve as soldiers in the guard, and direct appointments of nobles to the officer corps were forbidden. Non-noble noncommissioned officers would continue to be promoted on merit.[12]

This order laid the foundation of official policy on entrance into the officer corps until the end of Alexander's reign. It was patently impossible, however, for all young nobles to join the Guard, an elite formation requiring its members to be men of at least some means. Since no criterion was established, practice determined that guardsmen must be handsome, must come from established families, and must own at least twenty serfs.[13] Beginning in Anna's reign, it became a common practice to register children: the future marshal Rumiantsev entered the Guard at 5 in 1730, a son of General and Senator Bibikov was registered at 2 and became an officer at 9, and Alexander Balashov, the future Minister of Police, became a guardsman in 1776 at the age of 6. Guard officers, still in adolescence, then took advantage of the two-rank differential and transferred to the army to command battalions and regiments. The speed of further promotion depended on the importance of the patronage network to which the officer belonged. Other nobles, who entered the Corps of Cadets, created in November 1731, enjoyed similar preferential treatment. Those who had no choice but to join the army directly, and non-nobles who had been drafted had to await promotion through the ranks.[14]

Until 1797, promotions into and within the hierarchy of noncommissioned officers were made by the regimental commanders, who submitted to their divisional commanders candidates for promotion to the first officer rank. A distinction was already made at that level between nobles and non-nobles for whom a separate rank of *feldvebel—vakhmistr* in the cavalry—was established. Only nobles were guaranteed noncommissioned ranks. Colonels, who were the backbone of the army, thus determined the degree of mobility within their regiments and indirectly influenced the social composition of the apparatus. Divisional commanders also promoted to officer from within their staffs and retinues.[15]

There were limitations, however, at least in theory. Noble noncommissioned officers, who by virtue of their nobility already belonged to the ruling class, were promoted to officer without any required length of service. Sons of officers of non-noble origin had to have been noncommissioned officers for 4 years, military clerks—former civilian clerks or priests' sons—8 years, drafted soldiers 12 years. These requirements were forgotten in the 1780s and 1790s, when divisional commanders promoted lackeys, cooks, barbers, and musicians to ensign and then to higher ranks, a practice resulting in what General Langeron called the destruction of the Russian army by Potemkin, Zubov, and Suvorov.[16]

Promotions to higher officer ranks were governed until 1797 by the imperial order of April 1714. Junior officers were promoted by full generals to captains, and promotions to major and lieutenant colonel were made by field marshals and the president of the College of War, who recommended to the ruler candidates for promotion to colonel. Promotions were made on a regimental basis, with officers moving up to fill vacancies, but field officers were promoted on a divisional basis, transferring out from their regiment to wherever a vacancy occurred. Candidates for promotion were selected by the vote of their fellow officers (*balotirovanie*) until 1742. Thereafter, they were chosen on the basis of seniority and merit, a euphemism for the discretion of the commanders to select their favorites in the never-ending battle for patronage. Under Catherine, promotions were made on an armywide basis once a year, junior officers remaining 3 to 4 years in each rank, captains remaining 7 or 8. Junior officer commissions were signed by the president of the College of War, those of field officers by the empress. Mass promotions were made by divisional commanders after 1775 without regard to need: some regiments had up to twenty majors—instead of the authorized five—and Suvorov is said to have promoted 600 field officers in 2 years.[17]

The drastic reforms of Paul were directed against this fragmentation of the military apparatus among divisional commanders and the resulting lack of social discrimination in promoting noncommissioned officers into the officer corps. In November 1796 the College or War was ordered to give preference to nobles over non-nobles, and regimental commanders were rebuked in April 1798 for recommending non-nobles for promotion to officer. All noblemen in the ranks had to be promoted to noncommissioned officer within 3 months, and promotions into the officer corps required the tsar's confirmation. The reaction continued under Alexander. In December 1802, non-nobles were required to serve 12 years as noncommissioned officers before they could be recommended for promotion, while nobles had to serve only 6 years.[18]

Promotions to junior officer ranks were made once again on a regimental basis, to field-officer ranks on an armywide basis. All promotions henceforth required the ruler's confirmation, except in wartime. The Field Army Statute of January 1812 gave the commander in chief—a commander with far greater responsibilities than his Petrine predecessor—the right to promote only to captain. The War Ministry as the intermediary between the ruler and field commanders in personnel matters was replaced during the war by the army's Main Staff and after 1815 by His Majesty's Main Staff.[19]

Since the Russian nobility was also the ruling class of the country and found its identity in staffing positions that enabled it to govern the dependent population, it was taken for granted that service was for life. Military service, however, at a time when no logistical support system yet existed and landowners went to war hoping to subsist on their own resources and booty, was limited to campaigns in the field, usually of short duration. The general mobilization carried out by Peter after 1700 to face the Swedish danger, and the creation of a much larger standing army requiring an officer corps with a minimum of professional qualifications transformed military service into a permanent and lifelong occupation, as well as a heavy burden on the nobility, the treasury, and the economic health of the country. The Swedish war lasted 20 years and the Persian campaign another year. By 1724, with the return of peace in the midst of a fiscal crisis, the government was ready to accept not the demobilization of the officer corps but extensive leaves as a compromise. The imperial order of November 1724 allowed half of the army officers with country estates to spend every other year at home, of course without pay. Officers began to use the opportunity to enjoy a life of leisure (*na rekreatsiiu*), a welcome relief from the harshness and coarseness of army life. The order seems to have remained in effect after Peter's death but was suspended in wartime, during the Crimean campaigns of 1736–1739, the Swedish war of 1741–1743, and the Seven Years' War of 1756–1762.[20]

Extended leaves were the equivalent of a partial demobilization. Retirement, however, either partial or complete became permissible for some. Officers, as well as soldiers, who were old, crippled, or suffered from incurable diseases and were totally unfit for service but not invalids were allowed to return home in September 1725, after receiving passports from the College of War.[21] Those without resources (*sobstvennoe propitanie*) were sent to monasteries, there to be supported, like the monks, by the labor of serfs bound to church properties. Partial retirement took two forms. Officers unfit for the rigors of military service in the field—there were no barracks, and troops slept in tents in the summer and in peasants' huts and townsmen's quarters in the winter—were transferred to garrison service in the major towns, where the fortress became a permanent headquarters. Others, if they found an affinity for it, were sent by the College of War to the Heraldmaster's Office, from which they were assigned to positions in the civilian apparatus. The apparatus, indeed, seems to have been filled until well into the 1760s by retired officers. Retirement was usually accompanied by promotion to the next higher rank. Those who transferred to the civilian apparatus were promoted after 1735 to the next higher civilian rank.[22] A lieutenant in grade ten thus became a titular councillor in grade nine.

By the 1730s, the consequences of leaving the landed properties of the nobility and their large numbers of serfs without the supervision of their masters began to affect the productivity of agriculture, raise the level of insecurity in the countryside, and reduce the ability of the army to collect the capitation. The resulting pressures to counter this troublesome situation, combined with the resistance of Russian officers to Marshal Münnich's innovations in tactics and dress in the army, and their revolt against the haughtiness of the "German cohorts in powdered wigs" (*nemetskie pudrennye druzhiny*) compelled the government in December 1736 to rule for the first time that service was no longer universal—only sons and one of two or more sons were allowed to remain on the estate—and that officers could retire after 25 years in the service. Four years later, in August 1740, however, the Cabinet of Ministers made retirement dependent on Senate approval, and applicants had to be at least 45 years old. This seems to have remained the law until February 1762,[23] when the government at last decreed the final demobilization of the officer corps, insisting at the same time that it remained the duty of the nobility to fill officer positions. Retirement had ceased to be a privilege and had become a right, together with the refusal to enter the army in the first place.

For this right to be of any value, however, provision had to be made for veterans without landed property and serfs. The civilian apparatus remained open to those who applied for admission. Garrison forces were supplemented by local detachments (*shtatnye komandy*) for police duty in the countryside. The assignment of veterans to monasteries, however, was terminated in the wake of the secularization of church properties. Invalid officers and soldiers were assigned instead to various towns—thirty in 1764—with their wives and children, where they formed squads (*komandy*) of invalids used for light guard duty in return for a salary ranging from 120 rubles for a lieutenant colonel to 33 rubles for an ensign. Upon the veteran's death his widow and children continued to receive part of his salary.[24] The concept of an automatic pension was born.

This provision was not universally accepted, however. Individual officers had always been allowed to petition the ruler for a pension, which now replaced the *pomest'e* of old, on grounds of long and meritorious service. We find, for example, in the commissary budget for 1780 scattered references to pensions—500 rubles for a major general in Pskov, 300 for another, 180 rubles for a colonel in Orel gubernia, 125 rubles for a major in Simbirsk gubernia.[25] Regular military pensions would not begin to be paid until the reign of Paul, at the rate of half the officer's salary after 30 years of service, the full salary after 40 years, provided the officer had never been fined, never faced a court-martial, and did not request at the same time a promotion to the next higher rank.[26]

These general rules remained government policy until the end of Alexander's reign. Officers unable to remain in field army service were "retired" to the Internal Guard, which combined after 1811 the garrisons and the local and invalid detachments, or were appointed commandants in borderland fortresses manned by field army units. Those wishing to retire requested a pension from the ruler through their commanding officers, and these pensions were paid out from the general treasury.[27] Finally, officers who retired on grounds of disability retained the right to apply for a position in the civilian apparatus, and those wounded during the war of 1812–1813 were given the special privilege of collecting both a pension and their new salary. The so-called Committee of August 18, 1814, was created especially for the purpose of placing these officers, and in 1816 a list was published of civilian positions reserved exclusively for them. After 1807 the widows of officers killed in battle received their husbands' full salary. If they too had died, their children collected the pension, boys until the age of 16, girls until their marriage.[28]

The Civilian Apparatus

The civilian apparatus consisted of two strata, its leading members part of the ruling elite, in grades one to three, its executive agents among the managers in grades four to eight. Civilians in ranks below grade eight were not hereditary nobles and must be considered part of the secretarial and clerical staff.

At the very top stood the Chancellor, who represented the tsar in dealings with foreign envoys and was responsible for the day-to-day management of external relations as head of the College of Foreign Affairs. His role was often nominal, depending on the degree of the ruler's personal involvement, and the presence of a vice-chancellor was a source of constant rivalry. The post was established in 1709 but remained unoccupied between 1735 and 1740, during the entire reign of Catherine, between 1804 and 1809, and between 1814 and 1845, when the Vice-Chancellor in the eighteenth century, the Minister of Foreign Affairs during the reign of Alexander, became the government's only representative for foreign envoys.[29] Since there were always at least two or three field marshals who, as military men, enjoyed precedence over their civilian peers, it is obvious that the leaders of the high command were also dominant over the entire political apparatus.

The next two grades were not linked with any positions, with the sole exception of the procurator general in grade three. Those raised to the ranks of real privy councillor and privy councillor formed a loose group of members of the ruling families with some outsiders enjoying their favor, who were prominent at Court, in personal contact with the ruler, and functioned as social companions and advisers. That was indeed the reason why the Table of Ranks assigned no positions to them. They constituted an informal "grand council" of the Empire, which never met as a body but from which they retired after their tour of duty. Senators usually came from this pool of advisers. Thirteen of the nineteen members of the First Department in 1809 were real privy councillors and six privy councillors; its twenty members in 1823 were equally divided among the two ranks.[30] These men were never made "senators"; they were appointed "to attend (*prisutstvovat'v*) the Senate."[31] All five civilian ministers in 1802 and three of the four in 1823 were real privy councillors. In the State Council, eleven of its sixteen members in 1809 and ten of the seventeen in 1823 were in these two ranks; the others were generals and admirals. There were 40 real privy councillors and 120 privy councillors in 1796—civilian descendants of the boyars, *okolnichie*, and Duma nobles of Muscovite Russia, of whom there had been 144 in 1690.[32]

Positions in the next five grades—four down to eight—were managerial. Their holders made the system work or paralyzed it. They received instructions and decisions made at the higher level and channeled information on which these instructions a decisions were based. Some ran agencies, others supervised the work of agencies and watched over the execution of the laws. It is necessary, however, to distinguish between two levels, positions in grades four to six and those in grades seven and eight. They were sharply separated by the fact that all appointments in grade six and above were made by the ruler—on his own or on the recommendation of the Senate and ministers—while positions in grades seven and eight were filled by the Senate on its own authority and, increasingly after 1802, on the recommendation of individual ministers.

Presidents of colleges were usually in grade four (real state councillor), but we also find some in grade three, when it was found necessary to enhance the authority of the college. This was the case in the 1760s, for example, when the presidents of the Colleges of Justice, Landed Affairs, and Revenue were in grade three, while those of the Colleges of Audit, Mining, and Manufactures were in grade four. Heads of quasi-collegial agencies like the Expedition of State Revenues and the State Treasury were also in grade four. When colleges, reconstituted under their own or another name, were gathered to form ministries in 1802 and later became ministerial departments, their chiefs were logically placed in grade four and made accountable to a minister two grades higher. Senior procurators, the procurator general's delegates, who watched over the observance of procedures in each Senate department and guarded the legality of its decisions, were likewise in grade four.

Governors, like senators, were not included in the Table of Ranks. The early governors, indeed, belonged to the ruling group of councillors who, like the most important voevodas of the seventeenth century, sat in the Duma between tours of duty in various parts of the country. After Peter's death, most governors were real state councillors or majors general, hence their resentment at being subordinated to the colleges. By the end of the eighteenth century, they were all in grade four. Governors, presidents of colleges, and later departmental directors were thus, as a rule, in the same grade and filled the key managerial positions of the imperial government. There were 187 real state councillors in 1796.[33] This does not mean, however, that there were 187 positions in grade four. By then the Table of Ranks had ceased to be, despite its name, a table of positions and become truly a table of ranks. Individuals were promoted not only to fill vacancies but as a result of seniority or the recommendation of a powerful patron. A rank had become a badge of social achievement and had ceased to be an identification of administrative responsibility.

In the next two grades—five and six—of state councillor and college councillor, we find members of colleges, the chairmen and members of the three chambers in each gubernia after the local government reform, the provincial voevodas, procurators in colleges, and, after the reform, the "directors of economy," the gubernia procurator, and the gubernia marshal. These men were the assistant managers of the system, the collaborators of the presidents, directors, and governors. The entire administration of the country was in their hands. They did the staff work for the civilian high command, which could not function without their skills and assistance. Positions in the last two grades—court councillor in seven and college assessor in eight—were still managerial positions but of secondary importance. There were few positions in grade seven—the uezd marshal was one—but we find in grade eight the voevodas, the key links between the apparatus and the population, the assessors in the colleges, jacks-of-all trades who carried out whatever responsibilities were not included in the job descriptions of other members. After the reform we find in this grade the gubernia treasurer, the assessors in the chambers, the sheriff, and the uezd judge—this last an elective position. These men were the managers of the towns and uezds, subordinated in effect to the governor, the manager of the gubernia. There were 3,592 members of the apparatus in grades five to eight in 1796.[34]

Promotion to college assessor in grade eight was the equivalent of one to ensign in the army, six grades below. It gave non-nobles the status of hereditary nobility and secured for them a place in the apparatus. It was their ticket of admission into the ruling class. The downgrading of the civilian establishment by the Table of Ranks is obvious since the lowest-ranking officer was automatically co-opted into the hereditary nobility, which his counterpart, the lowest-ranking civilian, could not hope to obtain for many years, if ever in his lifetime. Only an army career was intended to offer the rewards of social mobility to ambitious commoners.

On the other hand, if young noblemen did not have the possibility of joining a civilian "guard" in order to earn promotion while remaining at home, some evidence of ability and the proper recommendation guaranteed an appointment by the Senate to a grade-eight position. Access to these coveted positions was also opened to army captains who retired from military service and took advantage of the one-rank bonus given upon retirement.[35] These retired officers were the major source of candidates for membership in the civilian apparatus. Finally, the local government reforms of the 1770s opened up access to these positions by election—after 1801 even grade-seven positions like assessor in the gubernia judicial chambers were filled by election. Tenure, however, was temporary, and holders of the post lost the rank attached to it when they left office.

Hereditary nobles, life nobles (after 1785), and non-nobles who began their careers as clerks or in the secretarial staff had to wait until they were recommended for promotion by senators, the procurator general, presidents of colleges, or ministers, and promotion was granted by the Senate in general assembly. There seem to have been no rules governing promotions until 1737, and members of the civilian apparatus did not even receive "commissions" (*patenty*), most likely because many kept using their military commissions as proof of status. The Senate order of November 1737 required civilians in "field-officer ranks"—that is, in grade eight and above—to obtain their commissions from the ruler, while those in "junior officer ranks" would receive theirs from the Senate. Six months earlier an imperial order took note of the Senate's generosity in promoting secretaries to grade-eight positions—notably assessors in colleges, town voevodas, stewards in *volosts* of court peasants—and required Senate nominations to be henceforth confirmed by the Cabinet and the ruler. The Senate regained its prerogative in May 1742.[36]

The first rules seeking to regulate access to the civilian apparatus date from September 1765. These rules must be understood against a background of increasing concern over the growth of the secretarial and clerical staff, which the rules of May 1762 and the general table of organization of December 1763 had tried to hinder. They did not regulate promotions within the apparatus but were directed at non-noble secretaries seeking access to the so-called *sudeiskie* positions, that is, those in grade eight and above where administrative and judicial decisions were made. Promotions had to be justified by the existence of a vacancy, and the three candidates recommended to the Senate had to have served at least 12 years in grade nine or ten; these were made on an agencywide basis. These restrictions did not apply to hereditary nobles, who retained free access to the apparatus by virtue of their social status and had to submit proof of it upon application. These rules of 1765 were incorporated into the statute of December 1790, although the experience of 25 years had shown that they had been ineffective.[37]

This statute, like the rules of 1765, did not apply to promotions within the apparatus. These depended on favoritism, and all members were not equal, those with a powerful patron being able to bring their case before the ruler. It is true that Catherine ordered a general promotion in April 1764 of all field officers who had been in the same post in the civilian apparatus for 7 years, and that a second such promotion took place in the fall of 1767 in favor of those who had been bypassed in 1764,[38] but there is no evidence that such apparatus-wide promotions continued to be made regularly. Indeed, the very use of the term *promotion as a reward* (*nagrazhdenie chinami*) instead of the simpler word for *promotion* (*proizvodstvo*) suggests that there were no established rules for promotions within the apparatus.

This relatively flexible but highly politicized system, which enabled ruling families to shape the apparatus in a constant interplay of intrigues and favors, was shaken by the introduction of seniority rules in December 1799.[39] They conformed to Paul's general policy, which sought to weaken the influence of those families by imposing rules to limit their freedom of action. The entrance of non-nobles into the apparatus continued to be regulated by the statute of 1790, but noblemen were now required to spend 4 years in grade nine or ten before their promotion to grade eight. Moreover, promotions to grade seven, six, and five were henceforth to take place after five, six, and four years, respectively, and all required the ruler's approval. Promotions to "general" ranks remained the prerogative of the ruler, as they had always been in the military as well.

The logical consequence of this policy of imposing restrictions upon the ruling group was the imperial order of August 1809, the product of Speranskii's fertile and subversive imagination. To the restrictions introduced in December 1799 it added the requirement of passing a university examination in literature, law, history, and mathematics; it even lifted some of those restrictions to speed up promotions to grade five for those who had passed with distinction but barred access to grade-five positions to those incapable of showing proof of intellectual achievements.

The order caused a storm among the ruling class, and with good reason. If the nobility was showing little interest in the "useful business of education," as the order noted, it was because it emphasized power and the control of decision making at the various echelons of the apparatus. But the constructive exercise of power at the higher levels increasingly required a knowledge of facts and a critical mind, especially in the administration of justice and finance, which only a well-rounded education could provide, the badge of westernization for an elite now committed to win its place on the vast stage of European politics and intellectual life. The order also favored those of non-noble origin, like Speranskii himself, or of modest origin without the proper connections in the network of ruling families. Intellectual achievement was becoming a substitute for the favor of the great. It gradually raised the educational level of the apparatus, but it was also a factor in the bureaucratization of the political world, which, in the long run, undermined the autonomy not only of the ruling families but of the ruler as well.[40]

The great demand for personnel to staff an overburdened civilian apparatus in the midst of war, the general mobilization of the nobility into the army and the resulting shortage of noblemen elsewhere, the admission of townsmen and peasants into the clerical staff and the subsequent promotion of the most capable into the apparatus—all these strengthened the traditional assumption that service was for life. Entering the ruling class in a society with so few other outlets meant gaining access to privilege; retiring from the apparatus presupposed the existence of independent resources that very few ever had. Since working conditions in the civilian apparatus were incomparably superior to those in the army—even if life in Petersburg in the 1720s had few amenities and costs were high—the question of unfitness was less urgent and less widespread. The very fact that service in it was a form of retirement for officers implied that it was largely a welcome second choice for those without a military vocation and the proper stamina.

Nevertheless, the civilian apparatus could not remain insulated from the pressures at work within its military counterpart, and the manifesto of December 1736 applied to both the officer corps and the civilian managers. The restriction introduced in August 1740 likewise applied to both, with the additional provision that members of the civilian apparatus could not retire before the age of 55, instead of 45 for the officers. Similarly, the famous manifesto of February 1762, usually referred to as the act of emancipation of the nobility from state service, was addressed to both military and civilians,[41] although its main object was the demobilization of the officer corps after the Seven Years' War. It did not emancipate the nobility from service for the simple reason that the officers, the politicians, and the managers in the first eight grades remained hereditary noblemen—it would be tantamount to saying that the nobility was emancipated from the nobility. What it did say in so many words was that the general mobilization of the nobility by Peter I, followed by the growth of education, had resulted in the training of enough capable officers and knowledgeable managers to eliminate the need for compulsion. The manifesto was not an act of emancipation but one of final demobilization of the ruling class. Civilians in the first eight grades who petitioned for retirement had to await the ruler's approval. Those allowed to retire were promoted to the next higher grade if they had been in their current grade for more than a year.

It was not enough to allow the civilians to retire: provision had to be made, as in the army, for the support of those who had no landed property to which to retire and essentially nowhere to go. The manifesto was followed by a decision of Catherine's government to set aside a pension fund for the old and crippled, and for those who remained without a position after the promulgation of the new table of organization of the imperial government in December 1763. A sum of 25,000 rubles was earmarked from the revenues of the College of Economy—the new agency just created to manage the secularized properties of the church—in June 1764, when rules were also announced to govern the grants of pensions. To be eligible, the applicant had to be at least 50 years old, to have served at least 35 years since the age of 15 (unless he suffered from some incapacitating illness—poor eyesight was a common cause), and had never been fined or tried during those years. Applicants could not be promoted to the next grade unless the ruler chose to grant both pension and promotion. The pension's amount was fixed at half the applicant's salary. Since the total sum could not be exceeded, the applicants had to wait for a vacancy if too many had applied. A pension was thus not automatic on retirement from the civilian apparatus, and its amount depended on the generosity of the ruler. It is thus obvious that the manifesto of 1762 and the rules of 1764 restricted the scope of the civil demobilization to those who possessed landed property and constituted, as we shall see presently, the political infrastructure of the ruling class. Pensions ranging from 100 to 600 rubles a year were also granted to holders of the Cross of Saint Vladimir, introduced in September 1782, who earned it for special distinction in the apparatus or simply for serving 35 years. It may have been reserved, however, for members of the ruling elite, since Saint Vladimir, fourth class (the lowest), placed the holder at public ceremonies and at court on the same footing as members of the apparatus in grade six.[42]

The grant of a civil pension and its amount remained the ruler's prerogative until the end of Alexander's reign. Two governors of Vitebsk, for example, retired in the 1800s, one with a pension equal to half his salary and a grant of villages for 12 years, the other on his full salary. If a pension was granted, the imperial order of March 1819 continued to allow the petitioner to collect half his salary but gave him a full pension if that salary did not exceed 100 rubles. A petition was addressed to the minister in whose jurisdiction the petitioner was serving and was submitted to the tsar only if approved by the minister and the Committee of Ministers. Such procedures strengthened the spirit of unconditional obedience binding members of the apparatus to their superiors no less than it did in the military, showing how little developed was the concept of an autonomous bureaucracy among the ruling class. Rewards, especially financial ones, so important in an economy of scarcity, continued to depend less on the performance of well-defined duties than on the arbitrary decisions of ministers who dispensed patronage as they saw fit. Those who for some reason ran afoul of their ministers were condemned to a life of poverty and degradation, like the 60-year-old man who, denied a pension, turned to the tsar directly and received from him 500 rubles but then made himself so obnoxious among the Petersburg ruling elite that he was banished to distant Tambov gubernia in 1822, where he was reduced to begging traveling noblemen for money until he died 2 years later. Widows and orphans too kept sending a stream of petitions for pensions or to be allowed to collect their husbands' or fathers' pensions, but nothing seems to have been done for them before Alexander's death beyond letting them rely on the mercy and generosity of the ruler.[43]

The Secretarial and Clerical Staffs

An analysis of the secretarial staff presents some difficulties. Secretaries, called *d'iaki* in Muscovite Russia, were essential to the process of governing yet were not quite an intrinsic part of the political apparatus. As stewards of the households of the ruling families, they often came from the very dependent population of townsmen and peasants that they administered on behalf of their masters, from the household itself, where they passed on their charges to their sons, and increasingly from sons of parish priests without prospect of appointment in the church. Marriage and promotion into the apparatus were neither unknown nor the rule, and secretaries became a buffer between the ruling class and the dependent population.[44]

Secretaries in the Duma, the *prikazy*, and the offices of the more important voevodas formed a natural hierarchy. The Duma *d'iaki* in the 1690s were equal in salary, that is, in the size of the *pomest'e* allotted as compensation for their services, to an *okolnichii*, and the salaries of the *prikaz d'iaki* corresponded to those of Moscow nobles. They were responsible for supervising the work of the clerks who copied and recopied documents, petitions, and decisions, submitting briefs to *prikaz* chiefs, presidents of colleges, or departmental directors together with the legal references serving to justify their proposals. They took an indirect part in decision making, especially when they served as deputies (*tovarishchi*) to *prikaz* chiefs and voevodas.[45] This role of the secretaries underscored the political importance of the apparatus. The drudgery of paperwork, the choice of options, and the shaping of decisions belonged to the secretaries, but the decisions themselves, whatever the factual and legal evidence compiled, were reserved for members of the apparatus. Its insistence on retaining power while secretaries controlled the flow of information and procedures generated a conflict within the Russian government lasting well into the nineteenth century.

When the Table of Ranks was drawn up, it was necessary to find a place in it for the secretaries and to retain the hierarchy among them. The senior (*ober-*)

secretary and the secretaries of the Senate—successors of the Duma *d'iaki*—were placed in grades six and eight, respectively, the senior secretary and secretaries of the three superior colleges in grades seven and nine (titular councillor), respectively. The titles given to the lower grades, outside and below the apparatus, show that these grades were seen above all as secretarial positions. Positions in grade ten were titled college secretaries—meaning secretaries in the other colleges—those in grades twelve and thirteen gubernia and provincial secretaries, that is, secretaries of governors and provincial voevodas, and those in grade fourteen registrars of colleges, who kept a ledger of all incoming and outgoing mail in a college. There were no positions in grade eleven.[46]

Since the Table of Ranks was a table of positions as much as a table of ranks, various positions were given titles that in no way corresponded to descriptions of their responsibilities. Postmasters in the larger cities and provincial treasures were titled registrars of colleges, foresters and treasurers in colleges, gubernia secretaries. On the other hand, a number of essentially secretarial positions in the broader sense were also given secretarial titles. Translators and recording secretaries (*protokolisty*) in the three superior colleges were called college secretaries; the Senate archivist and registrar were titled provincial secretaries. Sergei Troitskii estimates that there were 1,344 holders of positions in grades nine to fourteen in the 1750s, or 60.4 percent of the total in all fourteen classes.[47] The local government reforms multiplied the number of "secretarial" positions. Land captains and uezd treasurers were placed in grade nine, various assessors elected to local courts in grade ten, uezd procurators (*striapchie*) in grade eleven, and true secretaries in gubernia and uezd agencies in grades eleven to fourteen. No total figures are available for the number of people in grades nine to fourteen in 1796, but they must have exceeded 10,000.[48]

Giving the title of secretary to large numbers of people whose activities were far different from those of the traditional secretaries threatened to end their privileged status and diminish the distinction they had always enjoyed. Submerged in a mass of technical personnel and despised commoners, they would cease to be the collective stewards of the ruling class. The Table of Ranks incorporated only the Senate secretaries and the senior secretaries of the three superior colleges into the ruling class; all others were kept out of it. Pressure by the secretaries to be recognized as members of the apparatus was most likely behind Peter's order of January 1724.[49] The post of secretary was reserved for noblemen in order to block access to the apparatus by non-nobles who would normally have been promoted to college assessor in due time. The order, however, made an exception for clerks of exceptional talent and allowed the Senate to promote them to secretary and thereby admit them into the hereditary nobility. This explains the insistence with which the Senate later protected its exclusive right to appoint secretaries against the governors' encroachments. As a result, the holders of positions in grades nine to fourteen were divided socially into two kinds: true secretaries were noblemen, but the holders of other "nonsecretarial" positions remained non-noble, unless born noble. The order was still in force in 1758 when the Senate resolved that non-noble civilians in "junior officer positions"—except secretaries—did not enjoy a nobleman's privilege to buy and own inhabited land.[50] The decision immensely enhanced the status of secretaries vis-à-vis their nominal peers in the Table of Ranks.

The Charter of the Nobility of April 1785 took a narrower view and adopted a compromise that nevertheless downgraded the secretaries into the category of life nobles. It cited Article 15 of the Table of Ranks, which provided that the children of non-nobles serving in positions graded nine through fourteen were not nobles, discovered that the order of January 1724 said nothing about the children of clerks promoted to secretary, and concluded that secretaries were not hereditary nobles. The charter, however, also allowed an individual whose father and grandfather had served for 20 years in positions below grade eight to petition for admission to the hereditary ("real") nobility and thus enabled many a secretary to join the ruling class since clerkships had long been handed from father to son in families of clerks.[51]

For non-nobles who chose to become clerks, a promotion to secretary, even to registrar of college, was a giant step in social mobility. Secretaries and clerks were bound by many ties of common origin, common interest, and common ambition. Fortunate provincial clerks became Moscow clerks in the seventeenth century, by either promotion or marriage, and *d'iaki* were chosen from among them. Children of *d'iaki* succeeded their fathers or became *zhiltsy*, thereby entering the Moscow nobility from which they might be promoted to *stolniki* and Duma nobles.[52] Constant pressure was exercised from below for access to the apparatus, and the order of 1724 was an attempt, if not to close it entirely, at least to regulate it by concentrating the appointment of secretaries in the Senate. However, the growth of the clerical staff throughout the eighteenth century, together with the preference by noblemen for a military career, left the government on the defensive.

The order was not observed, and promotions to secretaries were made by presidents of colleges, governors, and provincial voevodas who used their authority to hire clerical personnel in order to build a bloated household staff of incompetent individuals unconcerned with "Her Majesty's interest" or any thought of the public welfare but shamelessly greedy and corrupt to the bone. This much we discover from the imperial order of October 1737 directing the Senate and colleges to cut their staffs to the 1725 levels, expel unworthy secretaries, and keep only those whose fitness was certified by all members of the agency. Governors and voevodas were ordered to stop the practice of hiring local clerks who had never been out of their towns and instead to hire clerks from the Senate and colleges as secretaries.[53]

This concern with regulating access to the apparatus by individuals from the dependent population was also evident in the Senate order of November 1737 requiring secretaries to obtain commissions from the Senate without which their frivolous appointment and promotions would be declared null and void. Thus the order hoped to carry out the injunction of 1724 that the entry of non-nobles be based on merit alone, so that secretaries, "who must have all business [*dela*] in their hands, carry it out, and submit recommendations to their chiefs, and remonstrate with them without fear in the event of violations of established procedures," might dedicate their talents to the "good of the State."[54]

Unfortunately, there was very little acceptance of the concept of state in eighteenth-century Russia, and the apparatus that set the tone in its exploitation of the dependent population and the glorification of greed could hardly expect its secretarial staff to behave otherwise. The order of October 1737 was simply ignored, a typical phenomenon of Russian political life in which the autocrat proposed and the apparatus disposed. In May 1742 the procurator general confirmed that governors and voevodas were still promoting local clerks to secretary and even dismissing secretaries sent to them by the Senate. This renewed attempt to concentrate the appointment of secretaries in the Senate may have been more successful, and the Senate order of June 1745 required clerks to be promoted on the basis of seniority and presumably only to fill vacancies.[55]

The reform of the 1770s added secretaries to all new gubernia and uezd agencies, some coming from the staff of the colleges closed in the 1780s, some still hired locally. Ivan Meshkov, for example, the son of a merchant who became a clerk in Saratov, was promoted from clerk to registrar in 1787 and to gubernia secretary in 1795, serving in the Saratov civil chamber. Appointments were made on the recommendation of governors and governors-general, themselves members of patronage networks headed by senators, who divided the spoils among their clients with the concurrence of the procurator general. When ministries were created in 1802, ministers gained control over the appointments of secretaries, each in his own ministry, but governors continued to recommend candidates to the Senate for appointment in their gubernias.[56]

Once a clerk had been promoted to registrar in grade fourteen, quick promotion was possible by petitioning the Senate with a personal recommendation (*attestat*) of his patron in the agency where he served, and such promotion would be granted if he could gain support of Senate secretaries and his patron's patron. To regulate promotions within the secretarial staff, the Senate had imposed in June 1760 a requirement of 8 years to be spent in grade fourteen, and forbidden individuals to petition for promotion without the approval of their agency. In addition, entrance into the secretarial staff had been further restricted by requiring clerks to have spent another 8 years in their post before their promotion to grade fourteen.[57]

Pressures were intensified by the demobilization of the ruling class that began in the summer of 1762. Young nobles—the so-called *iunkery*—who had been appointed to the staff of the Senate and colleges for training as secretaries were released, and secretaries would henceforth come almost exclusively from among the clerks, thus accelerating the process of caste formation that Gregory Freeze has studied among the clergy.[58] Seven years earlier, in August 1755, the Senate had forbidden children of secretaries and clerks of non-noble origin to serve anywhere outside the secretarial and clerical staffs unless granted an exemption by the Senate. This was upheld in April 1773.[59] The rules of

September 1765 had contributed nothing new, but the statute of December 1790 tried to regulate promotions above grade fourteen for the first time and end the chaos prevailing until then. Promotions were to take place every 3 years from one rank to the next up to grade nine. Those distinguished by skills and diligence were allowed to skip grades thirteen and ten and could thus reach grade nine within 6 years instead of 12 but then had to wait 12 years before being eligible for promotion into the apparatus in grade eight, a term reduced to 4 years in December 1799.[60]

On the other hand, the lower grades of the Table of Ranks were also being filled by a growing number of non-nobles with education and special skills, such as land surveyors during the general survey that began in the late 1760s and mining and medical personnel, especially during Alexander's reign. The University Statute of January 1803 placed holders of a candidate degree—the lowest university degree—in grade twelve, those of masters and doctoral degrees in grades nine and eight. Provincial schoolteachers were in grade nine and district schoolteachers in grade twelve. Students graduating from the provincial schools who wished to enter the secretarial staff began in grade fourteen. Their promotions followed the general rules of the 1790 statute.[61]

The great mass of what is indiscriminately called the Russian "bureaucracy" consisted of clerks. Called *podiachie* in Muscovite Russia, they formed the backbone of the *prikaz* organization and were the indispensable servants of the voevodas. It has been estimated that there were more than 2,637 *podiachie* in the central government in the 1690s, in contrast to ninety *d'iaki* and only twenty-two members of the apparatus ("judges"). To these must be added another 1,873 *podiachie* in local agencies compared with forty-five *d'iaki*.[62] In the eighteenth century the term *podiachii* was replaced in tables of organization by a hierarchy of copyists, subclerks, and clerks (*kantseliaristy*), collectively called *prikaznye liudi* or chancery personnel (*sluzhiteli*), but their total number remained unknown even to the government, as periodic calls for a census of clerks testify.[63] Hired and dismissed by agency chiefs, governors, and voevodas, they were not listed in the records of the Heraldmaster's Office. They were, of course, unpaid until the 1760s and subsisted on fees they were able to collect from petitioners and from the rewards of their own graft.[64]

The table of organization of December 1763 is the only published source giving a comprehensive estimate of the size of the clerical staff. It was most likely much larger, since presidents and governors could hire additional staff if they could find the funds—usually from unspent balances from their agency budget—to pay them. Although incomplete—some agencies were not included—it lists 7,502 individuals, 6,032 of them outside the Table of Ranks. The strength of the clerical element appears even more clearly when individual agencies are considered. In the College of Revenue, for example, there were 141 copyists, subclerks, and clerks in a total civilian staff of 218; in the College of Landed Affairs, 203 out of 246; in the College of Justice, 137 out of 182. The demand for clerks rose dramatically after the local government reform. If a province headed by a voevoda and including eleven uezd and town voevodas had an authorized staff of twelve secretaries and 124 clerks in the 1760s, a postreform gubernia divided, like Saratov, into eleven uezds, had a staff of thirty-seven secretaries and 320 clerks.[65]

These clerks came from the most varied social backgrounds. Young nobles, unfit for military service or unwilling to face its rigors, without connections and ambition, were found among them. One, in the 1760s, had been working in the chancery of the Ryl'sk voevoda and *magistrat* since the age of 12.[66] Others would seek work in the Senate and the colleges, where the practice of appointing *iunkery* gave them an opportunity to work in the capitals and obtain preferential treatment when promotions were made. This practice, discontinued in 1763, was restored 34 years later following the reopening of central agencies, and young nobles were invited in 1803 to fill the places allotted to each ministry, where they would acquire a form of on-the-job training before their promotion to grade fourteen or a secretary's post. It was also extended to other agencies, where these nobles would simply be called clerks.[67]

Clerks also came from among the urban population. Before its division into merchants and *meshchane* in March 1775, all townsmen registered on the rolls belonged to the dependent population, separated from the ruling class by the social stigma of being required to pay the capitation. Nevertheless, townsmen with a distant hope of rising in the world became clerks in a voevoda's or governor's office, or those who had already worked in municipal agencies were drafted into it, if no one else could be found, to the great outrage of townsmen.[68] To prevent what may have been a substantial drain from the families of average merchants and also to restrict their access to the clerical staff, only the children of first-guild merchants were allowed to become clerks after 1814. The restriction, however, was not completely effective.

Clerks even came from the peasantry, especially the peasants of the treasury, who, like the townsmen, remained on the capitation rolls while working in chanceries. They continued to be hired, despite repeated prohibitions. Soldiers' children were also employed as clerks until 1766, when it was forbidden to hire new ones. Yet the demands for clerks was so great in the 1780s that many an exemption had to be made. Increasingly, the major source of clerks became the growing number of priests' sons: those who did not succeed their fathers had become an unbearable burden for their families. They were occasionally drafted into the army, there to become military clerks. Governors were instructed, when they took office in their new gubernias, to contact the bishop for assistance in meeting their personnel needs.[69] Speranskii's success was symbolic of the rising status of priests' sons, who also became the major source of clerks in the ministries after 1802 and gradually displaced the nobles. By the end of Alexander's reign, the clerical staff had turned into a caste, recruited chiefly from sons of clerks and sons of priests.

There were no rules governing the promotion of copyists to subclerk and clerk, and all these scriveners depended on the goodwill of the governors and presidents of colleges under whom they served. The decisive event in a clerk's career was his promotion to "registrator," the lowest graded position in the Table of Ranks. Such promotions depended on the Senate and needed a formal recommendation (*predstavlenie*) from the governor or the president. Clerks increasingly sought to bypass their agency chiefs and turned to the Senate directly but were rebuffed in June 1760, when the Senate required them in addition to spend 8 years in their post before asking their chief to recommend a promotion. The rules of September 1765, however, allowed presidents and governors to promote clerks to "registrator" on their own authority, providing this was done only to fill a vacancy. After the reform of 1775 this right was extended to the three gubernia chambers, with the approval of the gubernia board. Another restriction was made in February 1803, when the Senate spelled out that a clerk promoted to fill a registrator's position was not thereby promoted to grade fourteen unless he had served the full 8 years as a clerk and a subsequent recommendation by the governor had been approved by the Senate's First Department—with the additional recommendation, after 1802, of the appropriate minister.[70]

The demobilization of February 1762 did not, of course, allow a clerk to retire, unless he also happened to be a nobleman, and the shortage of clerks after the local government reform was unlikely to change official policy. It did allow clerks, however, to petition for retirement on grounds of illness, provided the petition was supported by the results of a medical examination in the College of Medicine or, after the reforms, in the provincial board. The life of clerks was so miserable in general that retirement was a luxury they could not afford. Some, however, sought retirement in order to become agents (*poverennye*) offering their services to anyone in need of help to deal with the formalities and the delays attending any suit against a government agency or private individuals.[71]

The political apparatus of the ruling class thus consisted of a ruling elite and a managerial staff that did not yet constitute a bureaucracy because its internal mobility was not governed by formal rules until at least the beginning of the nineteenth century, when bureaucratization was, however, further retarded by the upheaval of war and the rapid growth of the ministries. It was instead a political formation unified by a common mission: to provide at all levels the key individuals who made decisions and exercised jurisdiction not only over members of the ruling class but also over any member of the dependent population. This apparatus, which acquired a separate identity as a political infrastructure came into being, continued to replenish its ranks by co-opting members from the dependent population who underwent a training stage in the secretarial and clerical staff and the noncommissioned ranks of the army. These men formed a human reserve, blurring somewhat the sharp distinction between ruling class and dependent population, but through them the ruling class multiplied its points of contact with that population and magnified its power over it.

II

INSTITUTIONS

4

The Foundations: 1689–1725

On the Road to Poltava

When Tsar Peter was carried to the throne at the age of 17 by the tumultuous events of the summer of 1689, the Romanov dynasty was three generations old, and the men who governed Russia were the grandsons of those who had guided its early steps, strengthened its confidence, and intermarried with it. They were for the most part the relatives of the two wives of Tsar Alexei, Peter's father, who had died when his son was only 4 years old and left the ruling elite in a state of disarray generated by the vicious struggle between the Miloslavskiis and the Naryshkins over control of the tsar's household and, by extension, of the political spoils. Peter's victory meant the triumph of the Naryshkins and their allies but also led to the recognition that even an uneasy consensus was necessary among the ruling families to guarantee a consistent and responsible dispatch of the public business, at a time when the young tsar openly deserted the royal chambers and customs of his ancestors for the heretical allurements and subversive inspirations of the German quarter.

Two constellations of ruling families crystallized gradually, each finding the legitimacy of its claims to rule in a marital tie with the Romanov house. The core of one was the Naryshkin clan, small but with powerful allies, notably the Streshnevs, and the ability to keep finding more; the core of the second was the Saltykov family, related to Peter's half brother and co-ruler, Ivan V, sickly and mentally incompetent, who died in 1696. The Saltykovs' position was strengthened by their close marital ties with the Dolgorukovs, related, like the Streshnevs, to Mikhail, the first Romanov tsar. These two constellations, which kept grooming their own members or adopted outsiders for positions of leadership and often absorbed occasional favorites thrust into the limelight following a fortuitous encounter with the ruler, remained the heart of the Russian political system for more than 100 years, until the massive circulation of elites in the wake of the Napoleonic Wars shattered their monopoly.[1]

If political power issued from a Romanov house whose autocracy was recognized and enforced by two constellations of ruling families because it served their ends and legitimized their practices, the channels through which it made itself felt were the Duma and the *prikazy*. The Duma was not so much a "constitutional" body with a well-defined membership and jurisdiction as a general council of the political leadership. The ruler referred to it matters that he felt required a general debate and a firm consensus. It discussed foreign policy, domestic legislation, jurisdictional disputes among *prikaz* chiefs, and whatever matters were submitted by these in search for guidelines.

Its membership mirrored the struggle of families for the control of patronage. It was relatively stable throughout the reign of Mikhail, then rose sharply during the early years of Alexei's reign. In 1676 it numbered 66 individuals, but 14 years later, after the crises of 1682 and 1689, it had risen to 153. Each successive phalanx of victors packed the Duma with its supporters, until its very size made it unfit for reflection and concentrated action. It became instead a general pool from which appointments were made to leadership positions— diplomatic envoys, military commanders, assignments on special missions, and chiefs of *prikazy*. Necessity, however, always creates institutions to cater to permanent needs, and the original function of the Duma—to discuss, coordinate, and set guidelines—gradually passed to a committee of the Duma of about twenty members, called the *blizhnaia* or *komnatnaia duma* because it met in the private apartments of the tsar, a kind of family council of the ruling house. By the end of the seventeenth century this smaller Duma, consisting largely of *prikaz* chiefs, had become a de facto committee of ministers. It remained in existence under the name of Privy Chancery (*Blizhniaia Kantseliariia*) until the creation of the Senate in 1711.[2]

Prikazy were the executive agencies of the ruling house and the Duma. Created in the course of more than a century by individual orders (*prikazy*) of the tsar to carry out a given task, they had proliferated to such an extent that even modern scholars cannot agree on their exact number and classification, and their overlapping responsibilities created an administrative nightmare.[3] Some were still responsible for a task, such as prosecuting banditry, but others had jurisdiction over only certain kinds of people or certain towns, while at least two possessed a universal competence over the vast territories of Siberia and what had been the khanates of Kazan and Astrakhan. There existed no hierarchy of *prikazy*, although one of them, the *Razriad*, achieved preeminence over the others when it was allowed to send them orders (*ukazy*) and not memoranda (*pamiat'*) in February 1677.[4] *Prikaz* chiefs were appointed by and subordinated to the tsar, and complaints against them were referred to the Duma. They sat alone or with a deputy (*tovarishch*), and there has been much debate over whether *prikazy* were collegial agencies.[5] In fact, the authority of a chief depended upon his place in the order of ruling families and his relationship with the ruler.

Secretaries (*d'iaki*) and clerks were the backbone of the *prikazy*. Some *prikazy* were small agencies of no more than a dozen people, others were large and well structured, and two had over 400 people. Secretaries ran the chancery and gave the *prikaz* its technical proficiency, while clerks followed the tedious ritual of registering petitions and reports, collating supporting documents, and preparing briefs, which the secretary submitted to the *prikaz* chief. In a system still so patriarchal despite its bureaucratic appearance, the clerks

were the "household people" (*dvorovye liudi*) of the tsar and the ruling families.[6] They belonged to a world of dependent servants, and although secretaries
were highly prized as stewards of the leadership, it was only in rare cases that
they married into the ruling families. However, their control of the paperwork
in a highly centralized system, together with the illiteracy and lofty detachment
of many a member of the leadership, gave them the means to swamp their
chiefs with an avalanche of reports and ready-made recommendations. As a
result, they often ran the *prikazy* in their own interests.[7]

On the eve of the great conflict with Sweden, there did not yet exist a
separate military establishment independent of the civilian government. Yet the
ruling class of Muscovite Russia was a nobility deriving its legitimacy and
dominant position from military service in the cavalry whenever Tatar raids or
tensions with Poland or Sweden required partial mobilization. Indeed, the two
most important *prikazy*, the *Razriad* and the *Pomestnyi*, were responsible, one
for military affairs in general, including the construction and upkeep of fortresses and the supply of their garrisons, as well as keeping the service records
of the nobles and assigning them to their units in wartime, the other for
distributing allotments of land among them and keeping files on the disposition of those lands.[8] But since the nobility was not only a class of warriors but a
ruling class with a monopoly over the political life of the country, these
two agencies were more than military agencies; they were the heart of a vast
patronage system extending over the entire country.

Since the nobility was mobilized for operations of usually short duration,
there was no need for supply agencies, and the real property (*pomest'e*) granted
a noble was traditionally considered adequate to sustain the cavalryman and
his horse; servants from his property kept supplying him with the necessities of
life, supplemented by requisitions in enemy country. However, cavalry charges
emphasizing the courage and cunning of part-time warriors had become obsolete by the end of the seventeenth century, professional armies had made their
appearance, and technical services required constant improvement. An infantry of *streltsy* troops had come into being to man the garrisons and for use in
the field, but it was without adequate training; a professional cavalry (*reitari*)
and mercenary troops had also become essential components of the Muscovite
armed forces, and the artillery had long been an object of special care. These
three formations were financed and supplied separately by three different
prikazy, although the fragmentation was deceptive—the artillery, mercenary
troops, and professional cavalry were commanded by a first cousin of the tsar,
the *streltsy* by his brother-in-law.[9]

Peter's decision in October 1699 to make war upon Sweden compelled a
reorganization of military administration. The tsar was thrust, both by his own
temperament and by the necessity to stand up to the military genius of Charles
XII, into the position of commander in chief in the field. The old-style cavalry
had demonstrated its limitations, a standing army was being created but could
not grow without a supply system, and the artillery was in need of expansion
and modernization in close connection with the development of the iron in-

dustry. These considerations called for the proclamation of a general mobilization of the ruling class to obtain the officers of the new army recruited from the
peasantry, the townsmen, and the surplus clergy.

The reorganization called for a new division of functions. The supply of the
army—of uniforms, equipment, provisions, and forage—which had been either
unnecessary or distributed among the *prikazy* commanding professional troops,
was concentrated in two new agencies, created in February 1700. One, called
Provision (*Proviantskii*) *Prikaz*, was made responsible for supplying provisions
to the troops in the field and forage to the horses; the other, unidentified, was
entrusted to Iakov Dolgorukov, the senior figure of the clan, with the title of
commissioner general (*General Komissar*). The agency was intended to assume
responsibility for the regular payment of the troops in the new standing army and
the supply of uniforms. These two agencies thus took over for nearly the entire
army in the field the supply responsibilities that had been those of the two
prikazy in charge of the professional cavalry and the mercenary troops. Unable to
justify their continued existence, both *prikazy* were merged in February 1701 into
a Military (*Voennyi*) *Prikaz* that took charge, in addition, of recruiting and
assigning soldiers to various army units, while the *Razriad*'s role was reduced to
record keeping, an important task nevertheless, as a military establishment
rapidly came into being that grew by leaps and bounds.[10]

Meanwhile, Dolgorukov had been taken prisoner at the first battle of
Narva in November 1700 and remained in captivity for the next 11 years. No
successor was appointed, and the Military *Prikaz* took over the supply of
uniforms and the payment of the troops. Moreover, the *streltsy* had been
abolished following their revolt of 1698, and their *prikaz* formally ceased to
exist in 1701. The consolidation of the military establishment became even
more obvious when both the Military *Prikaz* and the *Razriad* were placed
under the adoptive father of the tsar, Tikhon Streshnev, the leading figure in
the Naryshkin group, who thus became the chief of personnel and chief of the
commissary of the Russian army. At the same time, however, the artillery
regained its autonomy with the appointment of a separate chief (*General
Feldzeugmeister*), a post occupied for 22 years beginning in 1704 by Jacob
Bruce (Brius), a Scot of considerable scientific learning who later became a
major figure in the development of Russian industry.

Thus, as feverish preparations were made to recover the losses suffered at
the battle of Narva, in anticipation of the decisive encounter that would settle
the destiny of two great nations on a battlefield outside the fortress of Poltava
in June 1709, a military establishment with its own source of recruitment, its
supply organization, and its own technical service had been created. This basic
structure, despite many modifications caused by changing needs and the ambitions of powerful members of the apparatus, remained essentially unchanged
until the end of Alexander I's reign.

It was a principle of Muscovite administration that the functions of government must be centralized in the hands of the tsar and a political elite attracted
to Moscow by the perquisites of membership in the court society or brought
there against its will. Extreme centralization was the product of a patient

policy of gathering the Russian lands around the core of grand-princely power, an obsession with uniformity, and a fear of anarchy. Its corollary was the dispersion of these functions among an ever-larger number of central agencies not only in order to carry out the growing number of administrative tasks that a centralized government kept imposing upon itself but also to accommodate the ruling families and their patronage networks in sharing the spoils. Conversely, the removal of the territorial elites to the capital and the lack of urban development established a third principle of Muscovite administration: that all functions of government within any territorial unit be concentrated in the hands of a single agent of the central government.

This local agent was the voevoda, a title also given in the army to certain commanders. Indeed, the origin of the territorial voevoda was military, going back to the early years of the seventeenth century, when the country was placed under what was later called martial law, or the state of emergency.[11] Voevodas were appointed in almost all towns, some the center of an uezd—the basic administrative–territorial unit—some not. They were the local managers of the ruling class, chosen from among its members as a reward for services or because the state of their health required a less arduous assignment, or simply because a candidate sought a lucrative position and had the necessary connections to get it. A voevoda was not paid and was expected to "feed himself."[12] The lack of distinction between public service and private activity made the voevoda in principle no different from a large landowner. Both were given the use of services and wealth as a consequence of their membership in the ruling class, and voevodas and landowners who demanded services and payments in kind were partners in an enterprise founded on serfdom.

Voevodas had the assistance of a small staff of clerks, and the more important ones were also given a secretary (*d'iak*) who functioned as a kind of deputy. Their office was called the *prikaznaia* (or *s'ezzhaia*) *izba*, and they were about 300 at the end of the seventeenth century. Relationships with the *prikazy* were complex, since central and local government operated in accordance with opposite principles. *Prikazy* did not have their own local agencies, the voevoda being the collective agent of the entire central government, and their jurisdictions overlapped. A document of 1708, for example, lists 323 towns, of which 87 constituted two large regions under the Siberian and Kazan *prikazy*, and another 24 along the western and northern borders were dependent on the *prikaz* of Foreign Affairs because they were the point of contact between Russia and the outside world. The other 212 were under the jurisdiction of the *Razriad*, *Pomestnyi* and court *prikazy* but did not form compact territories, since neighboring towns depended on different *prikazy*. In addition, certain parts of towns, or certain categories of people, or certain types of cases depended on other *prikazy*.[13]

In this jurisdictional jungle there was, nevertheless, some order. Voevodas were appointed by the ruler on the recommendation of the *Razriad*, or of other *prikazy* channeled through the *Razriad*, and were subordinated primarily to the *prikaz* that recommended their appointment and, secondarily, in important matters, to the *Razriad* and the ruler. If yet another *prikaz* later required the assistance of the voevoda to carry out its responsibilities locally, it was first necessary to obtain from the *prikaz* to which the voevoda owed his primary allegiance a "command to obey" (*poslushnaia gramota*), without which voevodas would blissfully ignore such requests.[14]

It was a fourth principle of Muscovite administration that all voevodas, whatever the importance of the town to which they were appointed, were equally subordinated to the Moscow *prikazy*, and a fifth, that their competence was universal. Each received an instruction spelling out his responsibilities but also giving him wide discretion to act in accordance with circumstances or, as the phrase went, "as God will suggest."[15] Competence, however, is not necessarily power, and voevodas were not absolute masters in their towns and uezds. The long history of administration by voevoda and later by governor was one in which God's suggestions became increasingly restricted to ministerial circulars, leaving the local agent of the central government with considerable supervisory authority but little effective power, at least over the other agencies, with which he shared the administration of his territory.

The voevoda was chiefly a military and fiscal agent. Criminal cases were for the most part decided in Moscow on the basis of the voevoda's investigations; disputes over real property went before the *Pomestnyi Prikaz*, but other civil litigation was tried by the voevoda if the value of the suit did not exceed twenty rubles, unless the litigants enjoyed the privilege of being tried in their own courts or in Moscow itself. Serfs, more than half of the peasant population, were at the mercy of their owners.

The constant insecurity of the steppe frontier made it the first task of the voevoda to keep the fort and the defensive line in good condition, to keep a roll of local nobles, to send them to the army when the call came in, and, in the event of local hostilities, to command them in person, unless a military voevoda was available or was appointed by Moscow.

The major goal of fiscal policy was to extract as much as possible from the population without regard to its ability to pay, and personal greed went hand in hand with public necessity. As a general rule, direct taxes were collected by the voevoda, indirect taxes—chiefly from the sale of vodka and internal custom duties—by townsmen elected in their communities or farmed out, and the proceeds were deposited in Moscow; practices, however, varied greatly from place to place. At the turn of the century, a clear trend was noticeable to restrict the voevoda's role in tax collection, in obvious recognition that a private economy run under the cover of official policy was damaging to the treasury's interest.[16]

The Experiment with Regionalism

The defeat of Narva accelerated the restructuring of the Muscovite government announced by the military reforms of 1699–1701. The tsar became a peripatetic ruler, striding across the wide expanse of his domain with increasing nervousness as the inevitable showdown drew near. In 1701–1703 he spent much of his time in the Baltic sector, where the Russians reached the mouth of the Neva in April 1703 and took Derpt and Narva in the summer of 1704. His presence was also needed in Voronezh, until the shipyards were moved to Petersburg. Between 1705 and 1708 we find him commuting between Petersburg, Moscow, Kiev, and Vilno, elaborating a strategic defense against Charles XII and settling constant squabbles among his commanders.[17] Moscow was deserted as the seat of government, and Muscovite administration was being transformed into a civilian reserve cadre subordinated to the itinerant headquarters of the commander in chief. There followed two consequences: the *prikaz* organization became obsolete because it imposed a detour between the tsar and his agents in the field; and the multiplicity of voevodas, without any hierarchy existing among them, squandered energies requiring for maximum efficiency the creation of clear lines of command.

Precedents and ad hoc experiments gradually helped the government out of its predicament. There had emerged in the last decade of the seventeenth century ten small military regions called *razriady* along the western and southern borders run by the *Razriad* in Moscow. They ceased to be functional after 1700, but the tsar then proceeded to give his close collaborators, most of them his relatives, regional commands combining military and civilian functions. Thus, Fedor Apraksin was sent to Voronezh, Alexander Menshikov put in command of the occupied Baltic territories, Petr Saltykov sent to prepare the defense of Smolensk and Pskov, Dmitrii Golitsyn moved from Belgorod—the old headquarters of southern defense—to Kiev, and Petr Apraksin took over in Kazan the command of the eastern borderlands.[18] *Prikaz* chiefs, even those of territorial *prikazy*, had ruled from Moscow; the new territorial commanders were stationed in strategic outposts. The completion of this administrative-territorial reform took place in the course of 1708, at the very time when the king of Sweden was beginning the occupation of Lithuania. The tsar ordered the distribution of the 323 towns among eight gubernias—those of Moscow, Petersburg, Arkhangelsk, Smolensk, Kazan, Kiev, Azov, and Siberia—to which governors were formally appointed.[19]

These governors were regional voevodas—the two titles were used interchangeably at times between 1700 and 1708—new intermediaries between the tsar and the other voevodas. They were appointed by him; all belonged to the ruling families and were related to the tsar in various degrees of cousinhood. Their relationships with the *prikazy* remained undefined and perhaps needed no definition, as *prikazy* gradually shrank into regional agencies of Moscow gubernia.[20] In other words, the entire machinery of the civilian government became harnessed to the high command of the Russian army and the country was placed for all practical purposes under martial law—this only a few months before the battle of Poltava. The Swedish defeat eased the pressure but did not end the war, and a new sector in this interminable conflict opened in the south with the Turkish declaration of war of December 1710. The absence of the tsar at a considerable distance from his capitals, Petersburg and Moscow, necessitated the creation of a Senate, an executive committee of nine members, to which the governors were subordinated in 1711.[21]

As a result of these reforms, the principles underlying traditional central and local administration were considerably modified. Symmetry was introduced between the Senate and the governor's office: both exercised a universal competence over all sectors of public administration, now concentrated in their chanceries; a substantial decentralization of responsibilities was achieved, even though the respective spheres of Senate and governor remained to be determined; and the subordination of Senate and eight governors to the tsar simplified the chain of command.

The largest gubernias were large indeed—Arkhangelsk had 29 towns, Moscow 39, and Kiev 56—and governors became valuable dispensers of patronage. Voevodas were no longer appointed by the ruler but by the Senate, most likely on the recommendation of the governor, who substituted for the *prikaz* chiefs. What happened to the voevodas, however, is not clear. They may have been replaced beginning in 1710 by a network of commandants, military people chosen by the governors, at least in the more important towns. The ukase of March 1714 regulating the procedure for filing petitions made no mention of them. If the voevodas had been replaced by commandants, the country was indeed under martial law, since commandants were tried by courts-martial chaired by the governor.[22]

Like the Muscovite voevoda, the governor was chiefly a military and fiscal agent. With the help of his commandants he built fortresses and commanded the garrisons, billeted troops stationed in his gubernia, and negotiated contracts to supply them. Menshikov and the Apraksin brothers even commanded troops in person, but this was not the general rule—a separation was made in principle between governors and field commanders. Like the prefect of Napoleonic France 100 years later, the governor was above all the recruiting agent of the government. In wartime this was a demanding and thankless task.

The governor's financial responsibilities were much greater than those of the voevoda. Not only did he collect all taxes in his gubernia, he also became the chief budgetary officer of the government, and national budgets—to the extent that it was possible to elaborate them—were based on regional estimates submitted by governors summoned to meet in committee in Moscow. The creation of the Senate and its powerful chancery, however, reduced their autonomy in budgetary matters. Finally, the closing of the *prikazy* moved to the governor's office responsibilities for the prosecution of crime, the sentencing and execution of defendants, and even the settlement of land disputes.[23] Governors were on the way to becoming satraps, a radical departure from Muscovite tradition.

The appointment of governors also subverted the operations of the central military agencies. Gradually drained of the major responsibilities that were transferred to new gubernia capitals operating as headquarters of military regions, they virtually ceased to exist after 1711. The Military *Prikaz* was renamed Military Chancery and was subordinated to the Senate; the *Razriad* became a mere desk (*stol*) in the Senate Chancery. Tikhon Streshnev, who had headed both, was appointed the first governor of Moscow gubernia and a senator.[24] Recruiting had been made a major responsibility of the governors, and promotions henceforth took place within the command structure of a standing army.

On the other hand, the exigencies of military operations in an immense theater of war stretching from the Baltic to the Black Sea led to the practice of appointing two field marshals as commanders in chief over separate sectors, the tsar reserving for himself the supreme command of the entire army. The first marshal was Boris Sheremetev, promoted in January 1702 after his victory near Pskov signaled the end of the beginning for the Swedes. The second, Alexander Menshikov, was promoted in July 1709 for his part at Poltava. One was safely ensconced in the ruling families, the other a newcomer from the lower depths, both symbols of a new army of nobles and commoners.[25]

Promotions were granted much faster in wartime, especially after bloody battles; the most deserving were recognized, but protégés were never forgotten. We learn that much by reading between the lines of the imperial order of July 1714, which followed an earlier one, presumably ignored. The order was published in the midst of the Finnish campaign, while the war was winding down, just before the battle of Hangö broke the back of the Swedish war machine. Promotions were allowed only to fill vacancies and required a general recommendation of fellow officers. Generals granted promotion to captain, marshals, to major and lieutenant colonel, and the ruler, to colonel and above. Thus, as far as we can determine, responsibilities for personnel management had been removed from central agencies after 1711 since commanding officers promoted officers in their commands; artillery officers, however, depended on the chief of the artillery, who obtained in February 1715 an imperial order forbidding governors to interfere. The Military Chancery issued commissions to officers who presented evidence of their promotion.[26]

Supply agencies were likewise affected by the creation of the gubernias. The Military and Provision *Prikazy* appointed their own agents in the field army, but their gradual integration into the territorial structure of military regions undermined the hierarchical lines of command, which recent experience had consolidated. Despite the creation of a full-fledged commissary in July 1711, entrusted to Iakov Dolgorukov upon his return from captivity, governors became responsible for the supply of troops stationed in their gubernias, and commissary agents (*komissary*), to whom agents of the Provision *Prikaz* were subordinated in April 1713, were placed at their disposal. The concentration of financial resources in a gubernia treasury under gubernatorial control facilitated the collection of revenue and the allocation of funds to military units in accordance with a table of organization approved by the tsar in February 1711.[27] Not only the payment of salaries and the procurement of provisions were decentralized; even patterns were sent to the governors to help them supervise the manufacture of uniforms. Such extreme decentralization, together with the concentration of all supply operations in the office of governor and regional commissioner, reduced the new chief of the commissary (*General Kriegskomissar*) to a supervising authority without managerial responsibilities. When the army was on the move, supply operations were concentrated in the office of senior commissioner (*ober-krigskomisar*), subordinated to the Chief of the Commissary.[28]

In an economy of scarcity such a dispersal of fiscal and managerial power over an enormous territory was fraught with danger in the long run, above all in military administration where centralization and uniformity are the guarantee of discipline, and a reaction soon set in against its most harmful manifestations. The regional experiment had been the child of wartime conditions; it meant a rejection of Moscow with its cumbersome *prikaz* organization. Petersburg gubernia, where Menshikov was both governor and field marshal, was the most striking illustration of the emergence, for the first time since the destruction of Novgorod in 1478, of a political center outside of Moscow. Once war neared its end and the supremacy of Moscow had been broken, the reaction paved the way for the restoration of a central government around the Senate, which moved to Petersburg at the end of 1713. The commissary remained in Moscow because its central location made it the natural clearinghouse for the transfer of funds and the negotiation of contracts, but its chief and that of the artillery moved to the northern capital.[29]

The appointment of Iakov Dolgorukov, the Chief of the Commissary, to the Senate in August 1711—he was not one of the original nine senators—raised an issue destined to become one of the most contentious in the battle over turf between the Senate and the high command. The supply agencies were new—should they then become part and parcel of the military establishment or should they instead be subordinated to the Senate? At a time when the center of gravity in military administration had shifted to the governors and army commanders, the representation of those agencies in the Senate and their subordination to what was emerging as a new central but civilian leadership was not a logical step unless it was intended to prevent the high command from gaining an autonomy perceived as destructive of the unity of government.

The ultimate consequence of the appointment of governors of considerable military and fiscal power who were subordinated directly to a tsar constantly on the move was the abolition of the executive branch of government. The tsar's peregrinations, however, had been for the most part restricted to familiar country between Moscow, the Baltic, and the Polish border, within relatively easy reach of Moscow and his new "paradise" on the mouth of the Neva. The decision to go to war against the Turks and to lead the army in person in a distant, unchartered, and inhospitable territory against an enemy yet untested in the field threatened to leave a void at the center and raised the specter of a dynastic crisis should the tsar be taken prisoner.

The Privy Chancery, a committee of *prikaz* chiefs, thus had lost its raison d'être, and its president was informed in February 1711 that the tsar had appointed a committee of nine members to govern the country in his absence. Two imperial orders issued the following month, on the eve of the tsar's departure, announced that the committee, to be called the Senate, was a temporary agency for the duration of the war and that everyone, whether civilian, military, or clergy, must carry out its orders as if they were the monarch's own commands. By implication, governors were likewise subordinated to it. The Privy Chancery would remain in existence but as a chamber of audit until the creation of the colleges in 1718.[30] After the disastrous campaign on the Prut—where Peter barely escaped capture—the Senate, however, continued to function as a regency throughout the next 6 years when the tsar was traveling abroad. It became against all expectations a permanent institution but one without an organic statute, meeting 3 days a week in committee with a senator, rotated once a month, required to be in attendance every day. Petitioners were forbidden to turn to the tsar directly without first seeking redress in the Senate.

Its jurisdiction was clearly restricted to civilian affairs. In the wake of the abolition of the *prikazy*, the creation of the Senate meant a new concentration of functions in a single organ of government, a trend running parallel to the concentration of responsibilities in the governor's office but with this fundamental difference: the governor was seen as the agent of the entire government, the Senate as the embodiment of its civilian branch.

The Senate was a judicial agency, dispensing "impartial justice" to those appealing the decisions of governors. It was a fiscal institution charged with the collection of as much revenue as possible, "since money is the sinew of war," with pruning excessive expenditures, improving credit, conducting an inventory of revenues and goods farmed out to merchants, setting up a company to run the China trade, and encouraging Armenians to develop the Persian trade. It was also enjoined to form a reserve of young nobles to staff the officer corps.[31]

The integration of the *Razriad* into the machinery of the Senate made the latter into the chief personnel agency of the ruling class. The registration of noble sons from the ages of 10 to 30, which had been accompanied for a decade by physical inspection (*smotr*) by the tsar in person, was vested in the governors in distant gubernias, in the Senate in the central provinces, and all those without an assignment (*ne u del*) were kept on reserve lists from which candidates were selected for any position, civil or military.[32] Service had become—or at least was intended to become, since repeated references to objectors (*netchiki*) point to widespread evasion—a lifetime commitment, and the Senate took charge of the general mobilization of the ruling class that began after 1700.

The closing of the *prikazy*—save those in charge of foreign affairs, church properties, and the political police—left their secretaries and clerks available for employment with governors who received their share from the staffs of the central establishment. Those who remained in Moscow were appointed to the Senate's chancery divided into desks (*stoly*); some were responsible for certain matters like secret dispatches, relations with foreigners, or the persecution of Old Believers, others for two gubernias each.[33]

The emergence of a large chancery—it had eighty-seven clerks in 1711[34]—in a Senate with such broad responsibilities gave the household servants of the ruling families a stranglehold on the execution of national policies because it made them the guardians of the old procedures. Senators were required to reach decisions by unanimous vote—yet the "monthly senator" acted more often than not on behalf of the entire Senate.[35] The old Muscovite procedure maintained a strict division of labor between the preparation of briefs and even of a draft of decision and the discussion of the business brought before the senators. It gave the secretaries, still called *d'iaki*, control not only over the agenda but also over the substance of the deliberations by keeping out circumstances considered extraneous and damaging to their interests, especially in private litigation, from which they derived a substantial income in the form of fees paid by petitioners. The new order remained a patriarchal one, and great lords still managed the public business the way they ran their households—by leaving considerable leeway to their domestics, without realizing that they were often at their mercy.[36]

And, indeed, the Russian government of those years was a government of great lords who divided the administration of the realm among themselves, without the need to spell out their mutual relationships. The early governors, we know, were all related to the tsar, and Menshikov, the outstanding exception, was his closest companion. The original Senate contained the tsar's adoptive father, his illegitimate brother, and one of his first cousins; in 1717, one of his brothers-in-law and another first cousin by marriage. If Senator Apraksin ever wrote to the two governors Saltykov, he wrote to his distant cousins, and if Senator Streshnev wrote to Governor Golitsyn, he wrote to a man whose grandnephew married his—Streshnev's—granddaughter. In such a world, much was taken for granted, and little needed to be said, let alone printed.

The Restoration of Central Government

Nevertheless, the very informality of relationships among ruling families threatened to create anarchy in the governing of a large empire whenever rivalries and outright hatreds among great lords were unrestrained by a network of institutions. Moreover, the tsar's vision of a Russia brought into the mainstream of European developments led him to study the governmental structure of both friendly and enemy states, above all Sweden, whose high command he toasted as his teachers after Poltava. Preparations accelerated after the battle of Hangö to introduce a modified Swedish system into Russia, notably the colleges. In December 1717 a list of colleges and their presidents was published, the agencies began to operate formally in 1719, and a Statute of Governmental Procedures (*General'nyi Reglament*) was issued in February 1720.[37]

There were originally nine colleges: for foreign affairs, war, and navy; for revenue, treasury, and audit; for commerce, mining and manufactures, and justice. In 1722 a separate College of Manufactures was created, and the old *Pomestnyi Prikaz* became the College of Landed Affairs. Another four agencies must be included among the new executive agencies: the *Preobrazhenskii Prikaz*, the only leftover from the old Muscovite administration, the Secret Chancery, the Policemaster General's Chancery, and the Central (*Glavnyi*) *Magistrat*.[38]

The organization of the colleges retained the old distinction between members of the political apparatus and the clerks, the secretaries operating as the link between the two. Each college consisted (after 1720) of ten members; a president chosen by the ruler at discretion, a vice-president chosen among three candidates recommended by the Senate, and eight members chosen by the Senate from candidates recommended by the college. The chancery consisted of secretaries recommended by the president to the Senate and of clerks appointed by the college, that is, most likely by the president himself.[39] The procedure thus recognized two patronage levels, that of the ruler, who appointed the president and often the vice-president as well on his own authority, and that of the Senate, where the spoils were shared among the ruling families. The tsar was aware of this when he told the presidents in December 1717—they were senators as well at the time—not to select members from among their relatives and protégés (*sobstvennye kreatury*). That the order was repeated in November 1723—when they were no longer senators—was more than a hint that patronage was flourishing, and this at a time when the creation of the local agencies of some colleges multiplied the favors at the disposal of presidents and members.[40]

There was much ambivalence toward the authority of the president. On the one hand, he was to exercise only general supervision over the operations of the college; decisions were reached by majority vote, and the president only broke a tie. On the other, he appointed the chancery, which was subordinated to him, and he was the personal choice of the ruler. The two propositions were hardly compatible; in any conflict the president was bound to prevail, and it is doubtful that a Menshikov, an Apraksin, a Golitsyn, and later a Münnich tolerated much dissent among junior members, whose careers and those of their children depended on the good graces of their president.[41]

This new dispersal of functions among service chiefs reminiscent of the *prikaz* system did not at first affect the position of the Senate as the coordinator of governmental operations. The Senate became a committee of ministers, that is, of presidents of colleges in which the tsar took part whenever he could. The solution was hardly original, since there was a precedent in the *blizhnaia duma*. Once again, however, the ambivalent position of the presidents as the ruler's immediate executive officers undermined the very harmony and cooperation the statutes were designed to enforce. Colleges received their orders (*ukazy*) from the Senate, but nothing was said about the respective limits of competence between the colleges on the one hand and the Senate on the other. They also received their orders from the tsar, and presidents were thus empowered by statute and by their immediate dependence to appeal to him against Senate decisions and whenever they considered that a matter of general interest required his attention.[42] This procedure reflected the continued strength of the patriarchal state and the refusal of the political leaders to be bound by institutional devices. Personal rapport with the ruler did not so much strengthen his hand as it enabled ambitious figures among the ruling families to obtain his approval in order to bypass the joint decisions of their peers and legitimize their personal and group objectives in the sanctity of imperial commands. This was especially true of the presidents of the Colleges of Foreign Affairs, War, and Navy.

This uneasy situation, in which chiefs of executive departments sat in a committee but did not feel bound by its decisions, and disorderly proceedings compelled the tsar on at least one occasion to call his senators–presidents so many fishwives (*baby torgovki*),[43] were the chief causes of the reform of January 1722. It made three major changes. The posts of senator and president of a college were declared incompatible, and the senators were ordered to recommend candidates to head seven of the eleven colleges. Although their presidents continued to be appointed by the tsar, their importance in the hierarchy was clearly downgraded, and they were subordinated to the Senate; only in exceptional cases were their presidents authorized to appeal to the ruler.[44] The Senate thus became a higher council of government, consisting of great lords freed from day-to-day responsibilities and expected to coordinate the operations of the colleges. However, the continued refusal to demarcate the competence of Senate and colleges kept them inseparable parts of a single political machine, one increasingly unable to cope with a mass of details, with favoritism and bribery prevailing over expertise and justice.

The reform also created, in fact, two Senates. The presidents of the three colleges not immediately concerned with internal and civil administration were required to attend Senate sessions only when the tsar was present or when a law was discussed.[45] Not only did the reform thus create by implication an administrative and legislative Senate, it also recognized for the first time the existence of a separate military establishment. Finally, perhaps as a recognition that the tsar's absences and other responsibilities made it difficult for him to attend the Senate regularly, a procurator general was appointed between him and the Senate in order to keep order during debates, to enforce the rule that decisions must be unanimous, and even to suspend the execution of a decision if he objected to it, pending the tsar's confirmation.[46]

The existence of two Senates may not have been a workable arrangement during the last two years of Peter's reign. This attempt to concentrate in one body the coordination of domestic policy, military administration, and the conduct of foreign affairs was, in this respect at least, a return to the Muscovite government of the last decade of the seventeenth century. However, the transformation of Russia into a great power had created clusters of vested interests no longer amenable to pressures for joint deliberations within the framework of institutions restricting their freedom of action. Twenty years of war had shaped the high command into a political force seeking recognition and independence from the civilian leadership, and it was symptomatic of the new alignment of forces that Peter's death and Catherine's accession were announced by the Senate, Synod—and *generalitet*, a body of some fifty generals making up the high command.[47]

The institutional representation of the high command was the College of War. Marshal Sheremetev died in February 1719, and Menshikov, the only other marshal, became its first president. Henceforth, it became the practice to place one of the marshals in the presidency of the college. The college was the central personnel agency of the army, keeping records of men in active and garrison service, responsible for drawing up the military budget and for military planning. Its power over promotions was that of the field marshal in accordance with the order of July 1714, so that the co-optation of noncommissioned officers into the officer corps and promotions to captain remained the responsibility of commanding generals, with promotions to lieutenant colonel made in the college. It is not certain, however, whether recommendations for promotions to colonel, that is, to all regimental commands, were routed through the Senate or were submitted directly to the ruler. The college thus absorbed the functions of the Military Chancery, which was closed.[48]

From omissions in the Table of Ranks of January 1722[49]—published shortly after the Senate reform—we learn about relationships within the new political establishment created by the Petrine reforms. Presidents of colleges were placed in grade four, but that could not apply to the presidents of the Colleges of Foreign Affairs, War, and Navy, who were chancellor, marshal, and grand admiral, respectively, all in grade one, and senators were not graded. Conversely, grades two and three—real privy councillors and privy councillors—were not assigned to any post but one, that of procurator general, in grade three. Thus, the Table of Ranks and the sheer weight of the military establishment gave its chief a privileged position in the government. The Senate on the other hand, was seen not so much as an organ of government as a privy council outside the governmental structure. Yet developments had shown, and would continue to show, that the Senate could not reconcile its role as privy council with the coordination of domestic policy: it became increasingly bogged down in details of day-to-day administration. As a result, separate and informal privy councils (*tainye sovety*) began to meet during Peter's reign to discuss important problems of foreign policy, to which were summoned senators and other privy councillors. These privy councils and the Senate together cannot but remind us of the Duma: boyars had now become real privy councillors, *okolnichie* privy councillors, and Duma *d'iaki* senior secretaries (*ober-sekretari*), of whom there were only five, in the Synod, the Senate, and the three "supercolleges."[50]

The creation of the College of War reduced the importance of the commissary, whose chief lost his seat in the Senate; his agency became a subdivision of the College of War in June 1723, although with the right to appeal college orders to the Senate. However, the instruction of January 1724 placed the entire provisioning of the army under a separate provisionmaster general at the head of a Provision Chancery—which replaced the old *prikaz*—subordinated to the Senate and with the status of a college.[51]

This uneasy compromise between the Senate and the College of War over the accountability of the supply services among the two establishments added to the confusion created by the emergence of two capitals, Petersburg and Moscow, separated by 763 kilometers of forests and swamps. Colleges with headquarters in one capital set up a branch office (*kontora*) in the other. The commissary was in Moscow, but its chief was in Petersburg. The Provision Chancery was in the northern capital because the provisioning of troops in and around Petersburg was inseparable from that of the civilian population and required the presence of an authoritative agency to break bottlenecks and keep unhindered the flow of provisions. Its branch office in Moscow negotiated contracts with merchants and landowners. Since the Senate also had a branch in Moscow,[52] the possibilities for behind-the-scene manipulations by playing off one agency or one capital against the other were endless.

The artillery, however, managed to retain, if not its independence, at least a considerable amount of autonomy, with its own commissary, arsenals, and gun factories. In 1718 the Artillery *Prikaz* was renamed chancery, and its chief, Brius, became president of the College of Mining as well, the only one to combine two presidencies. In 1720, after all fortresses were removed from under army command and placed under him, he insisted on corresponding with Menshikov with memoranda (*vedeniia*) instead of reports (*donosheniia*) implying subordination, despite the fact that the chief of the artillery was in grade two. Menshikov took his case in November 1722 to the tsar, who compromised by ruling that the artillery was a separate service only under the "general supervision" of the College of War. This implied that the college became the intermediary between the artillery and the Senate or the tsar, and when Brius submitted his table of organization in 1723, the college refused to examine it and forward it to the Senate.[53] Battles over tables of organization were battles over turf and continued long after Peter's death. Moreover, since Menshikov was a relative of the Naryshkins and Brius one of the Dolgorukovs, such a battle had overtones of a struggle over the division of the spoils among the ruling families.

The restoration of a central government structured along functional lines, together with the concentration of responsibilities in the Senate operating as a committee of ministers between 1718 and 1722, was bound to affect drastically the governors' position. It reconstituted in Petersburg, and partly in Moscow, the cozy world of secretaries and clerks who could only have resented their dispersal among gubernia capitals, a threat to their traditions and esprit de corps, and were bound to see the creation of the colleges as their revenge against the decentralization of 1708–1718.

The instruction of January 1719 established principles of territorial administration in central Russia for more than 50 years.[54] It was addressed to the voevoda, thus implying the restoration of civilian administration and the end of martial law. It was issued 4 months before a new territorial division broke up the gubernias into provinces (*provintsii*). It may very well be that this reform was no more than the consecration of a de facto situation in which senior (*ober*) commandants were appointed in the major towns of the original gubernias sometime in 1711, combining civil and military powers and responsible for a group of towns.[55] In any case, the new territorial units run by civilian delegates of the central apparatus did not become official until 1719. Since copies of the instruction were sent to both voevodas and senior commandants, it is clear that it was addressed not so much to voevodas in general as to provincial voevodas, who now succeeded the military incumbents in most places.

That it was also addressed to the governors had more significant implications. A single instruction for all local agents implied the downgrading of the governor's office and the refusal to recognize regional agencies as intermediaries between the capital and modest uezd centers. When voevodas later replaced commandants in almost all towns—this may not have taken place until after Peter's death—the instruction was made to apply to them as well.[56] The restoration of this fundamental principle of Muscovite administration—that all local agents were equally subordinated to central agencies—had made a triumphant return. Although a compromise had to be made in giving the governors some powers that voevodas would not share, the governor was obviously being reduced to the status of a provincial voevoda in the province formed around the gubernia capital, with only "general supervision" over the remainder of his gubernia.

These implications, however, were not immediately apparent. The instruction said little about relationships, and incumbent governors remained in office or were replaced with men of equal standing. At any rate, it would take time before the colleges got their house in order, and until their requests for data and explanations compelled the pieces of the new system to fall into place. The issue was complicated by the fact that certain colleges, unlike the *prikazy*, spawned their own local agencies in gubernias and provinces, and that their agents were expected to give their first loyalty to their headquarters in the capital. Thus, there were provincial courts dependent on the College of Justice; tax collectors (*kameriry* and *zemskie komissary*) responsible, some to the College of Revenue, others to the College of War; treasurers (*rentmeistery*) depending on the treasury; provisionmasters, subordinated to the Provision Chancery.[57] Consequently, it was necessary to define relationships not only between the governor–voevoda and the central agencies but also between him and the local agents of the colleges.

Governors were appointed by the tsar, voevodas by the Senate. This, however, established a purely formal subordination. Beginning in 1722 both in fact became subordinated to the colleges to which they sent reports on the performance of their local agents. These were given instructions by their colleges spelling out their duties, but it was the responsibility of the voevoda to see to it that the instructions were followed. Only in important cases, and if no college was responsible for the matter, was he authorized to request a decision from the chancery of the Senate. If he was displeased with the performance of the agent, he dismissed him and sent him to his headquarters for punishment and appointed a replacement.[58]

Voevodas seem to have been little impressed by the authority of their government. It was taken for granted that the Senate had to repeat its orders twice before they were taken seriously. When Major General Hennin was sent by Peter to the Urals, where he would need the cooperation of local voevodas, he asked for orders signed by the tsar in person, knowing as he did from experience that voevodas regularly ignored instructions from the Senate and the colleges.[59] In a system where every local agent had an interest in claiming to be subordinated to central agencies, and central agencies to the tsar, everyone could claim the ruler's authority in obstructing everyone else's will. Nevertheless, the voevoda, like his Muscovite predecessor and the governor of 1708, was given universal competence over all the official business transacted in his province. He billeted army units among villages and towns. He watched over the quality of grain kept in stores for the military. He maintained order, suppressed banditry, supervised the administration of justice (in a vain attempt to prevent the proverbial long delays), carried out sentences, collected state revenues (except the capitation collected by army officers), drew up a budget for his province, but had no authority to spend without order from the central treasury.[60]

In conclusion, then, four of the five principles of Muscovite administration had once again become government policy on the eve of Peter's death.[61] Centralization was the order of the day, and responsibilities were dispersed among a network of central agencies that was beginning to grow out of control despite the creation of nine colleges. All voevodas were equally subordinated to the central government, despite the need to retain the governor as a regional agent, yet they were left without a direct hierarchical superior. And they still possessed universal competence. The appointments of local agents, however, meant that all local authority was no longer concentrated in their hands. A new symmetry, unknown in Muscovite Russia, had been achieved between a poorly coordinated central government and a poorly coordinated provincial government, to the greater detriment of both.

5

The Rule Of The Empresses: 1725–1796

Families and Councils

The death of the great tsar in January 1725 left a void in the Romanov house and intensified the rivalries between the supporters of the two courts, gathered around the Saltykovs and Dolgorukovs on the one hand, the Naryshkins on the other. Under a powerful ruler and in difficult circumstances, these rivalries were usually muted by the fear of dissension, the acceptance of his leadership, and association with his cause. They never disappeared, however, and the history of Peter's domestic reforms was largely a chronicle of the attempts by these two extended political families to place their supporters in key institutions from which they could develop their patronage networks. They were then in a good position in 1725 to test their strength in a battle for the control of the throne.

The tsar left a wife, model companion of his campaigns and tribulations but an illiterate empress, and it was common knowledge that Menshikov, her former lover, was the power behind the throne, and even signed imperial orders. He also sought to engage one of his daughters to Peter's grandson, then 10 years old. Menshikov's only son was married to a Golitsyna, a relative of the Naryshkins. His bitter enemy was Petr Tolstoy, nephew of a Miloslavskii and relative of the Saltykovs and Dolgorukovs. Tolstoy's banishment, engineered by Menshikov on the very eve of the empress's death in May 1727, left Menshikov facing the Dolgorukovs, who destroyed him a few months later. It became the Dolgorukovs' turn to seek a marital alliance with Peter II, as Menshikov had done when he convinced Catherine to write her will, but the unexpected death of the boy emperor in January 1730 brought to naught these attempts by one family to appropriate an autocracy that had become the common property of all.[1]

The settlement of 1730 was founded on a choice between the two courts.[2] For the first time since Kievan times, the only claimants were women. Anne, the niece of Peter I, was the granddaughter of a Miloslavskaia and the daughter of a Saltykova. Elizabeth was the daughter of Catherine I, despised by the ruling families for her origin—a maid taken prisoner by Sheremetev's troops—and herself considered illegitimate. Yet she was, through her father, the granddaughter of a Naryshkina and the great-granddaughter of a Streshneva.

In Peter I, who was coarse and brutal but inspired by the noble vision of his country's greatness and an ideal transcending special interests, including his own—witness his magnificent address to the Russian army on the eve of Poltava—the autocracy had found its unsurpassed practitioner. Between 1725 and 1730, its substance was dissipated by sterile struggles in search of a ruler. During the next decade it was embodied in a woman of good intentions whose personal development, perhaps already threatened by the imbecility of her father, had been stunted by Peter's callousness and her exile to Mitava, there to serve the interest of her house in Courland. By the time Anna was chosen to succeed Peter II at the age of 37, her cruelty, reminiscent of her mother's, had been sharpened by bitterness, and she had learned that the darker world of religiosity and dwarf baiting was preferable to participation in the public business, which she left to her advisers, whether relative or protégés. Her rule, overshadowed by the presence of "Germans" imported from Courland or the German states, but made possible by the support of her relatives from the Saltykov family, witnessed, nevertheless, the beginning of a reconciliation between the two extended families, if only because a consensus among them was a prerequisite for domestic peace.[3]

The empress Anna had no children, and her death in October 1740 created a succession crisis. It was to be expected that she and her German advisers should want the succession to pass to her niece, another Anna, married to a German prince, all the more since a son was born to them shortly before the empress's death. But the prospect of a long regency and foreign interference, the reaction against German influence, and the feeling that Elizabeth ought now to come into her inheritance combined to swell the nationalist wave that brought Peter's daughter to the throne in November 1741. The Saltykovs fell for a while under a cloud, and relatives of the Naryshkins, Nikita Trubetskoi and Aleksei Bestuzhev-Riumin, became, respectively, procurator general and vice-chancellor, then chancellor, for the greater part of the reign.[4]

The new empress was not equal to the task of taking up her father's burden. Beautiful and lazy, pleasure loving yet intensely religious, she saw the governing of her realm as an endless round of entertainments to dazzle foreign diplomats and smother dissensions in a sea of favors. Like Anna, she abandoned her government to her relatives and brought favorites into the inner sanctum of power. Toward the end of her reign, when poor health and a morbid fear of death led her into seclusion, not even the leaders of her government could gain access to her, and autocracy became synonymous with capricious denials and outbursts of temper. Favorites were men on the fringe of the network of ruling families, who gained access to the ruler by a stroke of good fortune or whose relatives had already paved the way by marrying into the ruling families. The Razumovskiis, for example, came from the Ukraine and the Shuvalovs from Kostroma; they then consolidated their positions by marrying into one or both of the ruling families. Thus, the daughter of one Shuvalov married Trubetskoi's niece; the son of another the daughter of Marshal Saltykov, Trubetskoi's brother-in-law.[5]

The crown passed to the last empress of the Romanov dynasty in June

1762. German by birth, trained in adolescence in the merciless school of court politics, but welcomed into it by the Saltykovs and the Trubetskois, Catherine II understood that the successful exercise of power rests on qualities of leadership and persuasion. The network of ruling families that were always in rivalry yet conscious of a common goal to support the ruler's autocracy in their own interest was never so strong as at the beginning of her reign. Yet its own success, together with the expansion of the empire and the impact of war, generated powerful forces working toward its dissolution and compelling a restructuring of the political leadership after the empress's death in November 1796.[6]

This reaction against the legacy of Catherine was in fact one against a practice of governing that took shape after Peter's death and adapted itself to changing relationships among the ruling families in the course of nearly three generations. The relative weakness of widowed or unmarried empresses necessitated the creation of councils for a dual purpose: to operate as surrogates for the ruler and to coordinate military and foreign policy with domestic affairs.

Catherine I's incompetence and Menshikov's ambition were the major factors accounting for the formation of the Supreme Privy Council in February 1726. Its composition—the senior field marshal, the president of the College of the Navy, the chancellor and vice-chancellor, and two real privy councillors—made it in a curious way a kind of committee of ministers, under which the Senate was reduced to the status of a college of internal affairs: the three "supercolleges" and the Senate now corresponded with memoranda, and all four received orders from the council, which governed in the ruler's name. The original council, wracked by dissensions over the choice of a ruler and weakened by the death or elimination of three of its members, was transformed between 1727 and 1730 into a family council of the Dolgorukovs and a regency for Peter II. After his death, this powerful clan sought to institutionalize its position by getting Anna to accept the famous "conditions" in which we find the gist of the autocrat's jurisdiction: the power to decide questions of war, peace, and finance, to grant estates as rewards for service, to appoint to positions above colonel (the council had already appropriated the right to appoint colonels), and to confirm death sentences on nobles.[7]

The restoration of the autocracy, when Anna tore up the conditions in February 1730, was above all a revolt against the hubris of a clan laying claim to the succession of the Romanov house. Anna's own incapacity to govern, however, compelled her to announce in November 1731 the creation of a Cabinet of Ministers "attached to Our Court," consisting of Chancellor Gavril Golovkin, Vice-Chancellor Andrei Osterman, and real privy councillor Aleksei Cherkasskii, who had played a major role in supporting Anna the previous year. This cabinet, which may have begun earlier as a private secretariat of the empress, was authorized in June 1735 to issue imperial orders over the signature of three members. It exercised the empress's jurisdiction over all matters of government and thus coordinated military and foreign policy with domestic administration. All reports addressed to the empress, including those of the Senate, were routed through the cabinet, which also sent orders directly to the colleges, ignoring the Senate. The president of the College of War, Marshal Burkhard Münnich, seems not to have been an ex officio member of the cabinet, and retained his own separate access to the empress, but he often took part in its deliberations; so did the chief of the political police, Andrei Ushakov. Joint sessions with the Senate were held occasionally. This informal council—informal because two of its three members seldom attended and it functioned as a council only when outsiders were invited—filled the void (*pustota*) between the ruler and the Senate, which so exercised Münnich and provided a forum where representatives of the two political families and of the German element sought a consensus on the governing of the empire.[8]

If the empress Elizabeth was able to govern without a council during the first 15 years of her reign and resisted the entreaties of her chancellor to set up a successor to Anna's Cabinet of Ministers in which he would repeat Osterman's performance, it was because the political constellation that coalesced around the throne after 1741 created an exceptional situation: an ambitious and energetic chancellor shared the governing of the realm with a procurator general to whom he was closely related, who was the de facto chairman of a Senate now in full command of the government and able to subordinate the military establishment to its leadership, as we shall see presently. Nevertheless, the imminence of war with Prussia compelled the empress to agree to the establishment of a "conference attached to the imperial court" in March 1756. Its nine members included the leaders of the foreign policy, military and naval establishments, the chiefs of the artillery and political police, as well as the procurator general. This conference, like the Supreme Privy Council in its early days, was a kind of committee of ministers, the Senate becoming once again a supercollege responsible for internal affairs.[9]

While these councils, under whatever name, served the dual purpose of filling a void created by the incompetence of the rulers and coordinating the operations of the entire government, the "secret councils" continued to meet from time to time to discuss important foreign policy questions. Under Anna they were called general assemblies. One, for example, met in February 1733 and resolved that Russia could not accept the election of Stanislas Leszczynski to the Polish throne. The nine participants were the three members of the cabinet, Münnich and his brother, the chiefs of the navy, commissary, and political police, and one of the chancellor's sons. The Polish question was also discussed in December 1745 at another such conference of eleven participants including, among others, the chancellor, the procurator general, the chiefs of the Artillery and Commissary, and the Governor-General of Moscow.[10]

Peter III thought he could govern without the Conference but set up a Council (*Soviet*). Catherine II was convinced she could do without it yet set up her own "Council attached to Her Majesty's Court" in November 1768, at the outset of the first Turkish war. If there was no longer any need for a council to stand in for an incompetent ruler—the Council was not an autonomous body like the Cabinet of Ministers or the Conference—the necessity for a joint committee bringing together the chiefs of the three supercolleges and the artillery, the procurator general, and a sprinkle of military commanders and diplomats had become not only imperative but permanent. The Council was not closed after the war and remained in existence until the end of the reign.

It never ceased to be, however, a nongovernmental agency, outside the hierarchy of institutions, consisting of representatives of families that had now governed Russia for over four generations, joined by the favorite—Orlov, later Potemkin—and, for the first time, by men from the borderlands. In its composition and the role assigned to it, it resembled the Senate of 1722–1725. Indeed, both the Senate of 1723 and the Council of 1791 had thirteen members.[11]

While families were jockeying for membershp on various councils that maintained some unity in the operations of the imperial government, bitter struggles were taking place within the military establishment in search of unity of command and independence from the Senate. In 1726, when Menshikov was at the height of his power, the Provision Chancery was removed from Senate control and placed under the College of War. The supply services were now combined with personnel management in a single agency. In 1731, however, both the Commissary and the Provision Chancery were returned to Senate supervision exercised by a newly appointed procurator accountable to the Senate. Moreover, the internal audit of the Commissary accounts, heretofore concentrated in a separate division of the Commissary—a procedure that guaranteed that irregularities would not be challenged—was to be conducted in the presence of a senator before they were sent to the College of Audit for final auditing. The College of War and the supply services were again separated.[12]

The artillery kept up its fight to remain autonomous but suffered from internal divisions. The growth of its responsibilities during Peter's reign bred a new service, the engineers, who won a major supporter when Münnich, an old enemy of Menshikov, was made Chief of Fortifications in March 1727. Two years later, however, artillery and fortifications were reunited under Münnich, appointed Chief of the Artillery in August 1729. Münnich, a relative of the Saltykovs, was the greatest empire builder of Anna's reign and a man not to be hindered by collegial procedures. His practice was to present the Chancery of Artillery and Fortifications with a "proposal" (*predlozhenie*), in fact a directive that was then dutifully repeated verbatim in a formal resolution (*prigovor*) of all members. In January 1732 he became president of the College of War, and the prestige of the Artillery was immensely enhanced. Three years later, however, his major rival, the prince of Hessen-Homburg, who later married into the Trubetskoi family, became Chief of the Artillery, although Münnich was successful in keeping the engineers for himself.[13]

This endless rivalry among families over control of the constituent parts of the military establishment was so detrimental to military efficiency that Münnich, who retained direct access to the empress, was able to impose the drastic reorganization of January 1736, as operations against the Turks and Crimean Tatars were about to begin. In this conflict that was to last more than 3 years, the president of the College of War and field marshal was also commander in chief of the army in the field.[14]

The reform created seven board (*kontory*), five of them responsible for the commissary, provisioning, artillery, fortifications, and accounting. Each was headed by a director running his board in collegial fashion in accordance with previous instructions and regulations. Any decision exceeding the authority of a board had to be brought before a general assembly of the College of War, consisting of the president, vice-president, and two councillors—the core membership of the college, responsible for personnel management—and the seven directors. Decisions were reached by majority vote. Moreover, the seven boards were located in Petersburg. Since Münnich had already won from the empress the right to refuse Senate orders that he found in violation of imperial orders, the entire central military establishment had become not only concentrated at last in the College of War but also independent of the Senate.

Such arrogance brought about a backlash after Münnich's dismissal in March 1741. The dismantling of his empire began in December. The Commissary and Provision Chancery were subordinated to the Senate. The engineers were placed under the Chief of the Artillery, which remained under the "general supervision" of the College of War. There began a close association between the Commissary and the Procurator General's office that lasted until 1764: at least three procurators general had been chiefs of the Commissary before their appointment.[15]

This concentration of the military establishment was accompanied by an extraordinary development. The new president of the College of War, Marshal Vasilii Dolgorukov, was too old to be more than a figurehead. Following his death in February 1746, no replacement was appointed for more than 14 years, and the vice-president was a weak and low-ranking general. Furthermore, no Chief of the Artillery was appointed after the death of Vasilii Repnin in July 1748. Thus, it is no exaggeration to say that the entire military leadership had been decapitated by 1748.[16] The beneficiary of this counterreform could only be Nikita Trubetskoi, the Procurator General. Münnich's achievement had been turned on its head, and the Senate had gained the upper hand over the military establishment, a trend matching the clear downgrading of military values during the reign of Elizabeth. A new Chief of the Artillery was not appointed until May 1756,[17] at the outset of the Seven Years' War; a new president of the College of War was not appointed until August 1760.

By the late 1760s a new independent military establishment had been restored, but its leaders and those of the Senate were closely related. The daughter of Zakhar Chernyshev, the vice-president of the College of War, married in 1768 the son of Marshal Saltykov, the Moscow Governor-General, brother-in-law of Nikita Trubetskoi, whose daughter was married to the Procurator General, Alexander Viazemskii. The Commissary and the Provision Chancery were placed under the College of War in April 1766, but the appointment of the favorite, Grigorii Orlov, Chief of the Artillery, set a precedent that enabled this skilled and stubborn service to retain its independence, although it was more apparent than real in view of the favorite's incompetence. After his death in April 1783, the fiction of the Artillery's independence was abandoned, and it responsibilities were given to the College of War. In October 1790 the president of the college, Potemkin, marshal and favorite, assumed command over the Artillery. This event presaged the reorganization of April 1791, inspired by the principles of 1736. The reform was announced 2 weeks before Potemkin learned of his loss of favor with the empress. The new favorite, Platon Zubov, became chief of the artillery but one as incompetent as Orlov had been.[18] The real power in the newly concentrated military establishment was Nikolai Saltykov, Potemkin's enemy. The Saltykov family, to which Münnich had been related, thus regained its hold over military affairs.

Senate, Procurator General, and Colleges

The announcement in March 1730, in the wake of the disbanding of the Supreme Privy Council, that the Senate was being restored to the eminence it had enjoyed under Peter I was destined to become part of the ceremonial accompanying almost every new accession until Alexander I.[19] No one seems to have asked which Senate was being restored, whether that of 1711, 1718, or 1722, but it was most likely that of 1722. Declarations of intentions in Russian administrative history, however, were very seldom synchronized with what was real and possible. If autocracy had been what it appeared to be, there would have been no discrepancy, but the ruler's will had to contend with a field of forces that only hard work, persistence, and leadership qualities could shape into a malleable instrument. In fact, the role of the Senate was about to be radically altered.

Membership was raised to twenty-one, larger than it had ever been, in order to accommodate Anna's supporters. In June the Senate was divided into five departments, one to take up church-related matters, another for military and naval questions, a third for fiscal and budgetary operations, a fourth and a fifth for justice and industry, respectively.[20]

There were two reasons for this departure from the Petrine model. One was the recognition that division of labor contributed to efficiency. It was also an attempt to break the hold of the clerks over Senate decision making. The clerks, the collective household staff of the political apparatus, had so imprisoned their masters in a web of reports, extracts, and minutes that senators came to a session like guests to a dinner, without knowing what dishes the cooks had prepared and what entertainment was in store.[21] Departments, consisting of four or five senators, were henceforth required to prepare briefs themselves, to be then discussed in general assembly, where the clerks were expected to become mere executors of their masters' will.

Whether such intentions could be realized was doubtful. The political apparatus was not interested in working long hours and learning the rules: instead it insisted on its ability to wield the power that comes with key positions in the patronage network from which the ruler's favor was sought, to expand connections, and to build empires in search of a social base that would guarantee permanence. The emergence of the cabinet in the fall of 1731, together with the removal of the procurator general, ended the experiment with departments—it had lasted hardly more than a year. The Senate's membership began to shrink, and there were often no more than two or three senators in attendance by the mid-1730s.[22] In one respect, however, the settlement of 1722 was preserved and expanded. The distinction made by Peter between the three supercolleges headed by presidents who were also senators and the remainder of the Senate brought about the subordination of the Senate to the army, navy, and foreign policy leadership.

The trend, we know, went in the opposite direction during the reign of Elizabeth, and the dominance of the civilian establishment, together with the lack of a cabinet-like intermediary, reflected the renewed strength of the Senate. Its membership fluctuated between nine and sixteen, including the presidents of the three supercolleges, but its working core was much smaller. Individual senators, however, took advantage of the empress's distrust of the institution and of her lazy detachment from day-to-day affairs to obtain imperial sanction to carry out their policies without having to clear them through the Senate. The best example was that of Petr Shuvalov, whose cousin was the empress's favorite and wife one of her closest confidants. His knowledge of political economy and managerial skills enabled him to build an empire that rivaled the procurator general's.[23] These tensions showed only too clearly that the imperial government was not a government of bureaucratic institutions but a collection of political clans vying for supremacy in the name of unconditional support for autocratic rule.

Despite its weaknesses, the Senate became under Elizabeth an indispensable agency of government. One of the major functions of the ruling class, the dispensation of patronage at all levels of government, was one of its major responsibilities. All civilian members of the apparatus from grade fourteen to five, the equivalent of an army lieutenant colonel, were appointed by the Senate. Civilian appointments were thus much more concentrated in the Senate than were military appointments in the College of War. The Senate was the highest court of civil appeals and the highest court of review in criminal cases. It confirmed contracts valued at more than 10,000 rubles for military supplies, construction, the sake of vodka, and other obligations undertaken with the private sector, and it sought to keep in existence a rudimentary national budget without which no government is possible. Its ability to compel all colleges and governors to carry out its orders made it the "keeper of the laws," and, in this sense, a more effective guardian of the integrity of the imperial government than the autocrats themselves.[24]

Another radical change in Senate procedures took place in December 1763, for reasons similar to those that inspired the reform of 1730. The Senate was divided into six departments, the first four in Petersburg, the other two in Moscow. Responsibilities for personnel management, budget making, and all administrative matters of the Senate were vested in the First Department. Judicial appeals and criminal reviews went to the Second and the Sixth; the confirmation of military contracts over 10,000 rubles to the Fourth; educational, postal, and police matters to the Third Department. The Fifth took over the old responsibilities of the Senate's branch office in Moscow, chiefly administrative matters. Thus, the departments, like those of 1730, took up matters exceeding the authority of colleges and chanceries. They reached final decisions by unanimous vote unless a new law or an amendment was required, in which case they forwarded their recommendation to the general assembly of the departments in either capital. In the long run, however, the reform had extensive implications for the Senate's role in the imperial government. With the closing of the colleges in the 1780s, the Senate became a high court of five judicial departments, while the First Department became the true government of the empire. By the end of Catherine's reign this department had eleven members, about the size of the old Senate, another forty senators sitting in the other six departments.[25]

The evolution of the Senate after 1722 was inseparable from that of the procurator general's office. This office, for more than 50 years after 1740 the single most important office in the civilian establishment, is an excellent case study of the importance of ruling families in the imperial government and of empire building by their more ambitious members.

From its inception in January 1722 the office was intended to be the intermediary between the ruler and the Senate, the latter functioning as a general council of representatives and protégés of the ruling families, sharing with the ruler in the distribution of the spoils and privileges among members of the apparatus in the capitals and provinces. Presented as "the eye of the Sovereign" in the Senate, the Procurator General was instructed to make sure that senators attended meetings, debated with proper decorum—our traditional view of the autocracy has caused us to forget they were often tumultuous—and that voting followed the proper procedures. Senate decisions had to be unanimous, a requirement intended to compel debate among insiders and to impose a facade of unchallengeable consentaneity to outsiders. If senators could not agree, it was the responsibility of the Procurator General to offer a proposal likely to reconcile divergent opinions and, if that was not possible, to bring the matter before the ruler. In addition, the Senate was bound by its precedents, which became the law of the empire. Should it become necessary to overturn a precedent, create new law, or amend existing law, the Procurator General sought imperial confirmation.[26]

He had his own agents and his own patronage network. In the Senate itself there was a senior procurator, who operated as his deputy. The reform of 1763 placed the Procurator General in the First Department—to underscore its importance—a senior procurator in the other five. A sixth was added in 1774.[27] Meanwhile, procurators had been appointed in almost all colleges and in the chanceries of governors and provincial voevodas. The administrative–territorial reform of the 1770s multiplied the size of the procuracy some fifteen times and gave the procurator general an unequaled ability to distribute favors in every corner of the empire.[28] Moreover, he became the chief dispenser of civilian patronage. Appointments and recommendations made formally by the Senate had to go through his office where the real bargaining over who was to get what took place, before they reached the general assembly.

The Procurator General also headed the Senate's chancery. The built-in antagonism between him and the senators was sustained by resentment— mitigated by the senators' refusal to do hard work and specialize—of the importance of the secretarial and clerical staff. The chancery had 87 people in 1711, and only 70 in 1743, when the Senate was just beginning to recover from its humiliation in the 1730s, but 193 in 1762 and 274 in 1796.[29] Senate procedures that gave the staffs such a deciding role in the preparation of briefs and the drafting of decisions transformed the procurator general in the course of three generations into the lord of the senatorial mansion to which senators by the end of the century did indeed come to be dined and entertained by the clerks.

Who were these procurators general? The first, Pavel Iaguzhinskii, through his marriage to a daughter of Chancellor Golovkin, was related to the Naryshkins.[30] The creation of the Supreme Privy Council made the post superfluous. Restored in October 1730 and headed once again by Iaguzhinskii, it was abolished a second time a year later, when the formation of the cabinet was announced, and no Procurator General was appointed again until April 1740. However, we know from Filippov's study of its minutes that the Cabinet often operated as a one-man council, Golovkin and Cherkasskii choosing to stay away or taking no part in its work.[31] It follows that Osterman became a de facto procurator general. He was related by marriage to the Streshnevs and Naryshkins; his wife was also a close cousin of Semën Saltykov, whom the Empress Anna affectionately called *mon cousin* and made majordomo of her court and her representative in Moscow.[32] The so-called rule of the "Germans" during her reign is very much in need of reassessment.

If we agree that Osterman was procurator general in all but name, the third procurator general, Nikita Trubetskoi, came from a family also closely related to the Naryshkins and married another daughter of Golovkin. He remained in the post 20 years, long enough to build a considerable following in the Senate establishment. The sixth and most remarkable, Alexander Viazemskii, married Trubetskoi's daughter, who was also the niece of Peter Saltykov, Semën's son. His 28-year tenure was the longest, and the post reached its apogee under him. His successor, Alexander Samoilov, married the grandniece of Trubetskoi and Saltykov. It thus appears that this crucial post was for 25 years the property of the Naryshkin–Trubetskoi families, shared for another 41 years with the Saltykovs. It is difficult to exaggerate the importance of such concentration of patronage power in these two political families, the Naryshkins and the Saltykovs, descendants of the two wives of Tsar Alexei, Peter the Great's father.[33]

The closing of the colleges removed the major rivals of the procurator general's office, and Viazemskii must have played a major role in guiding the reform through a maze of political intrigues. Presidents of colleges and chiefs of chanceries had been building empires for 50 years. They too, like the Procurator General, appointed large clerical staffs and channeled the flow of business through their agencies, the presence of assistant procurators as eyes of the Procurator General could not but breed resentment. Staffs were broken up; clerks were scattered; some of the colleges' functions were concentrated in satellites of the procurator general's chancery; and others were decentralized among provincial agencies under the supervision of governors subordinated to the First Department and of procurators directly dependent on the Procurator

General. All these shifts created for the first time in modern Russian history an institutional structure in which the relative, protégé, and representative of the ruling families became the ruler's immediate deputy in civil administration, with her favorite at the head of the military establishment. Never before had the imperial government reached such a degree of structural cohesion and political unity as in the 1780s.

The colleges were the executive agents of the imperial government. Their presidents had come in 1718 from the very top of the political leadership, but the reform of 1722 demoted them from immediate collaborators of the tsar to subordinate instruments of the Senate's will. The presidents of the three supercolleges remained, of course, the exception. It was intended in 1718 that the colleges responsible for internal administration would open their own local agencies in gubernias and provinces, and some did, although little must have been achieved by the time Peter died in January 1725. The financial retrenchment that began immediately after his death, together with the continuing reassertion of Muscovite traditions, caused the new leaders to close those agencies. By 1727 colleges resembled *prikazy* more than ever in their subordination to a higher council of government and in their lack of local agents.[34]

The size of the political apparatus was also sharply curtailed. The imperial order of July 1726, emanating from the Supreme Privy Council, reduced members from ten to six—a president, vice-president, two councillors, and two assessors. In fact, it even reduced it to three by providing that half should serve in the capital for a year while the other half was given a leave of absence without pay "to watch over their properties," a first step toward the demobilization of the ruling class.[35]

The colleges, however, were only the most visible past of the executive branch. The strength of the Muscovite tradition was evident in the proliferation of "chanceries" created for special purposes and given the status of colleges. Some were even called *prikazy*. They too were collegial bodies, but smaller, and their presidents were usually called "commanding officer" (*glavnyi komandir*), or chief judge. By the 1740s their number exceeded fifty!

The agenda of a college was set by its secretary, who drew up a brief for the members containing the essentials of the matter to be discussed and the laws under which it had to be decided. These briefs were debated on, and a vote was taken beginning with the member junior in rank. Decisions were made not by unanimous vote as in the Senate but by majority vote, the president breaking a tie. The prohibition of meetings held at the home of a president was a reminder of the persistence of patriarchal relationships in Russian politics and of the readiness to abandon formal procedures for cozier chats, where members would find the president's arguments irresistible.[36]

Colleges and central agencies in general were often called judicial (*sudeiskie*) bodies, for two reasons. Procedures were essentially judicial, collecting evidence, invoking precedents and the law. They also deserved to be called judicial bodies in the sense that they did not initiate cases but decided matters brought before them. When they were not trying to obtain data to draw up an endless number of tables (*vedomosti*), colleges took up cases sent by the ruler or the Senate (for reexamination), by governors and voevodas, or submitted by petitioners directly. There existed no clear demarcation of authority between the colleges and the Senate except in a few specific instances—colleges could not confirm death sentences or contracts exceeding 10,000 rubles. It was by no means clear that a demarcation existed between colleges and governors. The result was a constant upward flow of business that should have been decided at lower levels, but which the lack of jurisdictional stratification compelled members of the apparatus to refer to their superiors. This was further evidence of the nonbureaucratic nature of the Russian political order in which a highly politicized group of ruling families and their relatives insisted on remaining the last resort for agencies and private petitioners alike.

However, such traditional obsession with having the final say in matters great and small was realistic only if the political families were willing to increase their household staffs. It is tempting to call these staffs an imperial bureaucracy, but it is a temptation that must be resisted. Clerks without legal protection, without a guaranteed income, without pensions, without hope of regular promotion in accordance with definite rules, were no more than private staffs, protecting their master's interest but intent on bending it to serve their own. While great lords managed their estates as if they were regiments or governmental departments, political leaders managed government offices like private bailiwicks. The inability to separate public duty from private behavior was taken for granted by contemporaries, and petitioners resented the interposition of secretaries and clerks who behaved with the officiousness of domestics in private households.[37]

Petitioners from the provinces had other reasons for resentment: they traveled great distances for solutions to problems that could have been resolved locally and were forced to finance expensive stays in Moscow until their business was settled there. Further, the need for efficiency made crucial by the war served to break the hold of the *prikazy* over political life in the 1700s. A similar situation developed in the 1760s while the demobilization of the ruling class was in full swing and the settlement of frontier regions in the south and southeast of the Muscovite core placed an excessive burden on the ability of Moscow to redress grievances in distant provinces. It also fed the ambition of the Procurator General to make a clean sweep of these hordes of clerks, whose very existence was a painful reminder that the imperial government was still unable in 1762 to determine how much revenue was collected.

The first stage in the political offensive of the ruling class against the staffs was the Instruction of April 1764, which ended the subordination of the governors to the colleges and placed them under the First Department and the empress.[38] In the absence of a clear line of demarcation between the jurisdiction of the colleges and that of the governors, the Instruction at a single stroke made the colleges superfluous. The second stage was the creation in the new gubernias of fiscal and judicial chambers to take over, each in its gubernia, the managerial responsibilities of the colleges. The third was to vest the supervisory functions of the colleges in "expeditions" that were no more than extensions of the Procurator General's chancery. The fourth and final stage was the closing of the colleges in the 1780s.[39] The victory of the ruling class, however, came at a price, and the clerks would take their revenge during the reign of Alexander I.

Local Government

Nowhere was the return to principles of Muscovite administration so evident as in the reappointment of voevodas in all towns. The trend that began with the instruction of 1719 reached its completion in the late 1720s. In February 1727 the Supreme Privy Council ordered the Senate to dismantle the provincial agencies created by the reform of 1719 and restored the voevoda as the single agent of the entire central government. The tradition of military government, however, had by then become so well established that it was found necessary, in order to give the voevoda adequate authority in the eyes of the population and vis-à-vis military units and garrisons, to place him in provincial capitals in the rank of a colonel . . . while he was in office, even if his career had been in the civilian apparatus. Those appointed in other towns were placed in the rank of major. Voevodas thus belonged, as field officers, to the managerial level of the ruling class. To guide their operations, a new instruction was issued in September 1728.[40] They remained unpaid and, like their seventeenth-century predecessors, were expected to feed themselves off the population and the petitioners who turned to them for assistance.

Russia was governed after 1728 by nine governors, 28 provincial voevodas, and about 170 voevodas, some in uezd centers, others in ordinary towns.[41] Governors were still appointed by the ruler, but the Cabinet played a crucial role in their selection during the reign of Anna. All voevodas were appointed by the Senate, usually from candidates submitted by the Heraldmaster's Office, which kept records of both civilian members of the apparatus and retired officers—chiefly wounded veterans—waiting for civilian appointments in lieu of pensions. The post was a lucrative one and, like a regimental command, one much sought after by those needing to repair their finances, as well as those with an interest in staying away from the capital for a while. This much appears from the Cabinet orders of December 1733 and January 1734 warning the Senate to be more careful in selecting voevodas.[42]

Many voevodas were illiterate. Nikolai Vonliarliarskii, himself a provincial voevoda in the 1720s, noted that candidates were never asked whether they could read or write. Official documents were signed by one of the clerks, locally recruited, and justice was administered in Solomon-like fashion or for the sordid purpose of satisfying greed and currying favor with the strong. Even in the 1760s, when the educational level of voevodas seems to have risen, many were still illiterate "in the allegorical sense" as the author put it—that is, did not know the laws they were appointed to administer and treated petitioners with the same coarseness that military life had trained them to use toward recruits and soldiers.[43] Most voevodas had followed a military career; some, the sons of soldiers, who were former peasants or clergy or townsmen, had risen through the ranks, like the Alatyr voevoda in the 1770s. Prokhor Bavykin, for example, presumably from the nobility, entered the army as a soldier and rose to captain, retired and transferred to the civilian apparatus with promotion—as was the custom—to the next higher civilian rank, and was appointed voevoda in a small town of Kostroma province. Six years later, in 1765, he was transferred to one of the provincial capitals of the Ukraine of the Settlements.[44]

The significance of the lack of training for the post of voevoda—and that of governor—must not be exaggerated. Indeed, training was often irrelevant. Voevodas and governors were the managing officers of the ruling class. They owed their position to their political skills, to their ability to find a patron properly connected with the ruling group to make sure that his name would be among those recommended by the Heraldmaster's Office to the Senate. In return for loyalty they were given power to rule over a dependent population with very few restrictions and joyful expectations of substantial rewards.[45]

These appointments were not only patronage plums. They were also the equivalent of banishment for members of the apparatus who lost out in the rivalries of court politics. This seems to have been very much the case between 1725 and 1741, a period of great turbulence in the politics of the ruling class. Ivan Dolgorukov, for example, senator in 1728, was demoted to voevoda in Vologda 5 years later, before his further banishment to Pustozersk and execution in 1739. The more fortunate Ivan Bakhmetev, regimental colonel in 1726, became Alatyr voevoda in 1729 but was promoted to major general in 1733. He transferred in 1740 to the civilian apparatus as senator, reentered army service in 1742, and became a senator once again in 1753 in the rank of real privy councillor. If the banishment was to a distant town in Siberia—Policemaster General Divier and Senate Senior Procurator Skorniakov became voevodas in Okhotsk—it was the most severe form of punishment for a member of the apparatus, short of expulsion and trial as a common criminal.[46]

The evolution of the post of voevoda between 1725 and 1775 evinced two contradictory trends. As a rule, voevodas had not been appointed for any specific length of time, but the expectation that they would feed themselves handsomely had kept their tenure short. It was limited to 2 years by the imperial order of March 1730 and extended to 5 years by the Senate in October 1760. It is not without interest that the first order was issued 1 month after the restoration of the "autocracy." It essentially called for the removal of voevodas appointed by the Supreme Privy Council—the second order appeared 2 months after the major shake-up of August 1760. In both cases the apportionment of patronage was obviously a major factor.[47]

On the other hand, the government recognized that voevodas were becoming integrated into the local society of the ruling class. In June 1740, they were forbidden—once again—to acquire real property and peasants in the town or territory they administered. This unenforceable prohibition was lifted 24 years later. Beginning in the 1740s, we find references to local requests sent to the Senate to keep voevodas in office for longer terms.[48] Voevodas were gradually being transformed into local landowners with local interests, and their replacement after 1775 with a triumvirate of land captain, uezd judge, and uezd treasurer was the logical consequence of the demobilization of the ruling class and of the shift in the center of gravity from Moscow to the provinces.

The creation of colleges and the appointment of provincial voevodas in 1719 had marked a reversal of the reform of 1708 and the beginning of a concerted attack upon the office of governor and the concept of regional administration. The instruction of September 1728, however, sought to enhance the authority of the governor by vesting the power to impose sanctions in the Senate alone. It asserted that all voevodas in his gubernia were subordinated to the governor, that no appeals were to be taken from town to provincial voevodas, that complaints against any voevoda were to be addressed to the governor. Voevodas sent their reports to the governor; the governor sent his to the colleges and the Senate. Sanctions, such as fines and transfers, were imposed by the governor, although transfers required the Senate's approval.[49]

The governor thus emerged as the relaying agent of the entire central government to add compelling force to directives from above, to curb the voevodas' propensity to misuse their powers, and to make sure they would send in their reports on time. The instruction contained the crucial provision that all directives from the Senate and the colleges must be addressed to the voevoda via the governor, so that he might be kept informed of all current business conducted in his gubernia at the initiative of the central government, and exercise, in the military language of the day, direct command (*blizhniaia komanda*) over the voevodas. On the other hand, the instruction was ambiguous toward the position of the provincial voevoda in the hierarchy. Since the governor could not watch over the activities of the voevodas in distant towns, the provincial voevoda should assume over them the same responsibilities as those of the governor over his entire gubernia and be held accountable for their derelictions of duty. The instruction thus proclaimed that all voevodas were equal before the governor but at the same time that some were more equal than others. This ambiguity—the result of a compromise between Muscovite and Petrine principles—soon proved fatal to the attempt to shore up a regional structure in the administration of the Russian heartland.[50]

A renewed attack on the office of governor began in the spring of 1730. The instruction applied to territorial divisions, which varied considerably in size. Two of the nine gubernias were not divided into provinces, and the capital of the largest gubernia was also one of the country's two capitals. As early as March 1730, provincial and town voevodas of Moscow gubernia were ordered to forward civil appeals and criminal sentences to the branch office of the College of Justice, and no longer to the governor's office. We know from subsequent Senate orders that financial reports on tax collection and arrears were sent by provincial voevodas directly to the relevant colleges. An expression came into use, reflecting a new attitude toward the role of the governor: governors and provincial voevodas were to file reports, "each for his province separately."[51] In other words, the governor's effective jurisdiction was being restricted to the province around the gubernia capital.

A further blow to the authority of the governor was the Senate order of

June 1730 that all but annulled the requirement that all central directives must be routed through the governor's office. Wherever provincial centers were located between Moscow and their gubernia capital, directives to the provincial centers had to be routed through Moscow, causing delays and additional expenditures for couriers. Provincial voevodas in those centers were now authorized to receive these directives directly and to send their reports without going through the governor's office.[52] Ten of the twenty-eight provincial centers were in Moscow gubernia, where the order of March 1730 had already subordinated the provincial voevoda to the colleges. A glance at a road map shows that nine of the other eighteen were closer to Moscow than to their gubernia capitals, Arkhangelsk being a special case since the governor resided in Vologda. In other words, the regional structure created by the instruction of 1728 was declared inoperative in six of the nine gubernias and in the larger part of a seventh.[53]

Thus did the province emerge in the 1730s as the basic unit of the administrative–territorial division and its voevoda as the chief local agent of the central government. A final blow to the authority of the governor and a logical consequence of the reform of 1730 was the imperial order of May 1737 restoring the power of colleges to fine governors without seeking Senate authorization. The order was the answer to complaints by the Colleges of War and Revenue that financial reports were not being sent despite repeated reminders. Since chanceries enjoying equal status with colleges were given the same power, governors were soon deluged with humiliating threats of fines by some fifty-four agencies! The order was not annulled until April 1764, when a third instruction—the first specifically addressed to the governor alone—subordinated him once again only to the Senate and empress.[54] By then, however, the large territorial gubernia created by Peter was no longer considered viable, and governors as regional agents of the central government were about to be demoted to the status of provincial voevodas.

Very few changes took place in the territorial division of Russia between 1727 and 1775. On the eve of the reform introduced by the Organic Law of November 1775, there were ten gubernias and thirty provinces, excluding those around the gubernia capital. As the reform took effect in the span of a decade, the larger gubernias were systematically broken up into smaller ones, formed around provinces. Sixteen provincial centers became new gubernia centers, raising the number of gubernias to twenty-six. The other fourteen were incorporated into neighboring provinces.[55]

The new gubernia became the basic territorial division of the country until the Revolution, but the old ambiguity that had marred the relationships between governor and provincial voevoda persisted when governors-general were appointed over two gubernias. We find again the equation between the two posts and the expression "each in his gubernia."[56] The governor-general succeeded the old governor, who now replaced the provincial voevoda, higher in rank and prestige but with few additional powers. By the end of Catherine's reign governors-general were on their way out, and the governor became at last the undisputed single intermediary between the central government and the towns.

It remained a cardinal principle of Russian provincial administration that the local agent of the central government must possess a universal jurisdiction over all the public business conducted in the territory to which he was appointed. This universal competence, however, did not give discretionary power to reward or punish individuals, impose taxes, or disburse public funds. Moreover, the existence of two levels and the undeniably higher status of the governor required that he should be given specific powers that would not be shared by the voevodas. As a result, the governor continued to exercise the powers of a regional authority, while most of his responsibilities were being circumscribed to the province centered in the gubernia capital.

The dispensation of civilian patronage was highly centralized in the Senate and became more and more concentrated in the procurator general's office. Only the clerks were appointed in the colleges by their presidents, in the gubernias by the governors and voevodas, but promotion to secretarial positions—the lower grades in the Table of Ranks, which gave secretaries the status of hereditary nobles—was strictly forbidden because the co-optation of civilians into the ruling elite was the exclusive prerogative of the ruling group. This became a sore point with the governors following the instruction of 1764, when the contrast between proclaiming the governor to be the lord and master (*khoziain*, also *opekun*) of his gubernia responsible for its government (*pravlenie*) and his inability to promote anyone in the apparatus became more jarring than ever.[57]

This had not been the case in the 1730s, but governors and voevodas were reminded that their appointments of ordinary clerks to secretarial posts with promotion to the equivalent rank were unlawful, and the Senate order of May 1742 quashed all such promotions.[58] By then, governors and provincial voevodas had to contend with a powerful procurator general, who insisted that the Senate chancery and secretaries in gubernias and provinces belonged to his patronage network.

These agents of the central government had few other opportunities to influence the selection of local personnel once colleges closed their local agencies in the late 1720s. In most gubernias there remained only postal officials, field officers who helped the governor carry out his military responsibilities, stewards appointed over court peasants and *odnodvortsy*. The general rule, found in both the instructions of 1728 and 1764, was that the governor, and the governor alone, could fine officials as well as subordinate voevodas and request their transfer from the Senate or the College of War. Elected townsmen who met in municipal bodies called *magistraty* were subordinated to governors and voevodas between 1727 and 1743, to their Central *Magistrat* thereafter.[59]

A sharp distinction thus must be drawn between members of the apparatus on the one hand and the clerks and the dependent population on the other. Over the former, governors had few powers, voevodas even less; toward the latter, arbitrariness and violence were the norm, and murder was not unknown. The clerks, however, had their own network, and violence against a clerk well connected with other clerks in the capital could cause a governor or voevoda much anguish.[60] A similar distinction must be made when we discuss their judicial powers.

Governors and voevodas became judges again after 1727. Much litigation never went beyond the patriarchal world of townsmen and peasants, and was settled by the elders of the litigants' communities. Civil suits were filed with either provincial or town voevodas, and appeals were taken to the governor directly. In criminal cases, misdemeanors were punished by the *magistraty*, stewards, or landlords, but felonies were prosecuted before the voevoda or the governor. Voevodas at either level investigated and tried cases, and their sentences were carried out immediately unless the punishment was death or galley labor, which required the governor's confirmation. Members of the apparatus, however, were prosecuted in the College of Justice or its branch office in Moscow, and sentences on members of the ruling class entailing expulsion from that class required the ruler's confirmation.[61] These extraordinary powers vested in the governors to confirm death sentences on all but members of the ruling class, at a time when capital crimes were of the most varied kind, were little affected by the suspension of the death penalty in 1754. Its replacement by hard labor in ports and mines did not reduce the sweep of the governor's powers as punitive agent of the apparatus against clerks and dependent population.

To back up his authority as punitive agent of the government, the governor, and he alone, was given command of the garrisons. Garrison troops constituted the only national police force until the 1760s, when the *shtatnye komandy* were created and placed at the governor's disposal. In large gubernias like Moscow and Kazan he shared with provincial voevodas the maintenance of order, the collection of the capitation, the convoying of prisoners and funds, and the transportation of recruits to their assigned destination. As a rule, governors did not command regular troops, except in certain strategic locations and only at certain times, often with the title of governor-general. In case of need, they had to obtain the cooperation of military commanders stationed in the area. Voevodas sent their requests for military assistance to the governor.[62]

Finally, both governor and voevoda were fiscal agents. The prohibition on new taxes was absolute, but governors, and governors alone, were authorized to negotiate contracts for the lease of the so-called *obrochnye stat'i*, properties of the treasury made available for public use such as mills, fisheries, bridges, landings, and customs houses; for the supply of provisions to the army; and, most important, for farming out the vodka monopoly. Governors remained authorized to confirm contracts valued at up to 3,000 rubles. Other contracts were referred to the College of Revenue or were negotiated in the capital directly, those valued at more than 10,000 rubles requiring Senate approval. Proceeds from the capitation were sent by voevodas to the governor's office, from which they were dispatched to military units in accordance with instructions of the College of War. Other taxes were collected by provincial and town voevodas, who sent them directly to the relevant colleges, a procedure inherited from Muscovite days and one increasingly the source of chaotic accounting and budgetary legerdemain.[63]

6

Consolidating the Foundations: 1796–1825

The Military Establishment

The accession of Paul in November 1796 represented a military coup by the head of the Romanov house against an oligarchic government of ruling families. The tsar, an adult male for the first time in the 71 years since the death of Peter in 1725,[1] asserted his authority as commander in chief, proceeded to secure a political base in the army, began a buildup of the Guard, and created an institutional mechanism giving the military establishment an independence it had never before been able to achieve, even under Potemkin. The long conflict with revolutionary France facilitated this renewed transformation of the ruler into a commander in chief and the militarization of the imperial government, a phenomenon that outlived the war and reached its apogee during the reign of Nicholas I.

Paul introduced at the very beginning of his reign the practice of issuing imperial orders addressed to military personnel alone (*vysochaishie prikazy*), thus establishing a legal distinction between civilian and military orders originating in the ruler's cabinet, until then combined under the name of *ukazy*.[2] The number of adjutants general and aides-de-camp (*fligel-ad'iutanty*) increased dramatically from 50 at the end of Catherine's reign to 93 and reached 176 in 1825. They constituted His Majesty's Suite, ready at all times to transmit the ruler's orders to members of the high command and civilian chiefs as well, the first step toward the subordination of the civilian government to the tsar as commander in chief. As the suite expanded, it required an executive officer, who became the chief of a new Military Field (*pokhodnaia*) Chancery—a term well designed to emphasize the mobility of the ruler in the exercise of his military duties, a situation unheard of since the reign of Peter. Created in August 1806, it became the nucleus of a separate imperial headquarters, intermediate between the ruler and the College of War, and thus outside the formal governmental structure. Its chief, Christoph von Lieven from 1798 to 1808, announced imperial orders and reported to the tsar on their execution.[3]

The General Staff (*General'nyi Shtab*) fell victim to Paul's early impulse to remove command responsibilities from the college and concentrate them in his immediate entourage. Its origin went back to the 1760s, when the lessons of the

Seven Years' War exposed serious deficiencies in operational planning. It consisted of about forty officers, who received their instructions from the president of the College of War. They collected data, chiefly topographical, prepared war plans, wrote descriptions of battles, and trained regimental officers called quartermasters (*kvartirmeistery*) to read and correct military maps and scouts (*provozhatye*) to lead military units in wartime. In 1772 the General Staff was placed under a quartermaster general and began to be called a department of the College of War. Most officers were attached in wartime to various commanders in chief, whose auxiliary agents they became in securing troop movements, billeting, and conducting reconnaissance missions ahead of the troops. Its abolition in 1796—the education and professional training of General Staff officers had won them an independence and respect that did not sit well in the atmosphere of the new reign—did not thereby end the need for careful planning, and the General Staff reappeared in 1797 as a separate Suite for General Staff Affairs (*po kvartirmeisterskoi chasti*), placed the following year under Aleksi Arakcheev, a protégé of the Saltykovs and favorite of the tsar, with the restored title of quartermaster general.[4] These reforms, together with the curtailment of the powers of commanders in chief in the field of personnel and budgetary matters, undermined the authority of the College of War and the field army high command. They correspondingly enhanced that of the ruler, who thus centralized command and personnel responsibilities, which had become dangerously scattered among commanding generals in the field, and concentrated them in his suite.

The ministerial reform of September 1802 created a Ministry of Land Forces, also called simply the War Ministry. Nikolai Saltykov, who succeeded Potemkin in 1791 and became president of the College of War in 1796 when he was promoted to field marshal, was succeeded in 1802 by Sergei Viazmitinov, a Potemkin protégé, as the first minister. He remained in his post until 1808. That a field marshal was not appointed to succeed Saltykov must be seen as part of the same policy designed to enhance the authority of the ruler at the very time when the reform of 1791, which integrated the supply services into the structure of the College of War, was beginning to bear fruit. The integration of the Commissary was accelerated by its removal to Petersburg in 1797. In January 1798, the Commissary and Provision Expeditions were renamed Departments, but their chiefs retained their respective titles of Chief of the Commissary and Provisionmaster General, both subordinated to the War Minister.[5] Two new agencies appeared. The general auditor, who had been a member of the College of War since 1702, was appointed chairman of a new Court of Military Appeals (*General Auditoriat*) in January 1797. The new court was given independent status in September 1805, when it was subordinated directly to the tsar and the Senate. In the same year, a Medical Expedition was created in the War Ministry, headed by a Chief Medical Inspector,[6] raising the number of basic constituent agencies of the War Ministry from three to six—commissary, provisions, judicial, medical, and of course, the artillery, from which the engineers seceded in 1802.

The appointment of the favorite, Platon Zubov, Chief of the Artillery, in 1793 thwarted the full implementation of the reform of 1791, even though Zubov was a protégé and distant relative of Nikolai Saltykov. His dismissal in November 1796 was followed in December by yet another attempt to concentrate military administration in the President of the College of War. The Artillery became another department of the College—but the term *expedition* was retained until 1812. Its chancery was merged with that of the College, promotions were requested, and its correspondence was channeled through the office of the president. Despite this long-standing pressure to consolidate the military establishment into one agency, however, the Artillery continued to insist on a measure of autonomy. In December 1797, the chief of the Artillery Expedition was made Inspector of All Artillery, with the right to report to both the College of War and the ruler, and in January 1798 the newly born fourth son of the tsar, Mikhail Pavlovich, was made Chief of the Artillery (*Feldzeugmeister*)—a purely formal appointment, of course, but one that singled out the artillery as a service enjoying imperial favor; Mikhail kept his post until his death in 1849.[7]

The practice of appointing inspectors began in the 1780s but did not flourish until the reigns of Paul and Alexander.[8] Centralization, intensified by an obsession with details of military performance, compelled these two rulers to rely on trusted generals to carry out sudden inspections of regiments, battalions, and squadrons, fortresses, batteries, and depots. The purpose of these inspections was to determine whether the detailed instructions from the center were carried out to the letter, to check the actual strength of military units, and to impose an absolute uniformity on the appearance and performance of every separate formation of the Russian army. Inspectors recommended promotions and dismissals, and their direct access to the ruler gave them enormous power. Since their activities violated the chain of command, inspectors were usually appointed on an ad hoc basis. The appointment of a permanent inspector for the artillery was a compromise solution between the traditional insistence on independence and the necessity of effective fiscal management.

This compromise was embodied in the reform of September 1802. It barred the chief of the Artillery expedition from direct access to the tsar but let the Inspector report directly to him on the results of his inspections, an awkward compromise when the two positions were held by the same officer. Only two other military leaders had access to the ruler by virtue of the office they occupied. One was the War Minister, the other the chief of the Field Chancery—another awkward situation because the latter was empowered to issue imperial orders binding upon the entire military establishment.

Separatist tendencies within the artillery establishment, however, remained strong and found a spokesman in Arakcheev. The authority of an agency, then as now, was not founded in its statues but derived from the position occupied by its head in the power structure. Arakcheev had earned Paul's trust in his capacity as commander of the Gatchina troops before 1796 and had drawn close to Alexander during his father's reign. His career had been in the artillery, and his first post when he returned to the service in May 1803—after losing favor in October 1799—was that of Inspector of All Artillery. Four years later, in December 1807, he joined the ruler's Suite "for Artillery Affairs," with the title of Inspector General of the Artillery. His orders were given the force of imperial orders, and the Expedition, now accountable to Arakcheev, was placed under a new inspector without access to the ruler. The new appointment restored de facto the post of Chief of the Artillery with the nine-year-old Mikhail still unable to exercise his responsibilities. In the following month, January 1808, Arakcheev became War Minister while remaining Inspector General of the Artillery. It was a striking repetition of Münnich's coup of 1732—using the artillery as a power base from which to gain control of the military establishment, once more united under a single head, who became at the same time chief of the Field Chancery and thus the only intermediary between the tsar and the military establishment. When Arakcheev left the ministry 2 years later to fill a unique triple appointment to the Committee of Ministers, the State Council, and the Senate, his successor, Barclay de Tolly, was given full powers over his ministry with the abolition of the post of Inspector General of the Artillery and the reintegration of the Artillery Expedition into the ministry.[9]

Meanwhile, however, the Commanding General of the Engineers (*Enzhiner-General*), who had been subordinated to the Chief of the Artillery since 1756, gained his independence in October 1802 when he was placed at the head of a new Engineer Expedition of the War Ministry, with the title of Inspector of Engineers. The holder of the post, Petr van Suchtelen (1802–1812), whose son married Zubov's niece, had access to the tsar but worked closely with Arakcheev.[10]

The long-sought unification of the military establishment, however, remained an elusive goal, as it had been after 1736 and 1791, because it depended above all on the ability of a powerful individual to impose his will upon stubborn vested interests. Moreover, the imminence of a major war soon destroyed whatever unity had been achieved in 1808. On the eve of the fatal conflict with Napoleon, expected to be a war of movement in which military formations of unprecedented size would have to be moved from one sector to another without waiting for the authorization of Petersburg, with the tsar reserving for himself the right to accompany his army in the field, it was clearly understood that the old rivalry between a centrally based council and a mobile headquarters in the field could not be repeated. As a result, all Russian forces not required for military and police duties in the borderlands and the defense of the northern capital were combined into a Grand Active Army of some 210,000 men to face Napoleon's Grande Armée of about 600,000. This army was placed under a commander in chief, a post filled at first by Barclay, the War Minister, who left the ministry to assume his command in Vilno, where the invasion took tsar and commander in chief by surprise in June 1812.[11]

The statute of January 1812 on the Active Army, the first army statute since the Military Code (*Ustav*) of March 1716, declared the commander in chief—whose appointment was announced by an imperial *prikaz* to the troops and an *ukaz* to the Senate—"invested with His Majesty's power," which he relinquished, however, when the tsar was at military headquarters. His closest deputy was the chief of the Army's Main Staff. The administration of the entire army was concentrated in the Staff, including keeping tables of organization, preparing battle plans, and securing supplies. The tsar appointed to the post General Petr Volkonskii, a relative of both Nikolai Saltykov and the Kurakin brothers, who had been chief of the General Staff (Quartermaster General) since 1810. This position was now made dependent on the chief of the Main Staff. Artillery and engineer units in the army were placed under their own commanders (*nachalniki*), subordinated directly to the commander in chief. Responsibilities for the supply of uniforms and the payment of salaries were vested in a chief of the Field Commissary, those for the provision of food and forage in a Field Provisionmaster, both subordinated to the Chief of Supply (*General Intendant*), responsible to the commander in chief. The Court of Military Appeals was abolished and replaced by a court of appeal for the army (*polevoi auditoriat*), accountable, like the army medical services, to the General of the Day (*Dezhurny General*), whose major responsibility was the maintenance of discipline in the army. He also inspected army units at any time. The statute thus created a field army organization with hardly a link to the War Ministry. Its brain, the Main Staff, assumed ministerial powers over the army in the field, while the ministry retained jurisdiction over units not included in the Active Army. During the war of 1812–1815, the Main Staff became the single most important agency of military administration, following the tsar across Europe all the way to Paris, some 3,000 kilometers from the War Ministry in Petersburg, while Arakcheev, who never left the tsar, concentrated his energies on the formation of reserves and the flow of supplies.[12]

The War Ministry was reorganized at the same time as the field army command structure was created. It was divided into seven departments—the term now replaced "expedition," with its connotation of autonomy—each headed by a director subordinated to the minister. Those of the two supply departments—Commissary and Provision—retained their historical titles; those of the two technical departments—Artillery and Engineer—were headed by an Inspector of the Artillery and an Inspector of the Engineer Corps, respectively. These two inspectors also reported to the Chief of the Army's Main Staff on the results of their inspections of artillery and engineer units outside the field army. The creation of a Medical Department was a mere change of name. Court-martial cases requiring the tsar's confirmation, which in the field army went before the court of appeals and the commander in chief, were sent to a new Judicial (*auditoriatskii*) Department, to which the commander in chief also sent already decided cases for safekeeping in the ministerial archive. Its director was called the Judge Advocate General (*General Auditor*). Finally, a Personnel (*Inspektorskii*) Department, under the Ministry's General of the Day took over responsibilities for keeping tabs on all military units outside the field army, their actual strength and level of readiness. This War Ministry statute, modeled after the General Statute on Ministries of June 1811, also provided for the creation of a ministerial council (*soviet*) consisting of the seven departmental directors and a number of other generals appointed by the tsar, some on a permanent, others on a temporary basis. Its duties consisted in discussing matters of common interest to two or more departments, reviewing contract proposals before their submission to the Minister, and drafting legislative proposals.[13]

This structural symmetry between the Active Army and the War Ministry was misleading and concealed a complete reversal of the roles played in the eighteenth century by the central agency and the field headquarters. The concentration of the armed forces in a single army gave its Main Staff responsibilities incomparatively heavier than those of the ministry. When Barclay left for the army in March 1812, his successor, General Alexei Gorchakov, nephew of the great Suvorov, was given the title of "interim" minister, and the instruction of the same month declared the duties of the ministry to be of a strictly executive nature.[14] The War Minister thus became subordinated to the chief of the Army's Main Staff and, beyond him, to the commander in chief. He consequently lost his right of direct access to the tsar, and his reports had to be routed through the Committee of Ministers. This tended to relegate the ministry to the status of a supply agency for the field army responsible for preparing a military budget, drawing up contracts, and supplying uniforms, salary, and food to the troops.

The ministry performed poorly during the war, and Gorchakov, accused of corruption, was dismissed in December 1815. On the day of his dismissal, a new reform of the military establishment was announced, one, however, that merely brought to completion the trend begun in 1812 toward an institutional separation of command responsibilities from logistical support. The Active Army ceased to exist and was replaced by two armies stationed for the most part in the western provinces, each under a commander in chief with reduced powers. Other troops stationed in the borderlands were reorganized into "separate corps." Its Main Staff was moved to Petersburg and renamed His Majesty's Main Staff, Volkonskii remaining its chief until his replacement in 1823 by General Hans Diebitsch, the former chief of the First Army's Main Staff.[15]

The Main Staff became the central agency in which the administration of the entire military establishment was henceforth concentrated, and its chief the only intermediary with the tsar, even for commanders in chief. It was in fact a committee of military ministers consisting, under the chairmanship of its chief, of the War Minister, the Inspector of Artillery and the Inspector of the Engineer Corps—that is, the directors of the two technical departments. It was not a collegial agency, however, and all three were subordinated to Volkonskii. At the same time, each member was given a definite jurisdiction. The chief of the Main Staff retained responsibilities for personnel management and command matters (*frontovaia chast'*). To him were thus subordinated the Quartermaster General, the ministry's Personnel Department, and the restored Court of Military Appeals, while the Judicial Department passed under the General of the Day, likewise subordinated to the Chief of the Main Staff. The refusal to give the highest military tribunal the same independence from the command structure upon which the legislation of 1805 had insisted reflected a renewed emphasis on the unconditional obedience of the troops and the disciplinary powers of their commanders, an essential ingredient of the conservative reaction that set in after 1815. The distinction, never too clear in practice, made in 1812 between the troops assigned to the Active Army and other units was abolished, and the entire army—except the military settlements but including even the Suite—was placed under the administrative authority of the Main Staff.[16]

On the other hand, the financial management of the army (budget matters, contracts, purchases, and deliveries—the so-called *ekonomicheskaia chast'*) remained the responsibility of the war minister, to whom the Chief of the Commissary and the Provisionmaster General and their respective departments, as well as the Medical Department, were subordinated. The War Minister was thus formally downgraded to the status of chief of supply for the entire military establishment. The legislation of 1815, however, retained the link between the supply services and the civilian government that had been such a bone of contention in the eighteenth century between the College of War and the Senate. While the Chief of the Main Staff was barred at first from membership in the State Council, the Senate, and the Committee of Ministers, the War Minister was a permanent member of these three agencies. Jurisdictional conflicts between Volkonskii and Arakcheev, the chief of the tsar's chancery, were settled by the tsar in person.

The reform also affected the standing of the technical services. Both inspectors were given a considerable autonomy by being made accountable no longer to the War Minister alone as had been the case in 1802 but to three superiors: to the tsar for the results of their inspections, to the Chief of the Main Staff for administrative matters and the supply of guns and powder, and to the War Minister in financial matters. Their authority was further enhanced by continued imperial patronage. Paul's third son, Nikolai, the future tsar, was made Inspector General of Engineers in 1817, and Mikhail assumed the full title of chief of the artillery in 1819. Although these titles were still largely ceremonial, they gave the representatives of the two services on the Main Staff greater authority vis-à-vis its chief.[17]

The Civilian Government

The unprecedented concentration of political power in the office of Procurator General Viazemskii in the 1780s was the work of a skilled and tenacious politician, but it could not outlast him for at least three reasons. It placed an unbearable burden upon a single individual, even after the decentralization of management functions in the wake of the local government reform. It also gave a single individual, linked by marriage with the two most important political families until the end of the eighteenth century, undue influence in the distribution of civilian patronage, thereby creating jealousies and resentment among those without the proper connections. Finally, it was incompatible with the reassertion of autocratic power against oligarchic government at the very time when discontent in the provinces called for forceful action, a discontent fueled in part by the resentment of members of the apparatus and the clerical staff who had been shipped off to the provinces a decade earlier.

The result was the gradual disintegration of the imposing administrative edifice built by Catherine's procurator general. Financial administration—by far its most important building block—gained its independence in 1793 when the posts of Procurator General and State Treasurer ceased to be held by the same individual. This was followed in 1796 by a gradual reconstitution of some central agencies and the creation of new ones, such as the Department of Waterways and the Department of Imperial Properties,[18] rewarding spoils for those eager to make their way in the corridors of power and reestablish a residence in the capital. Two features, however, distinguished the new agencies from the former colleges. Their chief, whether called director or even minister, possessed great authority vis-à-vis the members, who referred to him the most important matters coming up before the agency, although decisions continued to be made, at least formally, by majority vote. And whenever a decision could not be reached or exceeded the agency's authority, the matter was referred no longer to the Senate but to the ruler.[19] This managerial deconcentration was thus accompanied by the establishment of direct channels of command with the ruler, a development emphasizing hierarchy and discipline but one that destroyed the coordinating role of the Senate's First Department and threatened to turn the Procurator General into an adjutant general announcing imperial orders, without managerial responsibilities outside the Senate.

The reform of September 1802 built upon the foundations laid by Paul. It created eight ministries, four of them—Foreign Affairs, War, Navy, and Commerce—the immediate successors of eighteenth-century colleges. Another three—Internal Affairs (or Interior), Finance, and Justice—resulted from the breakup of Viazemskii's empire, and one, Education, from the superimposition of a ministerial staff upon the School Commission created in 1782 and its expansion into a national agency responsible for university as well as secondary education. Indeed, Petr Zavadovskii, the first minister (1802–1810), had been chairman of the Commission for nearly two decades (1782–1799). This continuity, in fact, turned out to be the chief feature of the new ministries. Agencies, reopened or created under Paul, were grouped under a minister whose authority and jurisdiction remained for practice to determine. Certain principles, however, were clear from the beginning. Agencies no longer reported to the Senate but submitted regular memoranda to the minister on their activities, requested his decision whenever they encountered difficulties, and received from him directives (*predlozheniia*) against which there was no appeal. Ministers were appointed by the tsar and were accountable to him alone. They had the right of direct access (*lichnogo doklada*) and used it to submit to the ruler projects of new laws or amendments to existing laws in the form of *ukazy*, which, once signed by the ruler, were announced to the Senate for publication and dissemination among central and local agencies, as well as decisions exceeding their authority.[20] The elimination of the Procurator General—now transformed into a mere Minister of Justice—and the First Department as coordinating agencies in domestic administration seemed at first glance to enhance the authority of the ruler. In fact it paved the way for the ministerial despotism so characteristic of an increasingly fragmented imperial government in the nineteenth century. As early as 1803, Semen Vorontsov warned Viktor Kochubei, the first Minister of Internal Affairs, that this would occur. Such despotism was bound to follow the building of several empires, each with a monopoly of technical information, against which the tsars would soon become powerless. Kochubei himself became aware of the ominous trend after only 4 years in office.[21]

The centralizing trend that began in 1796 placed on the civilian ministries the duty to conduct an activist policy and on ministers that of integrating departments, boards, and chanceries into a single agency responsive to their personal initiatives. The statute of January 1811, drafted by Mikhail Speranskii, a protégé of the Kurakins and the civilian counterpart of Arakcheev in the degree of influence he exercised on the tsar at the time, streamlined the internal structure of the ministries and enhanced the minister's authority. The agencies, merely gathered under the umbrella of a minister in 1802, were reorganized into uniform departments headed by directors appointed and removed by the tsar on the minister's recommendation. All other appointments, except those of section heads, were made by the minister, who was empowered, also at discretion, to promote ministerial personnel all the way to grade seven, the equivalent of an army lieutenant colonel. To coordinate activities within the ministry, a council (*soviet*) consisting of the directors under the minister's chairmanship, was created to examine amendments to the laws and statutes, proposals to acquire and alienate property belonging to the ministry, budget estimates, and contracts and claims to the value of 10,000 rubles. The minister was not bound by the council's opinion, but it had to be included if he chose to submit a proposal to the Committee of Ministers, the Senate, or the State Council.[22]

In their eagerness to justify their existence and build patronage networks, ministers appointed large staffs and chanceries of clerks to handle the flow of correspondence, statistics, and position papers. It soon became obvious, however, that the clerks, banished in the 1780s, were reasserting their influence, not without creating some disquiet in the higher ranks of the ruling elite. The same Kochubei complained in 1814 that chanceries had taken over the ministries, determining the agenda, preparing briefs and projects of decisions, and effectively forming "a certain brotherhood" (*obshchestvo*), well aware of its interests extending beyond those of individual ministries.[23] The ruling elite had always been obsessed with the exercise of power, treating clerks as private servants to be used, patronized, and dismissed at will. However, the growing size of the ministries—that no table of organization was published would seem to show that each ministry had an interest in blocking statutory restrictions—was beginning to raise the specter of a bureaucratic monster out of control.

If the power of ministers rested on a patronage network and an army of clerks—Speranskii complained that each minister was treating his agency like a piece of bestowed property[24]—the power of the ruler, in spite of the assertion of his autocratic prerogative, was increasingly dependent on the ministerial core of the ruling elite. The right of access was used to obtain his assent in matters of little import, in order to mark every operation of each ministerial empire with the unchallengeable stamp of imperial approval. The glorification of the ruler's autocracy only served to strengthen each minister's despotism toward his subordinates and his independence of other ministers. Alexander's plaintive excuse in March 1812 that "they took away from me [*otniali u menia*] Speranskii, who was my right hand," the decision of the Committee of Ministers in August to send a delegation demanding the replacement of Barclay by Kutuzov,[25] together with the incredible confusion of jurisdictions after 1815 suggest that the "autocrat" was no longer the master of his own ministers.

The Senate reached its centenary at the very time the ministerial statute sanctioned its demise as the coordinating agent of the imperial government. This demise was the effect of two trends. The increasing volume of business transacted in the Senate—suffice it to say that the size of the chancery rose from 193 in 1762 to 1,185 in 1824[26]—compelled a separation of responsibilities and the transformation of the venerable institution into a supreme court of appeals. The reform of January 1805 created two new departments, raising their number to nine, six in Petersburg and three in Moscow, all but the first constituting separate courts of appeal for a number of gubernias. The number of senators rose, as a result, from forty-three in 1796 to ninety-one in 1809 and ninety-nine in 1823.[27]

This trend toward institutional specialization was rendered irresistible by the growing dissatisfaction of the rulers with an institution representing an oligarchy of families hiding behind a mask of servility to brake assertions of autocratic power and guard tradition against the innovations of impatient tsars like Paul and Alexander. The quasi-monopoly of the post of procurator general in the Saltykov and Trubetskoi families alternately or even jointly, as in the case of Viazemskii, had consolidated the oligarchy's hold on the Senate. Paul understood the source of the Senate's influence when he conducted a massive alteration of its membership, appointing 108 senators in 4 years compared with 132 appointed by his mother in 34 years.[28] He demanded in December 1796 that decisions be made only by senators present—without the need to circulate the minutes among the residences of the senators who had not attended the session—and in January 1797 that they be reached by majority vote in both departments and general assembly.[29] This order, abolishing what had by then become a hallowed tradition, reduced the Senate to a "big nonentity" (*bol'shaia nichtozhnost'*), as Aleksandr Vorontsov claimed, albeit with some exaggeration,[30] preventing as it did key members of the oligarchy from blocking decisions they opposed. The imperial order of September 1802, which preceded the manifesto on the creation of ministries, reflected Alexander's willingness to compromise by restoring the unanimity rule in the departments but requiring a two-thirds majority in the general assembly.[31] The role of the Procurator General in Senate procedure remained otherwise unchanged. Alexander's compromising attitude also became apparent in the fact that the post was occupied for 18 of the 23 years between 1802 and 1825 by relatives and protégés of the Kurakin clan, a subgroup of the Naryshkin–Trubetskoi political family.

Despite the transformation of the Senate, it remained an axiom of elite politics that the Senate was the supreme institution (*verknovnoe mesto*) of the empire, subordinated nevertheless to the ruler as the supreme power (*verkhovnaia vlast'*). After 1763, when departmental decisions were given the force of Senate resolutions, the "Senate" came increasingly to mean the First Department, to which nonjudicial cases were referred, chiefly personnel, financial, and various administrative matters, unless the Senate met in general assembly to discuss an issue that a department could not decide unanimously or that the procurator general chose to bring before a joint meeting of the Petersburg departments. Two Senates thus came into being—although this was never officially recognized—an administrative Senate (the First Department) and a judicial Senate (the other departments).

When the question naturally arose about relationships between ministers and Senate, the solution advanced in the legislation of 1802 defied common sense. Ministers were instructed to submit to the "Senate"—the First Department—a report on their activities at the end of each year, and the department was empowered to request "explanations" from the minister and required to submit in turn a reasoned opinion (*doklad*) to the tsar about the minister's performance. On the other hand, each minister was given direct access to the tsar to seek during the year the authorizations necessary to settle difficulties in his ministry, and ministers collectively were given a seat in the First Department.[32] Of its nineteen members in 1809, six were ministers—the Minister of Foreign Affairs and, of course, the Minister of Justice were not included—three were former ministers, one was a deputy minister, and four occupied quasi-ministerial posts. In other words, ministers were called upon to justify before a committee—in which they and their colleagues had a majority—decisions for which they had been careful to secure beforehand the approval of the "supreme power."

The First Department was thus unable from the very beginning to carry out its supervisory function, and ministers gained their independence from the Senate. At the same time, it provided a setting for the ministers to meet collectively. The Department was the agency where laws and *ukazy* were published, the fundamental principles of the social order preserved, and claims against the Treasury adjudicated. Ministers used it to obtain Senate *ukazy*, which had binding force on all government agencies, especially provincial ones to which they were not yet allowed to send circulars. If no unanimity could be reached, the Procurator General, as Minister of Justice, could bypass the general assembly and refer the matter to the Committee of Ministers, from which an imperial order would be requested to settle the case. The Department became, instead of a control agency, an enlarged committee of ministers and an extension of ministerial power.

The purpose of the eighteenth-century councils had been to discuss important foreign policy issues and, increasingly, to coordinate foreign policy, strategic initiatives, and domestic policy in wartime. The reassertion of auto-cratic power affected most strongly the conduct of foreign policy, which remained, in Russia as in other monarchies, a prerogative of the ruler, interna-tional relations still being essentially relations between ruling houses. Paul and Alexander, to a greater degree than their predecessors except Peter, became their own foreign ministers,[33] feeling no need for a Bestuzhev-Riumin or a Panin, let alone for a council to pass judgment on their family relations. Since military affairs were also the favorite interest of those two tsars, the coordina-tion of foreign and military policy became the personal responsibility of the ruler, leaving him at the mercy of transitory advisers and confidants, even foreign ones like the King of Prussia.

Such a departure from the post-Petrine tradition made the "council at-tached to His Majesty's Court" obsolete and explains its transformation—and demotion—in March 1801 into a State Council, that is, a permanent part of the governmental structure.[34] Its purpose was to provide a forum to thrash out constitutional and legislative issues and to propose legislation. This was not quite the novelty it was made out to be. The creation of agencies and new norms of procedural and substantive law had always required the ruler's approval. The Senate, however, always interpreted the law in the process of applying it but submitted a recommendation to the ruler whenever its resolu-tions introduced new norms, while individuals and committees drafted propos-als from time to time, outside the Senate, which became law upon receiving the ruler's approval. The Council fell prey to the same forces that were transform-ing the Senate from a coordinating agency into a supreme court. The ruler's distrust of a coordinating agency for policymaking at the highest level was strengthened by the recognition of a need for a specialized agency for legisla-tive questions that would inherit and expand a function the Senate was no longer able to exercise. The Council, however, was a phantom institution at the beginning. Ministers were made ex officio members in September 1802, and in 1804 eight of its fourteen members were ministers while the other six were either in retirement or occupied posts requiring their presence outside of Petersburg. Five years later, it had seventeen members under the unofficial chairmanship of Nikolai Saltykov.[35] Of the fifteen actually sitting, seven were ministers and three were senators in the First Department. The Council had become not so much an enlarged First Department as another enlarged com-mittee of ministers and the legislative function an after-hours hobby of the executive branch.

The reform of January 1810 and subsequent appointments sought to re-duce the stranglehold of the ministers over both the First Department and the council, loosen up the small directorate that had governed the country since the beginning of the reign, and open up the top positions to outsiders not related to the ruling families. That it was the work of Speranskii, an outsider and the son of a priest, was logical.[36] It was also a sign that the old network was beginning to dissolve, a process accelerated by the war of 1812.

The new council was much larger and consisted of two kinds of members, those assigned to departments and members-at-large. It was divided into four departments—Laws, Military Affairs, Civil and Ecclesiastical Affairs, and State Economy—of two or three members under a chairman. Saltykov remained chairman of the entire Council, a post now officially recognized, and combined during the war with the chairmanship of the Committee of Ministers. The Council had thirty members in 1823. The thirteen members-at-large included the Chief of His Majesty's Main Staff, the commanders in chief of the First and Second Armies, and the Military Governor-General of Moscow. Its chancery of twenty-four was placed under an Imperial Secretary (*gosudarstvennyi sekretar'*), a post that, in other circumstances, might have become a modern version of the eighteenth-century procurator general. Departments reached decisions by majority vote. Those creating new law or amending existing law were referred to the general assembly of all members, the others were submitted to the ruler through the imperial secretary. The same procedure was followed in the general assembly. Departments received their business from the tsar directly or from ministers, who were not made ex officio members of the new Council but took part without the right to vote in the debates of the department in which their recommendations were discussed.[37]

The reform of 1810 gave the appearance of creating a new coordinating agency for domestic administration, a modern version of the old Senate. It assumed that laws and organic statutes were superior to ministerial directives and even Senate *ukazy*. Ministers needed the sanction of the Council, and resolutions of the Senate's general assembly raising legislative issues were referred to the Council before they were submitted to the ruler. But Russia was not a government of laws, and appearances were misleading. While ministers were not members of the Council, the chairmen of its four departments were ex officio members of the Committee of Ministers, Council and Committee had a joint chairman after 1812, and the core of the First Department consisted of the eight ministers. The eight ministers and the four chairmen were thus the true government of Russia, like the nine senators in 1718 and the eleven senators of the First Department in 1796.

The Committee of Ministers was never "created." It was not mentioned by name in the reform of 1802, was ignored in that of 1811, and was not listed in the annual directory of imperial personnel. No statue defined its jurisdiction in any detail or spelled out its jurisdiction against that of Senate and council. The rules of September 1805 merely stated that it took up three kinds of business— the reports of individual ministers before they were submitted to the tsar, doubts about the scope of a minister's jurisdiction, and whatever the tsar might see fit to refer to its examination. Since the committee met very seldom, at least until 1812, ministers exercised their personal right of direct access without the intermission of the Committee. Beginning in 1812, however, ministers were required to submit their reports to the Committee when the tsar was away—a situation of increasing frequency and duration until the end of the reign—and the right of direct access became almost exclusively a collective one.[38]

The committee emerged, as a result, as the ultimate authority not only in executive but also in legislative and judicial matters whenever it chose to interfere in the statutory procedures of Senate and Council. Its recommendations went through Arakcheev, while those of the "committee of military ministers" went through the Chief of His Majesty's Main Staff. The symmetry, however, concealed the chaos that the arbitrary actions of the committee caused in the civilian administration. No wonder that Speranskii, who had done so much to introduce orderly procedures, complained that the imperial "bureaucracy" had created no "state" but conjured up the world of Muscovite boyardom with its concepts of tsar and *druzhina*.[39] Had not the ministers become the chief dispensers of patronage, distributing the spoils and altering "constitutional" relationships by common agreement, with the connivance of a master who hated the details of administrative work and could do nothing without their cooperation?[40]

Local Government

The local government reform of the 1770s has been studied elsewhere in some detail.[41] Suffice it to say here that it resembled in outline and content the territorial reform of 1708 and diverged considerably from the traditional principles of territorial administration, before and after Peter's reign. It was marked by a massive decentralization of managerial functions, the closing of central executive agencies, and the concentration of control functions in the Procurator General's office. As a result, the governor's office ceased to be the agency in which the execution of all centrally made decisions was concentrated. Managerial functions were dispersed among gubernia board, judicial and treasury chambers, while the governor became a control agent directly subordinated to the First Department and the Procurator General. He retained, however, the universal competence that had always been the prerogative of the local delegate of the ruling elite. The ministerial reform of 1802, by contrast, reaffirmed traditional principles yet also raised new issues, to which practice alone could give an answer.

Governors continued to be appointed by the ruler, but the large numbers of governors after 1775 devalued the importance of the post. The requirement introduced in December 1801 that the Senate submit a list of ten candidates, from which the tsar would choose one able to resist the pressures of the strong and respond to the entreaties of the weak, rang so hollow in a world obsessed with power and fragmented into rival patronage networks that it was never put into practice.[42] At the very beginning of Alexander's reign, it was already difficult to find competent governors, although it was true that no more experience or training was necessary then than in the eighteenth century, when Vonliarliarskii complained about the illiteracy of the voevodas. Governors were former generals who had retired, or been made to retire, from the army, individuals who did not get along with their ministers, relatives of grandees who wanted to get rid of their undesirable presence. Many were cynics, often Guard officers who, after commanding a regiment for a few years, sought another remunerative appointment in which extortion and embezzlement would help them pay their debts and save a bundle.[43] Ivan Bakhtin, an exception who became an outstanding governor, was appointed to Kharkov after Vasilii Karazin, at the time influential with the tsar for his work in education, casually mentioned his name. Alexander asked Karasin to write an *ukaz*, and Bakhtin was appointed without even being consulted.[44] After 1802, candidates were recommended by the minister of internal affairs, and after 1815, when a surplus of generals became a problem, by the chief of His Majesty's Main Staff and Arakcheev as well.

A governor was thus ultimately responsible to the tsar who had appointed him. In practice, however, he was subordinated to the Senate and the Minister of Internal Affairs. The gubernia board and the chambers remained subordinated to the Senate, and the reform of 1802 did not annul the provision of the Instruction of 1764, retained by default in the reform of 1775, making governors accountable to both the ruler and the Senate. Since the First Department was the government of Russia in all but name during Catherine's reign, the governors' accountability to the Department after 1775 created a symmetry between the First Department as coordinating agency in domestic administration and the governor's office as coordinating agency in the gubernia. When a governor's dereliction of duty was noticed by the judicial departments, the matter was referred to the First Department, which imposed a warning (*zamechanie*), a reprimand (*vygovor*), or a fine. The Senate usually exercised caution in imposing reprimands because the governor was appointed by the ruler and because the authority of the ruling elite had to be upheld in the provinces vis-à-vis both the apparatus and the dependent population. It was less constrained in reprimanding and fining chairmen and members of the chambers. This was noted in the imperial order of September 1809 when the tsar directed the Senate to reprimand governors as well whenever justified, subject to his confirmation.[45]

The growing strength of the ministerial apparatus was bound to introduce a disturbing element into the symmetry created by the reform of 1775. The breakup of the unity of government after 1802, the insistence of each ministry on being answerable only to the tsar, the jurisdictional conflicts among empire builders seeking to integrate all activities of government into the ministerial system raised persistent questions about the place of the governor. If the judicial chambers remained under the authority of the Minister of Justice—the former Procurator General—and the treasury chambers passed under that of the State Treasurer, it was logical to expect that the Minister of the Interior would seek jurisdiction over the gubernia board and the governor himself.[46] The logic of this argument was challenged by other ministries, however, because the governor's control function gave him a universal competence that every ministry had to covet but all others had to oppose. To subordinate the governor to the Committee of Ministers was neither possible, because the Committee did not meet regularly, nor acceptable, because this would give the governor the authority to bypass individual ministers and appeal to their collective decision.

Conflicting interests paved the way for the easiest solution. Governors, recommended for appointment by the Minister of the Interior—by the Minister of Police between 1810 and 1819—developed a primary allegiance to him. The Ministerial Statute of June 1811, however, placed the governor at the beck and call of every minister, who began to request information and assistance and give warnings and reprimands for nonperformance. Worse still, directors of departments joined the fray, placing the governor at the willful mercy of members of the apparatus equal to them in rank. The wheel had turned full circle back to the 1740s, when governors became acutely aware of the humiliation to which they were subjected by the luxuriant growth of specialized agencies asserting their authority on a national scale.

The inspection tours the tsar began to conduct at the end of the war brought him face to face with the dissatisfaction of governors resentful of the breakdown of the chain of command. The tsar considered the practice offensive and directed the Committee of Ministers in October 1816 to discontinue it. Requests for explanations and disciplinary measures against governors were henceforth to be issued over the signature of the minister, who had to inform the Committee each time. The order applied to the Minister of Justice as well, who complained that it stripped the Senate of its time-honored disciplinary power over governors, an authority it had used on occasions without seeking imperial approval. The tsar relented and allowed the Senate to continue to exercise its disciplinary power, but insisted that no sanction take effect without his approval. In the army, he added, no general might be punished without the tsar's consent.[47] Governors were equated with divisional commanders and the Committee of Ministers with the Main Staff.

The governor thus wore two hats, and not very comfortably. As representative of the Minister of Internal Affairs, he was chiefly a police authority; as executive officer of each individual minister, he was also the representative of the entire government and of the ruler himself. His effective power, however, rested in his ability to coerce other members of the apparatus to do his bidding. The existence of ministries made this more difficult than had been the case since 1775. We must distinguish here between the gubernia board, the chambers, and the elected representatives of nobles and merchants in the gubernia.

The Organic Law of November 1775 declared the board to be the agency responsible for the administration of the entire gubernia. The board disseminated laws and orders received from the Senate, settled nonjudicial (*bezspornye*) disputes, examined complaints against any other agency in the gubernia, and imposed sanctions. Its announcements were printed on its own press and distributed among sheriffs in towns and land captains in uezds, who brought them to the attention of the population in churches and public squares. It consisted of two councillors appointed by the Senate, and its meetings were chaired by the governor.[48] It was therefore subordinated to the Senate and functioned as a "provincial First Department." The symmetry was complete but unstable and broke down as ministries began to stake out their claims.

Councillors could not veto an order of the governor but could register their opposition in the minutes. The stage was thus set for the transformation of the board into a chancery of the governor—its predecessor, indeed, before 1775 had been called the gubernia chancery. In some cases, governors even put councillors in the guardhouse (*hauptwache*) for disagreeing with a governor's order. Since that transformation could not take place officially, however, governor and board began to grow apart, governors ignoring the board's status as the "first agency" (*pervoe mesto*) in the gubernia while they built up their own personal chanceries. The Minister of the Interior claimed jurisdiction over the board, but the law stubbornly refused to recognize it, and the Digest (*Svod Zakonov*) of 1832 still insisted that the board reported only to the Senate and the ruler and received orders only from them, although the councillors were by then appointed by the Senate on the minister's recommendation.[49] The result was an incredible confusion. Ministers sent orders to the governor but not to the board, which recognized only orders from the First Department. Unless a minister chose to work through the department—we can now understand the importance of making ministers ex officio members of the department— the latter did not know what orders a minister had sent and vice versa, and the same misunderstanding was repeated in the gubernia capital, where the physical proximity of the participants fanned institutional antagonisms.

If the board was able to retain a measure of autonomy vis-à-vis the governor despite the fact that both passed under the administrative authority of the Minister of the Interior, other gubernia agencies played off their ministerial headquarters against the governor's office to gain independence from the governor's orders. By the 1820s, the vice-governor and the councillors of the treasury chambers, the judicial chambers and the gubernia procurator, the commander of the Internal Guard and gendarmes, the administrator of crown properties, and the director of schools all claimed to be accountable to their respective chiefs in Petersburg and "pretended to see in the governor a person higher than themselves only out of courtesy."[50] The provincial delegate of the ruling elite thus found himself forced to play an active role in the treacherous currents of elite politics by siding with some agencies against others or by declaring war on all of them, while they tried to hide behind ministerial circulars not intended for publication, which began to bypass governor and board in increasing numbers.

It took more than a decade for the ministries—other than the Ministry of the Interior—to destroy the governors' powers to coordinate the activity of gubernia agencies. Ministers recommended the appointment of their local agents to the First Department and even appointed some themselves. Vice-governors and chairmen of chambers, being in grade five, were appointed by the tsar on their minister's recommendation. The governor had no power over them, and they in turn could complain to their minister, who then had the choice of bringing the matter before the Committee of Ministers. This was especially true of the gubernia procurator, who lost the great supervisory powers he had enjoyed during the tenure of Alexander Viazemskii but not his inclination to disparage the governor before the minister of justice.[51]

The governor, nevertheless, continued to possess significant powers over the personnel of the provincial apparatus. Its members needed a recommendation (*attestat*) from the governor when they came up for promotion and for a pension, and a poor one could kill an applicant's chances, despite the minister's support. Governor's were empowered to hand over local personnel for trial in the criminal chamber, but its decisions were automatically reviewed in one of the judicial departments—the minister could use his influence together and even protest the governor's action before the Committee of Ministers.[52] Here the governor had to tread carefully and avoid antagonizing powerful supporters of the accused. The gubernia apparatus thus remained, as it was bound to, a mirror image of the central apparatus. The unity of government at both levels created by the reform of 1775 made way, under the influence of the ministerial reform, for fragmentation, autonomy, and the creation of vertical chains of command that nearly destroyed the universal competence that had been the single most important attribute of the governor in his gubernia.

There had always existed beyond the apparatus, and increasingly so since the 1770s, a political infrastructure of noblemen in gubernias and uezds, which was gradually being infiltrated by the upper ranks of the merchantry, a force the governor could not afford to ignore for two reasons. Even if the governor received a salary, the tradition survived that required his predecessors and the voevodas to "feed themselves" off the local population. Local elections were introduced by the reform of 1775 to select a land captain to manage the uezd police, a uezd judge to try cases in the uezd, a *magistrat* to try those in the town, a court of equity, and—after 1802—assessors in the judicial chambers. Their election required the confirmation of the governor, who could hand them over to trial for dereliction of duty. It was taken for granted that these local people would make "gifts" to the governor, especially if he had many daughters, each in need of a dowry.[53] Moreover, governors were aware that local nobles often belonged to large family networks with bona fide members of the ruling elite among them. In each gubernia, uezd marshals—about twelve of them—won increasing independence from the governor when they were placed under the protection of the gubernia marshal.[54] His election required the tsar's confirmation and thus placed him outside the governor's jurisdiction. Indeed, the gubernia marshal became the local politician the governor had most to fear—some gubernia marshals were known personally to Alexander, while most governors were not. The Kursk governor complained in the 1810s to the Minister of Internal Affairs that a uezd marshal was making his life impossible, the "sensitive" Kazan nobility wanted only highly connected governors, and a retired cartographer retorted to the irascible Governor-General of Moscow that only the tsar could proceed against a real privy councillor.[55] Even though the governor was the delegate of the ruling elite, he found himself dealing in his gubernia capital with other members of the elite and their relatives or protégés, with whom demands of unconditional obedience fell on deaf ears. It is important to remain aware of two channels linking center and provinces—an administrative one running from tsar to minister and governor, and a political one linking members of the ruling elite in and out of the apparatus into a vast patronage network in which accommodation to the realities of power was a prerequisite for administrative advancement and administrative peace.

What, then, were the responsibilities and effectual powers of a governor? He remained ultimately responsible for the maintenance of order and remained the punitive agent of the ruling class against the dependent population and its chief fiscal officer, but with considerably less extensive powers than before 1775.

Garrisons were removed from the governor's jurisdiction in 1775. Their commandants were required to report to the governor-general and after 1796 directly to the College of War. *Shtatnye komandy* in gubernia capitals and uezd centers continued to operate under the governor's orders, but the consolidation of those forces into an Internal Guard in 1811 removed the governor completely from the direct command of police forces. From then on, the governor had to request assistance from the battalion commander stationed in the gubernia capital and wait for his approval.[56] Sheriffs in the towns were appointed by the Minister of the Interior and could be replaced only by him if they refused to cooperate with the governor. Land captains, however, had to be more responsive because they could be dismissed by the gubernia board. The governor was a dreaded police authority more as a result of the fact that the police played a pervasive role in the social, intellectual, and economic life of the gubernia, as we shall see in Part III, than of his capacity as the effective head of a police apparatus and police forces.

The dread he inspired among the dependent population was considerably magnified by his judicial role. The Organic Law of 1775 pretended to separate the dispensation of justice from the other responsibilities of the governor and declared him no longer a judge.[57] The institutional separation of the governor's office from judicial chambers—while the old gubernia chancery had handled the entire volume of business in the gubernia—made little difference in fact. The law provided that all sentences passed by the criminal chamber had to be referred to the governor. Sentences of death, the knout and public whipping, and expulsion from the ruling class and the privileged guilds had to be referred to the appropriate Senate department. Others were returned by the governor for immediate execution, but only if he agreed with them. If he did not, they too had to be forwarded to the Senate with the governor's opinion, and further disposition had to await a Senate and even an imperial resolution—as in the case of a nobleman expelled from the ruling class. Acquittals likewise had to be submitted to the governor, as did all investigations conducted in the lower courts, even if no defendant had been named. In the simplest possible statement that Russian justice was essentially political justice, the Senate declared in May 1803 that the governor, as lord and master (*khoziain*) of his gubernia— that is, as delegate of the ruling elite assigned to administer a gubernia in the interest of the ruling class—must be in a position to determine whether judicial sentences were "proper" and "just." The decisions of civil chambers too were sent to the governor and took effect immediately unless he quashed them and referred the case to the Senate. No wonder that the two chairman often preferred to bring the pending decisions of their chambers to the governor beforehand, in order to avoid later unpleasantness with governor and Senate.[58] The governor remained very much a "judge." Nevertheless, his powers were curtailed in two important areas. Beginning in 1797, the execution of civil decisions appealed to the Senate was suspended until completion of the appellate review, and governors were forbidden to quash them. Twenty years later, governors were forbidden to approve mass punishments: when "many people," later defined to mean ten or more, were sentenced to corporal punishment, sentences had to be sent to the Senate for submission by the Minister of Justice to the ruler through the Committee of Ministers.[59]

The creation of a treasury chamber headed by a vice-governor, appointed, like the governor, by the tsar and placed after 1811 under the jurisdiction of a powerful Ministry of Finance, substantially reduced the managerial responsibilities of the governor in fiscal and economic matters but left him considerable supervisory powers. At the same time, the development of a subsidiary economy of compulsory services after 1775—some delivered in kind, others in money—requiring the application of police compulsion, the appearance of municipal budgets in which police expenditures represented the largest outlay, and the expanding activities of the Boards of Public Welfare, which collected fines and loaned money, and, finally, public construction, gave the Ministry of Internal Affaris and the governor new fiscal responsibilities, not without creating some friction between the two ministries and between governor and vice-governor. The governor continued to be responsible for inspecting the gubernia treasury once a month, for confirming official (*spravochnye*) prices, which served as the basis in contractual negotiations, for confirming contracts, now negotiated in the treasury chamber, and for leasing state property, sometimes at scandalously low prices and without much concern for the public interest.[60]

By 1825 the governor was in a paradoxical situation. His universal authority had been shrunk by the concerted efforts of the ministries to carve it into separate spheres of competence for their own provincial delegates. On the other hand, the powers of the police were so extensive in the conduct of investigations and the execution of decisions made in other provincial agencies that he managed to retain the right to interfere in the internal affairs of the gubernia managed by those agencies, no longer as representative of the government but as delegate of the Minister of Internal Affairs.[61]

III

POLICE

7

Police Organization

Central Agencies

A command structure does not necessarily need an elaborate police organization. The possession of disciplinary powers by members of the apparatus and the political infrastructure, and by patriarchal heads of families, as well as by patrons over their clients, kept subordinates and individual members of communities on the path of obedience to authority and of respect for norms of behavior reflecting a consensus on the foundations of the political and social order. Only once such foundations are no longer taken for granted does it become necessary to define them explicitly and to defend their legitimacy with the help of police agencies, external to the social networks that had been adequate until then to enforce compliance on occasional dissenters.

Strains within the ruling elite, however, above all at times of rapid political transformation, could have dangerous implications for the ruling house, and any form of dissent could easily be magnified into a threat. This alone would justify the existence of a police agency to protect the security of the ruler. Moreover, the maintenance of order, essential in any society, could not always be carried out by simply invoking the disciplinary powers of superior over subordinates, especially in the towns, where it also included the provision of services benefiting members of the ruling class and the dependent population. This broader concept of police function, in part reflecting contemporary political thought on the well-ordered police state, in part the logical consequence of the rudimentary urban activity that does not yet recognize the need to establish separate departments for fire prevention, sanitation, and other services, required the creation of police forces and police agencies to provide them.

The maintenance of order at the end of the seventeenth century was divided among three *prikazy*. The *Razboinyi Prikaz* will be considered briefly in the following chapter, since it was as much a criminal court as a police agency. Within the city of Moscow its responsibilities were carried out by the *Zemskii Prikaz*, which also exercised jurisdiction over fire prevention, the paving of streets, sanitation, and zoning ordinances. Police forces, staffed with *streltsy* troops, operated under the *Streltsy Prikaz*, closed in 1699 following the uprising of the Moscow *streltsy* the previous year. After 1701, when the *Razboinyi*

Prikaz was also closed, voevodas became responsible for the maintenance of order in their towns under the overall jurisdiction of the *Zemskii Prikaz*, while various categories of people passed under that of the various *prikazy* to which they were subordinated—a confusing arrangement rich in jurisdictional disputes and hardly conducive to the efficient prosecution of felonies.[1]

When colleges were created in 1718, none assumed jurisdiction for policing the realm, but a Policemaster General was appointed in May and given duties in Petersburg similar to those of the *Zemskii Prikaz* in the old capital, where a senior policemaster was appointed in January 1722 and subordinated to the Policemaster General in the northern capital. His office, referred to from time to time as the "Central Police" (*glavnaia politsiia*), the immediate successor of the *Zemskii Prikaz* closed in 1719, was in effect an embryonic national police agency, which, however, never realized its potential in the eighteenth century. The post was held in the 1730s by Vasilii Saltykov, a distant cousin of the Empress Anna, and during most of Elizabeth's reign by Alexei Tatishchev, a relative of the Saltykovs and cousin by marriage of the Empress. Neither was subordinated to the Senate: they reported directly to the ruler. When policemasters were appointed in various towns in 1733, they were subordinated to the Policemaster General, who was thus placed in a better position than the presidents of other colleges to build an empire of his own, since colleges after 1725 did not have their own local agents in the gubernias and provinces. This no doubt was one reason why the network of local policemasters was gradually curtailed and ceased to exist in the 1760s, while the subordination of the Moscow senior policemaster to his Petersburg chief was seriously compromised by the allegiance he also owned to the Governor-General of Moscow, who was ultimately responsible for the security of the city.[2] Police forces at the time consisted almost entirely of garrisoned troops. These, however, were under the jurisdiction of the College of War.

The provision of rudimentary services was vested in local *magistraty*, also responsible, in the absence of policemasters, for maintaining order. Their subordination to the Central *Magistrat* created a built-in conflict of interest between the ambitions of the Policemaster General in Petersburg and the reluctance of the Central *Magistrat* in Moscow to sanction the appointment of policemasters who would have to be paid by the local merchant communities. Once the local government reform reached Petersburg and Moscow, the police of the two cities were subordinated to their governors-general in 1780 and 1782, respectively. The post of Policemaster General was abolished in 1780, a senior policemaster in each capital reporting thereafter directly to his governor-general or to the empress, depending on the circumstances, and the Central *Magistrat* was closed in 1782.[3] Even a nominal central police agency had ceased to exist.

The Senate, of course, was ultimately responsible for the police administration of the empire. All central agencies reported to it, including the policemaster general from the beginning of Catherine's reign and the College of War in matters of internal administration. When it was divided into departments in

December 1763, police matters came under the Third Department. So did censorship, conducted for the most part by the Academy of Sciences.[4]

The country, however, was never without a political police. Sometime in 1696, before Peter's departure for his grand tour of Europe in March 1697, the prosecution of political crimes, previously the collective responsibility of all *prikazy*, was vested in a *Preobrazhenskii Prikaz*, named after the village of Preobrazhenskoe, now a suburb of Moscow, where Peter had been banished with his mother 20 years earlier, and which had become the de facto seat of the government. This *prikaz* was also the headquarters for the two regiments of the Guard, a new formation serving as an elite force in battle and as security troops in peacetime. The Guard protected the person of the ruler and carried out sensitive political assignments. The *prikaz* was headed by Fedor Romodanovskii, a leading figure in the Saltykov group, whose position in the government was so strong that contemporaries often saw him as the first person after the tsar himself.[5]

Three events, however, undermined the position of the *prikaz*. Romodanovskii died in 1717, an old man steeped in Muscovite Russia, ill at ease in the new order. His son Ivan succeeded him but without the same authority. The government moved to Petersburg at the end of 1713, but the *prikaz* remained in Moscow, where the political situation remained sensitive. As a result, the prosecution of the great scandal of Peter's reign, the defection of tsarevich Alexei, was entrusted to a new agency, created in 1718 and called the Secret Chancery, a collegial body headed by Petr Tolstoi, another major figure in the Saltykov group. The Chancery was not abolished after the tsarevich's death from the tortures to which he was subjected and replaced the *Preobrazhenskii Prikaz* as the chief organ of political repression.[6]

The death of Peter in January 1725 made inevitable a power struggle within the ruling elite during which it was in every participant's interest to reduce the power of the political police. Tolstoi lost out to Menshikov and was ordered in May 1726 to turn over the Secret Chancery to Ivan Romodanovskii. The removal of the Court to Moscow in January 1728 enhanced the status of Romodanovskii, who had meanwhile been made Governor-General of the old capital. Illness, however, forced him to retire in April 1729, a year before his death, and the Supreme Privy Council assumed jurisdiction over the prosecution of the more important political crimes, the others being turned over to the Senate. The demise of the Council in March 1730 and the reassertion of the ruler's authority quieted the unrest among the ruling elite, while emphasizing the need for vigilance at a time of dynastic instability—the empress had no children, and her cousin Elizabeth was expected to become a focus of political opposition. In March 1731 the Secret Chancery was restored and entrusted to Andrei Ushakov, who had served with Tolstoi and was a distant relative of the Saltykovs. When the Court returned to Petersburg in 1732, a branch of the Secret Chancery was left in Moscow, doubly subordinated, like the senior policemaster, to Governor-General Semën Saltykov and to its Petersburg headquarters.[7]

The new Secret Chancery left bad memories, even though Ushakov was probably no more ruthless than Romodanovskii or Tolstoi. Its activities have been too easily blamed on the "Germans" by a school of Russian nationalist historians, despite the fact the Ushakov was an ethnic Russian and reported directly to the Empress, the daughter of a Romanov and a Saltykova. He received from her not only written orders but also oral commands in his capacity as Adjutant General, and dealt with Osterman on a footing of equality. He also commanded the Semenovskii regiment of the Guard, a number of Army regiments, and the Petersburg garrison. The chief of the political police obviously wielded considerable clout among the leadership, but no more than the Saltykov group was willing to tolerate. Even the coup of November 1741 did not shake his position—he was made a count in 1744—and he remained at the head of the Secret Chancery until his death in 1747. An imperial order of November 1743 instructed the Chancery to refuse to give any information or documents to the Senate, the Synod, or any other agency concerning cases in its jurisdiction without a written order signed by the empress. It thus became a kind of personal chancery of the ruler for political cases, outside the constellation of government agencies but with the right to report on their activities and to strike at any of their members suspected of political disloyalty, very much like the *Preobrazhenskii Prikaz* at the height of its powers. When Ushakov claimed in 1746 that he had the authority to send orders to the Policemaster General—who refused to accept them—he showed that he aimed at no less than the administration of the entire police establishment of the empire.[8]

The appointment of Alexander Shuvalov to succeed Ushakov turned the political police over to the Naryshkin group. This was to be expected, since the Empress was a granddaughter of a Naryshkina and her government was led by members of that group. The Shuvalovs were newcomers, but Alexander's daughter married the nephew of the Procurator General, Nikita Trubetskoi. Shuvalov continued the work of Ushakov in prosecuting the opposition and linked up with the Vorontsovs in supporting Elizabeth's nephew, the future Peter III, and opposing his wife, the future Catherine II. This meddling of the political police in the internal affairs of the ruling elite became, however, so disturbing that Peter III abolished the Secret Chancery in February 1762, less than 2 months after promoting Shuvalov to field marshal, a decision confirmed by Catherine in October.[9]

The fate of the political police agency during Catherine's reign established a pattern that would recur for the rest of the imperial period. The *Preobrazhenskii Prikaz* and the Secret Chancery had been personal chanceries of the ruler at a time of considerable ferment generated by endless intrigues among the ruling families, intrigues that gave rise to many rumors of political and religious dissent, mysterious events, and even witchcraft. They were the first line of defense of the ruling house and its immediate relatives and supporters, against whom the slightest dissent was perceived as a threat to the dynasty. When the ruler felt secure and the ruling elite was no longer racked by internal dissensions, the political police was integrated into the governmental machinery and its chief stripped of his exceptional prerogatives. It is not difficult to see a similar pattern during the Soviet period.

In 1763, a year after the abolition of the Secret Chancery, it was announced that a Secret Expedition had been created in the Senate. It was later subordinated to the First Department, in fact to the procurator general, the son-in-law of Nikita Trubetskoi. However, its chief, Stepan Sheshkovskii, did not belong to the inner circle; he was the son of a clerk, and had been secretary of the Secret Chancery under Shuvalov, and a secretary in the Senate itself after the Chancery's abolition. The enlightened empress appreciated his services, and the political police remained a dreaded instrument of rule during her reign. However, it was subordinated to the Procurator General, the guardian of "legality" and "prime minister" of the imperial government. The situation remained unchanged under Paul, but the Secret Expedition was abolished in April 1801, when Alexander decreed that political crimes be investigated by regular police agencies and tried in the Senate's Criminal Departments.[10]

The creation of ministries in September 1802 called for a radical reorganization of police administration. The recentralization of governmental functions and the gradual establishment of linear commands linking a small number of Petersburg headquarters with the gubernia agencies created by the local government reform of 1775-1785 required that police administration be integrated into the new structure. A separate judicial and fiscal administration had been a major contribution of the reform. A Ministry of Justice and a Ministry of Finance were established to coordinate and direct the judicial and treasury chambers. Education came into its own as well and was given a separate ministry. Everything else became "internal affairs," including the supervisory activity of the governors and, of course, the police.

The three essential forms of Russian police activity—the maintenance of order, the political police, and the provision of urban services—were now combined under a minister of internal affairs, a post first held by Viktor Kochubei (1802-1807), a Ukranian married to a granddaughter of Kirill Razumovskii, whose wife was the granddaughter of Kirill Naryshkin, governor of Moscow under Peter I. His successor, Alexei Kurakin (1807-1810), was the son of Elena Apraksina, whose grandmother married Ushakov after her husband's death. His clan was the most influential among the families constituting the Naryshkin group, which thus consolidated its control over the police. The ministry—the Ministry of Internal Affairs (MVD) of the Imperial and Soviet periods—was given four major responsibilities: to maintain order, to prevent food shortages, to manage state-owned industry (except mining, placed under the Finance Ministry), and to administer public construction. These functions were carried out by three expeditions: state economy; public welfare, including police; and medical. They were later combined in a Department of General Affairs, to which a Postal Department and a Central Board of Manufacturers were added. Governors, locally responsible for the maintenance of order, were made to report directly to the minister, who thus assumed control over local police forces (*shtatnye komandy*). As a result, the ministry took over from the governors the jurisdiction of both the old Central *Magistrat* and the policemaster general's office, closed in the 1780s.[11]

The political police, however, had a more checkered history in the same period. Alexander was wary of delegating it to a single agency, and Kochubei abhorred police work. Surveillance and censorship were carried out in the Second Expedition of the ministry as well as in the chancery of the governor-general of Petersburg and Moscow. When the tsar left Petersburg for the army, in September 1805, he entrusted the security of the capital to the governors-general, General Kuz'min Viazmitinov, and appointed an interministerial committee consisting of Kochubei, Minister of Justice Peter Lopukhin, and Evgraf Komarovskii, Viazmitinov's deputy, who represented the War Ministry. This committee drew up rules for secret police work patterned after French practices, which guided the special committee appointed in January 1807, ostensibly to carry out surveillance of French citizens in Russia. The Committee in fact prosecuted political crimes and counterfeiting, and tracked down political rumors, secret societies, and "harmful" books. It became the successor to the Secret Expedition, and its most active member was no other than Alexander Makarov, the Expedition's chief between 1796 and 1801. By then, censorship and sensitive cases had been removed from the Second Expedition of the MVD and transferred to a separate chancery reporting directly to the minister, which continued to operate alongside the Committee.[12]

A salient feature of Russian administrative history until the end of Alexander's reign was the absence of distinctions between the administration of the capital and that of the country as a whole. The most obvious case was that of the Policemaster General, whose jurisdiction had originally been restricted to Petersburg, then was extended to Moscow and later to other towns as well, but shrank again to include only the two capitals and a few other towns. The state of development—economic, social, and cultural—of Moscow and Petersburg was so far ahead of that of the rest of Russia that it was felt that one agency could be at the same time a local agency for the capital and a national one. The creation of the MVD could only be seen as a threat by the Petersburg police establishment. The governor-general's complicity in March 1801 had been a vital factor in the success of the conspiracy against Paul, and the security of the capital was the most sensitive assignment in police administration: it would no longer be subordinated to the tsar alone but to the Minister of Internal Affairs as well.

The creation of a Police Ministry in July 1810 therefore must be seen as a successful challenge by the Petersburg establishment against the MVD. The new ministry may have been patterned after Napoleon's, but the official announcement presented it as a restoration of the office of policemaster general. Moreover, its chief, Alexander Balashov, who had been senior policemaster in Moscow and Petersburg, was a protégé of Komarovskii and soon became a front for Viazmitinov, reappointed Governor-General of Petersburg in 1812 and made de facto chairman of the Committee of Ministers during the war of 1812.[13] The creation of the ministry left the MVD an empty shell. It incorporated its First and Second Expeditions, and its functions were divided in June 1811 into three departments: public security and liaisons with governors in the Department of Executive Police; public welfare, including provisioning and charitable establishments, in the Department of Economic Police; the supply of medical instruments to the government and the army in the Medical Department. Civilian censorship was removed from the Ministry of Education and vested in a committee accountable to Balashov, who, in his younger days, had given Catherine a copy of Radishchev's *Journey* and thus started the dismal process that ultimately destroyed the best-known critic of serfdom. The ministry, however, failed to gain control over the new police forces created in July 1811. They were placed under the War Ministry. The special committee of 1807 remained in existence, but after Makarov's death, also in 1810, secret police work was vested chiefly in the chancery of the Minister of Police, headed by Maksim von Fock, who later became executive secretary of the famous Third Section.[14]

Viazmitinov died in October 1819. By then, despite the tsar's continued reluctance to concentrate police administration in a single agency, the consolidation of ministerial power, the growing multiplicity of jurisdictions in the capital, and, most likely, the sheer inability of one man to combine such extensive responsibilities led to the final abandonment of the concept of policemaster general. The Ministry of Police was abolished in November, and Kochubei once again became Minister of Internal Affairs. Of its four departments created in June 1811, the new MVD lost the Department of Manufactures to the Finance Ministry, and the Postal Department became autonomous under a chief who was given ministerial status. The Ministry of Internal Affairs consisted of five departments: General Affairs for personnel matters, State Economy and Public Buildings, and the three departments of the former Policy Ministry. Jealousies, however, gave rise to competition among several agencies: the special chancery of the MVD; Arakcheev's own chancery; the office of Mikhail Miloradovich, the new and cantankerous Governor-General of Petersburg; the headquarters of the gendarme regiment; and the so-called Gribovskii organization, named after the director of the new police agency created in 1821 to carry out secret surveillance in the vastly expanded Imperial Guard.[15]

Local Agencies

Because towns represented territorial concentrations of people of various origins and were nodal points from which the ruling class exercised its dominion over the dependent population, they required a more elaborate police organization than the countryside, where order was maintained, even if not always successfully, by a network of chiefs of patriarchal households and locally chosen peasant wardens.

The seventeenth-century voevoda was responsible for the security both of his town and of the surrounding uezd. In the town, he might appoint a sheriff (*gorodnichii*), who operated with the assistance of elected *sotskie* representing

100 households and *desiatskie*, 10 households. The voevoda's office (*s'ezzhaia izba*) was also the police headquarters, equipped with the indispensable torture chamber run by the executioner (*palach*). After 1699, elected merchants called *burmistry* began to play a role in urban police administration, chiefly in the self-policing of the merchant population. The voevoda received his orders from the *Razboinyi Prikaz* and, after 1701, the *Zemskii Prikaz*, while the *burmistry* received theirs from the Moscow *Ratusha*.[16]

The gubernatorial reform of 1708 effectively placed the country under martial law and transformed voevodas into commandants, selected by governors and confirmed in office after 1711 by the Senate. Voevodas were restored by the provincial reform of 1719, and commandants thereafter assumed the role of garrison commanders, subordinated not to the provincial voevoda but to the governor alone, responsible to the College of War. By 1725 there were commandants in almost all gubernia capitals and in smaller towns with military significance. Police administration elsewhere must have been left to chance. In Tambov province, for example, there was in 1725 a voevoda in Tambov, a sheriff in one of the uezd capitals, and a regimental headquarters in another, its officers maintaining order in addition to their regular regimental duties. The creation of *magistraty* beginning in 1721 institutionalized the association of *burmistry* and made them responsible for both the maintenance of order and the provision of such elementary services as sanitation and fire prevention. No separate police organization was provided for the many small towns, even on paper. They were treated like mere villages.[17]

The first attempt to create a centralized network of urban police agencies took place in 1733, when the Policemaster General obtained the Empress's permission to appoint policemasters in seven of the nine gubernia capitals—all but Petersburg and Moscow—and eleven out of twenty-eight provincial capitals in Russia proper. These policemasters were selected by their chief in Petersburg and accountable only to him. The attempt failed, however, partly because the creation of linear commands ran against the prevailing principle of territorial administration but chiefly because the *magistraty*, which would have had to support the new policemasters, could not afford to do so. Most of the policemasters were withdrawn in 1737, and the urban police was once again vested in the *magistraty*, subordinated to the voevodas until 1743, autonomous thereafter. Those remaining were recalled in January 1762.[18] Meanwhile, there was a similar attempt to remove the commandants from under the governors' control. Fortresses in the empire were distributed in July 1731 among six regions called "departments," each headed by a senior (*ober*) commandant to whom the commandants were henceforth responsible. Both were appointed on the joint recommendation of the Senate and the College of War. The senior commandant, however, reported to the governor on the activities of his subordinates and was subjected to his orders. There were in central Russia in the 1760s five senior commandants—in Petersburg, Moscow, Smolensk, Kazan, and Arkhangelsk—and nineteen commandants, including five subordinated to senior commandants in Saint Dmitrii (Rostov-on-Don) and Astrakhan.[19]

In the 1770s the apparatus was about to fan out in the new gubernia capitals, and the political infrastructure saw uezd and gubernia capitals as social centers during the long winter months. An urban police was becoming necessary if living conditions were to reach a civilized level, and the treasury was finally willing to pay for the establishment of a uniform urban police. The local government reform created the post of sheriff (*gorodnichii*), to which retired officers were, as a rule, appointed by the Senate on the governor's recommendation. The Police Code of 1782 placed the sheriff at the head of a police board (*uprava blagochiniia*) consisting of two deputies chosen by the gubernia board and two members of the *magistrat*. Larger towns were divided into districts (*chasti*) and districts into wards (*kvartali*), run by appointees of the gubernia board to whom the network of elected *sotskie* and *desiatskie* was made accountable.[20]

Commandants were not affected by the reform: the subordination of the senior commandant to the governor-general simply adjusted the hierarchy of commandants to the new civilian hierarchy. Paul, however, believed in strict separation of military and civilian responsibilities. As a result, the post of senior commandant was abolished, and commandants were made to report directly to the ruler, and after 1808 to the War Minister. In garrison towns, where commandants had remained the chiefs of police over the entire population after 1775, their responsibilities were restricted to policing the fortress, and a separate policemaster, subordinated to the governor, was appointed, with responsibilities for the civilian population. A distinction was thus introduced for the first time between the policing of the fortress, including the glacis (*Vorstadt*), and that of the surrounding suburbs. This reform reflected the territorial expansion of the towns and the growing complexity of urban life, but it was likely to have generated rivalry and antagonism between commandant and policemaster, each now part of separate command hierarchies that met only in distant Petersburg. Conflicts between civilians and garrison soldiers were settled by the commandant or the governor. In the other towns sheriffs were retained, but the police boards were abolished in all but the largest towns.[21]

After 1802 the Ministry of Internal Affairs assumed jurisdiction over the urban police except between 1810 and 1819, when the Police Ministry took over the appointment of policemasters and sheriffs. Previous military service became an absolute prerequisite, and police chiefs could even continue to wear their military uniforms in retirement. After the war of 1812 they were no longer recommended by the governor but were selected by the minister from among candidates submitted by the Committee of August 18, 1814. They were paid from the municipal budget, in which the maintenance of police personnel and equipment was by far the largest single item. In some gubernia capitals and large uezd centers, policemasters began to dislodge sheriffs, at higher pay and with a larger staff, and the title of sheriff was increasingly reserved for police chiefs in the less important towns. By 1825 policemasters and sheriffs were appointed in every gubernia capital and uezd center; there were fifteen commandants in

Russia proper, all appointed by the War Minister, and over 300 police chiefs: an attractive patronage network for the Minister of the Interior and the Director of the Department of Executive Police.[22]

The reforms of Paul and Alexander built upon those of Catherine to make urban police administration more diversified, better adjusted to the condition of individual towns, and more responsive to the political imperatives of the ruling class. Sheriffs and policemasters in grade eight occupied the lowest rung of the system and were subordinated to the governor, the delegate of the ruling elite, and all were ultimately accountable to the Minister of the Interior, the corps commander of the Russian nobility, to whom gubernia marshals also reported on the condition of their flock, its interests, and its concerns. The urban police was thus turned, in an even starker fashion than under Catherine, into an instrument of the ruling class and the guardian of its position in the social and political order.

The beginning of the rural police in Russia goes back to the creation of land commissioners (*zemskie komissary* or *komissary ot zemli*) in 1719. Land-owners in each uezd were invited in December to elect a commissioner for 1 year. They might choose to reelect him if they were satisfied, fine him if they were not, or even turn him over to the voevoda in the case of a serious offense. This commissioner was the liaison between the nobility and the headquarters of the regiment stationed in one or more uezds, and if the regimental colonel and the voevoda found him unacceptable, they would dismiss him and ask the landowners to elect another. His function was to quarter the troops, help the regimental commissioner collect the amount of the capitation based on the number of souls registered in the census of the uezd, and find adequate provisions for the men and their horses. The commissioner was thus a tax collector, an arbiter of disputes between the army and the population—or at least the nobility—and, by extension, a sheriff of the countryside with an armed force at his disposal. He owed his existence to the attempt to create a territorial army living off and policing the countryside. When the attempt was abandoned after 1725 and regiments were marched from one place to another every summer, the post of land commissioner was gradually discarded, and the voevoda became once again responsible for policing his uezd and collecting arrears—one of the major responsibilities of the rural police.[23]

The unity of rural and urban police was first challenged by the creation of policemasters in the 1730s, but the experiment was limited and short-lived. It was definitely broken by the local government reform of the 1770s, which created the post of land captain similar in some respect to that of land commissioner. The noble *nakazy* of 1767 are replete with calls for the restora-tion of the land commissioner to function, once again, as representative of the nobility for the purpose of protecting it against depredations committed by passing troops, countering the arbitrary selection of quarters in villages of privately owned serfs, and taking the brunt of the latent rivalry between the apparatus headed by the governor and the political infrastructure. In this respect, land captains, who were placed in grade nine, were looked upon as expendable pawns in local politics. It was symbolic that the post did not give noble status, although it had to be filled by a local nobleman, while a sheriff was a "staff officer" of respectable standing in the nobility.[24]

On the other hand, the land captain, elected for 3 years, fulfilled an essential function in the new uezd. A small police force was available to maintain order, to help him with the investigation of important crimes, to carry out judicial sentences, to collect arrears, to keep an eye on the condition of roads, bridges, and ferries, and to keep the gubernia agencies informed about the price of commodities. Much of this could be done only superficially—uezds had a minimum population of 30,000 males in the 1780s, and the number kept growing during the next half century—but the organization was a beginning. These varied responsibilities, however, transformed the land captain into a hapless errand boy, forced to live a nomadic life by a governor who sent him on errands that a nobleman could only find demeaning. This explains why local noblemen were not eager to be elected land captain and why there were suggestions at the end of Catherine's reign that land captains be appointed from among army officers retired for disability.[25]

Alexander canceled his father's reforms of the rural police, notably the appointment of land captains and the elimination of peasant assessors, but the Minister of Internal Affairs failed to gain direct control over the land courts similar to that which he was achieving over the urban police. The election of the land captain, however, continued to require the confirmation of the governor, who followed the minister's instructions. Land captains remained subordinated to the governor, who did not hesitate to dismiss them and turn them over to the criminal chamber for trial and to appoint interim replacements. In four gubernias—Arkhangelsk, Olonets, Viatka, and Perm—where there were not enough nobles to conduct meaningful elections, land captains were appointed by the governor from among local nobles retired from the apparatus or from the army. The practice also developed of appointing additional noble assessors in various land courts, either to relieve overburdened assessors or to police parts of the uezd. These assessors, probably chosen by the governor, were recommended by the Minister of Internal Affairs—the Minister of Police between 1810 and 1819—who secured their appointment from the tsar. Finally, customs assessors were added in 1824 in thirty-two uezds along the western border and in Olonets gubernia to prevent the smuggling of vodka from the borderlands, where its production and sale were free, into Russia, where the sale was a government monopoly. They were chosen jointly by agreement of the governor and vice-governor, who headed the treasury chamber.[26]

This brief description of the urban and rural police does not exhaust the network of police agencies. It is obvious that the thousands of landowners scattered on their properties, large and small, who policed more than half of the peasant population directly or through their stewards, constituted a police presence much more real and oppressive than that of the land captains.[27] Moreover, landowners on large properties and land captains in areas populated by treasury-owned peasants depended on an extensive network of *sotskie* to report on events—suspicious deaths, fires, vagrants—and to carry out their decisions. These men were the delegates of the village elders, who ran the villages in accordance with customs tailored to suit their interests. Landowners were thus the real policemen of the uezd, and Derzhavin was perfectly justified in calling them in 1803 the policemasters of the countryside,[28] whose delegate, the land captain, was given jurisdiction over villages of the treasury-owned peasants. Since it is well known that elections to the noble assemblies were run, even from a distance, by the more influential landowners,[29] it follows that there existed an unofficial and looser police hierarchy run by members of the ruling elite and extending from the salons of Petersburg and Moscow to the land-owners' mansions in a few hundred uezds, parallel to the official hierarchy from Minister of Internal Affairs to land captain via governor, and no doubt much more effective.

The practice of farming out the sale of vodka in the eighteenth century—discontinued in 1817, when it became a government monopoly—turned tax farmers into the most diligent police agents. Their financial interest was at stake in the suppression of bootlegging, and they used their profits to hire men to patrol roads, search houses, and even imprison people. In the Iaroslavl of the 1780s, tax farmer Grigorii Shushin was the scourge of townsmen. In the Simbirsk gubernia of the 1810s the tax farmer's patrol (*otkupnaia strazha*) was so well known and useful that the governor borrowed it to search a paper mill producing counterfeit assignats.[30] Customhouses were also farmed out until October 1763 and kept their own police, later integrated into a customs guard (*tamozhennaia strazha*).[31] The land captain never had enough staff to police the roads and rivers of his uezd, yet the security of communications was vital to travel and commerce. When roads and waterways were grouped into regions in 1809, inspectors (*smotriteli*) and policemasters were appointed in the more sensitive areas. They were appointed by the director general of communica-tions on the recommendation of the regional director or the governor and chosen from among wounded veterans after the war of 1812.[32]

Censorship, finally, generated its own network of police agencies. It was at first vested in the urban police board in the 1780s, but censorship committees were created in October 1796 in Petersburg and Moscow—three more in the borderlands—consisting of representatives of the Synod, the Senate, and the Academy of Sciences. Following the creation of universities in Kazan in 1804 and Petersburg in 1819, for the first time since the founding of Moscow University in 1755, these committees were replaced by censorship committees for lay publications in each of the three universities, staffed with professors and responsible to the Minister of Education. Governors, however, remained or-gans of ex post facto censorship, and post offices, especially those in the two capitals, continued to censor newspapers and private correspondence.[33]

Police Forces

The forces deployed by the police were small and their presence was sporadic, especially in the countryside. That a relative order was maintained during most of the eighteenth century is eloquent testimony to the fact that Russia was still largely a self-policed society in which a consensus on the legitimacy of the existing social and political order, strengthened by a set of traditional assumptions to be examined presently, enforced obedience and stifled dissent without resort to formal structures of coercion.

In the seventeenth century order was maintained in the towns by the *streltsy* troops, who engaged at the same time in agriculture, trade, and handicrafts, and in the countryside, at least in emergencies, by the same *sotni* of landowners who were called into military service in wartime and whose cavalry was adequate to disperse unruly peasants.[34] The destruction of the *streltsy* after their revolt of 1698, the general mobilization of the landowners during the Northern War, and the draft of peasant recruits replaced those two decentralized forces with a regular army—divided into large formations commanded by the two commanders in chief, one the President of the College of War after 1718, or by separate corps commanders assigned special missions in strategic borderlands or garrisoned troops in major towns subordinated to the College of War. While garrisons were intended to maintain order in the towns, the regular army, which after the completion of the first census of 1719 Peter intended to transform into a territorial army living off the land, became the police force of the countryside, billeted in peasant houses, collecting its funds from the peasantry directly, and always at the disposal of the voevoda and the land commissioner to suppress peasant disturbances, transport funds, and convoy prisoners and recruits. In the south, along the Ukrainian border and the Don Territory, where defensive lines had been built in the seventeenth century to guard against Crimean Tatar raids, *odnodvortsy* were mobilized into a "land militia" beginning in the 1710s for better protection against the raids and to stop vagrants on their way to borderlands, where serfdom had not yet appeared.[35]

The regular army in 1725 was heavily concentrated in Russia proper: thirty-seven of the forty-nine regiments of infantry, twenty-nine of the thirty-three regiments of cavalry. An infantry regiment had a complement of 1,488 men, a cavalry regiment one of 1,250 men. This represented on paper a total force of about 90,000 men among a peasant population of 5.5 million males, or 1 army man to sixty-one peasants. Within Russia proper the army was very unevenly distributed. The territorial core around Moscow remained the demographic center of gravity, and forty-one of the sixty-six regiments were stationed there, in an almost complete circle around the old capital; there were eighteen regiments in Moscow and Vladimir gubernias alone, another seven regiments strung along the Volga in Kostroma and Nizhni Novgorod gubernias. In these nine central gubernias this meant an average of 1 army man to forty-five peasants. In the northern provinces the army, almost all infantry, was stationed in two clusters, six regiments in Novgorod and Pskov along the border of the Baltic provinces, another three in Viatka and Perm gubernias in the Urals. In the south, where fifteen regiments of cavalry alone were stationed, there were five regiments in Tambov gubernia, a strategic area on the line and a rough frontier country, another five in Kazan gubernia at the junction of the Ural and the mid-Volga regions—an unruly province with a heavily non-Russian population and a steady inflow of peasants seeking work on the riverboats and land in the southern Urals and Bashkiria. In these southern provinces, the army posted only 1 man for every ninety-one peasants.[36]

Forty years later, in 1765, the presence of the army in Russia proper had been much reduced. Despite an increase of the peasant population to 7.4 million souls in the census of 1762, only 47 of the 113 regiments were stationed there. This was a time, however, when auxiliary forces called *shtatnye komandy* were created, part of a conscious policy of reducing the role of the army as a police force and stationing a larger proportion of it in the Baltic and Ukrainian borderlands. The territorial acquisitions of 1771–1795 accelerated this trend, and by the end of 1796 only 29 of the 115 regiments—about 57,000 men—were stationed in Russia, while the peasant population has risen to 9.6 million in the 1795 census. By then, the south had become completely denuded of troops, and only fifteen regiments were stationed in the nine central gubernias, seven of them in Moscow and Vladimir, and four in Smolensk— 1 military man for every 116 peasants. In the northern gubernias eight of the twelve regiments were stationed in Petersburg, reflecting the tense military situation since the Swedish war and at the time of Catherine's death. This army had been distributed since 1763 among eight territorial "divisions" or regions, of which there were four in Russia, centered in Petersburg, Moscow, Smolensk, and Sevsk, the governors-general of Moscow combining the command of the division with his civilian responsibilities. The remaining three divisions (Sevsk's was abolished in 1769) were renamed "inspections" in 1796.[37]

The trend was reversed, however, during the peacetime years of Alexander's reign. By the 1820s about 80 of the 242 regiments—not including the Guard—were stationed in Russia proper, but this represented a force of about 235,000 men or 1 army man per forty-five peasants, a much more compelling presence than ever before in the eighteenth century. The inspections had been abolished in 1806, divisions had become tactical formations grouped into army and separate corps. After the war of 1812, the army corps—now called infantry and cavalry corps—stationed in the western borderlands were grouped into two armies, with commanders in chief in Mogilev and Tulchin (Podol'sk gubernia) who reported, like the commanders of the troops stationed in Russia, to the chief of His Majest's Main Staff.[38]

Garrisoned troops supplemented the regular army in the most important towns and relieved it of its police duties. They owed their origin to a natural division of functions within the army—not only to be a mobile force intended to project power against external enemies as circumstances and policy required but also to man fortresses and other fixed strategic points in the army's logistical network and to establish a strong military presence in areas of the national territory marked by endemic unrest. These troops also answered the need for a formation to absorb officers and men who had become unfit for the rigorous regimen of the army but were still able to bear arms and run military installations. They were better trained than the *streltsy* had been to operate a force of internal security troops for the new empire.

By 1725 garrisoned troops numbered 74,000 men in fifty-seven regiments of infantry and cavalry. They were distributed in three regions called *razriady*, each containing a small number of fortresses where the troops did guard duty and from which they carried out assignments that often resembled small-scale military operations. About forty-five of the fifty-seven regiments were stationed in Russia proper, either to reinforce a military presence in areas where army regiments were stationed or to create one where no regular troops were assigned. The largest garrisons at the time were in Petersburg and Vologda in the northern region, in Moscow, Smolensk, Vladimir, and Kostroma in the center, and in Kazan and Simbirsk in the south and east.[39]

Their function was not only to maintain order. They kept in permanent contact with villages in order to obtain information, serve summonses, carry out judicial decisions, and collect arrears. These services were also performed by certain non-nobles who were given land in return and were called *razsyl-shchiki*. Their number was raised in 1732 from 1,450 to 5,488, to be distributed among 201 towns and only in gubernias where no garrisoned troops were stationed.[40] These troops also provided a pool of relatively experienced and well-disciplined personnel for staff positions in the civilian administration, such as clerks and accountants, who were often in short supply at the time.

When army regiments returned from the battlefield in 1763 and took up permanent quarters in Russia, the Baltic provinces, and the Ukraine, a Military Commission, created to reorganize the army in peacetime, recommended the removal of the army, insofar as possible, from participation in civilian police responsibilities.[41] It was then, indeed, that a trend began to separate the military from a civilian establishment that was still amorphous and understaffed but soon to begin a rapid growth under Catherine. Paul's legislation would formalize that separation. As a consequence of the commission's recommendation, the police forces in towns and countryside were increased and diversified. Regiments—now larger and more cumbersome—were replaced in 1764 by battalions of 772 officers and men as the basic unit of garrisoned troops. Thirty-two of the eighty-four battalions were stationed in Russian towns, representing a force of about 24,700. The largest garrisons were now in Petersburg, Moscow, and Kazan. To guarantee that garrisons would thenceforth remain in the towns and no longer be scattered in the performance of duties unrelated to municipal administration, new units called *shtatnye komandy*—after the gubernia table of organization (*shtat*)—were created in 1763. They absorbed the *razsylshchiki* and were assigned to all three levels of local administration, the gubernia (a company of 132 men, including twenty-four dragoons), the province, and the uzed (57 and 29 men, respectively, including a small complement of mounted police). These *komandy* were created in Russia alone, where they constituted a force of 8,620 men—at least on paper.[42] A third police force was created at the same time. Disabled veterans, who until then had been retired in monasteries, were sent to various towns, chiefly in the eastern gubernias, where they were grouped into squads and companies and served as local guards (*storozhi*) in agencies, public squares, and churches.

Garrisons were subordinated to the governor until 1775, the regional ("divisional") commander thereafter, but *shtatnye komandy* and invalids remained subordinated to the governor.[43]

After the creation of the ministries in September 1802, a battle over territory developed between the War Ministry and the MVD. Garrisons remained, of course, part of the military establishment, but the *shtatnye komandy* and the invalids passed under the jurisdiction of the MVD, a division of responsibilities that did not augur well for efficiency, since the *shtatnye komandy* were plagued by corruption. It became increasingly incongruous, as the country prepared for war against Napoleon, that a large force of military men, even if retired from the regular army, should be subordinated to governors and sheriffs, under a civilian minister. When the tsar refused to place it under the new Police Ministry in 1811, a major reorganization of all police forces became necessary. Garrisons, *shtatnye komandy*, and invalids were combined in July in a military Internal Guard (*vnutrennaia strazha*) commanded by an army general with the title of inspector. Although he was made a deputy to the War Minister, the holder of the post, Evgraf Komarovskii, was also an Adjutant General, with direct access to the ruler. The commander of the Internal Guard thus became in effect a minister in charge of the internal security troops of the empire.[44]

The basic unit of the Internal Guard was the gubernia battalion, renamed garrison battalion in July 1816 and given a uniform complement of 1,091 officers and men in four companies in April 1817. Two battalions usually constituted a brigade, two or three brigades a region (*okrug*), with changes being made from time to time. There were twelve regional headquarters in 1818, four of them in Russia, for a force of about 32,000 men in thirty battalions.[45] Their territorial distribution appears in Table 7.1:

Battalions were distributed among the uezds of the gubernia and were placed at the disposal of the governor when he requested assistance from the regional commander (*okruzhnoi general*). Combined action by all the battal-

Table 7.1. Internal Guard Regions (in Russia alone)

Region	Headquarters	Battalion Headquarters		
I	Riga	Pskov		
II	Vitebsk	Smolensk*	Kaluga*	
III	Kiev	Kursk		
V	Arkhangelsk	Arkhangelsk*	Vologda*	Petrozavodsk
VI	Tver	Petersburg*	Tver	Vladimir
		Novgorod	Iaroslavl*	Kostroma*
VII	Tula	Moscow	Tula	Voronezh*
		Riazan*	Orel*	Tambov
VIII	Ufa	Viatka*	Perm	
IX	Kazan	N-Novgorod	Saratov*	Kazan*
		Simbirsk*	Penza	

*Brigade headquarters

ions in one region required the approval of the war minister. The Internal Guard's duties included those of the old garrison troops and *shtatnye komandy*, to which were added military responsibilities such as keeping track of all military units in the gubernia, tracking down AWOL military personnel, training recruits, and convoying them to gathering points before their assignments to army units.[46] As a result, the Internal Guard not only incorporated all existing police forces but also functioned as a kind of reserve cadre and military police. This marked a return to the Petrine situation and a reversal of the trend begun in the 1760s, with this difference: not only the regular army but one of its auxiliary forces had assumed responsibility for policing the country.

There were two other military formations with police responsibilities. The Imperial Guard was not, of course, a police force intended to maintain order, but it remained, at least in the first half of the eighteenth century, a security police and an instrument of political control in the hands of the ruler; as the social embodiment of the ruling elite, it was in a position to interfere in the order of succession and impose its candidate.[47]

When the Guard was founded in 1687 with the creation of two elite regiments of infantry, the Preobrazhenskii and the Semenovskii, the tsar himself was their colonel and they fought in the Northern War alongside other army regiments. Their officers, however, notably their majors, were often chosen by the tsar to conduct politically sensitive investigations, and the origin of the Secret Chancery has been traced to these various commissions and missions.[48] They were the tsar's *missi dominici*, sent out to gather information, conduct the census, and ferret out abuses; they were even empowered at times to place governors under house arrest until the abuses of which they had been accused had been verified and corrected. Even diplomatic envoys were selected from among guardsmen. The Guard thus became a cadre of talented and devoted individuals, who came from distinguished families already members of the ruling elite or even from families of non-noble origin.

The Guard was stationed in Petersburg and its outskirts. In the northern capital, where the palaces and gardens of the Court occupied such a prominent place, the Guard, to which their security was entrusted, was both a military presence and a police force, augmented by an increasingly large garrison and by army regiments rotated on an annual basis. Its strength totaled 10,250 men in the 1750s—the original two regiments, a third, the Izmailovskii, created in 1730; a small company of *chevaliers de garde* (*kavalergvardia*); and a horse guard regiment. During Catherine's reign, the Guard lost the role of security police and elite fighting force and was integrated into the Court establishment, enhancing the majesty of the ruler and adding to the trappings of power. It became a pool of well-connected but poorly qualified officers,[49] who used the two-rank differential to make a rapid career in the army and line their pockets before retirement—a Guard major became an army colonel following his transfer. It also became an agency of social mobility—sons of rich merchants were admitted on occasion and joined the upper reaches of the ruling class.

If the creation of two Guard regiments represented an assertion of the ruler's will within the constellation of power in which he had been raised,

Paul's incorporation of the Gatchina troops—those placed under his command when he was Grand Duke—into the Guard represented a challenge to families that had been ruling the country since Peter's reign. This new trend toward enlarging the Guard aimed at swamping it in a much larger formation that would neutralize opposition from the traditional core, create a new patronage network owing its allegiance to the ruler alone—a similar trend was noticeable in the army—and further enhance the majesty of the Romanov house. It continued under Alexander, and by 1812 the Guard complement exceeded 20,000 men. The following year, grenadier regiments were added to it as a reward for bravery in battle. In 1814 the old and the new (young) Guard became separate corps, each under a commander personally responsible to the ruler.[50] By 1825 the old Guard would number 60,000 men and the new 30,000, a total of 90,000 privileged officers and men. No longer would it be a political force capable of threatening the throne. Its very size would create a diversity of interests, and service in it would become a separate and self-contained career.

The extraordinary expansion of the military and civilian establishments under Alexander was bound to raise the question of the political stability of his reign. The new central and local police agencies were inadequate to watch over large formations scattered over an immense territory, and the Guard had outlived its role as a political police force. The descendants of the Guard majors of the 1720s were the Fliegel Adjutants of the Imperial Suite, whom the tsar sent on delicate missions from time to time. What was increasingly required, however, as the ruling class became more exposed to subversive ideas from western Europe, was a permanent force responsible for political surveillance, even within the Guard.

The first move was made in the army. In August 1815, one of the dragoon regiments was renamed gendarme regiment, and squads of new gendarmes were assigned to infantry and cavalry corps headquarters from which three gendarmes were assigned to each divisional headquarters.[51] The emphasis was placed on men of outstanding conduct, who reported to the corps commander on the political mood of the troops. Six years later, the commander of the (old) Guard corps, Adjutant General Illarion Vasil'chikov, won the tsar's permission to set up a secret police of fifteen individuals to listen in on conversations of guardsmen in their regiments, in public places, and at private gatherings.[52] Meanwhile, a force of gendarmes was taking shape alongside the Internal Guard. The dragoons who had been part of the *shtatnye komandy* remained subordinated to the governor. They were not integrated into the Internal Guard in 1811 but were placed under the Police Minister, another awkward solution typical of the endless compromises among members of the apparatus. In February 1817, however, these dragoons were transformed into gendarmes and subordinated in each gubernia to the battalion commander of the Internal Guard. A squad in each gubernia capital consisted of thirty gendarmes. In Petersburg and Moscow the gendarmes—two squadrons of 330 men each in each capital—remained subordinated to the senior policemaster and were considered on leave from the Internal Guard. The gendarmes thus made up a force of 2,080 men. Their role as a police force was not clearly stated at first.

They carried dispatches, served as a mounted police to maintain order at public gatherings, and were at the governor's disposal for special missions.[53] Two years after Alexander's death, however, they became yet another separate corps, organized, like the Internal Guard, into regional formations and responsible to a separate commander, who was also the chief of the Third Section, the new political police headquarters of the Russian Empire.[54]

8

Concept and Scope of
Police Authority

General Principles

Challenges to the legitimacy of the social and political order lacked any intellectual tradition justifying resistance to established authority, and only served to confirm the inflexible grip of the ruling class and its ideological apparatus on politics and society. As a result, that order remained, at least until the end of the eighteenth century, a self-policing world in which police attitudes permeated politics, administration, and social relations. The shattering of the traditional social order in the 1860s would generate a growing challenge to the legitimacy of the political order and, with it, the development of autonomous tendencies and the need for an ever more extensive police network to keep them in line.

There can be no understanding of that intellectual tradition without keeping in mind the insistence on the dual allegiance of man, so fundamental to Western jurisprudence.[1] Its roots were religious, grounded in the injunction to render unto Caesar what belongs to Caesar and to God what belongs to God, conceptualized in the theory of the two swords and transformed into an axiom of medieval politics by the rival claims of king and pope across the vast expanse of a continent. It developed into a secular creed when kings triumphed and laid claim to the total allegiance of their subjects, and it justified rebellion by keeping alive an allegiance to a higher standard against which the rulers' actions were to be judged.

Constantinople and Muscovite Russia lacked this permanent tension and disturbing dynamism. Even though the acceptance of man's dual allegiance was common to both East and West, the location of the metropolitan or patriarchal see in the secular capital fostered the belief in an organic unity of imperial and patriarchal power rather than in the need to constantly review their respective claims. A "rationalist" theology failed to develop within a church seeking to expound and teach an unfolding faith revealing itself in accord with the needs of each age:[2] the defense of an ideological status quo became instead its duty and its raison d'être. A similar intellectual sclerosis afflicted secular claims, and the so-called symphony of church and state[3]—assuming a happy balance between the two—became no more than a screen for the subordination of the church leadership to the ruling house, the ultimate transformation of the ecclesiastical structure into the ideological apparatus of the ruling class,[4] and a justification for the nearly total absence of political literature.

Seventeenth-century developments exposed the weakness of an institutionalized church that claimed preeminence over a new ruling house by invoking arguments strikingly similar to those of the medieval popes. Patriarch Filaret (1619–1633), ruling alongside his son, Tsar Mikhail, claimed that his office was higher than the tsar's since he had under his care the souls of all men including the tsar's, and Patriarch Nikon (1652–1666) used Innocent III's analogy between the sun and the moon to characterize relations between the ecclesiastical and temporal worlds. Nikon's claims, however, found no support within a church already weakened by the Schism, and these two attempts to introduce a vivifying dynamism in these relations ended in dismal failure.[5] Russian history never knew a conflict similar to that pitting Henry IV against Gregory VII in Germany, Henry II against Thomas à Becket in England, or Philip the Fair against Boniface VIII in France.[6]

It follows that a tradition of ideological opposition to the claims of the ruling house never developed in Russia and, by extension, that assertions of ideological uniformity were accepted by default. Peter's destruction of the administrative autonomy of the church in 1721 was no more than a footnote to the elimination of Nikon. The abolition of the patriarchate, created in 1589 and seldom a real, but always a potential, source of opposition to the ruler's policies, "left the emperor with no possible rival for his subjects' loyalty [and] left them with no independent court of appeal, no alternative source of justice, no room to escape from the tsar's power."[7] It also enhanced the religious role of the ruler, who became the head of church and country, to whom Russians now owed their undivided allegiance.

This now complete union of responsibility for the governance of a vast country and for the salvation of souls, coupled with the general mobilization of the nobility into an aggressive ruling class, increased immensely the Imperial government's awareness of its need to enforce a rigid political orthodoxy. The Synod—a committee of bishops—retained ultimate jurisdiction in matters of dogma, but the day-to-day administration of the church passed into the hands of the Senior Procurator (*ober-prokuror*), who played vis-à-vis the Synod the same role that the Procurator General developed so tenaciously toward the Senate in the course of the eighteenth century.

Rulers took their religious duties seriously. Anna was a traditional *boyarinia*, pious and stern, even with Biron at her side. The post of senior procurator was not filled during her reign; the Synod, like the Senate, was subordinated directly to the Cabinet of Ministers; and the activities of the Secret Chancery became so pervasive that they became the best-remembered feature of her reign. Pleasure-loving Elizabeth remained deeply religious, and the Secret Chancery retained pride of place in the network of governmental agencies. Catherine, Protestant by birth and Enlightenment cynic by education, understood the value of Orthodoxy as one of the main supports of her legitimacy, called herself the head of the church, and imprisoned in the most humiliating manner one of the few opponents of the final secularization of church properties. Paul, likewise as head of the church, continued the practice of crowning himself, and Alexander's piety and mysticism earned him the title of "Blessed," while his reign is also known for the growth of an unprecedented political police establishment and the close link between the Minister of Education and the Senior Procurator of the Synod.[8]

This debasement of religion from a guide to moral autonomy to an official ideology, emphasizing unconditional submission to the temporal power and the resulting deification of the ruler, justified—indeed mandated—the repression of any sign of intellectual independence as an offense against the majesty of the ruler, a sin against his holiness, and a heresy against the orthodoxy of the day.

If the union of religious and secular responsibilities in the ruler gave the process of governing an ideological intolerance that could not be challenged without jeopardizing one's salvation, the identification of Orthodoxy with the Russian people created a no-less-intolerant climate fostering suspicion, denunciation, and the systematic denial of privacy.

One of the most persistent assumptions of the Russians has been that their country is "holy," the land of salvation, blessed by its icons and its saints, and favored in the eyes of God by the qualities of its people.[9] The growth of an Orthodox community of believers had been the result of a *reconquista* against the Moslem world, and its continued independent existence after 1453, when other Orthodox lands fell under Ottoman rule, fostered a self-righteous identification of Orthodoxy with Russia, of a religious creed and a political ideology with the very existence of the Russian people.

The church's central role in the rise and consolidation of the Muscovite princely house and command society was buttressed by the necessity to express "national consciousness" in religious terms. Russian society was as great a melting pot as there ever was, assimilating a dozen eastern Slavic tribes, as well as Finns, Iranians, and Tatars, who needed common symbols and a common ideology to forge their acceptance of Moscow's leadership into a durable political allegiance.[10] As a result, a profession of Orthodoxy was the test for admission into the Russian political order and baptism its rite of passage. Thus, while Orthodoxy became for the Russians identified with "Russia," it also cemented the allegiance of non-Russians to a religious ideology transcending identification with a single ethnic group. Although it made for tension among the Orthodox ecumene, it provided the justification for a policy of assimilation in the borderlands and intolerance toward all outsiders.

Self-righteousness fed a strong xenophobic impulse born of enforced isolation and an unconscious fear of subversive influence from outside. The brightness of Holy Russia was contrasted with the darkness of "unclean Asiatic lands," and the term *busurman*, applied to Moslems in general and to Turks in particular, was also extended to all non-Russians.[11] When Ensign Lamp was sent in September 1725 to arrest Alexei Naryshkin, on whose estates crowds of highway robbers had been meeting with his connivance, Naryshkin upbraided him as a member of the "German Moslem faith" (*nemetskaia busurmanskaia vera*), who needed to be baptized and confessed before he could be admitted to the estate. This definition of the Russian people in religious terms was most striking in the use of the same word—*krest'ianin*—for a baptized man and a peasant. Military commanders addressed their men as "Orthodox," and a grenadier pretending to be the tsarevich could find no better way to enlist the support of his fellow soldiers than to call them "God's people."[12]

Russian culture remained throughout the eighteenth century essentially medieval, marked by conceptual simplicity, the absence of cultural pluralism, and a Manichaean attitude toward the outside world. Despite the inroads of Western influence, native books and manuscripts written in the course of the century were overwhelmingly devotional works keeping alive in Russian consciousness an awareness that intellectual endeavor was inseparable from religious meditation, if not synonymous with it. The continued permeation of the secular culture with religious concerns was confirmed with striking simplicity by the contemporary Soviet painter Ilya Glazunov, who stated in 1988 that "all Russian culture is Russian Orthodox culture."[13]

This culture, common to ruling class and dependent population, cemented the bond between them. It transcended social and economic differences and provided a common vocabulary that often made a public speech into a religious sermon. Anyone reading the speeches of Nikolai Dolgorukov to the nobility of the former grand duchy of Lithuania after the Polish revolt of 1831 must wonder whether he is listening to a governor-general's political message or to an archbishop threatening the black sheep of his flock with the fires of hell.[14] It also facilitated the transformation of the church hierarchy into obedient tools of the ruling class in estates and villages and into its political commissars in the army. The author of a book on military science wrote in 1823 that the advantage of the Russians was that religion was always on the side of the government. Chaplains, subject to the same military discipline as other officers, received their instructions from their generals, and the "rabble" (*chern*) followed their chaplains' interpretations as the will of heaven.[15]

Russian medieval literature showed no interest in the spiritual development of princes. They experienced bodily tortures but no spiritual torment, and remained unchanged throughout life, outside of time.[16] Russian literature has been poor in tragic heroes, who must be noble and great yet possess the tragic flaw that predetermines their downfall. Tragedy rests on rebellion, and rebellion gives dignity to those who brave the overwhelming odds of power and death. The message of a church that never accepted such odds was that humility, obedience, and the acceptance of fate are the finest adornments of a Christian son of the Fatherland. It was no coincidence that Athens and England, where tragedy flourished, were also the lands where individual freedom and the inquisitive mind were cherished and fought for.

The association of Orthodoxy with the Russian people facilitated enormously the task of policing society and repressing intellectual deviationism. Russia was a community of believers, of "baptized men and women," in which intellectual and social behavior that did not conform to the rules had to be denounced as ideological heresy and political subversion. Self-policing, then, was a constant preoccupation, and denunciations were acts of faith and self-justification. The salvation of each was the responsibility of all, and any assertion of the right of privacy and individual choice was bound to be seen as insufferable insolence and an incitement to sedition. There prevailed as a result at all levels of Russian society an oppressive atmosphere of communal self-righteousness and intellectual obscurantism. No other people, wrote Berdiaev, "has shown such an open hostility toward creative enthusiasm, a hatred so envious of any blossoming of the human individuality."[17]

A remarkably stable social and economic order strengthened the subordination of the church to the ruling class and protected a self-contained society against substantial internal differentiation and subversive influences. There was economic development between 1690 and 1825, but it remained a superficial and largely regional phenomenon. Despite the emergence of a textile industry around Moscow, of mining and metallurgy in the Urals, and of various manufactures on the banks of the Neva, Russia remained a world of self-sufficient estates, peasant communities, and anemic towns, cut off since the sixteenth century from the international trade routes that brought exotic products and precious metals to the vibrant towns of the Atlantic world that were eager to produce and exchange, and penetrated the countryside for the mutual benefit of townsman and peasant.[18] There is no better proof of the near stagnation of the Russian economy than the rigidity of the tax base: the revenue from the capitation and quitrent, from the sale of salt and vodka, and from custom duties contributed, as we shall see, 87 percent of the total tax revenue in 1724 and 83 percent in 1825.[19]

Such an economy did not keep pace with the growth of the country's responsibilities. It left Russia technologically backward at the beginning of the Industrial Revolution. It certainly did not foster the sprouting of commercial centers in an immense territory, while dependence on the Volga for transportation favored the concentration of economic activity in Moscow and, only later in the century, in Petersburg, the first port city capable of becoming a manufacturing center. This concentration in one capital city of political, ideological, and economic power intensified political considerations and blocked the emergence of autonomous tendencies among merchants and capitalists that were favored elsewhere by their geographical separation from the principal seats of military and political power.[20] This in turn precluded the development of political dialogue and intellectual diversity, which by their very nature would have checked the most extreme manifestations of intolerance and self-righteousness, the foundations of police power.

Serfdom grew upon an economy of scarcity, oblivious of a slow economic progress that did not reach the depths of an immutable peasant society. Indeed, its two most severe phases—the reigns of Peter and Catherine—coincided with the building up of an industrial infrastructure and an industrial spurt that made Russia the leader in the production and export of metal. In its starkest form, it placed more than 95 percent of the population at the disposal of a ruling class that extracted from it the resources needed to carry out its mission to make war and to govern. Even though serfdom was a complex arrangement whose assumptions often concealed a reality denying their validity—in property and contractual relations, for example—the principle that it was the foundation of the social order remained a non-negotiable issue beyond 1825. The treatment of Radishchev was understandable, and the so-called liberal censorship statute of 1804 could rationally equate criticism of serfdom, let alone support for emancipation, with crimes as pernicious as insulting the ruler and inciting readers against the ruling elite and its policies.[21]

Serfdom was a complete system of power. It was based on force—contemporary accounts are rich in examples of a pervasive coarseness and brutality at all levels of society, especially toward the dependent population.[22] It also rested on the use of compensatory power, not yet sharply distinguished from force. The slave could be beaten but could not be fired, and the reward of slaves was security of tenure, which the free worker in a free market did not enjoy. The protection afforded the serf by his master against the claims of other serfs and even those of other lords was a compensation for bondage to the ruling class. Finally, it made use of conditioned power, creating a situation in which the ideological apparatus made obedience and the acceptance of the status quo a natural and proper response.[23]

The union of these three forms of power in a society left fundamentally undisturbed by economic progress sealed the fate of any autonomous tendencies. Since Russian society was a command structure, within the ruling class, between the ruling class and the dependent population, and within the dependent population, any social criticism—and none was possible without ultimately raising the issue of serfdom—was bound to set into motion a train of subversive thoughts threatening power relationships at all levels. On the other hand, the lack of alternate sources of wealth and of opportunities outside serfdom made such criticism unrealistic and vulnerable. Serfdom thus facilitated the self-policing of society by imposing an intolerant consensus on the nature of the social order. The cooperation between those who policed and those who were policed, then, was based on the assumption that any deviation from the established path created a threat with repercussions across the entire order. It was the interdependence of all these acts and attitudes that created this most oppressive of all police states.

A Russian owed his undivided allegiance to the ruler and the ruling elite, and none could claim like Antigone that there were higher laws to justify dissent and sanctify disobedience. He was a member of an ethnic group, which was also a religious community in possession of the Truth, and his activities had to be those of a believer who must accept and obey but never question. He was part of a social order imposed and guaranteed by a ruling class, which he could not challenge without raising questions not only about his political loyalty but also about the strength of his faith. He could take no refuge in a private world of belief because there was no threshold that the community and its punitive agents might not cross. There was nothing original in the slogan "Autocracy, Orthodoxy, Nationality" expounded by the government of Nicholas I—it had been taken for granted for generations. By the 1830s, however, it had to be expressly formulated as a reassertion of principle against the first widespread challenge to the legitimacy of the traditional order. Policing society was thus the responsibility and sacred duty of all. The claims of political, social, and cultural orthodoxy were enforced by a community of believers who saw the salvation of their souls in the maintenance of tradition and the constant reinforcement of its unity. Policing was indeed the soul of the entire system.[24]

Police as Municipal Administration

The consolidation of the Romanov house by the end of the seventeenth century paved the way for the "organization of internal space"[25] in the territorial reforms of 1708 and 1775 and for the formulation of a program of municipal administration that was its natural corollary. Such a program made up much of what was called "police administration" at the time. The creation of the "well-ordered police state"[26] aimed at strengthening the power of the prince by creating a government machinery to administer justice, collect taxes, and provide logistical support for a large army of recruits. These were specialized activities whose increasing complexity helped them win a growing autonomy, while everything else became subsumed under the rubric of "police" or "internal affairs." This included the maintenance of order, to be sure, as well as the prosecution of offenses deemed by the ruling elite to be threats to their political dominion, but also the carrying out of sentences in judicial and fiscal cases, which thus deliberately reduced the courts to technical agencies.

This program of building up government machinery to satisfy the needs of a ruling class in full expansion was inseparable from the program of building towns. Successful towns, of course, could not be mere administrative creations; they also had to reflect the convergence of favorable economic circumstances. The dilapidated appearance of Russian towns and the primitiveness of urban life testified eloquently to their remoteness from the great currents of exchange vivifying the economic life of western Europe and North America. The building of an urban civilization in Russia became the responsibility of a ruling class steeped in an agrarian order, and the result remained an artificial creation well into the modern period.

The focus of the government's efforts was naturally Petersburg, built out of nothing by the iron will of a great ruler. The Instruction (*Punkty* in the administrative language of the day) given to the first Policemaster General in May 1718 did not give priority to the maintenance of order.[27] The first reference to it—apprehension of violators of the peace—is not to be found until "point" seven, sandwiched between sanitation and fire prevention. When the Policemaster General sought Anna's approval for the appointment of policemasters in a number of towns in 1733, he made his request on the grounds that summer heat and the lack of sanitation created such "harmful and poisonous stench" that separate police agencies had become necessary. Whether the appointment of policemasters and sheriffs under Catherine made a difference is another story. A general instruction of August 1803 would complain that sheriffs did not exercise proper supervision over the cleanliness of their towns.[28]

Sanitation, the lighting and paving of streets, construction, and fire prevention were the essential components of the urban program of "police administration." Its goal was to create a physical environment suitable for the flourishing of a modern society patterned after Western models, at least in Petersburg and to some extent in Moscow; to establish a substantial apparatus in the provincial capitals and a political infrastructure scattered in the countryside. By extension, the prosecution of criminals would be facilitated—the "policing" of Paris, for example, was based on such an assumption.[29] The failure to create a favorable environment was bound to retard the development of provincial centers capable of acting as a counterweight to a national capital moved to the distant shore of the Baltic while the country was expanding to the south and southeast. Kazan's location and history, for example, made it a major administrative, religious, and military headquarters, and the opening of a university in 1804 aimed at making it into one of Russia's three cultural centers, after Petersburg and Moscow. Yet its professors, many of them from the Germanic lands, were repelled by the city's unsanitary conditions, and the curator, Mikhail Saltykov—whose ancestor had been governor of Kazan exactly 100 years earlier—asked to be recalled in 1817, after 4 years of revulsion at such conditions, his wife having died in one of the epidemics they bred with alarming regularity.[30]

To improve sanitation by police measures alone was bound to have a limited effect. Standards could be raised only through a concerted effort by urban classes conscious of their towns as territorial complexes and not merely as microcosms of a command society in which subordination and obedience substituted for common interest and initiative sustained by adequate resources from a prosperous economy. Since that effort was lacking, there was a distressing repetitiveness in the government's instructions and circulars from the 1710s to the 1820s. Inhabitants were enjoined not to discard their trash in the street and to keep their houses clean, to have drainage ditches dug on both sides of the street, to keep wells free of litter, and slaughterhouses and tanneries out of the town. Obviously, very little was done.

Concern over unsanitary conditions, which gave the sheriff and policemaster, and beyond them the governor, who was an agent of the MVD, extensive rights to interfere in economic life, derived in part from the fear of disease, even though the link between disease and bacterial infection was only dimly perceived by medical science.[31] Outside the two capitals, medical personnel remained almost unknown until Catherine's reign, when a substantial effort was made to concentrate welfare activities in a Board of Public Welfare (*prikaz obshchestvennogo prizreniia*) chaired by the governor and consisting of two representatives each from the nobility, from the *magistrat* of the provincial capital, and from peasants of the treasury. A medical board (*vrachebnaia uprava*) was likewise created in gubernia capitals in 1797, headed by an inspector and consisting of a doctor and a midwife. The inspector became an ex officio member of the Welfare Board in 1818.[32] The creation of the MVD in

1802 and its absorption of the College of Medicine made the practice of medicine a branch of police administration. Doctors and their assistants— *lekari*, who did not have medical degrees—who had always been subordinated to the governor, became police agents in a dual capacity. When they ministered to the sick, ran hospitals, inspected markets for spoiled food, certified that enterprises met sanitary standards, and declared people insane, they operated as medical professionals and representatives of a ministry and a governor whose major function was the maintenance of order and the defense of political orthodoxy. Since the Welfare Board also ran madhouses, workhouses, and houses of correction, an unholy alliance developed between medical personnel and the repressive arm of the government, in which both stood to benefit financially from the operation of these enterprises.

Fire prevention was also a police responsibility. Every town built of wood because of the scarcity of stone was hostage to any careless inhabitant or determined criminal. Fires destroyed entire quarters and sometimes entire towns. Petersburg suffered extensive damage in 1736, Moscow in 1736 and 1737, Iaroslavl was almost entirely destroyed in 1768, Kazan burned down several times in the eighteenth century and once again in 1815.[33] A fire was an act of God against which there was little protection, especially when the wind was strong. Life was otherwise so peaceful that fires were often the only "event" worth recording in the semimonthly reports on events, which governors-general were required to submit to Catherine.[34] Pumps (*zalivnye truby*) were few in number—Moscow had only four on the eve of Catherine's reign. Their manufacture and maintenance were the responsibility of the *magistraty*, which could not find the funds because the urban economy was, like the Russian economy in general, one of scarcity, and because the registered merchantry remained unconvinced that the town's interests coincided with their own. When funds had to be found because conditions became acute, they were released by the Treasury as an emergency measure, without lasting effect.[35]

The Police Code of 1782 made a serious attempt to establish an administrative framework for combating fires, if not preventing them. In each district (*chast'*) into which the larger towns were divided, *brantmeisters* were appointed, subordinated to the sheriff, and local people were elected to contribute their services as a form of tax in kind (*povinnost'*). A contemporary document refers to 7,175 such people in the Moscow of 1785 whose duty was to run to the fires (*begaiushchie na pozhar obyvateli*). These fire-fighting forces, which would pass under MVD control in 1802, lacked equipment and uniform organization. An attempt to improve their performance was made in 1818 by training fire fighters in Petersburg for duty in other gubernia capitals, and the use of the Internal Guard was even considered to strengthen local resources.[36] Preventing fires, however, in private houses, in public baths, in markets and industrial enterprises remained a difficult task, but it gave the police a preemptive right to inquire into the operations of private enterprises and the conditions of private homes, which substantially enlarged its authority as the guardian of the public peace.

The government was aware that a solution to the problem of fire prevention was urban planning. Indeed, the first "point" of the 1718 Instruction called for the construction of stoves and chimneys in accordance with regulations and of buildings along straight streets of equal width for both utilitarian and aesthetic reasons, from which it followed that the appearance of buildings must also be regulated. In a country where private architects were few, those working for the government were placed on the staff of the police—another professional activity transformed into an extension of police work. Town planning reached its apogee in the 1770s and 1780s, when a Commission for the Construction of Petersburg and Moscow, created in December 1762, acknowledged that urban planning on a national scale went beyond the abilities and responsibilities of the Policemaster General and began to draw up plans for a systematic reconstruction of all gubernia capitals and uezd centers. The imposition of the plan over the old town plan shows that a radical transformation of the urban landscape was intended, with governors and sheriffs and the architects on their staffs to be responsible for carrying it out. How much was achieved is difficult to estimate, as the fiscal stringency imposed by endless war severely limited such a vast construction program.[37]

This intended reconstruction of Russian towns marked the last stage in the organization of internal space begun in 1708. Its purpose was not only to thrust broad and straight avenues through a maze of narrow and crooked streets— bordered by wooden houses patiently rebuilt after each fire, radiating from a central square graced by a church and the governor's office—but also to increase the amount of stone construction, a defense against fires. Yet by 1825 wooden buildings still prevailed over stone in all Russian towns. In Petersburg, surprisingly, the ratio of stone to wooden buildings was one to three; in Iaroslavl it was one to five, in Kazan and Saratov one to eight, in Novgorod and Kursk one to ten.[38] No matter how enlightened its program of urban renewal had been, the ruling class still presided in 1825 over a network of large "urban" villages that differed only in density from the kind of aggregates with which it had always been familiar on its rural properties. Town dwellers—who sometimes complained that straightening out the streets deprived them of their gardens[39]—were seen as no more than another category of peasants subject to the same kind of arbitrary police power.

Such a state of affairs explains not only why urban renewal after destructive fires could not significantly modernize the physical appearance of the buildings but also why conveniences were, in most cases, as nonexistent as they were in villages. Moscow in the 1750s, the abandoned ancient capital yet the center of Russian trade and industry, was little different from a big village, with its straw-covered houses and wells in the middle of streets. Petersburg in the 1820s was an "unfinished city," and the police was doing very little to raise the level of comfort and improve services to a level befitting an imperial capital.[40] The common complaint there and elsewhere was the deplorable condition of the streets: corduroy streets (*mostovye*)—a "pavement" of logs bound together and unable to resist for long the combined weight of wagons and the damage of frost—created quagmires of mud in the spring and dust bowls in the summer, and trash thrown away in the winter generated in the spring the stench associated with Russian towns. The lack of stone and the insufficiency of brick production made paving a hopeless task. As late as 1812, an order was issued to collect the ballast of ships coming in empty to Petersburg and use the stone to pave at least the public squares. Homeowners were made responsible for paving the street in front of their houses under the supervision of a police "well acquainted with the condition of every inhabitant." Other towns were to proceed likewise by requiring teamsters coming in from the countryside with empty wagons to fill them with stones.[41]

Since it bore a direct relationship to the maintenance of order, lighting the streets was the responsibility of the police. Darkness imposed a natural curfew, and life came to a standstill at sundown, as it did in the villages. The police were instructed to require inhabitants to burn candles in their windows or contribute money to maintain lampposts. These contributions were included in the town's police budget—in Petersburg, Moscow, Arkhangelsk during Catherine's reign, in Kazan during Alexander's. As a result, municipal administration became virtually identical with police administration and municipal budgets with police budgets.[42]

The major police responsibility, the maintenance of order, was limited largely to the towns: policing the countryside was required only in emergencies. Guard duty in the larger towns was done by troops from the garrison—at the post office, the church, and the storerooms containing funds, vodka, and provisions. These troops also patrolled the streets and public gardens. Detachments were often assigned to other towns, in violation of the original intent to keep the garrison troops concentrated in fortified towns. After 1764, guard duty became the responsibility of the *shtatnye komandy*. Inhabitants were required to elect a night watch to arrest suspicious individuals—if they could find them in the dark—and to be on guard for fires. In small towns the watch was responsible to the *starosta*, in large towns, divided after 1782 into districts and wards (*kvartaly*), to the ward supervisor (*nadziratel'*), elected by the population and responsible to the sheriff. In Moscow, for instance, divided by 1785 into twenty districts and eighty-eight wards for 121 avenues and 468 streets (*pereulki*), the night watch consisted of 1,056 individuals who warmed themselves at 320 bonfires kept burning during the long winter nights. The fires also attracted those in hiding whose only alternative was to freeze to death.[43]

In addition to guard duty, these police forces broke up street fights, inspected houses and enterprises, and provided the means for the sheriff to gain extensive knowledge about the activities, financial situation, and opinions of every inhabitant. They also kept a close watch on vagrants, defined as any stranger in town without a passport. The origin of the passport, going back to 1724, was fiscal—to bind all males registered in the census to a geographical location so as to guarantee their payment of the capitation. But passports came to be required of all members of the population when they traveled, except those serving in the apparatus. They were issued in written form by landowners to their serfs for travel up to 30 kilometers, and in printed form by voevodas beyond that limit and to peasants of the treasury, by *magistraty* to registered townsmen, and, after the local government reform, by uezd treasurers. A fee had to be paid according to the length of time for which the passport was issued. Retired members of the apparatus received their passports from the agency they had served, churchmen received theirs from their bishop.[44] The passport, which contained a short physical description, thus became an instrument of absolute control over the movements of the population, vagrants being subject to immediate arrest and banishment to Siberian settlement by administrative or court order.

Such a panoply of means at the disposal of the police was supplemented by a requirement that visitors entering the town report their arrival to the sheriff or the ward supervisor and that homeowners report outsiders staying with them.[45] As long as the legitimacy of the social order was accepted, such cooperation was given. How else to explain how runaway serfs or fugitives from justice were traced and returned with such remarkable efficiency? If cooperation was not forthcoming, punitive measures were resorted to: harboring vagrants was an offense no less serious than vagrancy itself. In addition, the sheriff's office functioned as an employment agency, a clearinghouse for almost any type of construction work, and a real estate agency. There was thus hardly any activity in the town that was not immediately known to the police.[46]

The sheriff and his agents also had a hand in policing markets. This took various forms, and graft provided handsome rewards. The quality of edible commodities required supervision for reasons of public health. Prices had to be kept "just" in the medieval sense, based on a moral judgment of what a commodity ought to cost at a given time; to let the law of supply and demand operate in an economy of scarcity would have been to run the risk of food riots easily associated in the mind of the ruling class with rebellion (*bunt*). Finally, rampant fraud had to be prosecuted for similar reasons. It resulted as much from the greed of merchants—adding sand to salt, water to vodka—as from the lack of standardized weights and measures that created confusion among sellers and buyers.[47]

The sheriff was thus more than a police chief. He was the chief architect of his town, the chief medical and sanitation official, and the chief welfare provider, acting always in accordance with the instructions of the governor and the MVD. The term *police* thus remained faithful to its etymological origin— to make policy (or policey, as it was spelled in the eighteenth century) in the *politeia*, a microcosm of the national community.[48]

Police as General Administration

Although certain *prikazy* were responsible for the suppression of crime, their responsibilities had been as much judicial as preventive, and the jurisdictional overlappings so characteristic of the pre-1700 system had precluded the creation of a clear division of function. Indeed, a conception of the interdependence of functions was lacking, each task requiring the formation of a self-contained agency armed with judicial powers and collecting its own funds. The reform of 1718 took the first step toward creating a central police agency—the political police, of course, had had institutional recognition since 1696—but it was one, as we have seen, that never spread its tentacles beyond Petersburg, Moscow, and a few towns.

In the provinces, the submersion of police responsibilities in a mass of activities—punishing convicted defendants, collecting money, recruiting soldiers, and filling out countless unsystematized forms—was characteristic of the governor's and voevoda's operations. The creation of the *magistraty* was an additional step toward a broader definition of the concept of police—the maintenance of order and the provision of services—but their uneasy relationship with the voevodas prevented the crystallization of a unified concept of police administration, even in the towns. The voevodas, however, the managerial agents of the apparatus established in a few hundred towns, saw it as their primary duty to maintain order, that is, to enforce the recognition of the ruling class's dominion over the dependent population. Many sins of omission and of commission could be forgiven in Moscow, but not disobedience and disorder. They raised an ideological and political challenge, which the ruling elite always magnified into a threat to its very existence.

The local government reform of 1775 broke the unity of local administration at the uezd level and carved out a police jurisdiction for the sheriff in the town and the land captain in the countryside. At the same time, it begged the question of who would become the head of the new uezd. As a result, an incipient conflict emerged between the new police chiefs and the agencies to which the reform assigned the administration of justice and the collection of taxes. The responsibilities assigned to the police made both the sheriff and the land captain the true successors of the voevoda.

At the gubernia level the reform made it possible to retain the governor as the delegate of the government as a whole, but one whose previous responsibilities for the dispensation of justice, the collection of taxes, and the policing of his gubernia were vested in judicial and treasury chambers and the gubernia board, while he exercised a general supervision over the proper course of their operations. The governor was formally responsible to the Empress and the Senate, but in fact to the Procurator General, who concentrated in his chancery almost the entire internal administration of the realm. After the creation of the ministries, the governor's superior position among gubernia agencies increasingly became a fiction. The refusal to subordinate him to the Committee of Ministers destroyed the symmetry that the application of the reform of 1775 had gradually shaped, and his continued subordination to the ruler and the Senate became a front behind which the MVD—the Police Ministry between 1810 and 1819—transformed the governor into a delegate of the police establishment whose personal chancery inexorably drew off the substance of the gubernia board's jurisdiction and left it an empty shell. As a result, the supervisory activities of the governor on behalf of the entire government were carried out by a political manager who was first and foremost a police official. Before 1802, governors exercised their police responsibilities as part of a broad mandate to carry out government policy in their gubernia. By the 1820s, they carried out their mandate as part of their police responsibilities. General administration had become an extension of police work, and those responsibilities not specifically assigned to specialized agencies responsible to the Ministries of Justice and Finance in Petersburg became part of a residual jurisdiction over "internal affairs" exercised by the governor in his gubernia, and by sheriffs and land captains subordinated to him in towns and uezds.[49]

Imperial commands and Senate orders, as well as laws and "opinions" of the State Council, were sent directly to the gubernia board for execution. Ministerial circulars were addressed directly to the governor. They were then distributed, if appropriate, by the board among the town sheriffs and police boards as well as land captains in the uezds. Those intended for publication were tacked on posts (*stolby*) in the public squares or were forwarded to parish priests to be read in churches on Sundays, holidays, and market days. The hierarchy through which the population was informed of the government's policies was thus the police chain of command, assisted by the clergy.[50]

Governor and gubernia board in turn issued their own regulations dealing with local problems in pursuance of central government orders. In the eyes of the populace, although not of the law, these were police regulations emanating from police agencies—distinguished from courts and fiscal agencies—which issued them, compelled their execution, and took measures against violators.

Conversely, any complaints against violations of the laws, against the nonfulfillment of contractual obligations, against the nonperformance of their duties by local agencies were sent not to the courts but to the gubernia board and the governor,[51] who possessed a monopoly over the use of force in the gubernia, who commanded the garrison or a *shtatnaia komanda*, and could call in the Internal Guard for assistance. Local agencies looked to the board as the government of the gubernia; their personnel were disciplined, suspended, and committed to trial with the governor's consent. Criminal sentences did not take effect without his approval. Funds deposited in the Board of Welfare and used for the operations of schools and philanthropic institutions were under his control. Such a concentration of responsibilities affecting the security and welfare of the population, as well as the proper functioning of the entire provincial administration, in the office of a political delegate whose major concern was public security and whose authority was based on the potential use of force, identified the governing of the gubernia with the policing of its inhabitants. This becomes clear when we consider the importance of investigations and examine the methods by which decisions were carried out: it will be shown that the police played a decisive role at the beginning and the end of the administrative process.

Investigations gave the police a means to settle the fate of almost anyone without a challenge. Until 1775, judicial procedure in serious criminal cases differed little from disciplinary proceedings or, perhaps more accurately, from court-martial proceedings, and voevodas and governors detained, interrogated, and sentenced prisoners in the same offices and with the same clerks who also collected taxes, processed recruits, and examined petitions. The reform created an institutional separation of functions that at first promised to vest the investigation in the land court and the sheriff's office and the trial in the uezd court or the *magistrat*. It soon became apparent, however, that the gubernia chambers were looked upon as technical bodies, created for the purpose of trying to find the appropriate law in an increasingly confused body of contradictory and overlapping jurisprudence, and applying its letter, subject to review by the governor. It was not until the 1860s, a century later, that the role of the police was confined to gathering facts and material evidence for the use of prosecutors unconnected with the police, who questioned witnesses and drew up an indictment for submission to the trial court.[52]

Instead, the land captain and the sheriff, both members of the ruling class, were called upon to investigate crimes, most of them committed by the dependent population. Some of these investigations were initiated on frivolous grounds, for purposes of intimidation. When they investigated other members of the ruling class, the sheriff and the land captain were apt to feel pressure from the local political infrastructure enmeshed in a patronage network extending all the way to Petersburg if the suspect was a prominent nobleman, unless the crime earned universal condemnation. Once an investigation had begun, it gathered its own momentum, and dropping it on grounds of unsubstantiated charges became the equivalent of a loss of face by a superior before a subordinate. The jurisdiction of the police was so extensive that material seemingly irrelevant to the case could always be added in an attempt to prove the impossible and in the last resort to justify initiating a new investigation.[53] These considerations, together with the presumption that any suspect was guilty of something, explain the practice of leaving in a state of suspicion (*ostavlenie v podozrenie*) suspects against whom nothing incriminating had been found, in the hope that new evidence would be found in the future, thus justifying the original assumption. Such a procedure was followed in the courts as well, and acquittals were not considered respectable.[54]

The police arrested not only the primary suspects of a crime but, in addition, those it chose to consider related to it in any way, as well as village *starosty* and *vybornye* and even stewards to be kept as hostages for the good behavior and cooperation of the suspects.[55] In a society where actions were above all collective, it was natural to assume that crimes could be committed only with the knowledge and the connivance of other members of the community. Hence the emphasis on implicating others,[56] a game played by suspects seeking to dilute their own guilt and perhaps even drown their own case in a larger conspiracy, in which they would become minor defendants, and by the police, for whom the investigation became an end in itself. Hence the practice of seeking a collective judgment from the community, not so much on the suspect's culpability as on his standing, on whether his behavior was "approved." A judgment of "disapproval" was a damning piece of evidence, expressing a desire to expel the suspect from the community and justifying his banishment, whether or not he was found guilty of the crime.[57]

Once a suspect had been arrested, the police could use two drastic weapons to secure a confession, proclaimed by the Procedural Code of Military Justice—which applied also to civilians—to be the best form of proof.[58] One was preventive detention, which was such a widespread source of abuse—scores of people held in each gubernia for several years and more—that procurators were repeatedly enjoined to press the police and the courts to speed up the resolution of cases. Preventive detention, not only until the completion of the investigation but until the final confirmation of the sentence, was the most feared instrument of police power. Peasants plucked from their fields, merchants from their stores, and artisans from their shops, as well as workers without passports were thrown into a common prison for men and women, children and old people, suspects and hardened criminals, and kept indefinitely while their businesses disintegrated and their families were ruined.[59]

The second weapon was torture. Practice made a none-too-subtle distinction between torture administered by traditionally recognized methods (*pytka*) and various forms of violence, including beating prisoners with sticks (*pristrastnyi dopros* or simply *istiazaniia*). It is customary to trace the abolition of all forms of torture to the influence of Catherine II, although it did not disappear from the police arsenal, since Alexander found it necessary in September 1801 to uphold the prohibition following the discovery of a pattern of abuse in Kazan. The very mistreatment of prisoners—feeding them salted herring with vodka, for example—and their total subjection to the whims of sheriffs and land captains, who sometimes forgot to turn over cases to their successors, became, however, a form of torture more suited to an enlightened age.[60]

Whether or not a confession was obtained, the police were required to draw up an indictment—a recapitulation of the circumstances of the case and the role of the suspects. This document was crucial. Criminal procedure was written, and there were no adversary proceedings to challenge the counts of the indictment, especially if there had been a confession. The initiative therefore belonged to the court that held the indictment. This record was all too often a statement of assumptions and prejudices, lacking in consistency and written unclearly. It stacked the cards against the suspect the police wanted punished, unless the uezd judge or the criminal chamber demanded a clarification or even a new investigation.[61] In all cases, except those in which nobles were accused, the police, having determined the issue and the guilt, turned the trial into a disciplinary proceeding. The fate of nobles depended on their position in the infrastructure, with the governor possessing the decisive power. That the police covered up investigations, either because they were bribed or because influential nobles did not want them to see the light of day (bribery and patronage always softened the harshness of the system) probably explains the Senate order of February 1789 requiring all investigations—even if no suspect was found, as in the case of fire or the discovery of a corpse on the road—to be sent to the criminal chamber via the lower courts. In December 1821 governors, instead of the chambers, were made the final judge.[62]

The execution of judicial decisions was likewise vested in the police after 1775. When sentence had been passed in the criminal chamber and confirmed by the governor, it was customary to order its execution in the town or village where the crime had taken place. The purpose of the procedure was to instill fear in the evil-minded (*v strakh zlym*) and to teach a moral lesson to the community that had allowed the crime to happen.[63] The same sheriff or land captain—unless he was no longer in office after the usually long judicial delays—who had conducted the investigation was called upon to administer the penalty that his own investigation had called for.

The suspension of the death penalty in 1754 made corporal punishment the heart of the penal law. Its most severe form was the knout, administered by an executioner who was on the police staff in the gubernia capitals or was hired by the police. Other forms included whipping the bare back of a prisoner in the public square and whipping at the police station a prisoner who remained dressed. This last punishment was used extensively on peasants and townsmen, and did not require a judicial sentence but was applied as the police saw fit. The police exercised a great deal of arbitrary power in the application of corporal punishment. Whipping could be administered savagely or gently, and bribes made the difference. Whipping a prisoner with the knout was not intended to kill, but it could, and the police were not held responsible for unforeseen consequences. In addition, a knouting was usually followed by banishment to hard labor. To make convicts easily recognizable, they were mutilated by the police—their nostrils slit and letters branded on their forehead and cheeks.[64] The extent of the police's authority and of its arbitrary use thus appears in all its starkness. Members of the dependent population and noblemen without resources and connections who ran afoul of the land captain and the sheriff could without much difficulty be represented as dangerous criminals, then handed to the courts, those organs of the apparatus and agents of the ruling class, then to the governor, the highest police representative in the gubernia, and finally returned to the police for chastisement.

Civil cases, which usually involved noblemen and merchants, did not activate the repressive policy of the ruling class toward the dependent population. These parties, however, were still part of a command society in which the ruling elite led a disciplined apparatus and political infrastructure, and the better-connected and wealthier individuals laid down the law to the less fortunate. In the towns, where almost all social and economic activity was regulated to some degree by the police, decisions handed down by the *magistrat* and the civil chamber required the cooperation of the sheriff and the police chiefs in districts and wards, receptive to offers of bribes by owners of enterprises and tax farmers. In the countryside, where it was taken for granted that land captains owed their election to the support of the most influential landowners, sometimes in league with tax farmers—the two having a common interest in neutralizing the restrictive provisions of the law on producing and selling vodka—the police played a decisive role in civil procedure as well, especially in property cases, since they affected the circulation of landed property within the ruling class.

One of the most troubling problems of civil procedure was ensuring the respondent's appearance in court. The plaintiff's inability to get a response accounted for both frivolous suits and endless delays.[65] Summonses were served by the land captain—an unpleasant duty if the respondent was an influential landowner. It might be necessary to turn to the gubernia board to obtain his cooperation. Gathering evidence required the participation of the police. Once the litigants had joined battle, however, civil cases proceeded on their own, and decisions of the civil chamber did not require the governor's confirmation. Nevertheless, their execution was turned over to the police. Granting title to property that had been purchased, inherited, or obtained in a civil suit took place in two stages, separated by a 2-year interval during which the land captain played a crucial role and might even force the prospective owner to file suit all over again.[66] The very fact that the police controlled both the initial and the final stages of the judicial process, and had to be induced— usually by bribery—to do what the law required them to do, made the police, not the courts, the arbiter of disputes among members of society and between them and the apparatus. In a command society, where the law did not embody a compromise between clashing interests but expressed the will of superior over subordinate, nothing else could be expected.

The courts were not the only specialized agencies depending on the police for the execution of their decisions. Treasury chambers and uezd treasuries lacked executive agents and had to turn to sheriffs and land captains. Much of the statistical information on which the chambers depended, notably prices of commodities in uezd centers and village markets, was gathered by the police and served as the basis for negotiating contracts, especially contracts for provisioning the army. This information, collected all over the country and collated in the gubernia boards, was sent to the Provision Chancery of the army and published by the MVD. The police thus exercised a critical influence on the initial stages of one of the most important operations of the Russian government nationwide. Governors were empowered to confirm contracts negotiated in the chambers up to a certain amount.[67]

At the same time, when treasury chambers noted an accumulation of arrears in the collection of the capitation and the quitrent, they requested the police to prosecute the delinquents. Small arrears called for low-level demonstrations of force, the land captain bringing several soldiers from the *shtatnaia komanda*; larger arrears led to *dragonnades* (*ekzekutsii*), with troops from the garrison or the Internal Guard quartered in villages and behaving as they pleased until the peasants paid up. The collection of arrears not only provided indispensable assistance to the fiscal agencies, it was also a lucrative operation in which land captains perfected their practice of collecting funds illegally from the peasants.[68] It can thus be seen that the police establishment, from the minister of the interior down to several hundred sheriffs and land captains, draped in a mantle of respectability by its duty to manage "internal affairs," moved in the wake of the local government reform of 1775 and the ministerial reform of 1802 into a central position in provincial administration, controlling access to the specialized agencies and the execution of their decisions.

9

The Political Police

Policing the Ruling Elite

Despite widespread social acceptance, a command society had to place a premium on political policing—even of the ruling order. Its object was to check threats against the ruler as the source of power around which the ruling elite operated and prospered, to correct manifestations of social deviancy, and to keep intellectual life within bounds considered ideologically safe by the ruler and the political leadership at any given time.

In the political world of eighteenth-century Russia, threats to the stability of the ruling house did not come from the dependent population. The "peasant movement," about which so much has been written, reflected the inevitable tensions pervading a command society but took place within a social consensus that recognized the legitimacy of the status quo. The great peasant revolts (Bulavin's in 1707–1708 and Pugachev's in 1773–1774) were predominantly borderland phenomena, breaking out in areas where the consensus had not yet crystallized and where the extension of the heartland's social order clashed with the freewheeling ways of a frontier society.

By contrast to the dependent population, the ruling elite was a highly unstable world. Whenever the ruler initiated controversial policies arousing strong emotions, he risked destablizing the entire system. Even personal conflicts snowballed into rivalries between clans and cliques, and became a threat to the political consensus so vital to their interests. Peter I, after long years of preparation outside the formal government structure run by the tsar's relatives, the core of the ruling elite, took over the effective leadership of the government when he led his army against Azov in 1696, made an unprecedented tour of western Europe in 1697–1698, and planned military operations against Sweden. These disturbing events provided the background against which the *Preobrazhenskii Prikaz* began formal operations in January 1697.[1] Its chief became the most powerful member of the government because his exclusive responsibility for public security gave him the right to arrest any member of the elite suspected of subversive activity.

Peter's policies created a paradoxical situation in which a powerful ruler presided over a government verging on anarchy, evidenced by the personal antagonisms that flared up when he was away and the succession of reforms never brought to completion.[2] The Lopukhin family, at the very heart of the ruling elite, since one of its members was the tsar's first wife, became the center of the opposition, strengthened by the support of the church, which objected, among other things, to accepting foreign experts and sending Russians abroad for study. Other supporters of the old order were drawn to the religious dissidents persecuted by the same church. The *Preobrazhenskii Prikaz*, kept well informed by denunciations, arrested and tortured a religious elder who had written a critique of Peter's program, a *stolnik* for raising questions about who the real tsar ought to be (Peter's half brother was the co-ruler at the time), another for supporting the Schismatics and seeking to form a conspiracy to assassinate the tsar, a Kostroma landowner for insulting him.[3] The insistence of the political police on finding ramifications in every case reflected an awareness of the subterranean links binding the elite into a ruling group. The major prosecutions of the reign were, of course, the investigations of the *streltsy* uprising in 1698, conducted by the *Preobrazhenskii Prikaz*, and that of tsarevich Alexei conducted 20 years later by the Secret Chancery.[4]

The more conservative climate of Anna's reign tempered some of those disputes, yet it is known, perhaps unfairly, as one of the most repressive reigns in modern Russian history. Two sources of instability poisoned the political atmosphere among the ruling group. The scars left by the battle of 1730 remained fresh. The Dolgorukovs had falsified the will of a boy emperor in order to usurp the throne and establish for all practical purposes a Dolgorukov dynasty, and Dmitri Golitsyn had contributed his share to a harebrained constitutional scheme, influenced by foreign ideas and certain to create anarchy among a ruling elite used to a discipline that restrained ambition but licensed the urge to power over subordinates.[5]

The second source of instability was the existence of a rival claimant to the throne who was a cousin of the empress and a daughter of Peter's second wife. Elizabeth became what Alexei had been during Peter's reign, a focus of potentially dangerous opposition. The result was the creation of a highly charged atmosphere in which innocuous remarks created political cases, and rivals denounced their opponents to the Secret Chancery in order to remove them from the scene.[6] A similar situation prevailed during the latter part of Elizabeth's reign, when the Secret Chancery maintained a constant surveillance over the heir to the throne and his wife, the future Catherine II. What strikes the student of the role of the political police during that period is that its operations were not so much directed by the ruler against political opposition to the Romanov house—there was hardly any because dynasty and ruling remained bound by a common interest—as it was used by ambitious politicians to eliminate their opponents in a never-ending power play that often destroyed outstanding individuals while keeping the system inviolate.[7]

Catherine's reign was politically stable, despite some uncertainties at the beginning, but the growing presence of Grand Duke Paul behind the scenes attracted those discontented with his mother's policies. His reign was marked less by a recrudescence of political prosecutions than by the wholesale dismissal of members of the elite and the promotion of others into it.[8] That his policies resembled a frontal attack on its privileges explains why a conspiracy could form against him under the leadership of Petersburg's chief of police and with the knowledge of his own son, the future tsar.

The uncertainty over the succession, despite the tragicomedy of December 1825, ended for the remainder of the imperial period with the reign of Catherine; so did the disruptive tug-of-war between factions seeking a return to Muscovite ways and those supporting a Western orientation. On the other hand, the enormous growth of the apparatus, the weakening of the network of families that had governed Russia since the 1680s, and the reassertion of the ruler's authority vis-à-vis the ruling elite created a new situation. Distrust and secrecy had always been the endemic plague of the system; they now became institutionalized as the ministerial empires began to take shape. Disputes over policies—toward Napoleonic France, the Continental System, the march to Paris after the liberation of Russia, the crackdown on the optimists who believed in the early "liberal" promises of the tsar, fiscal measures affecting the interest of the ruling class—could no longer crystallize into an opposition gathered around a leader. The tsar had no children, and his brothers were not politically active. This explained the tsar's confidence, in the face of evidence that dissatisfaction was spreading and unrest threatening, that no supragovernmental agency of political police was necessary[9]—and why his brother, who had to pay the price of Alexander's negligence, created the Third Section, a latter-day version of the *Preobrazhenskii Prikaz*.

Retribution for offending the ruler and for violating the unwritten rules of political behavior within the charmed circle of the ruling elite was swift and harsh. Political investigations, usually conducted with the generous application of torture, often resulted in the death of the accused. Such was the case, for example, of the Lopukhin brothers, relatives of the tsar's first wife, in 1694 and 1698. Others were formally indicted and tried by handpicked members of the elite, sitting as a high court, sentenced to death, and executed. Peter's son and only heir was treated by such a court, consisting of 126 members, but died from his tortures before the death sentence could be carried out.[10] In these cases, Peter acted as the patrimonial head of the ruling house, dispensing favors and punishments among his relatives, ordering the execution of his brother-in-law Avraam Lopukhin and the banishment of his uncle Semën Naryshkin to Arkhangelsk in 1718.[11]

Nevertheless, resort to the high courts reflected the fact that political trials were not only an expression of the ruler's will but an outcome of elite politics. Petr Tolstoi, for example, nephew of the Ivan Miloslavskii whose corpse was exhumed and desecrated at the order of a tsar who could not forget and forgive the humiliations he had suffered as a child, became the relentless pursuer of Tsarevich Alexei, the son of a Lopukhina related to the Naryshkins, the enemies of the Miloslavskiis. He asked for a high rank as a reward, the Cross of Saint Andrew, and the estates of Avraam Lopukhin.[12] Cynicism was the rule among members of the elite, who passed sentence on their former friends and colleagues for selfish purposes. The proceedings of the high courts of the first half of the eighteenth century were animated by the partisan spirit of families eager to get on the victors' bandwagon, whenever a change of rulers or good fortune and political footwork brought another family into the ruler's inner circle. They were also as often as not the result of a collective reflex on the part of a ruling elite turning against its own members who had deviated from the established path.

During Anna's reign the high courts were called "general assemblies" because they consisted of the cabinet ministers, senators, general officers (*generalitet*), admirals (*flagmany*), presidents, and some members of colleges. The elite on active duty was thus called upon to judge one of its equals. One such "assembly" of twenty members tried Dmitrii Golitsyn in January 1737, another two sentenced four Dolgorukovs and Artemii Volynskii to death in October 1739 and June 1740, respectively, a fourth headed by the procurator general, Nikita Trubetskloi, sat in judgment of Andrei Osterman in January 1742. The death sentences on Golitsyn and Osterman were later commuted, one to life imprisonment, the other to banishment to northern Siberia.[13]

Greater stability in elite politics resulting from the withering away of hatreds going back to the 1680s and the settlement of the succession question—the three chief counts against Osterman accused him of attempts at interfering with it—put an end to political trials by high courts. Radishchev was tried in the regular courts, Paul resorted to dismissals from the apparatus, and Alexander banished Speranskii.

While the ruler's personal security grew with each new reign until it became virtually unassailable because of the disappearance of legitimate rivals—this, paradoxically, at a time when the dynasty had become "germanized"—the expansion of the ruling elite that sustained his power required that he be kept informed of the moods, the ambitions, and the dissatisfactions of its members, as well as of their marriages and alliances that determined its texture and shaped its configuration.

Gathering information on the relatives of the very close family circle governing Russia at the end of the seventeenth century had been an easy task, all the more so since the bitter feuds pitting relatives of Peter's two wives produced a stream of rumors and denunciations. It is unlikely that the *Preobrazhenskii Prikaz* had to seek information on a regular basis about moods and activities at the court and in the government—the two still overlapped to a considerable extent—since the information was so liberally supplied.[14]

Relationships with the ruling elite became more subtle and more complex after Peter's death and Anna's coronation. There were in fact two courts. European governments had established diplomatic relations with the new Russian Empire, and their diplomats eagerly sought access to centers of influence and sources of information. Leading figures at Anna's court were not Russians but Germans raised in the Baltic provinces and even abroad. On the other hand, the victory of the Saltykovs under Anna and that of the Naryshkins under her successor Elizabeth paved the way for the reconciliation of these two core families and calmed the turbulent waters of elite politics. The adoption of favorites brought in ambitious outsiders representing important constituencies—the Baltic Germans in the 1730s, the Ukrainians in the 1750s, the polonized Smolensk *shliakhta* in the 1780s—all with a political agenda and a concept of empire.[15]

It is possible that a more elaborate and consistent surveillance of the apparatus began under Anna, at Osterman's instigation and with the active participation of the Secret Chancery. The existence of a de facto prime minister until the end of Catherine's reign, and especially during Prince Viazemskii's tenure, favored such a development. So did the continued existence of a Secret Chancery subordinated not to the Senate like most other governmental agencies but to the ruler alone. The relative weakness of the empresses, enmeshed in a growing network of interrelated families, compelled them to feel the pulse of the ruling elite before embarking on any new policy. Catherine's conversation with her secretary Vasilii Popov, not intended for publication and self-glorification like her correspondence with Voltaire, is remarkable for the frankness with which the "autocrat" confessed her dependence on the elite, euphemistically called "the enlightened part of the people."[16] Seeking its support with "prudence and circumspection" took the form not only of private discussions and listening to debates in her council but also keeping a discreet watch on the conversations and contacts of various individuals.

A helpful if not always reliable source of information was the interception of the mail. In a world without a partisan press, let alone a free press, gathering information outside of regular administrative channels was becoming a major problem by the reign of Catherine. Opening private and diplomatic correspondence was almost the only substitute. When some correspondents suspected their mail was being opened, the practice provided an opportunity to inform the ruler about developments she should know about. By the 1780s, one of Catherine's secretaries, Alexander Khrapovitskii, inspected the mail regularly once or twice a week, on the arrival or before the departure of the postal fourgon. One could thus learn, for example, that Potemkin might have plans to carve out of the lands acquired from Poland a separate principality independent of both Russia and Poland.[17]

Alexander's assertion of autocratic power, built on military support and facilitated by a prolonged military conflict the like of which had not been seen since the Northern War of 1700–1721, made it nonetheless of crucial importance that the ruler not lose the support of the ruling elite. The tsar did not yet know that a commander in chief of his army could be imposed upon him, as would occur with Kutuzov in 1812.[18] Yet as early as 1807 he found it necessary to defend himself against reproaches by Fedor Rostopchin, the future Governor-General of Moscow, that he had forgotten that the "wellborn nobility" was the support of the throne, and asked Rostopchin to keep him informed about the causes of the supposedly general contempt of "the people" for government and the laws.[19]

The interception of mail continued, carried out by the directors of the post offices in Petersburg and Moscow, responsible to the MVD and later to a separate chief, Alexander Golitsyn, the former Minister of Education and chief of censorship in the empire. Intercepted letters were copied, then forwarded to their addressee, and their contents were reported to the chief of the tsar's chancery, Arakcheev, and after 1815 to the chief of His Majesty's Main Staff as well, enabling these two close lieutenants of the tsar at the head of the civilian and military apparatus to gauge the mood of "public opinion." They may have been amused to read that Petr Chaadaev resigned from the service in 1821 and refused to become the tsar's aide-de-camp in order to show his contempt for people who despised everyone else, and especially for Vasilchikov, the "stupidly arrogant" commander of the (old) Imperial Guard.[20]

Meanwhile, it is clear that steps had been taken to provide the ruler with regular and systematic reports on the attitude of the ruling elite toward the government. These reports were prepared in the Ministry of Police between 1810 and 1819 and may have originated in the MVD afterward. One such report covering the period from August 1818 to May 1819 informed the tsar, who was abroad, that "society" was displeased with manifestations of "Teutonic Jacobinism" among German youth, was tired of war, and expected changes in internal administration, including greater coordination of governmental activities in the tsar's chancery. The report continued with a blistering denunciation of the ministers: the Minister of Education lived in "a fog of Western mysticism," the MVD's "fabrikomania"—a reference to his policy of developing native industry—was only less disastrous than the Finance Minister's laissez-faire policy, to which "public opinion" was "unanimously" opposed; the Minister of Justice had to make "much noise" to remind the public of his ministry's existence; the former (and next) MVD, Kochubei, a Ukrainian of Tatar origin, would wear any coat (*kaftan*) except a Russian one; and the Petersburg Governor-General's military ardor and rashness had finally been tamed by the "heavy dreariness" of chancery work.[21] These were sharp comments indeed about individuals whom the tsar had chosen and some of whom he would have to let go during the next 4 years. We also know that dissatisfaction among the ruling elite was so widespread that the same commander of the Imperial Guard received the tsar's approval in January 1821 to create a secret police to check on guardsmen. Although the tsar remained reluctant to take further action, it is obvious that a reaction was taking place within the ruling elite leading to the formation of the consensus on which Nicholas I would base his iron rule.

The emergence of the police as a source of information supplementing the rumors and petty gossip of busybodies and timeservers was a development of doubtful value for the ruler. If it gave him access to systematic information at regular intervals, it also put him at the mercy of those who compiled the reports, clients of patrons engaged in the politics of the elite, themselves embodying its moods, tensions, and yearnings. Their authors even succeeded in pressing the tsar to act against his better judgment and issue orders with which he disagreed in principle.[22] They destroyed his trust in people and suggested replacements whose policies were more in line with the general interests of the ruling elite at a particular time. In the peculiar conditions of Russian political life in the decade after 1815, when the tsar was often abroad or away, these reports acquired added influence from the fact that there was no way to check them.

Policing the Rest of Society

Any consideration of the policing of Russian society outside the ruling elite must begin with an assumption that it was not simply a matter of police agencies thrusting their agents into the midst of a refractory milieu. Mme Vigée Lebrun's comment at the end of the eighteenth century—that everybody's words and actions were watched to such an extent that there may have been no social circle without a spy[23]—testified no less to the efficiency of the police than to an unconscious acceptance of the need to be policed, reflecting the continuing symbiosis between the rulers and the ruled at all levels of the command society. Police agents, like fish in water and guerillas in towns and countryside, cannot operate without a life-supporting environment. The very nature of Russian society—the refusal to recognize man's dual allegiance, the subjugation of the individual to the collective, and the abject recognition of authority—facilitated police work by integrating the bearers of the ruling class's authority into the world of the dependent population. It was thus assumed that the behavior of individual members of the community of believers was rightly a matter of concern to the agents of authority as much as to the community at large.

The method by which the police was made aware of threats, real or imaginary, to public security was the denunciation. It was so common that it was taken for granted that anyone could denounce anyone else at any time. Trefolev, who examined the files of the Iaroslavl *magistrat* in the 1750s, discovered hundreds of names of accusers who had denounced their relatives and friends for a variety of faults, some trivial, some serious, and for purposes ranging from the acceptable (denouncing enemies of the social and political order) to the crass (getting rid of business rivals or personal enemies).[24] With the social and political order sanctioned by the religious ideology of a community of believers, any denunciation might become a political case. If it did not become one, it was either by chance or because the police were reluctant to take advantage of the opportunity. Denunciations were also anonymous, and the accused had no right to face his accusers. Increasingly, these denunciations fell out of favor. That they continued to be accepted, however, appears from the resolution of the Committee of Ministers of March 1818 confirming earlier legislation declaring them null and void.[25]

Overtly political denunciations were referred to until 1762 as cases involving the "sovereign's word and deed" (*gosudarevo slovo i delo*), a term already used in the *Ulozhenie* of 1649. Such cases brought before a Moscow *prikaz* had to be forwarded to the *Preobrazhenskii Prikaz* for final disposition, subject to the ruler's approval. Voevodas were required to do likewise, although they were given some freedom of action from time to time in view of the central agency's inability to process all such denunciations. Drunkenness was usually considered a sufficient mitigating circumstance for the voevoda to drop the case.[26] Nevertheless, it remained general policy throughout the eighteenth century and again during Nicholas I's reign—when gendarmes with blank forms authorizing them to send the suspect to the Third Section had only to fill in the suspect's name[27]—that suspects arrested on the basis of political denunciations had to be sent to the capital, where the investigation and punishment took place outside the normal procedural channels. If the declaration was made by a defendant in a criminal case, it suspended all proceedings and saved him from sentencing for his crime or from the penalty if he had been sentenced.[28]

"Word and deed" cases were usually those in which the ruler's dignity or safety, or the security of the ruling elite—rebellion, for example—were involved. The police prosecuted those who called Peter I the Antichrist and circulated rumors that the great tsar ate meat during Lent—and had he not killed his son, who was a true son of the Orthodox church? It was not more acceptable to tell the apocryphal story that the empress Anna had begged the tsar in vain not to marry her off to a "non-Christian *busurman*" prince but to a Russian general or boyar. Those who did not cross themselves in church when Elizabeth's name was read by the bishop were denounced by fellow parishioners, and a landowner was denounced by his domestic for telling his friends that Elizabeth was illegitimate and not a native (*prirodnaia*) princess. To object to the rule of a woman, whether Elizabeth or Catherine II, and to say "we have a lot of Catherines in Russia" was enough to bring the culprits before the Secret Chancery or its successor.[29]

The police needed volunteers to ferret out secret meetings of people who collected money and "preached," like the unfortunate ascetics who practiced self-mutilation in 1733 and had a network of supporters in various monasteries,[30] or of people like the future Decembrists, who plotted major changes in the political system.

Some political denunciations involved witchcraft.[31] Someone had been given a powder that, if spread on the ground where Elizabeth walked, would damage her feet. More serious, perhpas, were accusations that a copyist had skipped the "Her" in Her Majesty; that another had cut the word *imperatritsa* (empress) in two, carrying over *atritsa* to the next line; that a peasant had shown disrespect to a tax receipt bearing the imperial title.[32] This voodoo behavior,[33] attributing to an inanimate object the life of its subject, attracted the serious interest of the Secret Chancery. Other accusations were made to discredit and eliminate individuals in the apparatus, and investigations sometimes went back an entire decade to trace those unpunished offenses.

It is easy to imagine that if such denunciations were believed by those who made them, they were also made at times for purposes other than those for which they were intended. The abuses were so rampant that steps were taken at the very beginning of Catherine's reign to limit the damage caused to innocent people who could be influential: the former grand duchess had gone through the hard school of elite politics for more than a decade. These denunciations were often made by uprooted individuals. Indeed, the frenzy of denunciations during the first half of the eighteenth century must be seen in the context of a society shaken by 20 years of war during Peter's reign and reeling from the fiscal crisis of the 1730s. It was also a reflection at all levels of the anxiety pervading the elite during the same period and the ruling class as a whole until its demobilization in the 1760s.

Abuses took various forms and showed how blurred was the distinction between political and nonpolitical denunciations. Peasant and domestics denounced their owners, merchants their rivals, borrowers their creditors, and all too often clerics denounced other clerics to settle accounts with persons they disliked. A woman accused of theft alleged that those she had robbed had said that the grand duchesses lived in sin with singers of the court's choir and bore them children. A peasant dismissed by a cook of the court denounced him for spreading a rumor that the Swedes had stolen away the tsar. Accusers were sometimes tortured in the Secret Chancery to ascertain whether they told the truth; knowing this, Old Believers waited for religious holidays to denounce other Orthodox and used their tortures to satisfy their masochistic yearnings. Prisoners sentenced to the knout and soldiers to run the gauntlet seeking to avoid the execution of their sentences shouted "word and deed" and denounced anyone, only to get a reprieve. A townsman actually did this to stop the search of his house by the police! Children were taught by their mothers this simple and dishonorable performance[34]—evidence of the broad acceptance of the consensus and a willingness to play by its implicit rules.

Finally, exclaiming "word and deed" was resorted to in cases having nothing to do with policing society: it was a convenient way to gain the attention of someone in the central government. When a quarrel broke out in 1720 between the abbot of a Kazan monastery and his bishop, the bishop denounced the abbot to the Synod, which ordered an investigation, whereupon the abbott declared, "Word and deed," knowing that his case automatically would be sent to Moscow, where he expected to get a fairer hearing. There he denounced his bishop for tearing up petitions addressed to the ruler. The move backfired, but the intent was clear.[35] In the same year a prospector discovered copper deposits in the Urals and took ore samples to the voevoda, who refused to recognize his claim. The prospector went to the public square, shouted "Word and deed" for all to hear, and was sent to the *Preobrazhenskii Prikaz*, where he stated his case. He was then referred to the College of Mining, which gave him a patent.[36]

This pernicious climate was aggravated by a collective mentality that did not recognize the existence of solitary actions. The police always assumed there were accomplices, and Muscovite law often imposed collective punishments on the same assumption. Petrine legislation warned "those who knew but did not denounce" that they would be punished with the same severity as the wrong-doer.[37] This created an impetus to denounce among those who would not otherwise have done so. A monk once heard a drunken tailor say that a bishop had upbraided the tsar for wanting to take away the relics from the Kiev Monastery of the Caves. The monk thought the remark innocent enough, but since it had been made at a party he concluded that it would be reported by someone else and that he would be blamed for not being the first to report it. The tailor, sent to the *Preobrazhenskii Prikaz*, got twenty-three lashes of the knout.[38]

The manifesto of February 1762—repeated verbatim in October—abolished the Secret Chancery and prohibited in the strongest terms the use of the expression "word and deed."[39] But, necessity being the mother of invention, a new expression was substituted: the accuser was said to have a "secret" to tell.[40] This strategem, along with the establishment of the Secret Expedition, seemed to mean that little of substance had changed. Nevertheless, the strong feelings of the empress against unsupported denunciations, the reduction of tensions within the ruling elite, and the local government reform from which the ruling class and the merchantry derived considerable benefits seem to have reduced the flow of denunciations. The ruling class, from then on solidly implanted in the countryside, possessed agencies capable of distinguishing between frivolous denunciations and those deserving prosecution. Accusers could no longer obtain the automatic transfer of their case to Petersburg; cases arising from political denunciations began to be referred to the new local courts. In 1801, the manifesto abolishing the Secret Expedition specifically instructed the police to refer all such denunciations to the courts, there to be treated as state crimes punishable under the provisions of the penal law.[41] The consolidation of the dynasty and the social order gave the ruling class in town and countryside the opportunity to monitor locally those expressions of tensions within society that did not contain the clear expression of a political challenge.

Interrogators in the *Preobrazhenskii Prikaz* or the Secret Chancery used torture. Since torture was ordered by governors and voevodas in the normal course of investigations, the methods used by the central agency of political police were not unusual. In one respect, however, the procedure in the Secret Chancery before 1754 could be considered anomalous. At a time when governors and voevodas freely imposed death sentences—so much of the penal law consisted of capital crimes—the standard punishment in the chancery seems to have been the knout, followed by release or banishment. After 1754, when the death penalty was suspended, punishments meted out in the chancery no longer differed from those imposed by gubernia chanceries.

After the abolition of torture in the 1760s, the Secret Expedition acquired the sinister reputation of being the only agency where torture was still liberally applied, under the eyes of the enlightened empress who had banished it from the police agencies and the courts created by the reform.[42] There was thus a link between the abolition of the Secret Expedition in 1801 and Alexander's order that governors and criminal chambers instruct the police and the lower courts to observe the prohibition against torture. One justified the other, and the abolition of torture led to the demise of the Secret Expedition, with the MVD and the governors assuming full jurisdiction for the repression of subversive behavior. Moreover, the creation of the courts had separated the investigation from the trial, while sentences in the expedition had been imposed by administrative order. A further difference, of course, was in the fact that sentences passed on members of the dependent population were carried out upon confirmation by the governor, while decisions of the Expedition had been submitted to the ruler's approval. The Expedition had thus increasingly appeared as an archaic holdover of an administrative system thoroughly transformed by the local government reform.

Denunciations were not only the means by which countless individuals in the apparatus, the political infrastructure, and among the dependent population cooperated with the police in exposing anyone expressing opinions insulting or antagonistic to the person of the ruler, the imperial family, and the ruling elite; they also provided a vital source of information about prevailing popular sentiments. Tsar Peter was strongly given to understand that in the eyes of his people a policy of westernization was an apostasy that rendered his rule illegitimate and a threat to the integrity of his realm, however mitigated by his victories over the *busurmany* and other enemies of Christ. The empresses must have feared that dissatisfied elements in the ruling elite might find support among a population that resented seeing women on the throne and had occasional "visions" of their impending demise.[43] At a time when the politics of the realm was confined to the politics of the ruling elite, such information was used to exacerbate suspicions and magnify tensions within the ruling group. There was little concern about provincial society's opinion of government policies because such a "society" barely existed, the settlement of property disputes among the ruling class was concentrated in Moscow, and the only form of cooperation expected from the dependent population was the payment of taxes and delivery of services.

However, a political infrastructure in town and countryside developed steadily after 1760; commercial relations were extended, with ensuing rivalries among nobleman, merchant, and peasant; and a small educated constituency emerged in distant provinces that had only recently bordered on the nomadic world: Karamzin and Dmitriev came from Simbirsk, Derzhavin from Kazan, Bolotov from Tula. These developments coincided with the stabilization of elite politics to create an awareness that a provincial society existed and that the government could not afford to neglect it. This society had given expression to its yearnings and frustrations in its *nakazy* to the 1767 Legislative Commission, in which regional differences were already apparent.[44] The concentration of power in ministries based in distant Petersburg threatened by 1825 to cut off the ruling house and the government from a provincial society from which it derived its legitimacy and the source of its power. The necessity to maintain a command structure within a community of believers, in an age of growth and distention that spread doubts and subverted unconditional obedience, required the development of a more active policy to gather information and repress dissent.

Denunciations continued to play a major role. The government remained ambivalent about their value. Many of these were animated by the spirit of revenge and hatred, but many more reflected the cooperation between ruling class and dependent population, between authority and obedience, between the individual and the collective. Denunciations were called for and rewarded to combat counterfeiting, bootlegging, smuggling, and the harboring of vagrants.[45] They were naturally even more welcome in the struggle against dissidence. Informers remained the extension of a vastly undermannd police apparatus incapable of penetrating on its own the labyrinthine world of popular moods and intellectual dissent.

This cooperation between the police and society made the governor and the MVD the channels through which popular opinion expressed itself and in turn was repressed. The extensive jurisdiction of the police, with which we are now familiar, made it easy to collect information from a wide variety of sources. The police, like the government as a whole, had been largely passive in the eighteenth century, waiting to receive information in the form of denunciations before taking action it considered politically justified. Now it began to probe public opinion, with the help of eager informers, listening to conversations in clubs and gatherings, infiltrating religious and ethical societies, assessing the influence of new books. Conversely, intellectuals, noblemen, and townsmen, deprived of a free press, used police channels to bring grievances to the attention of the government. A secret society was even formed in the 1810s to create an "avenging" (*karaiushchee*) public opinion, bent on spreading word of "vulgar, evil, and unjust acts" far and wide until informers reported them to the police.[46]

To supplement this eager cooperation the police continued to open the mail. This practice may have been limited to Petersburg and Moscow in the late eighteenth century: it was understood that a general practice of opening private correspondence in the post offices of the gubernia capitals would be detrimental to the development of commerce.[47] But we know that the minister of police ordered governors by circular after the war of 1812 to obtain letters of "suspicious" persons from these post offices and send them to the ministry. After 1819 the Postal Administration continued the practice and learned, for example, that a petitioner needed 1,000 rubles to bribe a Senate secretary, that duels were taking place in Moscow, and that a corps of cadets was a prison where children were tortured.[48] The appointment of gendarme officers beginning in 1817 crowned a policy of systematic information gathering that bore fruit during the reign of Nicholas I. Not only had police agencies acquired a central position in provincial administration by 1825, they had also become the focal point of popular attitudes toward the government. The minister of police and the MVD became in turn the interpreters of those attitudes to the ruler, relaying thoughts safe for him to hear. These police reports thus created either a false sense of security or an exaggerated perception of danger, and perpetuated, paradoxically, the blindness to the real conditions of Russia that they were supposed to correct.

Policing the Printed Word

Policing the ruling elite and the rest of society, as we have seen, was a form of self-policing rather than the imposition of political surveillance by an almighty tsar on reluctant subjects. The same must be said about policing the printed word. One detects the same complicity and connivance between the police and those who were policed, the same consensus that ideological dogma, political authority, and social conformity not be challenged. This was not surprising, however. Thinking individuals, when carried away by the compelling power of reason, could not forget that they incarnated a culture that equated free thinking with apostasy and treason.

It was symptomatic that the first application of censorship was made to protect ideological purity. It was a basic tenet of the Russian church that the truth handed down by church councils and embodied in dogma and practice was indivisible, inviolate, and not subject to dialectical interpretation—hence the ignorance of the ideological establishment and it uncompromising defense of the status quo. Printing presses were rare and were often seen as an "unwelcome foreign guest."[49] After the printing presses of Kiev and Chernigov in the Ukraine refused to seek the imprimatur of the Russian patriarch for their books, they were forbidden in 1720 to print without the approval of Moscow, so that there would be no disagreements with "the Eastern Church and Great Russian policy (*pechat'*)." The Statute of January 1721 on the administration of the Russian church required the Synod to exercise preliminary censorship to prevent the distribution of "sinful violations" (*pogresheniia*) of Orthodox teaching.[50]

Meanwhile, the import of foreign books was permitted in 1700, subject to the proviso that they be useful and that they not denigrate the majesty (*prevysokaia chest'*) of the ruler and the greatness (*slava*) of Russia. The introduction of civil type (*shrift*) in 1704 established a permanent distinction between secular books printed on secular presses and religious books printed on the Synod's press. By the late 1720s there were only three printing outlets: the Synod's, the Senate's for the printing of laws and decrees, and that of the Academy of Sciences for everything else.[51] This distinction created the necessity for procedures to police the printing of books to insure they would not deviate from both religious and political orthodoxy.

Censoring secular books was easy under Peter because there were so few books, most of them of a technical nature, and the tsar read them all, correcting only "unfriendly" (*neprigozhie*) words and expressions. By the 1730s we find the first manifestation of ex post facto censorship—the seizure of material criticizing the "Germans" in the government and of Polish calendars circulating in the Ukraine in 1739 for containing "unfriendly passages on the future" (*nepristoinye passazhi o prognostikakh*) of the Russian Empire—a case that also attracted the attention of the Secret Chancery. By the 1740s, censorship became more alert, a response to the spread of Western books and the subversive effect of the critical thought of the Enlightenment as well as a manifestation of the rising influence of the church, cowed under Peter and Anna but triumphant under Elizabeth.[52]

It was then that the dilemma between the useful and the ideologically acceptable began to be felt. Books on naval science, fortification, and medicine were useful, but they could not be studied profitably without astronomical observations, mathematical tables, and anatomical studies—all anathema to the bishops, who feared with good reason that they would strike at the foundations of religion and, by extension, of the political order. Such scientific data were thus banned from the printed page in December 1754. Studying ancient Egypt and Rome might well inspire Russians to attempt great deeds and advance their own empire, but comparing Anna or Elizabeth with Cleopatra and Messalina was an unfriendly act against the person of the ruler. It even became dangerous to praise too highly the beauty of an Italian actress, lest Elizabeth take umbrage.[53] Yet such fears did not impede book publishing. The flooding of official presses by the 1750s with private orders for the publication of literary works they were not equipped to handle compelled the government to consider allowing private presses. Under such conditions, a project for a history of Russia could be carried out only in the Academy of Sciences, where the ugly fight between Mikhail Lomonosov and Gerhard Müller showed that "denunciations were already riding high on the crest of heated patriotism."[54] Censorship was assigned to the chancery of the Academy or individual academicians, as when two mathematicians were appointed by its president, the Ukrainian Kirill Razumovskii, to censor Alexander Sumarokov's *Busy Bee* (*Trudoliubivaia Pchela*). More often than not, it was the joint work of a "collective editorship" of academicians and members of the ruling elite, who sometimes interpreted the requirements of political orthodoxy with more tolerance and understanding that the writers themselves,[55] who competed with one another in denouncing the subversive ideas of their rivals. That Lomonosov should be known as eighteenth-century Russia's greatest scientist as well as poet and censor[56] speaks volumes about the tacit alliance between intellectual inquiry and self-censorship.

The reign of Elizabeth is also known for a first attempt to rewrite history. An order was issued in October 1742 to return for "editing" (*perepravlenie*) all books printed between October 17, 1740, and November 25, 1741—the reign of Anna Leopoldovna, considered a usurper. Religious books were to be sent to the Synod, secular books to the Academy of Sciences, from which they would then be sent back to their owners after comments unfavorable to Elizabeth were removed. It took 8 years for the order to take effect, but the response was so great in 1750 that the order was suspended, as the presses found themselves unable to cope with the number of books returned.[57]

The empress Catherine was a German by birth, whose infatuation with Voltaire had not yet taught her in the 1760s that the application of reason to human affairs was incompatible with the preservation of dogma and the doctrine of autocratic infallibility. This would later become the root of the tragic misunderstanding with Nikolai Novikov. The first 20 years of her reign reflected the glowing victories over the great Frederick on the eve of the coup and Rumiantsev's shining success on the banks of the Danube: enthusiasm and arrogance could blind a monarch to the danger of subversion. Both the ruling elite and the empress embarked on an unprecedented policy of *glasnost'*, allowed a periodical press, supported a broad program of translating foreign books and articles from the *Encyclopedie*, and allowed the import of foreign books, except those directed against ideology, good manners, the ruler, and the "Russian nation." The first private press was allowed in 1771, but only to print foreign books. Five years later, two German booksellers were authorized to set up a press to print books in Cyrillic but were forbidden to sell Cyrillic type to private persons. Another 7 years later, in January 1783, presses were declared a form of private enterprise no longer subject to government regulation. They began to sprout all over the country, as far as Penza and Tambov, where a Rakhmaninov specialized in printing the collected works of Voltaire.[58]

This was not to say that censorship had been lifted. It was no longer vested in the Synod, the Academy of Sciences, and Moscow University (established in 1755) but in the police boards created by the Police Code of 1782, made up of nearly illiterate people who were given no instructions on how to proceed with their new duties.[59] The policy may have loosened the grip of censorship by decentralizing it, enabling authors to shop for presses in gubernia capitals where the sheriffs were known to be more tolerant, indifferent, or susceptible to bribes. It may also have made publication depend on the arbitrary approval of the local delegates of the ruling elite, the governors and governors-general.

Reaction was not long in coming, and it began in Moscow, the old capital, guardian of Russia's political and ideological heritage, where Alexander Brius was appointed governor-general in 1784. Brius, the great-grandson of a Scot, was the son of a Dolgorukova, from a family distinguished by its arrogance and its piety, and he was known as a haughty and dour individual. Brius became the spokesman for those segments of the elite who felt that Catherine's policy was a betrayal of Russian tradition, as indeed it was.

A nascent Russian literature was welcome because it added to the greatness of Russia among European nations, but tragedy remained unacceptable. When Nikolai Nikolev's tragedy *Sorena and Zamir* was staged in Moscow in 1785, Brius objected to certain lines expressing the ruler's pride and other faults, and spearheaded an opposition to the play that took the empress by surprise and forced its closing. In 1794 Brius's successor, Alexander Prozorovskii, whose sister-in-law was another Dolgorukova, ordered the burning of Karamzin's translation of Shakespeare's *Julius Caesar*.[60]

If exposing the hubris and tragic flow of a foreign king or queen struck at the heart of the political creed of the ruling elite—a point Novikov seems to have missed in his undisguised baiting of Catherine—the expression of autonomous tendencies at home was intolerably damaging to the unity of leadership in a command society. Brius followed his attack on the hapless Nikolev with a frontal assault on the Freemasons and especially on one of their branches, the Martinists. These lay people, inspired by mystical books, were dedicating themselves to the service of society, to teaching and preaching outside the formal structures established by the ruling elite and even in opposition to its considered policy. Some Martinists belonged to the ruling elite, notably Nikolai Repnin, an impetuous military commander with broad ties in the army and a devotee of Grand Duke Paul, who was waiting impatiently for his mother to die. Others belonged to the new intellectual community—a recent and disturbing phenomenon in Russian history—linking members of the ruling class and the dependent population in a common endeavor to criticize, denigrate, and challenge the primacy of power. Masons also believed in secrecy, and secrecy served as a wall against denunciations from within and police prying from without. To these two cardinal political sins, which denied two fundamental tenets of Russian political life, the Masons added a third—their subordination to Swedish Masonry—the recognition of a supranational authority being tantamount to treason.[61]

In 1784 the empress forbade the printing in Moscow of a history of the Jesuit order, which she had taken under her protection—cynicism makes strange bedfellows. Its author, Novikov, became the prime target in the counteroffensive against the Masons. In 1786 Brius carried out an inspection of all hospitals and schools run in Moscow by Masons, whom he referred to as a "gang of new schismatics (*skopishche izvestnogo novogo raskola*)—a typical fusion of political and religious terminology. In 1787 all books considered Masonic propaganda were ordered withdrawn from circulation, but not before copies of some 313 titles were burned in Moscow under the eyes of an Orthodox clergy unruffled by the destruction of Psalters, prayer books, and admonitions of the Holy Fathers, together with French and German grammar books. An ideology that is not subjected to dialectical interpretation becomes a mere justification for the exercise of unrestrained power. The spectacle of Novikov, suffering the symptoms of a heart attack at the time of his arrest in April 1792 by a relative of Adam Olsuf'ev—one of the finest and best-educated members of the ruling elite—but denied permission to confess and take communion (was his political offense not a sin as well?) was brutal but eloquent testimony of the alliance of politics and religion. His arrest was followed by the burning of more than 18,000 books in Novikov's warehouse.[62]

Criticism of the social order was likewise a threat to the legitimacy of the ruling elite. If serfdom reached its apogee during Catherine's reign, it also met its first challenges, on both practical and ethical grounds. Alexander Radishchev was a member of the elite, and his *Journey from St. Petersburg to Moscow* a challenge to the legitimacy of its rule. He was thus a traitor to his class. In 1790 his confession of error (*zabluzhdenie*)—the term implies a conviction that one has sinned—his recognition that censorship was necessary to save people from their erroneous beliefs, and his repentance did not save him from the prosecuting zeal of Brius, now governor-general of Petersburg, and the enlightened empress's vindictiveness.[63] All this, it must be emphasized, took place before the outbreak of the French Revolution or at any rate before its implications became obvious. The elite's reaction, in which Platon Zubov and the Ukrainian Alexander Bezborodko took an active part, continued into the 1790s and led to the creation of censorship agencies in September 1796 and the closing of the private presses.[64] Thus ended an unprecedented experiment with *glasnost'*, which struck at the foundations of the elite's political power. Russians would have to wait until 1905 to experience again a similar freedom of the press that, this time, contributed to the final destruction of the old order.

Paul's reassertion of the autocrat's power, with its consequent upheaval in the ruling elite, exacerbated the reaction that had begun in the 1780s. The chief inquisitor in the policing of the mind was Fedor Tumanskii, the scion of another distinguished Ukrainian family who, with the help of informers, made the "Germans" tremble in Riga and seized books that called the ruler the first citizen, that denied the legitimacy of serfdom, and called bastards the children of love. Swift, for making fun of "great [tall] people," did not pass muster; neither did La Fontaine, for saying it was shameful to seek rank. The total ban on the import of foreign material in April 1800 created a "Chinese wall around Russia"[65] and returned the country to the more serene days of undisturbed ignorance of things of this world that had characterized pre-Petrine Russia. The country had changed, however, and no permanent turning back was possible. The ruling elite thus found itself face to face with the same problems that had so disconcerted the preceding generation.

The absence of specific rules to guide censors had been a sore point since the 1780s. The Code of July 1804, the first attempt to clarify the issue, was hardly a success. On the one hand, censors were encouraged to exercise "reasonable forbearance" (*blagorazumnoe sniskhozhdenie*) toward authors and to assume their intentions honorable. On the other, it established both a preliminary censorship of all manuscripts and an ex post facto censorship of printed books, making authors liable to prosecution for publishing something that they had been authorized to send to the printer. Moreover, not only did it ban the publication of manuscripts denying the existence of God, inciting readers against the faith and the laws, insulting the ruler, and "completely at variance with the spirit of the social order [*dukh obshchestvennogo ustroistva*]," but censors receiving such manuscripts were enjoined to turn them over to the police for investigation and to the courts for trial.[66] Such broad prohibition left to the ruling elite the definition of the acceptable, and the Code became a political weapon in the hands of factions fighting for power at a time of considerable stress over the future of Russian culture and national destiny.

The ideological apparatus fell under attack in the wake of the victory over Napoleon, as Catholic Jesuits and Protestant mystics, like the Encyclopedists in the 1760s, found a receptive ear in Russian society. Its determined defender was Fotii, the abbot of the Iur'ev monastery in Kaluga gubernia, supported by the Moscow Metropolitan and Arakcheev. The mystics, descendants of the Masons of the 1780s, won enough influence with the tsar to secure the appointment in August 1816 of Alexander Golitsyn—a former Voltairian!—as Minister of Education. Golitsyn chose as his deputy Vasilii Popov, of whom it was said that the "sectarian spirit darkened a weak mind." Their instrument, the Bible Society, with Golitsyn as president and Popov as secretary, certainly seemed legitimate.[67] The purpose of the Society, however—to make the Bible available in Russian translation to a wide public—struck at the heart of the official doctrine that the Scriptures must first be distilled into an ideology dedicated to upholding the sanctity of power.

Censorship provided the defenders of tradition with an opportunity to overthrow Golitsyn and Popov in 1824. When a German book providing a mystical interpretation of the Bible was published in Petersburg and passed by the civilian but not the ecclesiastical censor, it was burned and its author deported. When it was discovered that Popov had translated several chapters, a storm broke out—was it not perversity (*razvrat*) itself to claim that a true Christian has only one fatherland: the entire world? The Metropolitan secured an audience with the tsar and begged him on his knees to remove Golitsyn. The Bible Society was closed, all mystical books were banned, and even a catechism approved by the Synod was removed, because the Lord's Prayer was written in Russian instead of church Slavonic.[68] The first act of censorship, in 1720, and one of the last, in 1824, were thus directed at maintaining the political integrity and linguistic unity of the official ideology.

Censorship was used to ban the discussion of public affairs, such as the policies of the ruling elite. Alexander Kunitsyn's book *Natural Law* was withdrawn from circulation—there could be no standard against which to judge the positive law. Criticism of the existing tax system was unacceptable: since taxes were approved by the ruler, how could he do anything harmful? Members of theatrical troupes could not be criticized because they belonged to the apparatus. The publication of excerpts from judicial proceedings was banned in 1817, of judicial statistics on murders and suicides in 1824, the year of the great repression, when members of the ruling elite were forbidden to publish memoirs or anything else concerning the exercise of their duties. Publication of landowners' instructions to managers of their estates was also forbidden. When the Neva overflowed its banks in November 1824, causing a catastrophe in a city of 400,000 inhabitants, nothing was published about it for a year. And in 1825 Arakcheev obtained the tsar's permission to forbid publication of any comments or studies on the military settlements.[69]

The criticism of serfdom had always been considered subversive because "most influential people looked upon emancipation as a revolutionary attack on all the foundations" of the political order. A book published by Ivan Pnin, the illegitimate son of the Mason Nikolai Repnin, was withdrawn from circulation in 1806, chiefly because the author had expressed compassion for the fate of the peasants. The translator of a book published in Vilno in 1809, discussing voluntary agreements between landowners and their serfs, was expelled from the apparatus, and repression grew worse in the wake of peasant revolts in the 1820s, especially those taking place on the properties of Viktor Kochubei, the Minister of the Interior.[70]

It must be emphasized once again, by way of conclusion, that policing the printed word was largely a form of self-policing, in which writers and professors cooperated with the ruling elite in an effort to keep intellectual discourse within the safe limits set by the political imperatives of the day. The agencies created in September 1796 were closed in February 1802, and censorship became the responsibility of the governors. Preliminary censorship was then vested in censorship committees in each university, staffed with professors from that university, while ex post facto censorship remained the duty of the governor, and thus of the MVD (the Ministry of Police between 1810 and 1819). Ecclesiastical censorship was vested in the Synod. The superiors of the censorship committees were the curators of the universities and the Minister of Education, all leading members of the elite and usually men of culture. Alexander Shishkov, who succeeded Golitsyn, was a linguist of strong, if retrograde, views.[71] Despite the acceptance of self-policing, however, tension was inevitable between the ruling elite and the intellectual community. The purge of Kazan and Petersburg Universities in 1819 and 1821[72] must therefore be seen as a call to order, a reminder to the intellectual and teaching circles of their political and ideological responsibilities. When Pushkin, with the genius's disregard of tradition and restrictions, irritated certain members of the ruling elite, and was banished as a result to his estate near Pskov in July 1824, he was placed under the surveillance of the governor, the marshal of the nobility, and the abbot of a neighboring monastery[73]—representatives of the still-indivisible triad of apparatus, political infrastructure, and ideological establishment that had never ceased to rule the Russian Empire.

The police provided the methods by which a command structure became effective. That Russian society was a community of believers implied both the existence of a consensus without which orders would not be accepted as legitimate and a recognition of the need to maintain it at all costs. Without it, that society's self-image would be shattered and its sense of destiny dangerously compromised. That it was still a largely self-policed society shows how strong the consensus remained and explains why the relatively rare expressions of dissent were punished with great severity.

The emphasis on hierarchy and obedience within the ruling class and the systematic and undifferentiated subordination of all members of the dependent population to any member of the ruling class served to emphasize the essentially political and nonbureaucratic nature of the relationship. That is why the technical activities of government—tax collection and criminal justice—were clearly subordinated, as soon as the local government reform carved them out of general administration, to governor and police. The creation of an environment favorable to the constitution of a civil society, which Marc Raeff sees as the goal of the "well-ordered police state," was in Russia a clearly political act, unfolding without the beneficial influence of a generally accepted concept of the common good. It was therefore no more than a policy to maximize the resources at the disposal of the ruling class, to strengthen its security against autonomous tendencies in its ranks and against the potential rebellion of the dependent population at a time when serfdom was reaching its apogee and the alienation of the ruling class from that population was beginning its fateful course.

It will be objected that orders often were not carried out, that society devised at all levels mechanisms to neutralize their force, passive resistance the most important among them. If voevodas ignored orders from colleges, their success may be explained by the great distances from the center, a relaxed concept of time, and the persistent belief that subordination to the next higher level could be circumvented by insisting on one's own subordination to the ruler's absolute will.

Peasants certainly were resistant to orders from lords and stewards, and it may be contended that the effectiveness of orders stopped at the threshold of the village. It is important, however, to distinguish among the purposes of orders. It is true that interference with peasant customs, such as land repartition, crop rotation, and the various methods by which the peasant world met the demands of the ruling class for the supply of recruits, provisions, and money, could meet an insuperable wall of resistance. On the other hand, the absence of personal rights—the exercise of manorial police, the arbitrary arrangement of marriages, the all-too-common intrusion in the private life of the peasant family, the banishment of undesirables by the lord's will, the sale of peasants, the summary requisitions of peasant labor for public works at harvest time by land captain and governor—testified to the effectiveness of an apparatus of compulsion assuming unconditional obedience. The lack of personal rights in a community of believers bound by an intolerant consensus on the validity of the social and ideological order made Russian society a command structure incapable of resisting the exercise of arbitrary power.[74]

IV

JUSTICE

10

Courts and Procedures

Central Courts

Without a tradition of political and scholarly debate and a social and territorial differentiation favoring the emergence of conflicting interests seeking resolution in a national jurisprudence, the Russian judiciary remained in an amorphous state. The political order was no *Rechtsordnung*, a legal system in which the cultivation and the application of power had become secondary;[1] it was instead one in which the subjective and arbitrary preferences of ruler and ruling elite were accepted as legal norms, and those of the ruling class overrode the claims of the dependent population.

Agencies punished crimes and settled civil disputes among the other functions assigned to them when individual *prikazy* were set up. They did not so much initiate cases as wait until injured parties brought litigation before them.[2] It was brought, however, not to a court as such but to the *prikaz* with jurisdiction over the particular type of case or category of people involved; it was a source of incessant jurisdictional conflict, settled in the final analysis by the respective influence of patronage networks. The prosecution of serious offenders, their punishment, and the review of sentences enabled the apparatus to maintain order within its ranks and among the dependent population, but this judicial function, combined as it was with personnel management and tax collection, gave the apparatus a quasi-absolute power over the fate of defendants.

An attempt was made, however, to concentrate criminal repression in one agency with a truly national jurisdiction. Of the three categories of felony—murder, larceny with battery (*grabezh*), and highway robbery (*razboi*)—only the last was a truly national scourge, a threat to the security of travel by land and river. The task of the *Razboinyi Prikaz* was to fight it, and by extension to prosecute the other two felonies as well. Executioners—who carried out death sentences and whipped and branded lesser offenses—and prisons, used chiefly for preventive detention rather than for the incarceration of convicted criminals, were within its jurisdiction. Its jurisdiction, however, did not include the city of Moscow, except for a short period (1681–1686). There felonies were prosecuted in the *Zemskii Prikaz*. The *Razboinyi Prikaz*—called then the *Sysknoi Prikaz*—was headed in 1697 by Mikhail Lykov, who was related to the ruling house through the Streshnevs. It was closed in 1701, its responsibilities turned over to the voevodas individually, to *prikazy* with jurisdiction over certain categories of people, and to territorial *prikazy*.[3]

The *Prikaz* of Indentured Servants (*Kholopnyi*) had jurisdiction over household serfs' contracts with their masters, their transfers from one master to another, their emancipation, and those crimes they committed that did not come under the jurisdiction of the *Razboinyi Prikaz*. It was closed in 1704, its criminal jurisdiction presumably absorbed into that of the *Zemskii Prikaz* and the voevodas, its civil competence into that of the Moscow *Sudnyi* (Judicial) *Prikaz*. Other *prikazy* to which separate categories of people were subordinated were the *Razriad*, the Treasury, and the Postal *Prikaz*. Foreign merchants were tried in the *Prikaz* of Foreign Affairs.[4]

The emergence of the Moscow *Sudnyi Prikaz* reflected the progressive administrative unification of central Russia throughout the seventeenth century about to reach completion in the reforms of Peter the Great. There had been Ryazan, Dmitrov, Vladimir, and Moscow *Sudnye Prikazy*. All had been merged by 1699 into one Moscow *prikaz* for civil affairs (*iskovye dela*) for Moscow and satellites of the capital. Elsewhere civil justice remained in the hands of voevodas, part and parcel of the universal jurisdiction of these middle managers of the apparatus. The *prikaz* was headed in 1697 by Iurii Urusov, closely related to both the Saltykovs and the Naryshkin families at the core of the ruling elite.[5]

The most important *prikaz* after the *Razriad* was the *Pomestnyi Prikaz*, whose chief in 1697 was Petr Sheremetev, second cousin of the future marshal and related to the ruling house through the Dolgorukovs. It was by far the largest agency, with a complement of 446 clerks in 1687 compared with 125 in the *Razriad*, 76 in the *Sudnyi Prikaz*, and 58 in the *Sysknoi Prikaz*. It was responsible for keeping records of lands held by the ruling class in hereditary or conditional tenure; registering transactions involving them such as sale, exchange, and reassignment; and conducting periodic censuses of their population. By extension, it was the highest instance in inheritance cases and operated in close collaboration with the *Razriad*, which kept the service records of the ruling class, including births, marriages, and deaths of its members.[6]

These administrative–judicial *prikazy* suffered the fate of other *prikazy* in the wake of the gubernatorial reform. Its intent was to assign some key figures of the apparatus to a small number of territorial commands (gubernias) and to give each within his command the collective authority of all *prikaz* chiefs. Its consequence was the abolition of the *prikazy* and the scattering of their responsibilities among eight gubernia chanceries, with the territorial jurisdiction of the old *prikaz* reduced to Moscow gubernia. The files of the *Pomestnyi Prikaz* were sent to the relevant governors, but the *prikaz* remained officially in existence—as a temporary department to process old cases and as a reference desk. It was moved to Petersburg in 1715.[7] Governors became judges in addition to being military commanders and fiscal officials, and central courts ceased to exist.

This experiment in regional administration lasted, as we know, no more than a decade. By 1719 there had come into being the network of agencies called colleges, some headed by former governors, which lasted until the 1780s, when central executive agencies were again abolished and their responsibilities delegated to gubernia chambers. The new system retained a key feature of the old: central agencies combined judicial with other responsibilities, despite the existence of some with a distinctly judicial profile. Thus, the College of Commerce tried civil and criminal cases involving foreign traders, the College of Mining those involving mine owners (*zavodchiki*), the College of Manufactures those to which factory owners (*fabrikanty*) were a party, and the Central *Magistrat* and the Chancery of Court Peasants other townsmen and court peasants, respectively. Likewise, the two colleges that may be called almost exclusively judicial, Justice and Land Affairs (*Votchinnaia*), combined general responsibilities with the more specific task of dispensing justice to members of the civilian apparatus and the political infrastructure, while the officer corps depended in the last resort on the College of War.[8]

The College of Justice was for much of its life located in Petersburg but moved to Moscow in 1762. Like most colleges, it had a branch in the other capital. Its first president, Andrei Matveev, was the grandson of a *d'iak* close to the Romanov house; its second, Petr Apraksin, was a relative of Peter the Great; and its last, Alexander Iakovlev, was a descendant of Ivan the Terrible's first marriage. In order to speed up the handling of cases, it was divided in December 1763 into three departments, with the president chairing the first. Its staff numbered 152 individuals in Moscow and another 34 in the northern capital.

No general instruction was ever published for the College of Justice, and none may have been drawn up, despite a Senate order of July 1733. No doubt it was felt that the rights and duties of a judicial agency were better left unspecified if the claims of power were to remain free to assert themselves against procedural obstructions. Nevertheless, it is possible to form an outline of its jurisdiction, both civil and criminal.

Wills, to be lawful, required notarization by the college; so did sales and mortgages of personal property registered on certain forms (*kreposti*) if they exceeded a certain amount. Civil litigation involving these documents was tried in the college and required the presence of the parties in Moscow or in Petersburg, at least until 1762. The transfer of the college to Moscow was thus a first step in the decentralization of civil litigation based on the recognition that the political infrastructure was reaching into the provinces and that economic life had slowly expanded opportunities and rewards.

The college was also a criminal court chiefly for members of the apparatus, whose verdicts were then forwarded to the Senate for review. It also received complaints from all over the country about miscarriages of justice in the governors' chanceries. It thus functioned as a general overseer of the entire system of criminal justice. Finally, guardsmen stationed in Petersburg brought suit before the college in both civil and criminal matters after Romodanovskii was appointed governor-general of Moscow in 1727.[9]

The College of Landed Affairs was the successor of the *Pomestnyi Prikaz*, subordinated to the College of Justice in August 1718 and resurrected as a separate college in January 1721. Governors were ordered to return to it the records they had been sent a decade earlier, and the agency became once again the central repository for all transactions affecting the landholdings of the ruling class and the court of first resort for inheritance cases.

Like the *Pomestnyi Prikaz* a century earlier, it was the single largest agency of the civilian government in 1763, with a staff of 259 in four departments in Moscow and another 39 in Petersburg to serve the needs of the northern provinces. Its jurisdiction was more narrowly judicial—the national land survey ceased to be one of its responsibilities in the 1760s—and its chiefs ranked lower in the apparatus. Its first vice-president, Fedosei Manukov, had been *d'iak* in the *Pomestnyi Prikaz*, and its last, Luk'ian Kamynin, had been senior procurator in the Senate; neither had close family connections to the inner core of the ruling elite.

The college's efficiency was very much affected by strains resulting from the territorial expansion of the political infrastructure. As the number of landowners grew in distant provinces and districts, all real estate transactions had to be registered in Moscow. There was widespread fraud by those taking advantage of the ignorant and simpleminded, and a growing volume of litigation requiring the parties' presence in the old capital. Moreover, a great many records, housed in decrepit buildings, were deteriorating. For these reasons the government accepted the necessity of decentralization.[10] The reforms of the late 1770s, long in the making and delayed by the Russo–Turkish War of 1768–1775, satisfied both the needs of the political infrastructure for a more responsive machinery to redress grievances and those of the civilian and military apparatus for a more efficient machinery to collect information and taxes.

As a result, both colleges were closed,[11] their civil responsibilities distributed among the civil chambers in each of the new and smaller gubernias, and their criminal powers turned over to the gubernia boards and criminal chambers. Their administrative responsibilities—the maintenance and transportation of prisoners and the general supervision over the administration of justice—became those of the governors, governors-general, and the Procurator General.

This key member of the ruling elite during the reign of Catherine (Alexander Viazemskii, related by marriage to the Saltykovs and Naryshkins, was the chief dispenser of civilian patronage, head of the political police, and de facto minister of finance) possessed considerable powers of intervention in the judicial process, chiefly at the appellate level. The chancery of the Senate and the senior procurators in its departments were subordinated to him. All cases reaching the departments passed through their hands, and all departmental and senatorial decisions required his approval; if he refused it, the case was sent to the ruler. The stream of complaints reaching his office gave him the leverage to intervene anywhere at any stage—if he felt the case was worth his time. The institutional separation of justice from political management was one of the most laudable features of Catherine's reforms. There could be no question, however, of abandoning the traditional assumption that the dispensation of justice is a political act.

In September 1802 there emerged out of the Procurator General's office a new Ministry of Justice, but one without the same authority and power, since another two ministries—Internal Affairs and Finance—were also born out of the office's transformation. The two ministers with the longest tenures, Petr Lopukhin (1803–1810) and Dmitrii Lobanov-Rostovskii (1817–1827), were both safely ensconced in the Naryshkin political family, to which the eighteenth-century Procurators General, as a rule, had also belonged. Stripped of his predecessor's more burdensome responsibilities, the new Minister of Justice could afford to become an even more politically conscious watchdog over the administration of justice—over sloppy procedures in the chambers and the Senate, over the appointment of judges or the confirmation of their election, and over limiting the Senate's role to the narrow application of the law—while reserving the right to submit any doubt or interpretation to the Committee of Ministers or the State Council.[12]

Despite the many vicissitudes it underwent in its long history, the Senate was always the highest appellate court of the empire. Its judicial function, however, was only one of its many responsibilities as the chief coordinating agency of the entire government and was often lost in a sea of trivia. The division of the Senate into five departments, one of them judicial, in the summer of 1730 had been short-lived. By 1763, however, its chronic inability to keep abreast of its agenda, and the recognition that two major functions of government—drawing up a budget and making case law—required expertise and consistent application, compelled a new, efficiency-minded government to divide the judicial colleges and the Senate into departments.

The original six departments, created in December 1763, remained unchanged until 1805. A seventh (unnumbered) was added in 1794 when an "expedition" created in 1765 to adjudicate claims arising from the upcoming national land survey was raised to the status of a department. No distinction was made at the time between civil and criminal justice, and only one department was give a territorial jurisdiction. Both the Second Department in Petersburg and the Sixth Department in Moscow were appellate courts for decisions of the Colleges of Justice and Land Affairs, and litigants could file their appeals before either court. In the 1760s the Second Department had five senators, the Sixth had four; in 1796 both had eight senators. The Fourth Department in Petersburg had a less-pronounced judicial profile. It reviewed decisions of the Colleges of War and Navy, the supply services, and the two cadet corps, when higher confirmation was necessary or dissatisfied parties appealed, and had territorial jurisdiction over cases sent up from Smolensk gubernia and New Serbia, two strategic territories. Military contracts exceeding 10,000 rubles were negotiated in this department, which presumably took up any litigation over them. Five senators usually sat in it.

The other two departments were special cases. The Fifth, in Moscow, to which the Governor-General belonged ex officio, was intended to be an administrative department, capping the entire administration of the old capital and its huge gubernia, and a branch of the First and Fourth Departments. By 1796 it had seven members and had become, like the Sixth, a judicial department. The Third Department, finally, was distinguished by a definite territorial jurisdiction—it took up in Petersburg cases from the Baltic, Polish, and Ukrainian borderlands where Russian law did not apply, and reviewed decisions of the Academy of Sciences and other higher-education institutions, court agencies, the Postal and Policemaster's chanceries.[13]

The departments gained considerable experience, and the creation of two judicial chambers in all gubernias after 1775, which forced an institutional separation of civil from criminal cases, compelled a similar division of labor in the highest court. During Paul's reign a number of decrees stripped the Second and Sixth Departments of their criminal jurisdiction and concentrated it in the Fourth and Fifth. An imperial order of December 1802 then gave these two departments a territorial jurisdiction for the first time: thirteen of the twenty-six Russian gubernias under the Fourth Department in Petersburg, the other thirteen under the Fifth in Moscow. The Senate thus became six appellate courts—two civil and two criminal, another still combining civil and criminal jurisdiction over the western borderlands, and an unnumbered Department of Land Survey.[14]

The reorganization of January 1805 added two civil departments, shifted remaining administrative responsibilities to the First Department, and completely altered the numbering of departments in effect since 1763. There were thenceforth two criminal and six civil departments, including the Third Department, now without any criminal jurisdiction over cases from the western borderlands, and the Land Survey Department, both in Petersburg. The other four were the Second and Fourth in Petersburg, the Seventh and Eighth in Moscow. These departments had six or seven members in the 1820s. Another feature of the reform was to give all departments (except Land Survey) a territorial jurisdiction. By 1825 the twenty-six Russian gubernias had been divided among these four civil departments in the following manner:

Second Department:	Arkhangelsk, Iaroslavl, Kostroma, Novgorod, Olonets, Pskov, Smolensk, Tver, Viatka, Vologda
Fourth Department:	Kazan, Perm, Petersburg
Seventh Department:	Kaluga, Kursk, Moscow, N. Novgorod, Vladimir, Voronezh
Eighth Department:	Orel, Penza, Riazan, Tambov, Tula, Saratov, Simbirsk

The volume of criminal cases was obviously much smaller since only two departments were considered adequate to dispose of them. They were the Fifth in Petersburg, which also assumed jurisdiction over criminal cases from the Baltic, Polish, Ukrainian borderlands, and the Sixth in Moscow. Each department was further divided into sections responsible for smaller groups of gubernias. They were also much larger departments, with seventeen senators in the Fifth and fourteen in the Sixth in 1823. Each department reviewed cases from the following Russian gubernias:[15]

Fifth Department: Arkhangelsk, Iaroslavl, Kaluga, Kostroma, Kursk, Novgorod, Olonets, Petersburg, Pskov, Smolensk, Tver, Vladimir, Vologda

Sixth Department: Kazan, Moscow, N. Novgorod, Orel, Penza, Perm, Riazan, Saratov, Simbirsk, Tambov, Tula, Viatka, Voronezh

The reform thus completed the transformation of the roles of the Senate. No longer a committee of ministers, advisory legislature, and high court of review, it had become a civil and criminal tribunal charged with imbuing the entire judicial system with respect for procedures and systematically applying the relevant laws to cases under review. But this depoliticization of the judiciary was more apparent than actual. All decisions involving an interpretation of the law were no longer submitted directly to the ruler but went first to the Civil and Ecclesiastical Department of the State Council or its Department of Laws, which became a higher court of review between the ruler and the Senate. In addition, the Minister of Justice made ample use of his power to suspend the execution of Senate decisions and submit them to the Committee of Ministers.[16] The growth of the body of law and the greater expertise and specialization required by the increasing complexity of life had in no way modified the traditional assumption that any legal controversy raised essentially political questions.

Local Courts

There was no comprehensive network of local courts until the reforms of the 1770s, when the growth of the political infrastructure and its increasing presence in the towns and districts generated such a mounting volume of grievances that governors and voevodas were overwhelmed. In a society where popular aspirations were few and the demand for change negligible, there was no need for law to develop a concept of justice to be enforced by courts. Resort to a higher authority outside the immediate community was to be avoided because the voevoda, the delegate of the apparatus, embodied power goaded by greed and unrestrained by law. A society shaped into a command structure by consensus, poverty, and the need to extract resources from an economy of scarcity did not foster the development of objective standards and a legal tradition incorporating the concepts of justice and mercy.

The administration of justice, then, was diluted among families and social communities rather than concentrated in universally recognized agencies. Decisions to marry and leave the extended family, the distribution of personal property, and the appointment of trustees for minors were made and challenged within the family. The apportionment of taxes, the selection of recruits (as a rule the subject of heated exchanges), the repartition of land, permission to seek work in the towns—these decisions were made and accepted or challenged within the community without appeal to outside authority. Members of the apparatus took their disputes to their patrons, with patronage networks acting as extended families, in which disputes were settled in accordance with the respective strength of patron and client.[17]

In the peasant world—more than 95 percent of the population—disputes that could not be settled in families and communities were referred to land-owners, retired officers appointed to watch over peasants of the treasury, or to the abbots of monasteries. If a landowner lived on his property, he himself judged his peasants. If he did not, his steward followed his instructions. On large properties the steward's office sometimes resembled a voevoda's, the table covered with a red cloth, a copy of the *Ulozhenie* within easy reach, the mirror of justice on the wall.[18] The serf was defenseless before such a tribunal and had no recourse against its decisions, ranging from a fine or a flogging to banish-ment to hard labor without requiring further sanction. Denunciations by serfs of their owners were considered null and void by the apparatus unless they involved treason, attempts on the life of the ruler, or hiding male peasants from census takers.[19] Death sentences were forbidden, but the cruelty of corporal punishment was often such that it amounted to a slow death. In civil matters, lords married off their serfs and disposed of their property at will. As members of the political infrastructure, these landowners collectively exercised private judicial power over nearly two-thirds of the peasant population and were sometimes rebuked by the ruler and the core of the ruling elite for excessive cruelty. But their very existence denied their peasants access to the public power represented by the voevoda.

In villages of state peasants, the assemblies of heads of patriarchal house-holds—the *mir*—took up disputes affecting the welfare of the community; issues that could not be resolved were brought before retired officers whose appointment to supervise these communities made for a comfortable retire-ment. Following the reform of 1797 legalizing the *volost* as an intermediate level between those communities and the uezd, the *volost* chief (*golova*), chosen by the peasants for a 20-year term, performed the functions of a judge as part of his general responsibilities for the maintenance of peace and stability in his territory.[20] Disputes throughout the peasant world were settled and infractions punished without involving the apparatus and without recourse to formal legal procedures.

The situation in the towns was in some respects not very different. Elders and assemblies of patriarchal heads of *kuptsy* families decided the fate of members of their communities with the same finality as their village counter-parts. Town air did not make a man free in Russia but bound him to the other members of his community, who made his freedom of movement dependent on the general will. This absence of personal freedom—the essence of serfdom—militated for a long time against the development of local courts. Not only did it leave serfs at the mercy of their owners, it strengthened the communal bond chaining individuals into a mass collectively responsible for the private and public behavior of its members and the correction of their transgressions. Urban communities were similarly crushed by the lack of public life or legal equality between apparatus and dependent population conducive to the transference of disputes among individuals to the adjudication of public authorities.[21]

In other respects, however, urban life created conditions favorable to the intrusion of the apparatus in the settlement of disputes and the punishment of crimes. Voevodas lived in the towns, closer to the litigants and the scene of the crime. The apparatus drew a line between felonies that threatened public order and misdemeanors that did not, and reserved for itself the exclusive right to punish the former, more often reported in towns than in distant villages. Finally, while communities policed themselves and settled the overwhelming majority of disputes involving their members, disputes between members of scattered communities and those involving members of different social groups had to be referred to voevodas.

The seventeenth-century voevoda administered justice in the same office where he received petitions, tortured prisoners, and kept accounts of the taxes he had collected. He thus embodied political justice, with the *Ulozhenie* and various *ukazy* leaving him considerable discretion to assert the authority of the apparatus on the side of those it was important to please and against those it was convenient to exploit.

On the other hand, the fragmentation of Russian administration into competing vertical jurisdictions, leaving the voevoda little statutory power, preserved the ruling elite's ability to intervene at any stage in the judicial process. Consequently, while voevodas operated as courts of first resort, disputes and prosecutions also routinely began in the Moscow *prikazy*. Their closing in the wake of the territorial reform of 1708 established for the first time a "judicial" hierarchy in which governors became the only superiors of commandants and voevodas, and the appellate link with the central government was cut. The governors' place in the elite guaranteed that its discretionary control remained undiluted.[22]

A major feature distinguishing some of the Petrine colleges from the old *prikazy* was the creation of local agencies responsible to their collegial headquarters. This resulted in a dilution of managerial responsibilities of governor and voevoda, and was bound to foster mutual resentment. In January 1719, so-called *nadvornye* courts were created in seven gubernia capitals—Petersburg, Moscow, Smolensk, Voronezh, Nizhni Novgorod, Kazan, and Tobolsk—and in Kursk and Iaroslavl, each consisting of six judges appointed by the ruler and the College of Justice and subordinated to it. The experiment was short-lived. In April 1722 governors were ordered to assume the chairmanship of these courts, which became mere extensions of the governors' chanceries. At the same time, judges appointed in provincial capitals and various towns by the College of Justice were dismissed, and voevodas resumed their traditional judicial functions. However, in what resembled a return to the seventeenth-century practice of associating voevodas with so-called *gubnye starosty*—elected in theory by the local population, handpicked in practice by the voevoda, discontinued in 1679 but restored in the 1700s with the selection of *Landrichter*—governors and voevodas, where *nadvornye* courts did not exist, were ordered to administer justice with one or two assessors at their side chosen from the political infrastructure of the uezd. In addition, provincial voevodas were enjoined to appoint "commissioners" (*komissary*) in distant towns more than 200 kilometers from their capitals.[23] The outline of a court system had thus been created by the end of Peter's reign, but one embedded in the managerial hierarchy of the ruling class and responsive to its pressures.

This new judiciary was intended to settle disputes among members of the political infrastructure and clerks—members of the apparatus came directly under the College of Justice—among peasants of the treasury belonging to different communities, and between peasants and townsmen if the suit was filed by a townsman. It also prosecuted felonies by members of any social group. Suits among merchants, however, even those from different towns, and the punishment of misdemeanors, went before separate courts—the *magistraty*—set up in accordance with the instruction of 1724. With a network of *magistraty* under the jurisdiction of the Central *Magistrat* in Petersburg,[24] the apparatus created a hierarchy parallel to that formed by the College of Justice, the governor, and the voevodas, and invested it with an independent existence, although both the college and the *Magistrat* were subordinated to its ultimate authority, embodied in the Senate. Such a policy reflected a belief in the need to bolster the self-esteem of the registered urban population by raising its status above that of the peasantry, a belief that the desolation of the urban scene after the Swedish war neither justified nor encouraged.

Peter's successors faced the difficult task of reconciling the tsar's ambitious and costly administrative reforms with an intractable fiscal situation, and their solution was virtually a return to the Muscovite pattern of government. The abolition of the *nadvornye* courts, the dismissal of the assessors, and the subordination of the *magistraty* to the voevodas in 1727[25] ended even the pretense of rudimentary judicial machinery within the administrative hierarchy. There is no question that fiscal stringency played a role, but it must also be asked whether the tense political situation of the 1730s did not also convince the ruling elite that a reduced managerial setup would be easier to control. Governor and voevoda became the sole dispensers of justice and the dreaded instruments of a repressive policy designed to curb banditry and compel the dependent population to pay their arrears, although the government seems to have assumed that judicial decisions were not to be personal but collegial, arrived at with the participation of the governor's or voevoda's deputy and his secretary. Elizabeth's proclamation of December 1741 that Peter's governmental system would be restored at all levels did not result in the recreation of the mixed courts in existence between 1722 and 1727, let alone of the more independent courts of 1718–1722. The only reform was the restoration of the Central *Magistrat* and the removal of the local *magistraty* from under the governors' and voevodas' heavy hand in May 1743.[26]

The radical pruning of the managerial structure in 1727, however, created a major problem. It most likely compelled more litigants to bring their cases directly to Moscow or Petersburg if they could afford it, and to forgo justice if they could not. It also made imperative the restoration of separate agencies for the city of Moscow in order to relieve the gubernia chancery of the burden of cases tried in the old capital as well as those tried in its gubernia, the largest and most populous in the country. As a result, the government announced in March 1730 that a new *Sudnyi Prikaz* would hear the case of any litigants living in Moscow, irrespective of their social origin, and a new *Sysknoi Prikaz*, descendant of the *Zemskii Prikaz*, would prosecute felonies committed in the city. Appeals from these two courts would go not to the Moscow governor's chancery but directly to the College of Justice.[27]

The policy of administrative retrenchment inaugurated in 1727 was accompanied by a gradual demobilization of the military apparatus completed in February 1762 and a concurrent growth and territorial expansion of the political infrastructure. This alone can explain why several hundred officers were familiar enough with local conditions 4 years later to draw up lists of grievances to be discussed at a Legislative Commission. This perception of a local environment, which sustained the growing interest in geography so characteristic of Catherine's reign, made the ruling class painfully aware of the lack of administrative machinery to settle disputes among its members. Townsmen, even if the government still had difficulty accepting the fact, lived within a territorial framework with a definite profile and specific needs. What was more logical, then, than to use the *magistrat* as the model for a court to which noblemen would take their own disputes? Moreover, the implantation of a political infrastructure in the countryside required the creation of courts to translate a monopoly over the exercise of the political function into an effective tool for the settlement of disputes in a manner favorable to the interests of the ruling class.

This acceptance of the need for separate courts was relatively new. It was a tradition of long standing that agencies, central and local, performed judicial functions within the more general scope of the responsibilities for which they were originally set up. In other words, the judicial function was incidental to the process of governing. The creation of the College of Justice had been a first step toward the recognition of the specificity of the judicial function, perhaps under the influence of German thought. The Enlightenment, no doubt, played a major role in popularizing the concept of the separation of powers, but the beneficial consequences of such separation could have no appeal for a ruling class for which governing was inseparable from exploitation and inconceivable without the continuous assertion of the primacy of power. However, the existence of separate agencies with the specific task of dispensing justice in Moscow had taught that both the volume of business and the growing difficulty in finding the appropriate law in a mass of poorly coordinated and often contradictory legislation made specialization and the separation of functions inevitable. A similar awareness was compelling the ruling elite to allow fiscal administration an autonomy it had never known before.

Two additional developments combined to tear apart the archaic fabric of Muscovite administration. More nobles and their serfs were settling in provinces far from the old Muscovite core—toward the Don and the mid-Volga, in Voronezh, Tambov, and Saratov—and Petersburg, the political capital, was becoming an administrative capital as well, sapping Moscow's last claims to leadership. This distention of the old core threatened to paralyze the entire system. If access to Petersburg became prohibitive for rank-and file members of the infrastructure and disputes could no longer be settled peacefully, how would the ruling class retain its unity and the apparatus its legitimacy?

The reform of 1775 achieved three purposes. Not only did it create separate courts, it created an overabundance of them. By closing the Colleges of Justice and Landed Affairs, it eliminated the intermediate and often superfluous link between the governor's office and the Senate. And by a judicious combination of election and appointment it guaranteed that the punishment of crimes and the settlement of disputes within and among various groups of the dependent population would remain the monopoly of the ruling class.

Three courts at the uezd level—the uezd court, the *magistrat*, and the lower *rasprava*—each consisting of a judge and two assessors, where intended to administer justice to the nobility, the townsmen, and the peasants of the treasury. Three intermediate courts functioned as courts of review for cases on their way to the judicial chambers: the upper land court, the gubernia *magistrat*, and the upper *rasprava*. Each consisted of a chairman appointed by the Senate's First Department and assessors elected by members of whichever of the three social groups it was intended to serve. The judicial chambers in the gubernia capital, civil and criminal, were entirely appointed, their two chairmen by the empress, their eight assessors by the First Department. Eight courts to administer justice in gubernia and uezd in place of a governor and a voevoda busy with a multitude of other matters—such was the unprecedented scope of the reform.

Its most innovative feature was the court of equity (*sovestnyi sud*), the quintessence of the new system, since its chairman was appointed by the governor-general and its two elected assessors came from the nobility, the merchantry, or the peasants of the treasury, depending on the social origin of the defendants. Its justification was humanitarian: it tried cases involving chiefly juveniles and the insane, to whom it was felt the full force of the law must not apply. The recognition that the law was too severe and its procedures too rigid had led to the creation in 1726 of "oral courts" (*slovesnye sudy*) attached to the most important *magistraty* and customshouses. Their purpose was to avoid endless written depositions and challenges to documentary evidence. The link between urban precedents and this reform must not be overlooked.

There was no question that this proliferation of courts strengthened the power of the ruling class. It gave the population broader access to courts and thereby facilitated the penetration of the countryside, above all the world of the state peasantry, by the political infrastructure, now institutionally separated from the apparatus for the first time but extending immensely the range of its effective action. The chairman of the lower *rasprava* was most likely a local landowner. All assessors—to which all appeals from the lower courts were referred—were confirmed in office by the governor, and the judges of the chambers belonged to the upper management level of the ruling class. The judicial world of each gubernia became a microcosm of the political society—

ruling elite, apparatus, and political infrastructure governing townsmen and peasants.[28]

The short-lived reforms of Paul were a step backward, seeking as they did to obliterate the new autonomy of the infrastructure. The intermediate courts, the lower *raspravy*, and even the courts of equity were closed, and the election of assessors was canceled and replaced by the appointment of members of the apparatus on the waiting lists of the Heraldry. This self-defeating policy, amounting to a rejection of the infrastructure that alone could sustain the legitimacy of his rule, was a factor in the conspiracy against the tsar, and compelled his son to reverse it. What emerged was a compromise, one in which the position of the infrastructure was strengthened. Only the court of equity was restored, and assessors were once again elected. The result was a uezd court chaired by a landowner and consisting of two assessors elected from among landowners, and two peasant assessors—who were to take up only matters involving the state peasantry—the first civil and criminal court for both nobility and peasantry. Townsmen remained under their *magistraty*. The membership of the chamber became a mixed one: two assessors and two councillors still appointed by the Senate, four assessors elected by the nobles, and four by the merchantry, sitting together to try all cases, whatever the social origin of the litigants or defendants might be.[29] The chambers, then, became in each gubernia the common forum for apparatus and political infrastructure, into which the upper ranks of the merchantry were gradually drawn during Alexander's reign.

Judicial Procedure

One of the most striking features of Russian administration was the absence of a code of judicial procedure. Long before the general codification of 1832 there had been numerous administrative codes for separate agencies, and the General Code (*General'nyi Reglament*) of February 1720 systematized internal procedures throughout the Petrine government. Amended by decrees and practice, it nevertheless remained in force until the Ministerial Statute of June 1811. Judicial procedure was submerged in administrative ritual and only occasionally surfaced as the object of the legislator's hurried concern: the process of governing in a command society was largely limited to collecting information, examining petitions, and issuing binding orders, little allowance being made for adversary relationships and challenge to authority. Indeed, judicial procedure so lacked autonomy and recognition that it was not even clear whether a distinction existed between civil and criminal procedure.

An individual seeking redress at the end of the seventeenth century filed suit before the voevoda, who had no power to render a final decision in any case, and was expected to refer all proceedings to Moscow. It was thus preferable, if the litigants could afford it, to file suit in the capital. There they had to find the *prikaz* with jurisdiction over their person, or their case. The lack of clear demarcation between jurisdictions was the cause of this first hurdle. The

second was to get the respondent to accept the summons sent by the *prikaz*—
posting to a distant assignment and other forms of sudden "disappearance"
being common ways of avoiding summonses. If the respondent did appear
before the *prikaz*, both he and the plaintiff were required to sign a pledge to be
present on the date set for trial by agreement of "judges" and parties. Parties
could be represented by their agents (*poverennye*). If either the plaintiff or the
respondent did not appear, he lost the case. Since this provision does not seem
to have been applied to the letter, getting both parties to show up for the trial
was a third hurdle.[30]

This pretrial procedure was little affected by the creation of the colleges,
even though jurisdictional conflicts were much reduced. Parties continued to
go to Moscow, where their patrons or their clients represented them, and
colleges created to review the decisions of governors and voevodas found
themselves transformed into courts of first resort. Respondents continued to
disappear or simply used physical force to prevent delivery of a summons.[31]
Procedures had to take into account and accommodate power relationships
within the command structure. The famous decree of November 1723 (*o forme
suda*) was less concerned with trial than with pretrial procedure and devoted
much attention to securing the presence of all parties or their agents on the trial
date.[32] It was not, however, until the reforms of the 1770s that these pretrial
hurdles were almost entirely removed.

The "trial" went through five stages. It began with oral depositions of the
plaintiffs and the answers of the respondent, both taken down and organized
into pararaphs (*punkty*) by the secretary. These depositions made up the basic
record of the case. Because this record was often extremely long and confused,
it was necessary for the secretary to summarize it in the form of an abstract
(*vypiska*), likewise divided into paragraphs, submitted to the parties, who were
required to sign it if they acknowledged it as reliable. The third stage was
finding the laws relevant to the case—no mean task at the time and one better
left to the secretary. This indeed was one of the reasons militating in favor of
filing suit in Moscow rather than in the provinces, since the law was better
known in the central agencies. The abstract and citation from the laws were
then submitted to the voevoda's or governor's chancery or the judges of the
central agency or the local court (after 1775), where a vote was taken, the
junior members voting first and the president or chief judge breaking a tie. The
decision was then announced publicly to the litigants.[33]

This apparently simple and expeditious procedure was in fact often an
obstacle course that turned litigation into a nightmare. To substantiate their
claims, parties needed documentary evidence from a distant voevoda chancery
or a central agency. Whenever any of it was challenged or more was requested,
sometimes just for the purpose of delaying the decision, a summons had to be
issued and further inquiries made. Interlocutory appeals were permitted, adding interminable delays. Any party could raise endless objections to the abstract: depositions were not taken in front of the judges, who were thus not in a
position to settle the disputes without resorting to more written exchanges.

These flaws were inherent in a written procedure rejecting adversary proceedings before judges. They also brought into focus the crucial role of the secretarial and clerical staff in the large agencies and of the secretary in the local courts. Secretaries expected to be paid by petitioners for their services, even when that became illegal after 1763, and their well-known greed led to constant blackmail. Merely by sitting on his hands a secretary blocked progress—even prevented the announcement of a decision—and there was no recourse to the judges, who depended on him to draw up the abstract and cite the laws. It was as dangerous to antagonize the secretary as it was to run afoul of the domestic staff of a great household, where lords and servants were bound by ties of mutual dependence and suspicion.[34] Litigants were not bringing their disputes before courts administering justice in the name of abstract norms but before members of patronage networks linked with the ruling elite, and only through access to its members in the central apparatus could effective action be taken against a secretary's obduracy.

Secretaries and judges dealt with civil and criminal cases in like manner, but criminal prosecution dictated an even more nonchalant attitude toward procedural safeguards. The distinguishing features of criminal procedure in felony cases were preventive detention and torture in front of the judges, the secretary asking questions and taking down the answers. Torture for the purpose of obtaining a confession was declared by the Code of Military Justice of March 1716 to be the best form of proof, and it was used at all levels until 1763, when voevodas were forbidden to apply it; it was declared illegal shortly thereafter, except in the prosecution of crimes in the Secret Expedition. After the reforms, investigations were conducted by the police, but cases were often reinvestigated by the uezd court. In misdemeanor cases, the general rules of civil procedure usually applied.[35]

Appellate procedures made a greater distinction between civil and criminal cases. Civil suits tried by voevodas went to the *prikaz* with jurisdiction over the case, the town, or the social group to which the litigants belonged, and were decided there in the last resort. If vexed (*spornye*) questions were involved, civil cases were routed through the *Raspravnaia Palata* or went directly to the Duma sitting with the tsar and, after 1701, to the Privy Chancery sitting as a committee of ministers. In 1711 the Senate became the highest court of appeal, and the imperial order of December 1714 spelled out the appellate hierarchy from commandant through governor to Senate and tsar, and established the grounds for an appeal in decisions made contrary to law (*nepravdoiu vershenie*).[36]

The creation of colleges complicated the appellate hierarchy. Decisions of voevodas—provincial or local—were appealed to the governor. His decision, however, could not be appealed to the relevant college until a petition asking permission to appeal had been filed with and accepted by the college and it had issued an order to send up the case. Until 1762 no appeal to the Senate was allowed against the decision of a college unless the college voted to refer the case to it. Litigants wishing to see their case reviewed in the Senate filed a "complaint" to the *General Reketmeister*, a new post created in 1722. If enough influence was brought to bear upon him to accept it, he requested the case from the college and, if convinced that the complaint was justified, brought it to the Senate. No appeal was accepted against a Senate decision, but a similar complaint filed with the tsar's secretariat might result in the ruler's final review of the case. If the Senate could not reach a unanimous decision or if the procurator general or the Cabinet of Ministers objected to it, the case was automatically referred to the ruler. To discourage frivolous complaints, litigants were warned that if the ruler sided with the Senate, they would suffer criminal penalties.[37] Of course, the tendency for provincial litigants to take their cases directly to a college in order to avoid the delay and chicanery at each level eliminated the possibility of appeal. What is most striking in such a system is the absence of a recognized right to appeal decisions of the central apparatus, since an appeal was seen as an unacceptable challenge to the authority of those who made the decision. Judicial decisions, then, settled or failed to settle legal questions; they were also political decisions that the ruling elite felt free to make at its discretion, unaffected by the pressure of appellants and deadlines.

The economic revival that began in the 1750s—the territorial extension of the political infrastructure coupled with an offensive launched against the stifling influence of the clerical staff in the colleges—convinced the government to loosen these discretionary procedures and welcome the discussion, within the ruling elite, of substantive issues raised in civil appeals, at a time when an important debate was about to take place openly in the Legislative Commission. The imperial order of July 1762 was a landmark in the history of appellate procedures. Litigants thenceforth had a week to notify the governor's chancery or the college of their intention to appeal a decision, and all proceedings were then forwarded to the college or the Senate, where a formal appeal had to be received within 1 year. Appeals against Senate decisions were still forbidden, but it now became the *General Reketmeister*'s role to examine complaints and bring Senate decisions to the ruler's attention. The post was closed after 1810, when its role was taken over by a Commission of Petitions (*proshenii*). One of the commission's members, Petr Molchanov, was a descendant of the Ivan Molchanov who had been appointed in May 1720 to receive petitions, 2 years before the formal appointment of the first *General Reketmeister*.[38]

The decree of 1762 may well have increased the flow of indiscriminate appeals to the colleges: at least one purpose of the next procedural reform was to regulate it once again, an effort facilitated by the creation of gubernia chambers and local courts. A formal hierarchy of courts ended the traditional practice of filing suit in higher agencies and bypassing lower ones. All litigation had to be submitted to the uezd court—or *magistrat* or lower *rasprava*—and no appeal was allowed if the value of the suit did not exceed 25 rubles. If it did, an appeal was permitted to the corresponding intermediate court, from which no appeal was permitted unless the value of the suit exceeded 100 rubles. Appeals to the civil chamber were decided in the last resort, but suits for more than 500 rubles could be appealed to a Senate depatment. In all cases, the deadlines established by the decree of 1762 remained in effect. Appellants had 1 week to state their intention to appeal and 1 year to file a formal appeal. Decisions took effect 1 month after the declaration of intent. After the closing of the intermediate courts in December 1796, suits exceeding 25 rubles could be appealed directly to the civil chamber.[39]

The reform blocked small suits at the uezd level and sought to make the civil chamber the final court of appeal. An appeal to the Senate, for which it was necessary to deposit 200 rubles in the chamber, forfeited by an appellant who lost his case, was frought with uncertainties, entailed endless delays, and required much ready cash to stimulate the interest of secretaries and clerks. The provision that decisions take affect while the appeal was being processed— it could take years—induced appellants who felt they had been wronged to accept the chamber's decision against them: the winner would have squandered away his gains or so ruined the estate that gaining a reversal in the Senate was not worth the effort. Catherine's reforms, here as in much else, shifted the managerial center of gravity to the provinces and sought to create in each gubernia a community where ruling elite, apparatus, and political infrastructure settled disputes among themselves and gained the freedom and the ability to exploit the dependent population at will.[40]

Conversely, Paul's reforms were designed to encourage dissatisfied parties to turn to Petersburg. After August 1797, an appeal automatically suspended execution of the chamber's decision until all appellate remedies had been exhausted. Complaints to the ruler were thenceforth welcome. A favorable order by the chamber resulted in the sending of the case to the Senate, whose decision could not take effect until it had been confirmed by the ruler. Civil chambers became way stations en route to the Senate.[41] The creation in 1805 of departments with territorial jurisdiction and in 1810 of the Commission of Petitions could barely regulate the flow of appeals to Moscow and Petersburg.

Not only did governors and colleges until 1775 take up civil cases along with tax collection, investigations, and complaints of every sort (all processed in paragraphs, summarized in abstracts, and registered in *protokoly*), they knew no distinction between the trial of a case and its review on appeal. Each level had the right to reinvestigate, reexamine, amend, and cancel the decisions of a lower agency[42]—practices typical of a command structure in which judicial procedures differed little from disciplinary proceedings.

A trial court bases its decision on the facts, while an appellate court reviews procedures and scrutinizes the legal references that guided the lower court's decision. The facts of the case, however, without the benefit of cross-examination to clear up contentious points, could not be ascertained, and the abstract was unreliable. In any case, the absence of a scholastic and legal tradition expressed in dialectical debate and cogent prose made depositions an amorphous mass of undigested facts. Laws, as anyone familiar with the Collection of Laws of the Russian empire can attest, often established no clear norms but consisted of Senate reports leaving an issue half resolved, which the ruler had merely signed. These "laws," which often could not be quoted verbatim, were paraphrased, and misunderstandings compounded the confusion. As a result, the entire proceedings of the lower agency were sent to the higher court, and a new trial in fact took place, requiring the presence of the parties. No wonder cases lingered for years when no one showed up.[43] The requirement of the law of November 1775 that an (appellate) review (*revizia*) be "nothing but an examination of whether the case was handled in accordance with established procedures [*poriadochno*] and was based on the laws"[44] was bound to remain unrealistic as long as a basic record of facts remained incomplete and unreliable and no collection of laws in force was available to secretaries and litigants.

These administrative–judicial procedures were used in all agencies to examine and review all claims—between private individuals, between private parties and the treasury, and between members of the apparatus. During the last quarter of the eighteenth century, however, when the administration of justice emerged as a separate function of government in consequence of the growth of a political infrastructure autonomous from the apparatus, an effort was made to differentiate between judicial and administrative procedures and to open separate channels for the redress of nonjudicial disputes. For example, individuals claiming their rights had been violated, their property seized, their contracts not honored, their loans not repaid, or their share of a will not released—if their claims were uncontested (*bezspornye*)—had no recourse to the new courts but had to turn to the gubernia board chaired by the governor, which had the power to compel satisfaction of the claim.[45] On the other hand, it was found necessary to separate claims between private persons and the treasury—the so-called *interesnye dela*, the single most important type of civil cases—from other civil cases and try them under different, more cumbersome, procedures. The reform of 1775 concentrated the civil judiciary of each gubernia in the civil chamber, emphasized that neither the governor's office nor the treasury chamber was a judicial body, and required that *interesnye dela* be first on the agenda of each session of the civil chamber. The imperial order of August 1799 involved the treasury chamber in the decision of these cases, the Senate likewise needed the opinion of the procurator general, later the minister of finance, before reaching a decision, and even unanimous decisions required imperial approval.[46] This defense of the treasury's interests was another facet of a conscious policy in which Paul and Alexander reasserted the dominance of the ruling house against the encroachments and greed of the political infrastructure during the reign of Catherine.

If parties to civil cases were likely to belong to the ruling class and the upper merchantry, criminal cases were bound to involve chiefly members of the dependent population. Felony investigations were turned over to the relevant *prikaz—Razriad, Rasboinyi*, and so on—for sentencing, although sentences were imposed directly by the *Zemskii Prikaz* on felons captured in the capital. There was no right to appeal even death sentences, but, if the defendant was a nobleman, the tsar, as commander in chief of the ruling class, reserved the right to pass final judgment on the fate of one of its members.[47]

Governors inherited in 1708 the collective right of *prikazy* to confirm all sentences in their chanceries. After 1719 it devolved upon the chanceries of the provincial voevodas, who were required, however, to refer sentences of death or hard labor to the *nadvornyi* court sitting with the governor. After 1744, governors were required to send death sentences to the Senate and await confirmation, pending which felons were kept in detention.[48] Members of the ruling class serving in the army were tried by courts-martial, those in the civilian apparatus were tried by the College of Justice, and sentences of deprivation of noble status or death still required imperial approval.

This procedure of automatic review of the more severe sentences was modified by the local government reform of 1775. Lower courts had their sentences carried out locally excepting death, deprivation of status, and severe corporal punishment. These sentences were sent to the criminal chamber through the appropriate intermediate court, which merely added its opinion. The criminal chamber, unlike its civil equivalent, had no authority to order the execution of its own decisions. All sentences were submitted to the governor, who forwarded to the relevant Senate department those involving members of the upper merchantry and of the ruling class (members of the apparatus were now tried in the chamber), those with which he disagreed, and all death sentences. He had no right to reduce or increase a sentence, let alone reverse it. If he agreed with it, it was sent back to the lower court and carried out. Senate decisions were final unless the sentence was death or a member of the ruling class was stripped of his membership.[49]

Petitions for review ("complaints") to the College of Justice were allowed on the grounds of violation of the law, but sentences were carried out on receipt of the governor's confirmation. After 1775, such petitions against decisions of the lower courts were addressed to the criminal chamber. If the chamber heard a case, its decision could be appealed to the senate after May 1796, when the empress allowed defendants to file appeals under the provisions of the above decree of July 1762 after depositing 200 rubles with the criminal chamber. This privilege, however, did not apply in cases of death sentences, deprivation of status, or severe corporal punishment.[50] The governor, jointly with the chairman of the criminal chamber, both delegates of the ruling elite, thus remained for defendants from the dependent population the final judge of their destiny.

11

Crimes and Punishments

Attitudes and Sources

Another characteristic feature of the Russian political order—besides the absence of a code of judicial procedure—was the poverty of the legal tradition. Until the local government reform of the 1770s and the senatorial reform of 1805, no distinction was made between legal and other institutions; the dispensation of justice was ancillary to personnel management and fiscal administration. As a result, the ruling elite, perceiving political life as the exercise of power and the perpetual consolidation of patronage networks, saw the training of jurists as a challenge to its monopoly over political life.[1] *D'iaki* and secretaries were trained in the apparatus, and their knowledge of procedural intricacies was not the knowledge of a body of law growing by accretions and rejections in the searching criticism of a public debate. And although Russian law, like all law, borrowed from other legal systems, notably the Byzantine and the Lithuanian, it did not operate in competition with them within a single political order. Moreover, the insignificant development of towns did not foster the growth of mercantile law any more than serfdom favored the growth of manorial law.[2]

Finally, the absence of a tradition of conflict between church and ruling group, and the concomitant rejection of a higher allegiance before which secular rulers themselves must bend, deprived Russian political culture of that tension between ideals and realities that has been one of the fundamental features of Western civilization. The fusion of political community, church, and nation into one intolerant and xenophobic community of believers militated against the acceptance of natural law—the common reason of mankind—as a source of inspiration and a beacon of light for those who would rebel against the rampant injustice of the day.

This is not to say that there was no Russian law. The *Ulozhenie* of 1649, very much a digest of previous laws in 967 articles, was the fundamental law of late Muscovite Russia, and *prikazy* kept separate books of case law, developed in applying the *Ulozhenie* and decisions handed down by the tsar to settle conflicts, correct misunderstandings, and fill gaps. The *Ulozhenie* was enlarged following the publication of the Supplementary Articles (*novoukaznye stat'i*) of January 1669 for highway robbery and murder, those of March 1676 for *pomest'ia*, and those of August 1677 for *pomest'ia* and *votchiny*. The Mercantile (*Novotorgovyi*) Code of April 1667 and two more sets of Supplementary Articles in April 1684 and January 1686 completed an edifice of law that had been taking shape since the last codification of 1550.[3]

It was a paradox that much of this massive work would become obsolete within two generations, since Peter often enacted laws inspired by Western models, as if a legal system came from above and need not consider the customs and moral values of the population to which it was addressed. A period began during which an abundant positive law (*zakon*) often ran ahead of custom (*pravo*), limiting itself to specific issues and making the work of interpretation and coordination a nightmare for agencies. The imperial order of March 1714 introduced unigeniture; that of March 1731 annulled it. The rules of May 1725 governed inheritance in the collateral lines. The Military Code of March 1716 and the Naval Code of January 1720 contained a penal and a procedural code, while the order of November 1723 (*O forme suda*) contained another.[4] Since the apparatus consisted of officers, some on active duty, others retired, the country was governed de facto if not de jure by martial law, and military codes were applied to civilians when some of their provisions were found necessary to supplement inadequate or poorly edited civilian laws.

In the meantime, a number of colleges received an instruction, while others did not, but all, like the old *prikazy*, developed a body of case law. Its study should give us a most rewarding insight into lawmaking in Russia. Codes and regulations established guidelines, and separate *ukazy* settled specific questions but often raised new problems. Since all legislation issued from the ruler, it remained in force until specific provisions were annulled by imperial order. More often than not, they were never so annulled, and countless orders began to vie for the secretaries' attention—assuming they were known, since many were addressed only to the authority asking for clarification. In addition, many issues had never been addressed by legislation, such as recidivism, mitigating circumstances, and third-party responsibility; and agencies expressly limited to the strict application of the law found themselves without any law to apply. The well-known prevarication of voevodas and governors and their habit of referring all doubt and controversy to central agencies were often the result of their ambiguous position and the fear of fines for handing down the wrong decisions. The central apparatus had greater freedom of action, and the result was the growth of a body of unofficial law having little in common with the provisions of codes and decrees, yet one by which disputes were settled and crimes punished, one that imposed punishments for acts the law did not recognize as crimes and changed the sanctions of the law according to the perceived needs of the moment.[5]

This freedom of action may have been one factor behind the failure of attempts at codifying the law. Another was the infatuation with foreign models that produced, among others, the Great Instruction of July 1767, a mishmash of quotes from writings of the Encyclopedists designed by a publicity-conscious empress to catch the eye of western European progressive society. It had no influence on criminal legislation, and it was even forbidden later to refer to it, but its humanitarian ideals—of non-Russian origin—continued to inspire those desiring to taste the "forbidden fruit of free thinking" in an unfavorable environment. On the other hand, this infatuation was explained by the very lack of a legal tradition.[6] What had grown was not a single body of official law, an organic fusion of enacted law and the commentary of a legal community known at least to the better minds of the ruling class and the dependent population, but a subterranean maze of uncoordinated precedents in the cellars of colleges and chanceries ignored by the positive law, yet the law by which Russians were effectively governed.

Crimes, chiefly felonies, were not and could not be mere violations of objective norms embodied in legal paragraphs. The Russian world was a cosmic order in which social and even private acts acquired political and ideological content, and nonconformist acts were implicitly seen and, if circumstance required, openly advertised, as political disloyalty and religious heresy.[7] Russian criminal justice was, as a result, intensely subjective. It has been said that the harshness of the penal law under Peter was motivated by the tsar's assumption that crimes by members of the apparatus were violations of his trust,[8] especially if they involved embezzling public funds, collecting illegal taxes, or accepting bribes. On the other hand, the widespread collusion within the apparatus in the commission of these crimes assured that they would not be punished with the severity prescribed by law, unless it was necessary to make an example.

A criminal from the dependent population who murdered, stole, or (above all) committed highway robbery, was guilty of a political act if the victim of the crime belonged to the ruling class. Breaches of the peace, depending on circumstances and the perceptions of the moment, could easily be transformed into political crimes if they challenged the foundations of serfdom—no freedom of movement and absolute power of the lord over his serfs—since serfdom was the foundation of the political order. Likewise, any manifestation of intellectual autonomy reported by the self-appointed guardians of orthodoxy became a political crime if the ruling elite perceived it at a given time as a threat to its ideological monopoly.

Crimes of all sorts were often equated with sin. If the ruler was God's anointed and the head of the church beyond whom there was no appeal, dissent was blasphemy and active opposition was apostasy. Moreover, his representatives were thus doing God's work, and to oppose them was to commit an impious act (*Bogoprotivnosti*). Russian culture was so permeated with religious imagery and religious vocabulary that defendants themselves confessed their crimes as sins. Grigorii Dolgorukov and Dmitrii Golitsyn, expelled from the councils of the elite in 1723 following what was clearly a political frame-up, made an act of contrition and asked to be forgiven their sin (*pogreshenie*). The Senate in 1786 called an act of sodomy committed in Lifland a sin (*grekhopadenie*), yet one less serious than murder and disturbing the peace. Hence the emphasis on repentance (*raskaianie*) followed by unconditional acceptance of the status quo and submission to the political dominion of the ruling class and, for its members, of the ruling elite.[9]

Moreover, a sin could be not only a religious offense but a political offense too, a crime against the entire community of believers. Five guardsmen implicated in a plot to overthrow Catherine in 1762 found themselves accused of opposing God, betraying the fatherland, and making themselves outcasts from society. Pugachev was declared before his execution to have cleansed his soul by complete repentance before God, Her Imperial Majesty, and all humanity.[10] Such expansive interpretation of crime as violation of the cosmic order was applied not only to offenses against the ruler, the linchpin of the entire system, but also to lesser crimes. An imperial order of March 1727—one certainly not written by the empress herself—attributed self-mutilation among recruits seeking to be disqualified to the fact that "they do not have the fear of God and do not know what a great sin crime is," adding that those "ungodly rascals had so little respect for the faith and the fatherland that they would rather damn [*gubit'*] their soul in this way than serve their fatherland and obey their monarch."[11]

Russian law traditionally recognized two categories of offenses, felonies and misdemeanors, the latter outside the provisions of the penal law until the 1780s and considered by ruling class and dependent population as mere irritations properly disposed of by arbitration in the communities or by resort to general rules of procedure. Felonies (*zlodeistva*) were defined by the Senate order of May 1725 as offenses against the church—the ideological bulwark of the ruling class—and against the ruler and his family, to which were added rebellion and treason, as if to emphasize the personal union of ruling house and country. A third group of felonies consisted of murder, highway robbery, and theft from the treasury or from private individuals if the defendant was caught red-handed. Felons did not come under the provisions of the procedural order of November 1723 and would therefore be tortured. Suspected thieves were not considered felons unless a civil suit determined that they were.[12]

Crimes were next classified in the Police Code of April 1782, where felonies called "criminal offenses" (*ugolovnye prestuplenia*) included murder, highway robbery, larceny (degrees of which were established in April 1781), fraud, and violations of regulations on public order, public health, and trade.[13] These crimes were tried in the new courts; other violations came under the jurisdiction of the police boards. The creation of provincial courts and the considerable work of classification and diversification that also marked the reign of Catherine in fiscal administration further deepened the penetration of the apparatus into Russian life, and many misdemeanors that would never have fallen into the lap of a voevoda were now taken into police jurisdiction and summarily punished.

Another classification of crimes, announced in July 1811, bore the marks of haste and ran counter to the diversification sought in Catherine's legislation. It divided felonies—besides those directed against church and ruler—into three categories, to each of which a punishment was attached. Murder, highway robbery, public violence (*vozmushchenie*), and bribe taking, "etc. [*sic*]," were punished by death or hard labor; larceny in excess of 100 rubles, repeated theft, and vagrancy by settlement in Siberia or drafting into the army. "Other crimes" were punishable by light corporal punishment or detention in the workhouse. This rough classification may have been intended for the duration of the impending conflict with Napoleon and was followed by a military penal code included in the Field Army Statute of January 1812, the first of its kind since the penal code of March 1716.[14] For our purpose, crimes may be divided into three categories: those against the ruling class, those against persons, and those against property.

If crimes were implicitly political and sacrilegious acts, punishments pursued a political and religious goal. Retribution was an essential part of the penal code. The zeal with which superior punished subordinate and ruling class the dependent population was motivated by the belief that internal challenges would weaken the power of the ruling class, thereby threatening the stability of the whole system.[15] Retribution was one side of the coin, deterrence was the other. The striking display of cruelty in administering punishment not only exacted revenge but instilled—or was intended to instill—fear in the hearts of potential wrongdoers. Indeed, the Military Code of 1716 declared that the subject's reverence for the ruler should be motivated by fear and implied that the entire political order was a state of war of every man against every man.

It was no coincidence that Peter's reign marked the "point of greatest punitive severity in the entire history of Russian law."[16] The general mobilization of the ruling class, the consolidation of the dependent population into fewer and more clearly defined social categories, and the creation of a command structure that has persisted to our own day, made for extraordinary tensions. The law of the talion was still very much alive in the Military Articles, by which blasphemy was punished by cutting out the tongue, murder by decapitation, and perjury by cutting off two fingers.[17] The introduction of a new punishment, running the gauntlet in the army, added collective savagery to the executioner's solitary work.

Acceptance of the need for draconian punishment was widespread. Compassion is notably absent from the *nakazy* of 1767; noblemen, townsmen, and peasants alike called for the ruthless repression of banditry and even of lesser crimes.[18] The stress of the insecurity and poverty of life in town and countryside expressed itself in vengeful cries for the extermination of criminals. Elizabeth's generous heart, Catherine's discriminating intellect, and Alexander's mystical sensibility sought to introduce compassion into criminal justice but made only a superficial impact on a ruling class steeped in the tradition of repression as the bulwark of stability. Paradoxically, the ruler's generosity was most often bestowed on members of the ruling class, who could count on their cases being reviewed at the highest level. In the 1800s, Ivan Lopukhin in the Senate's Sixth Department complained against the thirst for revenge of his colleagues showed in confirming harsh sentences;[19] the military apparatus made a mockery of the tsar's yearning for decency by its systematic application of the gauntlet, and in Simbirsk province, which we have no reason to consider an exception, the chairman of the criminal chamber in the 1810s could not remember how many cases he decided in 1 year. He was sure, however, that he had no pity for criminals and imposed 1,000 blows of the knout and 2,000 lashes of the whip every year.[20] The ultimate revenge was not the death penalty but a declaration of insanity on social or political grounds.[21] It expelled the criminal in the most humiliating fashion from his social group, from his church, and from the political community.

Punishment also met the religious requirement of penance and redemption. The Russian word usually translated as "punishment" (*nakazanie*) actually meant "teaching a lesson" (*nauchenie*), while *kazn'* referred to severe punishment.[22] Punishments that taught lessons were called corrective (*ispravitel'nye*) in the nineteenth century. Until March 1775, *kazn'* included the death penalty (*smertnaia kazn'*) and the knout, also called *torgovaia kazn'* because it was carried out in the public square; beating with sticks and flogging with a whip, also in public, were added thereafter. In the 1750s the whip was still in wide use, and the Iaroslavl' townsmen, among others, thought it "corrective" rather than humiliating.[23] The knout and other corrective punishments were acts of penance, chosen to fit the seriousness of the crime. Penance was sometimes enough to wash away the stain of the crime, but it was often followed by redemption, which had to be earned far from the defendant's community, usually in the Far North or Siberia. This was the rationale of banishment, which also served the more mundane purpose of settlement. Banishment, in the pungent word of the day, was for eternity (*vechno*), but prisoners, if not sentenced to hard labor, had a chance to build a new life and create a new generation of hardy Siberians while remaining in the community of believers. Hard labor was both revenge and redemption; it expelled a criminal from his social group and the political community but not from the church.

The growth of a political infrastructure and its acceptance of the creed of the Enlightenment as part of the ruling class's attempt to win respectability in the concert of European nations modified its perception of the value of revenge as the motive for punishment. This new perception also reflected a higher self-consciousness and sensitivity, and was thus a defense against the ghastly effects of the severe penalities, to which even members of the ruling elite were subjected when the ruler chose not to pardon them. Immunity from corporal punishment, won by the ruling class and merchants of the first two guilds in 1785, proclaimed the obvious: that Russian justice remained political justice while proclaiming the quality of all before the law. On the other hand, if greater sensibility fostered in some a revulsion against the crueler forms of revenge, it also led them to emphasize penance. The fear of the knout and the whip, wrote an anonymous commentator at the beginning of the nineteenth century, compels criminals to hide their guilt and their accomplices. The abolition of their use, except for the more heinous offenses, would induce the defendant to confess and leave him "in a state of permanent spiritual contrition [*sokrushenie*] and repentance."[24] The lack of reference to the more severe forms of corporal punishment in the decree of July 1811 previously cited may have been an expression of this emphasis on penance—unless it was a mere oversight.

By 1825 the penal law recognized three major penalities—death, corporal punishment, and banishment, each subdivided according to severity. Detention still meant largely preventive detention and was not used widely as a punishment until the nineteenth century. There were few prisons for that purpose, and most detainees were kept in monasteries or in fortresses, which could not accommodate large numbers.

Crimes

Crimes against the ruling class were one of the three major categories of crimes, and consisted of offenses committed against the ruler and his family, those committed against the apparatus and the political infrastructure, and violations of the foundations of serfdom.

The very intent to inflict harm upon the ruler was punished by death, as was uttering words considered offensive to his "honor" (*chest'*). These offenses were investigated and punished by the political police, whose decisions required the ruler's confirmation. Harsher sentences were usually commuted inasmuch as many a culprit from the dependent population had cursed the ruler in a drunken state, and the exercise of the right to pardon and commute exalted the ruler's magnanimity. Such was his majesty, nevertheless, that any oral or written criticism of the political order or of governmental decisions— which in law all originated from him— could be termed offensive if the ruling elite decided that it was politically expedient to do so.

Words and intended acts directed against the ruler were lumped together with treason and rebellion (*bunt, vozmushchenie*) as crimes falling under the "first two points." This expression originated in the imperial order of January 1715 inviting every "true Christian and faithful servant of his lord [*gosudar*] and fatherland" to denounce those suspected of (1) evil intentions against His Majesty and treason, (2) rebellion, and (3) embezzlement of treasury funds. Since the procurator general on one occasion persuaded the tsar that the hanging of all embezzlers would deprive him of his apparatus ("Sire! Would you want to remain an emperor without servants and subjects?"), the third point was soon demoted to the much less serious category of crimes against property, and those who insisted on reporting evidence of embezzlement directly to the tsar found themselves threatened with the death penalty! Treason and rebellion were later combined to constitute the "second point."[25]

Treason was defined not only as taking up arms against the ruler, surrendering a town to the enemy, or espionage but even as leaving the country without permission. It could be stretched to warn senators not to "postpone until tomorrow" the execution of the tsar's will.[26] This, however, was a frontal attack upon the privileges of the ruling elite, and a tsar who made such a claim put his life on the line. Rebellion, of course, meant any uprising in any part of the country but usually referred to public violence by the peasantry. It later included the preparation and circulation of calls to violence and, by extension, anything throwing doubt on the "inviolability of the rights of the Supreme Power" as well as "arrogantly" (*derzostno*) rejecting the established form of government.[27] Any criticism, let alone a call to action directed against the ruling elite, thus came under the "first two points" and was punished by death, although sentences were often commuted to hard labor and banishment.

Crimes against the apparatus—officially called crimes against the government in the Digest of 1832—included the defamation of officials in the exercise of their functions, and obstructing the publication of laws and decrees, even if by an act of negligence. These crimes were usually punished by whipping and settlement in Siberia. More serious was the fabrication of spurious laws and decrees, especially those upsetting public order, the circulation of rumors, and the mailing of anonymous letters. Hard labor was the usual penalty, also applied to the counterfeiting of official seals, coins, and assignats. Before the suspension of the death penalty in 1753, these offenses had been capital, like those falling under the first two points. Refusal to obey orders, resistance to low-ranking members of the apparatus like policemen and land surveyors, breaking prison, or forming organizations without the approval of the governor,[28] as the delegate of the ruling elite in each gubernia, were not serious enough to come under the first two points and were punished by corporal punishment and banishment.

Relationships between the political infrastructure and more than half of the peasant population were not regulated by law. The most heinous offense that could be committed by a serf was insolence (*derzost'*) against his master—that is, a challenge to his master's dominion, which had to be met lest an isolated act become contagious and turn into rebellion. A lord disposed of troublemakers by sending them to the army, a form of banishment, and gained the right in December 1760 to banish them to settlement in Siberia without any review of his decision in the apparatus, and in January 1765 to hard labor. The right to banish to hard labor was later rescinded, but the authorization to banish to settlement—the landowner's decision was forwarded to the gubernia board, which confirmed it by administrative order—would remain a prominent feature of the Russian penal law throughout Alexander's reign.[29]

Finally, the ruling class collectively sought to protect itself against an endemic threat to the status quo by prosecuting vagrancy with the utmost vigor, although vagrancy also worked at times in the interest of important members of the ruling elite, who welcomed the settlement of vagrants on their sparsely populated estates. Since restriction of movement was the foundation of serfdom, every member of the dependent population wishing to leave his town or village had to possess an internal passport: anyone lacking a valid passport was a vagrant. Members of the ruling class also needed a passport, but only to prevent the adoption of false identities by the dependent population. Vagrants were deserters—soldiers deserted their commanders, serfs deserted their owners in the political infrastructure or those who kept them in trust as a source of funds for the military and civilian apparatus. Vagrants whose origins could not be traced, as a rule, were banished to the army or settled in Siberia after a public whipping.[30] Any offense against the political monopoly of the ruling class was thus punishable by the uprooting of the offenders. If they were sent to Siberia, their transportation to the distant glades and meadows of a vast hinterland, where climate taught humility and under-population made rebellion unthinkable.

The second major category of crimes consisted of crimes against persons—primarily homicide, bodily harm and violations of honor, and the mistreatment of the dependent population by the ruling class.

Homicide, of course, was a capital offense, but after 1753 the death penalty was usually commuted to beating with the knout and banishment to hard labor. The *Ulozhenie* already distinguished between murder and manslaughter, defined as unintentional (*bez umysla, neumyshlennoe*) murder. The most serious kinds of murder were those committed in church or in the ruler's presence, when someone drew a weapon and inflicted wounds resulting in death. If there had been a conspiracy (*skopom i zagovorom*) to use force with the intent to steal, and someone was killed, the killing was considered murder, even if there had been no intent. These provisions were developed in the Supplementary Articles of January 1669.[31]

Russian law distinguished between major criminals and their accomplices, even though the dividing line between commission and assistance seems to have remained vague. As a result, *prikazy*, governors, voevodas, and local courts had much freedom of interpretation when applying essentially political criteria to murder investigations. Moreover, individuals who knew but did not report that a murder had been committed were also liable to criminal prosecution, although they ranked below accomplices in the apportionment of guilt. The vengeful principle of old Russian law that all parties to a crime were equally guilty gradually gave way to a more discriminating application of revenge,[32] but the political implications of a crime were undiminished.

The Military Articles of March 1716 made a major contribution by listing the types of lethal wounds inflicted during fights or in a drunken state and clarifying the distinction between murder and manslaughter, mandating detention, corporal punishment, or cash compensation for manslaughter and decapitation for murder.[33] Finally, Russian law recognized accidental (*sluchainoe*) homicide, caused, for example, by a horse that cannot be controlled by its owner. No criminal penalties were attached to it, but the defendant, having committed a sin, was required to do penance in church.[34]

Bodily harm consisted of mutilation (*uvech'e*), defined as the loss of a limb, an eye, or an ear. Insults (*obidy*) made by word of mouth, in writing, or expressed in actions caused the insulted party to suffer "dishonor" (*bezchest'e*). Both types of offenses were redressed in the *Ulozhenie* by a cash payment, sometimes preceded by corporal punishment. The amount of the compensation was determined by a scale establishing the severity of an offense according to the victim's social position. Thus, anyone who insulted a member of the apparatus suffered the knout—without the number of blows being specified—and imprisonment. For insulting members of the *gostinnaia sotnia*, the compensation varied from twenty-five to ten rubles, for insulting a peasant one ruble, for mutilating him ten rubles. Insulted wives and unmarried daughters received twice or four times the compensation attached to their husband's or father's status, respectively.[35] Nowhere, however, was the word *insult* defined—

that was left to the agency trying the suit—but in one of its most curious yet logical invocations, an appeal to the tsar against a decision of the ruling elite was itself deemed an insult to that group's honor. Likewise, the provision of the Organic Law of November 1775 requiring appellants to deposit a substantial sum returned only if they won their appeal must be seen as a reflection of the view that any challenge of an official decision was an "insult," a milder form of "insolence."[36]

The Military Articles took a dim view of bodily harm and insults, and borrowed from German law a procedure that combined asking "Christian pardon" from the insulted party with the application of the law of the talion in its most hideous form, thus introducing a system of compensation totally different from that of the *Ulozhenie*. By 1825, however, it is clear that jurisprudence had borrowed from both systems, retaining only the requirement of Christian pardon and setting the financial compensation at the equivalent of a year's salary if the insulted party was a nobleman, or the annual amount of taxes paid by a townsman.[37] The law, it would seem, no longer recognized insults or bodily harm to the peasants, who constituted more than 90 percent of the population.

The Russian ruling class took pride in its contention that custom forbade a landowner to kill his serf, overlooking the fact that beatings, a starvation diet, and banishment to hard labor were often the equivalent of a delayed death sentence. Since private serfs—60 percent of the peasant population—were no more than chattel in the enlightened reigns of Catherine and Alexander, it was natural that manslaughter among them continued to be treated as a civil matter. The Senate, for example, took up a suit in 1805 in which the peasants of a landowner wounded the peasant of another, who later died of his wounds. The man who inflicted the lethal wound was not found, and the lower court invoked the Military Articles, imposing collective punishment on all those involved in the fight. The owner of the dead serf, however, filed a civil action under the *Ulozhenie*, which called for turning over the murderer to the injured party as compensation and, if he could not be found, for substituting another peasant, even one totally innocent. The Senate and the tsar accepted the claim that such cases should be treated as civil actions.[38]

Life in the provinces was coarse and brutal. The ruling class, raised among defenseless serfs and domestics and trained in an army where former peasants, townsmen, and sons of priests were expected to show their officers unconditional obedience, knew no restraint in its treatment of the dependent population. Beating peasants of all dominations or slapping townsmen and clergy and pulling their beards were common occurrences of bodily harm and "dishonor" left unpunished. The most celebrated case of mass murder—at least seventy-five killed by Daria Saltykova, née Ivanova—was punished by detention in a monastery, only because the enormity of the crime required some action, even against a cousin of Petr Saltykov, the Governor-General of Moscow and a pillar of the ruling elite. And Alexander, despite his exalted vision of his role as a Christian ruler, did not feel strong enough to take forceful action against landowners who felt the penal law did not apply to maltreatment of serfs.[39] To challenge one of the most cherished prerogatives of the ruling class was something not even a tsar could do as late as the first quarter of the nineteenth century.

The most widespread and incorrigible crime aginst property was larceny (*tat'ba, vorovstvo, krazha*) and its aggravated forms, larceny with battery (*grabezh*) and highway robbery (*razboi*). The *Ulozhenie* and the Supplementary Articles of 1669 lumped all forms of theft under the rubric *razboinye i tatinnye dela*. It distinguished between first and second offenses but not between grand and petty larceny based on the value of the stolen property, although "courts" may have taken such value into consideration before imposing sentences. For first and second offenses, the *Ulozhenie* provided for whipping with the knout, mutilation, a prison term, and finally banishment to settlement in the "Ukrainian towns." For third and subsequent offenses, or if the larceny was accompanied by murder or took place in a church, the penalty was death. First convictions for highway robbery were punished by torture, mutilation, and banishment to the Ukrainian towns, second offenses by death, whether or not accompanied by murder. The Supplementary Articles retained the knout, aggravated the mutilation (the loss of a foot or a hand replaced that of an ear), introduced banishment to Siberia, or simply ordered the defendant returned to his community. No change was made in the punishment of highway robbery, larceny with battery was not considered a separate crime unless committed by military personnel—battery in those violent days must often have been the equivalent of murder—and pickpocketing (*moshennichestvo*, which also included the acquisition of property by fraud) was treated as simple larceny.[40]

This legislation remained in force until the publication of the Military Articles of March 1716. Article 189 introduced the distinction between grand and petty larceny (but without using the terms) by providing for lesser penalties when the value of the stolen property was twenty rubles or less. The penalty was running the gauntlet through an entire regiment six times, twelve times for the second offense. For the third offense, the defendant was mutilated and was sent to hard labor for life. The article also retained the most vengeful provisions of the old Russian law, applying the same penalty to "those who helped," to those who knew about the crime and did not report it, to all those caught with the defendant, and to the receivers of the stolen property. If the value exceeded twenty rubles, or for a fourth offense, the penalty was death. Five years later, an imperial order restored the provisions of the *Ulozhenie* and the Supplementary Articles, but it was ignored by jurisprudence. Article 189 became the fundamental reference, applicable to both military and civilian trials. In the latter case running the gauntlet was replaced by whipping, a much less severe punishment.[41]

The suspension of the death penalty in 1753 reduced the penalty for grand larceny and modified the distinction introduced by Article 189. Henceforth, first and second offenders, when the value of the stolen property was twenty rubles or less, were whipped and returned to their communities on bail (*na poruki*), but all third and fourth offenders, whatever the value of the stolen property, were whipped or knouted and sent to hard labor. How these provisions were actually carried out in criminal sentences during the next 25 years would be the subject of a valuable study on the interaction between the written law and judicial practice.

The local government reform of the 1770s, which carved out of the undifferentiated structure of local administration a national network of local courts and police agencies, together with the influence of Beccaria and others who popularized the concept that the punishment must fit the crime, and, no doubt, the case law handed down in Russian agencies, notably the Criminal Expedition in Moscow—all these led to the promulgation in April 1781 of the first important legislation on theft since the 1710s.

Theft (*vorovstvo*) was said to consist of larceny with battery, larceny (*krazha*), and pickpocketing. Highway robbery, defined as assault on a village, building, or residence for the purpose of stealing, was not included and continued to be punished by whipping with the knout and hard labor. The number of blows was adjusted to fit the importance of the crime, at the courts' discretion. Larceny with battery was defined as the use of force against an individual for the same purpose. How it differed from highway robbery was not always clear. Indeed, both crimes were subject to the same penalty.[42]

The 1781 legislation returned to the definition of grand larceny in Article 189 as the theft of property valued at 20 rubles or more or any theft committed for the fourth time, and continued to classify it as a felony, punishable by whipping with the knout and hard labor, following confirmation by the governor of the criminal chamber's sentence. Whether the retention of 20 rubles as the line between grand and petty larceny did not in fact broaden the scope of grand larceny in the wake of inflation must remain a moot point. Suffice it to say for purposes of comparison that a horse sold for about 5 rubles in the 1760s, a thousand bricks for 4.50 rubles in Pskov in 1785, and a covered cart (*kibitka*) for 4.50 rubles in 1780.[43] Petty larceny was excluded from the jurisdiction of the courts and was punished by the police who sent the convicted to the workhouse, there to earn an amount equal to the value of the stolen goods, plus an additional percentage to be paid to the owner of the goods and to the workhouse. To earn 19 rubles at seven kopecks a day thus required 288 working days. Second and third offenders received two or three blows of the whip. Pickpockets had to earn two or three times the amount they had stolen and were kept on bread and water for 24 to 72 hours.[44] This legislation thus incorporated two leading principles in the evolution of penal law during Catherine's reign: increasing the number of misdemeanors to be punished summarily by the police, and the increasing differentiation of offenses pegged to a diminishing scale of punishments.

Subsequent legislation built upon these principles. In July 1799 the knout and hard labor were reserved for larceny with battery and highway robbery. For grand larceny, defendants were to be whipped at the police station, not by the executioner in the public square, then drafted or banished to settlement in Siberia. In May 1802 the threshold was raised to 100 rubles, just enough to keep in line with the rampant inflation that had begun in the 1780s. In May

1816, finally, petty larceny was divided into four categories, and fixed terms of detention in the workhouse, ranging from 90 to 180 days, were applied to each category.[45]

Punishments

Of all penalties available to the legislator, death has always been the simplest, the most final, and the most indifferent to inequalities of station and power. The consolidation of the ruling class after Peter's reign was bound to affect its attitude toward the ultimate penalty, and gradually to compel the government to establish a new scale of punishments recognizing its privileged status.

Unlike earlier codes, which reserved it for the most serious offenses, the *Ulozhenie* imposed the death penalty for sixty-three separate crimes and extended it to all political charges, the forging of official documents, the counterfeiting of coins, and certain forms of manslaughter, rape, and arson. It codified legislation promulgated at a time of extreme domestic stress, when the ruling house set about strengthening the autocracy of the ruler and added burying alive and burning to hanging, decapitation, and shooting. The half century following the *Ulozhenie* of 1649 witnessed the first implantation of a political infrastructure in the countryside since the reforms of Ivan the Terrible and the stabilization of the domestic political situation. The Supplementary Articles reflected this more relaxed atmosphere and deemphasized the death penalty in the repression of crimes.[46]

War and the mobilization of the ruling class once again created a highly tense domestic situation, exacerbated by the emergence of a tsar who assumed direct command over military operations and constantly felt his rear threatened by dissatisfaction and treason, even among his immediate entourage. The Military Articles of 1716, like the *Ulozhenie*, were the codification of attitudes and repressive measures characteristic of a period of political and social transformation in a climate of violence and fear. It was thus no wonder that the death penalty, to which new and barbarous forms were added—breaking on the wheel and quartering—became applicable to 122 charges not including additional ones provided for in other legislative acts.[47]

This orgy of capital charges and executions caused a reaction as early as October 1726, when the Supreme Privy Council resolved to suspend the execution of capital sentences. Agencies were ordered to submit abstracts to the council and to await the approval of the empress. In March 1727, however, the Senate restricted the application of the resolution to death sentences imposed in the Petersburg agencies and authorized governors to carry out their own.[48] The resolution may have been canceled after the restoration of the "autocracy" in 1730, but it pointed the way to the future: by requiring that all death sentences be sent to the ruler, which took a long time and might never be accomplished, the government would effectively make the death penalty obsolete. Fourteen years later, in March 1744, the Senate noted that the death penalty was being imposed indiscriminately everywhere, "even on innocents," and ordered colleges, governors, and military commanders to suspend executions until the Senate had examined their "detailed reports" on each case and the empress had confirmed them.[49] It took another decade for these reports to be collected and collated, while the Senate was obviously testing the reaction to its order. In March 1753 the empress confirmed its recommendation that the death penalty be thenceforth replaced by whipping with the knout, branding, and mutilating, followed by lifelong banishment to hard labor, but the circular of September 1754 made it clear that the death penalty had not been abolished.[50]

Banishment expelled an individual from the apparatus and his local community and transported him across vast distances into a different environment, where he became a second-class member of the community of believers, carrying for life the badge of his inequity and the burden of his sins. But banishment was also a method of transporting unwilling settlers to areas that were not attractive to the inhabitants of Russia proper, like the far north, the deep south, the southern Urals, and Siberia. Beginning in the seventeenth century, these two attitudes toward banishment—a form of ostracism (*iz zemli von*) and assignment to productive labor—became virtually inseparable except in specific cases.[51] On the other hand, banishment was not a single punishment but ranged from mild and temporary forms to harsh and "eternal" ones combined with hard labor, although these distinctions were not always clear and did not become so for a long time.

The mildest form of banishment was to "enforced residence" (*na zhit'e*). It was either temporary or for life ("eternal"—*vechno*); all other forms of banishment were for life.[52] Banishment to settlement (*poselenie*) expelled convicted criminals to various places on the rim of Russia proper. In the seventeenth century they lived as settlers and soldiers in border towns of the south ("Ukrainian"), and they formed the first Russian settlement in Azov after its conquest in 1696. In the 1750s, they were dispatched to Kazan gubernia, then a large and sparsely populated borderland. Bootleggers were banished to Orenburg gubernia in the 1760s. Criminals sentenced in Iaroslavl and Vologda gubernia were sent to the far north in the 1780s to help run the cod-fishing trade on the Kola peninsula and settle the coastline. But the largest contingent of those banished to settlement went to Siberia.[53] Banishment to Siberia gave rise to many abuses, but it was not until the promulgation of the Regulations on the Exile System of July 1822 that the government sought to eliminate them. Banishment was imposed by judicial sentence after 1775, but serf owners also possessed the right to banish their serfs for "insolence" after 1760. This right was suspended in 1773, during the Pugachev rebellion, but was restored unofficially in 1787 and not abolished until 1802, after which assemblies of peasants and townsmen in their communities continued to exercise the right to expel undesirables and turn them over to the gubernia board for banishment by administrative order.[54]

Another form of banishment was drafting into the army between the times of official levies of recruits. Those sentenced to serve in the army were often physically unfit, and by the end of the eighteenth century penal legislation began to equate banishment to settlement and serving in the army for the same offenses, those fit going into the army, the unfit to Siberian settlement. Recruits had to meet certain requirements—to be between 17 and 35 years old, stand 1.60 meters barefoot, and presumably be without physical disabilities. Others, whether vagrants, thieves, or "insolent" people, were transported indiscriminately to Siberia, which many never reached. As late as the 1810s, it remained clear that the government continued to view banishment as a punishment for less serious felonies. It became part of a broader policy of demographic resettlement as a means to populate Siberia with people "who had committed no crime" (these had to be under 45 years of age and accompanied by their families) and a handy way of enlarging the pool of recruits.[55]

A fourth kind of banishment was to hard labor within European Russia or in Siberia. This was an innovation introduced by Peter I, who needed manpower to carry out difficult and dangerous projects for which only outlaws could be used. At the time, the word for hard labor—*katorga*—meant a galley; Peter used a fleet of them with considerable success against the Swedes in the shallow waters of the Gulf of Finland. Besides manning the galleys, convicts were used to build naval installations in Petersburg, which required working in the icy waters of the Neva estuary. They were also used in Estonia, where the navy was hoping to build its first warm-water port at Rogervik (Baltiiskii port). Beginning in the 1770s, when it became necessary to support a military presence in the territories annexed in the south and the west and to provide a first line of defense, convicts were used in large numbers to build an extensive network of large fortresses. They were also used to mine salt south of Orenburg. Hard labor in Siberia was the harshest: convicts were transported in chains and assigned to the silver mines of Kolyvan in the Altai or the silver and lead mines of Nerchinsk beyond Lake Baikal. Hard labor, originally imposed for a term of years, became a life sentence that doomed the convict to die of cold and exhaustion—a delayed death sentence. A decision was made in July 1797 to commute hard-labor sentences to settlement if the defendant was over 45 years of age, but was annulled in May 1812.[56] Hard labor became the standard punishment for the more serious political crimes, and for murder, larceny with battery and theft over 100 rubles, and highway robbery.

After death and banishment, the third most important penalty was corporal punishment. The use of whipping and beating, whether with a whip, sticks, ropes, or birches, was so widespread in Russian society in the eighteenth century that it was part of a way of life. Andrei Bolotov recounts how, in 1784 at the age of 10, he was often birched by his German tutor for not learning his German vocabulary and was once promised 600 blows: the whipping stopped at 300 when the landlady of the house where his parents were staying called the tutor an "accursed infidel" (*busurman prokliaty*) and reported the deed to his father, who, however, took no action. Bishops had priests whipped or birched, and townsmen "winked affectionately at the whip" as a handy tool for teaching a lesson.[57]

The penal law distinguished between two major forms of corporal punishment, the knout and the whip, with a third, running the gauntlet, reserved for the military. The knout inspired universal fear.[58] Depending on the strength of the criminal and the zeal of the executioner, who could be bribed, ten blows were enough to kill a man, yet sentences of fifty or more blows were not rare. Whipping with the knout was applied to all, regardless of age and sex.[59]

The whip was used on criminals convicted of lesser offenses, for which the knout was considered excessive punishment. It was not administered in the public square; each agency carried out its own sentences behind closed doors. In March 1775, however, the whip was declared a severe punishment, not a mere corrective one, and it required the confirmation of the governor and administration by a public executioner. Following the creation of courts separate from police agencies, a distinction was made between a sentence to whipping pronounced by a court and carried out in public and light whipping over the clothing of the offender—not on his bare back—with a whip, a rope, a horsewhip, or birches, carried out at the police station, from a few lashes to perhaps a dozen. The number of lashes remained unregulated until the Penal Code (*Ulozhenie*) of 1845 abolished the use of the knout and limited lashes to 100. Whipping applied to men and women of any age, but in June 1765 birching was substituted for the whip when the offender was under 15.[60]

These punishments were combined in various ways and entailed legal disabilities. Only death, which had usually been preceded by torture during the trial, stood alone and was final. Corporal punishment was at the heart of Russian penal law and affected social status. Whipping with the knout was considered a shameful punishment, even though it made no distinction of social rank, and the Code of Governmental Procedures of February 1720 declared knouted offenders expelled from the society of "good people" and stripped of their civil rights.[61] The penalty was sometimes imposed alone but gradually became associated with banishment to hard labor, and after 1754 the two punishments together became the single penalty to which death sentences were commuted. Offenders sentenced to hard labor were declared dead to the world and had their marriage and parental rights dissolved, although wives had the option of asking permission to join their husbands.[62] By extension, members of the ruling class and its apparatus were expelled from it, and others lost those privileges to which the law entitled them. Public whipping, on the other hand, because it was so widely applied, entailed at first no disability but became associated with banishment to settlement after 1754. Offenders were thus subject to a double penalty, corporal punishment in each case resulting in expulsion from the community.[63]

What, then, were the reasons for the penal reform of 1753–1754? The suspension of the death penalty reflected the more stable relationships within the ruling elite after 20 years of acute tension during Peter's reign and its aftermath in the factious reign of Anna. Although Elizabeth's "refusal to shed blood"[64]—she may have meant no more at first than a refusal to let vindictiveness guide the purge of those bent on depriving her of her inheritance—has been credited for the new policy, it was in fact nothing more than a return to the resolution of 1726, which had failed only because it was premature. The new stability, embedded in the settlement of the dynastic question and the rapprochement between the Saltykov and Trubetskoi families, demanded an end to the death penalty for members of the growing ruling class: The Senate's concern over the execution of "innocent people" could hardly be construed as compassion for the dependent population. Exile was better than death, and a pardon was always possible. Moreover, at the very time the Senate was putting the finishing touches on the new policy, between March 1753 and September 1754, it submitted a recommendation, confirmed by the empress in July 1754, giving the nobility a monopoly on the production of vodka and compelling its merchant competitors to sell their distilleries or face confiscation,[65] thus granting the ruling class exclusive access to the most important source of cash in an economy of scarcity even more important than the quitrent. The years 1753 and 1754 must thus be seen, in both penal and fiscal legislation, as symptomatic of the growing consolidation of the ruling class.

From then on, as the ideals of the Enlightenment began to penetrate the ruling class and even to be taken seriously in its upper reaches, corporal punishment was seen as a degrading sentence offensive to the dignity of the "wellborn" (*blagorodstvo*), as the entire nobility was called for the first time, also in 1754.[66] It would be, however, a useful distinction of status between the ruling class and the dependent population. The clergy, the ideological apparatus of the ruling class, was the first to benefit from the new attitude: in June 1767 it was given immunity from corporal punishment. The spectacle of priests administering the sacraments between beatings by their "ecclesiastical commanders" (*dukhovnye komandiry*) was deemed unconducive to respect for those whose chief function was to maintain obedience and ideological purity.[67]

In March 1753 the Senate added to the penal code the penalty of civil death, a ceremony of public degradation later replaced by a simple declaration that the convict had been stripped of his civil rights and expelled from the ruling class.[68] Governors could not execute such sentences on their own authority, but condemnation to the knout and hard labor took effect immediately. The charter of April 1785 extended immunity from corporal punishment, including mutilation and branding used to identify hard-labor convicts, to merchants of the first two guilds and "distinguished citizens," as well as to the entire nobility, both life and hereditary. The Noble Charter, however, also provided that a nobleman be stripped of his status for committing treason, larceny in any form, highway robbery, perjury, or various other felonies, thus depriving him of immunity should he commit another crime. This became government policy, despite the attempt made in April 1797 to apply corporal punishment to nobles for the first offense.[69]

Penal reform under Catherine thus served to etch more clearly the privileged position of the ruling class. Peasants and *meshchane* were sent to their fate by order of the governor. Merchants sentenced to the loss of their new privileges had to wait for their fate to be resolved in the Senate, and noblemen, whose nobility could be revoked only by the ruler, had to await his or her sanction, on the recommendation of the Senate, the institutional core of the ruling elite. Peasants and *meshchane* were subject to the full severity of the law,

noblemen and merchants were immune from the double punishments general-
ized in 1754 and spared the indignity of corporal punishment, whose degrading
effect was further recognized in March 1799: it made Russians ineligible for
service in the army,[70] the backbone of the entire system, to which banishment
in the form of the draft had the paradoxical result of raising the status of a
member of the dependent population to that of a free man.

12

Civil Law

Property

Russian law distinguished between real ("immovable") and personal ("movable") property, and real property was in turn divided into patrimonial (*rodovoe*) and acquired (*blagopriobretennoe*) property.[1] Real property—land, whether settled with peasants or empty—included its fixtures, such as forests, orchards, gardens, hayfields, houses, church and factory buildings, saltworks, trade shops (*lavki*), barns and cellars (*pogreby*); and its appurtenances, such as rivers, lakes and swamps, roads, metals and minerals in the subsoil, mills, dams, bridges, and landings, as well as deeds, survey maps, and ledgers. Until 1714 real property held "in service" (*pomest'e*) was distinguished from that held "in demesne" (*votchina*), the chief difference being that the disposal of the former required the assent of the *Pomestnyi Prikaz*. Holders of both, however, belonged to the ruling class, and ownership "in demesne" did not carry exemption from the obligation to serve and command. The inexorable transformation throughout the seventeenth century, by the legal collective will of that class, of *pomest'ia* into *votchiny* rendered the distinction obsolete, although both terms remained in use in the eighteenth century despite the gradual abandonment of the granting of land in Russia proper as a reward for service.[2]

Real property was partible, but restrictions were imposed upon the conveyance of industrial property. Until 1721 merchants (*kuptsy*) were restricted to the conduct of trade and had few other outlets for their surplus capital, in a country whose industrial facilities were few and more could not be built without the grant of a charter by the ruler. Peter's industrial policy encouraged the development of private industry but only within the framework of a serf economy. Serf labor was therefore a necessity, and serfs were ascribed (*pripisany*) to industrial plants, chiefly in the Urals, built and managed by the government. Merchants who wanted to take part in the development of the Ural metallurgical base or build factories elsewhere were allowed in January 1721 to buy a labor force of serfs.[3] Since these serfs, however, appurtenances of privately held real property, could not be sold separately, merchant–industrialists could not become full owners of human beings.

It also became apparent that the division of property characteristic of a legal system that frowned upon unigeniture was bound to destroy the viability

218

of industrial enterprises, consisting as a rule of many mutually dependent components. The issue came to the fore in 1762, when the Senate took up a suit over the inheritance of the vast properties of Alexander Stroganov, who had died 8 years earlier, leaving a family fortune in saltworks, copper and iron mines, forests, and peasants. The Senate resolved that, in this and similar future cases, the widow's portion and the share of the co-heirs must be paid in cash by the principle (*glavnyi, starshii*) heir, the amount to be determined by a fair assessment, even if the inheritance consisted of several enterprises. In the Krapivnikov case (1825), the Senate further resolved that instruments, boilers and saltpans (*posuda*), and spindles (*stany*) were to be considered appurtenances of real property, to be owned only by noblemen, merchants of the first two guilds, and properly authorized peasants. Unqualified owners were given 6 months to sell. These elements of factory production, grouped together under the general term *fabrichnoe zavedenie*, were, however, considered separable from the factory building itself (*fabrichnoe stroenie*), although this interpretation may have later been challenged as contrary to the 1762 decision. Finally, single-heir legacies—rare before 1825—were ipso facto considered impartible.[4]

Personal property was simply that which did not come under the definition of real property—boats, agricultural tools and equipment, horses and cattle, and products severed from the earth, such as cut and threshed grain, extracted (*nalichnye*) metals and minerals, and those already processed (*vyrabotannye*). It also included incorporeal personal property—liquid assets (cash, creditors' notes, mortgages), as well as serfs not used in agriculture (without land). The digest of 1832 left unsettled the question of whether other serfs were real or personal property. The imperial orders of February 1797, May 1801, and January 1815 forbade the printing of announcements of the sale of serfs without land—because these serfs were treated by the law as chattels—and thus implicitly treated serfs settled on a nobleman's land as appurtenances to his real property. On the other hand, landowners who converted serfs into domestics and vice versa, or sent them to earn a living in a town or a factory, most likely continued to view all their serfs as so much personal property. Precious metals, stones, and china were considered imperishable personal property, as distinguished from perishables like pearls, furs, and dresses.[5]

The classification of messuages (*dvory*) caused some hesitation during the eighteenth century. Messuages varied in size, depending on the location and the status of the owner. Large ones, like country seats outside Moscow, had extensive grounds, granaries, artisans' shops, stables, and servants' quarters, but those of the nobility in Moscow itself had an average of only 1.7 habitable rooms in 1775, those of the merchants 2.9, and those of the clergy 1.9. The *Ulozhenie* equated messuages with real property; so did the imperial order of March 1714 on unigeniture. That of March 1720, however, concerned with the settlement of Vasil'ev island in Petersburg, let the Policemaster General's office issue title (*dannye*) to messuages, which were thenceforth considered personal property, no longer justiciable in the College of Justice, the successor at the time to the *Pomestnyi Prikaz*. This remained the law until the Stroganov case of 1762, when the Senate, faced with a dispute over the classification of messuages as part of a large estate, returned to the earlier definition. Thereafter messuages were considered real property.[6]

Patrimonial property was real property lawfully inherited, transmitted in accordance with the statutory law of inheritance if its owner died intestate or in accordance with a will, provided, however, that the intended heir was the same as that designated by the statutory law. Property purchased from relatives (*rodstvenniki*—members of the same *rod*) became part of the buyer's patrimony only if it had been part of the seller's as well, while property bought from outsiders (*chuzherodtsy*—those outside the *rod*) was considered acquired property. Likewise, patrimonial property sold to an outsider left the patrimony and became the buyer's acquired property. In *Sukhotin* v. *Verderevskii* (1807), one party sold patrimonial property to a relative, then bought it back. The Senate declared it still patrimonial property. Had it been sold to an outsider and later bought back, it would have lost its status and become acquired property, even though the seller and the new buyer were the same person. Acquired property included, in addition, grants of real property by the ruler, the statutory portions of widows, any other real property acquired by purchase and labor,[7] and property purchased by a father from a son who had inherited it from his mother; since fathers could not inherit from their sons, when the property left the *rod* of the mother to join that of the father, it thus went to an "outsider."

The concept of private property was not traditional in Russia[8] and began to take hold only with the beginnings of a political infrastructure in town and countryside during the seventeenth century, two or three generations after the massive turnover of landholdings under the brutal policies of Ivan IV, the havoc created by the succession crisis of 1605–1613, and the distribution of the spoils after the proclamation of the Romanov dynasty. Indeed, the ruler had always been assumed to own the spoils of war, including land, which he distributed among the members of his *druzhina*, who expanded over time into a ruling class. Some of the land was given away as *votchiny*, much of it as *pomest'ia*, rewards for loyalty and attributes of membership in the ruling class. But even *votchiny* were subject to confiscation until 1785, as patronage networks continued to fight for the allocation of the spoils and used confiscation of real property as a means of redistributing resources among the winners.[9] Nevertheless, it was no coincidence that *pomest'ia* became equated with *votchiny* in all but law toward the end of the seventeenth century and thenceforth were held in hereditary tenure, since a state of relative domestic peace favored the formation of a political apparatus with an interest in holding land and transmitting it to the next generation.

Real property, however, was conceived in the narrow sense of the surface of the land, without its most important fixtures and appurtenances—forests, metals, and minerals—over which the Treasury retained a preemptive claim. The status of the eighteenth-century landowner thus retained a feature of the old *pomest'e* law that made the holder no more than a tenant and the Treasury an absentee landowner. It was not until 1782 that the right of ownership (*pravo sobstvennosti*) was broadened by the Manifestoes of June and September to include subsoil and forests, a definition confirmed by the Charter of April 1785. The Charter, however, did not give landowners the right to dispose of their property at will, although it recognized the right to sell, mortgage, and exchange it. The law of inheritance imposed severe limitations, including the right of preemption (*vykup*), according to which "relatives" could block the sale of patrimonial property to "outsiders" and buy it themselves on the same terms. The most comprehensive restriction, however, was the legal prohibition against selling land outside the ruling class, as if the land in its entirety were considered the collective patrimony of that class.[10]

The prohibition, however, was often unenforceable, and we know from the imperial order of October 1730 that even peasants bought real property and serfs settled on it. Repeated prohibitions seem to have had little effect, and townsmen and peasants bought and sold real estate in the name of noblemen.[11] Even widespread violations, however, do not invalidate the law, and it remained a fundamental legal principle that land was inalienable to members of the dependent population and its ownership the prerogative of the ruling class. This is shown quite clearly by the surprise with which the Russian authorities discovered after the annexation of the Crimea in 1783 that non-nobles owned land, chiefly orchards and vineyards, and by their insistence that these properties ultimately be absorbed into the land fund at the disposal of the ruling class.[12]

The development of a money economy, however, inevitably brought about the commercialization of land, and the imperial order of December 1801 extended the right to acquire unsettled land and exploit its surface and subsoil to all Russian subjects—excluding private serfs but including peasants of the Treasury and emancipated serfs—and to sell, mortgage, and bequeath it.[13] As a result, private property became a legal concept understood at four levels: personal property belonged to all but serfs, who had no valid claims since anything could legally be taken from them by their owners, although it has been argued that the Manifesto of April 1797 allowing serfs to work on their plots 3 days a week for themselves implicitly recognized their ownership of part of the fruits of their labor.[14] Real property as land likewise belonged to all but serfs. Factories belonged only to landowners, merchants of the first two guilds, and peasants of the Treasury with the proper authorization. Land settled with serfs belonged only to noblemen.

With the Charters of 1785 Russian law began to recognize the holdings of associations, corporations, and social groups (*sosloviia*) as a separate type of private property. The nobles of a gubernia and the registered townsmen in each town formed associations (*obshchestva*), which were granted the right to own buildings, municipal lands and commons (*vygony*), and the revenues they had raised. Churches, likewise, owned real property, as did banks, charitable establishments, like the Golitsyn hospital in Moscow, and private schools, like the Demidov gymnasium in Iaroslavl, and commercial companies (*tovarishchestva*).[15] These holdings, however, were not a large part of the total aggregate of real and industrial property.

The property of the Romanov house must also be considered private. It was of two kinds. Court properties (*dvortsovye*) and the peasants settled on them, together with palaces like Tsarskoe Selo and Pavlovsk and the Altai mines, constituted the collective property of the imperial house acting as a corporation managed by the Cabinet and, until 1786, the Chancery for Court Peasants (*Dvortsovaia Kantseliariia*). The accession of Paul in 1796 witnessed the reappearance of an imperial family—parents and children—for the first time in at least three generations, and lands, peasants, and separate palaces were assigned for the maintenance of individual members, who were thus entitled to a "share"—hence the name of these properties (*udel'nye*)—managed on behalf of the grand dukes and grand duchesses by a minister who, during most of Alexander's reign, was also Director of the Cabinet and Minister of Finance.[16]

What was not recognized as private property came under the general rubric of "treasury-owned" (*kazennye*) properties, increasingly called "state domains" in the nineteenth century, with the exception of certain mixed properties— the so-called possessional factories to which treasury-owned peasants were "ascribed" while other peasants were purchased by merchant industrialists under the provisions of the imperial order of January 1721, suspended in March 1762, restored in March 1798, and allowed to lapse in the 1810s. State domains included lands, forests, rivers and their banks, coastlines, main roads, government buildings, state-owned factories and mines, all revenues from taxation, escheated properties, and all chattels incidental to these properties.[17]

It was not easy to define them in a legal sense in a country where the personalization of power was so extreme and the monopoly of political power in a ruling class obliterated the distinction between public and private activities. Indeed, the digest of 1832 was at a loss to find precedents in Russian law to sustain the concept of separate "state" property. It defined the right of private property as separate from that of state property (*sobstvennost'*)—that is, the "Supreme ownership" (*verkhovnoe obladanie*) of state domains, their use and disposal—but it departed from the usual practice of footnoting the statement.[18] The reference to "Supreme ownership" was a transparent allusion to the Supreme Power (*verkhovnaia vlast'*), the semimystic abstraction representing the ruler, the head of the Romanov house, who never recognized the existence of a state with interests separate from his or her own. Throughout the eighteenth century, treasury-owned properties—land, factories, peasants—were given to members of the ruling class and its ruling elite and confiscated (or returned by mutual agreement) by decree of the ruler (with or without the recommendation of the Procurator General, later the Finance Minister) or at the request of leading members of the elite.

There are two ways of looking at this state of affairs. The first is that "state domains" were still the private property of the ruler in 1825 but were kept in trust for the ruling class as the source of the considerable revenues that paid the salaries and perquisites of the military and civilian apparatus, from which the ruler authorized the sale of various holdings from time to time to improve the Treasury's cash flow. The second is that the private property of the ruling house had the same legal status as that of any member of the ruling class, making the entire land fund of Russia the collective private property of the ruling class and its leader. Kliuchevskii noted that in the seventeenth century the nobility concentrated in their hands the basic capital of the country—land.[19] This was still very much the case at the end of Alexander's reign, despite the intrusion of industrialists. An anonymous author wrote the tsar that it was an undeniable fact that all the land in Russia was the private property of the *pomeshchiki*, including the sovereign, who owned court properties and state domains. We certainly do not need Marxist theory to claim that the ruling class also owned most of the means of production throughout the eighteenth century.[20]

Property was conveyed in various ways: by wills, by inheritance, by gifts, and by sales. Treasury-owned property was sold to the highest bidder; private property changed hands on the conclusion of an agreement between its owner and the prospective buyer. Documents validating the conveyance of property were called deeds (*kreposti*) in general, while sale agreements were called deeds of purchase (*kupchie kreposti*). Personal property was sold with or without legal documents. By 1825, deeds were of two kinds. Deeds of purchase, mortgage agreements, and gifts, as well as emancipation certificates, were considered null and void unless they had been registered in the uezd court or the civil chamber. Wills, dowry settlements (*riadnye zapisi*), hiring contracts, and loan agreements (*zaemnye pis'ma*) constituted a second category of deed called *akty iavochnye*. These did not have to be copied word for word into official ledgers (*zapisnye knigi*), but were merely notarized in the same courts or by notaries elected by the townsmen or appointed by the *magistraty*. All deeds had to be written on stamp paper, however, the fee depending on the value of the property conveyed.[21]

Deeds of purchase had to be witnessed to guarantee that the parties present at the sale were the same as those undertaking the agreement, that no compulsion was involved, and that seller and buyer had agreed upon the price. Some limitations were introduced by the statute on stamp paper of November 1821, which imposed standard prices for the taxation of real estate transactions. Unsettled land was assessed per *desiatina* (2.7 acres), settled land per male serf registered in the census. In Iaroslavl gubernia, for example, a *desiatina* was assessed at 25 rubles, a peasant on settled land at 350 rubles.[22]

Until 1701, deeds were drawn up in the relevant *prikaz* where the fees were collected by clerks whose greed was a national scandal. At the time the government was seeking to concentrate revenue collection in a smaller number of agencies, and it was decided that deeds would thenceforth be written in the Armory (*Oruzheinaia Palata*), headed at the time by Petr Prozorovskii, the Chief of the Treasury. In the wake of the gubernia reform of 1708, deeds began to be drawn up in the governors' chanceries, where clerks were assigned for that purpose (*u krepostnykh del*). After 1718 all transfers of real estate had to be registered in the College of Landed Affairs, while wills were deposited in the College of Justice. In addition, transfers of factories with ascribed peasants and of mines required the confirmation of the Colleges of Manufactures and Mines, respectively. After the local government reform of 1775, the civil chamber took over in each gubernia the jurisdiction of the Colleges of Landed Affairs and Justice, the treasury chamber that of the industrial colleges.

Transfers could also be registered before the uezd court when the value of the transaction did not exceed 100 rubles, raised to 1,000 rubles by 1825. The creation of ministries made no fundamental changes but restored the requirement that the sale of factories and mines be confirmed by the Ministry of Finance. Agreements emancipating serfs in accordance with the law of February 1803 on "free agriculturalists" required the ruler's approval.[23]

The conveyance of property was completed when the buyer was given title. This was a two-stage process carried out by the voevoda's chancery until 1775 and by the land court after the local government reform. Thus, as in criminal procedure, the police had the final say, leading to much abuse. Although the police were legally the court's executive agent, litigants were in fact at the mercy of a land captain, who, for reasons of his own, might choose to delay indefinitely the execution of a judicial decision.

In the first stage, the buyer submitted a copy of the deed to the *magistrat* or the uezd court of the uezd where the property was located, or to the civil chamber of the gubernia if the property was located in different uezds. The land captain repaired to the property, gathered the local people, read the order of the court, admonished serfs on settled land to obey their new owner, and drew up a description of the property witnessed by neighbors (*storonnye liudi*). An announcement was then posted on the courthouse door that the property had changed hands. This was called granting possession (*vvodit' vo vladenie*).

If the transfer was not challenged within 2 years, the court asked the police to grant title (*otkazat'*). The same procedure was followed, neighbors being asked whether they knew of any changes in the interval. If not, their signed statement, called *skazka*, was added to the description of the property, and a copy given to the new owner. Failure to register sale agreements (*spravliat', spravka*) and to assume title in the legally prescribed manner—a common occurrence in the eighteenth century—subjected offenders to civil penalties between 1766 and 1801, and again after 1817.[24]

Inheritance

Inheritance is the intergenerational transfer of property and takes place either by testamentary disposition or through intestate succession. Property to which statute law established no heirs, and to which testamentary intent had not been expressed, escheated to the treasury, in affirmation of the right incidental to sovereignty.[25]

The law of inheritance was in a state of great confusion by the middle of the eighteenth century, as the *nakazy* of 1767 to the Legislative Commission amply testify.[26] In the nature of things, a legal system in which ownership rights had so long been the victim of confiscations and other vicissitudes of the political struggle left in doubt the extent of the owners' power to dispose of their property. Moreover, the provisions of the *Ulozhenie* and the Supplementary Articles, expressing the social situation of the second half of the seventeenth century, had by then become largely outdated. Two generations after the general mobilization of the ruling class began to weaken traditional concepts, notably that of the clan (*rod*), consisting of all the patrilinear descendants, male and female, of a common ancestor (*rodonachalnik*), a political infrastructure was reconstituting itself in the countryside. As a result, a true law of inheritance was pushing up for recognition out of what had been a family law, a law of blood inheritance.[27] Property rights were vague thanks to the common assumption that the true source of wealth and status was not property held in some distant and often insecure uezd of the Russian land but integration into a patronage network and proximity to the ruling elite and the ruler, which gave access to spoils in the form of lucrative appointments that were transitory forms of incorporeal property, to which sons and daughters could claim no heritable rights.

All Russian subjects possessed in theory the right to inherit property, but restrictions on its use were extensive. Serfs, more than half the population, although entitled to inherit even real property, were required to sell it to nobles or merchants within 6 months. Peasants of the Treasury and townsmen not registered in the first two guilds could inherit only personal property.[28] Thus more than 95 percent of the population was not covered by the law of inheritance when the transmission of real property was involved. Those sentenced to hard labor and loss of civil rights were denied all claim to inherit as well, since they were considered dead to the world. On the legator's side, testamentary freedom was limited to the disposition of acquired property, and the testator could not deprive an heir of the share of patrimonial property to which the law entitled him except by selling that property before his death to an "outsider," and only if the prospective heir did not invoke his right of preemption. In 1767 this restriction exercised the Vologda nobles, who lamented that their children, assured of their inheritance, mistreated their parents in various ways and made them prisoners on their own property. Other nobles wanted to leave their patrimony to "dearest and least provided for" outsiders, and in fact often did so, although they knew it was illegal.[29] The law, however, remained inflexible in this matter. Exceptions required the tsar's approval, at least among the ruling elite, as in the Khvostov and Nepliuev cases (1816–1817).[30]

Wills were of three kinds. Some were written by the testator in a *prikaz*—after 1704, in the *Sudnyi Prikaz*, later the College of Justice, and finally, after 1775, in the local courts—and a copy deposited there. The imperial order of February 1704, which had retroactive force, required that all wills be deposited in the *Sudnyi Prikaz* and a fee paid for their registration, thereby recognizing only one kind of will. An order of the Supreme Privy Council of July 1726, however, accepted wills written at home as valid instruments, provided they had been written on stamp paper and witnessed. Such wills, when presented for execution to the appropriate agency, were nevertheless challengeable if it was found that their provisions violated the statute law. Finally, testators left oral wills (*izustnaia pamiat'*, *slovesnoe zaveshchanie*) despite the 1704 order both in the countryside, from which access to the College of Justice was difficult, and among the elite in the capitals. These wills were "announced" after the testa-

tor's death by a father, mother, wife, husband, confessor, or any other designated or self-appointed witness, and had the force of law. The Senate declared
oral wills null and void in *Chaikovskaia* v. *Mokeeva* (1823), except in the event
of the testator's blindness or terminal illness, but the Sate Council ruled out all
exceptions on the grounds that wills could still be written at home before the
secretary of the local court and two witnesses.[31]

The property of individuals who died intestate and left no lawful heirs was
seized by the Treasury. Governors and voevodas were required to inform the
Chancery of Confiscations—created in May 1729, the successor of the *Prikaznaia Palata* and the Chancery of Arrears (*Doimochnaia*) set up in 1700 and
1727, respectively[32]—which then printed announcements three times in the
national *Viedomosti* and assumed title if no claimant appeared. After 1775,
announcements were printed at the request of the gubernia boards, and un-
claimed property was incorporated into the state domains of the gubernia
managed by the treasury chamber. The Town Charter of April 1785 allowed
municipalities to escheat in the property of townsmen not registered in the
guilds (*meshchane*)—obviously insignificant sums. Such right was also ac-
corded the church and the universities when their members left no heirs.[33]

The most troublesome question was at what point the law could refuse to
recognize the existence of an heir, and the controversy revolved around the
concept of *rod*. Peter's resolution of January 1712 forbade the last member of
his *rod* to bequeath or sell his real property to an "outsider." When Dmitri
Kantemir (the grandnephew of the Moldavian *hospodar* who settled in Russia
in 1711 and the last in the Kantemir *rod*) died in 1829, leaving a will bequeath-
ing his property—including that inherited from his mother, thus his patrimonial property—to an "outsider," the Finance Ministry claimed the right to
escheat and won its case after a suit by presumptive heirs was rejected in the
State Council. There were disagreements, however, when acquired property
was involved.[34]

Let us assume that a descendant left a widow and three sons. The first claim
on the estate was the widow's. Her share was left by the *Ulozhenie* (xvii:3) to
the discretion of her sons if she still lived with them, but was fixed—hence its
name, statutory portion (*ukaznaia chast'*)—by the imperial order of March
1731 at one-seventh of the real and one-fourth of her husband's personal
property. If her husband died while her father-in-law was still alive, she was
entitled to a similar share of the property her husband stood to inherit after his
father's death—this, however, only if the couple had children. Her dowry and
whatever property she had owned before her marriage (*sobstvennoe imenie*) or
acquired after it were not included in the statutory portion and were returned
separately.[35]

The remainder of the property was divided among the three sons in equal
shares. This has often been invoked as the cause of the nefarious partition of
landed estates, which left families with substantial holdings and several sons
destitute after three or four generations. Paradoxically, it also made it possible
for the sons to continue to live off their peasants in idleness, if in less and less
luxury, until they became "homesteaders" (*odnodvortsy*).

This, at a time when the mobilization of the ruling class was still official policy, was a cardinal sin in the eyes of Peter I, who invoked Holy Scriptures to declare idleness (*prazdnost'*) "the mother of all evil." As a result, it was decreed in March 1714 that fathers' wills must henceforth name one son the only heir to their real property, the personal property being divided among the other sons and the daughters. If the father died intestate, the property would pass to the oldest son (*bol'shoi syn po pervenstvu*).[36]

This order, like some of Peter's other reforms, was based on an unrealistic premise. It was assumed that the other sons, deprived of land and peasants, would seek careers in the service, trade, or the professions. To leave the ruling class, unless they chose service, and engage in activities that were either scorned or just getting started in Russia was more than they were willing to do. The order dealt a shattering blow to the communal and egalitarian spirit that remained a strong element in the national culture. The application of the order generated such hatred among children and such despair among parents that it was revoked in March 1731.[37] It again became a basic principle of Russian law that real property be divided equally among the sons.

The reality, however, was not so simple. The order of 1731 was addressed to situations in which the decedent died intestate, and it rejected both unigeniture and primogeniture. This did not affect, however, the testamentary freedom of an enterprising landowner to decide which of his sons would inherit his acquired property, although this property then became the son's patrimonial property, which he was required to divide equally among his own sons. Moreover, the imperial order of December 1736 allowed one son to remain on the estate while, say, the other two went to the army.[38] This was a partial return to the provisions of the 1714 order, since the property would be transferred inter vivos by mutual agreement to that one son, the chattels and the usufruct being shared among the others. Such a practice would have been a compromise between unigeniture and entail, to which the Russians seldom resorted. The entail bound ensuing generations to leave the estate impartible and transformed the owner into a de facto tenant for life. Such a departure from statute law required the ruler's approval. It was invoked only twice before 1825—by Zakhar Chernyshev in 1774 and Pavel Stroganov in 1817.[39]

If the decedent left no sons, the inheritance descended to the grandsons in accordance with the right of representation (*pravo predstavleniia*), also called right of entry (*Eintrittsrecht, pravo zastupleniia*). This right created a legal fiction in which the grandsons were entered in the place of their dead father, thus "representing" him in the division of the estate. If there were no grandsons, the great-grandsons, and so on, inherited the right to succeed, extending to the extinction of the descending line.[40]

Let us now assume that the decedent, who left a widow and three sons, also left two daughters. They too were entitled to a statutory portion, each daughter to one-fourteenth of the real property and one-eighth of the chattels, that is, one half of their widowed mother's share. This was bound to create embarrassing problems in large families, like that of Ensign Rachinskii, who left a widow, five sons, and six daughters: there were no chattels left for the sons. In

February 1815 the Senate declared that in such cases the remaining three-fourths of the chattels, after payment of the widow's portion, be shared equally by sons and daughters alike.[41] Daughters had no further claims on the estate as long as a brother or any male in a brother's descending line survived. Upon the extinction of all three descending lines, the two daughters would become co-heirs to the entire estate and divide it equally among themselves, whether married or single (*devki*).[42]

The transmission of inheritance in collateral lines took various forms. In the simplest case, if one of the three sons died without issue, the property passed laterally to his two brothers, who divided it equally. If then descended to the sons of these two sons (i.e., his nephews) and, if they had no sons, to their daughters (i.e., his nieces) until the extinction of the two sons' descending line.[43] In *Nelidova* v. *Kozina* (1750), a daughter claimed the inheritance of an uncle who had died without issue and that of her father following the death of her only brother, who left a married daughter, her niece. It took 22 years for the College of Landed Affairs and the Senate to settle the case, largely because of a controversy over title to the property and over whether the order of 1692—which allowed the equal division of property between aunts and nieces—had been annulled by the order of March 1731. The Senate upheld the *Ulozhenie* and the 1731 order, which gave preference to transmission downward instead of upward and laterally, to direct descendants over sisters and other collateral relatives. This remained the basic law, as shown in the Lutovinov case (1820).[44] The sisters' chance of inheriting thus would be extremely remote if their brothers had any issue.

Government Contracts

Government contracts were known as *podriady, postavki*, and *otkupy*. Although Russian law remained unclear into the nineteenth century about distinguishing them,[45] often used the first two terms interchangeably during the eighteenth, and admitted other forms of contractual obligations with the government, rough distinctions can easily be established.

Podriady were contracts for the delivery of services and were of the most diverse kinds. Some were contracts for construction and repairs: of government buildings to house offices, of stores to keep vodka, of postal stations, of roads and "hydrotechnical works" like canals, sluices, bridges, and towpaths. If these services were local, they were called in the nineteenth century "contributions from the land" (*zemskie povinnosti*) and increasingly became the object of contractual obligations between the governors and competent local people, as they replaced the more authoritarian levies (*nariady*) in force until then. Such local contracts were entered into to pave streets, remove refuse, maintain lampposts and fire equipment, and pay the night watch in towns. *Podriady* were contracts to transport bulky and heavy goods (*tiazhesti*) such as anchors, gun carriages, and artillery shells. Closely related to them were contracts for hire, as when the governor of Moscow asked the Central *Ma-*

gistrat in October 1769 to send sixty tailors to the garrison to sew uniforms because of a shortage of military tailors at a time of heavy demand in the midst of the Turkish war.[46]

Postavki were contracts for the delivery of goods, chiefly food and forage to the army and salt to government-owned stores for resale at a profit to the population. In the Urals they also regulated the supply of ores, like copper, from privately owned mines to smelters run by the College of Mining. The supply of provisions to the army was the single most important contractual activity of the imperial government and the most expensive. Rye and groats (*krupy*), the staples of army food, were purchased directly from producers who assumed the right to transport the goods to army units or military stores, or they were purchased through merchants who assumed the obligation to find the producers and transport the provisions from producer to consumer. Meat and salt were purchased locally but were supplied to the navy by contract.[47]

Contracts for services and contracts for the delivery of goods here became closely interrelated and created problems of legal definition. If a nobleman delivered produce from his estate to a regimental headquarters—clearly the preferred method—it was clearly a *postavka*, but a merchant who found grain in the Ukraine for delivery to Petersburg and had to hire workers and buy boats engaged in a *podriad*. Likewise, the rules of November 1809, which sought to regulate for the first time the construction and maintenance of a national network of roads and waterways, distinguished between the two types of contract, depending on the relationship between offeror and offeree. If the local director of "hydrotechnical works" signed a contract with a local land-owner to send his serfs not needed for agricultural work, the landowner was said to engage in a *postavka*. If he needed an intermediary to find the workers and bring them to the construction site, he signed a contract with a *podriad-chik*. It was altogether possible, in addition, that construction contracts were both *postavki* (of materials like timber, bricks, and iron) and *podriady* (when a merchant or factory owner delivered craftsmen and more materials from afar).[48]

Otkupy were "farms", that is, leases of profitable government properties to the highest bidder. They took various forms. Mills, fisheries, and landings were auctioned off by the government for a term of years and a definite payment (*otdat' v obrok*).[49] Consumption taxes, collected at the transportation stage, were deposited until the 1750s in internal customshouses farmed out to merchants, and the collection of a number of small taxes on trade at fairs and markets was left to local merchants in return for a pledge to remit the antici-pated amount of those taxes for a number of years. As we shall see in Part 5, the imperial government resorted increasingly in the eighteenth century to *otkupy* for the sale of vodka, from which it derived a considerable revenue. The vodka monopoly combined the three types of contract into one. The Treasury signed contracts with landowners, who had a monopoly on production, to supply vodka to local stores (*postavki*) or with merchants who pledged to deliver vodka from distant districts to Petersburg and towns in grain-deficient areas (*podriady*), and it paid the market price. It then signed contracts for the sale (*otkupy*) of that vodka from government-owned stores to tax farmers who pledged to sell it at a fixed price.[50] These sale contracts were made for 10 years in the 1740s and 1750s and for 4 years after 1767, at the end of which they were renegotiated for another term. Other contracts were usually signed for shorter periods.

Negotiating a contract raised three issues: competency, security, and the legal authority to confirm obligations. The issue of competency brought into focus the privileged position of the ruling class. Nobles were allowed to contract with the government without limitation on the amount of their obligation.[51] This not only marked a legal recognition of privileged status, it was also common sense. Since contracts for the most part were pledges to deliver workers, produce, and construction materials, it was cheaper to obtain them from landowners who, in an economy of serfdom, could obtain them at the lowest possible price. Hence the clear preference for *postavki* over *podriady*. Such government contracts were, in effect, less a public commitment to private individuals to pay a definite sum for the delivery of goods than a mutual agreement between members of the apparatus and the political infrastructure and even an internal arrangement among members of the apparatus. In such a case the distinction between public offer and private pledge disappeared altogether.

Members of the dependent population were nevertheless competent to bid for government contracts but were limited to certain types of activities. The Statute of the College of Revenue of June 1731, which included basic provisions on contracts, specifically forbade peasants to bid for *podriady* and *otkupy* and restricted their competency to the supply of boats and carts as well as their own manual labor. A century later the Statute on Bids (*torgi*) of October 1830 would confirm the long-standing policy on contractual segregation. *Meshchane*, craftsmen, and peasants of all denominations, including the serfs of landowners, were declared competent to contract with the government only in activities that were part of their trade.[52]

The participation of merchants (*kuptsy*) in government contracts raised some legal questions because they occupied the upper stratum of the dependent population and first- and second-guild merchants were in close social symbiosis with the ruling class. Their participation was less welcome than that of the landowners because they were intermediaries, and *podriady*, as a rule, cost the government more than the simpler *postavki*. It was, however, inevitable with the development of a money economy. Merchants of the three guilds were all legally competent to bid for contracts, but the amount of their obligations was limited to that of their declared capital; this was confirmed by Article 100 of the Municipal Charter of April 1785.[53] The privileged ones among these government contractors were the tax farmers (*otkupshchiki*), who were allowed to carry swords and often traded a higher bid for a rank giving them access to the ruling class, a privilege denied to other contractors because many among them were peasants while tax farmers had to be merchants.[54] The Supplementary Statute of November 1824 was more generous.[55] First-guild merchants, who had to declare a minimum capital of 50,000 rubles, could bid, like nobles, for any amount. Second- and third-guild merchants, who had to declare a minimum of 20,000 and 8,000 rubles, respectively, were allowed to bid for up to 50,000 and 20,000, respectively. If they chose to bid for higher sums, they had to pay the taxes, especially the tax on declared capital, incumbent upon the next higher guild. *Meshchane* were allowed to bid for up to 4,000 rubles. Peasants wishing to compete with *meshchane* and third-guild merchants for the award of government contracts had first to obtain certificates of competency (*svidetelstva*) in return for a fee.[56]

Anyone competent to bid for a government contract was required to put up security for his pledge. Three questions were involved here. It was first necessary to determine what kind of property was acceptable and how it would be assessed. Landowners pledged their serfs at a rate equal to that fixed by banking legislation for collateral notes. The Manifesto of December 1797 establishing the Auxiliary Bank for the Nobility placed on every male serf registered on the census rolls a value ranging from seventy-five to forty rubles, depending on the gubernia, to which fifty rubles was later added to cope with inflation. Unsettled land was valued at one-third of its taxable sale price.[57] In Iaroslavl gubernia, for example, where a *desiatina* of such land was valued at twenty-five rubles in taxing real estate transactions, it was worth only 8.33 rubles when offered as security for a government contract.[58] Residential stone houses and iron-frame stores, warehouses, and factory buildings, as well as boats, were also accepted, with the additional proviso after 1797 that they be insured. Cash and various negotiable instruments were welcome. Workers who merely contracted their manual labor did not put up security, even though their personal property was liable to confiscation in the event of default. Whatever property was pledged, its value had to equal one-third of the value of the contract. If cash was pledged, its owner had the option of depositing it in the Welfare Board, which paid 5 percent interest on such deposits.[59]

It was then necessary to identify the surety. Ever since their creation in the 1720s, *magistraty* were made to assume that responsibility. Any merchant seeking a government contract had to obtain from his *magistrat* a statement (*odobritel'nyi attestat*, also *svidetelstvo*) listing his assets (*sostoianie, pozhitki*) and other contracts for which his property might still be pledged. Those with a high credit rating (*vsegdashnaia ispravnost*) submitted a statement to that effect or evidence (*otpis, ochistka*) from a government agency that they had fulfilled their contractual obligations on previous occasions to its satisfaction. The *magistrat*'s statement represented an acceptance of collective responsibility for the loss incurred in the event of the principal's default.[60] These safeguards were insufficient to prevent abuses. In Belgorod, for example, the *magistraty* gave more than a dozen merchants statements for various amounts totaling nearly 300,000 rubles. An investigation began in the wake of default by several of those merchants disclosed that individual members of the *magistrat* had given statements as a favor to their friends without the knowledge of other members. The Senate reminded *magistraty* in October 1762 that such statements must be given over the signature of all members and must be countersigned by the contracting merchants in order to prevent their use for concurrent contracts.[61] Abuses continued, nevertheless, as we discover from other Senate decisions in December 1774 and April 1802.[62]

As a double protection against the dishonesty of merchants and the favoritism of *magistraty*, Russian law found it necessary—this is the third question—to require guarantors (*poruchiteli*), whose liability was secondary and collateral, while that of the *magistrat* was primary and direct.[63] The relative ease with which individual members of *magistraty* were willing to give inflated statements was based on the knowledge that if the *magistrat* could not cover the loss with the assets of its members, it would be charged against the property of the entire merchantry of the town. The 1762 decision therefore ordered a merchant to have guarantors, whose "approval" (*odobrenie*) was necessary before he submitted his request for a statement from the *magistrat*, and the 1774 decision required all registered townsmen (*gorozhane*) to state whether a given merchant would be able to carry out his obligations. This collective responsibility for the fulfillment of government contracts even extended to landowners who offered to supply food and forage to army units stationed in their gubernia.

Once the issue of competency and surety had been settled, it was possible to proceed to bidding, followed by the confirmation of the final offer. Before the local government reform of the 1770s, announcements were posted in gubernia chanceries and colleges and printed in the *Viedomosti*, published by the Academy of Sciences in Petersburg and Moscow University, asking for the submission of bids (*torgi*) on three separate occasions at 2-month intervals. When all bids had been submitted and the competency of the bidders and their surety verified, a formal offer was made by the governor's chancery or the college, and interested parties were invited to bid upon bid (*peretorgovat'sia*, *peretorzhka*), and the contract was awarded to the lowest bidder in *postavki* and *podriady*, to the highest in *otkupy*. Governors were empowered to confirm final bids if the value of the contract did not exceed 3,000 rubles. If it did, the contract required the confirmation of the relevant college in Moscow or Petersburg, where many contracts were also negotiated directly. If their value exceeded 10,000 rubles, they were sent to the Senate for confirmation subject to the empress's approval.[64]

After the reform, which closed the colleges and decentralized their operations among gubernia chambers, contractual negotiations were concentrated in the treasury chambers with the authority to confirm final bids up to 10,000 rubles. The regulations of December 1776 made no fundamental changes in procedures but were an attempt to codify past legislation and practices for the first time since the rules (*reguly*) on the provisioning of the army were promulgated in January 1758. The ministerial reform of 1802 and 1811, together with inflation and the increasing diversity of contracts, led to various amendments that were in turn codified in the Statute on Bids of October 1830. It retained the three announcements but combined the three separate bids into one followed by a bid upon bids three days later. Treasury chambers retained their authority to confirm final bids up to 10,000 rubles. Those between 10,000 and 25,000 rubles required the governor's confirmation. Those above 25,000 and those the governor refused to confirm were forwarded to the relevant minister, who submitted those over 50,000 rubles to the Senate's First Department for final confirmation. Two major exceptions were allowed: contracts for "contributions from the land" were confirmed by the governor irrespective of the amount, and all contracts for the sale of vodka required the confirmation of the Finance Minister.[65]

Executing a contract took place in three stages, and litigation over the nonperformance of obligations followed definite rules. The formal contract setting forth the mutual obligations of the parties often included, in the case of *podriady* and *postavki*, a provision for advances (*zadatki*), payable on signing the contract. Their purpose was to give the suppliers, in an economy where credit was either nonexistent or available at usurious rates, sufficient capital to buy an initial supply of provisions and materials as well as boats and carts. This was considered a last resort, however, and the rules of January 1758 allowed such advances to the amount of one-fifth, one-third, or at the most one-half of the value of the contract. A one-fifth advance seems to have become the rule in military contracts for the supply of provisions.[66] The statute of June 1731 made no provisions for advances, yet advances of one-half of the transportation costs may have become the rule in civilian contracts. This was still the case a century later. Peasants who contracted their labor were given advances of one-third to enable them to buy an adequate store of forage for their horses.[67]

Delivering the goods was the second stage in the performance of the contract, and store managers, when provisions and salt were delivered, for example, were enjoined to admit incoming shipments and to give receipts without delay, after verifying the contents of the shipments and the quality of the goods. A perverse refusal to recognize punctuality as an elementary virtue in business transactions and a pattern of dishonesty among suppliers were often major obstacles here. The supplier then submitted his receipt to the governor's chancery, the college, or the treasury chamber after the reform, and requested payment either locally or into his Petersburg or Moscow account. Failure to pay subjected the agency to a monthly fine of 2 percent of the value of the shipment.[68]

The nonperformance of contractual obligations entailed civil penalties, but the apparatus retained strict control over the procedure of redress and kept private litigants at the mercy of its prejudices and its whims. Default followed failure to deliver the goods, but there were other grounds for action, depending on the precision of the formal contract, which it was in the interest of the private parties to leave as vague as possible. That is why the rules of January 1758, the Salt Code of June 1781, and the Liquor Code of September 1781, among others, included model contracts for the guidance of local chanceries and commissions, which could be adapted to circumstances and reviewed in central agencies for the protection of the treasury's interest.[69]

Contractors who failed to deliver were fined the amount of the contract or its unfulfilled part and an additional half of 1 percent a month until a final settlement was reached. These contractors and those dissatisfied with the receipt they had been given on delivery brought suit in the governor's chancery of the province where the delivery had taken place, or in the relevant college, or in the commissary or the Provision Chancery if a military contract was involved.[70] The same central agencies that had approved the contract were thus the judges in their own case. The apparatus, which invited nobles and merchants to enter contractual obligations with it, remained the final judge of what constituted default, imposed collective penalties like the indiscriminate seizure of the property of sureties and guarantors, and even resorted to criminal penalties against merchants such as whipping, the draft, or banishment in the more serious cases.[71]

If we look back on the evolution of the Russian judiciary throughout the eighteenth century, it is easy to see that it was at all times the instrument by which the ruling class exerted its dominion over the dependent population. Before Catherine's reforms, a separate local judiciary hardly existed since the voevoda's managerial competence was universal. This indeed was the major factor establishing the dominion of the ruling class: only its members were invested by the apparatus with a political authority over all members of the dependent population. Toward them, as well as other subordinate noblemen, the voevoda was a regimental commander who instituted disciplinary proceedings against transgressors of the law, and his decisions were final against all but noblemen, who were entitled to higher review. Even merchants, who enjoyed at the time the protection of their own central agency, depended ultimately on the goodwill of the managers of the ruling class.

Catherine's local government reform reinforced the unity of the ruling class by associating apparatus and infrastructure in the settlement of disputes. Landowners and civilian managers, in many cases retired officers, reconstituted at the local level for the first time since the end of the seventeenth century a political alliance that controlled the fate of peasants and townsmen, with the exception of merchants of the first two guilds whose possession of cash qualified them for admission into the ruling class at the opportune moment. The Senate decided their fate, while that of noblemen depended on the ruler as the commander in chief of the ruling class. In criminal and civil cases and in the granting of contracts, peasants and *meshchane* were left at the mercy of the governors as civilian division commanders of an immense army of noble officers and peasant conscripts.

If the institutional forms of domination became very clear in the 1770s, it was no less obvious that the ruling class was also faced with the difficult task of shaping its internal structure. This development must not be seen as the creation of a civil society, unless it is made clear that it was a civil society *within* the ruling class. For how could there be a civil society where the law of real property and inheritance did not apply to 95 percent of the population? The underdevelopment of the civil law was the most important gap to be filled, once the legislation of 1754 on the vodka monopoly and the death penalty was promulgated. The next generation was a time of soul-searching, as the *nakazy* of 1767 well show, and the Charter of 1785 sought in part to satisfy their claims. It was not the autocrat's fault that the civil law remained inadequate, that the laws on the books were ignored, and the work of codification seemed to be going nowhere. It was precisely because the nobility had been a political formation, open enough to outsiders to avoid becoming a caste and impelled by its very monopoly of political life to manage a vast empire without the time to address itself to less pressing but no less fundamental problems, that the task of shaping its internal structure had been neglected. There was a direct link between the *nakazy* and the creation of the State Council nearly 40 years later to do the work that the final consolidation of the ruling class now made possible, a systematic work of legislation that led to the codification of 1832. Even then, however, the uneasy separation of the judicial function, first from administration, then from legislation, continued to show that the administration of justice remained subordinated to political imperatives, especially in the administration of criminal justice, which never quite freed itself from its origins in disciplinary proceedings by which hierarchy was maintained and dominion confirmed.

V

FINANCE

13

Financial Agencies

Management and Auditing

The management of public finances is the single most important function of government. Without adequate revenue, properly accounted for, a government's freedom of action is severely circumscribed, both in the conduct of foreign policy and in building the foundations of a civilized society. Taxation affects the well-being of the population, and tax policy is a powerful tool of social engineering. Great controversies over power relationships in government and society are inseparable from bitter conflicts over the apportionment of the tax burden. Moreover, competition for funds among government agencies is constant in government life, and battles over authority, which determine the shape and structure of political organization, are often battles over access to funds as well. The history of Russian fiscal agencies sheds substantial light on the workings of government and the forces shaping it from one reign to another.

We have seen that Muscovite *prikazy* were administrative agencies headed by members of the ruling elite, each of which dispensed justice as part of its overall responsibilities for a group of towns or a specific function of government. They were also revenue-collecting agencies. There thus existed no separate, distinct, and autonomous fiscal organization and hierarchy of offices: Miliukov lists thirty-five central agencies collecting funds, from a few hundred to nearly 300,000 rubles in 1680.[1]

Nearly all *prikazy* collected fees from petitioners seeking satisfaction of their claims. The *prikaz* of the Great Court (*Bol'shoi Dvorets*) collected the revenue from internal customshouses and the sale of vodka, the *Streltsy Prikaz* collected funds specifically assigned for the maintenance of *streltsy* troops, certain towns in the north and along the western frontier paid their taxes to the *Prikaz* of Foreign Affairs, others to the *Razriad*. Peasants of the church and the court paid their taxes to separate ecclesiastical and court *prikazy*, inhabitants of Moscow paid some of their taxes to a single agency—the *Zemskii Prikaz*—others to different *prikazy*. Such a system, which had grown piecemeal in the course of more than a century, was well designed to strengthen vested interests in the Muscovite government but ill-equipped to meet the wartime need for a simple fiscal machinery to channel funds into critical sectors with minimum delay.[2]

The territorial reform of 1708 marked a radical departure from the fundamental principle of Muscovite administration—that the management of the country should remain centralized to the utmost degree but deconcentrated among the key members of the ruling elite. It emphasized instead that all functions of government, including fiscal administration, be decentralized and concentrated in the hands of a few of those key members. Governors thus became fiscal officers as well, responsible for the collection of nearly all the revenue in their territory, and the management of public finance was considerably simplified as a result. Lines of communication between the eight governors and the Privy Council, later the Senate, were clear and simple, and the chain of command between the ruler and his eight or ten territorial commanders brooked no prevarication and no excuses. That it did not at the same time eliminate corruption was another matter.

Indeed, the danger inherent in making governors into tax collectors, treasury officers, and budget managers—epitomized in the case of Matvei Gagarin, governor of Siberia, hanged in March 1721 for falsifying accounts[3]—was one of the reasons for the recentralization of fiscal management in colleges after 1718. That six of the twelve colleges (in 1722) were either exclusively fiscal agencies or combined industrial management with revenue collection testifies to the importance of financial operations. The reform, then, while considerably simplifying the archaic Muscovite structure, did not make a clean break with it and retained as its cardinal feature the principle that revenue collection should not be the responsibility of a single agency, although a major effort was made to concentrate treasury operations and to create a national budget.

It was the intention of the reformers to establish the College of Revenue as the chief collecting agency of the government, and the statute of June 1731 sought to do so.[4] The persistence of traditional attitudes, however, together with the political infighting among the ruling families and the weakness of the empresses, guaranteed that this intention would never be realized. The College of Revenue collected the customs revenue, the Salt Board the revenue from the sale of salt, the College of Mining the revenue from the sale of metal and the tax on private sales, the College of Manufactures the revenue from the sale of stamp paper and from licenses to open factories.[5] Indeed, the original intent had been undermined from the very beginning, when the decision was made to assign the revenue from the capitation to the College of War. This fundamental distinction between military and civilian revenue set an example imitated by other sectors within the civilian administration, and the situation in the 1760s bore a striking resemblance to that of the 1680s.

Concern over ignorance at the highest levels of the true state of Russian finances—the secrecy of financial data served the interests of each revenue-collection agency—and the consolidation of a new leadership within the ruling elite under an inquisitive and hardworking empress brought about the reforms of the 1770s, which remind us of those of the 1700s. The decisive event was the creation of the Expedition of State Revenues in February 1773, formally subordinate to the Senate's First Department but directly under the Procurator General. This agency was not a new collection agency but a budget office, the first of its kind in imperial Russia. The next step was the creation of treasury chambers in each gubernia. The industrial-management and revenue-collecting responsibilities of the colleges were decentralized and concentrated in them, under the general supervision of the governor. The colleges were then closed, and the expedition, together with a new Treasury, became the only central agencies responsible for financial administration, as even the College of War ceased to be a collection agency. Moreover, both agencies were subordinated to the Procurator General, who emerged as the prototype of a modern minister of finance.[6] The Muscovite tradition was finally laid to rest by the 1780s, and a new, autonomous, and immensely powerful institution was beginning to take shape.

The reforms of Paul, hasty and inexpedient, did not shake the new structure built by Catherine's Procurator General, Prince Viazemskii. The Colleges of Mining, Manufactures, and Commerce were restored in November 1796, the College of Revenue and the Salt Board in February 1797. The Expedition of State Revenues and the Treasury were no longer headed by the same individual.[7] This new deconcentration of fiscal and industrial management was destined to be temporary, however. The creation of ministries in September 1802 reversed the trend and generated an intense rivalry among the Ministries of Finance, Internal Affairs, and Commerce. The Ministry of Commerce—officially still called a college but headed by a minister—assumed jurisdiction over foreign and internal trade, and was headed beginning in August 1808 by the Foreign Minister. Two years later, in August 1810, the management of foreign trade and customs was transferred to the Finance Ministry, and responsibilities for internal trade turned over to the Ministry of Internal Affairs. The College of Commerce was closed in November 1811.[8]

The Finance Ministry was likewise victorious in its rivalry with the Ministry of Internal Affairs (MVD). In August 1810 the management of Treasury lands, the farming out of the vodka monopoly, and the responsibility for mining and transporting salt were moved from the jurisdiction of Internal Affairs to that of Finance. Finally, the MVD's Department of Manufactures and Internal Trade was incorporated into the Finance Ministry in November 1819. By the end of Alexander's reign the recentralization of managerial functions begun in 1796 and their reconcentration after 1802 and especially after 1810 had recreated a massive fiscal–industrial apparatus, which the Expedition of State Revenues had supplanted in the 1780s. The Expedition's responsibilities were gradually distributed among the new agencies making up the Finance Ministry, and it was reorganized into a Department of State Treasury in February 1821.[9] The ministry emerged after 1811 as virtually the only tax-collecting agency in the country, the only Treasury, the chief architect of Russian economic policy, and the central budget office of the empire.

Credit must be given to Dmitrii Gur'ev (1751–1825) for this remarkable achievement, built on the solid foundation laid by Prince Viazemskii. Gur'ev was Director of the Cabinet during the entire reign of Alexander and Minister of Crown Properties between 1806 and 1825, thus the chief financial officer of the ruling house. He was Deputy Finance Minister for 8 years (1802–1810) and

Minister between January 1810 and April 1823. The patronage of Pavel Skavronskii, grandnephew of Catherine I, had given him entrance into the Vorontsov circle, whose interest in fiscal and economic questions was strong. He married a Saltykova, grandniece of Petr Saltykov, the Governor-General of Moscow in the 1760s, whose wife was Prince Viazemskii's aunt by marriage. This marriage linked him with the Shuvalov family—Petr (1710–1762) had been the architect of Russian economic policy in the 1750s, and his son Andrei (1743–1789), Director of the Assignat Bank for more than 20 years (1768–1789). Gur'ev's marriage also made him a distant descendant of Petr Prozorovskii, Peter the Great's Chief of the Treasury.[10] The management of public finance under Alexander I, Speranskii's original but short-lived contribution notwithstanding, clearly remained the preserve of the Saltykov family with which it had been closely associated for more than a century. His successor, Egor (Georg) Kancrin (1774–1844), the son of a German immigrant, had acquired considerable experience in budget making during the war of 1812, when he was Chief of Supply of the army in the field.[11] He had risen through the "German" patronage network in the army and became Finance Minister 2 days before Hans Diebitsch, a former Prussian officer, replaced Petr Volkonskii as Chief of His Majesty's Main Staff.

The Ministry was divided into four departments in June 1811. The Tax Department (*raznykh podatei i sborov*) had jurisdiction over the capitation and the quitrent, income taxes, postal revenues, fees charged for services, the sale of stamp paper, and municipal revenues. It was also responsible for the management of the vodka monopoly. The department thus assumed the financial responsibilities of the Commissary, the old Treasury, the College of Revenue, and the colleges that had collected their own fees. The Foreign Trade Department gathered statistics and information on commercial treaties and tariffs, and managed customshouses. In 1780 the treasury chambers in port cities had taken over those revenue-collecting responsibilities that the College of Commerce and the Chancery of Customs Duties had assumed in 1763.[12]

The other two departments combined revenue collection with broad managerial responsibilities. The Department of State Domains was the first establishment of its kind, claiming as it did jurisdiction over peasants and lands of the Treasury, the management of government-owned distilleries and the marketing of their production, the leasing of revenue-producing state properties, and the management of state forests. Never before had the management of the scattered properties of the government been so concentrated in a single agency, even though its operations would have been impossible without the support of the treasury chamber in each gubernia. The other department was that of Mining and Salt Affairs, which absorbed the responsibilities of the old College of Mining and the Salt Board. It managed government-owned metallurgical plants and mines, together with peasants and forests attached to them; provided assistance to private owners; gave instructions for the extraction of salt; and contracted for its transportation and sale. A fifth department, that of Manufactures and Internal Trade, added in 1819, assumed the responsibilities of the College of Manufacture; its major function was to encourage light industry. A sixth department was added in February 1821 with responsibilities for treasury operations, as we shall see presently.[13] As a result, at least eight colleges and agencies of equal status, abolished in the 1780s and recreated by Paul, were concentrated under the leadership of a single minister, an immense concentration of financial and industrial power that recalls Prince Viazemskii's empire in the 1780s.

Fiscal management consists of three distinct operations: collecting revenue, depositing it in a treasury from which it can be disbursed, and auditing both the revenue and the expenditures. This third operation was the most difficult and the most sensitive because it required reliable statistical information, which collecting agencies were for long both unable and unwilling to supply, and because it threatened to expose the fraudulent practices that everyone had an interest in concealing.

Nevertheless, an auditing agency was an integral part of the Russian government. There had been an Accounting (*schetnyi*) *Prikaz* in the 1650s, but it no longer existed in the 1690s, perhaps because the jockeying for power during the 1680s was not conducive to the maintenance of a mechanism of control over the operations of individual agencies. The chief purpose of the Privy Chancery, however, created at a time of national emergency, was precisely to correct this obvious institutional flaw. After the creation of the Senate, the Chancery became exclusively a chamber of audit and was followed in 1718 by a College of Audit, but one whose jurisdiction was restricted to the auditing of civilian accounts, while the College of War conducted its own internal audit. In 1722, however, the college was abolished and the auditing of both civilian and military accounts was vested in the Senate and its chancery, under the general supervision of the procurator general as the eye of the sovereign watching over the execution of the law.[14]

Vesting new responsibilities on an overburdened Senate was usually a prescription for nonexecution. By 1733, when it was found necessary to restore the College of Audit to handle current accounts, the situation was such that a separate commission had to be appointed to audit civilian and military accounts for the years 1719–1732—an acknowledgment that nothing had been done for more than a decade. The commission was abolished in 1736, and a branch of the college was opened in Moscow in 1737 to audit the accounts of Moscow-based agencies. Meanwhile, the military establishment had continued to carry out its internal audit, that of the Commissary vested in an accounting board (*schetnaia kontora*) subordinated to it, that of the Chancery of Artilley in the College of War to which it was subordinated. The reorganization of the central military establishment in 1736 made the board independent of the Commissary, giving the President of the College of War an opportunity to gain an insight into the secret dealings of the Commissary. The board also became independent of the Senate and the College of Audit, even though the Instruction of May 1733 gave the college jurisdiction over the accounts of the entire government. What happened during the reaction of the 1740s and 1750s is not clear, but the state of auditing in the 1760s was such that one may safely assume that it had become a forgotten science. To correct this dismal situation, the college, now based in Moscow, was divided into six departments in December 1763 in the hope that a rational division of labor would expedite the auditing of present accounts and eliminate the enormous backlog. The accounts of regiments and other military units were henceforth sent directly to the college, thus giving it access to those accounts without a preliminary audit in the Commissary and the College of War.[15]

The creation of the Expedition of State Revenues in February 1773 marked the beginning of a thorough reorganization of auditing as well, since realistic budget making was impossible without a reliable and comprehensive audit of all governmental revenues and expenditures. The creation of gubernias imposed a territorial framework on the auditing of accounts. What had been an indiscriminate operation (the auditing of large numbers of individual agency accounts) was replaced by the auditing of accounts submitted by the treasury chambers (twenty-six in Russia proper) for all agencies operating in their gubernia. In December 1779, as the territorial reform was approaching completion, an Expedition for the Auditing of Accounts was created in Petersburg. At the same time, the auditing of military accounts became once again an autonomous operation, with the creation of a separate Expedition (*schetnaia ekspeditsiia*) in the College of War with jurisdiction over the accounts of the Commissary, the Provision and Artillery Chanceries, as well as those of the regiments and garrisons. Potemkin's power was then at its height, and he and Prince Viazemskii were building their separate empires, a situation not without parallel in the post-1736 rivalry between Münnich and Osterman. Nevertheless, the Procurator General seems to have gained the upper hand, because the civilian Expedition was given authority in February 1781 to audit two types of accounts, those submitted by the treasury chambers and those submitted by the military expedition. The civilian Expedition was thenceforth required to review two major kinds of preliminary audits, a consolidated one for the military establishment and twenty-six separate ones for Russia alone, instead of several hundred separate and incomplete accounts.[16]

This remarkable achievement in cutting through what had become an administrative tangle improved the state of accounting and audit, yet considerable delays remained the norm at the beginning of the nineteenth century. This was especially true in the auditing of military accounts, unaffected by the territorial reform that so dramatically simplified the auditing of civilian accounts. Regiments, garrisons, units of every size, agencies of every kind and at all levels continued to send their account books pell-mell to the military Expedition, which found itself swamped by a mass of the most detailed unprocessed statistics—the number of rolls and eggs issued to every hospital patient every month—with which it could not cope. It was reorganized and divided into sections in July 1806, and its procedures were streamlined.[17]

Meanwhile, the ministerial reform of September 1802 did not at first affect the status of the civilian Expedition. It remained subordinated to the State Treasurer—who was thus in the crucial position of auditing his own accounts—but faced the possibility of being taken over by the Finance Ministry when Fedor Golubtsov was both Finance Minister and State Treasurer between 1807 and 1810. The takeover bid by an empire-building Finance Ministry failed, however. In January 1811 the civilian and military Expeditions were merged into a Main Administration for the Auditing of State Accounts, divided into two departments, one for civilian, the other for military accounts.[18] Its chief, called State Comptroller, had ministerial status. The first holder of the post, Balthasar von Campenhausen, had been the last State Treasurer in 1810–1811. Auditing thus became a single and indivisible operation, facilitated by the no-less-remarkable progress achieved in concentrating treasury operations in specialized agencies.

Treasury, Mint, and Banks

The concentration of all revenue in a single treasury is a fundamental prerequisite to responsible budget making. It enables the government to keep track of its revenue during the entire budget period, to project realistic expenditures, and to regulate the cash flow from collecting to disbursing agencies across the entire country.[19] The general acceptance until 1780 of the principle of specialization of revenues was incompatible with the creation of a single Treasury, suited as it was to autonomous *prikazy* and colleges managing people and property, dispensing justice, and keeping their own budgets.

There was a Grand Treasury (*Prikaz Bol'shoi Kazny*) in Moscow at the end of the seventeenth century, and it remained in existence until the creation of colleges in 1718. Its chief, Petr Prozorovskii, was a cousin of the tsar. Accounting procedures were so loose and the autonomy of key members of the ruling elite was so broad that he kept funds for emergencies in a secret reserve unknown to the tsar himself but agreed to show it to him at a critical time, providing Peter kept the secret from Menshikov.[20] Three generations later there were rumors that Prince Viazemskii was doing the same thing.[21] The major rival of the Grand Treasury was the Burgermasters' Chamber (*burmisterskaia palata* or *ratusha*), created for the purpose of collecting the revenue from the sale of vodka and from customhouses: by 1701 it had collected 1.2 million and the Treasury 700,000 rubles.[22] Its major rivals were all the other *prikazy* holding sources of revenue assigned to support their operations, each functioning as a minitreasury.

The reform of 1718 was intended to be a milestone in the history of the Russian treasury. It created a College of State Expenditures or Treasury (*Stats-Kontora*), intended to function as a single treasury in which all revenue, except the capitation, would be deposited and from which expenditures would be defrayed on presentation of an imperial order authorizing the release of funds. Its strong room was located in the Peter and Paul fortress in Petersburg.[23] The new college was thus the counterpart of the College of Revenue created for the purpose of drawing up a revenue budget—a task it was never able to carry out.

We have seen that a budget office called the Expedition of State Revenues was created in February 1773. Six years later, in December 1779, it expanded and divided into four expeditions, one for revenues, one for expenditures, a third for arrears, the fourth for auditing. The result was to concentrate in a single agency subordinated to the Procurator General the responsibilities of three colleges—revenue, expenditures, and audit—and render those bloated agencies superfluous. This was the first and decisive step in the general assault against the collegial organization that marked the first half of Catherine's reign, beginning as early as 1764 when governors were subordinated directly to the Senate and no longer to colleges. The logical corollary was then to concentrate in a single treasury all revenue collection, even the revenue from the capitation. This was done in the summer of 1780 with the creation of two treasuries, one for ordinary expenditures, the other for extraordinary expenditures to be defrayed from balances accumulated in the course of the year in every agency that had received funds for its ordinary expenditures. Each treasury in turn consisted of two agencies, one in Moscow, the other in Petersburg.[24] These agencies reported directly to a State Treasurer, who was not appointed until 1793 because the Procurator General became interim state treasurer until his retirement. As a result, the deconcentration of fiscal management, a characteristic feature of government by *prikazy* and colleges, made way for a determined concentration of budget-making and treasury operations under the leadership of a single individual.

Paul retained this arrangement, but the ministerial reform of 1802 raised the question of where the Treasury would fit in the new administrative structure characterized by the creation of an uncoordinated set of functional commands, each competing with all the others to extend its jurisdiction to the limits of the possible and seeking to create its own local organs. The new Finance Ministry did not emerge out of Prince Viazemskii's Expedition of State Revenues but was a new and therefore rival organization. From the very beginning, responsibility for preparing and executing the budget passed to the ministry, thus integrating three of the four expeditions into the ministerial structure. The Treasury proper succeeded in retaining semiindependence, although the first two finance ministers were also state treasurers at one time or another, sometimes concurrently. In June 1811, however, at the time of the second ministerial reform and shortly after Gur'ev took command of the ministry, the post was abolished, and the Finance Ministry assumed de facto jurisdiction over the Treasury. Its final integration took place in February 1821, when the four treasuries created in 1780 were merged into one Central (*Glavnoe*) Treasury in Petersburg and treasury operations were placed under the supervision of the Department of State Treasury in the Finance Ministry.[25] This meant the reconcentration of fiscal management under a single minister, as had been the case between 1780 and 1793, but with one major difference. The auditing of accounts had gained administrative autonomy.

The revenue was paid to collection agencies and was deposited in the Treasury after 1780. The payment of taxes, except those paid in kind, presupposed the existence of a money economy, and Russia suffered until the 1770s from a severe shortage of coins. It never benefited from the influx of gold and silver from South America that so stimulated the western European economies in the sixteenth century, although Russian silver coins in the eighteenth century were often former German thalers of various denominations, restamped with the two-headed eagle. There were no sources of precious metals in European Russia until Peter's reign, when the Ural mines began to operate, yielding gold and silver. Silver also came from the mines of distant Nerchisk, and those of the Altai, purchased from the Demidovs in the 1750s, produced small quantities of gold. Copper was more readily available.[26] With precious metals so scarce, the Russian mint pursued a dual goal—to mint coins from native metal or coins acquired as foreign exchange, and to increase the money supply by melting down existing coins and minting new ones with a reduced metal content.

The Muscovite mint (*monetnyi dvor*) was unaffected by Peter's reform until 1719 and continued to be headed by close relatives of the ruling house, including Petr Prozorovskii, the chief of the Treasury between 1714 and 1719. After the creation of the colleges, it moved to Petersburg and was subordinated first to the College of Revenue, then to that of Mining. In 1724 a second mint was opened in Ekaterinburg, the headquarters of the administration of the Ural and Siberian mines, and remained in existence until 1762. Its purpose was to mint coins for Siberia, which at the time began at Viatka and included the Urals.[27]

The supervision of the technical operations of the Mint was taken away from the College of Mining in 1727 and vested in a separate board (*kontora*), later called Chancery, which moved to Peterburg in 1754, leaving a branch in Moscow. In 1763, it was reincorporated into the College of Mining and became the responsibility of its Currency (*Monetnyi*) Department until the abolition of the college 20 years later. The Department remained, however, and was subordinated to the Procurator General until 1800, when the president of the restored college reassumed jurisdiction over it. It became part of the Finance Ministry in 1802 but was integrated into the Department of Mining and Salt Affairs in 1811. Meanwhile, a separate expedition for the reminting (*peredel*) of copper coins was created in October 1756 at the instigation of the Chief of the Artillery, Petr Shuvalov, in order to mint lighter-weight copper coins to facilitate the financing of military operations during the Seven Years' War. The conversion of the old coins was suspended in 1763, but the Expedition was not closed until 1780.[28]

The dependence on heavy coins imposed severe limitations upon the cash flow so essential to economic activity and budgetary operations. Suffice it to say that a ruble's worth of copper coins weighed 1 kilogram, or more than 2 pounds, and that transferring only 10,000 rubles from a gubernia capital to Moscow meant transporting 10 tons of metal,[29] often over considerable distances on bad roads unless water transport was available. As late as 1764, there were only 80 million silver rubles in circulation, or less than 4 rubles per capita,[30] and silver currency was usually reserved for foreign exchange transactions and to pay troops stationed abroad. Fear that this situation would become worse during the first Turkish war compelled the government to resort to the printing of paper money in 1768.

The idea was not new. It had been raised under Elizabeth but rejected in favor of minting new copper coins weighing half as much as the old ones.

Peter III had ordered the printing of 5 million rubles, but his overthrow had suspended the operation.[31] In December 1768, however, an Imperial Manifesto announced the creation of a bank of issue called the Assignat Bank in Petersburg with a branch in Moscow under a Chief Director. The first holder of the post was Andrei Shuvalov, Petr's son. After his death in 1789, the Procurator General took over the bank's management. As a result, the budget office, the Treasury, the auditing of accounts, and the creation of currency were concentrated in the hands of a single individual. After 1799 the bank regained its administrative autonomy, which it retained after the creation of the Finance Ministry.

The Assignat Bank became the government's main source of funds for its expansionist foreign policy and the protracted conflict with Napoleon. Unrestrained resort to the printing press, however, fueled unprecedented inflation,[32] and the depreciation of the ruble had gone so far by 1810 that Speranskii, then at the height of his influence with Alexander, proposed to reduce the amount of paper rubles in circulation by selling government-owned properties and destroying the withdrawn rubles. To carry out this operation, a Commission to Liquidate the National Debt (*pogasheniia dolgov*) was created in May, independent of the Treasury and the Finance Ministry and consisting of five directors, three of them elected by the merchantry, serving under a Chief Director. In February 1812 a council (*soviet*) was added to supervise the Commission's operations; it consisted of eighteen members, three of them members of the State Council, six senators, and nine merchants elected by their corporations in Petersburg, Moscow, and Riga. It met only once a year and submitted a report to the tsar on the progress of the redemption.[33]

The growth of the money economy in the wake of the Petrine reforms threatened eventually to undermine the commanding position of the ruling class. The acquisition of new tastes and habits, the transfer of the political capital to distant and inhospitable Petersburg, and the near cessation of land grants as a reward for political work compelled the ruling class to find sources of cash. The commercialization of estate management was a solution for some, hence the abundance of instructions addressed by absentee landlords to their stewards in order to maximize production, but for these and many less-enterprising landowners, credit became a necessity. Commercial credit, however, was nonexistent except at usurious rates from private sources, whether rich members of the ruling elite or successful merchants.

The two sources of ready cash, in a society still overwhelmingly agrarian and hardly stimulated by commercial exchanges, were government credit and the production of vodka for sale to the peasantry. It was thus no coincidence that a central Bank for the Nobility was established by the government in May 1754 or that landowners won a monopoly over distilling in July by barring merchants from competition. The Bank was not a bank of deposit: there were no savings to mobilize among the nobility. It was instead an administrative agency through which the elite withdrew funds from the treasury of the ruling class in order to help its ambitious, extravagant, or bankrupt members out of the clutches of "shameless robbers" (*bezsovestnye grabiteli*) charging interest of up to 20 percent—"something unknown in the entire world." Its original capital was 750,000 rubles—at a time when the revenue budget amounted to about 12 million rubles—and it made loans ranging from 500 to 1,000 rubles against the security of serf ownership, fifty serfs being the minimum collateral, not loans or revenue from the borrower's estate, as would have been the case if the loan had been a purely commercial transaction. The rate of interest was fixed at six percent.[34]

The Bank had branches in Moscow and Petersburg, and its activities were originally designed to benefit the nobility in the two capitals. The original capital was soon exhausted but was then increased to over 6 million to cope with demand, and loans were made to a broader group of the nobility. In 1770 it was allowed to accept deposits from private individuals, and its loans reached 4.3 million rubles 5 years later.[35] Its beneficiaries were nevertheless more likely to be members of the ruling elite, and the Bank became in fact the instrument by which this core of the ruling class financed its modernization.[36] In the 1770s its Chief Director in Petersburg, Ivan Viazemskii, was a relative of the Procurator General, and his counterpart in Moscow, Nikolai Sheremetev, was the son of Petr Sheremetev, whose marriage to Varvara Cherkasskaia in 1743 had created the largest private fortune in Russia.

After the completion of the local government reform and the grant of a charter to the nobility confirming its privileges as the ruling class of the country, more resources were placed at its disposal to help it maintain its status and avoid the usurers. In June 1786, debts were canceled on a large scale, and the Bank was reorganized as the Loan (*Zaemnyi*) Bank by adding to its assets 33 million rubles from the Assignat Bank, 22 of them for new loans to the nobility and the other 11 million for loans to towns against the security of stone buildings. Its first Chief Director was Petr Zavadovskii, concurrently one of the empress's secretaries. It was surbordinated in 1802 to the Finance Minister.[37]

Loans to the nobility served a dual purpose—some maintained the expensive habits of the ruling class, others were for agricultural development. Personal loans were suspended in 1811 at a time of extreme stringency on the eve of the French invasion, and the Auxiliary (*Vspomogatel'nyi*) Bank, created in 1797 to help the nobility redeem properties mortgaged with the Loan Bank, was incorporated into the latter in March 1812. Meanwhile, loans to agriculture began to come increasingly from the so-called *Sokhrannye Kazny*, credit offices attached to the Petersburg and Moscow Orphanages, created in 1772, which used endowments and deposits to make their loans.[38] These agencies did not depend on the Finance Ministry but were part of the empire built by the dowager empress, Maria Fedorovna, outside the governmental structure. In 1821 Gur'ev proposed to abolish the Loan Bank as superfluous, but the State Council took no action. His successor, Kankrin, who may have been more attuned to political realities because he was an outsider, proposed instead to reopen the inactive Loan Bank in May 1824, on the grounds that loans to the nobility were a necessity whether or not they were used productively, and even if the commercial sector had to be starved of funds as a result. His proposal

was accepted, and loans had reached 13 million rubles by the end of 1825.[39]
The primacy of political considerations was never forgotten.

By contrast, the merchants' lack of political power due to the insufficient
development of commerce made it difficult to obtain government credit without engaging in mutually profitable dealings with members of the ruling elite.
It was thus a break with tradition when a Commercial Bank was created in
May 1754, at the same time as the Bank for the Nobility. Its single purpose,
however, was to grant loans to Petersburg merchants engaged in foreign trade,
and it was therefore no more than a credit office of the College of Commerce.
Loans were made against merchandise warehoused in the port, but the government's insistence on short-term loans repayable within 6 months showed its
unwillingness to extend major credit and its ignorance of the real needs of
commerce. The Bank's first Director, Iakov Evreinov, was also president of the
college. In the 1760s the Director was Nikolai Golovin, the grandson in the
female line of Petr Shafirov, vice-president of the College of Foreign Affairs
between 1718 and 1723 and cousin of Nikolai Sheremetev. By then, however,
the Bank was moribund, and it ceased to operate in 1770, although it was not
closed officially until 1782.[40] The parallel between the expansion of credit to
the ruling class and the reluctance to support the commercial undertakings of
merchants was striking, more evidence of the exclusive access of the nobility to
government resources to serve its interests.

The reign of Paul, we know, witnessed a reaction against such a stifling
policy, in part because the economic development of the country was strengthening the upper layer of the merchantry, which now sought and gained recognition from a ruler trying to free himself from his dependence on the ruling
class in the name of the general interest. Beginning in 1797, the creation in
several cities of discounting offices (*uchetnye kontory*), subordinated to the
Assignat Bank, signaled a new attitude toward the interests of the commercial
classes. They remained in existence until the creation in May 1817 of a
Commercial Bank in Petersburg, its deposits personally guaranteed by the tsar.
But the ruling class opposed Bank credit to merchants and under Kankrin was
able, by insisting on stricter terms for commercial loans, to reassert the
primacy of its claims to scarce resources against those of manufacturers and
merchants.[41]

Local Agencies

The success of fiscal management did not depend solely on an efficient division
of functions among central agencies and the coordination of their responsibilities by a single individual. It depended to an even greater extent on the
existence of local agencies, in which the revenue extracted from the dependent
population was accounted for, held in reserve, and disbursed in accordance
with instructions. Without reliable accounting at the local level, the work of
central agencies remained an exercise in futility.

In the seventeenth century, voevodas were the government's tax collectors, sending to various *prikazy* the revenue assigned each of them by law, but a strict demarcation of responsibilities did not yet exist between the central agencies in Moscow and the voevodas, and revenue was also paid directly into the coffers of the *prikazy*. The concentration of commercial activity and legal transactions in the capital made this a natural practice. Moreover, expecting voevodas to "feed themselves" on the dependent population assumed that much of the revenue would never reach central agencies. The constant call to collect "arrears" concealed the recognition that they had in fact been paid but had disappeared on their way from the villages to the capital. The loss was compounded by the fact that taxes were not paid directly but through elected representatives (*vybornye*), whom voevodas bullied into submission without fear of retribution.[42]

It was therefore understandable that the government should seek to split revenue collection among different individuals and agencies. The resort to a deconcentration of fiscal operations, not a money-saving procedure in itself, reveals the ruling elite's concern over the fiscal liberties taken by its official delegates. After 1681, voevodas were stripped of the authority to collect the military tax (*streletskaia podat'*) and the proceeds from the sale of vodka. This revenue was instead collected by elected "headmen" (*vybornye golovy*) and *tselovalniki*, and deposited directly in the *Streltsy Prikaz* and the Treasury. Beginning in 1699, when the urban population engaging in trade and manufacture was removed from under the voevoda's jurisdiction and placed under its own "*prikaz*," the *Ratusha*, local representatives, now called *burmistry*, became at the same time tax collectors for yet another specialized agency, collecting the vodka and salt revenues and internal custom duties, and selling government property, while fees continued to be sent by the voevodas to Moscow or paid there directly.[43]

We remember that the administrative–territorial reform of 1708 radically changed the Muscovite administrative pattern. The revenue was no longer sent to Moscow but was kept in the gubernia capitals, where governors became territorial budget officers. Innovative and challenging in its far-reaching implications, the reform nevertheless threatened to reestablish on a much larger scale the scandalous abuses committed by the voevodas. Both governor and voevoda belonged to a ruling class for which no "constitutional" division existed between the national, "state," revenues and the collective revenues of its members. The occasional repression of corruption and bribery served only as a warning to the worst offenders that certain bounds must be respected. At other times the concept of corruption was incomprehensible to a ruling class used to extracting revenue from the dependent population to serve its interests and prestige and to keep up the patronage network that sustained its power.

The creation of colleges was a reversion to the late Muscovite pattern but improved on it by giving colleges local agencies responsible to both the governor or provincial voevoda and their headquarters in Moscow or Petersburg. The College of Revenue had its own tax collector (*nadziratel sborov*, also called *kamerir*) in each province with jurisdiction over all revenue, including proceeds from the sale of vodka and salt, and profits from government properties. In each uezd there was a land commissioner (*zemskii komissar*), at first appointed by the college, then elected by the political infrastructure of the uezd, who combined police and fiscal powers and was the dreaded agent of the ruling class in the countryside. *Magistraty*, created in 1724 under a Central *Magistrat*, assumed jurisdiction over the collection of revenue from the registered urban population but were no more than institutionalized *golovy* and *tselovalniki* now reporting to a member of the ruling elite in Petersburg instead of to the local voevoda. They sold vodka and salt in the towns, and individual merchants hawked these two revenue-rich commodities at fairs and in villages. The Treasury, too, had its own provincial agent called *rentmeister*, who received the revenue collected by the *kamerir* and deposited it in a local treasury (*renterei*), from which funds were disbursed at Treasury orders.[44] By 1725 a streamlined and efficient fiscal organization was taking shape, at least on paper. It concentrated revenue collection in the office of a single agent and treasury operations in that of another, and heralded the possibility of drawing up about two dozen territorial budgets from which a national budget could be assembled.

This new administrative structure, however, may well have been ahead of its time. Competent personnel were lacking; collectors and treasurers were no different from voevodas. *Magistraty* sometimes refused to collect revenue. Financial data were not sent or were incomplete and sent intermittently, so that no coherent revenue budget could be prepared. The return to Muscovite patterns could not be limited to the central government, and the difficult financial situation inherited by Peter's successors demanded curtailments of staff. As early as July 1726, the provincial treasurers were abolished except in Petersburg and Moscow, and tax collectors as agents of the College of Revenue were recalled a year later, when voevodas were restored as the local agents of the ruling elite with jurisdiction over all governmental operations in their provinces, uezds, and towns. The *magistraty* were also subordinated to them.[45]

Nevertheless, the specialization of revenues—the assignment of each source of revenue to a different agency serving a definite purpose—militated not only against the retention of the Petrine organization but also against the transformation of the voevoda and governor into the only revenue and treasury agents of the government. The capitation was not deposited in the provincial treasuries; the revenue from the sale of vodka, when farmed out, was paid in Moscow; the customs revenue in Arkhangesk and Petersburg was deposited in customshouses subordinated to the College of Commerce. This fragmentation of revenue collection, which Peter had sought to eliminate, rendered his reform ineffective and contributed to the waste and fraud that Catherine's government would find so disheartening in the early 1760s.

It is one of the most remarkable features of Russian administrative history between 1689 and 1825 that all major principles of territorial administration were tried in various combinations.[46] Such experimentation reflected the pressure and internal stresses in a ruling class consolidating its power in the midst of dramatic changes brought about by the country's transformation into a European power and a continental empire. By the late 1760s the pressures on the political infrastructure and the recognition that the concentration of fiscal management was the only way to bring order out of the chaos of Russian finances compelled the government to decentralize. The reform of 1708 was the obvious model, although perhaps an unconscious one. At that time the necessities of war had compelled the government to break the hold of the *prikazy* and to make the office of the governor a regional government in which tax collection and treasury operations were concentrated.

The local government reform of the 1770s created a treasury chamber (*kazennaia palata*) in each gubernia, headed by the vice-governor, subordinated to the governor. It originally consisted of a director of state domains ("economy"), a gubernia treasurer, one councillor, and two assessors, all appointed by the Senate. Its primary jurisdiction was to manage government properties, including factories, stores, mills, and fisheries, and to collect revenue from them and from peasants of the Treasury. This was the responsibility of the "director of economy," whose office was called an "expedition," obviously a favorite term of administrative practitioners during Catherine's reign. Gradually, the number of expeditions was raised to eight, some created only in appropriate gubernias. One assumed jurisdiction over bridges, ferries, and all public buildings; another kept the census books and records of recruit levies. The expedition of the director of the economy was a third. A fourth managed the salt and vodka monopolies, a fifth was found only in gubernias where government-owned and privately-owned mines and metallurgical plants required supervision and assistance. Even the customshouses were subordinated to an expedition of the chamber.[47]

As a result, management of the country's entire economy, until then overcentralized in Moscow- and Petersburg-based colleges, was decentralized and concentrated within each gubernia in a single agency. Whether this decentralization made possible a unified economic policy is doubtful, but it is certain that it subordinated such a policy to the interests of the political infrastructure in one gubernia after another at a time when credit was expanded for the ruling class and restricted for the merchant class. This was the heyday of Russian industry, when the country produced more iron than England and exported it in competition with Sweden.[48] Its decline in the first quarter of the nineteenth century may have been the price the ruling class had to pay for the consolidation of its power during the preceding generation.

The reform concentrated more than economic management in the chamber. A treasury expedition under a gubernia treasurer became the respository of all funds collected in the gubernia. The specialization of revenue ceased to be the guiding principle of treasury operations, and even the capitation was included in the general revenue, although still accounted for separately. The gubernia treasurer combined the function of the Petrine *kamerir* and treasurer, a logical development that did away with the separation of responsibility for collection and for holding funds, which had been those of the College of Revenue and the Treasury. He drew up a revenue budget for the gubernia and released funds from the gubernia treasury. Finally, an auditing expedition, the eighth, was added in 1782 to carry out a preliminary audit of economic management and treasury operations before the account books were forwarded to the Expedition of State Revenues in Petersburg.[49]

Local banks and credit agencies, however, remained outside the control of the chamber. By 1788 there were eight branches of the Assignat Bank in towns with substantial commercial activity. Likewise, the reform created in each gubernia a Board of Public Welfare (*prikaz obshchestvennogo prizreniia*) with an initial capital of 15,000 rubles to be loaned at interest against proper collateral and replenished by fines imposed as civil penalties. This credit agency consisted of six assessors from the intermediate courts representing the nobility, the townsmen, and the peasants of the treasury, but it met under the chairmanship of the governor only during the winter months.[50] At other times it was in fact no more than an informal meeting between the governor and the gubernia marshal, at which the delegate of the ruling elite and that of the infrastructure shaped the credit policy of their gubernia.

The reform substantially increased the number of uezds, from 177 to 321 in the twenty-six provinces of central Russia,[51] and created in each uezd the post of treasurer, descendant of the Petrine land commissioner whose police functions were taken over by the land captain. He was chosen by the chamber, sometimes from retired noncomissioned officers of the Guard, sometimes from local merchants with some familiarity with accounting, and he was confirmed in office—but only for 3 years at a time—by the State Treasurer, concurrently the Procurator General until 1792.[52] The uezd treasury was the crucial link in the new hierarchy: revenues collected from state peasant communities, on the estates of landowners, from towns, and from the lease and use of government properties were deposited in it. It was at this level that the concentration of revenue collection had to be the most thorough if the Expedition of State Revenues was to work effectively.

Such were the essential features of the reform. The creation of ministries, less than a generation later, we remember, marked a reaction against the ominous centrifugal tendencies that marked the end of Catherine's reign, a reaction by the central apparatus against the claims of the provincial infrastructure, a reassertion of the general over the particular, and the first groping for a definition of "state" interests. Its precedent was the reform of 1718, which had also sought to create a central organization based on specialized local agencies and had likewise weakened the existing unity of management control. The competition between the ministries exploded the imposing edifice of the treasury chamber. The governor increasingly became the delegate of the Ministry of Internal Affairs, the Board of Public Welfare its local agency, and public construction one of its responsibilities. The vice-governor represented the Finance Ministry, the audit expedition, now called section, was subordinated after 1811 to the Main Audit Administration, while remaining part of the chamber. Responsibility for the administration of customs and industrial management, as well as for the vodka and salt monopoly, was removed from the chamber and placed directly under separate departments of the Finance

Ministry, which began to behave like miniministries eager for empires of their own. By 1823, when a new table of organization was published for the chamber and the uezd treasuries—raising salaries for the first time since 1776—the chamber consisted, under the chairmanship of the vice-governor, of an economic section, the successor of the expedition of state domains, subordinated to the Department of State Domains; a treasury section, subordinated to the Treasury Department; and an audit ("control") section.[53] The chamber of 1775 had become a collection of independent fiefdoms.

The creation of a standing army paid by the government both in money and in kind and dressed in standard uniforms necessitated the creation of agencies and the building of stores to assure a sufficiently reliable flow of money and supplies to units in the field. The first step was the appointment in 1701 of commissioners (*komissary*) in each regiment, linked with a network of stores built in different sectors of the army's theater of operations and guided by the instructions of the chiefs of the Military and Provision *Prikazy*.[54] The reform of 1708 radically transformed military no less than civilian administration. Some governors were military commanders, others were not, but in either case the reform established an implicit distinction between a support structure anchored permanently in a small number of cities and mobile supply agencies accompanying the regiments on the move. A senior (*ober*) commissioner and a senior provisionmaster (*proviantmeister*), subordinated to the governor, who took over in each gubernia the responsibilities of the two central *prikazy* and worked with their two counterparts in each regiment, subordinated to the regimental commander, who was made accountable for the supply and provisioning of his men.[55] The activities of the eight governors were coordinated beginning in 1711 by the Senate, to which the Chief of the Commissary was appointed in August.

The reform was intended to speed up the supplying of the army in the field as the showdown with Charles XII was approaching, and governors, given full powers over the collection of revenue then deposited in a single treasury under their control, were expected to give priority to the needs of the army. As time went by, however, it became apparent that the new arrangement's major flaw was poor coordination between functional and area management, a characteristic feature in the administration, of large territories, military theaters, and naval commands in Russia and elsewhere. The army was subordinated to its commander-in-chief, and regiments were constantly on the move from one gubernia to another, while a governor's jurisdiction stopped at the boundaries of his gubernia. The need to plan the army's movement from one military headquarters or from the capital did not mesh easily with the regionalization of supply under governors not subordinated to a commander-in-chief, whose orders, unless he was the tsar himself, they felt no need to obey. By 1716 a central supply organization was being rebuilt, capped two years later by the creation of the College of War.[56]

The consequence of this counter-reform was to divorce the supply of the army in the field from the general administration of the gubernia, only governors retaining responsibility for the garrisons. When the capitation was introduced in 1724, its collection was not vested in the *kamerir* subordinated to the College of Revenue, but in regimental commissioners—not to be confused with the land commissioners elected in each uezd. After the return of peace in 1721—or in 1723 following the tsar's return from the Persian campaign— regiments were assigned permanent quarters in gubernias and uezds in such a way that a given number of males from the dependent population would contribute a fixed amount to support each regiment, and the task of the regimental commissioner was to collect the amount on his own, independently of the governor or provincial voevoda, but in cooperation with the land commissioner.[57] This reform was short-sighted, and took no account of the fact that the army, unlike a garrison, required mobility both to provide distraction to its officers and men and to project power in strategic areas in accordance with military and diplomatic imperatives. After Peter's death the collection of the capitation was vested in the voevoda and the proceeds were shipped to the gubernia capital, from which field officers appointed by the College of War forwarded them to regiments in the field pursuant to the Commissary's instructions.[58] Regimental commissioners received these funds and regimental provisionmasters used their share to buy provisions or pay contractors.

This situation remained unchanged until 1764, when the field officers were recalled, and governors assumed full jurisdiction over the collection of the capitation.[59] At the same time, however, commissary commissions were established, each attached to one of the eight "divisions" created a year before; they ignored gubernia boundaries and were purely military regional commands, headed by a senior commissioner assisted by a paymaster dependent on the Chief of the Commissary. Their locations varied with the territorial distribution of the army, but one was usually stationed in Petersburg, Moscow, Smolensk, and Kazan, the four major military headquarters of Russia proper. In 1766 provision commissions were likewise created, each under a senior provisionmaster responsible to the Provisionmaster General, located for the most part in the same city as the commissary commission. Funds collected by governors were now sent to these commissions. Since the commissions were required to follow the movement of troops, the army in the field acquired its own logistical organization for the first time.[60] A major handicap, however, was its continued dependence on the College of War in Petersburg, and the resulting difficulty of coping with the mobility of regiments transferred from one division to another and combined in wartime into various commands, which played havoc with the quasi-territorial jurisdiction of the commissions.

The enormous increase in the size of the army during Alexander's reign, the vast extension of its theater of operations, and the vital need to improve its maneuverability required the thorough reorganization of its supply management in the field. By 1815, at the close of the Napoleonic wars, the supply of regiments had become the responsibility of the commander-in-chief, the commanders of separate corps, and the War Minister, varying according to their location and affiliation. In each army, a chief of supply (*general intendant*), who received his instructions from the commander-in-chief and not from the center, operated through a chief of field commissary and a chief of field provision administration, and a network of commissary and provision commissions. Units not integrated into armies and separate corps continued to receive supplies and provisions from the commissions subordinated to the Commissary and Provision Departments of the War Ministry.[61] The reform thus regionalized military supply, which had remained so highly centralized since the beginning of the eighteenth century despite the reforms of 1764 and 1766. When we recall that the reform of 1812 had split the unity of the high command between a Main Staff and the War Ministry, it is obvious that a dangerous fragmentation of the army into functional and regional fiefdoms was in the making, a trend which the excessive centralization carried out by Nicholas I would seek to correct.

14

Taxation

Direct Taxation

A discussion of taxation in eighteenth-century Russia must consider three essential questions: Who bore the burden of taxation? What was the relationship between direct and indirect taxes? What was the role of taxation in kind? We shall see that taxation was the means by which an infinitesimal ruling class extracted enormous sums from the dependent population; that the share of direct taxes declined between 1725 and 1825 while that of indirect taxes grew, largely as a result of a systematic policy of extending alcohol consumption; and that compulsory labor and services constituted a substantial second economy not affected by the growth of a money economy until the reign of Alexander I.

Direct taxes are those paid by the taxable individual or communities directly to agents of the treasury, indirect taxes those, like sales taxes, paid to a third party in return for a service, then paid by that party to the treasury. Direct taxes are usually levied on personal income, indirect taxes on consumption and economic activity. The relative importance of these two kinds of taxes underscored differences in social and political systems, a point made long ago by Montesquieu, who declared that "a capitation is more natural to slavery, a duty on merchandise is more natural to liberty by reason it has not so direct a relation to the person."[1] For budgetary reasons, however, Russian terminology distinguished chiefly between taxes yielding a predetermined amount (*okladnye*) and the others (*neokladnye*). A poll tax had a definite rate (*oklad*), and its yield could be anticipated by multiplying the rate by the number of taxable heads. It was also a direct tax. It was not possible to anticipate the yield of an indirect tax on the sale of vodka because the number of customers was unpredictable, even though the rate was set. But if the sale of vodka was farmed out in a town or district, the government knew how much the tax farmer would have to deposit during the duration of his contract. Depending on the sale procedure, the same indirect tax would be *okladnyi* or *neokladnyi*.[2]

Until 1678 the basis of direct taxation had been the land tax, the unit of taxation being the *sokha*, a certain amount of cultivated land in the countryside, which varied in accordance with its quality. In the towns the *sokha* meant some 80 to 120 households (*dvory*), including houses and courtyards. Various direct taxes—to support the *streltsy*, to build postal houses, to ransom prisoners from the Tatars, for example—were assessed in accordance with the number of *sokhi* under the jurisdiction of a voevoda, and payments due from each family were established by the *mir*. One objection to making land the source of taxes was its unfavorable influence on agriculture, since peasants reduced the amount of cultivated land in order to keep their tax payment to a minimum. Another was that the lack of regular cadastration made it impossible to make a realistic measurement of taxable land.[3]

To prevent a potential crisis in agricultural production, the Muscovite government in September 1679 changed the object of direct taxation to the household, understood as the nuclear family, and imposed a tax of 1.30 rubles, combining all direct taxes into one, called the *streltsy* tax and deposited in the *Streltsy Prikaz*. The reform was important not only because of the simplification it introduced in the collection of direct taxes but because of the association it made between direct taxation and the support of the army. The new system, which required a census of households, had its own flaw. It promised to facilitate tax collection with a vengeance, but relatives began to gather under the roof of the nuclear family to form an extended family, thus reducing the number of households. This went so far that the Petrine government became alarmed, since direct taxes traditionally yielded over half the revenue.[4]

The major difficulty in shaping a program of direct taxation was to find a source, both easily identifiable and permanent, and capable of resisting tampering by those interested in avoiding the burden. Taxation by family represented progress over taxation of cultivated land and at first yielded higher revenue. It was to be expected, however, that the search would continue for a simple and permanent source of taxation and would ultimately focus on the individual member of the family, who could be known as a fixed entity. When he died, others were born. This would require a thorough census but one much simplified by counting only the males, on the correct assumption that nature maintains a nearly perfect balance between men and women. The decision was made in the fall of 1718 to base direct taxation on the individual "soul" and, in January 1719, to conduct a census of the entire male population.

Meanwhile, the tsar had already decided to retain a major feature of the reform of 1679—the use of direct taxation to support the army. In order to correlate direct taxation and ordinary military expenditures, it was necessary to know the exact size of the army and to know how much it cost to support a food soldier and a cavalryman. The new table of organization of the army of February 1720—it replaced that of February 1711—fixed military expenditures to support seventy-three regiments at 4 million rubles. When the results of the census became known in 1724, they showed a total dependent population of 5.4 million souls. The amount of the capitation was thus fixed at 74 kopecks.[5]

Concern over the economic situation at the time of Peter's death and the planned reduction of military personnel led the government of Catherine I to reduce the capitation to seventy kopecks in February 1725; the initial rate had most likely never been collected. However, it soon became apparent that letting the army collect its own funds led to widespread abuses, with military personnel and clerks demanding additional sums, and it was estimated in the 1730s that peasants were paying an average of ten extra kopecks per soul to accommodate the tax collectors' greed, although requiring peasants to pay more than the legal amount was a capital offense.[6]

The rate of the capitation remained unchanged until 1794, despite the fact that military expenditures kept growing. The correlation established by Peter consequently lost its meaning, as additional resources from various colleges were assigned to support the military establishment. Since to raise the capitation would have put an additional burden on the human property of the ruling class, even if that increase merely kept up with inflation, it was a decision to be avoided as long as alternative sources of funding were available. By 1794, however, rampant inflation in the midst of a financial crisis compelled the government to raise the capitation for the first time in 70 years to one ruble. Speranskii's "financial plan," which called for tax increases to finance the enormous expenditures of the war with Napoleon and asserted the fiscal integrity of the treasury against the claims of an infrastructure favoring the printing of more paper money, led to a second increase in February 1810 to two rubles, but it was recognized that such an increase barely kept up with the depreciation of the *assignats*. It was raised by another ruble on the eve of the war. After the war, a separate capitation of twenty-five kopecks was introduced to serve as a trust fund for the repair and maintenance of the major national roads, beginning in 1816, to which an additional five kopecks was added in March 1818 to improve internal navigation. The capitation, which had by then completely lost its original purpose, thus amounted to 3.30 rubles at the end of Alexander's reign.[7]

The nobility was exempt from paying the capitation, but townsmen were not. The exemption was thus at first the great divide between the ruling class and the dependent population, and it placed upon the latter, as time went by, a badge of social inferiority. The imperial order of April 1722 imposed a rate of 1.20 rubles upon townsmen registered in the merchant and craft guilds; this remained unchanged until 1794, when it was raised to two rubles. Fifty kopecks were added in December 1797, and the rate, doubled in February 1810 to 5 rubles, was raised to 8 rubles in 1812. The same thirty kopecks for the trust fund were added in 1816 and 1818 to bring it to 8.30 rubles, where it remained beyond 1825.[8] Meanwhile, merchants in the three guilds were granted the much-coveted exemption in March 1775, thus aggravating the social contempt in which the *meshchane* were held. It was extended in June 1787 to soldiers and noncommissioned officers retiring after 25 years of active service.[9]

The other major direct tax was the quitrent (*obrok*). Originally it was not a tax but a revenue collected for the use of treasury-owned lands and properties, the rate fixed by a contractual agreement for a specific, usually short, duration.[10] The *Plakat* of June 1724 transformed this fee into a universal tax binding on every peasant registered in the census as property of the Treasury.[11] This legislation drew a parallel between the Treasury as the fiscal agent of the apparatus holding more than a third of the peasantry in trust for the needs of its members and landowners in and out of the apparatus for whom the possession of human chattel was a major source of revenue. These landowners, too, collected a quitrent in money from the serfs they allowed to work in the towns, on riverboats, or in factories, and thus operated in the dual capacity of tax collectors when they helped gather the capitation from their serfs and rent collectors when they pocketed the quitrent. The Treasury likewise collected both the capitation from all peasants and the quitrent from its own peasants.

The *Plakat* described the official quitrent as the equivalent of the "land-owner's revenue" and assumed it equaled about forty kopecks per capita. As a result, the treasury-owned peasants paid a combined direct tax of 1.10 rubles in 1725. Thirty-five years later the government recognized that landowners were collecting an average of 1 ruble per capita and raised the official quitrent to that amount effective in 1761. From that time on, it was raised more and more frequently to keep up with the private quitrent, and the decision was justified each time by referring to the increased rent collected by landowners. These rates, of course, varied from estate to estate and from region to region, but Semevskii, whose figures are still accepted as reliable even though they have been challenged for oversimplification, estimated that the private quitrent amounted to 2 or 3 rubles in the 1770s, 4 rubles in the 1780s, and 5 in the 1790s. In July 1769 the official quitrent was raised to 2 rubles, and to 3 rubles in May 1783. By increasing the revenue from the quitrent from .7 million to over 14 million rubles between 1726 and 1796, the ruling elite could afford to leave the rate of the capitation unchanged for so long—its yield rose from 4 million to 10.4 million between those dates—and continued to subsidize the economy of serfdom. Beginning in 1797 the quitrent was even regionalized; it was raised to 3.50 rubles in Arkhangelsk, Novgorod, and Perm gubernias, to 4 rubles in Petersburg, Pskov, and Vologda gubernias, to 4.50 rubles in Moscow, Tver, and Smolensk, and to 5 rubles in the other fifteen gubernias. It was raised again in February 1810 and once more in February 1812, with some changes made in the classification of gubernias. By 1825 it ranged from 7.50 to 10 rubles.[12]

The capitation and the official quitrent were personal taxes in name only. They were in fact territorial taxes, exacted by voevodas and later by uezd treasurers responsible for meeting a quota determined by multiplying the rate of the tax by the number of souls registered in the census of the territory under their jurisdiction. For landowners on their properties and villages among the state peasantry, they were repartitional taxes, to be assessed not so much against individual males as against the smallest economic unit in the peasant world, the work team (*tiaglo*).

Censuses were conducted irregularly and at great intervals. The second census was that of 1744, 25 years after the first. The third took place in 1762, the fourth in 1782, the fifth in 1795, and the sixth in 1811, but the seventh came only 4 years later, in 1815. The number of souls registered in one census was considered fixed until the next, and demographic changes within the *uezd* or the gubernia were not taken into account. Males of all ages, from babies to old men, were registered, despite the obvious fact that some were unable to work and pay taxes. Recruits were not stricken from the rolls, nor were those who ran away, often in the thousands from a single gubernia, across the Polish border into Bashkiria, the Ukraine, or the Northern Caucasus. As a result, only those who stayed behind paid taxes—they were often the less able-bodied— and among them only those who could work or had something to sell. It is obvious, then, that the census soul became a mere unit of accounting unconnected with the taxable male, and that the fixed per capita rate, the characteristic feature of direct taxes, became a fiction, some paying very much more, others nothing at all.[13]

One can only speculate about the burden of direct taxation upon the dependent population. Miliukov's conclusion that the legislation of 1724 raised the revenue by 61 percent has long been accepted, but Arcadius Kahan has recently asked very pertinently why any government should tax its population in peacetime more than it ever had in wartime and surmised that the capitation and the quitrent may even have reduced the tax burden.[14] These direct taxes made a negative impression because they were introduced in years of famine and because the military was made responsible for collecting its own resources, while the insufficient amount of money in circulation often compelled tax collectors to resort to outright confiscation of grain. Later in the century, and especially after 1768, as more cash found its way into villages and households, the payment of direct taxes may have been a less distressing experience. In the late 1770s, when the capitation and the quitrent combined amounted to 2.70 rubles, a bucket (*vedro*: 12.3 liters) of vodka sold at government stores cost 3.50 rubles, a *pud* (16.4 kg.) of salt thirty-five kopecks. One could live well on bread and meat for five kopecks a day.[15]

Direct taxes, however, were not the only imposition on the dependent population: taxes in kind may have been a much heavier burden. Moreover, the lack of correspondence between the rate of direct taxes and what was actually paid by individual males makes it impossible to estimate their impact on the peasant budget. Landowners knew the amount of the capitation assessed against their estates beforehand. On large estates this amount was distributed among the communes encompassing several villages, each commune becoming responsible for delivering its quota to the steward's office. Communes in turn reapportioned their quotas among work teams, each usually consisting of a husband and wife. These teams had to perform the peasants' labor obligations—plowing, sowing, and harvesting, spinning and weaving—on the estate. On small estates, landowners themselves apportioned the tax among the teams. If one defaulted on its payments, the others had to make good the loss. In addition, the husband and wife assumed responsibility for the tax obligations of their sons and aged fathers and even uncles, and all teams assumed collective responsibility for fugitives and for the dead not replaced by newborn males.[16]

In such conditions it was inevitable that some teams had to pay double or treble tax. When fugitives were numerous, in times of scarcity, and in families with several small sons, tax obligations became a crushing burden, and arrears piled up. As a result, the personal taxes introduced in 1724 came to resemble in practice the household tax they had been intended to replace, with this major difference: the new "household" did not necessarily consist of relatives but of members assigned to it by the commune or the landlord. In communities of state peasants the assessment was made by villages and the commune apportioned it among work teams. Taxes were then paid—with money earned from the sale of products or obtained by commuting some services to a cash equivalent—to the landowner or his steward, or to the *starosta* in villages of state peasants, and taken to the voevoda's or uezd treasurer's office. The *Plakat* required them to be paid in three installments—in January or February, March or April, and October or November. In 1731 these were reduced to two— between January and March and between mid-September and December.[17]

These methods of distributing the supposedly equal burden of direct taxation had profound social consequences. They kept up a permanent struggle within villages between the more affluent serfs and the less affluent, who demanded a distribution of the burden according to each household's ability to pay, and thus the transformation of a personal tax into an income tax.[18] In some cases the compulsion imposed upon richer peasants to include in their work teams peasants who were unable to pay—besides the very young and the old—must have created relations of dependence similar to those between master and indentured servant, a miniserfdom within a larger one. Such a development may have been favored by some landlords who had an interest in creating on their properties a social infrastructure linking ruling class and peasant in a unified command structure.

In other cases, however, the egalitarian and communal spirit so much in evidence among noble families traditionally reluctant to admit unigeniture, and among the peasantry repartitioning land in a constant endeavor to give everyone an equal share, strongly militated against letting the assessment of direct taxes create a layer of kulaks. Both landlord and commune would use the distribution of the tax burden to maintain a radically egalitarian distribution of wealth and to destroy the initiative of the more ambitious peasants. Attitudes must have varied greatly from one estate to another, depending on the interrelationship of economic circumstances and social prejudices, but it is a fact that the principles governing the assessment of direct taxes on estates and villages had nothing in common with those that had inspired on a national level the Petrine legislation of 1724.

Indirect Taxation

Indirect taxes are chiefly taxes on consumption, and their share of the total revenue depends on the level of commercial exchanges and the ability of the Treasury to tap them at the most profitable stages, whether production, transportation, or sale of the taxable product.[19] Since the Russian economy retained throughout the eighteenth century strong features of regional autonomy, strengthened by a self-sufficiency of villages and estates that crippled urban development, the treasury was unable to derive considerable resources from commercial expansion. It was limited to taxing the consumption of vital

necessities such as salt, taking advantage of the ruling class's ability to flood
the market with vodka, and collecting export and import duties on what was
hardly more than an exchange of raw materials extracted or produced by the
dependent population on lands of the ruling class for finished and tropical
products intended for consumption by the same ruling class.

Since salt is scarce in nature yet vital to human and animal health, taxing its
consumption is one of the oldest forms of taxation and was one of the most
resented. There were few sources of salt in central Russia. In the distant Urals,
however, at Solikamsk north of Perm, enormous deposits of brine salt, worked
until then by the Treasury, were turned over in May 1697 to the "distinguished
merchant" (*imenityi chelovek*) Grigorii Stroganov. This supply was later supplemented by salt extracted by convict labor from Lake Elton, in the parched
steppe beyond the Volga south of Saratov. The two major sources of salt were
thus located along the periphery of central Russia, at considerable distances
from the mass of consumers.[20]

The eagerness to appropriate the profits of tax farmers who sold the salt
explains the decision in January 1705 to confiscate existing inventories in the
trade channels and to require that all salt be sold from salt offices and internal
customshouses at double the wholesale price at which it had been purchased in
various cities and regions. In this method of tapping commercial exchanges,
the apparatus intervened directly to eliminate the profit of the tax farmers and
to obtain in taxes from the consumer what had been obtained by merchants
selling their own stocks. This government monopoly remained in effect until
1728, when sale on the open market was reintroduced, the treasury deriving its
revenue from a moderate tax of five kopecks per *pud* collected at the major
locations to which salt was shipped from the Urals, Lake Elton, and other
places.[21] It is clear from the language of the Salt Code of December 1727 that
one reason behind the new policy was the shortage of cash among the dependent population—consumers who had to pay cash for salt under government
monopoly could thenceforth obtain it by bartering away their produce. Free
sale, however, turned into a disaster for the Treasury, the revenue falling by
two-thirds within 4 years, while merchants used their exclusive access to a vital
commodity to charge excessive prices in towns and villages, thereby threatening the public peace. In August 1731 all salt already on the market was once
again confiscated; the Central Salt Board, since 1720 a dependency of the
College of Revenue, was placed directly under the Cabinet of Ministers,
producers were required to deliver a definite quota—a hint that they may have
cut down production to reduce the tax and raise prices—and salt was thenceforth to be sold from voevoda chanceries and customshouses. This renewed
monopoly lasted until 1811.[22]

From then on, the size of the revenue depended on the difference between
the price paid by the Treasury to produce and the price at which it was sold in
different parts of the country minus transportation costs. But the rising price of
salt did not keep pace with inflation, and the monopoly became a deficit
operation beginning in 1794.[23-24] What had been almost without interruption
since 1705 a revenue-producing monopoly turned into a price-support mecha-

nism subsidized by the government, and Treasury losses had become so large by 1810 that a radical reform was imperative. When the government announced a series of measures to reduce the deficit in February 1810, it recognized the need to treat salt like any other industrial product sold on the free market but took no immediate action beyond raising the official price from forty kopecks to one ruble. The Manifesto of November 1811, however, introduced a mixed system, combining free sale with government regulation.[25] The new policy was incorporated into the Salt Code of August 1818 and was declared a temporary expedient until sale on the open market had become generally accepted. By 1823 its development had gone so far that the salt sections were merged with the vodka sections, and the excise became the major source of revenue from the sale of salt.[26]

The sale of vodka, much more profitable than the sale of salt, raised similar problems for a Treasury seeking to develop its revenue from indirect taxation. The difference, however, was that the product was distilled almost everywhere and consumed for the most part locally, and its shipment to the larger markets of Petersburg and Moscow generated only marginal costs easily absorbed by the suppliers.[27]

The first essential question was thus to determine who should be allowed to produce vodka. At the end of the seventeenth century, nobles and merchants were allowed to distill without restrictions. In January 1716 producers were ordered to declare their boilers and to pay an excise of twenty-five kopecks ("half a *poltina*") per bucket of capacity. By 1754, the marketable production of some 2 million buckets came from distilleries owned by the Treasury, landowners, and merchants, the share of the merchants amounting to just over one-fifth. In July the ruling class eliminated competition from the merchants when their distilleries were ordered sequestered until sold to noblemen or simply torn down. Treasury-owned distilleries were retained only in areas where the production of vodka distilled by landowners was inadequate to meet the demand. Meanwhile, it had been discovered that the excise on capacity was not being paid and was unfair to noblemen who owned boilers but did not distill. It was abolished in August 1744 and replaced by an excise of three kopecks on each bucket actually shipped from the distilleries. This proved impossible to collect, and the excise on registered capacity was restored in December 1749. It was abolished again by the Liquor Code of September 1781. The registration of boilers was reintroduced in November 1794 but without the excise.[28] As a result, the production of vodka became an untaxed monopoly of the ruling class. And, though scattered across the country, it was dominated by large producers who were all members of the ruling elite.

The second essential question was to determine how the vodka would be sold and how much revenue could be collected—a question that caused the ruling elite considerable headaches for more than a century. In the 1670s farming out the sale was the prevailing method, but bankruptcies and competition with government-owned outlets compelled a change of policy. Farms were canceled in September 1682, and their owners compensated by the government. In 1705 a mixed system was reintroduced. The basic outlet was the tavern (*kabak*, *piteinyi dom*). Where officially recognized taverns were farmed out, the farmer, who bought his vodka directly from the producer, was required to sell at the official price at least as much as had been sold before he took over the farm and deposit the proceeds in the internal customshouse. This was the Treasury's revenue, and the farmer then made his profit by selling additional vodka at whatever price the market would bear. Taverns not found attractive to farmers were handed over to collectors usually elected for 1 year, serving not without some compulsion on the part of the voevodas. These men were called *golovy* and *tselovalniki*, both having "kissed the cross" as a form of oath, the former being merely the foremen of the more numerous *tselovalniki*. This form of sale was called *na vere*—that is, the collectors were responsible for selling as much as the previous year, and the arrears were charged to those who had elected them. After 1699 they were renamed *burmistry*, and they sent the revenue to the *Ratusha* in Moscow, after 1718 to the College of Revenue.[29] Had not the ruling class enlisted the assistance of the dependent population in this form of compulsory service without remuneration, the collection of the revenue would have come to a standstill.

These two methods of collecting revenue from the sale of vodka continued to coexist until the 1760s, the farm, however, gradually attracting more and more merchants and becoming increasingly attractive for two reasons to the ruling elite. Each farmer bid for clusters of taverns, sometimes those of an entire uezd, province, or even a gubernia, and this for up to 4 years, thereby simplifying considerably the accounting of the revenue. And farmers had substantial bribes to offer at all levels of the apparatus. At the same time, the Treasury became concerned over the amount of vodka bought by farmers from producers and sold above the quota they had pledged to sell, it being in their interest to keep that quota as small as possible. The Liquor Code therefore forbade these private arrangements and required producers to deliver their vodka to gubernia and uezd stores managed by vodka "expeditions" of the treasury chamber. By compelling the merchants to buy all their vodka at the stores, the Treasury was trying to forge a coalition with the political infrastructure to transform the latter's monopoly into a government monopoly aiming at cutting into the tax farmers' profit. The policy failed, however, the higher interest of the "state" being of little concern to the ruling elite and its clients in the provinces, whose greed was amply satisfied by the interested generosity of the tax farmers. In November 1794 producers were once again allowed to sell directly to farmers, creating by 1817 a situation in which the real amount of vodka sold on the market had become a secret from the government and the amount of the revenue depended on the benevolence of the tax farmers.[30]

The official sale price of a bucket of vodka had varied from place to place—it was an average of 1.30 rubles in the 1740s. In February 1750 a uniform price of 1.88 rubles was introduced at the urging of the same Petr Shuvalov, raised to 2.23 rubles in September 1756 and to 2.53 rubles in December 1763. Thirty-one years later, it was 4 rubles, then up by 2 rubles in 1809, by another ruble in 1815, and finally reached 8 rubles in 1820.[31] These increases, however, barely kept pace with inflation and the higher price of grain, even though technological improvements reduced the cost of producing vodka. Despair at the Finance Ministry, caused by falling revenue and the collapse of the system of channeling vodka through the stores because producers bypassed them in favor of direct dealings with tax farmers, explains the reassertion of the Treasury's interest in the Code of April 1817, which took effect in January 1819.[32] It maintained the nobility's monopoly over production, but distilling was allowed only if the producer had signed a contract to deliver the vodka to a government store; and it let the ministry determine each year the level of consumption in each gubernia and uezd. Farms were abolished, and taverns had to get their supplies directly from the stores. Tavern keepers were forbidden to make a profit. The new policy thus marked a return to sale *na vere*, now a rigid system in which tavern keepers became agents of the vice-governors, the delegates of the Finance Ministry. Such a system, which was run by former agents of the tax farmers, was an invitation to fraud, and bootlegging, against which there was no defense because the land captains were on the take, became its major enemy.

The third major source of indirect revenue was foreign trade. For the ruling elite of a preindustrial society, in which commercial interests carried little weight and usually were framed in parochial terms, tariff policy was often seen not so much as assisting an industrial program, whether laissez-faire or protectionist, as a fiscal measure to increase the revenue and give the ruling class access to the commodities considered essential to its social westernization.[33]

At the end of the seventeenth century tariff policy was relatively liberal and the balance of trade active, stimulating an influx of specie into the country. The first tariff of January 1724, a codification of piecemeal legislation of the previous 20 years, marked a departure from tradition. It was less a protectionist tariff than one with strong fiscal overtones, designed to obtain revenue in order to overcome balance-of-payment difficulties. The next tariff, that of August 1731, was based on long-term considerations. It reduced import duties to a maximum of 10 percent ad valorem and on many items to 5 percent, while reducing export duties as well, in order to equalize prices for imported and domestically produced goods, the former taxed in the port customshouses, the latter in the internal customshouses, both manned by merchants. The abolition of internal customshouses in 1753 and the resulting loss of revenue from domestic commercial operations was compensated in the Customs Code of December 1755 by an across-the-board increase of duties on both imports and exports. The outbreak of the Seven Years' War necessitated the replacement of the tariff of 1731 with what has been called the most protective tariff of the eighteenth century, that of April 1757; in fact it was no more than a revenue-raising measure that merely accentuated the existing protection of domestic industries.[34]

The tariff of August 1766 likewise retained the protectionist intent of its predecessors by imposing a 30 percent ad valorem tariff on manufactured and processed goods having a domestic near equivalent, thus maintaining a price parity between the imported and the domestically manufactured product. But it also lowered export duties to enable Russian landowners to take full advantage of the rising demand for grain in western Europe. The 1760s were also a time when the westernization of the ruling class went into high gear, and tariff rates were manipulated to prevent excess consumption of luxury goods while guaranteeing continued access to the goods by landowners and members of the apparatus. The tariff of September 1782 went further and lowered both import and export duties, hoping to increase the revenue by taxing the rising level of exchanges that the incorporation of the Baltic customshouses into the all-Russian network was expected to stimulate. However, the inflation of the 1780s and 1790s stimulated the demand for luxury imports to such an extent that the trade balance nearly turned negative in 1793 for the first time in the century.[35] It was perhaps no coincidence that two of the three major sources of indirect revenue, the salt monopoly and foreign trade, turned into deficit operations at about the same time.

Russian exports were dominated by cash crops—hemp and flax—exported as raw materials (seeds) or as finished products (linen and rope). They were raised chiefly in the northwestern part of the country and exported through Petersburg. Cash crops also included grain, chiefly rye and wheat. The grain trade responded to Western demand in the 1760s and in turn generated pressure for the acquisition of Black Sea ports through which exports from the black-earth zone were more profitable than through the Baltic ports. Livestock products such as tallow and hides were also major exports. The third component consisted of industrial goods. Russian iron was much in demand in western Europe because low labor costs kept it cheap. By the 1780s, Russia had supplanted Sweden as the chief supplier of the British market. Linen was exported in the form of sailcloth and formed with rope and forest products like pitch, tar, and potash, the famous strategic naval stores exported mainly to England. The share of these three categories of exports amounted to 99.4 percent of total exports in 1710, 87.6 percent in 1793–1795.[36]

Imports, by contast, were dominated by high-quality and high-priced consumer goods, whether colonial goods like sugar, coffee, and chocolate or high-quality textile goods, as well as wines, foods, cotton, musical instruments, and paintings. Imports for the first three-quarters of the century are still terra incognita, but we know that the share of these products was 94.4 percent of total imports for the 4 years between 1790 and 1793. In short, Russian exports consisted of crops raised by peasants of the Treasury, serfs, and their owners, and iron produced by conscripted labor in the factories of the Urals belonging to the ruling elite and the top layer of the merchant class, while imports were intended to support the high level of consumption of the ruling class.[37]

After Catherine's death, the ruling class was forced to respond to the challenges of war and Napoleon's victories, but joining the Continental System became detrimental to its interest and therefore a factor that made the war of 1812 inevitable. Moreover, industrial interests began to make their weight felt, and the ruling class had to grant them increasing participation in public affairs, notably in the gubernia judicial chambers and in the advisory bodies of the Finance Ministry. The tariff of November 1819 was inspired by foreign-policy considerations, above all the desire for friendly relations with Prussia and

Congress Poland, and turned away from the protection of the domestic textile industry at a time when Russian iron no longer found favor on the English market. It thus created a backlash and forced a return to a now excessively protectionist policy in the tariff of March 1822, which coincided with warning signals that the Liquor Code of 1817 was not yielding the expected increase in revenue. Both the tariff and the Code were in conflict with smugglers and a ruling class intent on keeping its profits and its luxury goods.[38]

Taxation in Kind

Direct and indirect taxes collected in money represented only part of the revenue extracted from the dependent population. Vast additional resources were extracted by landowners and members of the apparatus alike, either for selfish ends or to finance essential services. These services were contributions in kind, because money was still relatively rare in Russian towns and villages until the end of the eighteenth century, and it was not until the reign of Alexander that systematic attempts were made, first to determine what services were rendered by the dependent population without remuneration, and second to commute some of these forced contributions into a tax, its proceeds to be used to hire free labor or buy supplies on the market.

The practice of feeding off the land (*kormlenie*) had a long history. Members of the apparatus, chiefly voevodas, were assigned without salary to towns across the vast expanse of the Russian land and left to their own devices—it was taken for granted that they would know not only where to find enough resources to support themselves but also how to turn their short tenures into profitable operations.[39] If a salary was paid regularly to voevodas and their successors after 1763—and certainly after 1775—the practice of *kormlenie* nevertheless remained very much alive because it was anchored in tradition and because positions of authority in a society that was a huge command structure gave the ruling class the power to demand the unconditional satisfaction of its wishes. Moreover, the lack of awareness of a clear distinction between the property of the collectivity as a whole and that of the ruling class broadened the practice of "feeding" to include siphoning off funds allocated to the central government. It has been estimated that in ancien régime France about 60 percent of the gross revenue never reached the treasury, and the "fabrication of arrears" was a common practice in Manchu China.[40] There is no reason to assume that extortion and embezzlement were any less widespread in the third and largest state on the Eurasian continent—in fact, it may have been worse.

If voevodas were given a town and an uezd, and colonels, their counterpart in the army, a regiment, in either case for short periods of time, landowners had their estates, often much smaller than a town or a regiment, for life and fed themselves off their serfs with the same lack of scruples as their colleagues in the civil and military apparatus.[41] Those who were also voevodas or regimental commanders got the best of both worlds. Both the apparatus and the political infrastructure derived their sustenance from enforced contributions in money, in kind, and in services, while the revenue from government taxation went to the army and central government agencies to buy uniforms, produce armaments, raise buildings, and create an environment facilitating the profitable exercise of power by the ruling class. This essential duality in the practice of "feeding"—on the part of the apparatus and of landowners and their stewards operating in a semipublic and semiprivate capacity—is usually overlooked, yet it explains why the practice was so general and hence so oppressive.

The resources thus extracted in kind from the dependent population can be divided into three kinds—services, corvée labor, and the supply of housing and food. Until the end of the eighteenth century, they did not represent a legally recognized category, but the term *contributions from the land* (*zemskie povinnosti*) gained circulation during the reign of Alexander. In 1802 their regulation became the responsibility of the Ministry of Internal Affairs, which proceeded to commute some of the contributions into cash payments, that is, a tax, while others remained beyond the ministry's ability to restrict their scope. In 1810 contributions levied in the form of a tax were transferred to the jurisdiction of the Finance Ministry, and a separate jurisprudence began to form around their assessment and payment, and the contracting for labor to replace compulsory services. In June 1816 they were divided into extraordinary, gubernia, and local contributions, and governors were enjoined to forbid the collection of contributions not included in the official list.[42] Contributions in kind remained unregulated.

Services were a heavy burden in the seventeenth and eighteenth centuries. The concentration of the apparatus in Moscow, the small size of the voevodas' clerical staff, and the insignificance of the political infrastructure left the ruling class at the mercy of the dependent population in the collection of direct and indirect taxes. This obvious paradox nevertheless pointed at the foundation of the legitimacy of the ruling class—its ability by the combined use of condign and compensatory power to enlist the support of merchants and even peasants. Collectors elected from among the dependent population "kissed the cross," then sold vodka and salt and collected customs duties in hundreds of towns. Merchants were found as accountants in voevodas' chanceries, in the uezd treasuries and treasury chambers. They guarded confiscated property, assessed its value, and sold it at auction when instructed to do so.[43] These services were not remunerated: merchants were compelled to elect representatives to discharge them, and they usually elected their wealthier colleagues, whose assets were pledged against defaulting. The ruling class thus not only obtained free services but sought to guarantee the integrity of tax collection—at least until it reached the coffers of the apparatus—by outright confiscation of merchant property when necessary. On the other hand, merchants who cooperated, even against their will (and many felt that working for the apparatus took them away from their businesses and ruined them) made valuable connections with the wielders of power who granted contracts, and tax farmers—who worked of their own free will—gained entry into the ruling class.

Fiscal services were of vital importance on a national scale but ceased to be compulsory after 1785, when the triumph of tax farming as a method of collection, the growth of a money economy, and the training of clerks, many the sons of merchants and other townsmen, paid by the state budget made them superfluous. Other services, such as manning local fire-fighting and police forces, were likewise replaced by local forces integrated into the lower echelons of the apparatus, but at the beginning of the nineteenth century the lighting of streets, the maintenance of pavements (*mostovye*), the cleaning of embankments, and the digging of sewers were still done by the free contribution of the townsmen's labor. Where this was no longer the case, the commutation of these services into a tax made it possible for townsmen to buy themselves out and be replaced by workers paid for from the proceeds of the tax.[44]

The widespread resort to corvée labor illustrates very clearly the dual aspect of the practice of feeding off the land. We already saw one of its manifestations in the collection of the quitrent levied by the Treasury on its peasants and by landowners on their serfs, with the private sector setting the pace at which the rent was raised. On their estates, landowners required their serfs to perform corvée labor, called *barshchina*—that is, to cultivate their demesne in addition to the peasants' own land. If the restriction of movement was the essential feature of serfdom, the use of peasant labor without remuneration was its inevitable corollary. The expansion of the Russian land created a shortage of labor, and a ruling class without a dependent population to feed it and till its service land (*pomest'ia*) would be neither viable nor fit to govern. There existed, therefore, a close connection between agricultural expansion, the spread of forced labor, and the continued exercise of power by the ruling class. The increase in grain production in the eighteenth century to satisfy the needs of the growing population and the army, of the urban market of Petersburg, and of foreign demand led landowners on the path of greater exploitation of their peasantry.

It seems to have been a general custom that serfs would devote 3 days of work tilling the demesne and harvesting the crops (*barshchina*) and another 3 days working on their own allotments, leaving Sunday a day of rest. But customs in a command society are seldom translated into legal norms, and when they are, such norms are never binding. It was therefore not unusual for corvée labor to occupy the entire week, leaving peasants only Sundays and religious holidays to catch up on their own work, at the risk of their souls' perdition and the ruin of their crops by inclement weather. To demand such a heavy contribution implicitly denied the existence of the peasant's property and asserted his status as mere chattel. It was part of Paul's program of reasserting the supremacy of the Romanov house over the ruling class to claim the right to interfere between the political infrastructure and its dependent population, even though the claim had to be made cautiously. That it should have been necessary to forbid Sunday *barshchina* in April 1797 showed both that it was widespread and that peasants considered it illegitimate—the final stage before open rebellion. The imperial order did not restrict *barshchina* to

3 days, as it is sometimes assumed; it merely stated that a workload of 3 days should be considered normal, and it seems to have had no effect on the landowners' behavior.[45]

Tilling the demesne was only part of the compulsory contributions of the serfs to their owners' welfare. They also had to cart seigneurial products to market and provisions from the estate to their absentee masters in Moscow or Petersburg, sometimes hundreds of miles away. They had to build sheds, ovens, and cellars, repair buildings and dams, maintain paths across fields and woods, scour streams, and dig ponds. Such was the system by which the political infrastructure squeezed resources from the peasant population. While it is true that landowners often commuted corvée labor into the quitrent in the northern gubernias and wherever soil, climate, and market conditions made it more profitable, it remains a fact that 57.9 percent of the serfs in eighteen of the twenty-six gubernias were on *barshchina* in the 1760s and 59.4 percent in the middle of the nineteenth century.[46]

The apparatus was no less demanding in extracting resources from the peasants of the treasury, and even from those of absentee landowners, when it struck the fancy of governors and land captains. Peasants had to supply horses, carts, and guides when regiments on the march passed their villages, and horses and carts to the police—the land captain was an elected nobleman—and members of the apparatus on active duty traveling within 30 kilometers of their official residence. Officers and soldiers billeted in towns and villages requisitioned them for pleasure trip or for trips to the regimental headquarters. Peasants also had to supply horses and carts to *shtatnye komandy* and later to the Internal Guard for the transport of criminals and vagrants on their way to their place of exile. At least until the 1770s their carts also transported barrels of copper coins from the uezd centers to the gubernia capitals. They contributed horses to the post office and built and maintained post offices, bridges, ferries and landings: these contributions were replaced by the hire of free labor at the beginning of the nineteenth century, financed by a tax on the declared capital of guild merchants. In emergencies, peasants were rounded up to transport heavy loads such as gun carriages, artillery shells, and anchors.[47]

The road corvée was the heaviest contribution in kind. The building of a national network linking all gubernia capitals with Moscow began in earnest after 1817 and was carried out with recruit labor organized into labor battalions. Its maintenance was financed by a surcharge on the capitation. However, the many secondary roads linking uezd centers with gubernia capitals and cross-country (*proselochnye*) roads linking estates and villages with local markets still had to be built and maintained by free contributions of peasant labor—one reason, no doubt, why Russian roads were such a nightmare for travelers. Distances, the sparse population, several months of slush, and intractable clayish soils caused the peasants great losses in time and animals. Levies (*nariady*) were ordered by governors, who showed supreme unconcern for the peasants' welfare, sending men 30 or 40 kilometers away to repair roads in the summer months when peasants were bringing in the harvest.[48]

Finally, the ruling class exacted another tribute not in money or in kind but in blood. Recruit levies were included among the "contributions from the land" but could not be carried out without an imperial order. They were apportioned, like the capitation, among gubernias, uezds, villages, and estates at the rate of one recruit per so many hundred souls on the census rolls. During Peter's reign these levies yielded 370,000 men, during Catherine's 1 million, and during Alexander's 2 million.[49] Those who made it to the battlefield and were not killed in pursuit of the ruling elite's imperial policy or by disease went on to build barracks, fortifications, and military roads, and to contribute their free labor to the welfare of their regimental commanders, whose claims were indistinguishable from those of voevodas in their uezds and landowners on their estates.

The dependent population also supported both the landowners and the apparatus with free housing and food. This was "feeding" in its most elementary sense. The lords had their serfs deliver eggs, ducks, carp, and honey to their residences. Land captains and other members of the apparatus traveling on inspection tours demanded the same from the peasants of the Treasury and requisitioned what was not freely given. Soldiers quartered in villages were fed by the peasants. If a company was fortunate enough to be stationed in a large estate, the officers ate at the owner's table, with the flour, groats, meat, eggs, and wine contributed by the peasants from the steward's office. When troops were stationed among peasants of the Treasury—defenseless because no one could intercede for them in the capital—they behaved as they pleased, like the regiment quartered among Tambov *odnodvortsy* in the 1780s, which requisitioned food and hay for 3 years ahead, leaving the peasants unable to pay their taxes.[50]

Feeding off the land, however, was such traditional behavior that it was taken for granted by ruling class and dependent population alike, illustrating the obvious truth that custom rests on a broad consensus. When the land captain took office in one of the uezds of Orel gubernia in the 1820s, peasants lined up in front of his house with so many cartloads of various provisions that he had to refuse them. Instead he summoned the *starosta* from each village and gave them a list of how much flour, groats, oats, and cloth he needed to support himself, his wife, his three sons and five servants, as well as his cow, his chickens, and three horses. He reckoned that this requisition would equal an annual cash payment of about two kopecks per soul. If the uezd had at least 30,000 souls, it meant an income of 600 rubles a year in addition to his salary of 250 rubles. Everyone was pleased, and the captain maintained such good relations with his "constituents" that they petitioned the tsar to let him stay beyond his 3-year term against the governor's wishes.[51]

Not only did the dependent population feed the landowners and members of the apparatus on active duty in the provinces, it also supplied firewood, no small requirement in such a cold country, and candles. Cutting wood and carting it was part of the serfs' obligations toward their masters. Heating and lighting not only the offices of the apparatus but also those of the marshals of the nobility and of the *volost* boards were vested in the peasantry, although it gradually became customary after the 1780s to include these items in the expenditure budget of the gubernia agencies. Where the supply was free, consumption knew no bounds. It explains why the inhabitants of Pskov asked for relief when they complained in 1767 that the officers quartered in their houses were squandering firewood in the kitchens and heating their rooms day and night.[52]

The most burdensome form of support, however, was the billeting of troops—members of the civilian apparatus had to rent their quarters. Except in Petersburg and possibly Kazan, where there were large fortresses, officers were billeted in urban houses, soldiers in peasant huts. Barracks did not begin to be built until the latter part of Alexander's reign. Troops trained for only 4 months of the year—from May 15 to September 15—during which time it was the peasants' responsibility to contribute the training grounds and the pastures for military horses. During the other 8 months of the year, regiments were scattered throughout the countryside. The regimental commander and his chancery settled in the uezd capital or a large village, and each company was distributed among several villages. Higher-ranking officers, the divisional staff, spent the winter in the gubernia capital. Though the behavior of the officers was not, of course, uniform, it was nevertheless reprehensible enough to induce privileged groups to seek an exemption. By the 1780s, nobles, priests, manufacturers, tax farmers, and all guild merchants who managed to combine some business activity with government contracts or with clerical work in a government office no longer had to open their dwellings to the military.[53] In the countryside, however, the presence of officers in the landlord's house may have been welcome, if only to provide some distraction, the opportunity to share memories, and perhaps to arrange a marriage—aside from the order guaranteed by a military presence.

Exemptions only transferred the brunt of billeting toops to the poorer sections of the urban population. Beginning in 1802, "committees to equalize the burden of contributions from the land" were created in the major cities, consisting of elected merchants and police representatives, to draw up inventories of the housing stock available to military personnel and to investigate the possibility of levying a tax to build barracks instead. To reduce the arbitrary powers of the military to select quarters at random on the arrival of troops, billeting commissions were formed of representatives from nobles having houses in the town, merchants, and *meshchane*, chaired by the policemaster. The commission issued tickets (*bilety*) to the policemaster, giving permission to occupy officially listed quarters, and these tickets were given to the officers, who presented them to the owners of the houses to which they had been assigned. The size of the quarters depended on the officer's rank, ranging from nine rooms for a married general with an additional two rooms for his servants to a single room for an unmarried junior officer.[54]

It can thus be seen that an extensive fiscal system based on contributions in kind supplemented the official collection of direct and indirect taxes. This network owed its existence to the scarcity of money, itself the consequence of insufficiently developed exchanges, and it gradually began to interlock with the Treasury's own fiscal apparatus after the war of 1812, when the extremely stable social and political order created a century earlier began to show signs of internal strain. The ratio of contributions in kind to total tax collections is probably impossible to determine, but it is obvious from the description of these contributions that without them the governing of Russia until the end of the eighteenth century would have been limited to the two capitals. They thus made it possible for the army, the civilian apparatus, and the political infrastructure to function by providing the essential services and the essential subsistence. They were the link, however coarse, between ruling class and dependent population, a link more direct and intimate than cash payments could ever be. In turning over food and contributing its labor, the dependent population willy-nilly was expressing its acceptance of the command structure, of which it was both the bottom and the indispensable part, and of the nobility as a greedy and demanding yet paternalistic ruling class.

15

Budget Making

The Budget in Figures

There was no national budget in Russia until the 1780s, and there could be none until funds collected by fiscal agents were deposited in a central treasury from which most, if not all, expenditures were defrayed until the traditional concept of the specialization of revenues was first abandoned in favor of their concentration in a single general fund: until the treasury had become, in Stourm's words, the banker of the budgets.[1] It is nevertheless true that the constituent elements of such a national budget were in place year after year, even if they were not collated and integrated into a single comprehensive document. This failure to complete the budget process and to establish a unified budgetary procedure reflects certain assumptions on how public funds should be collected and spent. It is possible, with the help of documents published by Miliukov and Kulomzin, to gain at least an approximate idea of the size of the national revenue and expenditure.

During a first period stretching from the beginning of the eighteenth century to the 1760s, the most striking feature of the expenditure budget was the share of military outlays not only in wartime but in peacetime as well. Estimates for 1701, when the military buildup was under way, show that the army already consumed over 50 percent of all expenditures. Had it not been for an exceptionally large expenditure to buy silver and recover old coins from the population, the share of military expenditures would have exceeded 78 percent. In 1710, the year after Poltava, it was almost 80 percent.[2] It is thus no exaggeration to say that the expenditure budget of the first decade of the century was hardly more than the budget of the army, to which funds for the navy were added beginning in 1702. By 1725, a year of peace, military expenditures were more than double those of 1710, lending credence to Miliukov's thesis, challenged by Kahan, that the introduction of the capitation to pay for them meant an additional burden on the peasantry, despite the cessation of hostilities.[3] The creation of the colleges, large-scale public construction, and the opening of embassies abroad, however, raised the share of nonmilitary expenditures to nearly 30 percent.

In the fiscal retrenchment that followed Peter's death, expenditures for local administration were drastically curtailed from .6 million rubles in 1725 to

.1 million in 1744, but those for the Senate and colleges remained stable at .2 million. Expenditures for public construction were cut in half—from .6 to .3 million—while expenditures for the Court doubled to .6 million rubles, a nearly perfect equivalent exchange. On the whole, nonmilitary expenditures went down to 20 percent; army and navy expenditures absorbed the difference. The army was the chief beneficiary of the increase, no doubt a consequence of Münnich's reforms, the Crimean campaigns of the 1730s, and the Russo-Swedish war of 1741–1743. The expenditure budget for 1762—the first year of peace after the Seven Years' War, which ended on the Russian front in February—resembled that of 1725 and began to exhibit a pattern that would become increasingly familiar, in which military expenditures continued to grow while their share decreased. Nonmilitary expenditures went up again to nearly 30 percent, with expenditures for central and military administration now exceeding the 1725 level, while expenditures for the court went up nearly 3½ times.[4] This evolution can be traced more easily in Table 15.1 below.

To cover these expenditures the ruling elite had at its disposal two major sources of revenue, direct and indirect taxes, supplemented by a wide array of miscellaneous rents and fees. Direct taxes made up only 20 percent of the estimated revenue budget for 1701, while indirect taxes, from trade and the sale of vodka, exceeded 40 percent. Most of the remainder came from the minting of new coins, which alone contributed 26 percent of the revenue. The deficit was covered by including arrears from previous years.[5]

The estimated revenue budget for 1724 was the first based on the two direct and three indirect taxes described above, although the total size of the revenue budget long remained a mystery even to the College of Revenue, responsible for drawing up such a budget, known at the time as the *okladnaia kniga*. Direct taxes yielded 4.6 million rubles, or 54 percent of a total budget of 8.5 million, indirect taxes contributed 32.6 percent, and miscellaneous revenue the remainder. The capitation and quitrent were thus the foundation of the last Petrine budgets, a foundation, however, incapable of sustaining a steadily expanding budget because the yield of these two taxes could increase no faster than the population and their rate was limited by political considerations.

The budget for 1751 reflected two major changes in the relative importance of the major sources of revenue and established a pattern that would remain characteristic for the next three generations. One was the declining share of direct taxes, the other the growing share of the revenue from the sale of vodka.

Table 15.1. Expenditures, 1701–1762 (in millions of rubles)

	1701	1725	1744	1762
Military	1.8	6.9	7.8	11.8
Share of Total	**51.4%**	**70.4%**	**80.4%**	**73.7%**
Civilian	—	1.6	.9	1.7
Other	1.7	1.3	1.–	2.5
Total	3.5	9.8	9.7	16.0

From that time on, the expansion of the revenue from taxation was financed by the cooperation of the ruling elite and the upper stratum of the merchantry seeking to maximize the production of vodka. Such a policy called for higher bids from farmers for quadrennial farms in return for numerous outlets planted at tempting locations and dispensation to drown the dependent population in towns and villages in a sea of alcohol.

A third change became noticeable during the 1750s. While the revenue rose by 135 percent in the 27 years between 1724 and 1751, it more than doubled in the following 18 years, from 11.5 to 24.1 million rubles in 1769. This accelerated growtn was caused by the rise of the quitrent in 1761 and increased customs revenues following the tariffs of 1757 and 1766. These changes notwithstanding, it remains a remarkable feature of the revenue budget that the two direct and the three indirect taxes contributed 86.7 percent of the total revenue in 1724 and 85.1 percent in 1769, as can be seen from Table 15.2.[6]

The second part of Catherine's reign, beginning in 1775 with the launching of the local government reform, was marked by two developments with major consequences for the size and structure of the budget. The streamlining of the central administration made it possible finally to draw up a national budget for the first time, and the creation of boards, chambers, and courts in every gubernia resulted in an enormous growth of expenditure for civil administration. On the other hand, the inadequacy of the tax base to support such a growth, the chronic deficits, and the inflation resulting from the heavy demand for services that an undeveloped urban economy could not adequately supply led to the systematic resort to the printing of paper money and to borrowing abroad.[7] These developments also resulted in the establishment of two complementary budgets, one the formal budget for "ordinary" expenditures, drawn up in accordance with the established rules of accounting, and the other for those "extraordinary" expenditures that ignorance and calculated policy kept separate. Figures, therefore, must be used with caution.

Military expenditures—those of the Colleges of War and Navy—despite doubling in size between 1781 and 1786 in the wake of Potemkin's reforms of the cavalry and the building of a Black Sea fleet and naval installations, which absorbed much of the increase, represented about half as large a share of total expenditures as it had in the preceding period. By contrast, civilian expendi-

Table 15.2. Revenue from Taxation, 1724–1769 (in millions of rubles)

	1724	%	1751	%	1769	%
Capitation and Quitrent	4.6	54.1	5.2	45.4	10.3	42.7
Vodka	1.0	11.3	2.3	19.8	5.–	21.0
Salt	.7	7.7	1.2	10.5	1.9	7.8
Trade	1.1	13.6	1.2	10.7	3.3	13.6
Total	**7.4**	**86.7**	**9.9**	**86.4**	**20.5**	**85.1**
Other	1.1	13.3	1.6	13.6	3.6	14.9
Total	8.5	100	11.5	100	24.1	100

Table 15.3. Expenditures, 1781–1796 (in millions of rubles)

	1781	1786	1796
Military	13.9	27.8	27.7
Share of Total	**33.9%**	**44.3%**	**35.4%**
Civilian	21.0	24.6	36.3
Other	6.1	10.3	14.2
Total	41.0	62.7	78.2

tures, almost exclusively for salaries with smaller sums for communications, construction, and schools, rose from less than 2 to 21 million in less than 20 years and kept rising until the end of the reign. Likewise, "other" expenditures, chiefly for the court, continued the steady progress begun during the reign of Elizabeth. The most significant change was the appearance and relentless growth of expenditures for debt servicing, from .6 million rubles in 1781 to 4.2 million in 1796. The growth of the expenditure budget and the changing relationships between its component parts did not, however, alter the basic fact that most expenditures went to pay the salaries of the military and civilian apparatus, the clerical staff, and the military suppliers who belonged to the merchantry of the first two guilds.[8] It was thus not much more than the collective, almost household, budget of the ruling elite and its immediate allies and underlings. (See Table 15.3.)

The budget for 1781 was the first one drawn up by the Procurator General on the basis of the new principles of treasury operations announced in 1780. The revenue budget had grown by 64.3 percent since 1769, at a much lesser rate than in the 1750s, while expenditures had more than doubled from 16 to 41 million rubles, a first indication that even anticipated revenues were not keeping pace with expenditures. The share of direct taxes continued to decline despite the increase in the quitrent, reflected in the 1786 budget, and that of the capitation, reflected in that of 1796. But then the capitation yielded 10 million rubles and the quitrent, 14.7 million. The quitrent overtook the capitation in 1784, following an increase to 3 rubles in 1783, as the most important direct tax. The revenue from the two taxes was just about enough to cover military expenditures in 1781. This was no longer the case by 1786, and the military establishment became more and more dependent on additional resources from the Treasury in the form of paper money from the Assignat Bank and foreign credit.

The reduced share of direct taxation was compensated by the growing contribution of the tax farmers, who sold vodka from the government-owned stores. These two sources of revenue continued to contribute just under two-thirds of the revenue from 1724 to 1796, a revenue extracted almost entirely from the dependent population. More disturbing was the declining share of the customs revenue, the combined result of the protective tariff of 1766, the slump caused by the first Turkish war, and the disruptions of the Pugachev rebellion. It was not until after the promulgation of the tariff of 1782 that its share began to rise, but it again fell under 10 percent at the end of the reign. "Other" sources of revenue were many but yielded little; they are usually subsumed under two categories, those from mining operations (*gornye*), and the so-called administrative revenues (*kantseliarskie sbory*) from various fees and the lease of government properties. The most telling commentary on the rigidity of the Russian fiscal system during Catherine's reign is the actual decline of the revenue from mining operations, from 3.6 million rubles in 1781 to 2.3 million in 1796. The total share of direct and indirect taxes, which had been about 85 percent during the preceding period, went down to about 80 percent, as Table 15.4 clearly shows.[9]

Despite the much-improved fiscal administration and the rise in the rate of taxation, revenue could not keep up with the expenditures generated by an ambitious foreign policy in Poland and on the Black Sea. Chechulin has calculated that expenditures reached 1.6 billion rubles during the entire reign of Catherine, while revenues did not exceed 1.4 billion, creating a deficit of 200 million rubles. Additional revenue had been generated in the past by reducing the metal content in silver coins and minting copper coins. This time-honored method could no longer yield the vast sums needed by the imperial government. In 1769, at the beginning of the first Turkish war, the first assignats rolled off the printing press, and their ceiling was fixed at 20 million in 1774; at the beginning of 1786 the amount in circulation had already reached 45 million. In June of that year, the momentous decision was made to resort systematically to the printing press rather than to taxation to finance the military expenditures of the second Turkish war, and the ceiling was raised by a stroke of the pen to 100 million. By the end of Catherine's reign, in 1796, 156.7 million assignat rubles had been printed. Resort to paper money in 1769 was supplemented by foreign borrowing for the first time, and the foreign debt reached 33 million rubles in 1796, much of it accumulated between 1787 and 1792. It was later consolidated under the name of the "Dutch debt" because most of the loans had been floated in Amsterdam. An additional 15.5 million came from domestic borrowing—including a 4-million-ruble loan from a Narva merchant in 1791—bringing the total debt to 205.2 million rubles at the end of 1796, an average of 7.3 million a year between 1769 and 1796.[10]

Table 15.4. Revenue from Taxation, 1781–1796 (in millions of rubles)

	1781	%	1786	%	1796	%
Capitation and Quitrent	13.4	33.8	20.3	39.5	24.7	33.1
Vodka	12.5	31.6	13.3	25.9	22.0	29.5
Salt	3.8	9.6	4.3	8.3	5.2	7.0
Trade	1.8	4.5	5.4	10.5	6.5	8.7
Total	**31.5**	**79.5**	**43.3**	**84.2**	**58.4**	**78.3**
Other	8.1	20.5	8.1	15.8	16.2	21.7
Total	39.6	100	51.4	100	74.6	100

Table 15.5.

	1805	1815	1825
Military	53.7	135.–	173.8
Share of Total	**47.8%**	**42.7%**	**44.2%**
Civilian	46.5	122.3	126.6
Other	12.1	58.7	92.6
Total	112.3	316.0	393.0

Alexander's fiscal policies merely extended Catherine's in an international context marked by constant war and territorial expansion. By 1805 the military budget of 1796 had nearly doubled; by 1815, following the decisive conflict with Napoleon that was comparable in importance to the culmination of the struggle with Charles XII in 1709, it had nearly quintrupled; and by 1825 more than sextupled. If we break down this last budget according to departmental estimates, it appears, as could be expected, that the lion's share of the army budget went to the supply services: Commissary and Provision Departments received a total of 135 out of 173.8 million rubles. Another 11.2 million went to the Artillery and the Engineers. The Navy received 12.4 million. Nevertheless, despite the enormous increase in the size of the military budget, its share of total expenditures never again rose to the levels reached during the first 75 years of the eighteenth century but stabilized at about 45 percent. This was higher, however, than during Catherine's reign, except during the second Turkish war, as shown in Table 15.5.

Civilian expenditures continued to grow but at a much slower pace. The 1796 budget had increased by less than a third by 1805, had only trebled by 1815, and barely increased during the next decade. The strict apportionment after 1802 of civilian expenditures among the ministries makes it possible to determine the importance of each ministry in the central government. The expenditure budget of the Finance Ministry amounted to 21.5 million rubles in 1805, or 46.3 percent of the total, 88.4 million in 1825, or 69.5 percent of the total. By contrast, the second most important ministry, that of Internal Affairs, spent 16.5 million in 1805 and only 15.2 million in 1825. By then, however, expenditures for communications and the post office (13.5 million) had become the responsibility of other agencies. As a result, the ministry's share had gone down in 20 years from 35.5 to 12 percent. If we remember that Dmitri Gur'ev had by far the longest tenure of any minister during Alexander's reign, the central position of the Finance Ministry becomes all to obvious. Other expenditures include those for the church, the Foreign Ministry, and especially the Court, where expenditures amounted to 9.3 million in 1805 and rose to 17.7 million in 1825, a year when the servicing of the debt demanded another 54 of the 92.6 million.[11]

During Alexander's reign the rising share of direct taxes represented a new dependence on the poll taxes, on which Peter had founded so many hopes. It also showed once again the permanence of a rigid tax base and the superficiality of an industrial development from which the government was still unable to derive substantial sums. The revenue from direct taxation represented in 1825 about the same percentage of the total revenue as it did in 1796. Using figures for 1815, the capitation and quitrent collected from peasants of the Treasury yielded 72.2 of the 128.2 million, or 56.3 percent, while the capitation alone paid by peasants of the Court, peasants attached to factories, and the serfs of landowners contributed 33.8 million, or 26.4 percent. The capitation on townsmen and the tax on declared capital yielded 17.2 million, or 13.4 percent.

The rigidity of the tax base was evident in another aspect—the revenue from the sale of vodka remained at between a third and a fourth of the total. The transition to a government-run monopoly obviously made little difference, and the combined revenue from direct taxation and the sale of vodka continued to yield about two-thirds of the total revenue, as it had throughout the eighteenth century. The customs revenue now exceeded 10 percent, except in 1815, when Russia had not yet recovered from the Continental System and the war of 1812–1813. The "other" revenue retained the same composition—a paltry 2.6 million in 1825 from industry but 16.6 million from the lease of government properties and 29 million from fees on commercial transactions (*kupchie kreposti*), passports, stamp paper, and licenses (*svidetelstva*) to trade in towns.[12] Table 15.6 shows growth of the revenue before 1805 and 1825.

The rigidity of the tax base, combined with Russia's determination to prove itself Napoleon's sole unbeatable antagonist on the Continent—a claim realized only with the victorious entry of the Russian army into Paris in March 1814—made a mockery of the neatly balanced ordinary budgets fed by taxation alone. The total debt rose to 275 million rubles during the reign of Paul, an average of 17.5 million a year, but 2½ times the rate during his mother's reign after 1769. By 1825 it had risen to 1.3 billion rubles, at an average rate of 42 million a year. The deficit continued to be financed from three sources—the printing of paper money, foreign borrowing, and borrowing—especially transfers from the *Sokhrannye Kazny*, which had nowhere else to invest their substantial assets. Assignats continued to be printed until 1817, by which time the amount in circulation reached 836 million. After that date they began to be redeemed at a fluctuating rate of exchange of about four assignat rubles to one

Table 15.6.

	1805	%	1815	%	1825	%
Capitation and Quitrent	45.–	43.9	128.2	40.5	126.1	32.–
Vodka	27.2	26.6	105.5	33.4	128.4	32.7
Salt	6.3	6.1	16.6	5.2	25.–	6.4
Trade	12.1	11.8	20.–	6.3	48.–	12.2
Total	**90.6**	**88.4**	**270.4**	**85.5**	**327.5**	**83.3**
Other	11.8	11.6	45.6	14.5	65.5	16.7
Total	102.4	100	316.–	100	393.–	100

Table 15.7.

	1796	%	1825	%
Foreign debt	33	16.0	357	26.9
Domestic debt	15.5	7.5	371	28.0
Assignats	156.7	76.5	595	45.1
Total	205.2	100.0	1323	100.0

silver ruble. Table 15.7 shows the size and composition of the national debt in 1796 and 1825 (in millions of assignat rubles).[13]

Budget Procedure: Drawing Up the Budget

A comprehensive budget did not exist in Russia until 1781—a most telling commentary on the fragmentation of the central government, the autonomy of its constituent agencies, and the helplessness of a ruler whose "autocratic power," manifesting itself through a "bureaucracy," should have been able to keep a tight rein on this crucial sector of government. The impossibility of drawing up a national budget was not peculiar to Russia: France, with a similar tradition of centralized government, did not have one until after the Revolution.[14] The reasons for this state of affairs, somewhat incongruous at a time when "absolute" monarchs were imposing their rule on families and institutions, were several, but three stand out, at least in Russia.

The machinery of government had grown piecemeal, as new agencies like the *prikazy* were created for special purposes and closed when these were achieved. The growth of the grand princely household, bent on assuming expanding responsibilities as the frontier advanced to the south and the east, created an administrative monster that inertia and vested interests conspired to defend. As new agencies were created, funds to pay their staffs were most readily obtained by taxing the operations they were created to regulate. Hence, the general acceptance of the principle of specialized revenues and the refusal to accept that of a general fund (*edinstvo kassy*), into which all receipts would be deposited and from which all outlays would be disbursed.[15] Finally, the level of education among the ruling elite, the state of accounting, the autonomy— despite appearances—of voevodas, along with sheer greed, made it impossible to determine the size of the revenue.

Peter's reforms represented a serious attempt to create an organizational framework capable of drawing up a national budget, but intentions foundered on the inability and unwillingness of voevodas to supply comprehensive data on the funds they collected. As a result, the College of Revenue, established for the specific purpose of drawing up a revenue budget, the so-called *okladnaia kniga*, could not carry out its purpose and had to admit defeat before the Senate, despite threats of punitive action. After Peter's death, a new attempt was made to obtain regular and consistent reports on the progress of tax collections by requiring governors to send quarterly statements for each town, each uezd, and each item of revenue, while colleges were required to send monthly reports of their revenues and expenditures. Unfortunately, there did not exist a comprehensive table of taxes and fees indicating how much it was legal to charge. Different names were used for the same taxes, and voevodas might combine several taxes under the same rubric. The same revenue was classified as *okladnyi* by some, *neokladnyi* by others. Standard forms were not sent out by the College of Revenue to help governors and voevodas sort out their funds. More serious were the refusal of all too many to submit their reports and the inability of Senate and colleges to compel them to mend their ways. Others sent incomplete reports, a subject of endless correspondence. The college confessed in 1767 that it was unable to cope with a backlog of 90,000 cases dealing with unanswered requests and unsettled problems.[16]

This dearth of accurate information also plagued the expenditure budget. The level of expenditure in any agency was determined by its table of organization, but these tables did not exist until the 1760s. In May 1762, when the "autocrat" gave the Senate 2 weeks to submit a short statement of revenues and expenditures, he was told that it was impossible because a commission created in 1756 to draw up a general table of organization had not yet completed its work. Nevertheless, the Senate assumed revenues of about 15 million rubles and expenditures of 16.5 million.[17]

The task of bringing order to this long-standing chaos was given to Catherine's procurator general, and its solution is Prince Viazemskii's claim to greatness. After an unsuccessful start, a table was drawn up of 192 items of revenue, based on reports from 256 central and local agencies—with 74, including 14 central agencies, still refusing to cooperate or sending incomplete reports.[18] Many of these items were later annulled, as yielding insignificant sums. The reform might not have proceeded much farther, however, without the creation of uniform territorial divisions in gubernias and uezds of approximately equal size, the elimination of voevodas, and the establishment of the governor as the only intermediary between the center and local authorities. These changes immediately reduced some 200 chanceries in Russia proper to 26. Moreover, the creation of treasury chambers and the appointment of a separate paid treasurer in each uezd—very often drawn from among local merchants, with some knowledge of accounting—shaped a new fiscal apparatus tightly controlled by the Procurator General and his successor, the Finance Minister. After each chamber was supplied with a register of taxes to be collected and detailed forms standardized for the entire country to guide its accounting, it became possible to draw up twenty-six consistent and reliable *okladnye knigi*, the building blocks of the national revenue budget, first published in 1781.[19]

The Procurator General's determined struggle to improve accounting procedures and ascertain with reasonable accuracy the size of the anticipated revenue (how much would actually be collected was another matter) went hand in hand with a no-less-persistent rejection of the principle of specialized revenues. At the end of the seventeenth century, some revenues were collected entirely by a single *prikaz*, others by different ones, depending on the *prikaz* to which the town and the uezd that contributed it were subordinated. Colleges refined the practice. The original purpose of the capitation was to finance the military establishment. It was the perfect example of a specialized revenue, but it soon proved inadequate to cover all military expenditures. It was collected by the Commissary. A Senate report of June 1762 shows very clearly how widespread remained the practice of assigning other revenues to their collecting agencies.[20] Each agency, like each voevoda, had an interest in underreporting its revenue. The Treasury reform of 1780 is therefore one of the most important administrative reforms in modern Russian history. The concentration of funds in a single Treasury accompanied by the creation of twenty-six treasury chambers established a separate machinery of fiscal management responsible for all revenue collection and all disbursements. This reform, carried out with the indispensable support of the Empress by a procurator general who was also one of the pillars of the ruling elite, reflected the latter's concern over a chaotic situation, as larger and larger sums were needed to finance an active foreign policy.

The first stage in the elaboration of a national budget—even if the process remained incomplete—was the preparation of estimates of revenue and expenditures in every agency. A perusal of what Miliukov somewhat inaccurately calls the state budget (*rospis'*) for 1680—there are no total figures and some agencies are not represented—shows how those estimates were reached. Each *prikaz* collected specific revenues and was responsible for specific expenditures deriving from the purpose for which it had been established. If the revenue exceeded the expenditure, the *prikaz* kept the balance, thus functioning as a minitreasury. One example, and one of the simplest, will suffice to illustrate the composition of agency estimates. The revenue of the *Pomestnyi Prikaz* for 1680 consisted of balances from the preceding year (656 rubles) and receipts from fees on commercial transactions (9,005 rubles). Its expenditures included internal outlay (2,098 rubles) and transfers to seven other *prikazy* (6,451 rubles), leaving a balance of 1,112 rubles.[21] In a system where *prikaz* chiefs were often relatives of the tsar, these procedures strengthened the autonomy of every agency and made impossible the preparation of a general and accurate budget.

The gubernatorial reform of 1708 radically altered the procedures for drawing up the estimates and distinguished more sharply between those of military and those of civilian revenue and expenditure. Military estimates remained agency estimates, civilian ones became territorial estimates. Governors were required to collect and hold, each in his gubernia, the revenue previously sent to separate *prikazy*, soon to be closed, but to continue sending the funds for military expenditures to central military agencies or directly to the army. This marked the acceptance for the first time, at least in theory, of the concept of a general fund in each of the eight gubernia treasuries and entailed the creation of eight territorial budgets in which each item of expenditure continued to require the tsar's authorization and each item of revenue was determined by past and current legislation. Balances would be forwarded to the central Treasury, in which a similar general fund would be kept for other and unexpected expenditures. The experiment failed, however, largely because the pressures of war destroyed every attempt to create regular budgets and because distances and the state of accounting facilitated the tendency among governors to underreport revenue.[22]

The collegial reform of 1718–1719 contained an ambitious but unrealistic program of budgetary reform. The creation of colleges was not intended to be a return to autonomous *prikazy* financed by their own revenues and by outside contributions. Each college, gubernia, and provincial chancery was to have its own table of organization, kept by a treasurer responsible to the central treasury, and a book of revenues kept by the tax collector. Each agency would therefore know beforehand how much it needed for the coming year and how much it could reasonably expect. In the military establishment, there were to be separate tables for each infantry and cavalry regiment, for the artillery and garrisons, and for the navy. The plan also retained the concept of a general fund, except for the capitation—admittedly a major exception since it made up 54 percent of the revenue in 1724. The reform was decisively flawed, however, because the tables of organization were never drawn up with the completeness necessary to make estimates credible, except perhaps those for the army and the garrisons.[23] Moreover, it was premature, introduced at a time of unmistakable reaction against the experiment with territorial administration and a reflexive return to Muscovite practices, which accelerated after Peter's death. After the mid-1730s colleges began to operate very much like the old *prikazy*. The example of the College of War in 1765 well illustrates the composition of agency revenues (in thousands of rubles):[24]

Capitation	5,246
From College of Revenue	1,069
From Salt Board	424
From College of Commerce	249
From treasury	336
From other sources	792
Total	8,116

Peter's attempts to reform budgetary procedures in 1708 and 1718 thus stand in stark contrast to the reality that preceded and followed them. They also help us understand the problems faced by Catherine II and her Procurator General, and why they succeeded where Peter's failed. The empress insisted at the very beginning of her reign on a return to the concept of a general fund.[25] This implied concentrating treasury operations in a single and effective treasury that would not be the shadow of a name, and meant stripping the colleges of revenue-collecting authority. This attack on the fiscal foundations of the college's autonomy coupled with the decentralization of their management responsibilities led to the closing of most central agencies and to the treasury reform of 1780. Thenceforth, all revenues, including the capitation, of course, were deposited in the gubernia treasury chambers. A breakthrough was achieved in the publication of a table of organization for the entire government, first in 1763, then in the 1780s, in the wake of the local government reform, which created an extensive network of provincial agencies.[26] The reform thus made it possible for each treasury chamber and for central agencies, especially the Commissary, to draw up estimates of expenditures for each gubernia. The reform succeeded not only because of improved accounting procedures and the creation of a civilian apparatus in the provinces capable of operating effectively since it had the support of a political infrastructure but also because the Procurator General became the chief of the Treasury, with unchallengeable control over the collection of revenue and the disbursement of Treasury funds.

It might have been expected that the ministerial reform of 1802 would mark a return to the pre-1780 situation, but the not-too-subtle attempts by ministries to reintroduce the discredited principle of specialized revenues was squashed by the tsar in March 1807 at the request of the Finance Minister.[27] At the same time, revenue estimates by ministries became superfluous, since all expenditures were to be defrayed from the general fund. The manifesto of September 1802 had little to say about budgetary procedure; ministers had to submit clear and comprehensive expenditure budgets to the Finance Minister by the beginning of October. The Ministerial Statute of June 1811 made the directors of departments responsible for preparing estimates for their departments and submitting them to the ministry's council for amendments and coordination. It was then the minister's responsibility to draw up an estimate of the entire ministry's expenditures and submit it to the Finance Minister.[28] Gubernia budgets, so important after 1780, seem to have been broken up into so many local agency budgets of the respective ministries.

The completion of agency estimates was followed by the second stage in the elaboration of a national budget—the preparation of a general statement of revenues and expenditures. Indeed, one of the reasons behind the creation of the Privy Chancery about 1700 had been to establish a coordinating body consisting chiefly of *prikaz* chiefs for the purpose of keeping close control over *prikaz* accounting procedures and monitoring the level of balances kept in the agencies. Governors were summoned to Moscow with their estimates in the winter of 1709 to discuss that year's budget with the chancery. When the Senate was appointed in 1711, one of its major responsibilities was "to examine all state expenditures and to cancel those not urgent (*nenuzhnye*) and especially those without a purpose (*naprasnye*)."[29] It can thus be said that beginning in 1700 a conscious effort was made, in the face of war and shortages, to break the budgetary autonomy of central agencies and, later, of governors' chanceries, and to subordinate them to the discipline of a national budget. On the other hand, the demands of war were so great and resources so scarce that neither the Privy Chancery nor the Senate could afford to consider itself bound by any budgetary plan it had adopted. War was not a propitious time to impose order upon chaos.

With the creation of the College of Revenue, a Treasury, and a Commissary, their chiefs at first members of the Senate and after 1722 subordinated to it, the administrative infrastructure was in place on which to base a national budget. Each college gubernia and provincial chancery was to submit expenditure estimates based on its table of organization to the Treasury, where these requests would be reviewed to determine whether any entries were unauthorized by the table or separate orders. If any were found, the Treasury would refer the matter to the Senate or the ruler for decision, making sure that "no one should be offended and everyone should receive his due" in accordance with "patents, orders, and agreements" made with the agency. Once the amendments had been approved, a combined table of organization (*general'nyi shtat*) for the entire government was to be drawn up by the Treasury, each separate table requiring the ruler's signature. This table of ordinary expenditures would become the official document authorizing the release of Treasury funds.[30]

The reform of 1719 thus stripped agencies of their authority to spend without obtaining an order from the central Treasury, in which all their balances had thenceforth to be deposited. We saw that the counterpart of this expenditure budget was the revenue budget for which the College of Revenue was made responsible. The coordination, however, never materialized, because the task of preparing a register of all revenues collected in the country was insurmountable at the time. Nevertheless, the reform assumed that such a register would become available. It was then to be submitted to the Treasury, where a truly national ordinary budget called the *opredelitel'nyi shtat* would be drawn up. A budget was to be prepared for each gubernia and province showing expenditures and revenue, both *okladnyi* and *neokladnyi*, and bringing out what province had a surplus or a shortage of funds. The Treasury and the College of Revenue would then collaborate to determine how the deficit of one province could be covered by the surplus of another. This budget was to be binding on all authorities, and no change was to be made without the approval of the Treasury. The Senate and the ruler were to have the last word in case of disagreement.[31]

The reform of 1719 thus contained a truly grand design for budgetary reorganization. It established budget making as a separate sector of administrative activity, vested in a separate agency, and carved out of the managerial responsibilities of central and local agencies. It also reflected the will to power of a ruler bent on asserting autocratic authority against the patronage networks of ruling families for which the budgetary autonomy of agencies had been a means to an end—sharing the spoils of taxation. Although it failed, it was obviously a model for Prince Viazemskii's own reform, 60 years later, when rising expenditures and the emergence of a powerful Procurator General combined to break, this time lastingly, the alliance of vested interests that had paralyzed budgetary reform for so long.

Once again, in the 1780s, gubernia budgets for civilian administration and the Commissary and Provision Chancery budgets for the military became the major building blocks of a national budget. Tables of organization approved and amended over the ruler's signature were kept in the Procurator General's office, and each treasury chamber received a copy of its own table and kept a register of estimated revenue. Estimates thus became purely formal at the gubernia level. A civilian ordinary budget was drawn up in the Expedition of State Revenues and especially in its two subdivisions, one for revenue, the other for expenditures, which took over the responsibilities of the old Treasury and the College of Revenue. The reform of 1780 thus carried out what Peter's reform had intended: the concentration of budget making in a single office—the Expedition, subordinated to the Procurator General, became the first budget office in modern Russian history. Military estimates of expenditures were submitted in the fall to the Expedition, and revenue estimates lost their importance as military and naval agencies began to receive all their funds from the Treasury. The first national budget was still, as we shall see, a budget of ordinary expenditures based on tables of organization and of expected revenues, and a wide gap soon developed between the ordinary and the year-end budget bloated with extraordinary expenditures. Nevertheless, a giant step had been made in imposing order on this complex and intractable sector of Russian administration.[32]

The recreation of central agencies in 1802, the growth of government, and the diversification of expenditures made things more difficult for the Finance Minister, who now had to cope with ministers enjoying direct access to the ruler. The Manifesto of September 1802 required the Finance Minister to submit to him a comprehensive budget by November of each year. The budget had to be balanced, and it was up to the minister to reject unauthorized expenditures and to find the revenue to defray expenditures included in a table of organization approved by the tsar. A major problem was the classification of expenditures so that different ministerial estimates could be collated and their subdivisions combined to draw up a topical expenditure budget. Accounting began to require the knowledge of statistics, but "statistics did not exist in the state economy" of Alexander's reign. Speranskii proposed a model budget (*obraztsovaia smeta*), which the State Council in 1811 compelled the Finance Minister to accept, over his objections that it could not be realized. Despite these and other difficulties, including delays by departmental directors in submitting their budgets, regular procedures became the norm after 1810: ministers had to submit their budgets to the Finance Minister in September; these budgets, together with his amendments, were discussed in the Committee of Ministers and submitted to the State Council in the fall. There, they were discussed, first in the Department of State Economy, then in the General Assembly. Finally, they were sent to the ruler for promulgation and returned to the Finance Ministry for execution.[33]

Budget Procedure: Executing the Budget

The execution of the budget depended, of course, on how it had been prepared. It was a fundamental principle that all expenditures be approved by the ruler. Once approved, however, items of expenditure became part of an agency's table of organization and were carried over from one year to the next without the need for renewed authorization. Expenditures in the seventeenth and eighteenth centuries were overwhelmingly outlays for personnel—salaries, equipment, and provisions. The budgets of *prikazy* were thus autonomous, authorized expenditures defrayed as the agency's own revenues came in, without the necessity of requesting treasury orders to release money from a general fund. Local expenditures hardly existed, since voevodas were not paid and *prikazy* did not have local agencies. Budgets were thus prepared and executed within each *prikaz* under the supervision of its chief.[34]

The reform of 1708 introduced the concept of a territorial budget and thereby imposed a distinction between expenditures to be defrayed locally and those for which funds were to be transported to the center or to the army in the field. Revenues, no longer assigned for specific purposes, were deposited in the gubernia general fund, from which the governor, operating with the authority of a territorial treasurer, released funds to defray specific expenditures, previously requiring the ruler's approval, for the governor's staff, the garrison, the shipyards of Voronezh or Arkhangelsk, the foresters employed by the Navy in Kazan, the government-owned factories, mines, and arsenals. Estimated balances from the eight territorial budgets constituted a sui generis national general fund from which monies were assigned at the tsar's command to meet the most urgent expenditures of the day and released at the governor's order.[35]

The creation of the colleges, some with local agencies, and the introduction of the capitation as a specialized revenue designed to cover the entire needs of the army and navy complicated the execution of the separate budgets, all the more so since the administrative and fiscal reforms were based on contradictory principles: one established a central Treasury with all-inclusive jurisdiction, the other removed more than half the revenue from its jurisdiction. Here it is possible only to present a view of how the reform of 1718 intended the execution of the budget to take place and how it probably did take place by 1725.

The reform, we remember, was based on the assumption that a combined table of organization for all agencies of government, both central and local, would be available, and that all treasury operations would be concentrated in the gubernia capitals and at the center. Central treasurers were forbidden to release funds without written orders from the chief of the Treasury, and such orders had to be based on the table of organization approved by the ruler. Treasurers in the gubernia capitals received their budgets from the Treasury and released funds for salary on a quarterly basis on receipt of a request by the governor that likewise had to be justified by the table of organization of the gubernia. Requests for so-called *neokladnye* expenditures—for construction and the maintenance of prisoners, for example—were honored by the treasurer if he was satisfied that there was a real need for them and if they could be justified in the accounts. Funds in excess of the requests for local expenditures were forwarded to the central Treasury from which funds were released to colleges and chanceries following the quarterly requests of their chiefs based on the agencies' tables of organization.[36]

The execution of the expenditure budgets of regiments and other military units followed the same rules. On the principles that funds should come from the closest possible source, units stationed in a given gubernia would receive their funds from that gubernia's treasury and their table of organization from the Commissary. A copy would be sent to the gubernia treasurer, who released funds upon requests by the military commanders based on the table—providing of course, that adequate revenue had been collected in the general fund of the gubernia. If not enough funds were available in the gubernia, the Commissary, College of Revenue, and Treasury would jointly determine the source of the additional funds. The introduction of the capitation in 1724 destroyed the concentration of treasury operations, which was the most remarkable feature of the reform. This tax was collected by specially appointed officers who attended to the needs of units stationed in their gubernia and forwarded the balances to other gubernias for the needs of other units in accordance with the commissary's instructions. The military budget was thus the first to become autonomous after 1718. Even though the rate of the capitation was fixed in such a way that its yield would cover military expenditures, there was no need to abandon the concept of a single general fund—unless it was felt that a partial return to specialized revenue would better guarantee that the army would be paid, or unless the creation of the colleges was considered a first step toward a restoration of Muscovite practices.

The elimination of most local agencies after 1725 and the proliferation of central chanceries with their own sources of revenue and without even tables of organization restored the autonomous agency budgets of the pre-1708 period. The reform of the 1780s built on the experiments of 1708 and 1719. The Expedition of State Revenues provided each treasury chamber with its expenditure budget and the Commissary provided each regiment with its table of organization. Funds were released on request by local agencies or regimental commanders, based on the tables of organization, and the capitation, which ceased to be collected by army officers after 1764, was merged with other revenues into a general fund. By then the progress of accounting and the creation of an elaborate local administrative machinery of interdependent parts made it possible to execute the budget at both central and local levels with relative ease. The major difficulty remained the shortage of cash caused by delays in revenue collection and the resulting inability to satisfy requests for the release of funds.[37]

The ministerial reform made no fundamental changes here, but it placed a heavier demand on the central Treasury, from which the new ministries received their funds. Continuing cash shortages forced the Treasury to borrow from the Loan Bank and to juggle accounts: more than 15 million rubles collected in copper coins still reached the Treasury with a 2-year delay in the 1800s. Once the budget had been passed by the State Council, a line of credit was opened in the Treasury for each ministry in the amount shown on the budget. Ministers were required to submit monthly credit balances and estimates of projected claims for the following months. Funds were released over the signature of the Finance Minister.[38]

It must be emphasized that this long search for reliable procedures to draw up a national budget represented only a minimum program—to estimate revenues and, above all, foreseeable expenditures. Hence the persistent emphasis on the table of organization as the fundamental document legitimizing all expenditures and rendering null and void those not based on it. Nevertheless, the table was by definition a fixed and rigid frame of reference, while public life kept making new demands on the Treasury in the course of the budget period. Even if the revenue had been punctually collected—and it was not, as peasants remained in arrears and tax farmers went bankrupt—the government would have had to work out procedures for deficiency appropriations to cope with unforeseen expenditures. When cash shortages developed, the apparatus was simply not paid. The bribery so often associated with Russian officialdom was in fact no more than the continuance of the time-honored practice of feeding off the population, necessitated by the absence of a reliable source of income.

These unforeseen expenditures were of at least three kinds. Additions to the table of organization were made from time to time during the calendar year. Other expenditures were temporary or fluctuated, like those for construction and repairs. Finally, some expenditures grew out of all proportion because the table of organization on which they were based established basic prices for the purchase of provisions and materials that were not adjusted to keep pace with inflation. This was the case above all with the expenditure estimates of the Provision Chancery. Its ordinary budget was based on a price list included in the table of organization 20 or 30 years earlier. Its real budget contained "extraordinary" yet permanent expenditures, which had to be defrayed from separate sources. This explains why Russian budgets were usually presented as balanced: ordinary expenditures were made to match ordinary revenues. The real budgets had large deficits financed by resorting to "extraordinary" revenues, paper money, and borrowing.[39]

How deficiency appropriations were financed at the end of the seventeenth century is not clear. The problem was in any case much simpler. The effects of inflation were mild, and there was no standing army requiring a steady flow of provisions. It seems likely that whenever a new item of expenditure was added to the table of organization of a *prikaz*, a new source of revenue was assigned to the agency in the form of a next tax or a transfer from the balance of another *prikaz*. Such operations had to be approved by the ruler and presupposed a knowledge of the disposable surplus in each *prikaz*. A general statement of all available balances may have been kept in the *blizhniaia* duma, and was certainly kept in the Privy Chancery after 1700. Each new item became a permanent part of the table of organization until removed with the tsar's approval. Shortages of both revenue and cash, together with the inexhaustible demands of war, obliterated for more than a decade any distinction between estimated expenditures and deficiency appropriations. Money was seized to support the war effort wherever it was available, whether for current expenditures or to build a reserve.

The Treasury reform of 1719 recognized the need for deficiency appropriations because "it is impossible to know all state expenditures at the beginning of the year." Whenever an agency requested additional authority to spend or was instructed to exceed its estimated expenditures, a separate (*osoblivyi*) written order had to be sent by the ruler or the Senate to the Treasury, without which no separate authorization (*osoblivaia assignatsiia*) to release the funds to the spending agency could be given. Since such an authorization assumed that the funds were available, the Treasury had to turn to the College of Revenue to speed up the collection of arrears when they were not.[40] We know that the reform failed and that agency budgets recovered their autonomy after 1725. Whenever a deficiency appropriation was necessary, the Senate had to find the funds in whatever college they could. It is likely that colleges had to submit to it an annual statement of their balances—obtained in part by omitting staff from the table of organization—and that these balances were frozen until a college received written orders to release some part of them.

By the late 1770s, the gap between ordinary and extraordinary expenditures had become so great that the Treasury reform of 1780 created two treasuries, one for ordinary (*shtatnye*), the other for extraordinary (*ostatochnye*—literally, from balances) expenditures. The execution of the ordinary budget remained automatic and was financed from one treasury. The budgets sent by the Expedition of State Revenues to treasury chambers specified the amount each treasury would receive, and contributions to the Treasury for Extraordinary Expenditures built up a national reserve from which funds were released to finance deficiency appropriations during the year. The second innovation was to combine the posts of Procurator General and State Treasurer and provide that all orders to release funds issuing from the ruler be addressed to him, thus preventing all but a very small number of members of the ruling elite from turning directly to the empress for separate orders.[41] Never before had the execution of the budget been so concentrated in a single office.

The execution of the budget during the reign of Alexander I amounted to a long battle by the Finance Ministry to preserve Prince Viazemskii's achievements. Ministers with direct access to the tsar soon began to treat their ordinary budgets as a bare minimum and deficiency appropriations as a handy way to build empires behind the back of the Finance Minister. The harm caused by this tactic—essentially the misappropriation of the ruler's authority vis-à-vis the Treasury—convinced Alexander in February 1810 to require ministers to submit their requests first to the new State Council, which called on them in August to refrain as much as possible from exceeding their estimated expenditures. An exception was made, however: half a million rubles, a relatively small sum at the time, were placed at the disposal of the finance minister for "extremely urgent" needs and allowed ministers to request imperial commands directly authorizing the expenditure and ordering the Finance Minister to release the funds. These restrictions did not have the intended effect: in 1811 alone, requests for 11 million rubles of extraordinary expenditures went through the Council; requests for another 15 million bypassed it altogether. Ministers had become so powerful that the "autocrat" could not even compel them to follow the regulations he had approved a year earlier. After the war, Gur'ev fought to restrict the fiscal autonomy of the ministries and won in February 1822, when ministers were ordered to submit their requests for deficiency appropriations to the Finance Minister, who would then seek imperial approval. The State Council no longer played any controlling role.[42]

The third stage in the execution of the budget—after the release of funds for ordinary expenditures and the approval of deficiency appropriations—was the audit. Without it, determination of how much was actually collected and spent and how much remained available in the national accounts for use during the following budget period was impossible, and illegality and fraud were bound to go unnoticed and unpunished. Nevertheless, auditing remained the least-effective procedure in budget making until at least the 1780s. The neglect it suffered was due in part to the need to first concentrate on the elaboration of revenue and expenditure budgets and above all a comprehensive table of revenues, without which there was simply nothing to audit. The disappearance of the *Prikaz* of Audit by the end of the seventeenth century, remedied only in part by the attempts of the Privy Chancery and the Senate to maintain some control over agency accounts, and the closing of the College of Audit after fewer than 4 years in existence can only testify to the inability of the government and the "autocratic" ruler to obtain a final statement on the execution of a national budget, which continued to be no more than the aggregate of agency and territorial budgets.[43] The first Procurator General, Pavel Iaguzhinskii, admitted as much in 1726, when he wrote that agencies were not sending their accounts to the Senate "despite many reminders," and that no one had yet been appointed to take charge of the audit. When the College of Audit was restored and given an instruction in 1733, it was stated that the audit existed in Russia "in name only" and that, in fact, "there had never been a general statement [*schet*]" on the execution of past budgets.[44] It was only then that a concerted, if largely futile, effort began to audit civilian and military accounts.

It is necessary to bear in mind what an audit sought to achieve and how it was carried out. It sought above all, and in the eighteenth century almost exclusively, to control "regularity," that is, the conformity of all accounts with existing laws, regulations, and procedures. This left a broad gray area where the definition of what was irregular was by no means obvious, short of outright fraud. Its main purpose was thus to maintain fiscal discipline and to enforce it with the threat of sanctions. It did not yet concern itself with the merits of administrative policy or administrative efficiency and assumed, for example, that prices paid for the purchase and delivery of goods were acceptable if supported by documentary evidence, even if they were unfair and obsolete. Such an audit was thus a formal operation, satisfied with matching decisions against legal provisions and authorizations, without passing judgment on the merits of the case. It was similar to appellate review, and indeed the word *reviziia* was common to both.[45] An audit was internal—conducted in agencies—or general, when carried out in a separate agency of government, independent of the collecting and spending agencies. The Instruction of 1733 required the Senate and all colleges to conduct their internal audits by checking all their sources of revenue and items of expenditures against laws (*ukazy*) and payment orders (*assignatsii*), and to draw up a statement (*schet*), guaranteed accurate by the signature of all members of the agency. These provisions applied to the governor's and voevoda's chanceries as well. The most complex statement was that of the College of War, based on the accounts of each regiment of infantry and cavalry for salary, equipment, and provisions. Statements had to be sent to the College of Audit within from 3 to 10 months from the end of the year under review, and sanctions ranging from fines to hard labor were imposed on delinquent agencies. The College was responsible for conducting the general audit. This was to be done on receipt of a statement by checking whether each expenditure had been vouched for by the table of organization or by separate orders. To make this possible, the Treasury was required to submit each January 1 a copy of the general table of organization for the previous year and the College of Revenue a copy of its *okladnaia kniga*. Statements were checked against these two fundamental documents, and no resort to the original agency books was required unless a dispute arose between the college and an agency. If the college discovered "unvouched-for" (*pristrastnye, neporiadochnye*) expenditures, it required an explanation, which could lead to an investigation and a demand for repayment. Proved embezzlement was punished by death—surely the most unrealistic provision of the Instruction. Governors and voevodas who showed a permissive attitude (*slabost', upushchenie*) toward the collection of arrears were fined 10 percent of the arrears until they were fully paid. After the College completed the auditing of all agency statements, it was expected to draw up a general statement on the executions of the budget, showing all revenue collected, all expenditures, balances, and arrears, and submit it to the Senate.[46]

These general provisions remained in effect for more than a century, with occasional amendments concerning deadlines for submitting statements, the size of fines, and the nature of the documents used for internal auditing. They were not necessarily effective, however. The completeness of the audit depended on both the reliability of the accounts and the collaboration of the agencies, since each was unwilling to recognize another college as a superior agency with a right to control its most sensitive transactions. In the absence of a general table of organization and of a national table of revenues, a general audit remained impossible, and no general statement ever saw the light of day, since the "autocrat" still did not know in the early 1760s how much money was collected and spent in her realm. The reforms of the 1780s therefore represented a watershed in the history of Russian auditing, as in so much else. The concentration of national accounts for revenues, expenditure, and arrears, and of auditing in four subdivisions of the Expedition of State Revenues under the Procurator General made possible the preparation of a general statement. The reason may have been that the reform in a paradoxical way eliminated the general audit and transformed the auditing of Russian budgets into an internal audit of Prince Viazemskii's empire[47]—a development that alarmed other members of the empress's entourage.

The Finance Ministry succeeded in absorbing the Treasury in 1821 but failed to complete the reconcentration of all stages of budget making in a single agency. Speranskii felt that no responsible budget procedure could do without an independent audit, and his views prevailed when the Main Administration was set up in 1811. Its status was not that of a full ministry, however, even though the State Comptroller sat on the Committee of Ministers. It incurred the enmity of Gur'ev, the Finance Minister, who could not accept outside control and did all he could to defeat proposals to tighten the rules governing accounting. Seven years earlier, in 1804, the Committee of Ministers had ruled that general statements on all revenues and expenditures be considered secret and not be submitted to the Senate. They were most likely not submitted to the State Council either.[48] By preventing discussion of the statement by an outside body, another form of general audit, the core of the ruling elite protected the vested interests of its members and made the ruler the unwitting accomplice of their ambitions.

A survey of the finances of a command society brings out some outstanding features. Fiscal agencies were the most numerous and the most important agencies of the imperial government, and their concentration, after the reforms of the 1770s, in an "expedition," later a Ministry of Finance, gave them an even greater weight in the councils of government. They gained an operational autonomy that only the military could match. But it is just as obvious that fiscal administration more than any other required the participation of a large number of individuals from the dependent population to sell vodka and salt, to keep the accounts, and to contribute their labor where money was scarce and services had to be rendered in kind, even if compulsion was involved. In the Finance Ministry itself, the need for expertise was bringing about a dialogue between the upper management level of the ruling class and the top stratum of the merchantry; in provincial towns, the ministry's personnel was entirely of civilian, and overwhelmingly non-noble, origin, in sharp contrast to the administration of police and justice.

Fiscal administration reveals at the same time the deep chasm between the ruling class and the dependent population. The hereditary nobility was exempt from direct taxes, but it is true that the privilege was extended to the personal nobility and merchants of the first two guilds, both unstable social groups, forming together with the clergy the reservoir from which the ruling class kept rejuvenating itself and reaffirming its legitimacy. Beneath this intermediate stratum the capitation was the great social leveler and most likely contributed to restricting the economic opportunities of the most enterprising peasants. Moreover, those members of the ruling class with land and peasants benefited in their private capacity from two legal subsidies of their privileged status: the quitrent and the proceeds from the sale of vodka to their brethren in the apparatus. Both cemented the alliance between apparatus and infrastructure.

Finally, fiscal administration sheds light on "the inherent tension between law and autocracy."[49] We know that law in Russia was a flexible instrument of rule not grounded in the consensus of a community striving after a common good but a principle of order to contain rivalries within the management of the ruling class—the only political community in the Russian political order—in order to facilitate the execution of its mission. By 1825, however, it appears that fiscal legislation, in both its normative and procedural aspects, was emerging as a rigid body of rules increasingly assuming the nature of abstract norms binding upon both ruling elite and ruler alike. The bureaucratization of the apparatus began in fiscal administration,[50] and fiscal jurisprudence was the first successful development in modern Russian history capable of containing the arbitrary exercise of power, everywhere else the hallmark of ruling class politics.

16

Conclusion

On the eve of Peter's assumption of the full powers of his office in 1696, Russia was governed by a Romanov house a mere three generations old and by a constellation of families revolving around it. The leading families were the Dolgorukovs, the Saltykovs, and the Golitsyns on the one hand; the Streshnevs, Naryshkins, Lopukhins, and Kurakins on the other. These families, supported by relatives and clients, made up the core of the Russian ruling elite, filled the ranks of the Duma, and staffed the executive agencies of a government still indistinguishable from the extensive household of the ruling family. The remainder of the ruling elite consisted of the Moscow nobles, notably the *stolniki*, who formed a pool from which candidates were chosen for the most diverse positions in the machinery of government.

This ruling elite governed with the help of a still-loose political infrastructure of nobles in towns scattered across the sparsely populated countryside, whose place in a single ruling class was sealed by a common interest and mutual dependence: the extraction of resources from a population living in an economy of scarcity and reliance on provincial nobles to police the countryside on the one hand; dependence on the ruling elite for a share of the booty of war and the spoils of peacetime government, as well as to uphold the nobles' exclusive ownership of other human beings on the other. This emerging ruling class represented a conglomerate of patronage networks, the logical extension in time and space of the medieval *druzhina*, for which the undisguised purpose of ruling had always been to live off the population without a concept of duty toward a general good and the recognition of a higher allegiance to which all must subscribe. The conglomerate's administrative backbone was the network of *prikazy*, which meted out justice, collected revenues, and distributed spoils in the form of lucrative appointments to the post of voevoda and recommendations for grants of land and peasants.

The ruling class clung obsessively to the assumption that power could not be shared, and that political society had no room for outsiders unless they were already admitted into the ruling class and subjected to its internal discipline, or unless the terms of their association had been set by the ruling elite and were enforced by the rank and file. Such an association was a form of probation before admission into the ruling class. Moreover, the ruling class needed a large clerical staff to govern, and freely co-opted secretaries of non-noble background on a nearly equal footing with its other members. This monopoly over political power, together with an openness toward outsiders when they were needed to replenish its ranks and accepted its terms, was the source of the Russian nobility's strength, legitimacy, and ability to meet challenges from within and without. Clerks, children of townsmen, priests, and peasants collectively represented the domestic staff of the ruling class. They were scorned yet indispensable and possessive, and used the authority and privileges of their masters to serve their own interests.

The end of the seventeenth century marked the culmination of a process of ruling class formation. There had been tension between the Moscow-based ruling elite and the provincial middle service class, between this service class and other groups required to provide military support, and between foreigners imported to create a modern army and Russian nobles whose once-efficient cavalry was becoming obsolete. These strains resulted from the fusion of socially disparate elements into a ruling class conscious of its leadership role and bound to the ruling house by a compact of domination for the extraction and distribution of resources from the dependent population and for the maximization of military power. It was precisely this feeling of completion and awareness of broader horizons and more challenging possibilities that created a sense of "crisis," of the inadequacy of the lopsided and poorly integrated political and social order of the seventeenth century. Without that self-confidence and without a consensus on the foundation and purpose of the new order, Peter's plans would have fallen on barren ground and his reforms would have been inconceivable.

Despite the looseness of its social constitution and the tangle of its administrative machinery, both products of its haphazard growth after the establishment of the Romanov dynasty, the Russian political order was disciplined, unified, and intolerant. The transformation of the church into the ideological apparatus of the ruling class, long in the making and completed with the degradation of Nikon in 1666, left the tsar the sole vicar of Christ in his realm, against whom disobedience, let alone rebellion, could hope for neither organizational support nor ideological justification. Dissidents were doomed to a marginal existence. Identification with Orthodoxy made the Russian melting pot a community of believers, in which any individual act could be charged with ramifications in the spiritual, moral, political, and social environment, spreading the poison of suspicion and informing. The resulting conservatism, bordering on obscurantism at a time when superstition so often guided human behavior, sanctified a social order based on serfdom.

This political order, which already may have begun to show disquieting evidence of caste-forming tendencies, found a field of action in the challenge created by the propinquity of three large territorial formations, then at the height of their expansion: the Swedish, Polish, and Ottoman empires. The Poles had occupied Moscow and the Swedes Novgorod during the Time of Troubles, and the honor of the ruling elite gathered around a new dynasty demanded that they be rolled back, in a process similar to the eastward *reconquista* that had brought the khanates of Kazan, Siberia, and Astrakhan into the fold a century earlier. The Swedes were confined to their Baltic provinces in 1617, Smolensk was captured from the Poles in 1654, Kiev was annexed in 1686, and the first campaign against the Turks was launched in 1687, "when Russia crossed over permanently into the orbit of European power politics."[1] As the rollback gathered momentum, Western ideas, filtered through Poland, penetrated Russia, and Vasilii Golitsyn, who prodded the Ottoman dragon in 1687,[2] was the most distinguished representative of a ruling elite slowly and with many reservations treading the fateful path on which the enemies of yesterday were becoming the teachers of tomorrow.

It took two decades of war and diplomacy to shake the Swedish empire to its foundations and devastate Poland, disasters from which neither ever recovered; after 1725 their fate came increasingly to depend on Russian self-restraint or on the ability of other European powers to counter Russian ambitions. These victories were not achieved, however, without a thorough systematization of the Muscovite political, social, institutional, and fiscal order, the first round of reforms designed to bring Russia into the modern age.

A long war and an ambitious program of reforms could not have been carried to a successful conclusion without a stable political leadership. The men who governed Russia in the 1690s remained at the helm until their deaths in the 1710s, and their colleagues and successors were their relatives or clients. However confused the search for solutions to unprecedented problems, the great tsar could always rely on a tribe of relatives with its own patronage networks in the ruling elite, willing and able to sustain his vision and counter hostile forces. His assumption of power represented a coup d'état against the traditional Kremlin-bound Muscovite government of tsar and Duma and a challenge to the more conservative factions within the ruling elite who were rallied around the relatives of his first wife and her son to save them from the Antichrist and Russia from damnation. The coup was realized in the move to Preobrazhenskoe and the creation of Guard regiments with administrative headquarters that functioned at the same time as an agency of political police. Guardsmen, drawn from various patronage networks, became political inquisitors investigating threats of subversion, trusted and ruthless agents to break bottlenecks in the administrative machinery. This emergence of the tsar, both a personal phenomenon and an institutional development, was facilitated by his assumption of supreme command in the field at a time when the army was about to face the invincible Swedish king. The new leadership was not only drawn from the inner sanctum of power, it also looked benevolently upon the rise of outsiders—plebeians and converted foreigners—into the ruling elite in the continuous process of rejuvenation that was one of the most remarkable characteristics of the Russian ruling class in the eighteenth century.

The nobility, still without a generic name at the end of the seventeenth century, had always been an incipient ruling class, since its raison d'être was to serve, and to serve is not only to obey but also to command. Its territorial organization, set up around nodal points that projected power over a large and sparsely populated territory, was replaced by a regimental one, combined and stratified into formations of various strengths to fight the external enemy. The general mobilization of the ruling class after the first battle of Narva, which demonstrated the upreparedness of the army and the obsolescence of the administrative machinery, was followed, later in the reign, by a similar gathering of the merchantry. Finally, the peasant world, diverse thanks to regional differences and historical transformations, was forced into a single integrated administrative and fiscal framework, which assigned peasants as so much booty to the ruling house, the ruling class, its ideological apparatus, and their common treasury.

Disagreements over methods to carry out a program, battles over turf among powerful members of the ruling elite engaged in often ephemeral empire building, resistance and inertia among the lower ranks annoyed by the demands of conscription and war must not be construed as lack of unity among the ruling class vis-à-vis the dependent population. This is a fundamental point. The unprecedented struggle to bring Russia into the concert of European states and rationalize its administrative system in order to improve efficiency strengthened that unity. Militarization gave the ruling class a formal rigid hierarchy; uniforms and Germanic terminology enhanced its separateness from the dependent population; promotions on merit strengthened its legitimacy; and the systematic forcing of various dependent groups into a simplified and legally more uniform dependent population facilitated the extension of a command structure governed by martial law. Newcomers brought no challenges to the legitimacy of the compact of domination but only hoped to benefit from it, and merchants who sought admittance but were not chosen had no alternative to offer. That Peter's program of westernization was a key political choice arousing passionate opposition there is no doubt. That its opponents within the ruling class, who only wanted to return to an ancien régime whose crisis had generated that very program, were brutally disposed of testifies to the existence of a strong consensus on the validity of Peter's course among the ruling elite and the elite's ability to impose it on the rank and file of the ruling class. It was then that the ruling class was even given a collective name (*shliakhetstvo*).

The result of these social reforms was to transform a society of rough contours and disjointed elements into a command structure of well-defined parts, equipped with procedures and penalties to compel obedience. Although a desire appeared from time to time to give the merchants and other townsmen their separate hierarchical channels, the urban world was made, in fact, more subject to discipline and more subservient to the fiscal interests and political directives issuing from the ruling elite. This reshuffling of the constituent elements of Russian society in the midst of a long and bloody war released the energies of those seeking new goals for their ambitions[3] and restored a social mobility threatened by the consolidation of that society three generations after the ordeal of the Time of Troubles.

The same urge to streamline and systematize was evident in the reform of institutions. The *prikaz* system, which had grown haphazardly during the preceding century, had become the victim of overlapping jurisdictions and excessive centralization. It paralyzed whatever inclination voevodas might have to go beyond the pursuit of their private interests, and the growth of the clerical staff, favored by budgetary autonomy, created a bloated army of servants over whom the ruling elite was in danger of losing control. The dismemberment of the *prikazy* was thus motivated by a dual purpose. The inevitability of a showdown with Charles XII and the concentration of the Russian government in Peter's field headquarters required bypassing Moscow and establishing direct lines of command with territorial commanders who governed the country as if it were under martial law. This, in turn, required scattering the clerks among the territorial commands, weakening their esprit de corps, and making them more responsive to directives from the ruling elite and its agents in the field. The closing of the *prikazy*, together with the abandonment of the Kremlin and the building of a "paradise" on the banks of the Neva,[4] was part of the rejection of Muscovy and of a policy designed to break up the old order before building on new foundations.

Such a radical reform was bound to be temporary—born in exceptional circumstances and motivated by a desire to cut through red tape by giving selected members of the ruling elite extraordinary powers. In a political order lacking the acceptance of a concept of state against which actions are measured and ambitions restrained, governing with a *druzhina* posted at strategic points in such a large territory was a prescription for disaster. Reducing the governors' powers, on the other hand, meant restoring central agencies. The Swedes, whose generals the tsar toasted as his teachers after the battle of Poltava, produced a model, and a compromise did the rest.

The reforms of 1718–1719 embodied a comprehensive but unrealistic vision. Whether the colleges ever operated in true collegial fashion must remain moot. Their apparatus, larger than that of the *prikazy*, was at least a handy source of patronage for members of the ruling elite, now without an active command. The apparatus, however could not come to dinner—to paraphrase Nikita Panin—if the cooks had been dismissed.[5] A clerical staff was reconstituted under the leadership of the presidents of colleges, who had ample opportunity to practice patronage. A more-than-partial return to the old order was evident. The question of how best to organize Russia's internal space also became the object of a compromise between Muscovite practices and the reforms of 1708. The innovation that gave the vision its focus and power was the treasury reform of 1719, a total break with Muscovite procedures and a giant step toward the modernization of the Russian government. Indeed, the concentration of resources in a single treasury and the assumption of supreme command in the field were the fundamental prerequisites to the exercise of full autocratic power. These reforms, however, failed to anticipate the strength of the reaction against Peter's innovations and the nostalgia for the Muscovite order felt by a ruling class exhausted by war and domestic tensions. Moreover, they were based on an unstated premise: that their success depended on the development of an educated political infrastructure in town and countryside to raise the quality of government outside the capitals. The return of peace

accompanied by extended leaves and the refusal of nobles to present themselves for inspection after the peace of Nystad seemed to promise such a
development, but it matured much too late for Peter's reforms to succeed.

To crown Peter's reforms, a codification of the new legislation would have
been in order. The completion of another *ulozhenie*, however, remained elusive
for one more century, and for good reason. A considerable amount of partial
codification took place—witness the various *ustavy, reglamenty, nakazy*, and
instruktsii prescribing procedures, outlining jurisdictions, specifying powers,
and creating substantive law. Some of these were based on foreign models but
took Russian practices into account as well. They codified a large number of
managerial activities, but a complete codification remained beyond reach
because the system created by Peter remained highly unstable. If we cling to the
view of the Russian political order as one ruled by a tsar and governed by a
bureaucracy, nothing should have been simpler than to codify its organization,
procedures, and substantive norms. But it was a highly politicized system in
which laws drafted by some elements of the ruling elite and promulgated by the
tsar were ignored by other elements, with the ruler perennially unable to
compel obedience. Codification became possible and was indeed carried out
during the stable reign of Nicholas I, after the reforms of Catherine II and
Alexander I transformed Peter's vision into reality.

The two generations that followed Peter's death were a period of hesitation
and transition, marked by an increasingly repressive social order, the virtual
enslavement of more than half of the peasantry, and the regression of urban
development. At the same time, war and negotiations with the Swedes, the
Poles, and the Ottomans, together with an increasingly complex network of
diplomatic alliances, were bringing foreign influences to bear on the formation
of a national consciousness and national culture with which even those
members of the ruling elite—and they were many—who remained steeped in
Muscovite tradition had to come to terms. The occupation of Finland, even if
temporary, the gradual transformation of Poland into a Russian protectorate
and its first partition, as well as the first victorious war against the Ottomans
nearly completed the reconquest begun in 1617. But ambition fed on success,
and plans were already being discussed at the highest levels to annex the whole
of Prussia, so that the occupation of its Rhineland enclaves would give Russia
veto power over any change in the European balance of power, and to
strengthen the role of Orenburg as a staging area for commercial expansion
toward Afghanistan and India.[6]

Peter's death brought rivalries among patronage groups to a dangerous
level, as the uncertain succession maintained an atmosphere of crisis for more
than 5 years. It has been very tempting to see the events of 1730 as an attempt
to engage in a constitutional experiment. Such an experiment would have
revealed a split among the ruling elite on the issue of power sharing. That was
not the case. Proposals to institutionalize participation in the decision-making
process were part of a yearning for the days of the Duma, but the Duma had
already lost its authority and power by the time Peter took over the reins of
government. They were symptoms of that same nostalgia for a simpler world

that fiscal stringency now seemed to justify. On the other hand, the leading proponents of the reform were so obviously seeking to undermine the authority of the Romanov house and raise their own that their ambition discredited the attempt. An experiment brought to an end when the ruler publicly tears up a sheet of paper, without any opposition being registered and without the attempt ever being tried again, would belong to the realm of political farce had the stakes not been so high.[7] The accession in 1730 of the Empress Anna, the daughter of a Saltykova, gave that family, slighted during the latter part of Peter's reign, the dominant influence over the dispensation of patronage and precipitated a showdown with the Dolgorukovs, guilty of the most arrogant violations of the elite's political creed. They suffered the fate that, a decade earlier, had befallen the Lopukhins, who embodied the resistance of certain elements to Peter's reforms. A school of nationalist historians has painted the role of the "Germans" in dark colors, apparently unaware that the chief of Anna's household and Governor-General of Moscow was a Saltykov, the Policemaster General another, and that the chief of the political police and the President of the College of War—a German to be sure— were their relatives.[8] The accession in 1741 of the Empress Elizabeth, granddaughter of a Naryshkina and cousin of Nikita Trubetskoi, turned the tables on the Saltykovs and brought the Trubetskois to the center of influence and power, until the coup of 1760 displaced them in favor of the Vorontsovs, Elizabeth's others cousins. Behind this jockeying for the dominant influence under the ruler, who alone bestowed legitimacy and held in abeyance the anarchy latent among the ruling elite, an alliance was forming between the rival Saltykovs and Trubetskois that gave the government a stability it could not otherwise have had. The days of uncompromising hatred between the Miloslavskiis and Naryshkins that had so marked the young Peter were giving way among their grandchildren to a political alliance aimed at governing Russia under two weak empresses. This alone explains the emergence of Russian "prime ministers," Osterman, Trubetskoi, and Viazemskii—the latter under a strong but German empress—all three related to the Saltykovs and Trubetskois.

Despite this compromise to stave off a destructive struggle, the 1730s and 1740s continued to be marked by rivalries between powerful personages. Münnich's ambition to build a military establishment with its own supply agencies and budget office, the consistency with which Nikita Trubetskoi dismantled that structure and reduced the College of War to a personnel agency, the battle for the unification of revenue collection lost in the 1730s soon after it seemed to have been won, the unwillingness to draw up a general table of organization that would limit the size of the clerical staff—all these are landmarks in the incessant struggle over the allocation of patronage, of which the purge of August 1760 was the high point. It is therefore not surprising that the political police were so active during that period, flourishing on a sea of denunciations made for the most sordid motives, and adding to the insecurity of the political world, which the future Catherine II learned to dread, despite her closeness to both the Saltykovs and the Trubetskois.

The decision was made in 1727 to scrap some essential elements of the 1718–1719 reforms. The local agencies of colleges were closed, voevodas were restored in small towns and given a new instruction emphasizing their universal jurisdiction, the separation of justice and finance from general administration was abandoned at the local level, and colleges subordinated to the Senate came increasingly to resemble the *prikazy* subordinated to the Duma. A political infrastructure of landowners began to take shape in the late 1730s, after service was limited to 25 years. This partial demobilization of the officer corps, into which so many of the ruling class had been pressed in the 1700s that the civilian apparatus was largely staffed with veterans retired for reasons of health, was announced at a time when extended leaves and the refusal of nobles to serve, coupled with a conviction that the existing pool of officers was adequate to cope with ordinary needs, made it possible to look favorably on the reconstitution of a provincial nobility as an extension of the civilian apparatus.

This development has not been studied, but it deserves to be, and without the assumption that there were no nobles outside the two capitals and their provinces. Since the nobility never constituted more than half of 1 percent of the population, its visibility outside the capitals must have remained very low. Yet these nobles, members of patronage networks and related by common memories of regimental life, began to raise issues connected with the maintenance of order, the settlement of disputes, and their own status vis-à-vis local merchants, which they or their children would formalize in the *nakazy* to the Legislative Commission of 1767. The final demobilization of the officer corps and of the ruling class in February 1762 only marked the completion of the trend toward the recreation of a political infrastructure and the tripartite division of the ruling class into an officer corps, a civilian apparatus, and landowners on their estates, a division, of course, with overlapping elements.

That is why it cannot yet be said that the ruling class was losing its unity. The captains, majors, and lieutenants who signed the *nakazy* had only recently been the backbone of a successful army. For those who did not become voevodas or enter some central government agency, a new field of action was opening up in the provinces and districts: the close management of the peasantry and the constitution of a civil society within the ruling class. This explains why the *nakazy* expressed so much concern about the need to create a local administrative infrastructure more responsive to the interests of landowners and to modernize legislation on property and inheritance. They did not call for a change in the constitution of the ruling class—opposition to the arbitrary power and bribe taking of the voevoda was balanced by a conscious desire to absorb the public function and thus spread those same abuses more evenly among the elected delegates of the landowning nobility. If anything, the *nakazy* were a call to strengthen the command structure of Russian society—witness the demands for draconian punishment of vagrancy and "disorder" in general. The ruling class of the 1760s remained a unified ruling class but one engaged in a process of transformation from an officer corps into a civil society, entering an accelerated stage of "westernization" in dress, speech, and education, and more than ever conscious of its compact of domination over the peasantry, whether privately held serfs or those owned by the Treasury.

This transformation, however, raised important problems for the ruling elite. Was Russia's status as one of the great powers, no longer contested by anyone after the Seven Years' War and the first Turkish war but threatened by fiscal stringency, consistent with ignorance of the actual revenue the government was entitled to collect and was willing to spend? Was the existence of an army of clerks in Moscow and Petersburg favorable to the stabilization of an infrastructure requiring the decentralization of managerial and judicial functions to save nobles and others endless trips to Moscow to settle their disputes, especially those involving transfers of property? If the Russian government needed to overhaul its managerial practices, should it remain centralized in Petersburg and Moscow or decentralize its operations, helping the political infrastructure to consolidate its power? The very fact that the interests of administrative efficiency and those of the political infrastructure coincided helps explain the success of Catherine's reforms and reflects the continuing unity of ruling elite and the rest of the ruling class.

The next two generations—from the celebration of the peace of Kuchuk Kainardji in 1775 to the end of Alexander's reign in 1826—may be viewed as a separate and self-contained epoch, during which a second round of reform, strikingly similar to that projected by Peter I, was launched and carried to completion. Like Peter's time, it was a period of nearly constant war, including a campaign for political survival, and one of territorial expansion in which Russia took final revenge on the Swedes, the Poles, and the Ottomans, and became the neighbor of Prussia and Austria, whose cooperation and rivalry were destined to dominate the history of Europe to the banks of the Rhine until the end of the Romanov dynasty.

Unless we look at successful reforms as the brainchild of a ruler who gathered a few advisers, including the inevitable contingent from the Baltic provinces, wrote an elaborate statute in longhand, and simply ordered its execution—this, presumably, is for some *wie die Geschichte eigentlich gewesen war*—they must be assumed to be the product of long-held grievances and coalescent ambitions, and to aim at satisfying them. If that were not the case, they would have remained paper reforms, without substance and without support among those who had to carry them out and live with them. The reforms of Catherine II and Alexander I were successful because they provided a satisfactory solution to a controversy that had not ceased to agitate the ruling class since the beginning of the eighteenth century over the organization of internal space, the relationship between capital and province, and the concentration of power.

It would take a revolution in France to carry out a territorial division as systematic and durable as that which took place in Russia in the late 1770s, well grounded, despite its uniformity, on physical geography, economic considerations, and historical evolution. It brought to an end, finally, the Muscovite patchwork, which the reform of 1719 had only partially improved. This territorial division, and the table of organization based on it, were the prerequisite to Catherine's other reforms. The creation of uniform gubernias and uezds established a territorial framework upon which to build the administrative structure that dislodged the top-heavy colleges in Moscow and Petersburg and distributed administrative functions among twenty-six gubernia capitals so that the managerial reponsibilities of the colleges were decentralized and simplified.

The reform, it is obvious, whatever the contribution of the Baltic Germans may have been, so much resembled the reform of 1708 with some elements of that of 1718–1719 that it could only have been inspired by them, above all in the mind of an empress who saw herself as the worthy successor to the great tsar, as she stated unambiguously on the granite pedestal of Peter's equestrian statue.[9] The closing of the colleges, reminiscent of the dismantling of the *prikazy* 70 years earlier, followed. Both reforms represented a reaction by the ruling class against the suffocating hold of the clerks on the process of government, an "antibureaucratic" reform designed to give a freer hand to the more dynamic elements of the ruling elite, to scatter the clerks once again among provincial capitals, and to place them under closer surveillance by apparatus and political infrastructure. Like Peter's early reforms, they accentuated the politicization of government and brought out the leadership roles of the procurator general, the president of the College of War and—in Russia alone— some fifteen governors-general, the successors of Peter's governors, all members of the inner circle of the ruling elite. In both cases the reforms of 1708 and 1775 replaced a cumbersome and impersonal machinery of government with a strikingly simple and highly political regional organization

Both reforms, however, suffered from the same flaw. By emphasizing the personal element on a territorial foundation, they released on the realm a *druzhina* whose ambitions, arrogance, and anarchistic tendencies could be held in check only when its members remained gathered around the ruler. This lack of restraint has been the bane of Russian government from the eighteenth century to our own day and the cause most certain to derail any long-term decentralization. The regionalization of government had particularly scandalous consequences in the army, where regional commanders promoted as they pleased and even openly disregarded instruction from the College of War. The reaction that began under Paul was therefore motivated by considerations similar to those that inspired the reforms of 1718–1719—a rejection of the experiment with regionalism, a removal of administration from the province to the center, and the dispensation of patronage on a large scale. Indeed, it may not be wide of the mark to see most Russian reforms as the victory of one patronage network over the others, confirming the well-established fact that the Russian government was one of men and not of laws.

The reign of Paul certainly witnessed one of the most thorough purges of the political apparatus in Russian history. Its purpose was to create what might be called the tsar's personal patronage network, in order to support what was essentially a coup d'état against the political establishment of his day. Both Peter's reign and those of Paul and Alexander were marked by the prominent role of the Guard—its size, fairly constant throughout the eighteenth century, began to grow by leaps and bounds after 1796. The emphasis was placed once again on the creation of functional, not territorial, commands held by ministers directly subordinated to the ruler and beyond senatorial control, who then proceeded to build their respective patronage networks in their ministries and local agencies in the provincial capitals. The role of the household staff in lobbying for the restoration of central executive agencies and building support for the autocratic tsar, an important factor in the politics of the ruling class, remains to be studied. The ministerial reform of the 1800s succeeded because it was built on foundations established by the local government reforms of the 1770s; the partial failure of Peter's reforms of 1718 may be traced to the absence of such foundation.

The political infrastructure, which began to express grievances in the 1760s and was given a charter in 1785, gained the most from the reforms. To claim that the nobility did not win "power," did not gain autonomy from governor and later minister, took little initiative in local government, is to miss the point. The charter gave the nobility—or formalized what had already been granted—formal access to the resources needed to sustain its education in foreign ways. It established a mechanism by which its control over the peasantry and the townsmen could be systematized and created procedures to fill the posts that made this mechanism effective. It mattered little whether elections were well attended or not—their results were often predetermined by the will of the more influential landowners or the prejudices of the governor, all members of the ruling elite. The command structure of the ruling class cut across institutional and sociopolitical formations to assert the principle of authority and the virtue of obedience, in return for giving the infrastructure a free hand in exploiting the peasantry.

The creation of the ministries did not affect this political compromise, but it reflected concern among the ruling elite over leaving the management of finance, industry, and even education in the hands of an apparatus notoriously unable to distinguish between private interest and public responsibility—a distinction difficult to make in any ruling class with a monopoly of power. By 1802—a considerably simplified central government had learned to work for an entire generation with a provincial apparatus considerably more complicated than the governor's or voevoda's chanceries. The ministries were grafted onto an already tested provincial administration, supported by a well-organized political infrastructure. In 1718 the colleges had been built on sand.

These extensive reforms, consistent and complementary, which elsewhere would have followed a political upheaval or might have caused one, were drafted and carried out with what must have been considerable support among the apparatus and the political infrastructure. The downgrading of the importance of the police must be seen as evidence of a consensus. Even though an agency of political police never ceased to exist in Russia, it was integrated into the machinery of government after 1763 and ceased to be the supragovernmental agency it had been since 1696. The scope of police repression, among the ruling class at least, was sharply reduced until near the end of Alexander's reign, when the spread of education and direct exposure to foreign influence began to sow poisonous seeds in a self-contained and self-righteous political environment and to expose dangerous delusions among officers who joined secret societies.

Whatever the importance of the police in different reigns, the Russian political order remained well into the 1810s the playground of families and their patronage networks. The rulers, who were the major players in the game, always required the support of at least one of the three constituent elements of that order: the army, the civilian apparatus, and the political infrastructure. Peter threw in his lot with the army, into which he mobilized the landowners. His successors and their "prime ministers" built up a civilian apparatus served by an extensive clerical staff and took the first steps toward recreating a political infrastructure. Catherine's antibureaucratic reforms favored the landowners and the army. Paul antagonized all three and lost his life as a result. Finally, Alexander sought to bolster his legitimacy in the army and the civilian apparatus while distancing himself from the political infrastructure.

These shifts in the internal balance of the ruling elite and the ruling class, especially strong between the 1770s and 1820s, at the very time the political apparatus was undergoing uncontrolled growth, especially after 1796, raised essential questions about the future of the ruling class. The reign of Paul saw the reappearance of an imperial family with an interest of its own stimulated by a close association with Germanic courts and no longer identical with or even dependent on those of the ruling elite. The triumph of Petersburg as the only capital of the empire after the 1780s likewise created a perception of a state interest superior to that of the ruling class. The reforms of Prince Viazemskii laid the groundwork for the emergence of a concentrated and powerful fiscal establishment embodied 20 years later in a quasi-autonomous and professionally separate Finance Ministry. Paul's insistence on the separation of the military from the civilian establishment, with which it had been so closely associated since Peter's days in a unified political apparatus, initiated a trend leading during much of Alexander's reign to a new emphasis on professionalism. In the civilian establishment, the growth of the ministries depended on bringing more civilians into the apparatus, and their efficiency on raising the educational level. The army and the ministries were command hierarchies within a command structure, and the development of ministerial empires integrated the local managers of the ruling class into a vertical structure destructive of their association with the political infrastructure that had been one of the major features of Catherine's reforms. Professionalism narrowed vision, created new interests, and nurtured new loyalties. Can we then say that the ruling class was losing its characteristic features and becoming an aggregate of elites?

It took much more than a generation for the ruling class to disintegrate. One reason for ending this narrative with Alexander's death is that these new trends were only beginning. The ruling class that crystallized after the *Ulozhenie* of 1649 was still the ruling class in 1825. It was still the only civil society in Russia, distinguished from the dependent population by its privileges, including a monopoly over the ownership of human beings—which is not to say that all its members were necessarily serf owners—and over management positions. But it had lost, in the wake of fiscal necessities, its quasi-monopoly over the ownership of unsettled land. It continued to depend on social mobility, limited but real, to replenish its ranks, and continued to draw from the same three major sources—the noncommissioned officers, the secretarial staff, and the upper ranks of the merchantry. The merchants began to be associated with political managers in the courts and the Finance Ministry to discuss and settle common problems. But no challenge was in sight to its monopoly over the exercise of power, and too much freethinking, as in the universities, was still put down without regard for the consequences. Serfdom remained in Russia proper the foundation of the social order, and the ruling class's fitness to rule had received its triumphant confirmation in 1815 with the victory over Napoleon.

The year 1825, however, marked the beginning of a fateful change. The reign of Nicholas I, as Paul Dukes rightly points out, "far from marking the apogee of autocracy, constituted a descent from a high point that had been reached during the reign of Catherine."[10] The Decembrist uprising revealed much discontent, but it was without a social foundation. Nevertheless, it placed the new tsar on the defensive because its members came from families in the ruling elite. He anchored the legitimacy of his rule in the army, which he politicized in order to stem the trend toward professionalization and autonomy begun during the reign of his brother and predecessor, and in the civilian apparatus run by ministers as so many "chiefs of staff." The bureaucratization of the apparatus, begun under Paul, was now in full swing, as automatic promotions on grounds of seniority swamped all levels with newcomers and further weakened traditional patronage networks, already crippled by the extinction of old ruling families or the withdrawal of their members from active politics. The incipient rift between apparatus and political infrastructure began to widen, leaving the ruler increasingly at the mercy of a bureaucratized apparatus, estranged socially from the provincial nobles and isolated in distant Petersburg. The abolition of serfdom, even if it guarded the interests of the landowners, would challenge for the first time the legitimacy of the entire political order created by the *Ulozhenie* during the recovery from the Time of Troubles. After 1861 the ruler, traditionally the first landowner in his realm, would continue to govern with an officer corps and a civilian apparatus increasingly divorced from the political infrastructure, whose legitimacy as part of the ruling class had been shattered by the Emancipation[11] and further challenged by the emergence of other social groups that the ruling elite insisted on excluding from the exercise of power. Russia thus would enter the modern age at about the same time the legitimacy of its traditional order began to be questioned. Less than two generations later, the challenge had gone so far that a revolution would shake the foundations of the dynasty, and the First World War would then expose the ruling elite's unfitness to rule. It was no surprise that the dynasty collapsed in February 1917 without even a revolution[12]— without a political base, ruler and ruling elite had become superfluous, and its ruling class had disintegrated.

NOTES

Preface

1. Notably by Dukes, Lentin, and Pipes.

2. *Ruling Russia: Politics and Administration in the Age of Absolutism 1762–1796* (Princeton, 1984).

3. Mosca's *Ruling Class* and von Stein's *History* have been the dominant influences on my thinking. The essays are in Jaher: on Athenian society by R. Seager (7–26), on Roman society by R. Mitchell (27–63), on Victorian England by W. Arenstein (203–57). Paul Dukes (4) quotes Klyuchevskii's statement that 1613 marked the beginning of modern Russian history characterized by "a new dynasty, new enlarged territorial boundaries, a new class structure with a new ruling class at its head, and new economic developments." Miliukov understood that "the Charter of the nobility served to perpetuate the power of the ruling class until the liberation of the serfs in 1861": *Encyclopaedia Britannica*, 1965 edition, vol. 19:691–701, here 697. Dukes clearly identifies the nobility with the ruling class: see 20, 103, 144, 155–56, 165. It should be added for the benefit of the doubtful reader that neither von Stein nor Mosca was a Marxist. The theory of the ruling class is not part of Marxism, which is but a variation on the theme of the ruling class.

4. Keller, *Beyond the Ruling Class*, 57. For an illustration see LeDonne, "Ruling Families."

5. Hellie, *Enserfment*, 22.

6. Dahl, R., "A Critique of the Ruling Elite Model," *American Political Science Review* 52, no. 2 (1958): 463–69; Aron, "Social Structure," 9–10, 143. Although she criticizes Mosca, Suzanne Keller recognizes that "the absolute predominance of an elite is possible under fairly simple social conditions, when a core elite enjoys diffuse, overall superiority by virtue not of its specific functional contribution to society but of its general attributes and characteristics": *Beyond the Ruling Class*, 11–13, 124.

7. Cf. Field (19): "For a social stratum, as distinct from individual members, the principal goal of political action is control of men and goods." For him, "the Russian nobility was defined by serfdom" (11).

8. Bendix, R., "Bureaucracy," in *International Encyclopedia of Social Sciences*, vol. 2 (1968): 206–19, here 212.

9. Safonov, 114.

10. Weber, 3:956–60; Bendix, Ibid., 214, 217, and Bendix, *State and Society*, 308–20; Sjoberg, 237–44. For example, Isabel de Madariaga states that of the 209 "chinovniki" employed in local administration in 1738 only 26 were in receipt of salary (*Russia*, 54): how can we speak of a "bureaucracy" of "officials" without salaries and rules of promotion? On the other hand, I agree with Hans-Joachim Torke, who quotes A. Lotz (*Geschichte des deutschen Beamtentum* [Berlin, 1914], 7) as saying that "it is impossible to provide a theoretical definition of officialdom and to prove it scientifically once and for all": Torke, "Russische Beamtentum," 11.

11. See Part 1, Chapter 3. Madariaga has taken me to task for underestimating in *Ruling Russia* the growth of the number of "officials" during Catherine's reign. Unfor-

tunately, she is confused about terminology. No definition of "official" is given. Much of the growth was due to the introduction of elections to fill a number of new provincial posts. These elected people were not officials, as the procurator general himself recognized in 1784 or 1785 when he called for eliminating their salaries from the national budget: they worked only 2 or 3 months a year, lived at home, and continued to engage in their occupations. A salary was only a favor (*milost'*), not a compensation for service (*sluzhenie*): *SIRIO* 28 (1880): 262. Madariaga also accepts without discrimination in the midst of a discussion of "officials" and "officialdom" the total figure of 16,504 "civil employees." If she had looked at the source more closely (the table of organization of December 1763), she would have found that more than half consisted of retired and invalid soldiers used to carry messages and stand guard at government offices: such people cannot possibly be considered officials. They were not even "civil employees" since they were paid from the budget of the College of War: see "Readings of Reform," *Times Literary Supplement*, June 21, 1985, 700; and *Russia*, 56.

12. Mousnier, 157, 159.

13. Cf. Richard Pipes's discussion of what he calls the "partial dismantling of the patrimonial state": Pipes, 112ff.

14. Anderson, 333–37; Vernadsky, 2:405–8; Vernadsky, "Serfdom," 262–64; Pipes, 100–103.

15. This became quite obvious a century later: Troitskii, *Rossiia*, 195. For a somewhat different perspective on early Russian absolutism see Torke, *Staatsbedingte Gesellschaft*, 267–98.

16. Donnert, 79. Dukes emphasizes the unity of the period 1649–1861: *Making of Russian Absolutism*, 48.

17. See his article on the nobility in *Ocherki . . . XVII v.*, 139–59, esp. 142–43, 152–54, 156.

18. Hellie, *Enserfment*, 48.

19. Davies, 2:82.

20. Hellie, *Enserfment*, 181–201.

21. Raeff, "Seventeenth-Century Europe," 612–613; Raeff, *Comprendre*, 37; Cracraft, *Petrine Revolution*, 42, 56, 70.

22. Anderson, 18. Cf. Yaney: "The systematization of Russia was accompanied by the institutionalization of serfdom": 141. Dietrich Geyer comes close to a similar conclusion: 176, 180–81.

23. Beik, 31.

24. Anderson, 54. For a clear statement by the Russian historian Bochkarev of the contractual relationship between Catherine's autocracy and the nobility see Dukes, *The Making of Russian Absolutism* 158–59.

25. Semevskii, *Krest. vopros* 1:236–512.

26. This book focuses on Russia proper, defined as the twenty-six provinces of the heartland created by the reform of 1775. They are: Arkhangelsk, Iaroslavl, Kaluga, Kazan, Kostroma, Kursk, Moscow, Nizhni Novgorod, Novgorod, Olonets, Orel, Penza, Petersburg, Perm, Pskov, Riazan, Saratov, Simbirsk, Smolensk, Tambov, Tula, Tver, Viatka, Vladimir, Vologda, and Voronezh.

Chapter 1

1. Aristotle, 126, 135, 295–96.

2. Castoriadis, 38, calls Russia a "cynical society."

3. Some illustrations of the confusion are in Dobrynin, 219, 314–26, 655, and "Potemkin, G.," *RBS* 14 (1905): 649–70, here 667; see also Dubrovin, 1:507.

4. Solov'ev reached a similar conclusion and traced the emergence of this tripartite division to the 1730s: *Istoriia* 10:471. Hans-Joachim Torke writes that from the end of the seventeenth century "officials" (*Beamten*) ruled over the populace not only in their official capacity but at the same time as noble landowners, and that this situation led to the consolidation in the first half of the eighteenth century of the "true dominion of a class" (*wirksame Herrschaft einer Klasse*) over the remainder of the population: why not simply call this dominating class the ruling class? See "Russische Beamtentum," 24.

5. Shepukova, "Ob izmenenii," 390; Confino, 281–82.

6. According to Shepukova, "Ob izmenenii," 58,835 *pomeshchiki* owned between 1 and 100 serfs (41.1 percent of the total serf population) in the 1720s: ibid. Troitskii (*Russkii absoliutizm*, 170–75, 213–15, 298) gives the following figures on the relationship between rank- and landholding in the 1750s. I combine figures for the central and local apparatus:

Grade	100+ serfs	100–21	20–1	Total	None	No data	Total
1–5	61	14	6	81	14	15	110
6–8	198	144	80	422	58	17	497
9–14	76	212	303	591	430	20	1,041
Total	335	370	389	1,094	502	52	1,648

7. Pavlov-Sil'vanskii, 186, 225; Semevskii, I, 1–2, 4–5; Rubinshtein, 242–43; Trefolev, "Iaroslavl'," 281, 282; Rieber, 36.

8. Semevskii, *Krest'iane*, I, 2; *PSZ*, 1721, N. 3711; 1730, N. 5633; 1758, N. 10796; 1785, N. 16187, art. 26, 91, pt. 19; 1804, N. 21481; 1814, N. 25604; *SZ*, IX[1], 165.

9. Hellie, *Enserfment*, 27–28, 45, 115–16; Vladimirskii-Budanov, 565–73; Kahan, "Costs," and *Plow*, 65; Liashchenko, 267–69. See also Vodarskii, *Dvorianskoe*, 219–301.

10. *PSZ*, 1762, N. 11490; 1782, N. 15447, 15518.

11. *PSZ*, 1785, N. 16187, art. 28, 30, 33–34; Aksenov, 88–89.

12. *PSZ*, 1754, N. 10261, pt. 3; see also 1765, N. 12448, I, pt. 1.

13. *PSZ*, 1785, N. 16187, art. 12–13, 15; 16188, art. 107, 113; LeDonne, *Ruling Russia*, 201.

14. Turgot, 2:504.

15. Kotoshikhin, 26; Blum, 345. Brown writes about the consciousness of a more common identity between the higher and lower strata of the nobility in the late seventeenth century: 521–524. Centers emphasizes the element of consciousness, calling social classes "psycho-social groupings"; 27, 139.

16. Voslensky, 9, 70–72; Wickham and Crignard, 33. The Soviet concept of *nomenklatura* is very useful to gain an understanding of the working of the ruling elite.

17. As the governor of Vitebsk in the 1800s put it, the poor bring petitions, but the wellborn serve (*prosiat nishchie, a blagorodnyi chelovek sluzhit*): Dobrynin, 345.

18. Pavlov-Sil'vanskii, 163; Glinka, 92, 203.

19. Dubrovin, 1899, no. 1, 539–40; Vinskii, 188–89. As late as the reign of Nicholas I, education spread in the countryside "at a very modest pace" (*shlo ves'ma tikhim shagom*): Gloriantov, 662. See also Flynn, "'Russia's University Question,'" 31–32.

20. Belliustin, 133, 136. Cf. Lentin's statement that one of the paradoxes of cultural westernization was "that its recipients largely ceased to think of the common man as a fellow human-being": 122.

21. Klochkov, "Dvorianskoe," 372.

22. B-va, 56–57; Romanovich-Slavatinskii, 22.

23. Hellie, *Slavery*, 4, 11.

24. Pavlov-Sil'vanskii, "Prashchur," 837–38; TsGADA, f. 10, d. 545, l. 232–33; Aksenov, 77; Ch. says such intermarriages were "not rare": 492–94, 496, 502. .

25. Rummel and Golubtsou, 1:85; "Bumagi," 57; Kurmacheva, 118, 124–26. Such a situation, "so common in our time," greatly incensed Prince Shcherbatov: 67. There was no contradiction between the consolidation of serfdom and continued social mobility: cf. Raeff, *Comprendre*, 81–82.

26. *PSZ*, 1807, N. 22726; 1814, N. 25740. On the "many" such marriages between serf girls and "officials" (*chinovniki*) see 1805, No. 21847. See also 1785, N. 16187, art. 3–4.

27. Dobrynin, 665; Vorontsov, "Primechaniia," 99; Shcherbatov, 79–80; Pavlenko, *Istoriia*, 495–517; Aksenov, 91, 143; Kahan, *Plow*, 70; Fenster, 67–85. For a list of noble families of merchant origin see Fenster, 292–99, 319–21. On Saint Vladimir see *PSZ*, 1782, N. 15515, art. 7, 11; Rieber, 37–38. Cf. the complaint of merchants during Peter's reign that members of the elite, some of them of non-noble origin like Menshikov, were using their privileged position to ruin the merchant class: Solov'ev, "Razkazy," 101.

28. *PSZ*, 1785, No. 16187, art. 67, 85–88; 1796, N. 17608; 1801, N. 19769, 19820; 1803, N. 20608; 1813, N. 25376; Dubrovin, 550–51; Romanovich-Slavatinskii, 52–55; *PSZ*, 1834, N. 7007, II, art. 1, 3.

29. As he put it in his inimitable laconic style: "Social eminence is to depend on fitness to serve" (*znatnoe dvorianstvo po godnosti schitat'*): *PSZ*, 1724, N. 4589.

30. Rabinovich, "Sotsial'noe," 138–39. See also Indova, 277.

31. Vorontsov, "Zapiska," 350.

32. *PSZ*, 1722, N. 3890, art. 15.

33. Dobrynin, 570–71; "Volneniia," 35; *SIRIO* 5 (1869): 240–41; Atkin, 70–71.

34. Dobrynin, 209; Vorontsov, "Primechaniia," 99; Shelekhov, 514.

35. Vorontsov, "Zapiska," 360.

36. Narezhni, I:228.

37. Nikolaeva, 175.

38. *PSZ*, 1724, N. 4449; Troitskii, *Russkii absoliutizm*, 134.

39. Troitskii, *Russkii absoliutizm*, 137. He also shows (213–15, 181) the extent of social mobility in the civilian and military apparatus in the 1750s. I combine figures for the central and local civilian apparatus.

Grade	Noble Origin	Non-noble Origin	Total
1–5	99	11	110
6–8	384	113	497
9–14	368	673	1,041
Total	851	797	1,648
Officers*	1,402	649	2,051

*Sample. I combine figures for those who gave their origin as noble and those who gave no information but whose origin is established as noble. These incomplete figures show that while 31.6 percent of the officers were of non-noble origin, only 20.4 percent of the civilians in grades one to eight (the ruling elite and the managers) were of similar origin. Troitskii's failure to distinguish between a political apparatus from a secretarial and clerical staff creates misleading impressions.

40. D. Korsakov, "Volynskii," 292; *PSZ*, 1772, No. 13760. Rychkov began his career in the secretarial staff, as an accountant: Rychkov, 301.

41. TsGADA, f. 248, d. 6515, I, 42.

42. Meshkov, passim; Dobrynin, passim, 665, 5–6, 19. The reference to the cemetery comes from Gofshtetter, 228. Note that Dobrynin falsified his social origin in his service record, declaring that he was the son of a "Little Russian nobleman": 378.

43. Komarovskii, editor's note, v.

44. "*pervyi voevoda bol'shogo narodnogo velikorossiiskogo polka*," Kliuchevskii, *Duma*, 528.

45. *Brassey's Quotations*, 70; Cracraft, *Church Reform*, 6.

46. Solov'ev, *Izbrannye*, 14–17, 199–201; Gradovskii, 48–49; Willis, 11–17, 310, 316; Djilas, 38–46, 59, 62. See also Yaney, 135–37. Cf. this characterization of the Russian nobility by Pavel Stroganov in the early 1800s: a class without "aucune éducation et dont toutes les idées ont été portées à ne voir rien au-dessus du pouvoir de l'Empereur.

Ni droit ni justice—rien ne peut leur faire naitre l'idée de la plus petite résistance. C'est la classe la plus ignorante et la plus crapuleuse et dont l'esprit est le plus bouché": Nikolai Mikhailovich, 2 (1903): 111.

47. Behrens, 83. A Frenchman who grew up in Russia during Catherine's reign and wrote his memoirs in the 1810s declared that serfdom (*l'esclavage*), by isolating the tsar from the nation, "fit naitre une faction formidable qui usurpa bientôt le pouvoir du souverain et des lois, sous prétexte de les défendre l'un et l'autre": Passenans, 1:194.

48. LeDonne, "Ruling Families," 307; Shepukova, 397.

49. Clarkson, 196.

50. Hellie, *Slavery*, 85, 710; Blagovidov, 110; Man'kov, "Krepostnoe," 147. The testimony of a serf against his master was not acceptable in court: for a case from the late 1810s see "Uzhasy," 131.

51. "O sostoianii," 6.

52. Beyrau, 117–18. Cf. Prince Nikolai Viazemskii's belief that "the utmost submission and obedience of the people [*narod*] to the authorities (is) the secure foundation of a great and powerful [*velichestvennaia*] Russia:" Dubrovin, 1904, 2:262.

53. Hoch, 128–29, 182–83, 189. Barbara Engel quotes a Russian woman describing her father: like most people in the prereform era, he believed that "the head of the family must keep his children and chattels in a state of unconditional subjection" ("Mothers and Daughters: Family Patterns and the Female Intelligentsia," in Ransel, *Family*, 44–59, here 47), and Peter Czap quotes the poet Nekrasov on the life of a peasant woman in the serf era: "married, mated and subjugated to a slave" ("Marriage and the Peasant Joint Family in the Era of Serfdom," in Ransel, ibid., 103–23, here 105).

The ruling class was a society of ranks, and the dependent population was kept outside the hierarchy since it was collectively subordinated to the ruling class. Members of the secretarial staff were ranked for life only, and clerks were no more ranked than peasants. On some occasions, when townsmen were allowed to constitute public bodies, their members were given ranks only so long as they remained in office. So were professors. That noblemen who earned their military ranks by serving in the army or the guard were later treated, when they returned to their estates, with little consideration and even with contempt by members of the provincial apparatus is not at all inconsistent with the fact that they all belonged to the ruling class in which military ranks determined everyone's place and worth. If a land captain was arbitrarily dressed down by a governor, he was treated no differently than an army captain by a major general, and only members of extended political families or patronage networks gained immunity from the tyranny of hierarchical superiors.

The essential point is that Russian society was a hierarchical society in which everyone except at the very top and the very bottom was subordinated to and had authority over somebody else, and that this authority was unlimited by statutory or corporate rights. This is no doubt what A. Koshelev, who was active in the emancipation debate, meant when he wrote that "the despotism of the commune is only a weak reflection of the general despotism that prevails in our society": quoted in H. Seton-Watson, *The Russian Empire 1801–1917* (Oxford, 1967), 402.

54. Keep, *Soldiers*, 1–7.

55. Rosenberg, 9, 28, 40. Cf. this statement of Clausewitz's: "Thus, if the Prussian army cannot attach itself to the state without falling with it, if the loss of the state is inevitable, then it seems to me that we can detach the army from the state and prove that it is wiser to entrust the powers of the monarch to the former than to bind them to the latter": quoted in Aron, *Clausewitz*, 26. I do not think a Russian could have made such a statement.

56. Gofshtetter, 223; Blagovidov, 106–7; Keep, *Soldiers*, 57, 275, 307.

57. Keep, *Soldiers*, 4, 311.

58. The unconditional obedience of Russians to orders—the reverse side of their anarchism—has often been noted by observers of the Russian scene and has been the subject of anecdotes, some not doubt apocryphal. Passenans mentions two. During the Swedish war of 1808–1809 the captain of a sinking warship ordered his men to save the officers. The sailors manning the lifeboats asked every man swimming for his life whether he was an officer and kicked back into the sea all those who answered in the negative. In a second case, a French geographer was on his way to a site in the countryside accompanied by two soldiers with instructions not to stop on the way. He was unable to relieve himself because the soldiers refused to stop the carriage until they met a superior officer who told them to accept the Frenchman's entreaties.

A third anecdote was about Catherine II, who, learning of the death of her pet dog Sutherland, ordered the Petersburg policemaster "to have Sutherland stuffed." The policemaster, who remembered only one Sutherland, presented himself to the house of the court banker, also called Sutherland, and declared to his face that he had orders to have him stuffed: see Passenans, 2:196–98; and *The Memoirs and Anecdotes of the Count Segur* translated by Gerard Shelley, (New York, 1928), 196–98.

59. *PSZ*, 1722, N. 3890, introduction and art. 11, 15.

60. Keep, *Soldiers*, 310, 210; Dubrovin, 12, 665.

61. "Rumiantsev, A.," in *RBS* 17 (1918): 460–77; Bolotov, 1:56–57, 62–63, 77–78.

62. Shuvalov, 116; LeDonne, "Evolution," 94–96; *PSZ*, 1785, N. 16187, art. 64.

63. Based on *Miesatseslov* for 1823. Almost all uezd treasurers were civilians; most sheriffs, land captains, and uezd marshals were retired officers. Uezd judges were drawn from both sources. This concept of Russian society as a command structure is also evident in an opinion of Karazin, who had been active in the educational reforms of the early part of Alexander's reign. He wrote in 1816 that people cannot be without their commanders (*nachalniki*) under a tsar "to whom God gave Russia in service" (*v pomest'e*). Since all sectors (*chasti*) of administration and society must have their commanders, those of the peasantry are the landowners. He even proposed a division of Russia into *pomest'ia*, thus rationalizing and strengthening what was already a command structure in all but name: Karazin, 220–21.

64. See Burkolter and Burkolter-Trachsel; Orlovsky, "Political Clientelism"; Beik, 15, 234; Mousnier, *Social Hierarchies*, 87–88; Williams, A., 59, 158–62.

65. Nikoleva, 111; "Derzhavin, G.," *RBS* 6 (1905): 263–322, here 265–66; "Arak-cheev, A.," *ES* 2 (1890): 7–10; Raeff, *Michael Speransky*, 14, 17. (Nikoleva tells the story of the governor of a southern province who sent his two young sons to Petersburg, accompanied only by an old serf-tutor, with instructions to find a respectable way to educate them. The serf was advised by another, a domestic in a noble household, to go to Tsarskoe Selo and try to enter the park where the empress took her daily walk unescorted. When he met the empress, he mistook her for someone else, told his story, and asked for help. The empress ordered the two boys registered in the Corps of Cadets, in the same class with her grandsons Alexander and Constantine. One later became a general close to the tsar.)

66. Mertvago, 92–93; Dobrynin, 139; "Bezborodko, A.," *RBS* 2 (1900): 634–43, here 634; "Rumiantsev, P.," *RBS* 17 (1918): 521–73, here 549, 556, 569; Derzhavin, 551–58, 560, 562, 568, 573–74; "Tutolmin, T.," in Bantysh-Kamenskii, 5 (1836): 172, "Kak-hovskii, M.," *RBS* 8 (1897); 565–73, here 572.

67. Baranov, *Opis'*, 3 (1875): N. 11660–11662, 11664–11666; Ransel, *Politics*, 39–41.

68. Following Turkestanov, passim.

69. Nikoleva, 151, 154.

70. I follow here Beik's thesis that the creation of a royal patronage network in France explained the support the nobility gave to Louis XIV and the acceptance of his "absolute" rule: Beik, 15, 234, 239, 244.

It may be objected that the concept of a command society is too rigid in a preindustrial society where there were only occasional intrusions of the police, the treasury, and the army in the life of urban and rural communities, and strategies for evasion and noncompliance were many and refined by long experience. It is not argued here that such a command society was in a permanent state of turmoil, harshly driven by repeated orders from above to perform against its will operations it resisted on the ground of tradition or self-interest. What is argued here is that Russian society was not a society of estates protected by rights that had to be taken into consideration by the apparatus because they embodied a collective compromise among all social groups.

Kurt Mayer and Walter Buckley define an estate system as "a hierarchy of several social strata, which are clearly distinguished and rigidly set off from one another by law and custom. . . . Each estate has clearly defined rights and duties, and social position is generally inherited." They add that intermarriage is rare (Mayer and Buckley, 14). Russian society was a social hierarchy sanctioned by institutional and procedural devices discussed in Parts 3 and 4, not by rights inherited and protected by law and custom. Only the ruling class and a small fraction of the merchantry had any rights; the remainder of the urban population and the peasantry had none. They were therefore defenseless against the exercise of power whenever this exercise was considered oppor-tune by members of the ruling class. Its despotism was amplified—it is true that in certain circumstances it could also be checked—by the despotism of the leaders of communities in the dependent population, whether heads of households or elected elders, and it suffused the entire social and political order. When priests were beaten and humiliated by landowners in front of their parishioners, when land captains placed in preventive detention any townsman or peasant for weeks, months, and sometimes years, when corporal punishment on the estate or at the police station was taken for granted, and when men and women were banished to distant Siberia by administrative order for "insolence," must we still doubt that Russian society was a command society? Although patronage networks were based on self-interest, the relationship was not of equal strength to the contracting parties. These networks also contained a large dose of despotism, as the loss of favor could entail serious consequences. Only if he had a powerful patron in the capital could a local noble free himself from the despotism of the voevoda, a merchant or a peasant from that of the land captain or sheriff. But patrons were in a privileged position and had great powers over their clients. Patronage networks provided relief against despotism because they cut across social and institutional despotisms, not because they were not command structures of a kind. One could play off one despotism against another.

Chapter 2

1. Kliuchevskii, *Kurs* 4:76; Kabuzan, *Narodonaselenie*, 154. Figures for 1782, 1795, and 1816 are from Kabuzan and Troitskii, passim. It is more difficult to find satisfactory data for the end of the seventeenth century. Vodarskii, *Naselenie*, 153, gives a total population of 3.9 million in 1678. He estimates (64–65) the noble population at 140,000 *individuals* in 1719, or about 70,000 males, which is hard to reconcile with figures for the later part of the century. He recognizes, however, that a large number of nobles without serfs were reclassified as state peasants. His figure of 22,000–23,000 landowners for 1700 is more acceptable and comparable with figures for 1744: 23,000 nobles would constitute .58 percent of a population of 3.9 million males. Elsewhere he estimates the size of the nobility of 30,000 (males): Vodarskii, "Sluzhiloe," 237. Richard Hellie assigns the figure of 6,385 to the upper service class and estimates the size of the middle service class at 25,000, a total of over 31,000. This seems a bit high if we want to see a correlation between the pre-1700 "nobility" and the figure for 1744: *Enserfment*, 22, 24, 232. The sharp increase in 1816 is due to the inclusion of personal nobles. Without them, the percentage of the nobility would drop to .41. Total population figures are from Kabuzan, *Izmeneniia*, passim. The average number of hereditary nobles per gubernia in 1816 was 1836.

2. Hellie, *Slavery*, 6–8, 591, 596; Pavlov-Sil'vanskii, *Gosudarevy*, 166–71, 222, 258; Clarkson, 197–98; Romanovich-Slavatinskii, 6–8; P. Brown, 521–24. On the *stolniki* see Airapetian, 69 (1,307 in 1682, 1,938 in 1686).

3. Romanovich-Slavatinskii, 3–4, 72; Hellie, *Enserfment*, 22–24, 28–29. What I call the general mobilization of the ruling class Richard Hellie calls "the second service class revolution": "Structure," 5.

4. *PSZ*, 1722, N. 3890, esp. art. 11, 15.

5. *PSZ*, 1785, N. 16187; Romanovich-Slavatinskii, 21. When a life nobility was created, however, is not clear. Romanovich-Slavatinskii quotes Article 19 of the 1785 charter (p. 357) where the term (*lichnoe dvorianstvo*) seems to have been used for the first time. Article 15 of the Table of Ranks, however, stated that the children of individuals of non-noble origin serving in positions below grade eight were not (hereditary) nobles. But what were the fathers? Even assuming that the text meant fathers *and* children were not noble, why was it necessary to mention the children if their fathers were not noble? One is left with the impression that Peter contemplated a form of personal nobility but refused to commit himself, hence later misunderstandings.

6. Kabuzan and Troitskii, passim. On the antagonism between hereditary and personal nobles see Romanovich-Slavatinskii, 22–23. See also Raeff, *Imperial Russia*, 103–12.

7. Pavlov-Sil'vanskii, *Gosudarevy*, 267; "Gorodovye dvoriane," 314; Torke, *Staatsbedingte Gesellschaft*, 51–61; *Ocherki*, 152–55.

8. Hellie, *Enserfment*, 185–201, 229–34.

9. What Richard Hellie calls "truly put[ting] the gentry back into harness": *Enserfment*, 232.

10. Pavlov-Sil'vanskii, *Gosudarevy*, 268–70. On *Landraty* and *Landrichter* see Dmitriev, *Istoriia*, 443–44; Grigor'ev, 56–58; *PSZ*, 1707, N. 2135; 1713, N. 2673.

11. Grigor'ev, 67–69; Bogoslovskii, *Oblastnaia*, 140–44, 404–10; *PSZ*, 1724, N. 4533.

12. Pintner, for example, claims that only 17 percent of the nobility was in military and civil service on the eve of the Seven Years' War; "Burden," 256.

13. *PSZ*, 1762, N. 11444. That the drafting of the manifesto was treated as a joke (Dmitrii Volkov locked up for the night by Peter III with an order to write "some important legislation"—see Shcherbatov, 69) shows that it obviously sanctioned an existing state of affairs.

14. The electoral law is in *PSZ*, 1766, N. 12801.

15. *PSZ*, 1785, N. 16187, art. 38, 46, 63–64.

16. Dubrovin, 1899, no. 1, 562; and *PSZ*, 1809, N. 23513. This particular decision, however, was motivated by disorders in the western, polonized, borderlands. But see also, for Russia proper, Dubrovin, 1899, no. 2, 557–58, 561–62; and *PSZ*, 1811, N. 24546.

17. *PSZ*, 1785, N. 16187, art. 62, 39; see also 1778, N. 14816.

18. *PSZ*, 1766, N. 12801, art. 11–15.

19. Romanovich-Slavatinskii, 490–96. Yet 200 Tula nobles attended the 1811 elections, not a small number: Dubrovin, 1899, no. 1, 563.

20. *PSZ*, 1766, N. 12801, art. 29; 1768, N. 13119; 1775, N. 14392, art. 50; 1781, N. 15220; 1785, N. 16187, art. 39. Romanovich-Slavatinskii, 460; *Opis' del*, 9; and Savelov, 77–78. On relationships between the gubernia and uezd marshals see *PSZ*, 1808, N. 23128, and 1824, N. 30104.

21. Kochubei (1814), 16.

22. Dubrovin, 1899, no. 1, 557–58.

23. Dubrovin, 1899, no. 1, 551–55.

24. Good surveys are in Rozman, 66–73, 86–92; Hittle, 34–85; *Goroda feodal'noi Rossii*, passim; and Jones. See also Rieber, 10–11, 19; and Kahan, *Plow*, 27–29.

25. These figures are from Kabuzan, *Izmeneniia*, passim. See also Kahan, *Plow*, 25–26.

26. Hittle, 26–28. On the *gostinnaia sotnia* see Aksenov, 45–55; Zaozerskaia, 247–63. See also Ch., 489–90.

27. Baron, "Fate," 488; and "Who Were," 9.

28. The expression is used in the introduction to the *Reglament* of the Central *Magistrat*, *PSZ*, 1721, N. 3708. For the transition from the 1670s to the 1720s see Prigara.

29. Instruction to *magistraty*, *PSZ*, 1724, N. 4624.

30. Imperial order published in Senate order of October 1723, *PSZ*, 1723, N. 4336. See also Kahan, *Plow*, 276.

31. On *raznochintsy* see Clarkson, 218–19.

32. *PSZ*, 1775, N. 14275, art. 47; Klokman, 91.

33. *PSZ*, 1785, N. 16188, art. 132; 1807, N. 22418, art. 15; 1824, N. 30015, par. 21, 34, 78. For an original interpretation of Catherine's policies toward townsmen see Hudson. On the 1824 reform see Ryndziunskii, 107–28.

34. *PSZ*, 1785, N. 16188, art. 102–7; 1824, N. 30015, par. 1–3, 14, 18, 21–35; Hittle, 98–100, 102–4, 108–9, 111–13.

35. *PSZ*, 1785, N. 16188, art. 108–13; 1824, N. 30015, par. 5–6, 11–12, 14, 18, 34–35. On fairs see Rozman, 117–29; Kahan, *Plow*, 269–272.

36. *PSZ*, 1785, N. 16188, art. 114–19; 1824, N. 30015, par. 7–14, 19–20, 34–35; Hittle, 119–20.

37. *PSZ*, 1785, N. 16188, art. 123; 1824, N. 33015, par. 7; Hittle, 126–29.

38. On trading peasants see Morrison, esp. 74–100, 115–45; Prokof'eva, 164–79; Blum, 289–92.

39. Kahan, *Plow*, 264.

40. "Posadskie liudi," 656; Kizevetter, 630–37, 648–53; *PSZ*, 1773, N. 14045.

41. *PSZ*, 1699, N. 1674, 1683. Instructions to *burmistry* in 1700, N. 1813, 1816; 1703, N. 1922. See also Hittle, 78–80; Ditiatin, 1:146, 151, 170, 180–81.

42. *PSZ*, 1718, N. 3208, pt. 8; 1721, N. 3708; 1724, N. 4624; Amburger, 279.

43. *PSZ*, 1785, N. 16188.

44. Ibid., art. 156–58; Ditiatin, 1:392, 401, 416, 434, 438–41.

45. Klokman, 119.

46. Kabuzan, *Izmeneniia*, passim.

47. The best work on the peasantry remains Semevskii, *Krest'iane*. For a general survey see 1:iii. See also *SZ* 10[1], 386–87; Blum, 268–70, 475–85; Shepukova, "Izmenenie," 124, 127.

48. Rabinovich, "Odnodvortsy" 138–41; Tkacheva, 134–39; Dmitriev, *Istoriia*, 491–92; Esper. Catherine II thought they were all rich peasants: "O sostoianii," 3.

49. *PSZ*, 1789, N. 16741; Epifanov, 158.

50. Blum, 308–17; Kahan, *Plow*, 141–44; Vagina, 148, 153.

51. Semevskii insists that church peasants must not be considered serfs: *Krest'ianskii vopros*: 1:xxviii–xxix; Blum, 362–66.

52. Blum, 488–93; Druzhinin, 84–89. In a refreshingly new approach to terminology, Kahan applies the term *serf* to both privately owned and treasury-owned peasants: *Plow*, passim.

53. Blum, ibid.; Druzhinin, 78–83; *SZ*, 10[1], 413, 422–31. Among the free men we must also include the peasants emancipated under the provisions of the imperial order of February 1803, the so-called "free agriculturalists" (*khlebopashtsy*): *PSZ*, 1803, N. 20620. For the background of the decision see *Gos. Sovet*, 12, and for a comment by a contemporary and opponent, Derzhavin, 811–17.

54. On court peasants see Blum, 493–99.

55. Hellie, *Slavery*, 713; Blum, 455–60; Kolchin, 161, 352–56; Vinskii, 181–82. On the serf intelligentsia see Kurmacheva. On harems kept by landowners see Neverov, 433–35.

56. Kolchin, x.

57. "O sostoinaii," 6. Serfs, it seems, did not swear allegiance to the ruler until after 1861: Field, 15. Alexander I expressed his "surprise" at the beginning of his reign in a project of circular marked "secret" that governors paid no attention to serf complaints that their lords seized their "property," demanded excessive work and taxes, and tortured (*istiazat'*) them. Governors were ordered to report abuses to the ruler but to keep it secret: "Poveleniia."

58. Lincoln, 132.

59. Semevskii, *Krest'ianstii vopros*: 1:169–72, 325–28; Romanovich-Slavatinskii, 286–92, 306–17, 346–47, 382–87; Kolchin, 111–19. On the prohibition to complain see "Pis'ma imp. Ekateriny Velikoi," 61. On the legal status of serfs see *SZ*, 10[1], 571–72, 577, 611, 664. On various cases of abuses see "Bumagi," 55; "Pis'ma imp. Aleksandra Pavlovicha," 452–54; Dela Fliz, 599–601; Puparev, 416–19. Rulers took a benevolent

attitude toward abuses because they could do little about them; neither could governors: see Dunin, 554–60. In the two most famous cases of monstrous abuses the punishment certainly did not fit the crime: on the Saltykova case see "Saltychikha" and Studenkin; on General Izmailov see Slavushchinskii. On banishment see below, 312–17. On the murder of serfs by other serfs or by their masters see TsGADA, f. 16, d. 200, l. 20 (1770s); *PSZ*, 1798, N. 18395; 1805, N. 21961.

60. Semevskii *Krest'ianskii vopros*, 1:328, 341–56. When the Free Economic Society put the question in the 1760s whether peasants should own real and personal property, one answer stated that in Russia peasants have no real property and may have only whatever personal property their lord does not take away from them: "Mnenie ob osvobozhdenii," 289.

61. Romanovich-Slavatinskii, 299–303, 337–43, 536–37; Mansurov, "Iz provintsial-'noi zhizni," 320–23; *PSZ*, 1797, N. 17809; 1813, N. 25385.

62. Romanovich-Slavatinskii, 166 (referring to Haxthausen) mentions villages divided among 30 to 40 owners and one of 260 souls divided among 83!

63. Alexandrov, 123–28, 135–46, 166–69; Zaitsev, 1, 12, 18.

64. Semevskii, *Krest'ianskii vopros*, 1:xix; Confino, 81–91, 93–94; Korsakov, "Volynskii," 382–83; Prokof'eva, 24–27, 31–45, 128–38.

65. Litvak, 70–77; Confino, 10, 44, 57–58, 74; Shchepetov, 35.

66. *PSZ*, 1764, N. 12226; 1770, N. 13487; 1774, N. 14133; 1797, N. 18082; 1809, N. 23686; 1824, N. 30117. For the administration of court peasants see Indova, 301–4, 308–14, 329–31.

Gregory Freeze would disagree with such a simple division of Russian society. He rightly emphasizes its complexity. On the other hand, he also notes ("Soslovie," 23) that the government "lacked the conceptual and semantic categories for systemic social policy" until well into the nineteenth century. Is it not to say that contemporaries had difficulty distinguishing categories among the great mass of the peasantry and even between townsmen and peasants? *Muzhik* was a general term of opprobrium. When landlords called their parish priest peasant, as Freeze himself points out elsewhere ("Orthodox Church," 383), were they aware, and did they care to be made aware, that there were Court peasants, Church peasants, peasants attached to factories, and so on? Legislation refused to recognize complexity and insisted that guild merchants must engage in trade, as it was their function to do. If peasant traders had finally to be recognized, it was not as townsmen but as yet another subcategory of the peasantry whose primary function remained to till the land. And merchants who insisted in their *nakazy* to the Legislative Commission of 1767 that peasants must not be allowed to trade were well aware of the functional division of their society. In such a society, not truly a class society but one in which one ruling class dominates a population reduced to the level of dependents, "categories for systemic social policy" were irrelevant and superfluous. As late as 1900, for example, "about nine-tenths of urban workers were still designated as belonging to the peasant estate in their passports": H. Rogger, *Russia in the Age of Modernization and Revolution 1881–1917* (New York, 1983), 112. See also Coquin, who emphasizes the insignificance of urban society (*la médiocrité du fait urbain*), the "quasi-total silence" of the urban deputies to the 1767 Legislative Commission in any question of a political nature, and their defense of serfdom: *La Grande Commission Législative*, 36, 171, 175, 182. M. Hildermeier makes a similar point, referring to urban corporations not as "social estates" (*ständish-gesellschaftliche Institutionen*) but merely as "administrative, fiscal, and juridical categories." He also sees Russian society as a command structure (*Herrschaftsstruktur, administrative-herrschaftliche Praxis*): see *Bürgertum*, 604, 607.

Chapter 3

1. *PSZ*, 1716, N. 3006; 1722, N. 3890; Keep, *Soldiers*, 23, 104, 118–20, 121–28; Hellie, *Enserfment*, 229–34.

2. Pintner, "Burden," 253. Pintner assumes a ratio of 3.02 officers per hundred men. Beskrovnyi writes there were about 12,000 officers in 1803 and 25,919 in 1826. I assume these figures apply only to officers in active service: Beskrovnyi, *Russkaia armiia . . . XIX veke*, 81.

3. LeDonne, "Outlines. II.," 192.

4. Cracraft, *Church Reform*, 6.

5. LeDonne, "Outlines. III.," 193.

6. *PSZ*, 1720, N. 3511 (vol. 43¹, p. 15–37, here 15–16); 1763, N. 11735 (vol. 43¹, 4–10).

7. "Beschreibung," 79; LeDonne, "Outlines. II.," 189–90.

8. *PSZ*, 1799, N. 18968.

9. *PSZ*, 1798, N. 17857; see also 1722, N. 3890; 1725, N. 4809; 1748, N. 9536; 1763, N. 11818; Vorontsov, "Zapiska," 350–51.

10. *PSZ*, 1722, N. 3890; Romanovich-Slavatinskii, 220; *PSZ*, 1797, N. 17716; 1798, N. 18746; 1796, N. 17666; 1797, N. 17799.

11. See, for example, the degradation to the ranks of General Nikita Repnin in 1708: *RBS* 16 (1913): 74–83, here 79.

12. *PSZ*, 1714, N. 2775; Rabinovich, "Sotsial'noe," 164.

13. Romanovich-Slavatinskii, 131.

14. Romanovich-Slavatinskii, 128–30, 217, 220; on Rumiantsev see *RBS* 17 (1918): 521–73, here 521; on Bibikov see Romanovich-Slavatinskii, 129, and Pavlov-Sil'vanskii, *Gosudarevy*, 273; on Balashov see Shelekhov, 515. See also Vinskii, 98–99, 163.

15. "Beschreibung," 102–3.

16. "Beschreibung," 100–102; Langeron, 186–87; LeDonne, "Outlines. II.," 190–92.

17. *PSZ*, 1714, N. 2795; 1722, N. 3997; 1717, N. 3120; 1736, N. 7022; 1738, N. 7487; 1740, N. 8274; Romanovich-Slavatinskii, 216; LeDonne, "Outlines. II.," 192.

18. *PSZ*, 1796, N. 17534; 1798, N. 18486; 1802, N. 20542.

19. *PSZ*, 1796, N. 17570, pt. 4–5; 1812, N. 24975, art. 9; 1815, N. 26021, 26022, art. 4.

20. *PSZ*, 1724, N. 4595; Romanovich-Slavatinskii, 132–33.

21. *PSZ*, 1725, N. 4778.

22. *PSZ*, 1735, N. 6836.

23. *PSZ*, 1736, N. 7142; Korsakov, "Volynskii," 221; Solov'ev, *Istoriia* 10-173–76, 466–71; Bagramov, 366; Romanovich-Slavatinskii, 133. See also *PSZ*, 1762, N. 11444.

24. *PSZ*, 1764, N. 12060.

25. LeDonne, "Outlines. III.," 191–92, 204.

26. Langeron, 147–48. See also *PSZ*, 1803, N. 20770.

27. On staffing the Internal Guard see *PSZ*, 1817, N. 26937.

28. *PSZ*, 1813, N. 25361; 1815, N. 25931; 1816, N. 26209.

29. Amburger, 130. One also finds at least one "real privy councillor first class" (Alexander Kurakin) during Alexander I's reign. This rank, in grade one, seems to have been given as a mark of special favor and was not included in the Table of Ranks: see Zaionchkovskii, 35.

30. Based on *Miesiatseslov* for 1809 and 1823.

31. Its occasional ranking member was called the "first in attendance" (*pervo-prisutstvuiushchii*): Bestuzhev-Riumin in 1762, for example: *RBS* 2 (1900): 770–87, here 785. See also Troitskii, *Russkii absoliutizm*, 29–30.

32. Crummey, *Aristocrats*, 177; Zaionchkovskii, 66.

33. Zaionchkovskii, 66.

34. Ibid. For the title of positions in various grades see the tables of organization in *PSZ*, 1763, N. 11991 (vol. 44²), 59–71; 1796, N. 17494 (ibid.), 253–68; 1812, N. 24985 (ibid.), 219–51; and 1825, N. 30516 (ibid.), 194–224, among many others. Madariaga states that 70 percent of the 185 voevodas in 1745 had fewer than 100 serfs. They thus fitted perfectly in the second tier of the ruling class, as I have defined it, below that of the ruling elite, among those in lower-management positions: *Russia*, 53.

35. *PSZ*, 1735, N. 6836; 1762, N. 11444, pt. 1, 3; 1775, N. 14235.

36. *PSZ*, 1737, N. 7437, 7262; 1742, N. 8550. By the late 1820s, generals' commissions and those of civilians in the first six grades were signed by the ruler, those of officers were granted by the Personnel (*Inspektorskii*) Department of His Majesty's Main Staff, and those of other civilians by the Senate's First Department: *PSZ*, 1824, N. 30015.

37. *PSZ*, 1765, N. 12465; 1762, N. 11540; 1763, N. 11991 (vol. 44²); 1790, N. 16930.

38. *PSZ*, 1767, N. 12973. See the discussion of this point in Pipes, 135.

39. *PSZ*, 1799, N. 19219.

40. *PSZ*, 1809, N. 23771; Raeff, *Comprendre*, 140; Torke, "Russische Beamtentum," 58–63.

41. See above, nn. 30–31.

42. *PSZ*, 1764, N. 12175; 1782, N. 15515.

43. Dobrynin, 341–42; "Tarbeev, P.," *RBS* 20 (1912): 310; *PSZ*, 1819, N. 27739; 1817, N. 26682; 1825, N. 30418; Dubasov, 38.

44. Plavsic, 38–45; Demidova in *Absoliutizm*, 209, 214–21; Troitskii, *Russkii absoliutizm*, 132–40, 239–40, 246–59.

45. Pavlov-Sil'vanskii, *Gosudarevy*, 182; Crummey, *Aristocrats*, 4, 12. He lists nine Duma *d'iaki* in 1690: 177.

46. *PSZ*, 1722, N. 3890; 1712, N. 2521 refers to Senate *d'iaki*.

47. Troitskii, *Russkii absoliutizm*, 175, 179.

48. Zaionchkovskii (66–67) estimates that the number of individuals in the first eight grades (3,941) was about one-fourth of the total number in all fourteen grades (15,764). The number of those in grades nine to fourteen would thus be 11,823. Such a growth of the secretarial staff takes into account not only the increase of positions in the wake of the administrative–territorial reform of 1775–1785 but also the opening of Russian agencies in territories annexed after 1775. The total figure for 1796 thus exaggerates the real growth of the staff.

49. *PSZ*, 1724, N. 4449.

50. *PSZ*, 1758, N. 10796.

51. *PSZ*, 1785, N. 16187, art. 21 (pp. 357–58).

52. This was rare, however: Pavlov-Sil'vanskii, *Gosudarevy*, 179. See also Plavsic, 39–41.

53. *PSZ*, 1737, N. 7410.

54. *PSZ*, 1737, N. 7437, 7410.

55. *PSZ*, 1742, N. 8550; 1745, N. 9164, 9177.

56. Meshkov, 191–92, 195–96; *PSZ*, 1802, N. 20314.

57. *PSZ*, 1760, N. 11066. On *attestaty* see Meshkov, 204, 213.

58. On *iunkery* see *PSZ*, 1720, N. 3534 (*General'nyi Reglament*), xxxvi; on the clergy see Freeze, *Russian Levites*, 1–4, 184–217.

59. *PSZ*, 1773, N. 13972. The order of 1755 is not in the Collection of Laws.

60. *PSZ*, 1790, N. 16930, art. 1–5; 1799, N. 19159, 19219.

61. *PSZ*, 1803, N. 20597, art. 25–26; 1790, N. 16930, art. 11.
62. Demidova, "Gos. apparat," 124, 136.
63. See, for example, *PSZ*, 1746, N. 9279; 1769, N. 13268.
64. See the introduction to the Manifesto of December 1763 (N. 11988) announcing various fees to help pay the clerks.
65. *PSZ*, 1763, N. 11991 (vol. 44²), 59–71. The total civilian staff does not include the military detachment assigned to each agency. Unfortunately, the general table of 1796 does not include the number of clerks. Figures for Saratov came from a report of Governor Ivan Polivanov to the procurator general (March 1781): TsGADA, f. 248, d. 6515, I, 42.
66. Dobrynin, 1871, no. 1, 662–63. Nobles in clerical positions remained the exception in Russia; hence Senator Alexander Vorontsov's surprise at finding most clerks in some agencies of Vitebsk gubernia in 1785 to be of noble origin: Zhurkovich, 329. This was the case, however, in the Ukraine and the "western provinces."
67. *PSZ*, 1763, N. 11989, pt. 23; *Istoriia Senata* 2:394; 1797, N. 17707; 1803, N. 20852, pt. 4; 1811, N. 24601.
68. See, for example, the complaint of the Bolkhov and Kursk merchants in *PSZ*, 1738, N. 7620.
69. *PSZ*, 1766, N. 12723; 1771, N. 13596; 1772, N. 13760; 1779, N. 14831; 1782, N. 15401; TsGADA, f. 16, d. 21, 1. 37; f. 248, d. 6515, I, 1. 41–42. On the children of priests see 1769, N. 13306. See also Shtrange, 261–64.
70. *PSZ*, 1720, N. 3534, xxxiv–xxxv; 1763, N. 11989, art. 27; Meshkov, 188–92; Vorontsov, "Primechaniia," 109–11. See also 1760, N. 11066; 1765, N. 12465; 1803, N. 20608; 1817, N. 26706.
71. *PSZ*, 1763, N. 11767; 1765, N. 12535; 1775, N. 14325; 1771, N. 13617.

Chapter 4

1. LeDonne, "Ruling Families," 233–58; Crummey, "Peter and the Boiar Aristocracy," 274.
2. Crummey, *Aristocrats*, 177; Ikonomov, 102–9; Demidova, 138.
3. See Chernov, "O klassifikatsii," Vasilenko; Demidova, "Gosudarstvennyi apparat," 120. The most comprehensive study of the *prikazy* is that of P. Brown; a list of *prikazy* is on 583–609.
4. *PSZ*, 1677 (7185), N. 677.
5. Blagovidov, 99–101. See Bogoiavlenskii for a list of *prikaz* chiefs.
6. The order of July 1720 pointed to this similarity between service in the apparatus and service in private households: it stated that following the appointment to military and civil positions in the colleges and in the provinces, large numbers of clerks (*prikaznyi chin*) remained without employment and "they seek domestic employment in various households" (*vstupaiut v dvorovuiu sluzhbu k liudiam raznykh chinov*): *PSZ*, 1720, N. 3613. Richard Wortman strongly emphasizes the social differences between the apparatus and the clerks: *Development*, 21–25.
7. Tikhomirov, 352–53; Vasilenko, 187–88; Plavsic, 30–44. See Veselovskii for a list of *d'iaki* in the seventeenth century. I agree with Robert Crummey that bureaucracy "had a stranglehold on Russian government and society" but disagree on the meaning of "bureaucracy": "Peter and the Boiar Aristocracy," 285.
8. On these two *prikazy* see Hellie, *Enserfment*, 37, 71, 119, 143, 178, 218, 229; Brown, 448–79, 519–20.

9. Hellie, *Enserfment*, 170, 188.

10. *PSZ*, 1701, N. 1859; Strukov, 25; Shelekhov, 9–15; Avtokratov, 164–65, 171.

11. Got'e, "Otdelenie," 184.

12. Andreevskii, *O namestnikakh*, 40–41.

13. Chicherin, 99–104; "Viedomosti," 11–24.

14. Andreevskii, *O namestnikakh*, 47–48, 50; Chicherin, 262–64, 266–67, 334–37; Pokrovskii, xxiii–xxiv.

15. Pokrovskii, xxiii.

16. Andreevskii, *O namestnikakh*, 51–55, 58–59, 103–5, 121–26; Chicherin, 88–90, 104–5, 114–29, 135–53, 176–178, 187–256.

17. Schuyler, 2:1–5, 29–33, 37, 43, 63, 81.

18. Miliukov, 255–65.

19. Miliukov, 184–209, 270–83, 294; Brown, 550–57; LeDonne, "Ruling Families," 240–42.

20. Brown, 508, 556, 558.

21. *PSZ*, 1711, N. 2321. It was suggested by a contemporary, for example, that one reason for the reform of 1722 forbidding senators to be concurrently presidents of colleges was that senators were grandees (*velmozhi*) and those sitting with them did not dare contradict them but, instead, danced to their tune: cited in Gradovskii, 140. On Münnich's dictatorial ways see Strukov, 139–43.

22. *Min. Finansov*, 6–7; Bogoslavskii, *Oblastnaia reforma*, 47; Dmitriev, *Istoriia*, 442–43; *PSZ*, 1712, N. 2848; 1714, N. 2787.

23. Blinov, "Iz istorii," 127–28, and *Gubernatory*, 354. See also Korsakov, "Volynskii," 1877, no. 2, 27; Korf, "Ocherk," 133; Grigor'ev, 58–59.

24. Brown traces the evolution of the *prikazy* after 1700 in 507–13, 534–37, 560–64. See also LeDonne, "Ruling Families," 255–56; Bogoslovskii, *Materialy*, 4 (1948): 259–75.

25. "Menshikov, A.," in Bantysh-Kamenskii, 2 (1847): 378–423, here 384.

26. *PSZ*, 1714, N. 2795; 1715, N. 2887.

27. *PSZ*, 1711, N. 2412; 1713, N. 2671. The table of organization is under 1711, N. 2319.

28. Shelekhov, 17–18; *PSZ*, 1711, N. 2412.

29. Shelekhov, 9–12, 16, 19–20; Strukov, 49, 52.

30. LeDonne, "Ruling Families," 242–43; Petrovskii, 37–39; Miliukov, 82–85.

31. *PSZ*, 1711, N. 2330; Ivanov, "Senat," 47–48; Zavadovskii, 100–102; Petrovskii, 33–34.

32. Ivanov, "Senat," 45–46; *PSZ*, 1707, N. 2181; 1714, N. 2845; 1712, N. 2593.

33. *PSZ*, 1712, N. 2521; 1713, N. 2683; Ivanov, "Senat," 51–52.

34. *Istoriia Senata* 1:137–45, 147–49. Ivanov, "Senat," gives seventy-one persons, citing the table of organization of 1720, but it was probably much higher. Another source gives eighty-three clerks for 1711: *PSZ*, 2453.

35. On the "monthly senator" see *PSZ*, 1714, N. 2797; 1716, N. 2982. On Senate procedures see Ivanov, "Senat," 49–51, 55–59; *Istoriia Senata* 1:332–41.

36. See, for example, Münnich's comment in a letter to Catherine II: "The vast Russian Empire is administered and governed by the senior secretaries and secretaries and not, as a rule, by the governors and presidents of the various colleges, as the appearances suggest": cited in Gradovskii, 130.

37. Peterson, 61–70, 84–94, 113–21; *PSZ*, 1717, N. 3128–3129, 3133; 1720, N. 3534.

38. LeDonne, "Ruling Families," 256–57.

39. *PSZ*, 1720, N. 3524, art, xi, xxviii–xxxv, xl; Dmitriev, *Istoriia*, 497–98.

40. *PSZ*, 1723, N. 4342.

41. *PSZ*, 1720, N. 3534, vi, viii, xi, xxiv–xxvi; Dmitriev, "Speranskii," 1560.

42. *PSZ*, 1718, N. 3205; 1720, N. 3534, ii, lvi.

43. *PSZ*, 1718, N. 3231.

44. *PSZ*, 1722, N. 3877, 3978, 3934. The original nine colleges to which the Colleges of Landed Affairs and Manufactures were added in 1722. The four, whose presidents remained in the Senate, were the Colleges of Foreign Affairs, War, Navy, and Mining. See Dmitriev, *Istoriia*, 504–7; Petrovskii, 40–49, 56–61.

45. *PSZ*, 1722, N. 3877, pt. 2.

46. *PSZ*, 1722, N. 3877, pt. 4, 3979; LeDonne "Ruling Families," 248–49.

47. Cracraft, *Church Reform*, 6. For a list of the *generalitet* in 1730 see Meehan-Waters, *Autocracy*, 170–202, and "Muscovite Noble Origins." It includes 125 Russians and 54 foreigners because it combines civilian and military personnel in the first four grades and it includes all those alive at the time, not just those in active service.

48. "Gos. sanovniki," 3–4; *PSZ*, 1718, N. 3255. From the context of the imperial order of December 1731, it seems that recommendations for promotion to colonel were routed until then through the Senate: *PSZ*, N. 5920.

49. *PSZ*, 1722, N. 3890.

50. Solov'ev, "Imp. sovety," 464; *Istoriia Senata* 1:349–56; *PSZ*, 1723, N. 4353; Minikh, 7 (editor's note).

51. Shelekhov, 24–26, 31–32; *PSZ*, 1723, N. 4257; 1724, N. 4430, 4621.

52. Ivanov, "Senat," 66–67; *PSZ*, 1722, N. 3887; 1724, N. 4482.

53. Strukov, 54–55.

54. *PSZ*, 1719, N. 3294. The reform is the topic of Bogoslovskii's extensive monograph, *Oblastnaia reforma*, passim.

55. Grigor'ev, 55–56.

56. *PSZ*, 1719, N. 3294, introduction.

57. Blinov, *Gubernatory*, 84; Grigor'ev, 64–65.

58. *PSZ*, 1719, N. 3294, art. 41–42, 46; 1722, N. 3978, pt. 3. Between 1722 and 1728 governors were fined by colleges, no longer by the Sentate alone: 1737, N. 7240.

59. Iukht, 49. Cf. the voevoda who signed papers as "voevoda of the State of Pskov"; he got into trouble with the Secret Chancery, however: V., 195–96.

60. *PSZ*, 1719, N. 3294, art. 5–8, 10–14, 19–36.

61. See above, pp. 83–85.

Chapter 5

1. For a general survey of the struggle for leadership positions after 1725, see LeDonne, "Ruling Families," 295–306.

2. The succession crisis of 1730 has been the subject of an extensive literature: for a discussion see Meehan-Waters, *Autocracy*, 132–48. See also LeDonne, "Ruling Families," 307–8.

3. On Anna's reign see Curtiss. On her personality see Shubinskii, 336–38; Korsakov, *Votsarenie*, 214, 217; and Shcherbatov, 40, 43–44. I trace the beginning of a reconciliation of the two extended families to the central position of Osterman (see below, 90) and to the marriage of Praskov'ia Trubetskaia to Petr Saltykov (LeDonne, "Ruling Families," 297–98, and tables, 292). The full effect of their alliance was felt during Catherine II's reign and the tenure of her procurator general, Alexander Viazemskii.

4. For the reign and character of Anna Leopoldovna and the coup of November 1741, see Pikul', 2:156–61, 340–49, 382–87, 434–35, 578–82, 585–95.

5. An excellent survey of the political situation in the 1750s is in Anisimov, *Rossiia*. Popular surveys of Elizabeth's reign are in Olivier, Coughlan, and Rice. On her love of luxury and fear of death see "Russkii dvor 1761," 188–93. See also Shcherbatov, 51–52, and (on Shuvalov) 57–60.

6. Madariaga's *Russia* is the most recent, complete, and scholarly survey of Catherine's reign. See also J. Alexander, *Catherine the Great*.

7. *PSZ*, 1726, N. 4380, 4862; 1727, N. 5078; Korsakov, *Votsarenie*, 8; *Istoriia Senata* 1:345–49, 356–83, 472–75.

8. *PSZ*, 1731, N. 5871; 1741, N. 8480. See also 1735, N. 6745; Korsakov, "Volynskii," 219–21; Minikh, 63, 95–96; and *Istoriia Senata* 1:500–47, 611–14. For the proceedings of the Cabinet see *SIRIO* 104 (1898), 111 (1901), 124 (1906), and 128 (1912). For a general survey see Slany.

9. See Bestuzhev-Riumin, A.," in *RBS* 2 (1900): 770–87, here 775, 783–84; *Istoriia Senata* 2:25–27, 32–34, 94. For Nikita Panin's criticism of the Conference see Ransel, *Politics*, 81–84.

10. Solov'ev, "Imp. sovety," 464–65; *Istoriia Senata* 2:8–10.

11. *Istoriia Senata* 2:315–18, 359–63, 383–87, 510; Ransel, *Politics*, 76–98, 117–24, 134–38, 280.

12. *PSZ*, 1726, N. 4837, 4874; Beskrovnyi, *Russkaia armiia*, 50–51; Amburger, 313; "Viedomosti," 5–7; Shelekhov, 38–40, 44–46.

13. Strukov, 72, 81–95, 107, 113–23, 137–43. On Münnich see Manstein, 54–56, 62–64, 263–64, 283–88, 331–34.

14. *PSZ*, 1736, N. 6872; Beskrovnyi, *Russkaia armiia*, 69–71; Gradovskii, 180; Strukov, 167–79; Slany, 144–46, 155–56, 161–65, 302–5, 433–37.

15. Nikita Trubetskoi, Iakov Shakhovskoi, and Alexander Glebov.

16. Strukov, 190–99, 204, 209; Danilov, 30–32.

17. Strukov, 225, 243.

18. *PSZ*, 1766, N. 12612; 1791, N. 16959; Strukov, 287, 295, 302–12; Danilov, 40–42; Glinka, 79.

19. *PSZ*, 1730, N. 5510. See also 1741, N. 8480; and 1802, N. 20405, art. 1–5.

20. *PSZ*, 1730, N. 5570.

21. Gofshtetter, 227 (quoting Nikita Panin). On the social distance between Senate secretaries and clerks on the one hand and procurators and senators on the other during Alexander's reign see Przhetslavskii, "Vospominaniia," 458.

22. *PSZ*, 1731, N. 5871; *Istoriia Senata* 1:500–14, 2:12, 85–88; LeDonne, "Ruling Families," 297–98.

23. "Shuvalov, P.," in *RBS* 23 (1911): 490–503, here 496–97.

24. *Istoriia Senata* 1:431; Gradovskii, 192–204, 214–19.

25. LeDonne, *Ruling Russia*, 31–32, 146–48, 206, 271. By 1796 there were six numbered departments and a Department of Land Survey.

26. *Istoriia Senata* 1:203–11, 213–18; Gradovskii, 236–39, 255–56, 264–68; LeDonne, *Ruling Russia*, 34–36.

27. *PSZ*, 1774, N. 14192. Thereafter the Procurator General ceased to sit in any particular department.

28. LeDonne, *Ruling Russia*, 75–79.

29. *Istoriia Senata* 2:394–97, 708–9.

30. "Iaguzhinskii, P.," in *RBS* 25 (1913): 7–28; *Istoriia Senata* 1:218–25, 601–3.

31. *SIRIO* 104 (1898): 53–54; 111 (1901): introduction; and 124 (1906): introduction.

32. LeDonne, *Ruling Russia*, 298.

33. On Trubetskoi see Korsakov, *Votsarenie*, 199–201; Bantysh-Kamenskii, 5 (1836): 164–67; *Istoriia Senata* 1:609–10, 2:12–14; on Viazemskii see LeDonne, *Ruling Russia*, 35; *Istoriia Senata* 2:354, 366–82, 414–15; on Samoilov see Ivanov, *Opyt*, 57–64. The fourth and fifth procurators general remained in office for short periods of time: Iakov Shakhovskoi (1760–1761) and Alexander Glebov (1761–1764).

34. *Istoriia Senata* 1:290–92, 313–15, 322–24.

35. *PSZ*, 1726, N. 4934.

36. *PSZ*, 1720, N. 3534, iv–vii, xiv–xxi, xxx; Dmitriev, *Istoriia*, 497–98.

37. Dubrovin, 1899, no. 1, 4; "Sotvorenie sekretaria" (a satire on the "prince of Hell" looking for a name to give his creation at whose beauty he marveled—until he hit upon the name "secretary"); Vinskii, 181–82.

38. *PSZ*, 1764, N. 12137. Speranskii later wrote that the Instruction reduced the authority of the colleges to zero: Speranskii, "O gos. ustan.," 30.

39. LeDonne, *Ruling Russia*, 82, 162, 223.

40. *PSZ*, 1727, N. 5017, 5053; 1728, N. 5333; Dmitriev, *Istoriia*, 457–58.

41. The Senate order of May 1766 refers to an "official list" (*shtatnoe chislo*) of 165 towns and a number of additional towns where voevodas were appointed: 1766, N. 12641. In 1727 there were 186 such towns: LeDonne, "Territorial Reform, I.," 152. See Got'e, *Istoriia*, 1:108–10 for a list of gubernias, provinces, and towns.

42. *PSZ*, 1733, N. 6384; 1734, N. 6538; 1744, N. 8865; Got'e, *Istoriia*, 2:181–82.

43. TsGADA, f. 16, d. 190, l. 1–21.

44. Mertvago, 25–34; *PSZ*, 1773, N. 14040.

45. Got'e quotes the anonymous author of a memoir who wrote that voevodas, even provincial ones, were appointed "on the recommendation of and for services rendered to well established people" (*znatnye persony*): Got'e, *Istoriia*, 2:181.

46. "Dolgorukov, I.," *RBS* 6 (1905): 537; "Bakhmetev, I.," *RBS* 2 (1900): 603; "Divier, A.," *RBS* 6 (1905): 370–76, here 375.

47. *PSZ*, 1730, N. 5522; 1760, N. 11131; Got'e, *Istoriia*, 1:149–53.

48. *PSZ*, 1740, N. 8145; 1764, N. 12181; 1744, N. 9084.

49. *PSZ*, 1728, N. 5333, art. 6–8, 11, 20, 51; n. , Got'e *Istoriia*, 1: 89–90, 96, 184–85, 214.

50. *PSZ*, 1728, N. 5333, art. 5–6.

51. *PSZ*, 1730, N. 5521; 1734, N. 6649; 1735, N. 6633, 6676.

52. *PSZ*, 1730, N. 5585.

53. LeDonne, "Evolution," 105–8.

54. *PSZ*, 1737, N. 7240; 1764, N. 12137, I. See the complaint of the Smolensk governor in 1739 about the number of central agencies with the right to fine governors: *SIRIO* 130 (1909): 610–12; Got'e, *Istoriia*, 1:188–94.

55. I have traced the course of the reform in LeDonne, "Territorial Reform, I.," passim. See also Got'e, *Istoriia*, 1:103, 105–10, 113–19, 122–25.

56. See, for example, *PSZ*, 1775, N. 14395.

57. *PSZ*, 1729, N. 5399, 5412; TsGADA, f. 16, d. 374; Got'e, *Istoriia*, 1:49–53, 59–63, 331.

58. *PSZ*, 1742, N. 8550.

59. *PSZ*, 1764, N. 12137, XI; 1727, N. 5017; 1743, N. 8734.

60. For relations between the governors and members of the apparatus see the Golokhvastov case in "Vsepod. doklad." For an example of the treatment of the secretarial staff see Beliaev (a conflict between a voevoda and a clerk. The voevoda beat the clerk to death, but the clerk was the brother-in-law of another clerk serving in the

Secret Chancery, who used the resources of his agency against the voevoda. The voevoda was sentenced to death and decapitated in 1739).

61. *PSZ*, 1728, N. 5333, art. 9–10, 12–13, 16; Dmitriev, *Istoriia*, 462–63; Got'e, *Istoriia*, 1:56–57, 387–91, 422. See below Part 4, 199.

62. *PSZ*, 1727, N. 5017, pt. 2; 1728, N. 5292, 5333, art. 5, 15; 1761, N. 11347; Got'e, *Istoriia*, 1:53–56, 63–64, 348.

63. *PSZ*, 1731, N. 5789, art. 14, 24; Got'e, *Istoriia*, 1:57–69, 423, 431–32, 441–47, 463, 465.

Chapter 6

1. I overlook Peter II, who was a child, and Peter III, who ruled only 6 months.

2. "Gos. sanovniki," 5.

3. "Gos. sanovniki," 5–6; Amburger, 300; "Svita Ego Velichestva," *ES* 29 (1900): 157–58; *PSZ*, 1806, N. 22235.

4. Glinoetskii, "Russkii gen. shtab . . . Ekateriny II;" Beskrovnyi, *Russkaia armiia*, 329, 343; Danilov, 43–49. On the growing importance of staff work toward the end of the eighteenth century and during the Napoleonic Wars see VanCreveld, 35–38, 109–13.

5. *PSZ*, 1797, N. 17750; 1798, N. 18308; Shelekhov, 493–94.

6. *PSZ*, 1797, N. 17757, 17775; 1805, N. 21904; Amburger, 155–56, 323.

7. Strukov, 318, 323–24, 343, 355.

8. *PSZ*, 1785, N. 16260; Amburger, 311–13. Inspectors seem to have been first appointed in 1731 but only for a short time. Beginning in 1796, military regions called "divisions" under Catherine were called "inspections." The duties of an inspector (*inspektor voisk*) are spelled out in *PSZ*, 1805, N. 21628. A precedent was probably the Instruction of December 1731: N. 5900.

9. Strukov, 372–74, 378, 394, 424–25, 431–32; Danilov, 118, 129, 155–56.

10. Amburger, 317–18; Strukov, 372–74.

11. Andolenko, 176.

12. *PSZ*, 1812, N. 24975; Glinoetskii, "Russkii gen. shtab . . . Aleksandra I," 187–250, 5–43.

13. *PSZ*, 1812, N. 24971.

14. *PSZ*, 1812, N. 25049; Danilov, 211–12.

15. *PSZ*, 1815, N. 26021; Danilov, 221; "Gos, sanovniki," 14–18.

16. Shelekhov, 493–94.

17. Danilov, 223, 232, 256–57, 261, 281; Glinoetskii, "Russkii gen. shtab . . . Aleksandra I," 189ff. Military financial agencies are discussed in Part 5, pp. 392–95.

18. The Department of Waterways, however, was based in Novgorod. The Department of Imperial Properties (*udelov*) was headed by a "minister."

19. Pokrovskii, lxxix–lxxxi; Gradovskii, 288–89.

20. *PSZ*, 1802, N. 20406; Speranskii, "O gos. ustan.," 42, 48. For a background of the reform and Derzhavin's opinion of it see Derzhavin, 761–64, 776–81, 796–99.

21. Vorontsov, "O vnutren. upravlenii," 158, 161; Kochubei (1806), 208–9.

22. *PSZ*, 1811, N. 24686, par. 19, 25–26, 49–56, 209, 297; Speranskii, "O gos. ustan.," 44: Raeff, *Michael Speransky*, 1–28.

23. Kochubei (1814), 11. See also "Dmitriev, I.," *RBS* 6 (1905): 438–454, here 449.

24. "*pozhalovannaia derevnia*": Dmitriev, "Speranskii," 1641. See also Jacob, 535; and Orlovsky, *Limits*, 4.

25. Dmitriev, "Speranskii," 1645; Komarovskii, 198.

26. *PSZ*, 1824, N. 29725. Another source gives the total of 1,295: *Istoriia Senata* 3:264.

27. See *Miesiatseslov* for these 2 years.

28. Figures obtained from the alphabetical list of senators in *Istoriia Senata* 5:109–61.

29. *PSZ*, 1796, N. 17600, 17615; 1797, N. 17760.

30. Vorontsov, "Primechaniia," 97.

31. *PSZ*, 1802, N. 20405, par. 13–14, 17–18.

32. *PSZ*, 1802, N. 20405, 20406.

33. On Alexander's ministers see Grimstead.

34. *PSZ*, 1801, N. 19805, 19806.

35. *PSZ*, 1802, N. 20406, XV. A list of members is in *Gos. Sovet*, 7–13.

36. *PSZ*, 1810, N. 24064; Dmitriev, "Speranskii," 1601–2; Jacob, 535; Raeff, *Michael Speransky*, 115–17.

37. *PSZ*, 1810, N. 24064.

38. *PSZ*, 1805, N. 21896; Tel'berg, 32; Dmitriev, "Speranskii," 1608–9; Speranskii, "O gos. ustan.," 45; *Isto. obzor* 1:4–8. The appointment in December 1815 of Arakcheev to the Committee of Ministers "to watch over its activities and to report to the ruler" (*dlia doklada i nadzora po delam Komiteta*) effectively restored the post of procurator general. For the text of the order see Dubrovin, 1 (1904): 22. There is a striking similarity here with the reforms of 1718 and 1722.

39. Dmitriev, "Speranskii," 1623.

40. For comments on Alexander's dislike of administrative work see Metternich, 168, 173, 180. See also Vorontsov's prophetic comments on the role of ministers operating without the restraining influence of a council chaired permanently by the ruler himself: "Sinon sa majesté sera trompée volontairement ou involontairement traitant en tête à tête avec tous les chefs de départements, qui deviendront des despotes et le despotisme ministériel est mille fois pire que celui du souverain seul, et par dessus il n'y aura plus d'ensemble dans l'administration de l'état," and "il est dans la nature de l'homme d'augmenter sa propre importance, de la s'ensuit peu à peu le despotisme ministériel des chefs de départements, ce qui produit une obligarchie incompatible avec un gouvernement monarchique": Vorontsov, "Dva pis'ma," 985, 1005. On Karamzin's criticism of the ministries see Karamzin, 149–51, 153–54. See also I. Lobanov-Rostovskii, 1915–16; Speranskii, "O gos. ustan.," 47, 59. As John Keep put it in a nutshell: "The tsars felt insecure on their imperial throne": "Military Style," 63. Cf. Pavel Stroganov's comment in the early 1800s: "Puisqu'il [the tsar] a un caractère mou, le moyen d'avoir sur lui l'empire nécessaire pour faire le bien est de le subjuguer": Nikolai Mikhailovich, 2 (1903): x.

41. LeDonne, *Ruling Russia*, 67–75, passim.

42. *PSZ*, 1801, N. 20071; Andreevskii, *O namestnikakh*, 136–37.

43. Dubrovin, 1904, no. 1, 494–95; Kochubei (1914), 15.

44. Karazin, 278–79. Aleksei Kozhukhov, the governor of Kursk in the 1810s, complained of the same treatment. It is significant that he turned for assistance to three individuals: the Minister of the Interior (Kochubei), the chief of the tsar's Chancery (Arakcheev), and the Chief of His Majesty's Main Staff (Volkonskii): "Bumagi," 60.

45. Gradovskii, 235; *PSZ*, 1809, N. 23855.

46. Indeed, Kochubei claimed in 1806 that the gubernia board was subordinated to the Ministry of the Interior: Kochubei (1806), 199.

47. *PSZ*, 1816, N. 26493; *Isto. obzor*, 459–61.

48. *PSZ*, 1775, N. 14392, art. 4–5, 103, 95–98.
49. Blinov, "Iz istorii," 128–29; *PSZ*, 1814, N. 25738; 1816, N. 26407; *SZ*, 2:314, 330.
50. Strakhovskii, 61–62. This is also evident from a governor's lament about being "persecuted" both from Petersburg and in his own gubernia: "Bumagi," 58.
51. *PSZ*, 1804, N. 21189; 1828, N. 2309; "Mysli o uspekh," 139–41.
52. *PSZ*, 1799, N. 19158; 1802, N. 20179; 1803, N. 20719; 1812, N. 25255; *Isto. obzor*, 457; Dubrovin, 1898, no. 1, 493–94.
53. Dubrovin, 1898, n. 4, 498.
54. *PSZ*, 1808, N. 23128.
55. "Bumagi," 55–56; "Gubernator," 189–92; Valuev, 50.
56. Blinov, "Iz istorii," 128; Beskrovnyi, *Russkaia armiia*, 340. See below, pp. 182–83.
57. *PSZ*, 1775, N. 14392, art. 85–86, 113.
58. *PSZ*, 1797, N. 17900; 1803, N. 20745; Dubrovin, 1898, no. 4, 497.
59. *PSZ*, 1797, N. 18097, 18966; 1818, N. 27281.
60. Andreevskii, *O namestnikakh*, 144–46.
61. Blinov, *Gubernatory*, 157.

Chapter 7

1. Ustiugov, 139, 145; "Zemskie prikazy," *ES* 12 (1894): 499.
2. *PSZ*, 1718, N. 3203, 3883, 4013; *St.-Peterburg. stolichn. politsiia*, 45–46; *PSZ*, 1732, N. 6164; 1733, N. 6378; 1734, N. 6529, 6591; 1746, N. 9283; 1762, N. 11478.
3. LeDonne, "Ruling Russia," 90–91.
4. *PSZ*, 1763, N. 11989, pt. 1.
5. Golikova, "Organy," 250–52; Golikova, *Politicheskie protsessy*, 9–20; Veretennikov, 22–29, 51–52, 67–75. On Romodanovskii see *RBS* 17 (1918): 130–39; Schuyler, 1:223, 276; 2:132, 135.
6. Golikova, "Organy," 255–58, 260–62; Veretennikov, 76–91, 93–105, 109–42, 187–88; Pavlov-Sil'vanskii, "Prashchur," 863–64.
7. *PSZ*, 1726, N. 4892; 1729, N. 5397; 1731, N. 5727; 1732, N. 6151.
8. On Ushakov see Bantysh-Kamenskii, 3 (1847), 438–45; Korsakov, *Votsarenie*, 212–13; *PSZ*, 1736, N. 6911, pp. 763–764; 1743, N. 8825; 1746, N. 9323; "Delo o bogoprotivnykh," 65.
9. "Shuvalov, I.," *RBS* 23 (1911): 468–72, here 469; *PSZ*, 1762, N. 11445, 11687.
10. LeDonne, "Ruling Russia," 86–88; *PSZ*, 1801, N. 19813; 1802, N. 20113.
11. *PSZ*, 1802, N. 20406, IV; 1803, N. 21105; 1780, N. 15074, pt. 8–11; Orlovsky, *Limits*, 17–23.
12. Squire, 23–24, 27, 43; *PSZ*, 1807, N. 22425; Komarovskii, 137–42.
13. *PSZ*, 1810, N. 24307; 1811, N. 24686, par. 14, 2487; Komarovskii, 139; Squire, 32–36. On Viazmitinov see "Gos. sanovniki," 8–9.
14. Kochubei (1814), 12; Squire, 32–37. On Balashov see Shelekhov, 515; Kulakova, 229.
15. *PSZ*, 1819, N. 27632, 27964; Squire, 43–45, 55; *Miesiatseslov* for 1823; "Proekt."
16. Ditiatin, 1:311–14; Amburger, 278–79; V., 194–95.
17. *PSZ*, 1719, N. 3294, 3381; 1721, N. 3708, xxii; 1724, N. 4624; Dmitriev, *Istoriia*, 483–86; Bogoslovskii, *Oblastnaia reforma*, 89; Esipov, 783–86.

18. *PSZ*, 1733, N. 6378; 1737, N. 7211; 1743, N. 8734; 1762, N. 11401, 11628, and 11724; Trefolev, "Iaroslavl'," 366–68; Ditiatin, 1:355–60.

19. *PSZ*, 1731, N. 5803, xiv, xvi; 5864, xiv; 1763, N. 11818; 1764, N. 12135; LeDonne, "Ruling Russia," 93.

20. LeDonne, "Ruling Russia," 96–97.

21. *PSZ*, 1797, N. 17767; 1808, N. 22941. The responsibilities of a commandant were spelled out in the field infantry regulations of November 1796: N. 17588, pp. 26–129, here 62–64. On the various types of municipal police administration after 1802 see 1803, N. 21007, and 1804, N. 21551.

22. See, for instance, tables of organization under *PSZ*, 1808, N. 22992 (vol. 44², 98–102), and 1812, N. 25048 (vol. 44², 254–70). A list of commandants is included in the general table of organization of the engineers: 1825, N. 30521 (vo. 43², 280–336, here 328–30). For the appointment of wounded veterans see 1816, N. 26255.

23. Instructions to the commissioners in *PSZ*, 1719, N. 3295; 1724, N. 4533–4536. See also Keep, *Soldiers*, 130, 133–34; *PSZ*, 1727, N. 5017, 5056. They were still mentioned in 1734 (N. 6649) but as collectors of the capitation. See also Grigor'ev, 262–64.

24. See, for instance, *SIRIO* 4 (1869): 237–39 (Borovsk *nakaz*), XIV 14 (1875): 270–73 (Pskov *nakaz*); Grigor'ev, 256–66; LeDonne, "Ruling Russia," 93–94.

25. Dubrovin, 1899, no. 1, 566–67.

26. *PSZ*, 1800, N. 19418; 1801, N. 20004, art. 7, pt. 6; 1805, N. 21648; 1824, N. 29953. For one example of additional assessors see 1821, N. 28527.

27. "Razgovor," 491; Dubasov, 31–34; Mansurov, "Okhrana," 352; Dobrynin, 328–32; *Isto. obzor*, 449–50; "Sud i sud'i," 408–9; Dubrovin, vol. 482–83, 498–506. One of the rare testimonies by former serfs tells us about a noble of Catherine's days who kept two chained bears and six hunting dogs trained not to bite but to frighten and tear clothing to pieces: "The police did not dare show its nose on the property:" Zapiski, 140.

28. Romanovich-Slavatinskii, 382.

29. See, for example, Dubrovin, vol. 561–62.

30. See various contracts with tax farmers beginning with *PSZ*, 1765, N. 12448, III, 1, 7; and 1770, N. 13549, art. 12; Trefolev, "Iaroslavl'," 300; Morozov, 246.

31. *PSZ*, 1763, N. 11955; 1782, N. 15522. The table of organization of the customs guard is under 1825, N. 30467 (vol. 44², 166–194), 176.

32. *PSZ*, 1809, N. 23996; 1816, N. 26273; 1826, N. 769.

33. *PSZ*, 1783, N. 15634; 1796, N. 17523; 1804, N. 21388, art. 4–5, 9.

34. On the *streltsy* see Hellie, *Enserfment*, 161–65, 201–8; Chernov, *Vooruzhennye sily*, 126–28, 162–65.

35. On the land militia see *ES* 17 (1896): 324–25; *PSZ*, 1725, N. 4670.

36. Beskrovnyi, *Russkaia armiia*, 40–44; Kirilov, 368–80. For the number of peasants I follow the census results in Kabuzan, *Izmeneniia*.

37. LeDonne, "Outlines, I.," 327, 342–44.

38. *PSZ*, 1806, N. 22176; 1814, N. 25723; Amburger, 334–35. Figures are based on von Stein, 359–63, and *PSZ*, 1821, N. 28841.

39. Beskrovnyi, *Russkaia armiia*, 44–46, 48–49; Kirilov, 368–80.

40. *PSZ*, 1732, N. 6233.

41. Beskrovnyi, *Russkaia armiia*, 306.

42. *PSZ*, 1764, N. 12135; Beskrovnyi, *Russkaia armiia*, 326. For the *shtatnye komandy* see *PSZ*, 1763, N. 11991 (vol. 44²), 70.

43. *PSZ*, 1764, N. 12135; 1765, N. 12385; Beskrovnyi, *Russkaia armiia*, 339–40.

44. *PSZ*, 1808, N. 23250; 1809, N. 24034; 1811, N. 24486; Komarovskii, 131–32, 183–86.

45. *PSZ*, 1811, N. 24074; 1816, N. 26356b; 1817, N. 26784; 1818, N. 27284; Komarovskii, 219–21.

46. *PSZ*, 1811, N. 24704, par. 11–17, 23–24.

47. This section is based on *ES* 8 (1892): 196–97; Langeron, 172–74; Keep, "L'elitism," and "Secret Chancery," 178–93.

48. Veretennikov, 30–67.

49. Langeron calls the Guard in the 1790s the "shame and scourge" (*pozor i bich*) of the Russian army: 172. See also Beyrau, 187–98.

50. Amburger, 336–37.

51. *PSZ*, 1815, N. 25929; 1816, N. 26448.

52. "Proekt."

53. *PSZ*, 1812, N. 24986; 1817, N. 26650, 26784; 1823, N. 29596.

54. *PSZ*, 1827, N. 1062; Amburger, 145.

Chapter 8

1. Carlyle and Carlyle, 1:175–93, 252–90; 3:6–9, 129; 4:384–95; Berman, 44–45, 536–37.

2. Oliva, 142; Ware, 203–15, 318; Berman, 553.

3. Vernadsky, *Tsardom*, no. 2, 560. See also Hellie, "Structure," 12.

4. Gregory Freeze asserts the "state" excluded the parish clergy from lord–peasant affairs and that this "categorical exclusion, not a theology of submission, was the principal reason for the clergy's failure to play a more active role in secular affairs": "Handmaiden," 94. Is this not to say that the political apparatus determined the extent of permissible religious activity? To claim, as I do in this book, that the church was the ideological apparatus of the ruling class is not to imply that the church was actively enrolled to change popular attitudes in favor of the political order, since there existed a widespread consensus on its foundations at least until the 1830s. In a highly conservative society, unaffected for so long by currents of irreversible change, the withdrawal of the church from secular affairs was in itself a form of submission. And to the extent that a theology of submission was involved, was it not the ideal tool of the ruling class bent on conserving the social order of serfdom?

Freeze also criticizes "traditional historiography" for taking laws at their face value, including the orders of 1762 and 1797 obliging priests to exhort parishioners to obey their masters. He himself, however, agrees that "most clergymen's vision of the 'social compact' underlying the serf order" was that "peasants must not resist on their own": see Freeze, "Orthodox Church," 367, 374. If we agree with Buss that a central tenet of Russian Orthodoxy was that one must "not resist evil," the injunction "not to resist on their own" made the church the accomplice of every landowner and member of the apparatus who abused his power. Whether that was done wittingly is irrelevant; the effect was the same: Buss, 49.

5. Vernadsky, *Tsardom*, no. 2, 557–608; Neubacher, 22, 60–61, 142–79.

6. These conflicts can be traced in Carlyle and Carlyle, 4:165–258; 5:374–440; and Berman, 255–69, 287–88.

7. Cracraft, *Church Reform*, 306. Cf. Raeff, *Comprendre*, 16, 22, on the church and state symbiosis; and Besancon, 129–44.

8. On the early Synod see Cracraft, *Church Reform*, 165–215. For later periods and the role of the senior procurator, see Smolitsch, 129–30, 191–286. Catherine II called herself "*chef de l'Eglise grecque*" in a letter to Voltaire dated December 27, 1773 (January 7, 1774): *SIRIO* 13 (1874): 377–78.

Gregory Freeze has made a valiant attempt to modify the traditional perception of the Russian Orthodox Church as the agent of state power. He has succeeded in showing the existence of a separate collective interest among the ecclesiastical hierarchy but has failed to demonstrate the hierarchy's political independence and freedom of action. To say that the church was not a branch of the state bureaucracy because the Synod enjoyed considerable "operational autonomy" and disbursed its own revenues (who collected them?) is simplistic and begs the issue. The Ministry of the Interior and the Ministry of Finance also enjoyed considerable operational autonomy: this indeed was one of the major weakness of the imperial system. And to say that the church had its own rules of appointment, promotion, and transfers merely confirms that it was but another semibureaucratic empire, like the army and the political apparatus: see Freeze, "Handmaiden," 87–88, 92. The issue of church autonomy is much more complex than Freeze makes it out to be. Buss (31) uses the imagery of the lever (*archimedischer Punkt*) and says the Orthodox Church never had one "either outside or above" the political leadership.

Two incidents, taken at random, tell us something about the "operational autonomy" of the episcopacy and other church hierarchs. When Nicholas I visited Fotii's monastery in 1835 (on Fotii see 174). He had by then been transferred to Novgorod), accompanied by, of all people, the chief of the Third Section, the abbot received him without the proper vestments and presented his hand to be kissed without being asked. The tsar turned to Benkendorf with the comment "You will agree that I can keep my temper," and kissed the hand. The next day, however, Fotii was summoned to Petersburg and incarcerated in the Alexander Nevsky monastery, from which he won his freedom with a 30,000-ruble bribe and where he suffered "a deadly wound to his pride": "Iz zapisok," 530. In a more serious case, the opposition of the Metropolitan of Rostov and Iaroslavl to the secularization of monastic properties in 1764 caused him to be declared a nonperson by Catherine, imprisoned for life in a casemate of the Revel fortress, with a gag in his mouth to keep him from talking. With such examples before them, how many churchmen would dare to transgress the limits of acceptable behavior? The acquiescence of their peers—even their complicity—in such shoddy treatment was hardly a legacy to be proud of: Barsov and Trefolev, "Iaroslavl'," 271.

9. Cherniavsky, 101, 114, 123. See also Besancon, 38–59.

10. Hellie, *Slavery*, 390–93. Cf. LoGatto's statement that Moscow transformed the concept of national ethnicity into one of political unity and thereby established its material supremacy on the basis of a spiritual supremacy: 52–53. On the relationship between church and nation see Cracraft, "*Empire.*"

11. V. Dal', *Tolkovyi slovar' zhivogo velikorusskogo iazyka*, I (A–Z), (Moscow, 1978), 53 ("basurman"); Kartashev, 192.

12. Esipov, 786–91; Kartashev, 197; "Tainaia Kantseliariia," 532.

13. *New York Times*, July 30, 1988. Cf. Kartashev's statement that Orthodoxy is possible outside Russia but that there can be no Russia without Orthodoxy: 182. See also Rothe, 11–14, 34–85: he emphasizes the importance of manuscript literature as "the foundation of literary culture" (34).

14. Dolgorukov, "Rech," and "Ob'iavlenie."

15. Skabichevskii, 182. The situation was similar in the countryside. While no one will deny that priests felt a community of interests with peasants, especially state

peasants, who supported them with fees and other contributions, those practicing in parishes of privately owned serfs were at the mercy of the landlord. One in Poshekhone uezd (Iaroslavl' gubernia), for example, wrote to the landlord (sometime in the first half of the nineteenth century) that he was told when he assumed office 12 years earlier to be "quiet and meek" (*tikh i unizhen*) and wondered why he had upset the landlord's mother, asking: "I need to know what qualities I must have according to her and how I must behave toward her in my quality of priest and henceforth toward all (*voobshche vpred*)": "Pis'mo sel'skogo sviashchennika," 173, 176.

16. Likhachev, 33–34, 39.

17. Berdiaev, 83. See also Marc Raeff's perceptive comments in "'Iz pod glyb'" on the relationship between the intelligentsia and the state. Owen Lattimore cites a nineteenth-century entry in a church register in Buryat Mongolia: "Born a Buryat. Baptized a Russian": *Studies in Frontier History: Collected Papers 1928–1958* (Paris, 1962), 512.

18. See, for example, Wallerstein's challenging theory of peripheralization: 22, 129–45; Gille, 130. The negative influence of Orthodoxy must also be recorded. It is the theme of Buss's monograph, influenced by Max Weber.

19. See Part 5, pp. 278, 282; Kahan, *Plow*, 364.

20. McNeill, 1112–13. It also cemented the unity of the ruling elite and, as Aron put it, "a unified elite means the end of freedom": Aron, "Social Structure," 143.

21. *PSZ*, 1804, N. 21388, art. 19. A proposal to regulate lord–serf relations and raising the question of emancipation provoked the hysterical but understandable comment that emancipation threatened "our existence and that of our posterity, the existence of the State, and that of Russia" (*delo idet . . . o tselosti nashei i vsego potomstva nashego . . . o tselosti gosudarstva, o bytii ili ne bytii Rossii*) and aimed at the destruction of an "invincible and impregnable" (*nepreodolimaia i nepristupnaia*) Russia: "Vozrazhenie," 195, 201.

22. *SIRIO* 108 (1900): 278–79; *PSZ*, 1797, N. 17964; Romanovich-Slavatinskii, 353; Belliustin, 132–33, 138–39.

23. Galbraith, 4–6, 18.

24. The Instruction to the Central *Magistrat* declared the police to be "the soul of the municipal polity" (*dusha grazhdanstva*): *PSZ*, 1721, N. 3708, X. Cf. Raeff, *Comprendre*, 27; and Besancon, 99 (on treason being the key word in the Russian political vocabulary).

25. LeDonne, "Territorial Reform. II.," 434.

26. Raeff, *Well-Ordered*, 19–23, 45, 72–88, 154–56; Williams, A., xv–xvii, 6–10, 16.

27. *PSZ*, 1718, N. 3203.

28. *PSZ*, 1733, N. 6378; 1803, N. 20881.

29. Williams, A., 22, 26–28.

30. *PSZ*, 1773, N. 14027; 1825, N. 30552, p. 564; Flynn, *University Reform*, 58, 85, 93.

31. Alexander, 56, 292–93, 295.

32. Alexander, 36–40, 51, 280–81; *PSZ*, 1775, N. 14392, art. 24, 70, 38–39, 380; 1797, N. 17743; 1818, N. 27292a.

33. Solov'ev, *Istoriia* 10:498–500; Trefolev, "Iaroslavl'," 257, 260–61; Korsakov, "Volynskii," 28.

34. Those of Tutolmin, governor-general of Arkhangelsk and Olonets, are in TsGADA, f. 16, d. 804, II. They began to be sent in 1782 or 1783 following the imperial order of August 1782: N. 15821.

35. Ditiatin, 1:364–66.

36. *PSZ*, 1782, N. 15379, art. 76–78, 84, 134–35, 142; 1816, N. 26482; 1818, N. 27221; "Moskva 1785 goda," 63–64; Komarovskii, 122–26. For Novgorod see 1786, N. 16335.

37. A separate volume of the Collection of Laws (*PSZ*) containing old and new town plans for most gubernia capitals and uezd centers was published in 1839, unnumbered: *Kniga chertezhei i risunkov* (*Plany gorodov*). See also Jones and Brower.

38. Ditiatin, 2:316–18, 320–22.

39. TsGADA, f. 16, d. 806, l. 46 (Arkhangelsk).

40. Ditiatin, 1:369–70; Przhetslavskii, "Vospominaniia," 465–70.

41. *PSZ*, 1805, N. 21660a; Salias, 103–8.

42. Ditiatin, 1:364–66; *PSZ*, 1825, N. 30552 (Kazan).

43. *PSZ*, 1764, N. 12135; 1782, N. 15379, art. 137; Trefolev, "Iaroslavl'," 264–66; 1786, N. 16335 (vol. 442, 190–93), 193 for Novgorod as a model for other towns; "Moskva 1785 goda," 63–64.

44. *PSZ*, 1724, N. 4533; 1754, N. 10233, art 22; 1763, N. 11988, pt. 10; 1792, N. 17031; LeDonne, *Ruling Russia*, 125–27.

45. *PSZ*, 1782, N. 15379, art. 157; 1808, N. 23258, pt. 3.

46. *PSZ*, 1763, N. 11750, art. 4; 1782, N. 15379, art. 179–89. So many vagrants were being arrested in the late 1810s that the authorities did not know what to do with them: Dubrovin, 1 (1904): 599–600.

47. *PSZ*, 1782, N. 15379, art. 113–16; 1784, N. 16023. Paul's government sought to introduce uniform weights and measures in 1798: *PSZ*, 1797, N. 17938. For Paris see Williams, A., 74–75, 93, 202–10.

48. Wolzendorff, 9–15, 49–52; Maier, 14–49, 79–83. One wonders to what extent this legislation on police responsibilities was consciously borrowed from Germanic precedent: see Marc Raeff's detailed analysis of seventeenth- and eighteenth-century ordinances in the German states in *Well-Ordered*, 88–128. For Catherine II's efforts to follow a similar policy see 229–39, 246–50.

49. See Part 2, pp. 112–18.

50. *PSZ*, 1774, N. 14231, art. 3; 1775, N. 14392, art. 95; 1782, N. 15379, art. 48, 50–55, 108–11; Salias, 94–95; *PSZ*, 1837, N. 10305, par. 30, I, pt. 1–3.

51. These were the so-called noncontentious cases (*bezspornye dela*); see SZ 10¹, 1472–543. For examples see *PSZ*, 1778, N. 14829; 1815, N. 26004; 1820, N. 28334.

52. Separate "judicial investigators" were created by the reform of January 1860 (*PSZ*, N. 35890), which paved the way for the general reform of the judiciary in 1864.

53. Investigative procedures are described in SZ 15², 791–1006. For a general survey see LeDonne, "Criminal Investigations." See also *PSZ*, 1782, N. 15379, art. 99–106; Vinskii, 119–21, 150–62. Criticisms of these procedures and recommendations for their improvement are in *PSZ*, 1817, N. 27075; 1824, N. 30028; "Mysli o uspekh," 136–38; Lopukhin, 51–59, 206.

54. For illustrations of this practice see *PSZ*, 1765, N. 12424; 1780, N. 15000; Trefolev, "Iaroslavl'," 286. The anonymous author of "Mysli o uspekh" even speaks of "semisuspicion" (*polupodozrenie*)!

55. Got'e, "Otdelenie," 194; *SIRIO* 108 (1900): 278–79.

56. "Ogovarivat'": see *PSZ*, 1763, N. 11750, pt. 2, 7.

57. The procedure was called "*poval'nyi obysk*": see SZ 15², 982–93, 1053–4. For examples see Studenkin, 502–4; *PSZ*, 1776, N. 14539; 1780, N. 15032; 1817, N. 27075.

58. *PSZ*, 1716, N. 3006, Gl. II, art. 1.

59. *PSZ*, 1763, N. 11750; 1767, N. 13040.

60. LeDonne, *Ruling Russia*, 133–34, 168–69; Lebedev, 335–36; Trefolev, "Iaroslavskaia," 206–8, "Iaroslavl'," 369; Dubrovin, 1898, no. 4, 486–88; see also *PSZ*, 1801, N. 20022; Puparev, 418; "Mysli o uspekh," 151; "Razskazy," 631.

61. For criticism of the quality of the indictments see *PSZ*, 1800, N. 19622; 1823, N. 29599; 1824, N. 30028; Dubrovin, 1899, no. 2, 68.

62. Hoch, 142–43; *PSZ*, 1798, N. 18386; 1821, N. 28852.

63. *PSZ*, 1768, N. 13108; 1779, N. 14838; 1775, N. 14392, art. 113; 1799, N. 18933; "Mnenie Gos. Soveta," 408.

64. 4, Timofeev, 292; Selivanov, 87.

65. *SIRIO* 14 (1875): 255, 260–61; 68 (1889): 355–56; TsGADA, f. 16, d. 190, l. 11–14; f. 248, d. 6560, II, 273–76.

66. See Part 4, pp. 337–38.

67. *PSZ*, 1776, N. 14501, III-12; 1797, N. 17800; Shelekhov, 107–8; 1825, N. 30490. See also 1817, N. 26819, pt. 5.

68. *PSZ*, 1782, N. 15357, 15405, par. 19–20; 1797, N. 18051; 1811, N. 24633; 1820, N. 28080; 1811, N. 24704, art. 14; Grigor'ev, 267; *Tsto. obzor*, 452–53.

Chapter 9

1. A handy way to trace Peter's activities is the chronological survey of his reign in Schuyler, here 1:250ff. See also Wittram, 1:124ff.

2. LeDonne, "Ruling Families," 250.

3. Golikova, *Polit. protsessy*, 71–78, 90–92, 147–53, 189–90, 206–8, 294–96.

4. For the investigation of the *streltsy* see Golikova, *Polit. protsessy*, 101–9, 119–20, 123–28; and *Vosstanie*. For the trial of the tsarevich see Ustrialov, vol. 6, and Schuyler, 2:338–47. See also Cracraft, "Opposition," 24–28, 32.

5. LeDonne, "Ruling Families," 307–8; Meehan-Waters, *Autocracy*, 150–60.

6. See "Egor Stoletov" for a good introduction to the mood of the period. Pikul's *Slovo i Delo* is an overlong and poorly focused historical novel on the politics of Anna's reign, but it is very good on the investigation of Volynskii: Pikul, 2:492–509, 521–28, 530–35.

7. This was the case of Menshikov and Tolstoi, for example, two of Peter I's most capable collaborators.

8. Ransel, *Politics*, 222–26, 289.

9. Squire, 44.

10. Ustrialov, 6 (1863), 529–36: the sentence of June 1718 was signed by 161 individuals; see also Solov'ev, *Istoriia* 9:181–88; Schuyler, 2:343–44.

11. Schuyler, 2:341.

12. Schuyler, 1:277–78; Pavlov-Sil'vanskii, "Prashchur," 845.

13. For Golitsyn see Korsakov, "Sud," 39; for the Dolgorukovs see "Kniaz'ia," 741–43; for Volynskii see Korsakov, "Volynskii," 224, 238; and for Osterman see Solov'ev, *Istoriia* 11:131–32, 134–42. See also Marc Raeff on the concept of insecurity in Russian political life: *Comprendre*, 91–99.

14. Cracraft, "Opposition;" Golikova, *Polit. protsessy*, 69–101.

15. LeDonne, "Ruling Families," 297–301, 310–11.

16. LeDonne, *Ruling Russia*, 2.

17. Brückner, "Vskrytie," 75–76, 79; Lopukhin, 28–29.

18. The scene is described briefly but vividly in Komarovskii, 198.

19. Alexander I, 634.

20. "Cherty," 471–73.

21. Mal'shinskii, 168–74.

22. Mal'shinskii, 166.

23. Squire, 18; for the 1820s see Przhetslavskii, "A.S. Shishkov," 385.

24. Trefolev, "Iaroslavl'," 353.

25. *PSZ*, 1818, N. 27308. For the denunciation of "usurers," see 1817, N. 26759.

26. *Sobornoe Ulozhenie* 2:12, 14. A recent translation of that document has been published by Richard Hellie: *Muscovite Law Code*. See also Veretennikov, 11; *PSZ*, 1722, N. 3984; Ogloblin, 14–15, 17; Got'e, *Istoriia*, 1:53–54, 333–34; Pipes, 109–10.

27. Shompulev, 262, 268–69.

28. V., 193; "Sheshkovskii, S.," *RBS* 23 (1911): 268–70, here 269.

29. "Tainaia Kantseliariia," 526–27; 531, 534, 538; Esipov, 770, 791; V., 198.

30. "Delo o bogoprotivnykh," 3, 5, 41, 61, 65–67.

31. For a rather ghastly case see "Donoshenie," and for an amusing one see "Rozysk."

32. "Tainaia Kantseliariia," 524; V., 198.

33. Very traditional, too, since the painted icon was assumed to incarnate the saint it represented. I owe this comment to Daniel Rowland.

34. Esipov, 777–81; "Pis'ma imp. Ekateriny Velikoi," 32–33; *PSZ*, 1762, N. 11445, pt. 5; V., 195; "Tainaia Kantseliariia," 525; Korol"kov. In the 1830s mothers were praised for turning in their fugitive sons: Kolchin, 282–83.

35. Korsakov, "Volynskii," 30–32.

36. Shakinko, 188.

37. *PSZ*, 1722, N. 3984; 1728, N. 5333, pt. 15; 1781, N. 15174. On Peter's demand that priests report suspicious information heard during confessions, see Cracraft, "Opposition," 29–31. See also Besancon on the lack of distinction between commission and omission: 119.

38. Esipov, 771–76.

39. *PSZ*, 1762, N. 11445, pt. 2–5; N. 11687, pt. 2–5.

40. Lopukhin, 113–15.

41. *PSZ*, 1801, N. 19813. Note, however, the requirement to send these cases to the ruler for final decision: 1802, N. 20113; Lopukhin, 116.

42. Efremov, 510–11.

43. Ogloblin, 17; "Tainaia Kantseliariia," 526–27; LeDonne, *Ruling Russia*, 106–7.

44. For good surveys of the contents of the *nakazy* see B-va and Augustine.

45. See, for example, *PSZ*, 1754, N. 10233, pt. 16; 1763, N. 11750, pt. 4; 1764, N. 12178; 1765, N. 13448, III:4; 1781, N. 15174, art. 91, 94, 97; 1786, N. 16479, art. 65–66.

46. Mal'shinskii, 165–66.

47. This may have been the reason for the Procurator General's circular letter of January 1782 forbidding local agencies to open the mail: "Pis'mo gen.-prokurora."

48. "Perliustratsiia," *ES* 23 (1898): 328–29, "Cherty," 472–73, 475.

49. Skabichevskii, 2.

50. Lemke, 35; Skabichevskii, 5; Muller, 52.

51. Skabichevskii, 5–6; Cracraft, *Church Reform*, 301–2. Rothe (26) also mentions the Naval Academy's Press opened in 1722. For the period 1756–1755 Marker (77) lists these presses: In Moscow, those of the Senate, the Synod, and the university. Most Russian-language titles were published by the last two. In Petersburg, those of the Academy of Sciences; the Infantry Corps of Cadets; the Naval Corps of Cadets; the Artillery Corps of Cadets; the College of War; the Synod; and the Senate. Most titles were published by the first three.

52. Lemke, 35–36; Skabichevskii, 8–9, 12; Luchitskii, 577–78.

53. Skabichevskii, 14–15, 18, 20, 24; Lemke, 36–37.

54. Skabichevskii, 25–26, 31–33.

55. Black, 126–27; Skabichevskii, 27–28, 32.

56. See, for example, Black, 100, 116, 124.

57. Lemke, 37–39.

58. Skabichevskii, 33–37, 40; LeDonne, *Ruling Russia*, 110–11. On local presses see Marker, 135–51, and on the 1783 law, 105–9. See also Rothe, 26–27.

59. Skabichevskii, 38; Marker, 33–34, 41–42, 76–77.

60. Skabichevskii, 39–40, 54.

61. Skabichevskii, 41–43; Ransel, *Politics*, 255–59.

62. Skabichevskii, 45–52, 54, 56.

63. Skabichevskii, 56, 59; Lemke, 39–41; Kulakova, 139–95, 227–53; *PSZ*, 1790, N. 16901. See also Shtrange, 139–40.

64. LeDonne, *Ruling Russia*, 111–12; Marker, 49, 67, 79, 90, 212–32.

65. Lemke, 41–43; Skabichevskii, 69–85.

66. *PSZ*, 1804, N. 21388; Lemke, 56–59; Skabichevskii, 92–98.

67. Skabichevskii, 125–26. On Golitsyn see *ES* 9 (1893): 50–51; Mal'shinskii, 168–69, 174–75. On Fotii see "Iz zapisok," 529–30; and Sturdza, 283.

68. Skabichevskii, 195–206; Sumarokov.

69. Skabichevskii, 131, 142, 156, 211–12; on Kunitsyn see Yaney, 84.

70. Skabichevskii, 99–104.

71. Skabichevskii, 115–16; Przhetslavskii, A.S. Shishkov," 383–90, 401–2.

72. Skabichevskii, 135–42; Flynn, *University Reform*, 90–103, 110–12; Shishkov, 1355–58.

73. Skabichevskii, 171, 173.

74. We know that soldiers kept a company fund to which they contributed some of their meager earnings intended for the collective needs of the company, such as the purchase of carts and vegetables, and that the same officers who robbed soldiers of their pay and provisions could not touch that fund on pain of seeing their authority questioned and being degraded to the ranks. Does such resistance, when a collective custom was threatened, imply that the army was not a command structure? See Langeron, 147–50.

Chapter 10

1. Gagliardo, *Reich and Nation*, 45, 304. For a fine discussion of Russian attitudes toward law see Wortman, *Development*, 8–14, 17–21, 35–37, 284–89.

2. This seems to have been typical of ancien régime political systems: Beik, 225; Esmein, 493.

3. *ES* 25 (1898): 193–94; 12 (1894): 499; *PSZ*, 1701, N. 1859. The chiefs of the various *prikazy* are listed in Bogoiavlenskii, passim.

4. Ustiugov, 138, 145, 159; Hellie, *Slavery*, 30–31; Vasilenko, 193.

5. Ustiugov, 137, 160; *ES* 25 (1898): 195; Amburger, 348; *PSZ*, 1730, N. 5521.

6. Ustiugov, 136, 159; Demidova, "Biurokratizatsiia," 216; *ES* 24^A (1898): 520; Chernov, "O klassifikatsii," 197, 198, 201; "Viedomosti," 9–10.

7. *PSZ*, 1714, N. 2788.

8. Speranskii, "O gos. ustan.," 19.

9. Peterson, 311–17; for the list of its presidents see Amburger, 171; "Apraksin, P.," in *ES* 1^A (1890): 927–28. See also *PSZ*, 1763, N. 11989, pt. 7, 9–11, 13; 11991 (vol.

44²), 60–62; 1733, N. 6459; 1727, N. 5146. A summary of its jurisdiction is in TsGADA, f. 16, d. 334, 25–26.

10. *PSZ*, 1721, N. 3881; 1722, N. 4084; 1763, N. 11989, pt. 7, 9–11, 14–15; 11991 (vol. 44²), 60–62; 1765, N. 12371; 1785, N. 16270; LeDonne, *Ruling Russia*, 150–51; B-va, 71–73.

11. *PSZ*, 1786, N. 16307, 16419.

12. *PSZ*, 1802, N. 20406, 20409; Amburger, 171; Efremova, 27–50.

13. LeDonne, *Ruling Russia*, 146–48, 151–52, 206, 271; *Istoriia Senata* 2:383–411.

14. *PSZ*, 1796, N. 17639, 1800, N. 19589; *Istoriia Senata* 3:277, 282–83, 291, 295–97; Lopukhin, 89–91, 100–103; *PSZ*, 1802, N. 20561.

15. *PSZ*, 1805, N. 21605; 1808, N. 22901; 1809, N. 23436, 23815; 1821, N. 28524; 1824, N. 29725.

16. Yaney, 250–51.

17. See, for example, Hoch, 10–11, 127–28, 155, 163–64; Kolchin, 68–78, 120–28. Peterson quotes Heinrich Fick, the German who did much to familiarize the Russians with Swedish agencies and procedures in the 1700s, as saying that the institution of serfdom made lower courts superfluous: 332.

18. Semevskii, Kres'tianskii vopros, 1:241; Alexandrov, 144–46; Romanovich-Slavatinskii, 309–10.

19. *Sobornoe Ulozhenie* 2:13; *PSZ*, 1767, N. 12966; 1722, N. 3984; 1754, N. 10233, pt. 8, 16.

20. *PSZ*, 1797, N. 18082, art. 2–3, 12: 1808, N. 22982. See also Prokof'eva, 157–63.

21. Dmitriev, *Istoriia*, 489–90; Hittle, 150–54; Got'e, *Istoriia*, 1:390–91; 2:407–8, 415.

22. Chicherin, 135–39, 148–53, 178; Got'e, "Otdelenie," 184–85.

23. Dmitriev, *Istoriia*, 445–50; Bogoslovskii, *Oblast naia reforma*, 186–94, 198–214, 237–39, and Annex, 3–39; *PSZ*, 1722, N. 3917, 3935.

24. See above, pp. 40–42.

25. *PSZ*, 1727, N. 5017, 5033.

26. *PSZ*, 1727, N. 5212; 1743, N. 8734.

27. *PSZ*, 1730, N. 5521, 5597, 1763, N. 11989, pt. 7–12.

28. LeDonne, *Ruling Russia*, 153–65.

29. *PSZ*, 1800, N. 19418 and 19763 (vol. 44²), 394–95; 1801, N. 20004, pt. 7; 1802, N. 20284, pt. 3 and 7.

30. For a brief summary of procedures in the *prikazy* see Vasilenko, 189–90; also Chicherin, 139–42; Popov, 125.

31. This was one of the most sensitive issues in any reform of civil procedure: see TsGADA, f. 16, d. 190 (memoir of Vonliarliarskii) for a thorough criticism and various *nakazy* of 1767, notably those of Novgorod and Voronezh: *SIRIO* 14 (1875): 255, 260–61; 68 (1889): 355–56.

32. *PSZ*, 1723, N. 4344; Wortman, "Peter the Great."

33. *PSZ*, 1714, N. 2865; 1723, N. 4344; 1778, N. 14829; Dmitriev, *Istoriia*, 532–33. Voting procedures followed the General Code: 1720, N. 3534, vi. The insistence during Peter's reign on breaking up records into paragraphs seems to have been an innovation for the sake of consistency and clarity. Judicial records were, and often continued to be, an unbroken succession of phrases taxing to the utmost the patience of the reader.

34. Dubrovin, 1899, no. 2, 62–69; "Mysli o uspekh," 136.

35. LeDonne, *Ruling Russia*, 168–70.

36. "Raspravnaia Palata," *ES* 26 (1899): 318, *PSZ*, 1714, N. 2865; Brown, 529–31.

37. Speranskii, "O gos. ustan.," 31; *PSZ*, 1722, N. 3900, 3978; LeDonne, *Ruling Russia*, 175, 179–81.

38. *PSZ*, 1720, N. 3643; 1762, N. 11629; 1816, N. 26141, 26403; 1820, N. 28343; see also 1810, N. 24064, par. 88, 92–94; Amburger, 83–84; *Gos. Sovet*, 22.

39. LeDonne, *Ruling Russia*, 173–75, 177; *PSZ*, 1799, N. 18932.

40. For a case where the center refused to interfere see LeDonne, "Local Politics."

41. *PSZ*, 1797, N. 18097; Speranskii, "Zamechaniia," 98; "O gos. ustan.," 34.

42. Dubrovin, 1899, no. 2, 68–69.

43. There was even a term for this practice: *nekhozhdenie* (*za delom*): see TsGADA, f. 16, d. 190 (Vonliarliarskii's memoir), 19–21, 22; *SIRIO* 4 (1869): 258; *PSZ*, 1786, N. 16307.

44. *PSZ*, 1775, N. 14392, art. 116.

45. *SZ*, 10¹, 1473–1543; *PSZ*, 1775, N. 14392, art. 118; 1797, N. 17963, pt. 2; 1800, N. 19394; 1804, N. 21572; 1815, N. 26004; 1820, N. 28334.

46. *PSZ*, 1775, N. 14392, art. 86, 118–19; 1799, N. 19090; Speranskii, "O gos. ustan.," 34–35.

47. Chicherin, 143–53.

48. Bogoslovskii, *Oblastn. reforma*, 214–17; *PSZ*, 1744, N. 8944.

49. LeDonne, *Ruling Russia*, 173–75, 201.

50. *PSZ*, 1796, N. 17465; 1802, N. 20561; and especially 1815, N. 25770.

Chapter 11

1. Cf. Richard Wortman's statement that the "tsarist state held the judicial function in disdain" and "did not need the corporation of jurists that Western monarchs utilized . . . [because] military concerns remained paramount": *Development*, 3.

2. See Harold Berman's introduction to the Western legal tradition in *Law*, 7–10.

3. Vladimirskii-Budanov, 222–26. Until 1700, years were counted from the "beginning of the world," assumed to have taken place 5,508 years before the birth of Christ. The year 1700 would thus have been 7208. The 7 is usually skipped, and the Supplementary Articles of 1676 and 1677, for example, are cited in documents simply as "the articles of the years 184 and 185."

4. Vladimirskii-Budanov, 261–65, 368–69.

5. See Lipinskii for a very valuable introduction to the topic of case law. In the absence of a code it is obvious that even senators and their secretaries did not always know what law remained in force or had been superseded by more recent legislation: for example *PSZ*, 1820, N. 28270; Lopukhin, 195. See *PSZ*, 1791, N. 16993, for the distinction between a decision settling an individual case only (*separatnyi ukaz*) and one applicable to all similar cases. For the refusal "to find the law" see LeDonne, "Local Politics." On fines for reaching the wrong decision see *PSZ*, 1764, N. 12140; 1773, N. 14089; 1800, N. 19490, among many others; and Lopukhin, 144–47.

6. Grigor'ev, 184–85, 189–91, 197–98; Fel'dshtein, 285, 288–94. On Speranskii's attitude toward codification in the 1800s, see Jacob, 531; and Raeff, "Codification," 7, 9.

7. On crimes as violations of the cosmic order see Bodde and Morris, 3–6, 11, 43. See, for example, the manifesto of January 1797 ordering rebellious peasants to obey their masters "since the law of God teaches to obey those who hold power [*vlast'*], all of whom are God's representatives" (*postavleny ot Boga*): *PSZ*, 1797, N. 17769.

8. Shelekhov, 30–31.

9. *PSZ*, 1762, N. 11667, 11678; Ivanov, "Sudebnoe delo," 55–56; *PSZ*, 1786, N. 16308; LeDonne, *Ruling Russia*, 184. See also Besancon, 52.

10. *PSZ*, 1762, N. 11693; 1775, N. 14233, 14294.

11. *PSZ*, 1727, N. 5050.

12. *PSZ*, 1725, N. 4713.

13. *PSZ*, 1782, N. 15379, art. 191–274; 1781, N. 15147.

14. *PSZ*, 1811, N. 24707; 1812, N. 24975; pp. 75–84.

15. I borrow this from Galbraith's discussion of the sources of power: 58–59; see also Vladimirskii-Budanov, 361.

16. Vladimirskii-Budanov, 369–70.

17. *PSZ*, 1716, N. 3006, art. 3, 154, 196.

18. Brückner, *Katerina*, 490–91; Papmehl, 285–86.

19. Lopukhin, 10–11, 13–14, 166.

20. Morozov, 245, 247. On the discretionary powers of the apparatus to impose punishment, see Jacob, 531.

21. LeDonne, *Ruling Russia*, 197–98. Some local people who felt that the Orthodox must not wear "German" dress were declared "*bezumnye liudi*" under Peter I, and a Perm noble who believed that all men were created equal and that serfs should as a result be emancipated was declared insane on Catherine's order: Ogloblin, 17; Semevskii *Krest'ianskii vopros*, 1:201.

22. Dobrynin, 1871, no. 2, 181.

23. *PSZ*, 1775, N. 14275, art. 2; Trefolev, "Iaroaslavl'," 354–55, 359; Lebedev, 325, 327, 330–32.

24. "Mysli o uspekh," 147–48.

25. *Sobornoe Ulozhenie* vol. 2; *PSZ*, 1715, N. 2877; 1718, N. 3261; "Iaguzhinskii, P.," *RBS* 25 (1913): 7–28, here 26. See also *PSZ*, 1723, N. 4196; 1822, N. 29245; and Cracraft, "Opposition," 23.

26. *PSZ*, 1718, N. 3264, pt. 12; *SZ* 15:250–51.

27. *Sobornoe Ulozhenie* 2:2, 19–22; 1716, N. 3006 (Military Articles), art. 19–20, 68, 133–34, 137, 139; *SZ* 15:223–24, 226.

28. *SZ* 15:229–49.

29. *PSZ*, 1760, N. 11166; 1761, N. 11216; 1765, N. 12311.

30. There are countless references in the *PSZ* to the struggle against vagrancy: see, for example, 1712, N. 2467, pt. 8; 1754, N. 10233, pt. 7, 9, 11, 13–14; 1763, N. 11750, pt. 4; 1797, N. 18244; 1818, N. 27271a.

31. *Sobornoe Ulozhenie* 1:4; 3:3, 5; 7:30; 10:198; 21:3, 69–73, 28:17, 19; *PSZ*, 1669, N. 441, art. 11, 76–86; Man kov, *Ulozhenie* 220–23.

32. Vladimirskii-Budanov, 361–67, 369–70; Lipinskii, 4–5.

33. Those who died of other wounds were considered victims of manslaughter, not murder.

34. *PSZ*, 1716, N. 3006, art. 154–64; *SZ* 15:336–40. See also *PSZ*, 1780, N. 15029.

35. *Sobornoe Ulozhenie* 1:5–7; 3:17–18; 10:93–99, 134, 136, 142, 162–63. Most of these provisions were superseded by *PSZ*, 1787, N. 16535, or earlier.

36. *Sobornoe Ulozhenie* 10:9, 14, Vonliarliarskii seems to have recommended that litigants who lost their appeal should pay a fine for "insulting" the trial judge: TsGADA, f. 16, d. 190, l. 22–24.

37. See "Obida" in *ES* 21ᴬ (1897): 505–7; *SZ* 10:380–86; 15:367–88. For a case in which no less a personage than Sievers, the governor of Novgorod, was ordered to ask

for "Christian forgiveness," See "Vsepod. doklad." Another case is the *PSZ*, 1754, N. 10332.

38. *PSZ*, 1805, N. 21961. See also 1798, N. 18395, for a precedent and 1823, N. 29507.

39. Studenkin, and "Pis'ma," 452–54. There were apparently quite a few similar cases at the court of the enlightened empress: see Riabinin.

40. *Sobornoe Ulozhenie* 21:9–18; *PSZ*, 1669, N. 441, art. 8–12, 17–20; Kaiser, 71.

41. *PSZ*, 1716, N. 3006, art. 189; 1721, N. 3847; Lipinskii, 13–18.

42. *PSZ*, 1781, N. 15147.

43. See, for example, *PSZ*, 1764, N. 12244; TsGADA, f. 16, d. 384, l. 2; Vinskii, 174.

44. *PSZ*, 1816, N. 26295.

45. *PSZ*, 1799, N. 19059; 1802, N. 20263; 1816, N. 26295.

46. Vladimirskii-Budanov, 359–61.

47. LeDonne, *Ruling Russia*, 186.

48. *PSZ*, 1726, N. 4964; 1727, N. 5026, 5218.

49. *PSZ*, 1744, N. 8944.

50. *PSZ*, 1753, N. 10086; 1754, N. 10306; LeDonne, *Ruling Russia*, 187–88; Pikul', 2:605. For later legislation providing for the death penalty see *PSZ*, 1755, N. 10486, IV:3; 1766, N. 12570, art. 130; 1771, N. 13676; 1812, N. 24975, pp. 80–84; 1818, N. 27490, par. 230–38.

51. "Katorga," in *ES* 14ᴬ (1895): 756–57.

52. Ivanov, "Sudnoe delo," 50. For examples see "Egor Stoletov," 25; *Krest. voina*, 359; Vinskii, 164, 173–74; "Dolgorukov, M.," *RBS* 6 (1905): 543–44; "D. Volkov," 478; "Mel'gunov, A.," in Bantysh-Kamenskii, 3 (1836): 304–6; Gribovskii, *Materialy*, 1–2; *PSZ*, 1762, N. 11616, 11693.

53. Schuyler, 1:264; *PSZ*, 1754, N. 10233; Gribovskii, 24–26; 1765, N. 12448, I:3, II:1–2, III:3; 1772, N. 13846; 1781, N. 15124; 1785, N. 16227. On the transportation and assignment of exiles see 1767, N. 13010; 1783, N. 15709; 1784, N. 15976; 1785, N. 16295. See also Coquin, 45–59, 60–84, 108–17.

54. *PSZ*, 1822, N. 29128; 1760, N. 11166; 1773, N. 14091; Semevskii *Krest'ianskii vopros* 1:189; Romanovich-Slavatinskii, 287–89; Madariaga, "Catherine II," 38–47. On banishment by sentence of the *mir* see *PSZ*, 1812, N. 25170.

55. *PSZ*, 1754, N. 10233, pt. 15–16; 1765, N. 12396; 1797, N. 18244; 1798, N. 18705; 1803, N. 20757; 1807, N. 22441; 1810, N. 24467; 1811, N. 24707.

56. "Katorga," in *ES* 14ᴬ (1895): 756–57; Vladimirskii-Budanov, 372; *PSZ*, 1753, N. 10113; 1760, N. 11123; 1769, N. 13253; 1773, N. 13975; 1797, N. 18038; 1798, N. 18452; 1812, N. 25123.

57. See Lebedev for the use of corporal punishment by ecclesiastical authorities; Bolotov, 67, 72–73; Trefolev, "Iaroslavl'," 355.

58. "Telesnye nakazaniia," in *ES* 34 (1902): 290–95, here 292. For a striking description see Pikul', 2:353–55.

59. *PSZ*, 1802, N. 20115.

60. *SZ*, 15ⁱ, 29, 31–32; *PSZ*, 1765, N. 12424; 1845, N. 19283, art. 21–22.

61. *PSZ*, 1720, N. 3534, LIII; 1721, N. 3760.

62. *PSZ*, 1720, N. 3628.

63. *SZ*, 15ⁱ, 33.

64. Pikul', 2:589, 605.

65. *PSZ*, 1754, N. 10261.

66. Romanovich-Slavatinskii, 72.
67. *PSZ*, 1767, N. 12909; 1796, N. 17624; 1801, N. 19885; 1808, N. 23027.
68. *PSZ*, 1753, N. 10087, 10101. In fact, it had been in use before 1753: *SZ*, 15^i, art. 19; see also art. 20–24.
69. *PSZ*, 1785, N. 16187, art. 5–6, 15; 16188, art. 107, 113, 135; 1797, N. 17916.
70. *PSZ*, 1799, N. 18898.

Chapter 12

1. *SZ*, 10, no. 1, art. 230, 240.
2. *SZ*, 10, no. 1, 231–35, 327; *PSZ*, 1714, N. 2789, pt. 1. On *pomest'ia* and *votchiny* see Man'kov, *Ulozhenie*, 58–93; and El'iashevich, vol. 2.
3. *PSZ*, 1721, N. 3711.
4. *PSZ*, 1762, N. 11511; 1825, N. 30574. On the Stroganov case see Shakhovskoi, 225–28. See below p. 227.
5. *SZ*, 10, no. 1, art. 244–47; *PSZ*, 1748, N. 9504; 1797, N. 17809; 1801, N. 19892; 1815, N. 25775; 1816, N. 26202.
6. *PSZ*, 1714, N. 2789, pt. 1; 1720, N. 3541; 1740, N. 8190; 1762, N. 11681; 1773, N. 14056. For a description of messages see Alexander, *Bubonic Plague*, 76–78. See also Vladimirskii-Budanov, 569–70 (on the so-called "*dannye*" or *dvory* in towns); Hellie, *Slavery*, 491.
7. *SZ*, 10, no. 1, art. 243, 241; *PSZ*, 1807, N. 22700; Vladimirskii-Budanov, 547–51.
8. Semevskii 1:325.
9. Pavlov-Sil'vanskii, *Gosudarevy*, 197–220. On the Chancery of Confiscation see Andreevskii "Kantseliariia." See also Vladimirskii-Budanov, 372; *PSZ*, 1785, N. 16187, art. 24.
10. *PSZ*, 1782, N. 15447, 15518; 1785, N. 16187, art. 33–34. On the right of preemption see Vladimirskii-Budanov,, 551–54; and *SZ*, 10, no. 1, art. 828–49.
11. *PSZ*, 1730, N. 5633; Semevskii *Krest' ianskii vopros* 1:325–27, 341–56.
12. *PSZ*, 1794, N. 17265.
13. *PSZ*, 1801, N. 20075; 1817, N. 26649. The background of the 1801 decision is in Safonov, 182.
14. Speranskii, "O krepostn. liudiakh," 6–7.
15. *SZ*, 10, no. 1, art. 255–57.
16. *SZ*, 10, no. 1, art. 253–54; LeDonne, *Ruling Russia*, 223, 237; *PSZ*, 1797, N. 17906, esp. par. 80–96. On the size of court properties in the first half of the eighteenth century see Indova, 18–21, 41–47, 56–86, 318–20.
17. *SZ*, 10, no. 1, art. 248–52. On the "possessional factories" see *PSZ*, 1721, N. 3711; 1762, N. 11490; 1798, N. 18442; 1816, N. 26504; 1825, N. 30574. See also Baburin, 66–68, 96–99, 111–13, 143–46, 215–19, 251–54.
18. *SZ*, 10, no. 1, art. 263.
19. Kliuchevskii, *Kurs* 4:78.
20. "Zapiska," 138. Richard Wortman comments that "the establishment of civil rights in (the Russian) political culture . . . did not confer high ethical value on the right of property. In early twentieth-century Russia, property rights and civil rights belonged to antagonistic and irreconcilable political doctrines": "Property Rights," 32. Can we not explain this apparently paradoxical situation (from a Western point of view) by the fact that the right to own (real) property was for so long associated with a despotic

ruling class and that the struggle for civil rights was a struggle against both a unified ruling class and property rights?

21. *SZ*, 10, no. 1, art. 928, 940, 404–6, 424–27, 481, 494, 885.

22. *SZ*, 10, no. 1, art. 474; *PSZ*, 1821, N. 28814.

23. *PSZ*, 1701, N. 1833, and 1850. When the *nadvornye* courts were in existence, the clerks were attached to them: 1725, N. 4668 (vol. 44²), 6. On the registration of wills see 1704, N. 1970. See also "Viedomosti," 8–10, 15–19; *SZ*, 10, no. 1, 408–13, 425, 462–64; *Gos. Sovet*, 12–13.

24. The procedure is described in *SZ*, 10, no. 1, 555–60. On the many abuses connected with it see B-va, 71–73; *PSZ*, 1810, N. 24102; *AGS-DZGO* 4:11–12; and judicial cases in TsGADA, f. 248, d. 6560, I, 95–96, 112, 120; d. 6512, 19–20; TsGVIA, f. 44, d. 50, 37–40. In towns the *magistrat* simply gave the new owner of a house or a plot of land a copy of its decision to *otkazat'* the property and informed the police.

25. In the writing of this section I have greatly benefited from my reading of Huebner, Stone, Chester, and Ditz.

26. B-va, 80; *SIRIO* 4 (1869): 227–28.

27. Huebner, 694.

28. *SZ*, 10, no. 1, art. 678, 805.

29. *SIRIO* 14 (1875): 459–60; B-va, 80.

30. *PSZ*, 1817, N. 26678.

31. For a general background see Vladimirskii-Budanov, 492–95. *PSZ*, 1704, N. 1970; 1726, N. 4937, 4953; 1823, N. 29373. For examples of "oral wills" see 1804, N. 21405; and Garshin, 625.

32. Andreevskii, "Kantseliariia," 168–70.

33. *PSZ*, 1698, N. 1616; 1730, N. 5601, pt. 7–8; 1763, N. 11913; 1785, N. 16188, art. 148; *SZ*, 10, no. 1, art. 728, 730–31, 733.

34. *PSZ*, 1712, N. 2467, pt. 15–16; A. Lobanov-Rostovskii, 1st ed., 1:53 (for Kantemir); *PSZ*, 1823, N. 29511.

35. *PSZ*, 1731, N. 5717, art. 1–2. The legislation followed the old Muscovite practice of defining shares as percentages of landholding: 15 out of 100 *chetverti* of land. This was later translated as one-seventh: *SZ*, 10, no. 1, art. 717–19. The *Ulozhenie* 17:1 already gave the widow a fourth of the movables (*pozhitki*).

36. *PSZ*, 1714, N. 2789; Vladimirskii–Budanov, 503–5. The question must be raised whether Peter, who spent much of 1713 and 1714 in northern Germany and at war in the Baltic, was not influenced by a practice of unigeniture called *Anerberecht*, widespread in the northern German states at the time: Huebner, 763–64. The provisos of the order of March 1714 were developed in the extensive Supplementary Articles of May 1725: N. 4722.

37. *PSZ*, 1731, N. 5717; Meehan-Waters, *Autocracy*, 118–23.

38. *PSZ*, 1736, N. 7142.

39. Stone, 47–48; *PSZ*, 1774, N. 14117; 1817, N. 26995.

40. *SZ*, 10, no. 1, 696–99; Huebner, 726; *PSZ*, 1823, N. 29357.

41. *PSZ*, 1815, N. 25784.

42. *SZ*, 10, no. 1, 701, 703, 705.

43. *SZ*, 10, no. 1, 706–9.

44. *PSZ*, 1750, N. 9728; 1820, N. 28270.

45. See "Podriad," in *ES* 24 (1898): 110–11; and "Postavka," ibid., 702–3.

46. For examples see *PSZ*, 1782, N. 15379, art. 139, 141; 15479; 15511; 1789, N. 16778; 1823, N. 29508. The order for tailors is in TsGVIA, f. 291, d. 15405, l. 1–5.

47. *PSZ*, 1758, N. 10788; 1792, N. 17077; 1806, N. 22230; Shelekhov, 105; Beyrau, 75–94; and Keep, "Feeding the Troops," 25–31.

48. *PSZ*, 1809, N. 23996, par. 225; *SZ*, 10, no. 1, 1160.

49. See, for example, *PSZ*, 1782, N. 15511.

50. For a description of the operation see LeDonne, "Indirect Taxes. II."

51. *PSZ*, 1830, N. 4007, par. 4.

52. *PSZ*, 1731, N. 5789, art. 22; 1830, N. 4007, par. 7, 14.

53. *PSZ*, 1785, N. 16188, art. 100.

54. *PSZ*, 1768, N. 13206.

55. See above, p. 30.

56. *PSZ*, 1824, N. 30115, par. 1, 5, 7, 12, 87–88, 118, 121–26.

57. *PSZ*, 1797, N. 18274, art. 3; 1830, N. 4007, par. 45.

58. See above, pp. 223–36.

59. *PSZ*, 1830, N. 4007, par. 43, 45; 1816, N. 26325.

60. *PSZ*, 1731, N. 5789, art. 22; Shelekhov, 102; *PSZ*, 1776, N. 14544, art. 4.

61. *PSZ*, 1762, N. 11692.

62. *PSZ*, 1774, N. 14226; 1802, N. 20251.

63. For the distinction between surety and guarantor see "Surety" in *Black's Law Dictionary*, 5th ed., (St. Paul, Minn., 1979), 1293.

64. *PSZ*, 1731, N. 5789, art. 14, 17, 19, 24; 1765, N. 12362.

65. *PSZ*, 1776, N. 14544; 1782, N. 15511; 1825, N. 30380; 1830, N. 4007, par. 39, 41, 61–66, 72–81.

66. *PSZ*, 1758, N. 10788, art. 11. For examples see TsGVIA, f. 18, d. 184, l. 67, 205–7.

67. *PSZ*, 1772, N. 13784, pt. 12.

68. *PSZ*, 1776, N. 14544, art. 11; 1801, N. 19958, 1830, N. 4007, par. 27–32, 44, 49.

69. *PSZ*, 1731, N. 5789, art. 23; 1758, N. 10788, art. 11, 32.

70. *PSZ*, 1758, N. 10788, art. 10–14; 1781, N. 15174, art. 52–53; 15231, art. 64, 97.

71. For an example see *PSZ*, 1773, N. 14071.

Chapter 13

1. Miliukov, 551–68.

2. Miliukov, 78, 219–21; *Min. Finansov*, 1–15; Ustiugov, 137, 140, 148–49, 160–61.

3. "Gagarin, M.," *RBS* 4 (1914): 75–82, here 81.

4. Peterson, 140–79; *PSZ*, 1731, N. 5789.

5. Senate report of June 1762 cited in Kulomzin, "Gos. dokhody," 347–48.

6. LeDonne, *Ruling Russia*, 206, 217–25.

7. *PSZ*, 1796, N. 17567; 1797, N. 17793; 17849; 17894; 17936.

8. *PSZ*, 1802, N. 20406, VI; 1810, N. 24326, pt. 11; 1811, N. 24938.

9. *PSZ*, 1810, N. 24326; 1819, N. 27964; 1821, N. 28542.

10. Amburger, 105, 107, 208; "Gur'ev, D.," in *ES* 9^A (1893): 919–20; LeDonne, "Ruling Families," 284, 304; *Min. Finansov*, 31–34.

11. On Kankrin see *Min. Finansov*, 189–99; and Pintner, *Economic Policy*, 10–19.

12. *PSZ*, 1811, N. 24688, par. 111–115, 120–129.

13. *PSZ*, 1811, N. 24688, par. 6–33, 42–71; 1821, N. 28542.

14. Amburger, 218–19, 294; Miliukov, 307–12; Peterson, 209–22; *PSZ*, 1722, N. 3877.

15. *PSZ*, 1727, N. 5017, pt. 9; 1733, N. 6391, 6392; 1736, N. 6872; Shelekhov, 46–47, 50; 1763, N. 11989, pt. 16; 1806, N. 22220, p. 652.

16. LeDonne, *Ruling Russia*, 220–31, 241–43; *PSZ*, 1781, N. 15120, par. 72.

17. *PSZ*, 1806, N. 22220. This is a very useful document to help trace the evolution of military auditing agencies in the eighteenth century.

18. *PSZ*, 1810, N. 24307; 1811, N. 24686, 24502; Amburger, 221.

19. Miliukov, 219–21; Stourm, 267–71.

20. "Prozorovskii, P.," *RBS* 15 (1910): 20–22, here 21.

21. Derzhavin, 603.

22. Miliukov, 78, 85–87; Amburger, 199–202; Bogoslovskii, *Materialy*, 3 (1946): 283–93.

23. *PSZ*, 1719, N. 3308; Amburger, 221–22; Peterson, 179–209.

24. *PSZ*, 1779, N. 14957; 1780, N. 15039, 15074, 15075.

25. *PSZ*, 1796, N. 17609; 1802, N. 20406, V; Amburger, 201; 1821, N. 28542, and 28544. On Gur'ev's drive to subordinate the treasury to the Finance Ministry, see Jacob, 522.

26. Kahan, *Plow*, 81–86, 108–9.

27. Amburger, 221–23.

28. Ibid.; *PSZ*, 1727, N. 5101; 1754, N. 10224; 1763, N. 11991 (vol 44²), 59–71, here 63–64; 1797, N. 17934; 1800, N. 19710; 1811, N. 24688, par. 44, 54–57, 228–31. On the reminting expedition see 1756, N. 10623; 1762, N. 11439; 1763, N. 11741, 11907; 1780, N. 15074.

29. The Senate orders of July 1762 and January 1763 fixed the weight of a ruble at 1.02 kg of copper (16 rubles to a *pud*, or 16.4kg): *PSZ*, 1762, N. 1619; 1763, N. 11741.

30. Dukes, *Catherine the Great*, 109.

31. *Min. Finansov*, 17.

32. LeDonne, *Ruling Russia*, 263–64.

33. *PSZ*, 1810, N. 24244, 24287; 1812, N. 24992; Raeff, *Michael Speransky*, 82–105.

34. Kahan, *Plow*, 313–14; *PSZ*, 1754, N. 10235.

35. Kahan, *Plow*, 314.

36. Kahan, *Plow*, 311–12.

37. *PSZ*, 1786, N. 16407; Amburger, 211–12; Kahan, 315.

38. *PSZ*, 1797, N. 18274; Amburger, 211–12; McGrew; 1802, N. 20336; 1812, N. 25056; Kahan, *Plow*, 314. On the *kazny* see Ransel, *Mothers*, 43–44.

39. Pintner, *Economic Policy*, 35–39, 43.

40. *PSZ*, 1754, N. 10235; 1764, N. 12127; Kahan, *Plow*, 316–18.

41. *PSZ*, 1817, N. 26837; Kahan, *Plow*, 316; Pintner, *Economic Policy*, 38–39.

42. Miliukov, 66; *Min. Finansov*, 2–3.

43. Miliukov, 66, 85–92, 121–22, 219–21; *Min. Finansov*, 8; Bogoslovskii, *Materialy* 3 (1946): 293–302.

44. *PSZ*, 1719, N. 3294, art. 23–34; N. 3304; 1724, N. 4624, art. 10, 18–21, 23–26, 41, 43, 47–48; 1726, N. 4928; *Min. Finansov*, 6–7.

45. *PSZ*, 1726, N. 4928; 1727, N. 5017.

46. See above, Part 1.

47. LeDonne, *Ruling Russia*, 217–19.

48. Lyashchenko, 303–4, 329–31; Kahan, *Plow*, 109–14, 183–86.

49. *PSZ*, 1781, N. 15141, par. 66–81; 1782, N. 15318.

50. *PSZ*, 1788, N. 16626; 1775, N. 14392, art. 38–39, 380, 383, 393, 429.

51. LeDonne, "Territorial Reform, I.," 185.

52. *PSZ*, 1775, N. 14392, art. 134, 122; 1776, N. 14435; 1781, N. 15301.

53. *PSZ*, 1823, N. 29694; 1825, N. 30516 (vol. 44²), 194–224, here 203–4.

54. Shelekhov, 9–12, 14–15; Avtokratov, 176–78, 186–87.

55. Shelekhov, 16.

56. Shelekhov, 17–20.

57. Keep, *Soldiers*, 130–35.

58. *PSZ*, 1727, N. 5017; 1731, N. 5789, art. 5.

59. *PSZ*, 1764, N. 12138.

60. LeDonne, *Ruling Russia*, 215–16; LeDonne, "Outlines. III.," 195; Shelekhov, 54.

61. Shelekhov, 58–59, 61–62, 69–70, 75–76, 80; *PSZ*, 1816, N. 26206, 26547 (vol. 43²), 46–48; 1817, N. 26547.

Chapter 14

1. Buehler, 320–30; Ardant, 1:217–20, 407–12; Montesquieu, 215.

2. Miliukov, 3–4, 10–11; LeDonne, *Ruling Russia*, 246.

3. Ikonomov, 180–82; Kabuzan, *Narodonaselenie*, 46–47; Got'e, *Zamoskovnyi krai*, 54–56, 61–83. On the meaning of *dvor* for taxation purposes see Hellie, *Slavery*, 705–6; Hoch, 77–90.

4. Miliukov, 61–64, 78; Shepukova, "K voprosu ob itogakh;" Anisimov, *Podatnaia reforma*, 21–44.

5. Miliukov, 478–80; Anisimov, *Podatnaia reforma*, 45–105.

6. *PSZ*, 1725, N. 4650; 1736, N. 6872, pt. 8.

7. *PSZ*, 1794, N. 17222; 1810, N. 24116, X:1, 3; 1812, N. 24992, art. 25; *Min. Finansov*, 72–73, 75–76.

8. *PSZ*, 1722, N. 3983; 1724, N. 4565; 1794, N. 17222; 1797, N. 18278, art. 4; 1810, N. 24116, X:3; *Min. Finansov*, 72–73, 75–76. Note the different rate paid by peasants and townsmen.

9. *PSZ*, 1775, N. 14275, pt. 47; 1785, N. 16188, art. 93; 1787, N. 16551, pt. 3.

10. Miliukov, 6–7.

11. *PSZ*, 1724, N. 4533, II: 18.

12. *PSZ*, 1760, N. 11120; 1768, N. 13194; 1783, N. 15723; 1797, N. 18278, art. 5 (there were only twenty-four gubernias at the time, following the temporary closing of Olonets and Penza gubernias); 1810, N. 24116, X:2; 1812, N. 24992, art. 25; *Min. Finansov*, 73, 78–81; Milov, 271, 279, 308.

13. For a discussion of the issue see Kahan, *Plow*, 71–72. See also Iaguzhinskii, 270; Miliukov, 515–16.

14. Kahan, *Plow*, 328–32. See also Anisimov, *Podatnaia reforma*, 266–67, 272. Cf. James Cracraft's cryptic comment: Peter's "tax reform . . . went well beyond the requirements of the Swedish War" in "Kliuchevskii," 379.

15. See below for the price of salt and vodka. Sale prices for various commodities are in Meshkov, 182–85. See also Vinskii, 174.

16. Alexandrov, 114, 209, 225; Confino, *Domaines*, 48, 107–13; Hoch, 16, 41; *PSZ*, 1797, N. 18082, art. 8.

17. *PSZ*, 1724, N. 4535, II:2; 1731, N. 5789, art. 5. This remained the law for more than a century. The digest of 1832 required a deposit of half of the capitation between January 1 and March 1, and of the other half between October 1 and December 15: *SZ* 5:33.

18. Prokof'eva, 147–51.

19. Ardant, 1:435-42; Buehler, 330; Beloff, 75-76, 93.

20. For a general introduction see LeDonne, "Indirect Taxes. I." See also *PSZ*, 1697, N. 1584.

21. *PSZ*, 1705, N. 2009; 1727, N. 5219; Kahan *Plow*, 326.

22. *PSZ*, 1731, N. 5827; Kahan, *Plow*, 325-26.

23. Kahan, *Plow*, 95, 326-28; LeDonne, "Indirect Taxes. I.," 164, 185-86.

24. LeDonne, ibid., 188-89; *Min. Finansov*, 121-22; Kahan, *Plow*, 95, 328.

25. *PSZ*, 1810, N. 24876; 1811, N. 24851 and 24876.

26. *PSZ*, 1818, N. 27448; *Min. Finansov*, 123-24; 1823, N. 29694, art. 2.

27. See LeDonne, "Indirect Taxes. II.," for a general survey of the vodka monopoly. For the first half of the eighteenth century see Volkov.

28. *PSZ*, 1716, N. 2990; 1754, N. 10261; 1755, N. 10446; 1781, N. 15321; 1794, N. 17271; *Svedeniia* 1:22-26, 28; Pavlenko, *Istoriia*, 437.

29. *Svedeniia* 1:7-22; *Min. Finansov*, 3-4, 9, 107-8; Miliukov, 9-10; *PSZ*, 1705, N. 2074.

30. LeDonne, "Indirect Taxes. II.," 195, 198-99, 201-2; *PSZ*, 1794, N. 17271; *Min. Finansov*, 113-14; Lebedev, 10-11; *Svedeniia* 1:31-37. Catherine had already told Diderot in 1773 that the "countless laws" on the vodka monopoly were observed in the breach and that the situation was "a mess" ("c'est un dédale que cette affaire-là"): "O sostoianii," 9.

31. *Svedeniia* 1:26-31; Kahan, *Plow*, 322-24; *Min. Finansov*, 108-13, 117. New contracts were renegotiated with producers and tax farmers in 1809 for the 4 years from 1811 to 1815 and in 1815 for 1815-1818. The treasury took over the sale of vodka in 1817.

32. *PSZ*, 1817, N. 26764; *Min. Finansov*, 110-12, 117, 119; Lebedev, 12-14.

33. Kahan, *Plow*, 240.

34. *PSZ*, 1724, N. 4452; 1731, N. 5820; 1755, N. 10486; 1757, N. 10722. A separate volume of the *PSZ*, entitled *Kniga tarifov* (vol. 45) was published in 1830 to compare the tariff rates on individual items. See also Kahan, *Plow*, 236-38, 245-46; Semenov, 1:72-73, 134-38, 161-65, 168-70; Lodyzhenskii, 61-95.

35. *PSZ*, 1766, N. 12735; 1782, N. 15520, and *Kniga tarifov*; LeDonne, *Ruling Russia*, 257-58; Kahan, *Plow*, 239; Semenov, 2:22-30; Lodyzhenzkii, 98-156.

36. Kahan, *Plow*, 168-84; Lodyzhenskii, 146, 195; Firsov, 217-24.

37. Kahan, *Plow*, 192-97, 265-66; LeDonne, *Ruling Russia*, 259; Lodyzhenskii, 147, 196.

38. *PSZ*, 1819, N. 27988; 1822, N. 28964, and *Kniga tarifov*; *Min. Finansov*, 131-34, 136-40; Semenov, 2:131-40; Lodyzhenskii, 156-96; Pintner, *Economic Policy*, 44-47.

39. Chicherin, 84-86, 90-92, 310-18.

40. Beloff, 75-76; Godard, 246; Zelin, 47, 241.

41. Langeron, 159-64.

42. *Min. Finansov*, 75, 88-89; Skalon, 514-15; *PSZ*, 1816, N. 26316.

43. Murav'ev, Iz istorii, 254-59; *PSZ*, 1785, N. 16188, art. 101.

44. Kankrin, 129-32.

45. Kolchin, 5-6, 22-23, 69, 106-10, 142, 147, 204; Kolchkov, *Ocherki*, 529-69.

46. Kolchin, 63, 65; Shepukova, "K voprosu o chislennosti," 407-8.

47. *PSZ*, 1724, N. 4533, I:3; 1728, N. 5333, art. 14; 1785, N. 16262; 1790, N. 16839; 1809, N. 23497a; *SIRIO* 4 (1869): 239.

48. Dubrovin, 1904, no. 1, 483-85; Kolchin, 64; *PSZ*, 1812, N. 24992, par. 31; 1817, N. 26785.

49. Beskrovnyi, *Russkaia armiia v 18 veke*, 22–27, 294–97; and *Russkaia armiia v 19 veke*, 71–75. On the horrors of recruiting see Langeron 148–50. On the process of selection see Bohac.

50. Iudin, "Zhaloba;" Dubasov, 30–33; Salias, 112; Zhirkevich, 575. See also Anisimov, *Podatnaia reforma*, 234–37, 239–42.

51. Golitsyn.

52. *SIRIO* 107 (1900): 279.

53. *PSZ*, 1723, N. 4312, pt. 9; 1756, N. 10649; 1790, N. 16868; Klokman, 69; Langeron, 151–54; Ditiatin, 2:135–40; Meshkov, 187–88.

54. *PSZ*, 1808, N. 23114.

Chapter 15

1. Stourm, 269.

2. Miliukov, 614–19; Kulomzin, "Gos. dokhody v Rossii," 340–41.

3. Miliukov, 540–42, 546; Kahan, *Plow*, 330. See above, p. 402.

4. Kulomzin, "Gos. dokhody v Rossii," 344–45, 348–50.

5. Miliukov, 115–17.

6. Troitskii, *Fin. politika*, 214.

7. Gagliardo, *Enlightened Despotism*, 45.

8. Chechulin, 314–16.

9. Chechulin, 261–62.

10. Chechulin, 319–20, 323–26, 344, 365, 369, 372–73; Kankrin, 118. Firsov traces the collapse of the value of the assignat as increasing amounts were printed: 113–24, 158–65. See also Jacob, 516–19, 536–37.

11. Kulomzin, "Finansovye dokumenty," 121–33, 242–47, 344–53.

12. Ibid., 118–22, 239–42, 340–44.

13. *Min. Finansov*, 60, 62–66, 69, 71, 170–74, 185, 617–19. The rate of exchange was 4 to 1 in 1817. It was fixed at 3.5 to 1 in July 1839: *PSZ*, 1817, N. 26995; Pintner, *Economic Policy*, 210. For a general survey of Catherine's and Alexander's monetary policies, see Richard Pipes's comments on Karamzin's *Memoir*, 238–47.

This short review of the imperial budget in figures for an entire century is meant to be no more than a general introduction. Questions must be raised about the value of these figures—do they represent estimates or real collections, and what do they mean in real rubles, taking the 1720 ruble as a base, for example. These and many other questions are still awaiting a specialized monograph.

14. Stourm, 4–5.

15. Miliukov, 499–500.

16. *PSZ*, 1724, N. 4546; 1731, N. 5781, art. 1–3, 33, 35; Miliukov, 445–47; Iasnopol'skii, 73–75; Dukes, 142; Kulomzin, "Gos. dokhody v Rossii," 341.

17. Iasnopol'skii, 69–70.

18. LeDonne, *Ruling Russia*, 246: fifty-four agencies did not answer, and the reports of another twenty had to be sent back because they had been damaged in transit.

19. The forms were published as annexes to *PSZ*, 1782. N. 15405, 1795, N. 17298.

20. *SIRIO* 28(1880):25–9.

21. Miliukov, 560.

22. Miliukov, 283–94.

23. Miliukov, 482–83; *PSZ*, 1719, N. 3303; Iasnopol'skii, 73. Troitskii traces the difficulties in drawing up a budget in "Iz istorii."

24. *PSZ*, 1765, N. 12472.

25. Report of Petr Panin to Catherine II (January 1765) in *SIRIO* 28 (1880): 106–13, here 109 ("if it is Your Majesty's intention" to place all state revenues in the administration of a single agency . . .).

26. *PSZ*, 1763, N. 11991 (vol. 44²), 59–71; 1796, N. 17494 (vol. 44²), 253–68; LeDonne, *Ruling Russia*, 234–36.

27. *PSZ*, 1807, N. 22477.

28. *Min. Finansov*, 165; *PSZ*, 1810, N. 24335; 1811, N. 24686, par. 244–46.

29. Miliukov, 82–85, 283–84, 482–83; *PSZ*, 1711, N. 2330.

30. *PSZ*, 1719, N. 3303, art. 4.

31. *PSZ*, 1719, N. 3303, art. 5.

32. LeDonne, *Ruling Russia*, 236–37, 243.

33. *Min. Finansov*, 165–66, 176–80, 183–84; *PSZ*, 1811, N. 24688, par. 159–61; Pokrovskii, 227–38, 240–42. A Financial Committee (*Komitet Finansov*) existed in 1806–1809 and 1822–1825. It was created to draw up the budget in especially difficult circumstances and it even discussed financial legislation in the 1820s. It was a restricted Committee of Ministers (finance, internal affairs, justice) with a few other members: *Min. Finansov*, 39, 46–47.

34. This appears quite clearly from the 1680 budget of various central agencies in Miliukov, 551–68.

35. Miliukov, 285.

36. *PSZ*, 1719, N. 3303, art. 2–3, 14–15.

37. For a detailed examination of how a departmental budget was carried out, see LeDonne, "Outlines. III.," 199–203.

38. *PSZ*, 1811, N. 24686, par. 196–99, 248–51; *Min. Finansov*, 172–73.

39. *PSZ*, 1725, N. 4787; LeDonne, *Ruling Russia*, 240–41, 263. For a similar situation in ancien régime France, see Stourm, 146–57.

40. *PSZ*, 1719, N. 3303, art. 10–11, 18.

41. LeDonne, *Ruling Russia*, 234–36.

42. *PSZ*, 1810, N. 24116, VII, and 24164; 1811, N. 24686, par. 188, 200–1, 252–56; Pokrovskii, 239–40; *Min. Finansov*, 166, 178, 183–85; Iasnopol'skii, 114–15.

43. Miliukov, 307–12, 444–45, 447–49.

44. Iaguzhinskii, 272; *PSZ*, 1727, N. 5017, art. 9; 1733, N. 6391.

45. For a valuable introduction see Normanton, 17, 22–23, 56–57.

46. *PSZ*, 1733, N. 6391; 1735, N. 6855; 1736, N. 6872, art. 3.

47. This is what Bezborodko, Catherine II's chief secretary, complained of in so many words: LeDonne, *Ruling Russia*, 244. The "internal audit" of the military establishment (Potemkin's empire) remained, however, considerably less efficient: see the general survey in *PSZ*, 1806, N. 22220.

48. *PSZ*, 1811, N. 24502; 1823, N. 29348; *Min. Finansov*, 166; Iasnopol'skii, 119.

49. McDaniel, 153.

50. LeDonne, *Ruling Russia*, 265.

Chapter 16

1. E. Williams, 219.

2. On his life and career see Hughes, passim.

3. Raeff, "Seventeenth-Century Europe," 614.

4. Cracraft, *Petrine Revolution*, 147: Peter's letter to Menshikov (1706): "From paradise, that is, St. Petersburg."

5. See above p. 87.

6. D. Volkov, "Materialy," 481; D. Volkov, "Zapiska;" "Prisoedinenie."

7. Paul Dukes (104–7) goes to the heart of the issue.

8. An error that a contemporary Soviet historian acknowledges at last: Pikul', 2:560.

9. Mikhail Volkonskii, the governor-general of Moscow in the 1770s, was one of those aware of the Petrine precedent: see his project of reform in Popov. On Catherine II's attitude toward Peter I see Riasanovsky, 35–37; and Rasmussen.

10. Dukes, 182.

11. The Crimean disaster "called into question the very bases of society and challenged the legitimacy of all authority figures, including the patriarchal father. Emancipation of the serfs in 1861 undermined his role further": B. Engel (see above, p. 315, n. 53), 55.

12. Cf. Solzhenitsyn's statement that "the Russian army perished because of *seniority*," cited in Pipes, 136. See also Raeff, "Russia's Autocracy," 282. Allan Wildman (245) quotes the following entry from the diary of a Russian officer after the February Revolution: "Between us [the officers and the soldiers] is an impassable gulf. No matter how well they get on with individual officers, in their eyes we are all *barins*. When we talk about the *narod*, we mean the nation; when they talk about it, they understand it as meaning only the democratic lower classes. In their eyes, what has occurred is not a political but a social revolution, which in their opinion they have won and we have lost."

BIBLIOGRAPHY

AE	Arkheograficheskii Ezhegodnik
AHR	American Historical Review
C-ASS	Canadian-American Slavic Studies
Chteniia	Chteniia v Imperatorskom Obshchestve Istorii I drevnostei Rossiiskikh
CMRS	Cahiers du monde russe et sovietique
CSS	Canadian Slavic Studies
DNR	Drevniaia i Novaia Rossiia
EAI	Ezhegodnik agrarnoi istorii
ES	Entsiklopedicheskii slovar (Brokaus i Efron)
FOG	Forschungen zur Osteuropäischen Geschichte
IV	Istoricheskii Vestnik
IZ	Istoricheskie Zapiski
JGO	Jahrbücher für Geschichte Osteuropas
RA	Russkii Arkhiv
RB	Russkoe Bogatstvo
RR	Russian Review
RS	Russkaia Starina
RV	Russkii Vestnik
SEER	Slavic and East European Review
SIRIO	Sbornik Imperatorskogo Russkogo Istoricheskogo Obshchestva
SR	Slavic Review
TsGADA	Tsentral'nyi Gosudarstvennyi Arkhiv Drevnikh Aktov
VE	Vestnik Evropy
VI	Voprosy Istorii
VIRGO	Vestnik Imperatorskogo russkogo geograficheskogo obshchestva
VMU-I	Vestnik Moskovskogo Universiteta—Seriia Istoriia
VP	Vestnik Prava
VS	Voennyi Sbornik
ZhMNP	Zhurnal Ministerstva Narodnogo Prosveshcheniia

Absoliutizm v Rossii (*XVII–XVIII vv.*). Moscow, 1964.

AGS-DZGO. Arkhiv Gosudarstvennogo Soveta, IV: 1810–1825 (SPb, 1874–1875, 1893): *chast'* 3 (1893): *Zhurnaly po delam Departamenta Zakonov po grazhdanskomu otdeleniiu* (*1818–1820gg.*)

Airapetian, I. "Stolniki kak odna iz kategorii feodal'noi aristokratii v 80-kh gg. XVII v."*VMU-I* 6 (1980): 67–80.

Aksenov, A. *Genealogiia Moskovskogo kupechestva XVIII veka.* Moscow, 1988.

For additional bibliography see LeDonne, *Ruling Russia*, 371–92.

Alexander I. "Reskript Aleksandra I grafu Rostopchinu po povodu pis'ma ego o slukhakh i bezporiadkakh v provintsii (1807)." *RS*, 1902, no. 3 (July–Sept.): 634.

Alexander, J. *Bubonic Plague in Early Modern Russia*. Baltimore, 1980.

———. *Catherine the Great: Life and Legend*. New York, 1989.

Alexandrov, V. *Sel'skaia obshchina v Rossii* (17-nachalo 19 vv.). Moscow, 1976.

Amburger, E. *Geschichte der Behördenorganisation Russlands von Peter dem Grossen bis 1917*. Leiden, 1966.

Anderson, P. *Lineages of the Absolutist State*. London, 1974.

Andolenko, S. *Histoire de l'armée russe*. Paris, 1967.

Andreevskii, I. *O namestnikakh, voevodakh i gubernatorakh*. SPb, 1864.

———. "Kantseliariia Konfiskatsii 1729–1780gg." *RS*, 1881, no. 2 (May–August): 167–86.

Anisimov, E. *Podatnaia reforma Petra I*. Leningrad, 1982.

———. *Rossiia v seredine XVIII veka*. Moscow, 1986.

Ardant, G. *Théorie sociologique de l'impôt*. 2 vols. Paris, 1965.

Aristotle. *Politics*. New York, 1943.

Aron, R. "Social Structure and the Ruling Class." *The British Journal of Sociology* 1 (1950): 1–16, 126–43.

———. *Clausewitz Philosopher of War*. Englewood Cliffs, N.J., 1985.

Atkin, M. *Russia and Iran 1780–1828*. Minneapolis, 1980.

Augustine, W. "Notes toward a Portrait of the Eighteenth-Century Russian Nobility." *CSS* 4, no. 3 (1970): 373–425.

Avtokratov, V. "Pervye komissariatskie organy russkoi reguliarnoi armii (1700–1710 gg.)." *IZ* 68 (1961): 163–88.

Baburin, D. *Ocherki po istorii Manufaktur-kollegii*. Moscow, 1939.

Bagramov, I. "Kratkii istoricheskii obzor otbyvaniia voennoi sluzhby nashim dvorianstvom i obrazovaniia gosudarstvennogo opolcheniia." *VS*, 1899, no. 10 (Oct.): 346–72; no. 11 (Nov.): 170–93; no. 12 (Dec.): 386–408.

Bantysh-Kamenskii, D. *Slovar' dostopamiatnykh liudei russkoi zemli*. 5 vols. Moscow, 1836; 3 vols. Moscow, 1847.

Baranov, P., ed. *Opis Vysochaishim ukazam i poveleniiam, khraniashchimsia v. S.-Peterburgskom Senatskom arkhive za XVIII vek*. 3 vols. SPb, 1872–1878.

Baron, S. "The Fate of the *gosti* in the Reign of Peter the Great." *CMRS* 14, no. 4 (1973): 488–512.

———. "Who Were the *Gosti*?" *California Slavic Studies* 7 (1973): 1–40.

Behrens, C. *Society, Government, and the Enlightenment*. New York, 1985.

Beik, W. *Absolutism and Society in Seventeenth-Century France*. Cambridge, Mass., 1985.

Beliaev, I. "Bytovye ocherki proshlogo: Voevodskaia goriachnost'." *IV*, 1906, no. 3 (July–Sept.): 869–83.

Belliustin, I. *Description of the Clergy in Rural Russia: The Memoir of a Nineteenth-Century Parish Priest*. G. Freeze, transl. and ed. Ithaca, 1985.

Beloff, M. *The Age of Absolutism 1660–1815*. New York, 1962.

Berdiaev, N. *Un nouveau moyen age*. Paris, 1930.

Berman, N. *Law and Revolution: The Formation of the Western Legal Tradition*. Cambridge, Mass., 1983.

Besancon, A. *Le tsarevich immolé*. Paris, 1967.

"Beschreibung der Russisch-kaiserlichen Armee." In *Nordische Miscelleneen*, edited by A. Hüpel. Vols. 5–6. Riga, 1782, 62–78.

Beskrovnyi, L. *Russkaia armiia i flot v XVIII veke (Ocherki)*. Moscow, 1958.

———. *Russkaia armiia i flot v XIX veke*. Moscow, 1971.

Beyrau, D. *Militär und Gesellschaft im Vorrevolutionären Russland*. Köln, 1984.

Black, J. *G.-F. Müller and the Imperial Russian Academy*. Montreal, 1986.

Blagovidov, F. "Kharakter preobrazovatel'noi deiatel'nosti Petra I." *IV*, 1895, no. 3 (July–Sept.): 81–111.

Blinov, I. "Nadzor za deiatel'nostiu gubernatorov." *VP*, 1902, no. 7 (Sept.): 37–77.

———. "Iz istorii dolzhnosti gubernatora posle uchrezhdeniia guberniiakh 1775 goda." *VP*, 1903, no. 4 (April): 120–70.

———. *Gubernatory: Istoriko-iuridicheskii ocherk*. SPb, 1905.

Blum, J. *Lord and Peasant in Russia*. Princeton, 1962.

Bodde, D., and Morris, C. *Law in Imperial China*. Philadelphia, 1973.

Bogoiavlenskii, S. *Prikaznye sud'i XVII veka*. Moscow-Leningrad, 1946.

Bogoslovskii, M. *Oblastnaia reforma Petra Velikogo: Provintsiia 1717–1727 gg*. Moscow, 1902.

———. *Petr I: Materialy dlia biografii*. 5 vols. Moscow, 1940–1948.

Bohac, R. "The Mir and the Military Draft." *SR* 47, no. 4 (1988): 652–66.

Bolotov, A. *Zhizn' i prikliucheniia Andreia Bolotova, pisannye samim dlia svoikh potomkov 1738–1795*. 4 vols. SPb, 1870–1873.

Brassey's Soviet and Communist Quotations. A Weeks, ed. Washington, D.C., 1987.

Brower, D. "Urbanization and Autocracy: Russian Urban Development in the First Half of the Nineteenth Century." *RR* 42, no. 4 (1983): 377–402.

Brown, A. "The Father of Russian Jurisprudence: The Legal Thought of S. E. Desnitskii." In Butler, 117–41.

Brown, P. "Early Modern Bureaucracy: The Evolution of the Chancellery System from Ivan III to Peter the Great, 1478–1717." PhD. diss., University of Chicago, 1978.

Brückner (Brikner), A. "Vskrytie chuzhikh pisem i depesh pri Ekaterine II." *RS*, 1873, no. 1 (Jan.–June): 75–84.

———. *Katarina die Zweite*. Berlin, 1883.

Buehler, A. *Public Finance*. New York, 1940.

"Bumagi Kurskogo gubernatora Kozhukhova." *RA*, 1909, no. 1:1–4, 52–60.

Burkolter, V. "The Patronage System: Theoretical Remarks." In *Social Strategies*, edited by P. Trappee. Vol. 4. Basel, 1976.

Burkolter-Trachsel, V. "Strukturelle Bedingungen für das Entstehen und die Transformation von Patronage." *Schweizerische Zeitschrift für Soziologie*, 1977, no. 1 (March): 3–30.

Buss, A. *Die Wirtschaftsethik des russisch-orthodoxen Christentums*. Heidelberg, 1989.

Butler, W., ed. *Russian Law: Historical and Political Perspectives*. Leyden, 1977.

B-va, S., "Obshchestvennye idealy v Ekaterinskuiu epokhu," *VE*, 1876 (Jan.): 49–83.

Carlyle, R., and Carlyle, A. *A History of Medieval Political Theory in the West*. 6 vols. London, 1962.

Castoriadis, C. "The Social Regime in Russia." *Telos*, 38 (1978–1979): 32–47.

Centers, R. *The Psychology of Social Class*. Princeton, 1949.

Ch. "Moskovskoe kupechestvo XVIII i XIX vekov (Genealogicheskie zametki)." *RA*, 1907, no. 4 (N. 9–12): 489–502.

Chechulin, N. *Ocherki po istorii russkikh finansov v tsarstvovanie Ekateriny II*. SPb, 1906.

Cherniavsky, M. *Tsar and People*. New Haven, 1961.

Chernov, A. *Vooruzhennye sily russkogo gosudarstva v XV–XVII vv*. Moscow, 1954.

———. "O klassifikatsii tsentral'nykh gosudarstvennykh uchrezhdenii XVI–XVII vv." *Istoricheskii Arkhiv*, 1958, no. 1:195–201.

"Cherty k kharakteristike russkogo obshchestva." *RS*, 1882, no. 1 (Jan.–March): 471–80.

Chester, R. *Inheritance, Wealth and Society*. Bloomington, 1982.

Chicherin, B. *Oblastnye uchrezhdeniia Rossii v XVII-m veke*. Moscow, 1856.

Clarkson, J. "Some Notes on Bureaucracy, Aristocracy, and Autocracy in Russia, 1500–1800." In Ritter, 187–200.

Confino, M. *Domaines et seigneurs en Russie vers la fin du XVIIIᵉ siècle*. Paris, 1963.

Coquin, F.-X. *La Sibérie: Peuplement et immigration paysanne au XIXᵉ siècle*. Paris, 1969.

———. *La Grande Commission Législative (1767–1768): Les cahiers de doléances urbains*. Paris-Louvain, 1972.

Coughlan, R. *Elizabeth and Catherine*. London, 1974.

Cracraft, J. *The Church Reform of Peter the Great*. London, 1971.

———. "Empire Versus Nation: Russian Political Theory under Peter I." *Harvard Ukrainian Studies* 10, no. 3 (1986): 524–41.

———. "Kliuchevskii on Peter the Great." *C-ASS* 20, nos. 3–4 (1986): 367–81.

———. "Opposition to Peter the Great." In *Imperial Russia 1700–1917: Essays in Honor of Marc Raeff*, edited by E. Mendelsohn and M. Shatz, 22–36. DeKalb, Il., 1988.

———. *The Petrine Revolution in Russian Architecture*. Chicago, 1988.

Crummey, R. "Peter and the Boiar Aristocracy 1689–1700." *C-ASS* 8, no. 2 (1974): 274–87.

———. "Russian Absolutism and the Nobility." *Journal of Modern History* 49, no. 3 (1977): 456–67.

———. *Aristocrats and Servitors: The Boyar Elite in Russia, 1613–1689*. Princeton, 1983.

Curtiss, M. *A Forgotten Empress: Anna Ivanovna and Her Era 1730–1740*. New York, 1974.

Danilov, N. *Istoricheskii ocherk razvitiia voennago upravleniia v Rossii (Stoletie voennogo ministerstva, I)*. SPb, 1902.

Davies, N. *God's Playground: A History of Poland*. 2 vols. New York, 1982.

Dela Fliz, "Pokhod velikoi armii v Rossii v 1812g." *RS*, 1892, no. 1 (Jan.–March): 51–68, 339–63, 575–604.

"Delo o bogoprotivnykh sborishchakh i deistvakh." *Chteniia* 1887, no. 2:1–89.

"Delo o E. Stoletove, Gofmeistere A. Elagine, Poruchike kniaze M. Belosel'skom, Mundshenke S. Nesterove i zhene ego, Marfe, 1736 goda." *Chteniia* 1864, no. 1 (Jan.–March): smes', 8–10.

Demidova, N. "Biurokratizatsiia gosudarstvennogo apparata absoliutizma v XVII–XVIII vv." In *Absoliutizm v Rossii*, 206–42.

———. "Gosudarstvennyi apparat Rossii v XVII veke." *IZ* 108 (1982): 109–54.

Derzhavin. *Zapiski* in *Sochineniia Derzhavina*. SPB, 1871 (Reprint, ORP, 1973).

Ditiatin, I. *Ustroistvo i upravlenie gorodov Rossii*. 2 vols. SPb & Iaroslavl, 1875–1877.

Ditz, T. *Property and Kinship: Inheritance in Early Connecticut 1750–1820*. Princeton, 1986.

Djilas, M. *The New Class*. New York, 1957.

Dmitriev, F. *Istoriia sudebnykh instantsii i grazhdanskogo appeliatsionnogo sudoproizvodstva ot Sudebnika do Uchrezhdeniia o Guberniiakh*. Moscow, 1859.

———. "Speranskii i ego gosudarstvennaia deiatel'nost." *RA*, 1868, 1527–656.

Dobrynin. "Istinnoe povestvovanie ili zhizn' G.I. Dobrynina im samim pisannaia (1752–1827)," *RS*, 1871, no. 1 (Jan.–June): 119–60, 247–71, 395–420, 562–604, 651–72; no. 2 (June–Dec.): 1–38, 97–153, 177–222, 305–78.

Dolgorukov, N. "Ob'iavlenie ot general'-ad'iuntanta kniazia Dolgorukova." *Chtennia*, 1864, I (Jan.–March): 200–202.

———. "Rech' general'-ad'iuntanta kniazia Dolgorukova." *Chteniia* 1864, I (Jan.–March), 1988–1999.

Dolgorukov, R. *Rossiiskaia rodoslovnaia kniga.* 4 vols. SPb, 1854–1857.

Donnert, E. *Politische Ideologie der russischen Gesellschaft zu Beginn der Regierungszeit Katharinas II.* Berlin, 1976.

"Donoshenie v Sibirskii Prikaz o d'iavol'skom navazhdenii." *Chteniia*, 1880, no. 4 (Oct.–Dec.): 1–14.

Druzhinin, N. *Gosudarstvennye krest'iane.* 2 vols. Moscow, 1946–1948.

Dubasov, I. "K istorii otzhivshogo chinovnichestva." *RA* 1878, no. 1:30–39.

Dubrovin, N. "Russkaia zhizn' v nachale XIX veka." *RS*, 1898, no. 4 (Oct.–Dec.): 481–516, 1899; no. 1 (Jan.–March): 3–38, 241–64, 539–69; no. 2 (April–June): 53–75, 481–508; 1904, no. 1 (Jan.–March): 5–28, 241–74, 481–515; no. 2 (April–June): 5–34, 241–64.

Dukes, P. *Catherine the Great and the Russian Nobility.* Cambridge, 1967.

———. *The Making of Russian Absolutism 1613–1681.* London, 1982.

Dunin, A. "'Neprilichnaia' kompaniia." *IV*, 1910, no. 3 (July–Sept.): 554–60.

Dvorianstvo i krepostnoi stroi Rossii XVI–XVIII vv. Sbornik statei posviashchennyi pamiati A.A. Novosel'skogo. Moscow, 1975.

Eeckaute, D. "Les brigands en Russie du XVIIᵉ au XIXᵉ siècle: mythe et réalité." *Revue d'histoire moderne et contemporaine* 12 (July–Sept. 1965): 161–202.

Efremov, P. "Stepan I. Sheshkovskii." *RS*, 1870, no. 2 (July–Dec.): 510–12.

Efremova, N. *Ministerstvo iustitsii rossiiskoi imperii 1802–1917 gg.* Moscow, 1983.

"Egor Stoletov, 1716–1736: Razskaz is istorii Tainoi Kantseliarii." *RS*, 1873, no. 2 (July–Dec.): 1–27.

El'iashevich, V. *Istoriia prava pozemel'noi sobstvennosti v Rossii.* 2 vols. Paris, 1948–1951.

Epifanov, P. "Komaritskie burmistry pri Petre I." *VMU*, 1956, no. 2:157–61.

Eroshkin, N. *Krepostnicheskoe samoderzhavie i ego politicheskie instituty.* Moscow, 1981.

Esipov, G. "Gosudarevo delo." *DNR*. 1880, no. 1 (Jan.–April): 770–92.

Esmein, A. *A History of Continental Criminal Procedure, with special reference to France.* New York, 1968 (Kelley reprint).

Esper, Th. "The Odnodvortsy and the Russian Nobility." *SEER*, 45, no. 104 (1967): 124–34.

Fel'dshtein, G. *Glavnye techeniia v istorii nauki ugolovnogo prava v Rossii.* Iaroslavl', 1909.

Fenster, A. *Adel und Ökonomie im vorindustriellen Russland*, Wiesbaden, 1983.

Field, D. *The End of Serfdom: Nobility and Bureaucracy in Russia, 1855–1861.* Cambridge, Mass., 1976.

"Filaret pod tsenzuroiu (1824)." *RA*, 1905, no. 1 (Jan.–April): 306–11.

Firsov, N. *Pravitel'stvo i obshchestvo v ikh otnosheniiakh k vneshnei torgovle Rossii v tsarstvovanie imp. Ekateriny II.* Kazan, 1902.

Flynn, J. "'Russia's University Question': Origin to Great Reforms 1802–1863." *History of Universities* 7 (1988): 1–35.

———. *The University Reform of Tsar Alexander I 1803–1835.* Washington, D.C., 1988.

Freeze, G. *The Russian Levites: Parish Clergy in the Eighteenth Century.* Cambridge, Mass., 1977.

————. "Handmaiden of the State? The Church in Imperial Russia Reconsidered." *Journal of Ecclesiastical History*, 36:1 (1985), 82–102.

————. "The Soslovie (Estate) Paradigm and Russian Social History." *American Historical Review*, 91:1 (1986), 11–36.

Gagliardo, J. *Enlightened Despotism*. New York, 1967.

————. *Reich and Nation: The Holy Roman Empire's Idea and Reality 1763–1806*. Bloomington, 1980.

Galbraith, J. *The Anatomy of Power*. Boston, 1983.

Garrard, J., ed. *The Eighteenth Century in Russia*. Oxford, 1973.

Garshin, E. "Odin iz russkikh grakhkhov proshlogo stoletiia." *IV*, 1890, no. 3 (July–Sept.): 621–28.

Gettun. "Zapiski V. N. Gettuna (1771–1815)." *IV* 1880, no. 1 (Jan.–April): 26–27, 253–96, 473–504.

Geyer, D. "Der Aufgeklärte Absolutismus in Russland." *JGO* 30, no. 2 (1982): 176–89.

Gille, B. *Histoire économique et sociale de la Russie du moyen-âge au vingtième siècle*. Paris, 1949.

Glinka, N. *Derzhavin v Peterburge*. Leningrad, 1985.

Glinoetskii, N. "Russkii general'nyi shtab v tsarstvovanie imp. Ekateriny II." *VS*, 1872, no. 1 (Jan.): 5–64; no. 2 (Feb.): 157–94.

————. "Russkii general'nyi shtab v tsarstvovanie imp. Aleksandra I." *VS*, 1874, no. 10 (Oct.): 187–250; no. 11 (Nov.): 5–43; no. 12 (Dec.): 189–272.

Gloriantov, V. "Potomstvennye dvoriane kantseliarskogo proiskhozhdeniia." *RA*, 1905, no. 1 (Jan.–April): 662–74.

Godard, Ch. *Les pouvoirs des intendants sous Louis XIV*. Geneva, 1974.

Gofshtetter, I. "Russkie chinovniki." *IV*, 1897, no. 3 (July–Sept.): 222–29.

Golikova, N. *Politicheskie protsessy pri Petre I*. Moscow, 1957.

————. "Organy politseiskogo syska i ikh razvitie v XVII–XVIIIvv." In *Absoliutizm v Rossii*, 243–280.

Golitsyn, N. "Neobyknovennyi ispravnik." *RS*, 1890, no. 4 (Oct.–Dec.): 368–74.

Goroda feodal'noi Rossii: Sbornik statei pamiati N. V. Ustiugova. Moscow, 1966.

"Gorodovye dvoriane i deti boiarskie." *ES* 9 (1893): 314.

"Gosudarstvennye sanovniki upravliavshie voennoi chast'iu v Rossii s 1701 goda." *VS*, 1866, no. 9 (Sept.): 3–24.

Gosudarstvennyi Sovet 1801–1901. SPb, 1901.

Got'e, Iu. "Iz istorii peredvizheniia naseleniia v XVIII v." *Chteniia*, 1980, no. 1:3–26.

————. "Otdelenie sudebnoi chasti ot administrativnoi." In *Sudebnaia Reforma*, 181–204.

————. *Istoriia oblastnogo upravleniia v Rossii ot Petra I do Ekaterniy II*. 2 vols. Moscow, 1913–1941.

————. *Zamoskovnyi krai v 17 veke*. 2d ed. Moscow, 1937.

Gradovskii, A. *Vysshaia administratsiia Rossii XVIII st. i general-prokurory* in *Sobranie Sochinenii*. Vol. 1. (SPb, 1899), 37–297.

Gribovskii, V. *Materialy dlia istorii vysshego suda i nadzora v pervuiu polovinu tsarstvovaniia imp Ekateriny Vtoroi*. SPb, 1901.

Griffiths, D. "Catherine II: The Republican Empress." *JGO* 21, no. 3 (1973): 323–44.

Grigor'ev, V. *Reforma mestnogo upravleniia pri Ekaterine II*. SPb, 1910.

Grimstead, P. *The Foreign Ministers of Alexander I: Political Attitudes and the Conduct of Russian Diplomacy 1801–1825*. Berkeley, 1969.

"Gubernator dobrogo starogo vremeni." *RS*, 1907, no. 3 (July–Sept.): 188–96.

Hellie, R. *Enserfment and Military Change in Muscovy*. Chicago, 1971.

————. "The Structure of Modern Russian History: Toward a Dynamic Model." *Russian History* 4, no. 1 (1977): 1–22.

————. *Slavery in Russia 1450–1725.* Chicago, 1982.

————. transl. *The Muscovite Law Code (Ulozhenie) of 1649.* Part 1: Text and Translation. Irvine, Calif., 1988.

Hildermeier, M. *Bürgertum und Stadt in Russland 1760–1870.* Koln, 1986.

Hittle, J. *The Service City: State and Townsmen in Russia 1600–1800.* Cambridge, Mass., 1979.

Hoch, S. *Serfdom and Social Control in Russia: Petrovskoe, a Village in Tambov.* Chicago, 1986.

Hollingsworth, B. "A. P. Kunitsyn and the Social Movement in Russia under Alexander I." *SEER* 43 (Dec. 1964): 115–29.

Hudson, H. "Urban Estate Engineering in Eighteenth-Century Russia: Catherine the Great and the Elusive 'meshchanstvo'." *C-ASS* 18, no. 4 (1984): 393–410.

Huebner, R. *A History of German Public Law.* Boston, 1918 (Kelley reprint, 1968).

Hughes, L. *Russia and the West: The Life of a Seventeenth-Century Westernizer, Prince Vasily Vasil'evich Golitsyn.* Newtonville, Mass, 1984.

Iaguzhinskii. "Zapiska P. I. Iaguzhinskogo o sostoianii Rossii." *Chteniia*, 1860, no. 4 (Oct.–Dec.): 269–73.

Iasnopol'skii, L. *Ocherki russkogo biudzhetnogo prava.* Vol. 1 Moscow, 1912.

Ikonomov, V. *Nakanune reform Petra Velikogo.* Moscow, 1903.

Indova, E. *Dvortsovoe khoziaistvo v Rossii: Pervaia polovina XVIII veka.* Moscow, 1964.

————. "K voprosu o dvorianskoi sobstvennosti v Rossii v pozdnii feodal'noi period." In *Dvorianstvo*, 272–92.

Istoricheskii obzor deiatel'nosti Komiteta Ministrov. S. Seredonin, ed. Vol. 1 SPb, 1902.

Istoriia Pravitel'stvennogo Senata za dvesti let, 1711–1911. 5 vols. SPb, 1911.

Iudin, P. "Zhaloba Saratovskikh krest'ian na zemskii sud." *RA*, 1908, no. 3 (N. 9–12): 215–17.

Iukht, A. *Gosudarstvennaia deiatel'nost V. N. Tatishcheva v 20-kh-nachale 30-kh godov 18 veka.* Moscow, 1985.

Iuzefovich, M. "O znachenii lichnosti u nas i na Zapade." *Starina i Novizna* 11 (1911): 7–33.

Ivanov, P. "Senat pri Petre Velikom." *Zhurnal Ministerstva Iustitsii*, 1859 no. 1 (July–Sept.): 34–70.

————. "Sudnoe delo nad DTS baronom Shafirom i ober-prokurorom Senata Skorniakovym-Pisarevym." *Zhurnal Ministerstva Iustitsii*, 1859, no. 1 (July–Sept.): 3–62.

————. *Opyt biografii general-prokurorov i ministrov iustitsii.* SPb, 1863.

"Iz perepiski imp. Aleksandra Pavlovicha s V. S. Popovym." *RA*, 1864, 319–21.

"Iz zapisok barona (v posledstvii grafa) M. A. Korfa." *RS* 1899, no. 2 (April–June): 371–95, 511–42.

Jacob. "M. M. Speranskii as Viewed in L. N. Jacob's Unpublished Autobiography." Translated and edited by D. and K. Griffiths, with an introduction by E. Winter. *C-ASS* 9, no. 4 (1975): 481–541.

Jones, R. "Urban Planning and the Development of Provincial Towns in Russia, 1762–1796." In Garrard, 321–44.

Kabuzan, V. *Narodonaselenie Rossii v XVIII-pervoi polovine XIX veka.* Moscow, 1963.

————. *Izmeneniia v razmeshchenii naseleniia Rossii v 18-pervoi polovine 19 v.* Moscow, 1971.

Kabuzan, V., and Troitskii, S. "Izmeneniia v chislennosti, udel'nom vese i razmeshchenii dvorianstva v Rossii v 1782–1858gg." *Istoriia SSSR*, 1971, no. 4 (July–August): 153–69.

Kahan, A. "The Costs of 'Westernization' in Russia: The Gentry and the Economy in the Eighteenth Century." *SR* 25, no. 1 (1966): 40–66.

————. *The Plow, the Hammer and the Knout: An Economic History of Eighteenth-Century Russia.* Chicago, 1985.

Kaiser, D. *The Growth of the Law in Medieval Russia.* Princeton, 1980.

Kalachov, N. *Arkhiv istoricheskikh i parkticheskikh svedenii otnosiashchikhsia do Rossii.* 4 vols., SPb, 1859.

Kankrin, E. "Kratkoe obozrenie rossiiskikh finansov (1838)." *SIRIO* 31 (1881): 3–161.

Karamzin, N. *Memoir on Ancient and Modern Russia.* A translation and analysis by R. Pipes. Cambridge, Mass., 1959.

Karazin, V. "Mnenie odnogo ukrainskogo pomeshchika, vyrazhennoe posle besedy s svoimi sobratiiami o ukaze 23-go maia, 1816 goda, i ob estliandskikh postanovleniiakh." *Chteniia*, 1860, no. 2 (April–June): 218–27.

"V. N. Karazin. Osnovanie Khar'kovskogo universiteta, 1803–1804 gg." *RS*, 1875, no. 3 (Sept.–Oct.): 268–79.

Kartashev, A. "Pravoslavie i Rossiia." In *Pravoslavie v zhizni*, edited by S. Verkhovskii. New York, 1953.

Keenan, E. "Muscovite Political Folkways." *RR* 45, no. 2 (1986): 115–81.

Keep, J. "The Secret Chancery, the Guards and the Dynastic Crisis of 1740–1741." *FOG* 25 (1978): 169–93.

————. "L'élitisme militaire en Russie à la fin du XVIIIe siècle." *Slovo* (Paris), 3 (1980): 165–76.

————. "The Military Style of the Romanov Rulers." *War and Society* 1, no. 2 (1983): 61–84.

————. *Soldiers of the Tsar: Army and Society in Russia 1462–1874.* Oxford, 1985.

————. "Feeding the Troops: Russian Army Supply Policies during the Seven Years' War." *Canadian Slavonic Papers* 29, no. 1 (1987): 24–43.

Keller, S. *Beyond the Ruling Class: Strategic Elites in Modern Society.* New York, 1963.

Kirilov, I. *Tsvetushchee sostoianie vserossiiskogo gosudarstva.* Moscow, 1977 (reprint).

Kizevetter, A. *Posadskaia obshchina v Rossii XVIII stoletiia.* Moscow, 1903.

Kliuchevskii, V. *Boiarskaia duma dreveni Rusi.* 5th ed. Petrograd, 1919.

————. *Kurs russkoi istorii.* 4 vols. Moscow, 1937.

Klochkov, M. "Dvorianskoe samoupravlenie v tsarstvovanie Pavla I." *ZhMNP*, 1912 (Nov.–Dec.): 329–75.

————. *Ocherki pravitel'stvennoi deiatel'nosti vremeni Pavla I.* Petrograd, 1916.

Klokman, Iu. *Sotsial'no-ekonomicheskaia istoriia russkogo goroda.* Moscow, 1967.

"Kniaz'ia Dolgorukovy v 1730–1740gg. Zametka." *RS*, 1878, no. 3 (Sept.–Dec.): 735–46.

Kochubei (1806). "Zapiska grafa V. P. Kochubeia ob uchrezhdenii ministerstv, March 1806." *SIRIO* 90 (1894): 199–211.

————. (1814). "Zapiska grafa V. P. Kochubeia o polozhenii Imperii i o merakh k prekrashcheniiu bezporiadkov i vvedenii luchshogo ustroistva v raznye otrasli, pravitel'stva sostavliaiushchiia, Dec. 1814." *SIRIO* 90 (1894): 5–26.

Kolchin, P. *Unfree Labor: American Slavery and Russian Serfdom.* Cambridge, Mass., 1987.

Komarovskii. *Zapiski grafa E. F. Komarovskogo.* SPb, 1914.

Korf, S. "Ocherk istoricheskogo razvitiia gubernskoi dolzhnosti v Rossii." *VP*, 1901, no. 9 (Nov.): 130–48.

Korol'kov, M. "Chertovye litery (Iz del Tainoi Kantseliarii)." *IV*, 1907, no. 3 (July–Sept.): 172–79.

Korsakov, A. "Dva prozhetera." *IV*, 1892, no. 4 (Oct.–Dec.): 538–44.

Korsakov, D. "Artemii Petrovich Volynskii. Biograficheskii ocherk." *DNR*, 1876, no. 1 (Jan.–April): 45–60; 1877, no. 1 (Jan.–April): 84–96, 289–302, 377–85; 1877, no. 2 (May–August): 23–38, 97–114, 214–34, 277–95, no. 3 (Sept.–Dec.): 224–54.

———. "Sud nad kniazem D.M. Golitsynym (1736–1737)." *DNR*, 1879, no. 3 (Oct.–Dec.): 20–62.

———. *Votsarenie imperatritsy Anny Ioannovny.* Kazan, 1880.

Kotoshikhin, G. *O Rossii v tsarstvovanie Alekseia Mikhailovicha.* SPb, 1906.

Krest'ianskaia voina 1773–1775gg. v Rossii: Dokumenty iz sobranii gosudarstvennogo istoricheskogo muzeia. Moscow, 1973.

Kulakova, L., et al. *Radishchev v Peterburge.* Leningrad, 1976.

Kulomzin, A. "Gosudarstvennye dokhody i raskhody v Rossii XVIII-ego stoletiia." *VE* 1869, no. 3 (May–June): 336–51.

———. "Gosudarstvennye dokhody i raskhody v tsarstvovanie Ekateriny II." *SIRIO* 5 (1870): 219–74; 6 (1871): 219–304.

———. ed. "Finansovye dokumenty tsarstvovaniia imp. Aleksandra I." *SIRIO* 45 (1885): 1–623.

Kurmacheva, M. *Krepostnaia intelligentsiia Rossii: Vtoraia polovina XVIII-nachalo XIX veka.* Moscow, 1983.

Langeron. "Russkaia armiia v god smerti Ekateriny II." *RS*, 1895, no. 1 (Jan.–June): 147–66; (March): 145–77; (April); 185–202 (May).

Lebedev, A. "Primenenie nakazanii v srede dukhovenstva i mirian Belgorodskoi eparkhii v XVIII veke." *RS*, 1892, no. 1 (Jan.–March): 331–38, 696.

Lebedev, V. "Piteinoe delo." *Zhurnal Iuridicheskogo Obshchestva*, 1898, no. 9 (Nov.): 1–46.

LeDonne, J. "Criminal Investigations before the Great Reform." *Russian History* 1, no. 2 (1974): 101–18.

———. "Indirect Taxes in Catherine's Russia. I. The Salt Code of 1781." *JGO* 23, no. 2 (1975): 161–90; II. "The Liquor Monopoly," Ibid., 24, no. 2 (1976): 173–207.

———. "The Evolution of the Governor's Office 1727–1764." *C-ASS* 12, no. 1 (1978): 86–115.

———. "The Territorial Reform of the Russian Empire 1775–1796. I. Central Russia 1775–1784." *CMRS* 23, no. 2 (1982): 147–85; II. "The Borderlands 1777–1796." Ibid., 24, no. 4 (1983): 411–57.

———. "Outlines of Russian Military Administration 1762–1796. I. Troop Strength and Deployment." *JGO* 31, no. 3 (1983): 321–47; II. "The High Command." Ibid., 33, no. 2 (1985): 175–204; III. "Military Finance: The Commissary Budget of 1780." Ibid., 34, no. 2 (1986): 188–214.

———. *Ruling Russia: Politics and Administration in the Age of Absolutism 1762–1796.* Princeton, 1984.

———. "Local Politics in Catherine's Russia: The Gorokhov Case." *CMRS* 27, no. 2 (1986): 153–72.

————. "Ruling Families in the Russian Political Order 1689–1825." *CMRS* 28, nos. 3/ 4 (1987): 233–322.

Lemke, M. "Propushchennyi iubilei." *Russkaia Mysl'*, 1904, no. 11 (Nov.): 34–62.

Lentin, A. *Russia in the Eighteenth Century.* New York, 1973.

Leshkov, V. "Imushchestvennye i lichnye prava po ukazam Petra Velikogo." *RV*, 1861 (Dec.): 393–415.

Liashchenko, P. *History of the National Economy of Russia to the 1917 Revolution.* New York, 1949.

Likhachev, D. *Chelovek v literature drevnei Rusi.* Moscow, 1958.

Lincoln, W. *In The Vanguard of Reform: Russia's Enlightened Bureaucrats 1825–1861.* DeKalb, Ill., 1982.

Lipinskii, M. "K istorii russkogo ugolovnogo prava XVIII v." *Zhurnal grazhdanskogo i ugolovnogo prava,* 1885 (Dec.): 1–54.

Litvak, B. "Pomeshchich'ie instruktsii kak istochnik po istorii votchinnogo deloproizvodstva." *AE za* 1975 g. (Moscow, 1976), 70–81.

Lobanov-Rostovskii, A. *Russkaia rodoslovnaia kniga.* SPb, 1st ed., 3 vols., SPb, 1873–1878; 2d ed., 2 vols., 1895.

Lobanov-Rostovskii, I. "Mnenie kniazia I. A. Lobanov-Rostovskogo." *RA*, 1871, 1914–19.

Lodyzhenskii, K. *Istoriia russkogo tamozhennogo tarifa.* SPb, 1886.

LoGatto, E. *Histoire de la littérature russe des origines à nos jours.* Bruges, 1965.

Lopukhin, I. *Zapiski.* London, 1860. (ORP reprint, Newtonville, Mass., 1976).

Luchitskii, I. "Sekretnoe delo ob odnoi gazetnoi avizii, 1732." *IV*, 1889, no. 3 (July–Sept.): 577–87.

McDanile, T. *Autocracy, Capitalism and Revolution in Russia.* Berkeley, 1988.

McGrew, R. "The Politics of Absolutism: Paul I and the Bank of Assistance for the Nobility." *C-ASS* 7, no. 1 (1973): 15–38.

McNeill, W. "The Eccentricity of Wheels, or Eurasian Transportation in Historical Perspective." *AHR* 92, no. 5 (1987): 1111–26.

Madariaga, I. *Russia in the Age of Catherine the Great.* New Haven, 1981.

————. "Catherine II and the Serfs: A Reconsideration of Some Problems." *SEER*, 52, no. 126 (1974), 34–62.

Maier, H. *Die ältere deutsche Staats- und Verfassungslehre (Polizeiwissenschaft.* Neuwied, 1966.

Mal'shinskii, A. "Vysshaia politsiia pri imperatore Aleksandra I." *IV*, 1889, no. 1 (Jan.–March): 165–79.

Man'kov, A. "K istorii vyrabotki zakonodatel'stva o krest'ianakh na rubezhe XVII i XVIII vekov." *AE za* 1958 (Moscow, 1960), 350–86.

————. "Krepostnoe zakonodatel'stvo v Rossii pervoi chetverti XVIII v." *EAI*, 1971, 146–55.

————. *Ulozhenie 1649 goda: Kodeks feodal'nogo prava Rossii.* Leningrad, 1980.

Manstein, C. von. *Contemporary Memoirs of Russia From the Year 1727 to 1744.* London, 1968.

Mansurov, A. "Okhrana rekruta." *RS*, 1890, no. 4 (Oct.–Dec.): 352.

————. "Iz provintsial'noi zhizni proshlogo stoletiia." *RA*, 1895, no. 3 (Sept.–Dec.): 319–23.

Marker, G. *Publishing, Printing, and the Origin of Intellectual Life in Russia, 1700–1800.* Princeton, 1985.

Martynov, A. "Kleimenaia bumaga." *RA*, 1879, no. 2 (May–August): 488–89.

Mayer, A. *The Persistence of the Old Regime: Europe to the Great War.* New York, 1981.

Mayer, K., and Buckley, W. *Class and Society.* 3d ed. New York, 1969.

Meehan-Waters, B. "The Muscovite Noble Origins of the Russians in the Generalitet of 1730." *CMRS* 12, nos. 1/2 (1971): 28–75.

———. *Autocracy and Aristocracy: The Russian Service Elite of 1730.* New Brunswick, N.J., 1982.

Mertvago. "Zapiski D. B. Mertvago, 1760–1824." *RA*, 1867, 1–335.

Meshkov. "Zapiski Ivan Ivanovich Meshkova 1767–1832." *RA*, 1905, no. 2 (vyp. 5–8), 177–242.

Metternich. "Imperator Aleksander I." *IV*, 1880, no. 1 (Jan.–April): 168–80.

Miesatseslov s rospis'iu chinovnykh osob v gosudarstve. SPb, 1809, 1823.

Miliukov, P. *Gosudarstvennoe khoziaistvo Rossii v 1. chetverti 18 stoletiia i reforma Petra Velikogo.* 2d ed. SPb, 1905.

Milov, L. *Issledovanie ob 'ekonomicheskikh primechaniiakh' k general'nomu mezhevaniiu.* Moscow, 1965.

Minikh (Münnich). *Zapiski fel'dmarshala grafa Minikha.* SPb, 1874.

Ministerstvo Finansov 1802–1902. 2 vols. SPb, 1902.

"Mnenie Gosudarstvennogo Soveta o meste nakazaniia prestupnikov." *RS*, 1904, no. 1 (Jan.–March): 408.

"Mnenie o osvobozhdenii krest'ian," *RA*, 1870, 288–291.

Montesquieu. *The Spirit of the Laws.* New York, 1949.

Morozov, P. "Moe znakomstvo s M. L. Magnitskim." *RA*, 1875, no. 3:241–50.

Morrison, D. "'Trading Peasants' and Urbanization in Eighteenth-Century Russia. The Central Industrial Region." Ph.D diss., Columbia University, 1981.

Mosca, G., *The Ruling Class*, A. Livingston ed., New York, 1939.

"Moskva 1785 goda." *Sovietskie arkhivy*, 1968, no. 5: 63–65.

Mousnier, R. *Peasant Uprisings in Seventeenth-Century France, Russia and China.* New York, 1970.

———. *Social Hierarchies 1450 to the Present.* London, 1973.

Muller, V., ed. *The Spiritual Regulation of Peter the Great.* Seattle, 1972.

Murav'ev, A. "Iz materialov po istorii klassovoi bor'by v russkom gorode nachala XVIII veka." *AE za 1959* (Moscow, 1960), 157–63.

———. "Iz istorii obrazovaniia finansovogo apparata v Rossii v 20-kh godakh XVIII veka. *AE za 1962* (Moscow, 1963), 254–59.

Murav'ev-Apostol'. "Mnenie senatora Murav'eva-Apostola po delu DSS Popova o tsenzure." *Chteniia*, 1959, no. 4 (Oct.–Dec.): 37–42.

"Mysli o uspekh i tochnosti v sudoproizvodstve i o umerenii nakazanii za viny i prestupleniia." *Chteniia*, 1959, no. 2:134–52.

Narezhnyi, V. *Sochineniia v dvukh tomakh.* Moscow, 1983.

Neubacher, H. *Car und Selbstherrscher: Beiträge zur Geschichte der Autokratie in Russland.* Wiesbaden, 1964.

Neverov, Ia. "Stranitsa iz istorii krepostnogo prava 1810–1826." *RS*, 1883, no. 4 (Oct.–Dec.): 429–46.

Nikoleva, M. "Cherty starinnogo dvorianskogo byta." *RA*, 1893, no. 3 (Sept.–Dec.): 107–20, 129–96.

Nikolai Mikhailovich. *Graf Pavel Aleksandrovich Stroganov (1774–1817).* 3 vols. SPb, 1903.

Normanton, E. *The Accountability and Audit of Governments: A Comparative Study.* Manchester, 1966.

Ocherki istorii SSSR. Period feodalizma. XVII v. Moscow, 1955.

Ogloblin, N. "Bytovye cherty nachala XVIII veka." *Chteniia*, 1904, no. 1 smes': 1–21.

Oliva, L. *Russia in the Era of Peter the Great.* Englewood Cliffs, N.J., 1969.
Olivier, D. *Elisabeth de Russie.* Paris, 1962.
Opis' del arkhiva Vladimirskogo gubernskogo upravleniia. Vladimir, 1902.
Orlovsky, D. *The Limits of Reform: The Ministry of Internal Affairs in Imperial Russia 1802–1881.* Cambridge, Mass., 1981.
———. "Political Clientelism in Russia: The Historical Perspective." In Rigby, Harasymiu, 174–99.
"O sostoianii Rossii pri Ekaterine Velikoi. Vopros Diderota i otvety Ekateriny II (1773)." *RA*, 1880, no. 3 (Sept.–Dec.): 1–29.
Papmehl, K. *Freedom of Expression in Eighteenth-Century Russia.* The Hague, 1971.
Passenans, P. *La Russie et l'esclavage, dans leurs rapports avec la civilisation européenne.* Paris, 1822 (reprint, 2 vols. in 1, Leipzig: Zentral-antiquariat, 1977).
Pavlenko, N. *Istoriia metallurgii v Rossii XVIII veka.* Moscow, 1962.
Pavlov-Sil'vanskii, N. *Gosudarevy sluzhilye liudi: Proiskhozhdenie russkogo dvorianstva.* SPb, 1898.
———. "Prashchur grafa L'va Tolstogo. Graf P. A. Tolstoi." *IV*, 1905, no. 2 (April–May): 835–70.
Pazhitnov, K. "Remeslennoe ustroistvo v Moskovskoi Rusi i reforma Petra." *IZ*, no. 8 (1940): 163–73.
Peterson, C. *Peter the Great's Administrative and Judicial Reforms.* Stockholm, 1979.
Petrovskii, S. *O Senate v tsarstvovanie Petra Velikogo.* Moscow, 1876.
Pikul', V. *Slovo i delo* in *Izbrannye proizvedeniia v 4-kh tomakh.* 2 vols. Moscow, 1988.
Pintner, W. *Russian Economic Policy under Nicholas I.* Ithaca, N.Y., 1967.
Pintner, W., and Rowney, D. *Russian Officialdom: The Bureaucratization of Russian Society from the Seventeenth to the Twentieth Century.* Chapel Hill, N.C., 1980.
———. "The Burden of Defense in Imperial Russia 1725–1914." *RR* 43, no 3 (1984): 231–59.
Pipes, R. *Russia under the Old Regime.* New York, 1974.
"Pis'ma imp. Aleksandra Pavlovicha k I. I. Bakhtinu (1802)." *RS*, 1870, no. 1 (Jan.–June): 451–54.
"Pis'ma imp. Ekateriny Velikoi k fel'dmarshalu grafu P. S. Saltykovu 1762–1771." *RA*, 1886, no. 3:5–105.
"Pis'mo gen.-prokurora kniazia A. A. Viazemskogo." *RA*, 1889, no. 1 (Jan.–April): 397.
"Pis'mo sel'skogo sviashchennika." *RA*, 1898, no. II (N. 5–8): 172–76.
Plavsic, B. "Seventeenth-Century Chanceries and their Staffs." In Pintner and Rowney, 19–45.
"Pokazanie kn. I. A. Dolgorukova i mnenie o tom Tainoi Kantseliarii." *Chteniia*, 1864, no. 1 (Jan.–March): smes', 1–7.
Pokrovskii, S. *Ministerskaia vlast' v Rossii.* Iaroslavl', 1906.
Popov, A. "Proekt kn. M. N. Volkonskogo o luchshem uchrezhdenii sudebnykh mest, podannyi imperatritse Ekaterine II v 1775 g." *SIRIO* 5 (1870): 122–27.
"Posadskie liudi." *ES* 24^A (1898): 656–57.
"Poveleniia imperators Aleksandra I. Ob obrashchenii s krest'ianami (1802)." *RS*, 1872, no. 2 (July–Dec.): 281–83.
Prigara, A. "Opyt istorii sostoianiia gorodskikh obyvatelei pri Petre Velikom." *ZhMNP*, 1867, Sept., 671–735, Oct., 82–114, Nov., 578–616.
Prisoedinenie Prussi k. Rossii. Proekt 1760g." *RS*, 1873, no. 1 (Jan.–June) 705–716.
"Proekt o ustroistve voennoi politsii pri gvardeiskom korpuse 1821g." *RS*, 1882, no. 1 (Jan.–March): 217–19.

Prokof'eva, L. *Krest'ianskaia obshchina v Rossii vo vtoroi polovine XVIII-pervoi polovine XIX veka.* Leningrad, 1981.

Przhetslavskii, O. "Vospominaniia (1818–1831)." *RS*, 1874, no. 3 (Sept.–Dec.): 451–77.

———. "Alekandr Semenovich Shishkov." *RS*, 1875, no. 2 (May–August): 383–402.

Puparev, A. "Rasprava s dvorovym chelovekom 1818–1819gg." *RS*, 1871, no. 2 (July–Dec.): 416–19.

Rabinovich, M. "Odnodvortsy v pervoi polovine XVIII v." *EAI*, 1971, 137–145.

———. "Sotsial'noe proiskhozhednie i imushchestvennoe polozhenie ofitserov reguliarnoi russkoi armii v kontse Severnoi voiny." In *Rossiia v period reform Petra I.* Moscow, 1973, 133–71.

Raeff, M. *Michael Speransky: Stateman of Imperial Russia 1772–1839.* The Hague, 1957.

———. *Imperial Russia 1682–1825.* New York, 1971.

———. "*Iz pod glyb* and the History of Russian Social Thought." *RR* 34, no. 4 (1975): 476–88.

———. "Russia's Autocracy and Paradoxes of Modernization." *Ost-West Begegnung in Österreich. Festschrift für E. Winter zum 80. Geburtstag.* Wien, 1976, 275–83.

———. "Codification et Droit en Russie impériale." *CMRS* 20, no. 1 (1979): 5–13.

———. *Comprendre l'ancien régime russe.* Paris, 1982. English edition: *Understanding Imperial Russia: State and Society in the Old Regime,* translated by A Goldhammer. New York, 1984.

———. "Seventeenth-Century Europe in Eighteenth-Century Russia?" *SR* 41, no. 4 (1982): 611–19.

———. *The Well-Ordered Police State: Social and Institutional Change through Law in the Germanies and Russia 1600–1800.* New Haven, 1983.

Ransel, D. *The Politics of Catherinian Russia: The Panin Party,* New Haven, 1975.

———. *Mothers of Misery: Child Abandonment in Russia.* Princeton, 1988.

———. ed. *The Family in Imperial Russia.* Urbana, Ill., 1978.

Rasmussen, K. "Catherine II and the Image of Peter I." *SR* 37, no. 1 (1978): 51–69.

"Razgovor uezdnykh dvorian o vybore sud'i." *RA*, 1902, no. 2:489–91.

"Razskazy iz prezhnei sudebnoi praktiki." *RS*, 1874, no. 1 (Jan.–April): 191–97, 777–80; no. 2 (May–August): 628–31.

Reisner, M. "Dukhovnaia politsiia v russkom tserkovnom stroe." *RB*, 1907, no. 9 (Sept.): 132–65; no. 11 (Nov.): 107–37.

Riabinin, D. "Kniaginia A. V. Kozlovskaia." *RS*, 1874, no. 1 (Jan.–April): 383–90.

Riasanovsky, N. *The Image of Peter the Great in Russian History and Thought.* New York, 1985.

Rice, T. *Elizabeth: Empress of Russia.* New York, 1970.

Rieber, A. *Merchants and Entrepreneurs in Imperial Russia.* Chapel Hill, N.C., 1982.

Rigby, T., and Harasymiw, B., ed. *Leadership Selection and Patron-Client Relations in the USSR and Yugoslavia.* London, 1983.

Ritter, G., ed. *Entstehung und Wandel der modernen Gesellschaft: Festschrift für Hans Rosenberg zum 65. Geburtstag.* Berlin, 1970.

Romanovich-Slavatinskii, A. *Dvorianstvo v Rossii ot nachala XVIII veka do otmeny krepostnogo prava.* SPb, 1870.

Rosenberg, H. *Bureaucracy, Aristocracy and Autocracy: The Prussian Experience 1660–1815.* Cambridge, Mass., 1958.

Rosovsky, H. "The Serf Entrepreneur in Russia." *Explorations in Entrepreneurial History* 6 (1954): 207–33.

Rothe, H. *Religion und Kultur in den Regionen des russischen Reiches im 18. Jahrhundert.* Opladen, 1984.

Rozman, G. *Urban Networks in Russia 1750-1800 and Premodern Periodization.* Princeton, 1976.

"Rozysk o Moisee Churine i o- volshebnykkh ego pis'makh (1724)." *Chteniia,* 1880, no. 2 (April–June): 23–35.

Rubinshtein, N. "Ulozhennaia Komissiia 1754-1766gg. i ee proekt novogo ulozheniia 'o sostoianii poddanykh voobschche'." *IZ* 38 (1951): 208–51.

Rummel, V., and Golubtsov, V. *Rodoslovnyi sbornik russkikh dvorianskikh familii.* 2 vols. SPb, 1886–1887.

"Russkii dvor v 1761 godu." *RS,* 1878, no. 3 (Sept.–Dec.): 187–206.

Rychkov, P. "Zapiski Petra Ivanovicha Rychkova." *RA,* 1905, no. 3 (Sept.–Dec.): 289–340.

Ryndziunskii, P. *Gorodskoe grazhdanstvo doreformennoi Rossii.* Moscow, 1958.

Safonov, M. *Problema reform v pravitel'stvennoi politike Rossii na rubezhe XVIII i XIX vv.* Moscow, 1988.

St.-Peterburgskaia stolichnaia politsiia i gradonachal'stvo: Kratkii istoricheskii ocherk. SPb, 1903.

Salias, E. "Poet Derzhavin, pravitel' namestnichestva (1785-1788)." *RV,* 1876 (Sept.): 66–120, (Oct.): 567–627.

"Saltychikha." *RA,* 1865, 247–55.

Savelov, L. *Rod dvorian Savelovykh (Savelkovykh).* Moscow, 1895.

Schuyler, E. *Peter the Great, Emperor of Russia.* 2 vols. New York, 1890.

Selivanov, A. "Delo o podlozhnoi pros'be ob uvolnenii ot sluzhby Penzenskogo gubernatora F.-L. Vigelia (1807-1809)." *RS,* 1893, no. 3 (July–Sept.): 84–88.

Semenov, A. *Izuchenie istoricheskikh svedenii o Rossiiskoi vneshnei torgovle i promyshlennosti s poloviny XVII-go stoletiia po 1858 goda.* 3 pts. SPb, 1859 (ORP reprint, 1977, in 2 vols.).

Sementkovskii, R. "Siluety russkikh adminstratorov." *IV,* 1892, no. 1 (Jan.–March): 499–523.

Semevskii, V. *Krest'ianskii vopros v Rossii v XVIII i pervoi polovine XIX veka.* 2 vols. SPb, 1888.

———. *Krest'iane v tsarstvovanie imperatritsy Ekateriny II.* 2d ed. SPb, 1901–1903.

———. "Vopros o preobrazovanii gosudarstvennogo stroia Rossii v XVIII i pervei chetverti XIX veka." *Byloe,* 1906, no. 1 (Jan.): 1–53, no. 2 (Feb.): 76–120; no. 3 (March): 150–98.

Shakhovskoi, Ia. *Zapiski, 1709-1777.* SPb, 1872 (ORP reprint, 1974).

Shakinko, I. *Vasilii Tatishchev.* Sverdlovsk, 1986.

Shchepetov, K. *Iz zhizni krepostnykh krest'ian Rossii 18-19vv.* Moscow, 1963.

Shcherbatov, M. *O povrezhdenii nravov v Rossii.* SPb, 1906.

Shelekhov, F. *Glavnoe Intendantskoe Upravlenie: Istoricheskii ocherk.* SPb, 1903 (*Stoletie Voennogo Ministerstva,* vol. 5, pt. 1).

Shepukova, N., "Izmenenie udel'nogo vesa chastnovladel'cheskogo krest'ianstva v sostave naseleniia Evropeiskoi Rossii (XVIII-pervaia polovina XIXv.) *VI,* 1959, no. 12, 123–136.

———. "K voprosu ob itogakh podvornoi perepisi 1678-1679gg. v Rossiiskom gosudarstve." *Istoriia SSSR* 4, no. 3 (1960): 145–47.

———. "Ob izmenenii razmerov dushevladeniia pomeshchikov evropeiskoi Rossii v pervoi chetverti XVIII-pervoi polovine XIX v." *EAI,* 1963, 388–419.

———. "K voprosu o chislennosti barshchinnykh i obrochnykh pomeshchich'ikh krest'ian evropeiskoi Rossii vo 2-i polovine XVIII veka." *EAI,* 1964, 400–408.

Shishkov, A. "Mnenie Admirala i Prezidenta Rossiiskoi Akademii A. Shishkova o razsmatrivanii knig, ili o tsenzure." *RA*, 1865, 1339–58.

Shompulev, V. "Iz dnevnika zhendarma 30-kh godov." *RS*, 1897, no. 2 (April–June): 261–69.

Shtrange, M. *Demokraticheskaia intelligentsiia Rossii v XVIII veke*. Moscow, 1965.

Shubinskii, S. "Imperatritsa Anna Ioannovna, pridvornyi byt i zabavy 1730–1740gg." *RS*, 1873, no. 1 (Jan.–June): 336–53.

Shuvalov, I. "V Pravitel'stvuiushchii Senat imperatorskogo Moskovskogo Universiteta ot kuratora Shuvalova donesenie." *Chteniia*, 1858, n. 3 (July–August): 113–21.

Sjoberg, G., *The Preindustrial City*. Glencoe, Il., 1960.

Skabichevskii, A. *Ocherki istorii russkoi tsenzury (1700–1863 g.)*. SPb, 1892.

Skalon, V. "Zemskie finansy." *ES* 12A (1894): 514–31.

Slany, W. "Russian Central Governmental Institutions 1725–1741." Ph.D diss., Cornell University, 1958.

Slavushchinskii, S. "General Izmailov i ego dvornia." *DNR*, 1876, no. 3 (Sept.–Dec.): 38–50, 157–70, 255–83, 349–84.

Smetanin, S. "Razlozhenie soslovii i formirovanie klassovoi struktury gorodskogo naseleniia Rossii v 1800–1861gg." *IZ* 102 (1978): 153–82.

Smolitsch, I. *Geschichte der Russischen Kirche, 1700–1917*. Leiden, 1964.

Sobornoe Ulozhenie 1649 goda. Moscow, 1961.

Solov'ev, S. *Istoriia Rossii s drevneishikh vremen*. 15 vols. Moscow, 1960–1966.

——. *Izbrannye trudy: Zapiski*. Moscow, 1983.

——. "Razskazy iz russkoi istorii XVIII veka." *RV*, 1861 (Jan.), 93–126.

——. "Imperatorskie sovety v Rossii v XVIII veke." *RS*, 1870, no. 2 (July–Dec.): 463–68.

"Sotvorenie sekretaria (satira XVIII stoletiia)." *RS*, 1884, no. 4 (Oct.–Dec.): 222.

Speranskii, M. "O gosudarstvennykh ustanovleniiakh." In Kalachov, III, 3:15–59.

——. "O krepostnykh liudiakh." In Kalachov, 3:1–15.

——. "Plan finansov (1810)." In Kulomzin, "Finansovye dokumenty," 1–72.

——. "Zamechaniia o gubernskikh uchrezhdeniiakh." In Kalachov, 4:92–104.

Squire, P. *The Third Department: The Establishment and Practices of the Political Police in the Russia of Nicholas I*. Cambridge, Mass., 1968.

Stein, F. von. *Geschichte des russischen Heeres vom Ursprunge desselben bis zur Thronbesteigung des Kaisers Nikolai I. Pawlowitsch*. Hannover, 1885.

Stein, L. von. *The History of the Social Movement in France 1789–1850*. Totowa, N.J., 1964.

Stone, L. *An Open Elite? England 1540–1880*. Abridged ed., Oxford, 1986.

Stourm, R. *The Budget*. New York, 1917.

Strakhovskii, I. "Gubernskoe ustroistvo." *Zhurnal Ministerstva Iustitsii*, 1913, no. 7 (Sept.): 28–92; no. 8 (Oct.): 70–120; no. 9 (Nov.): 122–71.

Strukov, D. *Glavnoe artilleriiskoe upravlenie: Istoricheskii ocherk*. SPb, 1902 (*Stoletie Voennogo Ministerstva*, VI, chast' i, kn. 1).

Studenkin, G. "Saltychikha, 1730–1801." *RS*, 1874, no. 2:497–548.

Sturdza. "O sud'be pravoslavnoi tserkvi russkoi v tsarstvovanie Aleksandra I-go. (Iz zapisok A.S. Sturdzy)." *RS* 1876, I (Jan.–April), 266–88.

Sudebnaia Reforma. Edited by N. Davydov and N. Polianskii. Vol. 1. Moscow, 1915.

"Sud i sud'i v nachale XIX veka. Rukopisnaia satira 1807 g." *RS*, 1891, no. 3 (July–Sept): 408–10.

Sumarokov. "Mnenie senatora Sumarokova po delu DSS Popova o tsenzure." *Chteniia*, 1859, no. 4 (Oct.–Dec.): 43–48.

Svedeniia o piteinykh sborakh v Rossii. 4 pts. SPb, 1860–1861.

"Tainaia Kantseliariia v tsarstvovanie imp. Elizavety Petrovny 1741–1761." *RS*, 1875, no. 1 (Jan.–April): 522–39.

Tel'berg, G. "Proiskhozhdenie Komiteta Ministrov v Rossii." *ZhMNP*, 1907, no. 8 (March–April): 38–61.

Tikhomirov, M. *Rossiiskoe gosudarstvo XV–XVII vekov.* Moscow, 1973.

Timofeev, A. "Telesnye nakazaniia." *ES* 34 (1902): 292–95.

Tkacheva, N. "Iz istorii odnodvortsev v XVIII v." *EAI*, 1968, 133–41.

Torke, H.-J. "Das russische Beamtentum in der ersten Hälfte des 19. Jahrhunderts." *FGO* 13 (1967): 7–345.

———. *Die Staatsbedingte Gesellschaft im Moskauer Reich.* Leiden, 1974.

Trefolev, L. "Iaroslavl' pri imperatritse Elizavete Petrovne." *DNR*, 1877, no. 1 (Jan.–April): 255–89, 353–77.

———. "Iaroslavkaia starina." *RA*, 1896, no. 1: 206–19; no. 2:147–55; no. 3:88–100; 1897, no. 1:189–212.

Troitskii, S. *Finansovaia politika russkogo absoliutizma v XVIII veke.* Moscow, 1966.

———. *Russkii absoliutizm i dvorianstvo v XVIII v.* Moscow, 1974.

———. *Rossiia v XVIII veke.* Moscow, 1982.

———. "Iz istorii sostavleniia biudzheta v Rossii v seredine XVIII veka." *IZ* 78 (1965): 181–203.

Troshchinskii. "Zapiska D. P. Troshchinskogo o ministerstvakh." *SIRIO* 3 (1868): 1–162.

Turgot, *Oeuvres.* 2 vols. Paris, 1844.

Turkestanov, N. *Gubernskii sluzhebnik.* SPb, 1869.

Ustiugov, N. "Evoliutsiia prikaznogo stroia Russkogo gosudarstva v XVII v." In *Absoliutizm v Rossii,* 134–67.

Ustrialov, N. *Istoriia tsarstvovaniia Petra Velikogo.* 6 vols. SPb, 1858–1863.

"Uzhasy krepostnogo prava v tsarstvovanie Aleksandra Blagoslovennogo." *RA* 1907, 4: 119–35.

V—, K. "Provintsial'naia kantseliariia i cherty narodnoi russkoi zhizni (1719–1777)." *IV*, 1884, no. 4 (Oct.–Dec.): 191–200.

Vagina, P. "O nekotorykh prichinakh otmeny instituta pripisnykh krest'ian v kontse XVIII veka." *EAI* 1968, 148–53.

Valuev, P. "Ssory moi s tremia ministrami." *RS*, 1901, no. 2 (April–June): 43–52.

VanCreveld, M. *Command in War.* Cambridge, Mass., 1985.

Vasilenko, N. "Prikazy." *ES* 25 (1898): 186–96.

Veinberg, L. "Ocherki starodavnogo mestnago byta." *RA*, 1887, no. 2 (May–August): 289–306; no. 3 (Sept.–Dec.): 417–23.

Veretennikov, V. *Istoriia Tainoi Kantseliarii Petrovskogo vremeni.* Khar'kov, 1910.

Vernadsky, G. "Serfdom in Russia." *Relazioni del X Congresso Internatzionale di Scienze Storiche* 3 (1955): 247–72.

———. *The Tsardom of Moscow, 1547–1682.* 2 vols. New Haven, 1969.

Veselovskii, S. *D'iaki i pod'iachie XV–XVII vv.* Moscow, 1975.

"Viedomosti iz Sinoda, iz Senata i iz dvukh voinskikh kollegii o ikh Kontorakh i kakie v nikh dela otpravliaiutsia." *Chteniia,* 1905, no. 4: smes', 1–24.

Vinskii. "Zapiski Vinskogo." *RA*, 1877, 76–123, 150–97.

Vladimirskii-Budanov,, M. *Obzor istorii russkogo prava.* 6th ed. SPb, 1909.

Vodarksii, Ia. "Sluzhiloe dvorianstvo v Rossii v kontse XVII-nachale XVII veka." In *Voprosy voennoi istorii Rossii—XVIII i pervaia polovina XIX vekov,* 233–38, Moscow, 1969.

———. *Naselenie Rossii v kontse XVII-nachale XVIII veka.* Moscow, 1977.

———. *Dvorianskoe zemlevladenie v Rossii v XVII-pervoi polovine XIX veka.* Moscow, 1988.

"Volkov, D. Materialy k ego biografii." *RS*, 1874, no. 3 (Sept.–Dec.): 478–96.

Volkov, D., "Zapiska D. V. Volkova ob Orenburgskoi gubernii 1763g." *VIRGO* 1859, N. 9, 49–60.

Volkov, M. *Ocherki istorii promyslov Rossii.* Moscow, 1979.

"Volneniia krest'ian v Lifliandii v 1777 godu." *Pamiatniki novoi istorii* 1, otd. 2 (1871): 17–38.

Vorontsov. "Primechaniia na nekotorye stat'i, kasaiushchiiasia do Rossii, grafa A. R. Vorontsova, imperatoru Aleksandru I-mu predstavlennye." *Chteniia*, 1859, no. 1 (Jan.–March): smes', 89–102.

———. "Primechaniia o pravakh i preimushchestvakh Senata." *Chteniia*, 1864, no. 1 (Jan.–March): smes', 108–11.

———. "Dva pis'ma grafa S. R. Vorontsova." *RA*, 1874, no. 2:971–1025.

———. "Zapiska grafa S. R. Vorontsova o russkom voiske (1802)." *RA*, 1876, no. 3:345–61.

———. "O vnutrennem upravlenii v Rossii: Zapiska grafa S. R. Vorontsova (1803)." *RA*, 1881, no. 2:155–62.

Voslensky, M. *Nomenklatura. The Soviet Ruling Class. An Insider's Report.* Garden City, N.Y., 1984.

Vosstanie Moskovskikh streltsov v 1698 godu: Materialy sledstvennogo dela. Edited by V. Buganov and Kazakevich. Moscow, 1980.

"Vozrazhenie neizvestnogo na knigu sochinennuiu grafom Stroinovskim o usloviiakh s krest'ianami (1811)." *Chteniia*, 1860, no. 2 (April–June): 195–202.

"Vsepoddaneishii doklad Pravitel'stvuiushchogo Senata po delu kapitana Golokhvastova v zakliuchenii ego v ostorg Novgorodskim gubernatorom Siversim." *SIRIO* 2 (1868): 419–24.

Vvedenskii, S. "Cherty nravov v Voronezhskoi eparkhii pri sv. Mitrofane (1682–1703)." *RV*, 1903 (Nov.–Dec.): 699–713.

Wallerstein, I. *The Modern World-System II.* New York, 1980.

Ware, T. *The Orthodox Church.* New York, 1963.

Weber, M. *Economy and Society.* Edited by G. Roth and C. Wittich, 3 vols. New York, 1968.

Wickham, A., and Coignard, S. *La Nomenklatura française: Pouvoirs et privilèges des élites.* Paris, 1986.

Wildman, A. *The End of the Russian Imperial Army.* Princeton, 1980.

Williams, A. *The Police of Paris 1718–1789.* Baton Rouge, 1979.

Williams, E. *An Ancien Régime in Europe: Government and Society in the Major States 1648–1789.* New York, 1970.

Willis, D. *Klass: How the Russians Really Live.* New York, 1985.

Wittram, R. *Peter I: Czar and Kaiser.* 2 vols. Göttingen, 1964.

Wolzendorff, K. *Der Polizeigedanke des modernen Staates.* Breslau, 1918.

Wortman, R. "Peter the Great and Court Procedure." *C-ASS* 8, no. 2 (1974): 303–10.

———. *The Development of a Russian Legal Consciousness.* Chicago, 1976.

———. "Property Rights, Populism, and Russian Political Culture." *Civil Rights in Imperial Russia*, edited by O. Crisp and L. Edmondson. Oxford, 1989.

Yaney, G. *The Systematization of Russian Government.* Urbana, Ill., 1973.

Zaionchkovskii, P. *Pravitel'stvennyi apparat samoderzhavnoi Rossii v XIX v.* Moscow, 1978.

Zaitsev, K. *Ocherki istorii samoupravleniia gosudarstvennykh krest'ian.* SPb, 1912.

Zaozerskaia, E. "Skazki torgovykh liudei Moskovskogo gosudarstva 1704g." *IZ* 17 (1945): 245–64.

"Zapiska dlia sostavleniia zakonov rossiiskikh," *Chteniia*, 1858, 3 (July–Sept.), 137–41.

"Zapiski krepostnoi." *RS*, 1911, no. 1 (Jan.–March): 140–151.

Zavadovskii, P. "Mnenie o pravakh i preimuschestvakh Senata." *Chteniia*, 1864, no. 1 (Jan.–March): smes', 100–07.

Zelin, M. *The Magistrate's Tael.* Berkeley, 1984.

Zhirkevich. "Zapiski Iv. S. Zhirkevicha, 1789–1848." *RS*, 1874, no. 1 (Jan.–April): 207–44; no. 2 (May–August): 633–66; no. 3 (Sept.–Dec.): 411–50, 642–64; 1875, no. 2 (May–August): 554–80; 1876, no. 2 (May–August): 627–48; no. 3 (Sept.–Dec.): 127–44, 251–66, 771–86; 1878, no. 2 (May–August): 401–22; no. 3 (Sept.–Dec.): 33–54.

Zhukovich, P. "Upravlenie i sud v zapadnoi Rossii v tsarstvovanie Ekateriny II." *ZhMNP*, 1914, no. 1 (Jan.–Feb.): 265–315; no. 2 (March–April): 88–120, 314–55; no. 3 (May–June): 1–60.

Zhuravskii, D. *Statisticheskoe obozrenie raskhodov na voennye potrebnosti s 1711 po 1825 god.* SPb, 1859.

INDEX

Abakumov, A., 13
Absolutism, ix–x, xii
Academy of Sciences, 123, 171, 172, 186, 232
Alenin family, 27
Alexander I, xiii, 8, 45, 87, 108, 110, 125, 126, 131, 142, 155, 161, 162, 209–10, 308
Alexei Mikhailovich, 63, 90
Alexei, tsarevich, 123, 159, 160
Anna Ivanovna, 81–82, 161
Anna Leopoldovna, 171
Apparatus, civilian, 4–5, 8, 46, 48–54, 176, 193, 230, 234, 260. *See also* Ruling class
Apparatus, military. *See* Officer corps
Appeals. *See* Judicial procedure
Apraksin family, 9, 69, 70, 74, 75, 125, 183
Apukhtin, M., 10
Arakcheev, A., 20, 100, 101–2, 103, 105, 107, 112, 127, 163, 174, 175
Army, 12, 17, 25, 102, 104–5, 133–34, 255
Army supply, 255–57
Aron, R., viii
Arrears, 157, 251, 269
Artillery, 43, 65, 66, 78, 85–86, 101, 103
Audit, 243–45, 254, 294–95

Bail, 210
Bakhmetev, I., 94
Bakhtin, I., 112–13
Balashov, A., 44, 126
Banishment, 32, 205, 207, 213–14
Banks, 10, 231, 242, 248–50, 291
Barclay de Tolly, M., 102, 108
Barshchina, 271–72
Bavykin, P., 94
Beccaria, 211
Belliustin, 8
Bestuzhev-Riumin, A., 82, 110
Bezborodko, A., 173
Bibikov family, 44
Bible Society, 174
Billeting. *See* Taxation, in kind
Biron, 9
Board of Public Welfare, 118, 147, 153, 231, 254
Bogdanov, F., 12

Bolotov, A., 18, 214
Boyars. *See* Nobility
Brius (Bruce) family, 66, 78, 172–73
Budgets, 70
  procedure, 283–96
  size, 276–83
Bureaucracy, ix, xiii. *See also* Clerks; Secretaries
Bureaucratization, 9, 296, 309
Burgermasters' Chamber, 245
Burmistry, 33, 40, 128, 251

Cabinet of Ministers, 47, 83, 87, 93, 104
Cadet corps, 8, 20, 44
Campenhausen, B., 245
Capitation, 13–14, 31, 38, 98, 252, 256, 259–60, 291. *See also* Revenue
Catherine I, 81, 83
Catherine II, xiii, 16, 83, 84, 141, 155, 159, 162, 165, 171, 203, 286, 303
Censorship, 145, 162, 169–75
Census, 259, 262
Chaadaev, P., 163
Chaikovskaia v. *Mokeeva*, 226
Chambers, judicial, 26, 113, 117, 154, 193, 196–99. *See also* Courts
  treasury, 113, 118, 232, 253, 255, 284. *See also* Treasury, Local
Chancery/chanceries, 91, 96
  of Arrears, 226
  of colleges, 75
  of Confiscation, 226
  for Court Peasants, 41, 183, 222
  Military, 70–71, 77
  Military Field, 99, 101
  Policemaster General's, 74
  Provision, 77, 79, 85–86, 157, 255. *See also* Provisioning
  Secret, 74, 123–24, 137, 141, 159, 165, 167. *See also* Prikazy, Preobrazhenskii
  Senate, 70, 73, 89–90, 108
Charter of 1785. *See* Nobility; Townsmen
Cherkasskii family, 83, 249
Chernyshev, Z., 12, 86, 227
Clergy, 13–15

371